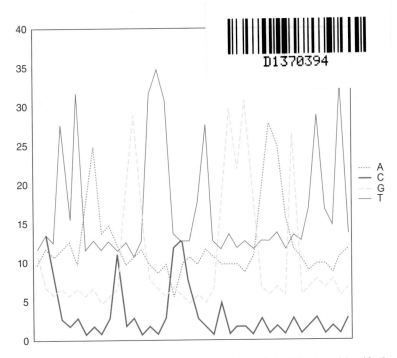

**FIGURE 9.2** One graph for all four columns of data. It is difficult to identify the nucleotides corresponding to a consecutive sequence of peaks.

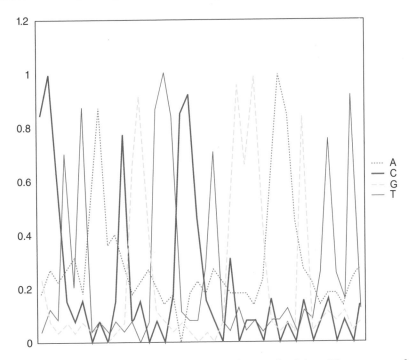

**FIGURE 9.3** One graph for all four columns of normalized data. The sequence of bases is fairly discernible.

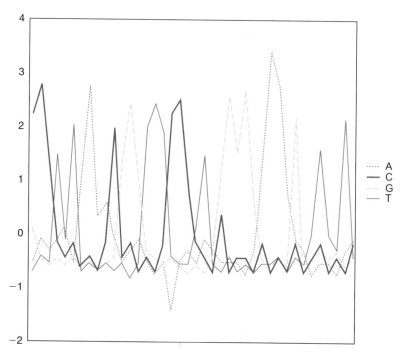

**FIGURE 9.4**   One graph for all four columns of data normalized to the same mean and standard deviation. The sequence of bases is readily discernible.

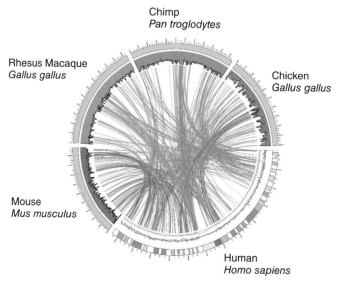

**FIGURE 9.5**   An image from Circos. This emphasizes gene similarities between human, rhesus monkey, chimp, chicken, and mouse genomes. Shaded arcs connect similar regions. Line charts and bar charts indicate the degree of similarities.
© M. Krzywinski (2005) Circos http://mkweb.bcgsc.ca/circos

# Bioinformatics
# A Computing Perspective

# Bioinformatics
# A Computing Perspective

**Shuba Gopal**
*Rochester Institute of Technology*

**Anne Haake**
*Rochester Institute of Technology*

**Rhys Price Jones**
*George Washington University*

**Paul Tymann**
*Rochester Institute of Technology*

**McGraw-Hill Higher Education**

Boston   Burr Ridge, IL   Dubuque, IA   New York   San Francisco   St. Louis
Bangkok   Bogotá   Caracas   Kuala Lumpur   Lisbon   London   Madrid   Mexico City
Milan   Montreal   New Delhi   Santiago   Seoul   Singapore   Sydney   Taipei   Toronto

# McGraw-Hill
# Higher Education

BIOINFORMATICS: A COMPUTING PERSPECTIVE

Published by McGraw-Hill, a business unit of The McGraw-Hill Companies, Inc., 1221 Avenue of the Americas, New York, NY 10020. Copyright © 2009 by The McGraw-Hill Companies, Inc. All rights reserved. No part of this publication may be reproduced or distributed in any form or by any means, or stored in a database or retrieval system, without the prior written consent of The McGraw-Hill Companies, Inc., including, but not limited to, in any network or other electronic storage or transmission, or broadcast for distance learning.

Some ancillaries, including electronic and print components, may not be available to customers outside the United States.

This book is printed on acid-free paper.

1 2 3 4 5 6 7 8 9 0 DOC/DOC 0 9 8

ISBN 978–0–07–313364–5
MHID 0–07–313364–7

Global Publisher: *Raghothaman Srinivasan*
Director of Development: *Kristine Tibbetts*
Senior Project Manager: *Kay J. Brimeyer*
Senior Production Supervisor: *Laura Fuller*
Associate Design Coordinator: *Brenda A. Rolwes*
Cover/Interior Designer: *Studio Montage, St. Louis, Missouri*
(USE) Cover Image: *Illustration Figure 4.7 and Photodisc Vol. 6 - Nature, Wildlife and the Environment*
Senior Photo Research Coordinator: *John C. Leland*
Photo Research: *Evelyn Jo Johnson*
Compositor: *Newgen Imaging Systems*
Typeface: *10/12 Times Roman*
Printer: *R. R. Donnelley Crawfordsville, IN*

Photo Credits: *Tymann Bioinformatics 1/e*
*Fig. 1.1: © Pixtal/age Fotostock, Fig. 1.2: © Science Source/Photo Researchers, Inc., Fig. 1.4: © Image Select/Art Resource, NY, Fig. 1.6: © CAIDA/Photo Researchers, Inc., Fig. 2.24B: © ISM, Fig. 3.13: © Scott Camazine/Phototake—All rights reserved., Fig. 3.24: Photos reprinted Courtesy of Ming Jin, et al, Two-dimensional gel proteome reference map of blood monocytes, Proteome Science 2006, 4:16; licensee Biomed Central Ltd., Fig. 3.26: © Dr. Cecil H. Fox, Fig. 3.27 © Dr. Cecil H. Fox, Fig. 8.2: Courtesy of the Center for Array Technologies at the University of Washington, Fig. 9.19: © Stephen Gerard/Photo Researchers, Inc.,*

**Library of Congress Cataloging-in-Publication Data**

Bioinformatics : a computing perspective / Shuba Gopal ... [et al.]. – 1st ed.
   p. cm.
  Includes index.
   ISBN 978–0–07–313364–5 — ISBN 0–07–313364–7 (hard copy : alk. paper)
1. Bioinformatics. I. Gopal, Shuba.

QH324.2.B546   2009
572.80285–dc22                                   2008004080

www.mhhe.com

# Dedication

*I Mam, Laurel, Sara, Caroline a Claire*
*—Rhys Price Jones*

*For Bill, Peter and Scott*
*—Anne Haake*

*For Sridhar, Sanjeev and Mara*
*—Shuba Gopal*

# Brief Contents

# Contents

# Preface

> "...we seem to agree that [bioinformatics is] an interdisciplinary field, requiring skills in computer science, molecular biology, statistics, mathematics, and more. I'm not qualified in any of these fields...though I spend most of my time writing software, developing algorithms, and deriving equations..."
>
> — Sean Eddy[1]

One of the challenges of writing a textbook in an interdisciplinary field as fluid and rapidly evolving as bioinformatics is that no one is an expert in all aspects of the field. We all come to the table with different backgrounds, a collection of skills accrued along the way, and a set of ideas of what to study and how to go about doing so. To be successful you need to communicate your ideas to people who share neither the background nor your vocabulary, and to do so in a way that fires the imagination. That's what we have tried to do in this book. We are a disparate group: formal training in mathematics and computer science for two of us; formal training in biology for the other two; all of us using, developing and evaluating new computational methods for the analysis of biological problems. What gets us out of bed in the morning is the idea that we can design an algorithm or computational method that will help us better understand the miracle of life. Along the way, we discovered that together we could create a textbook that blends computing and biology in an engaging and unique way.

In fact, we believe this book is as close to a stand-alone text as possible in the field. The book is aimed at those with a computing background, but it contains enough background from both the biological and computing angles that students from either discipline should feel comfortable starting with this text. Of course, no text can cover everything in equal depth, so when push comes to shove, we slide to the computing end of the scale rather than the biology end. Thus, we assume that students have already acquired about a year's worth of programming experience and are conversant with Java or a similar object-oriented programming language.

To help keep students focused on material that is often complex and detailed, we used one long-running example throughout the text. Specifically, we provided worked examples and discussed the ways in which computing approaches have elucidated key aspects of the biology of the human immunodeficiency virus (HIV), the virus that causes AIDS. Threading a single example through many topics is meant to enable computing students to ground themselves as they explore the complexities of biology. In turn, the HIV example gives biology students a chance to return to a familiar place even as advanced computing concepts are introduced.

---

[1] Eddy, Sean. (2005). "Ante disciplinary Science," *PLoS Computational Biology*. 1(1):e6.

We made a conscious decision not to talk about the application of common bioinformatics tools, although we highlighted interesting methods that are embedded in well-known programs. This book is not a "how-to" guide to bioinformatics, and its intended audience is not computer scientists hoping to pick up a little biology or biologists hoping to get a few computing clues. Rather, we hoped to engage the next generation of scientists. We wanted to inspire individuals to design the breakthrough algorithms and compuational approaches that will provide novel and valuable insights into biological phenomena. Ambitious as this is, we have learned from our experiences teaching undergraduates that if you demand the world of them, some will produce amazing results. Indeed, we wrote this book for just those undergraduates who over the years have surprised us with their ingenuity, tenacity and enterprising approach to the field. This is a book aimed at all the undergraduates and possibly first year graduate students who are just itching for the chance to try out their skills on a whole new set of problems.

We purposely took a conversational tone in the text, keeping things relatively lighthearted even as we engaged in rigorous analysis. We hoped in doing so to entice students into learning and thinking.

We did not think in such lofty terms when we began this process several years ago. We started at a much more prosaic level: Anne Haake and Rhys Price Jones were offering a pair of courses titled "Introduction to Bioinformatics Computing" and "Advanced Bioinformatics Computing" for undergraduates at the Rochester Institute of Technology (RIT). None of the textbooks on the market had the right blend of computing and biology for the courses. We identified many textbooks that were merely procedural guides describing how existing computational tools could be applied to specific biology problems. Another set of textbooks was so overwhelmingly focused on the algorithmic aspects that they lost sight of the biology that motivated them. We wanted to achieve that happy medium: a textbook that would emphasize the theoretical underpinnings and logic of the algorithms while also highlighting the biological knowledge that drives the algorithm development in a unique direction. Since no one else was writing the textbook we wanted, we wrote our own. The fruits of those labors reside in your hands now.

We will not tell you how to use this book because we think there are many ways to use it. What we do suggest is that you feel free to pick those chapters that most suit your tastes and the needs of your students. For example, if you or your students need a little extra biology background, you will find that Chapters 2 and 3 provide a very good primer on basic molecular biology. If, on the other hand, your students need a gentler introduction to some of the algorithms, chapters 3, 4, and 5 are designed to help them understand the spirit of bioinformatics algorithms. These chapters do, however, expect a familiarity with written explanations of algorithmic ideas, such as would be encountered in most introductory computer science courses at the college level.

You can certainly work through all the chapters in the book over the course of a semester or year-long course depending on the level of detail you wish to pursue. You can customize students' experience by selecting from the exercises included in each chapter. Many of these exercises require students to develop code and programs to accomplish specific tasks. Most of these tasks have a biological basis or are motivated by a specific biological phenomenon. For a faster paced, less involved course, you might omit some of the more detailed programming exercises. Additional instructional material and solutions to the exercises will be made available at www.mhhe.com/gopal.

Chapter 9 encourages you to give your students free rein to explore some fascinating new areas of bioinformatics where computing challenges loom large – areas in which the extant solutions come in an intriguing variety and the open questions are just as numerous. Rather than try to cover all the details of ongoing research, we leave the door open for innovative students to investigate the issues for themselves, either on their own or in small groups. This provides an important pedagogical tool: the motivation and context within which students can become independent investigators in their own right.

In the end, we want this book to be a gateway to new and exciting discoveries. We invite you to explore, to investigate and then to roam free through the field. If our experiences are any indication, what you produce from these explorations will surprise even you. We hope you will enjoy the journey as much as we have.

Shuba Gopal
*Rochester, NY, May 2008*

Anne Haake
*Rochester NY, May 2008*

Rhys Price Jones
*Washington, D.C., May 2008*

Paul Tymann
*Rochester, NY, May 2008*

# Acknowledgment

"Knowledge is in the end based on acknowledgment."

—Ludwig Wittgenstein

Many contribute to any endeavor such as this not just those whose names appear on the cover. These individuals deserve the real credit for bringing this work to fruition. Our students have been the primary motivation for this work, and we remain indebted to them. Transforming that inspiration into reality required the skills of our excellent editorial team at McGraw-Hill. Kelly Lowery and Emily Lupash helped us get started writing, and we were then ably guided by Alan Apt. Melinda Bilecki has been a steady source of support through our darkest hours. Kris Tibbets and Raghu Srinivasan helped us put the final touches on our manuscript.

We were fortunate to have numerous peer reviewers of our chapters, and their feedback provided much needed reassurance and valuable suggestions for improvement. Our student collaborators, Guy Paddock and Eric Foster, provided some of the code in the text, on the website, and in the Solutions Manual, while Brendan Dahl helped ensure that exercises were a good fit for the text. Dr. Robert Parody contributed material and guidance for the statistical analysis of gene expression data. The students of the Introduction to Bioinformatics Computing and Advanced Bioinformatics Computing courses in Winter 2005 and Spring 2006 reviewed many of the chapters and offered specific suggestions. Their enthusiasm for this project has buoyed us throughout.

Last but hardly least, we would like to acknowledge the unflagging support of our near and dear ones. To Laurel, Bill, and Sridhar: you made it easy for us to dream big.

# Road Map

*"Dealing with these system properties, which ultimately must underlie our under-standing of all cellular behaviour, will require more abstract conceptualisations than biologists have been used to in the past. We might need to move into a strange more abstract world…"*

—Paul Nurse (Nobel Prize in physiology or medicine, 2001), A long twentieth century of the cell cycle and beyond, *Cell.* 2000, 100:71–78.

## 1.1 WHAT IS BIOINFORMATICS?

Since the thirteenth century scientists have been using the scientific method to formulate a model of the world around us. The scientific method defines a cycle that starts with an observation of some phenomenon, the development of a hypothesis that describes the phenomenon, and performance of experiments to test the validity of the hypothesis. Although the hypothesis is the main focus of the scientific method, what really drives scientific advancement is the collection, analysis, and interpretation of the data generated by the experiments performed to test the hypothesis.

Gregor Mendel (1822–1884, Figure 1.1), the first person to trace the characteristics of successive generations of pea plants, used the scientific method to test his theories of heredity. During the middle of his life, Mendel performed hundreds of experiments on pea plants and observed changes in seven basic characteristics of the plants, carefully recording the results from each of these experiments in notebooks. After analyzing the data he collected in his notebooks, Mendel discovered three basic laws[1] that govern the passage of a trait from one generation of a species to another. Although Mendel's laws are very important in a study of genetics, what is really important here is the process that Mendel used to develop these laws, namely, he collected the data produced after performing several experiments, stored the data in his notebooks, and then analyzed the data to develop his laws.

The basic scientific work being done in laboratories around the world today follows the same principles that Mendel followed in the 1800s. One thing that has changed significantly from Mendel's time is the scale at which we can perform our

---

[1] Mendel's laws are: the law of dominance, the law of segregation, and the law of independent assortment.

**FIGURE 1.1**
Gregor Mendel.
(© Pixtal / age
Fotostock)

experiments. Mendel's data were based on the changes that he could observe in the characteristics of his pea plants from one generation to another. Today biologists are able to observe the cells and subcellular components of the organisms they are studying and collect data on the structure of the DNA and other molecules in these cells. This has not only changed our understanding of some of the basic processes in living organisms but it has also resulted in a flood of data. Instead of recording seven characteristics, modern scientists record tens of thousands. It is no longer possible to use simple notebooks to record the results of these experiments, let alone analyze the data they produce.

Like scientific experimentation, computers and how they are used have evolved over time. Charles Babbage (1791–1871, Figure 1.2), a mathematician and inventor, grew tired of calculating astronomical tables by hand and conceived of a way to build a mechanical device to perform the calculations automatically. In 1822, Babbage started work on a computing device—the difference engine (Figure 1.3)—to automatically calculate mathematical tables. During the course of his work on the difference engine, he conceived of a more sophisticated machine he called the analytical engine. The analytical engine was meant to be programmed using punch cards and would employ features such as sequential control, branching, and looping. Although Babbage never built a complete working model of either machine,[2] his work became the basis on which many modern computers are built.

---

[2] One of Babbage's earlier difference engines was eventually constructed from drawings by a team at London's Science Museum in the 1990s. The machine weighs 3 tons and is 10 feet wide by 6 feet tall.

**FIGURE 1.2**
Charles Babbage.
(© Science
Source / Photo
Researchers, Inc.)

**FIGURE 1.3**
A difference engine.
(© Bettman / Corbis)

When electronic computers were first built in the 1940s, they were large, cumbersome devices that were only capable of performing simple operations. These machines were typically very expensive to build and maintain and were designed for a specific purpose. Like many of the technological advances in the twentieth century, initially computers were primarily used for military purposes. The face of computing changed forever with the invention of the transistor, followed by the integrated circuit. These devices allowed computer engineers to build more powerful, smaller, and inexpensive machines. These breakthroughs ultimately led to the development of the personal computer.

In tandem with the development of more powerful, and useful, computer hardware, computer scientists were also learning more about the basic theories that underlie computation. Ada Lovelace (1815–1852, Figure 1.4), who also

**FIGURE 1.4**
Ada Lovelace.
(© Image Select / Art
Resource, NY)

was a mathematician, worked with Charles Babbage on the analytical engine. Unlike Babbage, who was interested in building a computing device, Lovelace sought to understand the methodology of computing. She studied these methods, implementations, and the properties of implementations. Lovelace developed a program that would have been able to compute the Bernoulli numbers. It is because of this work that many consider Lovelace to be the world's first programmer. It is interesting to note that both Ada Lovelace and Gregor Mendel were doing their groundbreaking work around the same time.

As computer hardware became more useful and powerful, our understanding of computing and programming increased as well. New programming languages, such as Smalltalk, Pascal, and C++, were developed that allow programmers to write more sophisticated programs. Groundbreaking work at Xerox Palo Alto Research Center (PARC) produced a computing environment that made it easy to display information in a graphical form. Computer scientists were developing an understanding of the basic properties of computation.

The stage was now set for computing and biology to come together. The curation of the amino acid sequences of proteins begun by Margaret O. Dayhoff (1925–1983) marked the beginning of modern bioinformatics. Curation involves the maintenance and annotation of the data, a task well suited to modern databases. In the *Atlas of Protein Sequences*, Dayhoff and her colleagues initiated the formal publication of known sequence data with yearly releases of the *Atlas* in the mid-1960s [3]. In 1970, S. B. Needleman and C. D. Wunsch developed the first algorithm that made it possible to align DNA sequences. The Needleman–Wunsch algorithm forms the computational basis of sequence alignment and represents the first major contribution by computer scientists to the field of bioinformatics. Over the years, computer scientists working together with biologists have developed faster, more effective algorithms to analyze the data collected during experimentation.

Computational and quantitative analysis of biological phenomena did not truly blossom until the explosion of sequence and other biologically derived data in the mid-1990s. Since then an ocean of biological data has been created. Modern scientists, unlike Mendel, routinely perform experiments that result in tens of thousands of data points. For example, using rapid DNA sequencing, scientists can unravel an entire genome, which typically consists of billions of nucleotides. A scientist can use a microarray to simultaneously measure the activity levels of tens of thousands of genes (Figure 1.5). As biotechnology brings ever more effective techniques to measure biological phenomena, the amount of data produced by experiments in a laboratory will become even larger, which in turn will require the development of sophisticated techniques to manage the data, to analyze the results, and to aid the scientist in interpretation.

Due to the amount and the nature of the data being collected in laboratories today, biologists are finding more and more that they need to collaborate with colleagues in different fields such as computer science, information technology, mathematics, and statistics in order to manage, store, analyze, and visualize the data produced by experiments they perform in their laboratories. This collaborative work is what makes it possible to interpret the results of modern biological

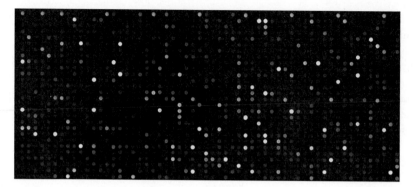

**FIGURE 1.5**   A microarray. A color version of this image is shown on the inside cover of this book.
(Courtesy of the Center for Array Technologies at the University of Washington)

experiments and, in turn, develop a better understanding of the nature of living organisms. This work, done by teams of biologists, chemists, computer scientists, information technologists, mathematicians, physicists, and statisticians, has given birth to a new field called bioinformatics.

**Bioinformatics** is a field of study in which these diverse fields merge into a single discipline. Working together bioinformaticists develop algorithms and statistical methods that can be used to analyze and further our understanding of large collections of different types of biological data, such as nucleotide and amino acid sequences, protein domains and structures, and the evolutionary relationship between organisms. During the past decade bioinformaticists have developed and implemented tools that enable efficient access to and management of different types of information.

Most of the work in bioinformatics to date has focused on the study of genomic sequences to provide insight into the function of a cell. Genomic sequence data is used to predict protein coding regions, amino acid sequences, and, ultimately, the structure and function of proteins. Although impressive advances have been made within the past two decades, there is still much that we do not know or understand. It is clear that advances in the field of bioinformatics rely on a multidisciplinary effort. In the next section we will look at the challenges faced by those working in this field.

## 1.2  A BIOINFORMATICS TEAM

Bioinformatics by its very nature requires experts in the various disciplines that make up this new field. Unfortunately putting together a successful bioinformatics team is not as simple as throwing a few biologists, chemists, computer scientists, and mathematicians into a room and asking them to work together. Individuals in these various fields often do not speak the same scientific language and often only have a basic understanding of the fundamental concepts of the other disciplines. If the members of a bioinformatics team cannot communicate, and do not understand or appreciate what the other disciplines offer in terms of techniques and tools to develop solutions to common problems, the team will not be successful.

Another way to look at this issue is to consider the spectrum of interests of the members of the team. In bioinformatics, as in all the sciences, a spectrum exists that spans the realms of theory, development, and application. The entire spectrum of both the computational and biological sciences contributes to the field of bioinformatics, but the boundaries of the realms within the spectrum of the new science are far from clear. An interesting challenge faces those working at the interface between the established sciences: If any aspect of the spectrum of either science is downplayed, then the eventual spectrum of the new discipline will be deficient.

As an example, consider how the boundaries of theory, development, and applications come together in a different field—the science of motor mechanics. Principles of combustion and equations governing energy release in combustive processes contribute to the realm of the **theoretical.** How to harness this energy through an internal combustion or a jet engine falls into the realm of **development.** The **application** realm involves the test pilot or the racing driver. The science of motor mechanics requires all three aspects of the spectrum. Additionally, any effective participant in the process—no matter their particular specialty—must have some knowledge of the rest of the spectrum. The developer needs to know the theory and the expected eventual use of the product; the test driver needs an appreciation of the limits of the engine and the processes enabling its power. Theoreticians must study the consequences and directions of their industry.

For a biologist or a chemist, the creation, study, and analysis of algorithms are within the theoretical realm. Program design, creation, and testing constitute the developmental realm. Some users of those programs, particularly testers, participate in the application spectrum of the science of computing. Users who know and understand the application area will contribute to the modification and maintenance stages and will need an understanding of the theory and development aspects in order to work effectively with the rest of their team. Likewise, for the computer scientists, information technologists, and statisticians, the chemical basis of the flow of information within a cell lies in the theoretical realm. However, a basic understanding of this theory is necessary, to build computational and statistical models of these processes.

It is important to distinguish the **users** of motor mechanics—the everyday drivers and commuters—from the application scientists. Similarly, we distinguish ordinary users of the computational sciences. Most users of word-processing programs do not need to know about the underlying representation of their keystrokes nor about the selection of the algorithms that implement their design wishes. The term **application scientist** describes users who contribute to the next generation of word processors: those who understand the needs of literary composition and presentation and who can knowledgeably communicate with the theoreticians and developers of the products.

Now consider the science of bioinformatics. Where on the spectrum does the conduct of sequencing experiments belong? What about the design of an efficient database for publishing the results of biological experiments? Is the search for common features among entries in such a database solely an application? Where in the science spectrum of bioinformatics does the design of an improved alignment program lie?

The truth is that we are as yet unable to specifically identify the boundaries of the spectrum of this new science. Nor do we need to. What is important is that all the scientists participating in bioinformatics need to know the entire potential extent of that spectrum in order to be effective. And the only way to be certain that you have covered the entire spectrum is to cover the spectra of both parent sciences: computational science as well as life science. As the disciplines represented in a bioinformatics team merge, participants in the merged science whose backgrounds are primarily in one of the parent sciences may be insufficiently versed in the entire spectrum of the other. And this is a danger even for those primarily interested in the application aspects of the new sciences. Application scientists must understand the underlying principles from the realms of theory and development. Many of the computational applications available for use today by experimental biologists allow for default assumptions about the nature of the input and its relevance to the application being used.

For example, the popular basic local alignment search tool (BLAST), used for sequence similarity searching, is often treated as a "black box" tool that will work unfailingly regardless of the input and underlying assumptions. To effectively use BLAST and especially to understand the results it can return, the user needs to understand principles of evolutionary relatedness and distance as summarized in the Dayhoff, or point accepted mutation (PAM), matrices (see Chapter 5). Users who understand the underlying heuristics used to speed up the execution and the effects of modifying window sizes and thresholds on the usefulness of the results gain insights into the results returned as well as power, or robustness, in manipulating the input data correctly. And users with a good understanding of statistics can have better confidence in their results. Therefore, we emphasize that bioinformaticists can only benefit from understanding principles across the entire spectrum of both the biological and computer sciences.

Bioinformatics has come into existence as part of our curiosity to understand how a biological organism functions. For millennia, humans have been trying to understand what life is. From Aristotle to Francis Crick and James Watson, some of the greatest minds have tried to answer this question. Yet, we still do not have a definitive answer. The next section of this chapter will discuss how an entire area of science has developed around attempts to define life and identify its components—the field of biology.

## 1.3  WHAT DEFINES LIFE?

Because of the nature of the question and the great diversity of life, one aspect of biology has been largely focused on collecting and describing all the instances of life available for study. This has led some, Ernest Rutherford in particular, to dismiss the biological sciences as mere "stamp collecting." But stamp collecting can be a valuable activity in this context because it provides the basis for making broad generalizations. For example, we can make general statements about groups of stamps: some have artwork, some are miniaturized photographs, some are commemorative, and others are decorative, and so on. From these, we might go on to a theory of stamp "evolution" in which we notice that the cost of stamps increases over time, or that stamps become more varied in color and tone across geographical regions. The same approaches are used in biology to draw long-range inferences about groups of organisms and the changes they undergo across time and space.

If we ask the question "what is life?" in a different way, we can move past merely descriptive discussions of what life could be. Let's ask the question this way: What defines life?

The answer here is a little bit easier to find. We can say that there are three features which are common to all living systems: they are capable of **self-reproduction;** they are **complex systems;** and as a result, they are **robust.** Self-reproduction is relatively easy to define; it is the property of being able to create a new copy of oneself. This, of course, does not mean an exact replica of oneself, and it is, in fact, the variation between parent and offspring that gives rise to diversity and drives the changes across time and space known as **evolution.** This aspect of life is what best separates it from, say, computers and the common cold virus. Neither of these can replicate themselves in the absence of direct assistance from a large cohort of other, possibly living, systems.

It is not difficult to see that most living systems are complex. So, for that matter, is your desktop or laptop computer. Your computer is made up of millions of logic circuits and transistors that together create a complex network capable of sophisticated processing and computation. Similarly, whether you consider a bacterium in your stomach or the human brain, each is a complex system capable of receiving and processing information. This occurs as a result of many small parts (whether silicon chips or cells) coordinating their responses and communicating through **complex networks** to transfer information and responses across time and space. Unlike computers, which are composed of large numbers of relatively simple and similar parts, biological systems have large numbers of diverse elements, many of which can function in more than one way.

**Robustness** is a more loosely defined concept. When we say that a system is robust, we mean that it is able to tolerate fluctuations in the environment or amongst its subcomponents [1]. For example, database management systems are designed to be robust to the demands of multiple users accessing and writing information to the database roughly simultaneously. To take a similar example from biology, human beings are able to maintain body temperatures at about 98.6° F regardless of the outside temperature. A high degree of interaction with the environment is one of the hallmarks that distinguish living systems from most physical systems. Living organisms require interaction with the environment for the most basic necessities of life on the one hand and must protect themselves from harmful environmental influences on the other. Consider the sun, one of the most important environmental factors. For humans, exposure to sunlight is essential for vitamin D production yet can cause adverse changes in the skin.

Just because a system is robust does not mean that it cannot fail. In our example, humans can only maintain a normal body temperature within a particular range of outside temperatures; if it gets too hot or too cold, then the system fails. Similarly, databases can fail if there is a massive power outage or a catastrophic incident that damages the storage system directly. However, in each of these examples, the system fails only when something goes dramatically wrong. These systems are able to maintain a stable state most of the time. In other words, robust systems can account for and manage anticipated perturbation events but are sensitive to unanticipated and potentially catastrophic failures [2].

Computer systems, such as database management systems, are designed to be robust. Living systems are continually "reengineered" by evolutionary processes. In some ways, this is the key definition of living systems: they have evolved to manage common, "anticipatable" disasters through complex networks designed to adjust for such fluctuations. Yet the complexity required to manage these potential disasters leaves them open to rare, albeit dramatic, failures [5, 2]. Take the case of the dinosaurs. For nearly 300 million years, they dominated the planet. And then, a single, catastrophic event—the collision of an asteroid—ended their existence. No matter how robust a system you build, chances are that a single, extremely low-probability event can completely destroy it. But this leaves the way open for a new solution to the problem: in the case of the dinosaurs, their extinction created room for mammals to evolve. Now we humans dominate the planet. There is no guarantee, however, that we will always remain at the top. New, more robust organisms might be in the making, just waiting for a chance to take over as the dominant mode of life.

So how do systems manifest complexity and robustness? The answer is that many systems are **modular** in nature. A **module** is a self-contained unit that can be modified or evolved, can retain integrity when removed from the larger system, and that has a clear protocol or method for interfacing with other modules [2, 4]. In the next section we will see how living organisms can be viewed as a collection of interconnected modules, and how a network of these modules can result in a complex and robust living organism.

## 1.4  A SYSTEMS APPROACH TO BIOLOGY

*So I went to the librarian in the zoology section and asked her if she could find me a "map of the cat." "A map of the cat, sir?" she asked horrified. "You mean a zoological chart!" From then on there were rumors about a dumb biology student who was looking for "a map of the cat."*
—Richard P. Feynman, *Surely You're Joking Mr. Feynman!*

Living systems utilize networks of interconnected modules to manifest complexity and robustness. As an analogy, you can think of a computer as being one module in the large network of such modules that are the Internet. Computers "interact" with one another through the hypertext transfer protocol (http) or through other, clearly defined, well-ordered protocols. The Internet is an expansive series of such interconnected modules, and the resulting network is an information transfer system that is both vast in size and complex in terms of its connections and responses to changes.

The Internet is a robust system in that it can tolerate perturbations within the network. Each computer connected to it is a node, and when a node fails, routers are able to find other ways to transfer the information around that failed node. In order to disrupt the entire system, a catastrophic event is needed. For example, a large swath of nodes and routers are suddenly disabled and no re-routing mechanism can be identified. It is hard to imagine a scenario in which so many routers and nodes would be disrupted that the entire Internet would fail. So, by most standards, the Internet is a robust system.

It is even, to some extent, self-replicating in that it grows and expands in complexity through the addition of new nodes, protocols, and modules. As a result the Internet is "evolving" across time and space. From an external perspective, the Internet is constantly changing and adapting to various pressures and demands, some of which are easy to identify and others more mysterious.

If you were an alien from Mars faced with the challenge of figuring out how the Internet works, where would you start? You might start by trying to document all the components of the network and account for the ways in which each component interacted with other components. Essentially, what you would be doing is building a "map" of the Internet. This is exactly the approach used in the Internet mapping project started at Bell Labs in the summer of 1998. The mapping consists of frequent probes to registered Internet entities. From these data a tree can be built that shows the paths to most of the nodes on the Internet. An example of such a map is shown in Figure 1.6.

So, where is the map of the cat or the dog or even of a single cell? It is still a work in progress. Most of twentieth century biology has been focused on trying to understand biological phenomena such as development and disease by studying the behavior of, and more recently by identifying, the underlying molecules. We have made tremendous progress and have generated huge volumes of data that remain to be translated into information. Figure 1.7 shows some of the pathways within an eukaryotic cell such as ours.

A major challenge facing scientists today is to try and assemble the map of the cellular intra- and internets: the networks that pass information around and between cells. This is the challenge that you will begin exploring through this text as we traverse the hierarchy of biological data and examine the computational approaches to mining the data. The cellular internet is at least as, if not more, complex than the Internet, and it has had millions of years of tinkering (evolution) to develop and optimize its connections. The challenge now is essentially to reverse-engineer this network.

So where are the modules in this biological network? In the context of our bodies, a cell might be considered as a module because groups of cells create tissues and organs that result in a human body. But we can zoom into the cell itself, and it is in here that we find the most astonishing array of modules, networks, and sophisticated mechanisms for communicating across modules. This is also the frontier of a new field called **systems biology,** which today attempts to model

**FIGURE 1.6**   Internet map circa 1998. A more recent version of an internet map is available at numerous locations, including http://chrisharrison.net/projects/InternetMap/ (© CAIDA / Photo Researchers, Inc.)

the modules within and across cells and to develop a computational replica of these modules so they can be studied in depth.

What kind of modules would we expect to find in cells? Since self-reproduction is a crucial aspect of all living organisms, we might expect that every cell contains a **replication module.** And indeed, all cells do have such a module. It is based on the information-carrying molecule in cells, known as **DNA (deoxyribonucleic acid).** DNA on its own can't replicate so there is an associated set of machines (biologists call these proteins) that are part of a specific network. The replication module in cells includes DNA, these proteins and all the other parts required to make a copy of DNA.

We could also think of cells as miniscule computer chips. That is, at every point, they are receiving input, making decisions as a result of this input, and generating output (in biology, this is known as responding to a signal, [4]). In cells, the most common output (response) is to make a machine (protein). Input from outside the cell is received at the surface of the cell and then transmitted to the DNA by signaling modules. Thousands of such modules occur in the cell, and all their signals converge at the DNA. This is where the decisions are made, usually

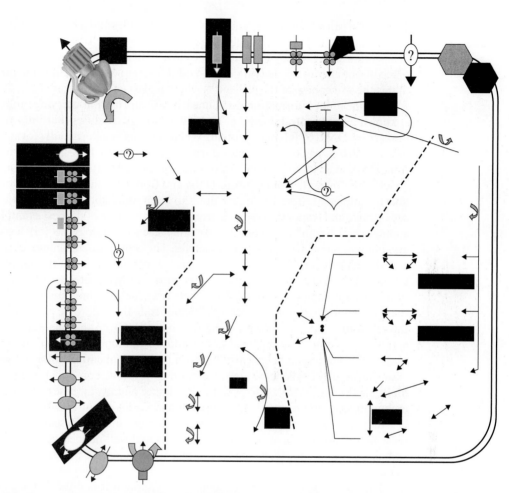

**FIGURE 1.7**    Schematic pathways within an eukaryotic cell, as visualized by the VisANT software package. The software package is described in Hu, Z., Mellor, J., Wu, J. and DeLisi, C. (2005) "VisANT: data-integrating visual framework for biological networks and modules," Nucl. Acids Res. 33: W352–W357. The data for this image was drawn from MouseNet v.1.1 (Kim, Wan K., Krumpelman, Chase, and Marcotte, Edward M. (under review)). "Inferring mouse gene functions from genomic-scale data using a combined functional network/ classification strategy," Genome Biology.
(Credit: Courtesy of Zhenjun Hu.)

as a result of combined inputs on the DNA. When a "decision" has been made, the DNA directs the generation of a short piece of information contained in a molecule known as **RNA (ribonucleic acid),** through a process of **transcription.** The information in DNA is essentially "transcribed" into another form—the RNA molecule. The information in the RNA will direct the creation of a protein through a "protein generation" module in a process known as **translation.** Rather than being simply an information-carrying molecule, the resulting protein has its own unique function and, thus, the information in RNA has been "translated."

The protein can then interact with many other molecules and modules to influence the behavior of the cell or its neighbors. The output of cells is a change in their behavior, or the way they respond to the environment. Although today we focus much of our energy on studying DNA and RNA sequence data, it is the protein that is the workhorse of the cell and is what "makes us what we are."

The idea that information flows linearly via information-carrying molecules is known as the **central dogma of molecular biology.** It states that information flows from DNA to RNA to protein. When this idea was originally formulated in the 1950s, it was thought that information could only flow in one direction: from DNA to RNA to protein. We've since discovered that information can flow "backwards" as well, from RNA to DNA and from protein to RNA, and we can take advantage of these alternative flows to learn more about the ways in which cells receive and respond to their environment. This is one of the best examples of an important "truth" in biology. Unlike other sciences, biology has very few clear and unambiguous never-violated principles. The central dogma comes close.

Once a protein is created, the information content inherent in that protein is transferred when the protein *interacts* with another protein. These interactions create complex networks. These networks include the signaling modules that allow information to be received from outside the cell, to be passed around the cell, and to be transferred to neighboring cells. Given that the web of interactions is so complex and involves thousands or millions of interactions among diverse, multifunctional elements, the effort to model an entire biological system is an enormously challenging task. The good news is that, somewhat surprisingly, molecular biologists have discovered a high degree of unity in these modules, even among diverse organisms. That is, we can learn a lot about how humans work by studying fruit flies, worms, or even simpler organisms. Research efforts in these model organisms, which have fewer cells and well-defined genetic compositions, contribute greatly to the task of piecing together the puzzle of molecular interactions.

This also is where computers come in. Although it is difficult for a single person to track these interactions across time or space, computers can be used to model what might happen when thousands of proteins interact. In order to model a biological system, however, we need to know something about each component of the system as well as how they interact with one another. In Figure 1.8 we summarize some of the ways in which biologists learn about the components of a biological module and some of the ways in which computer scientists model these modules. As you'll see, the more complex the system gets (e.g., tissues or organs), the less we know about them from either a biological or computational standpoint. The future challenges for both computer scientists and biologists lie in these areas.

What is at stake? Just as computer systems can be engineered to improve their performance, biologists are attempting to engineer molecular networks, cells, tissues, and even organs in order to improve the quality of life. Take for example, a cancer cell, which divides uncontrollably and has developed mechanisms to escape cell death and so keeps on dividing even under adverse environmental conditions (robustness is not always a good thing). An understanding of the

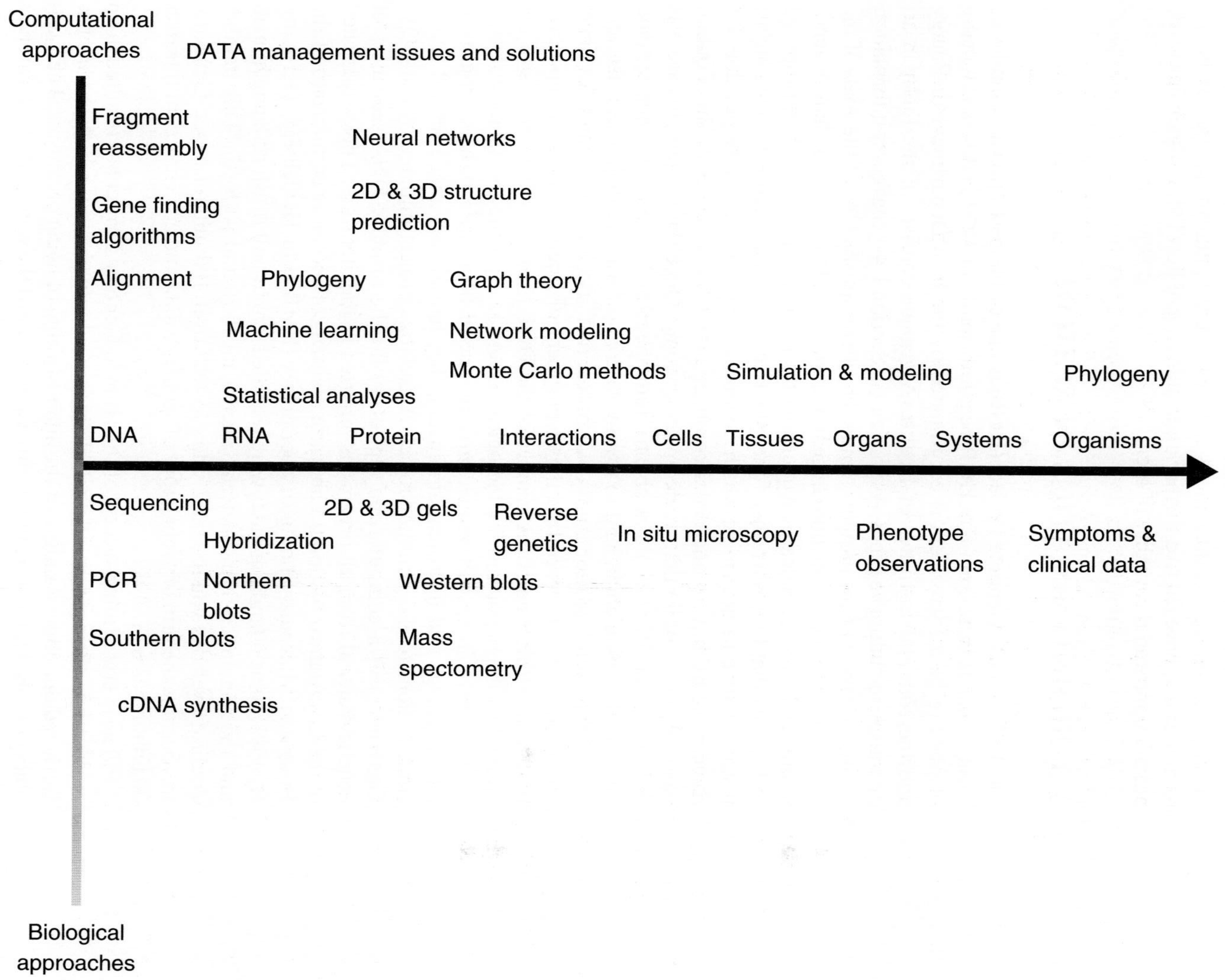

**FIGURE 1.8** Computational and biological approaches to modeling organisms.

15

modules that control cell division and cell death opens a window for pharmaceutical intervention that will lead scientists to develop new treatments and cures. In the next section we will take a look at some of the significant projects in bioinformatics that have led to a further understanding of how living organisms work or have improved the quality of life.

## 1.5  BIOINFORMATICS IN ACTION

The U.S. Human Genome Project (HGP) is one of the best known examples of bioinformatics in action. The HGP began formally in 1990 and was originally planned to be a 13-year effort coordinated by the U.S. Department of Energy and the National Institutes of Health. A **genome** consists of the DNA in an organism, including its genes. As you read in Section 1.4, genes carry information for making most of the proteins required by an organism. One of the goals of the HGP was to sequence the human genome, which could be used to identify genes in human DNA. The idea of sequencing the human genome was first proposed in 1985. At that time portions of the human genome were mapped, which meant it was possible to determine which portion of the genome was responsible for some proteins, but no one had a complete list of the sequence of the 3 billion bases (A, G, C, or T) that made up the genome. Once the human genome was sequenced, scientists would be able to study the effect of DNA variations among individuals, which could lead to revolutionary new ways to diagnose, treat, and someday prevent the thousands of disorders that affect human beings. You may find it interesting to learn that the Department of Energy played an important role in the HGP. One of the charges of the DOE is to study the residues of the atomic bomb project and the biological effects of exposure to radiation. Using their expertise in engineering technology derived from their massive projects in atomic energy and its potential dangers, they had already made several major contributions to the genome project. A previous project initiated by the DOE, GenBank, was a computerized repository for the primary DNA sequences of genetic material from all organisms reported in the literature. This was located at the Los Alamos National Laboratory with a collaborating counterpart at the European Molecular Biology Laboratories (EMBL) in Heidelberg, Germany. By 1991, some 60 million bases were recorded, about half of which being human and the remainder from bacteria, mice, fruit flies, and so forth. This number doubled over the subsequent 2 years to well over 100 million bases. GenBank has become the primary repository of sequence data and currently contains over 30 billion bases.

The overwhelming success of the Human Genome Project has resulted in an explosion in the amount of available biological information, which in turn has furthered our understanding of the inner working of living organisms. The availability of this information has dramatically changed the way in which researchers have been able to do their work. For example, in pharmaceutical research the traditional pipeline for drug development is a long and expensive one, usually involving the screening of a large number of potential compounds. Now new strategies in the process have emerged from our increased understanding of molecular biology and the rapidly growing data on gene sequence, predicted proteins, and their structures. As opposed to the traditional screening strategies, rational drug design is a more focused, high-tech, knowledge-based approach. The basic idea is that if you know exactly which gene and protein is responsible for a disease, you can custom-make a drug to combat it. Rational drug design uses the tools of bioinformatics to identify and validate genes and proteins as potential drug targets. The pharmaceutical industry has embraced genomics as a source of drug targeting and recognizes that bioinformatics is crucial for validating these potential drug targets and for determining which ones are the most suitable for entering the development pipeline. How successful will this be? Time will tell, but the tremendous potential for success of a rational approach to drug design is exemplified by the anticancer drugs imatinib mesylate (Gleevec) and trastuzumab (Herceptin), and the protease inhibitors that are part of the drug cocktail given to treat individuals infected with HIV. Gleevec, a revolutionary drug, developed by Novartis Pharmaceuticals and pioneered by Dr. Brian Druker is highly effective in managing chronic myelogenous leukemia (CML) and has few side effects. It specifically targets and inhibits a tyrosine kinase, an enzyme that functions incorrectly in cancer cells. Although the identification of the enzyme inhibitor and Gleevec's development relied on more than 10 years of research in the "wet lab" and clinic, the success of the targeted approach has created a huge amount of excitement about enzyme inhibitors specifically and about the rational approach, in general.

## 1.5.1  Deciphering a Killer: HIV and Bioinformatics

The human immunodeficiency virus (HIV) is the causative agent of AIDS (acquired immunodeficiency syndrome) and has brought tragedy to millions of lives. Figuring out the biology of HIV and the secrets of its genome have helped us develop drugs to fight this deadly agent, but it remains the source of a global humanitarian and medical crisis. Throughout the book we will examine some of HIV's biological complexity and how bioinformatics has helped us decipher some of its mysteries.

In Chapter 2 we include a description of the biology of HIV. We highlight the many unusual features of HIV: its RNA genome, its use of reverse transcriptase, its ability to integrate into the host genome, and its high mutability. Mutability allows HIV to evade the host immune system. In Chapter 3 we will learn about some of the laboratory techniques that scientists use to study HIV and its effects on human cells.

In Chapter 4 we will discuss how retroviruses like HIV are believed to be the source of many of the repeat regions in the human genome and transposable elements in many genomes. Although HIV itself has a small genome that was not difficult to sequence and reassemble, the integration of retroviruses into genomes bedevils the reassembly process in host genomes.

HIV and its retrovirus compatriots also impinge on the process of sequence alignment discussed in Chapter 5. Because of their high mutability, different strains of HIV will have slightly different sequences. By subjecting those strains to multiple alignment, researchers have obtained useful and valuable insights into where and how HIV originated. The origins of HIV are further explored in Chapter 6, where we look at methods for determining the evolutionary history of HIV. We also consider how mutations occur over time in HIV and use this to build a model of mutation rates.

In Chapter 7, we use HIV as an example of how to identify signals in host genomes, including our own. HIV integrates itself at specific points within the host genome, and we will explore the signals that might allow it to select a given point within the genome as appropriate for integration. This is an example of how HIV interacts with its host, and these interactions are central to its ability to infect and spread in a population.

Similarly, in Chapter 8, we consider how HIV influences the gene expression patterns of a host cell. Because it interferes with host cell protein synthesis, HIV has a profound effect on gene expression within host cells. Microarray and other recent technology can track changes in host cell gene expression as a consequence of HIV infection.

The study of HIV underlies many of the issues raised in the projects detailed in Chapter 9. In Section 9.2, we consider the secondary structures of RNAs, including some generated by HIV. These secondary structures are crucial for the transport of the HIV genome within the cell, and recent work in predicting the structures of these RNAs has yielded some insights into the biology of HIV. In Rational Drug Design through Protein Structure and Function Prediction (Section 9.3), we look at how a computational prediction of the structure of an HIV protein, the HIV protease, helped to develop a new class of drugs—the protease inhibitors.

Our hope is that learning about HIV will help you appreciate the many ways in which bioinformatics can elucidate the mysteries behind a complex biological system. As we discuss different aspects of HIV biology, you will see that both computational and experimental methods were used. The study of HIV exemplifies the kind of results that can arise when a team of interdisciplinary scientists bring their skills to bear on a specific problem.

## 1.6 THE ROAD AHEAD

As we have seen, a successful bioinformatics team is a synergistic combination of researchers from multiple disciplines who seek insight into the biological processes at work in a living organism. Although it is vital that all the members of a bioinformatics team work together, it is possible to discern two major focus areas within bioinformatics. The more established of these two areas concentrates on the biological processes at work within an organism and the use of existing computational tools to analyze and interpret these data. The second area focuses on the development of new computing approaches to interpret, manage, and distribute collections of biological data. The first focus area is biologically motivated and emphasizes collecting information on the state of an organism. The second studies computing techniques for converting biological data into biological information. Biologists and chemists are primarily interested in the first focus area, and computer scientists, information technologists, physicists, and mathematicians are drawn to the second.

In this book we will follow a "roadmap to systems biology," taking you on a journey of discovery from data to information, which is moving us ever closer to understanding biological problems. You will learn how biological laboratory science and computational sciences synergistically have enabled a data-driven, bottom-up approach to extracting information from the data at increasing levels of complexity. In many cases, computational strategies have greatly accelerated the extraction of information from the data. Just as important, you will see how effective computational approaches rely on input from the scientific knowledge base that has been generated from decades of ongoing biological research.

This book is written for individuals who have already had some training in the computational sciences. Specifically we assume that you have mastered basic programming skills and have already encountered basic algorithms and data structures before starting to read this book. We do not expect that you will have more than a passing familiarity with biological concepts; these will be developed in the course of presenting computational concepts. In the chapters that follow we will introduce both the computational issues, and the biological principals they rely on, in tandem. The chapters in this book can be divided into three broad categories: what we term the "kernel" (Chapters 1–3), the "classical" (Chapters 4 and 5), and the "avant-garde" (Chapters 6–9) of bioinformatics.

The first section will cover the requisite background needed by any bioinformaticist. The kernel will develop concepts from molecular biology, methodologies such as sequencing technology, and other aspects of biology relevant to bioinformatics. In addition, we will review computing concepts and techniques from mathematics and statistics. A discussion of database design and use will be part of this section as well, although databases and their uses, development, and implementation will be addressed in other chapters as appropriate.

From the kernel you will proceed through the classical bioinformatics section. This section covers many of the most frequently used bioinformatics tools. We will focus primarily on the algorithms that define these tools. A secondary emphasis will be on the biological justifications that motivated the design and development of the algorithms. Chapters in this section will devote attention to algorithms involved in fragment reassembly, pattern matching, and dynamic programming. Many of these methods focus on sequence analysis, an area within bioinformatics that has seen the greatest pace of development in the past decade.

In the third section of the text, we will extend the analysis to more recent developments. Some of the topics we cover within the avant-garde bioinformatics section include phylogenetics and tree building (Chapter 6), gene finding (Chapter 7), clustering of gene expression patterns, and development of gene networks (Chapter 8). More advanced topics, such as protein structure modeling and the modeling of cells, tissues, and organs will also be touched on (Chapter 9). These represent the "future" of bioinformatics and do not yet have formal algorithmic solutions—the area where the most active research will develop in the years ahead.

When you finish reading this book, you will be conversant with key concepts in the biological sciences and knowledgeable about current bioinformatics tools and approaches. Our purpose is not to train you to use those tools. Rather, you will be able to identify and understand the algorithms that underlie existing bioinformatics tools and be able to evaluate algorithms and their implementation, within the context of the relevant biological phenomena.

## SUMMARY

Bioinformatics is a new field in which several disciplines work together to manage, store, and analyze the data being produced in laboratories around the world. Although the process being used to advance our understanding of living organisms is similar to what Gregor Mendel used in the 1800s, the scale and scope of what is being done today is dramatically different.

For this new discipline to be successful all members of a bioinformatics team must have a basic knowledge of the fundamental concepts of the disciplines represented by the team and an understanding and appreciation of what each discipline brings to the project. We have seen that not only is it important for the biologist to understand computer science, it is equally important for the computer scientist to understand the basic biological process at work within a living organism.

Although bioinformatics is a relatively new discipline, after four decades two focus areas of the discipline have emerged. Biologists and chemists focus on the biological and chemical processes at work in an organism and concentrate on improving the ability to collect information on the state of an organism. Computer scientists, information technologists, and mathematicians working in a second focus area concentrate on the development of computing techniques that convert biological data into biological information. Working together scientists in both of these focus areas are improving the understanding of the biological processes at work within an organism.

This text will focus on the computing side of bioinformatics, but it will also introduce basic biological principles as needed. In the next chapter you will learn about the central dogma of molecular biology and the basic molecular structure of DNA and RNA. You will also obtain a basic knowledge of the science of evolution and a general understanding of the concepts related to biological information storage, a general overview of gene regulation, alleles, SNPs, and genome structure.

## KEY TERMS

bioinformatics (1.1)
theoretical (1.2)
development (1.2)
application (1.2)
user (1.2)
application scientist (1.2)
self-reproduction (1.3)
complex system (1.3)

robust (1.3)
evolution (1.3)
complex networks (1.3)
robustness (1.3)
modular (1.3)
module (1.3)
systems biology (1.4)
replication module (1.4)

DNA (deoxyribonucleic acid) (1.4)
RNA (ribonucleic acid) (1.4)
transcription (1.4)
translation (1.4)
central dogma of molecular
    biology (1.4)
genome (1.5)

# BIBLIOGRAPHY

1. J. M. Carlson and John Doyle. Complexity and robustness. *Proc. Natl. Acad. Sci. USA,* 99:2538–2545, 2002.

2. Marie E. Csete and John C. Doyle. Reverse engineering of biological complexity. *Science,* 295(5560):1664–1669, 2002.

3. M. O. Dayhoff. *Atlas of Protein Sequence and Structure,* vol. 5, supplement 3. National Biomedical Research Foundation, 1978.

4. H. L. Hartwell, J. J. Hopfield, S. Leibler, and A. W. Murray. From molecular to modular cell biology. *Nature,* 402(SUPP):C47–C52, 1999.

5. H. Kitano. Systems biology: a brief overview. *Science,* 295:1662–1664, 2002.

# 2

# Biological Basics

*"The difference [between biology and physics] is one of complexity of design. Biology is the study of complicated things that give the appearance of having been designed for a purpose . . . Man-made artefacts like computers and cars . . . are [also] complicated and obviously designed for a purpose . . . They [can be] treated as biological objects."*

—Richard Dawkins, *The Blind Watchmaker*

## 2.1 THE BLIND ENGINEER

When humans set out to build something, whether it is a skyscraper or a computer, we start by laying out a set of plans. These **blueprints** have several levels of detail from the wiring and organization of each constituent part up to the final appearance of the product. Once the plans are laid out, each part is designed and built by a team of engineers and specialists. These people are not necessarily concerned with the final product; what they do best is create one little part of the larger whole. When that larger whole is finally assembled, it can appear much greater than the sum of its parts. A good example would be the supercomputer, Deep Blue, which has taken on mythic qualities since it beat the reigning world chess champion in a rematch in 1997. (Deep Blue lost the first confrontation with Gary Kasparov in 1996 and underwent many upgrades.)

In Chapter 1, we talked about how living systems are defined by this kind of complexity, in which the whole seems to be much more than the sum of the parts. In biological systems, the engineers, architects, and design consultants are replaced by one process: **evolution.** Whereas human engineers start with a purpose and design a machine to support that purpose, evolution proceeds with existing materials with the long-term aim of continued survival. If there is a purpose to evolutionary processes, then it is simply to propagate life in some form across time and space.

Success in evolution is defined by the long-term survival of a **species** or *group* of organisms. The important point here is that evolution does not usually operate on the level of the individual organism, but rather over long periods of time on groups of organisms that form a species. Of course, for a species to survive, individual organisms are vital. Each individual organism represents a combination of features that help it survive in a particular environment. These features are passed from generation to generation across many organisms.

In each generation, some organisms will be better adapted to their environment, and they will reproduce faster than their less-adapted peers. Over time, the progeny from the better adapted organisms will begin to dominate the population. They will continue to reproduce faster than their less-adapted peers, and eventually the whole population may exhibit those adaptations that are best for a particular environment. This is not to say that the population will remain static; environments do change, and generally those organisms that are flexible enough to change with their environment will succeed over time.

## 2.1.1  The Case of the Peppered Moth

A good example of this is a species of moth common in England, *Biston betularia*. Prior to the Industrial Revolution, the majority of moths had white wings with small black dots. The peppered moth, as these moths were called, could hide against the bark of the many light-colored trees that are common in England. As a result, they were not easily picked out by birds, their main predators.

Occasionally, a peppered moth might have a variant pattern of entirely black wings. These moths were easily picked out by birds and often eaten before they had a chance to reproduce. We would say that the all-black wing feature was a poor adaptation for the preindustrial environment of England.

Things changed dramatically for these moths when the Industrial Revolution began spewing coal dust into the air. Now many trees were covered in soot, and those moths with white wings were distinctive against the blackened bark of trees. As a result, these moths were easily spotted and picked off by birds. In contrast, the occasional moth with black wings was perfectly camouflaged and avoided its predators. Over time, the majority of moths became black-winged because this was an advantageous adaptation.

Recently, scientists have observed a decline in the numbers of black-winged moths and a resurgence of white-winged moths. Scientists speculate that the enforcement of clean air standards in the last half century has once again made it advantageous to have white wings rather than black wings [9].

So you can see how a feature that is advantageous in certain conditions can suddenly become deleterious and vice versa.[1] Although individual organisms cannot change their particular set of features, the species as a whole can adapt to these changes and survive. So when we say that evolution operates on species

---

[1] Recently debate has arisen about this particular example because there is some evidence that the shift in coloring of the moths cannot be sufficiently explained just by changes in air pollution. For more on why this might be an oversimplified example, consult Michael Majerus' book *Melanism: Evolution in Action*.

and not on organisms, we mean that it can drive the adaptations of the species as whole, but it cannot make a huge difference at the level of the individual organism.

## 2.1.2  How Evolution Works

So how does evolution operate? Two processes drive evolution in species: mutation and natural selection. **Mutation** is the tendency for organisms to change just a little bit over time. This is the raw material for evolution. In the case of the peppered moth, a mutation or set of mutations led to the black-wing feature that was so advantageous during the polluted years prior to clean air laws.

How does evolution use these mutations? Through a process known as **natural selection.** This was first described in 1859 by Charles Darwin in his seminal text, *On the Origin of Species.* What Darwin noticed is that tiny differences between individuals can be magnified over time if a particular difference helps one individual adapt better to an environment than another of its counterparts. We would say that the black-wing feature of peppered moths was **selected** for during the years when pollution was high. The white-wing feature is now being selected for because of the cleaner air.

You might ask, "Who or what is doing the selecting here?" The answer is "It depends." In the case of the peppered moth, the selection comes from the predators: the birds. The black- or white-wing feature is protective under certain conditions because it allows the moths to hide from their natural predators. So, in a sense, the birds are doing the selecting. The same sort of idea applies to many species: Adaptations that make an organism weaker or less able to adapt will make these organisms prime targets for predation. So over time the species as a whole becomes better adapted and better able to avoid its predators. Of course, the predators are evolving too, so the equilibrium between prey and predators is constantly shifting.

Juxtaposed with this are the changes to the environment. No environment is stable over long periods of time. On a geological scale, environments are always changing: deserts become grasslands that become forests, oceans rise or fall, mountains are raised up and then eroded. All these changes put pressure on species: they must adapt to the changes or face extinction. Sometimes, an environment suddenly becomes isolated. For example, a species spread out across a large area might be split in two by floods or volcanic activity. When these sort of dramatic changes occur, the two populations may begin to evolve separately. That is, they begin to adapt to their local environments. Eventually, they may evolve in such different ways that they no longer resemble each other. This is the process of **speciation,** or the process of producing new species.

For example, cows and whales actually share an unexpectedly recent common ancestor. Many millions of years ago, that common ancestor diverged into two distinct populations: one adapted to the land, the other to the sea. The result today is two groups of animals that appear to be very different from each other. Yet, these species share a great deal of the same information and are closely related biologically.

## 2.1.3  Evolution's Palette

What do we mean when we say that cows and whales are related? What we are actually talking about are the sets of heritable information that each organism within the species has. In the case of cows and whales, they share much of the same heritable information. In biology, units of heritable information are called **genes.** The mutations that evolution uses to select organisms occur within genes. Because genes are inherited from one generation to the next, the mutations in the genes are also passed across generations. Adaptations are the result of sets of mutations within genes that allow organisms to survive in their particular environment. Think of the peppered moths. The coloring of their wings is driven by specific genes, and mutations in those genes cause the coloring to change.

Although changes in genes are necessary to make visible changes to an organism's appearance, not all changes at the gene level lead to visible changes. Changes can occur on two levels, and both levels are utilized by evolution. Small changes in the content of information are achieved by changing the letter sequences that make up genes. These changes are known as **genotypic** changes. Big changes in the appearance of an organism, such as flippers on a whale as it evolves away from its cow ancestor, are known as **phenotypic** changes.

We usually think of evolution as occurring in a slow, steady manner across millions of years. This is because we look at phenotypic changes, which tend to take a long time to appear. However, at the genotypic level, changes occur all the time. Each generation will have slight mutations in its genes, and not all of these will lead immediately to a change in phenotype. For example, you and your siblings probably share many phenotypic features such as the color of your eyes and hair with your parents. Yet, at the genotypic level, differences between you and your parents and even your siblings also exist. Some of these were the result of mutations, but many are the result of a "shuffling" of genetic information at your conception. Every one of your cells contains information from each of your parents, but some of the parts were mixed and matched when you were conceived. As a result, you are genetically unique, even though you share many genetic similarities with your parents. The combination of mutations and genetic variation in each generation might eventually lead to dramatic phenotypic changes, but probably not for another few millenia.

This is a key feature of evolutionary processes: on the one hand, mutations accumulate slowly at the genotypic level. On the other hand, the dramatic phenotypic changes are seen every now and then. Evolution is what is known in physics as a **stochastic process.** That is, small, random changes can be made through a process such as mutation until a large and dramatic change occurs. At each point, **selection pressure** is exerted so that some features are selected for or against. The easiest examples of selection to understand are phenotypic changes such as the coloring of peppered moths, but some pressures select for or against certain genotypic changes that do not have obvious phenotypic effects. We will return to this in later chapters.

## 2.2 COMPUTE MACHINE PAR EXCELLENCE

*"The uniformity of earth's life, more astonishing than its diversity, is accountable by the high probability that we derived, originally, from some single cell, fertilized in a bolt of lightning as the earth cooled."*

— Lewis Thomas, *The Lives of a Cell*

Leaps of evolution can be seen all across the biological spectrum. One of the most striking is the apparently sudden switch from single-celled organisms like bacteria to multicellular ones including humans. We do not fully know why single-celled organisms suddenly banded together to form multicellular ones. In other words, we do not yet understand all the pressures that might have favored selection for multicellular organisms. What we do know is that today, living organisms come in essentially two flavors: single-celled or multicelled.

The separation of organisms into these two categories also roughly follows a division of complexity: single-celled organisms are much less complex than multicelled ones. This does not mean that bacteria are by any means elementary systems: we still do not understand much of how bacteria function. Figure 2.1 shows a subset of all organisms that we know about today.

Of the three domains of life shown in Figure 2.1, the bacteria and archaea can be grouped together into a cluster called **prokaryotes.** The remainder are members of a separate cluster called **eukaryotes.** Traditionally, biologists differentiate between groups of organisms based on the complexity of their cells.

### 2.2.1 Cellular Organization and Complexity

The distinction between prokaryotes and eukaryotes lies in how their cells are organized. Eukaryote cells are divided into lots of little compartments, much

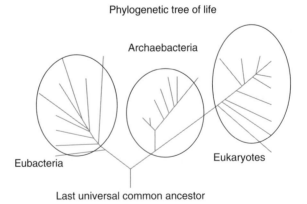

Phylogenetic tree of life

Archaebacteria

Eubacteria

Eukaryotes

Last universal common ancestor

**FIGURE 2.1**    The tree of life is a representation of how we think organisms are related to one another. It presupposes a universal common ancestor, a single organism from which every living species has evolved. That is shown at the center of the tree. Since that original ancestor, life has evolved into three main domains: eubacteria, archaebacteria, and eukaryotes.

like modern day computers with multiple hardware bays. Each compartment is called an **organelle,** or "little organ." Each organelle has a specific function, and eukaryotic cells have specialized mechanisms for transporting substances between their organelles as needed.

Every multicellular organism is made up of eukaryotic cells. All of our cells are eukaryotic, as are the cells that make up insects, animals, and plants. Many single-celled eukaryotes are deadly parasites, such as the organism that causes malaria (*Plasmodium falciparum*). Many other single-celled eukaryotes are benign. If you have ever looked at pond scum under a microscope, much of what you see are single-celled eukaryotes, such as algae, dinoflagellates, *Paramecium* and other species. A sampling of single-celled eukaryotes, also known as *protozoa*, is shown in Figure 2.2. You may already know of some single-celled eukaryotes: yeast, for example, is used in baking and in the making of beer.

In contrast to eukaryotes, prokaryotes have just one "hardware bay": all the contents of the cell are jumbled up in a single compartment. Prokaryotes have no organelles. Rather, the organization of the prokaryotic cell occurs through **complexes** or clusters of substances. Prokaryotes include organisms like the bacteria in your gut and the myriad disease-causing bacteria. The archaeabacteria are also prokaryotes, although many of them have highly unusual biology that is not seen in any other organisms.

All cells, whether prokaryote or eukaryote, share certain noteworthy features. You can think of each of these features as a component in a parts list. By the time you finish this section, you will have a preliminary understanding of the parts that make up cells and allow them to perform their functions.

Before we can start talking about cells, we need to review some basic chemistry specific to living systems. In this section, we will review the nature of atomic bonds, the basic atoms and molecules that contribute to life, and a little bit about how cells regulate the interactions between these molecules.

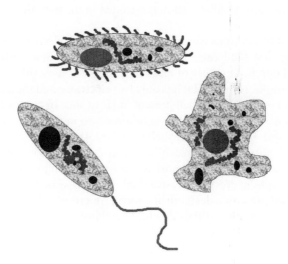

**FIGURE 2.2**   A sampling of some single-celled eukaryotes.

## The Discovery of Archaeabacteria

The archaebacteria, as they are sometimes known, are believed to be some of the most ancient organisms on the planet. However, they were discovered only 30 years ago. In 1977, two researchers, Carl Woese and George Fox, stumbled on a set of organisms that did not easily fall into either the bacteria or eukaryote divisions. These organisms appeared superficially to resemble bacteria: they lacked organelles, had circular DNA genomes, and had many of the same enzymes that bacteria do. However, they also showed certain features that had until then only been seen in eukaryotes.

The archaeabacteria are primarily characterized by the extreme environments in which they are found. Archaeabacteria live around the edges of sulfur vents many miles below the ocean surface; archaeabacteria "breathe" methane and die in the presence of oxygen; and they can survive extreme cold (up to $-20°C$) and heat (over $100°C$). The more exotic the places researchers have looked, the more archaeabacteria they have found. One reason we now think that archaeabacteria may be the most ancient forms of life is that they seem uniquely adapted for the very harsh conditions that we think must have existed when life first appeared on this planet [4].

A number of Websites provide additional information about these unusual organisms. One excellent place to start is:
http://www.ucmp.berkeley.edu/archaea/archaea.html

## 2.2.2  Chemistry and Life

All atoms are composed of protons and neutrons, which together form the nucleus of an atom. Surrounding this nucleus are electrons, which reside in a series of concentric orbits known as shells. The number of protons and electrons is exactly equal in all atoms, but different elements have different numbers of protons and electrons. This observation is encoded in the periodic table of elements (Figure 2.3).

Each shell of electrons can hold as many as eight electrons, with one exception: the very first shell can only hold two electrons. Since different types of atoms have different numbers of electrons, they will have different numbers of shells. For example, helium (He) has only two electrons, and these are both found in the first and only electron shell present in He atoms. In contrast, sodium (Na) has 11 electrons. These are divided as follows: two in the first shell, eight in the second shell, and one in the third shell (Figure 2.4).

In general, atoms like to have full electron shells as this is energetically favorable. In other words, atoms are most stable when they have two electrons in the first shell and eight in every successive shell. In the case of Na, the extra electron in the third shell presents a destabilizing force. As a result, Na atoms are willing to shed the eleventh electron if they can find a willing recipient. One such recipient might be chlorine (Cl), which has 17 electrons. How would these electrons be distributed across its shells (Figure 2.5)?

Legend: ■ Metal  ■ Semimetal  □ Nonmetal

Key: 6 / C / 12.01 — Atomic number / Symbol / Atomic weight

| 1 | 2 | 3 | 4 | 5 | 6 | 7 | 8 | 9 | 10 | 11 | 12 | 13 | 14 | 15 | 16 | 17 | 18 |
|---|---|---|---|---|---|---|---|---|----|----|----|----|----|----|----|----|----|
| 1 H 1.000 | | | | | | | | | | | | | | | | | 2 He 4.000 |
| 3 Li 6.941 | 4 Be 9.012 | | | | | | | | | | | 5 B 10.81 | 6 C 12.01 | 7 N 14.01 | 8 O 16.00 | 9 F 19.00 | 10 Ne 20.18 |
| 11 Na 22.99 | 12 Mg 24.31 | | | | | | | | | | | 13 Al 26.98 | 14 Si 28.09 | 15 P 30.97 | 16 S 32.07 | 17 Cl 35.45 | 18 Ar 39.95 |
| 19 K 39.10 | 20 Ca 40.00 | 21 Sc 44.96 | 22 Ti 47.55 | 23 V 50.94 | 24 Cr 52.00 | 25 Mn 54.94 | 26 Fe 55.85 | 27 Co 58.93 | 28 Ni 58.69 | 29 Cu 60.55 | 30 Zn 65.39 | 31 Ga 69.72 | 32 Ge 72.61 | 33 As 74.92 | 34 Se 78.96 | 35 Br 79.90 | 36 Kr 83.80 |
| 37 Rb 85.47 | 38 Sr 87.62 | 39 Sy 88.91 | 40 Zr 91.22 | 41 Nb 92.91 | 42 Mo 95.94 | 43 Tc 98.91 | 44 Ru 101.1 | 45 Rh 102.9 | 46 Pd 106.4 | 47 Ag 107.9 | 48 Cd 112.4 | 49 In 114.8 | 50 Sn 118.7 | 51 Sb 121.8 | 52 Te 127.6 | 53 I 126.9 | 54 Xe 131.3 |
| 55 Cs 132.9 | 56 Ba 137.3 | 71 Lu 175.0 | 72 Hf 178.5 | 73 Ta 180.9 | 74 W 183.8 | 75 Re 186.2 | 76 Os 190.2 | 77 Ir 192.2 | 78 Pt 195.1 | 79 Au 197.0 | 80 Hg 200.6 | 81 Tl 204.4 | 82 Pb 207.2 | 83 Bi 209.0 | 84 Po 209.0 | 85 At 210.0 | 86 Rn 222.0 |
| 87 Fr 223.0 | 88 Ra 226.0 | 103 Lr 262.1 | 104 Rf 261.1 | 105 Db 262.1 | 106 Sg 263.1 | 107 Bh 264.1 | 108 Hs 265.1 | 109 Mt 268 | 110 Uun 269 | 111 Uuu 272 | 112 Uub 277 | 113 Uut | 114 Uuq 289 | 115 Uup | 116 Uuh 289 | 117 Uus | 118 Uuo 293 |

6
| 57 La 138.9 | 58 Ce 140.1 | 59 Pr 140.9 | 60 Nd 144.2 | 61 Pm 146.9 | 62 Sm 150.4 | 63 Eu 152.0 | 64 Gd 157.3 | 65 Tb 158.9 | 66 Dy 162.5 | 67 Ho 164.9 | 68 Er 167.3 | 69 Tm 168.9 | 70 Yb 173.0 |
|---|---|---|---|---|---|---|---|---|---|---|---|---|---|

7
| 89 Ac 227.0 | 90 Th 232.0 | 91 Pa 231.0 | 92 U 236.0 | 93 Np 237.0 | 94 Pu 244.1 | 95 Am 245.1 | 96 Cm 247.1 | 97 Bk 247.1 | 98 Cf 251.0 | 99 Es 252.0 | 100 Fm 257.1 | 101 Md 258.1 | 102 No 259.1 |
|---|---|---|---|---|---|---|---|---|---|---|---|---|---|

**FIGURE 2.3**   The periodic table of elements summarizes some of the features of each element. Elements are each made up of just one kind of atom, and the properties of these atoms determine the properties of the element.

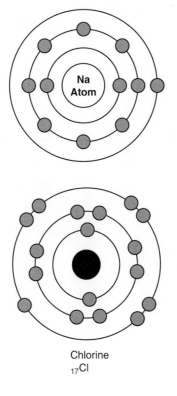

Na Atom

Chlorine
$_{17}$Cl

**FIGURE 2.4**   This schematic shows the 11 electrons of sodium (Na) as they would appear if we could see the electron shells. Each shell is a concentric orbit around the nucleus, which is made up of protons and neutrons.

**FIGURE 2.5**   The chlorine atom has 17 electrons distributed across three shells. The lack of a complete outer shell makes chlorine atoms "greedy" and willing to take electrons from other atoms.

When a Na atom and a Cl atom encounter each other, the Na atom gives up one of its electrons (the outermost one in the third shell) to Cl (which has only seven in its outermost shell). The result is that now both atoms have a complete outer shell (Na has eight in its second shell, which is now its outer shell, and Cl has eight in its third shell, which is its outer shell). However, the Na atom now has 11 protons with positive charges but retains only 10 electrons. As a result, it acquires one positive charge and is denoted as a $Na^+$ ion. The Cl atom now has one extra electron, giving it a negative charge, so it is denoted as a $Cl^-$ ion. Together, the two form an **ionic bond,** and the formula NaCl indicates the joining together of these two atoms to create a molecule that is neutral, or does not have a charge. NaCl, by the way, is the chemical formula for table salt.

In an ionic bond, electrons are fully transferred from one atom to another. However, in some instances, electrons are shared between atoms rather than fully transferred. For example, water ($H_2O$) is made up of two hydrogen atoms and one oxygen atom. Each hydrogen atom has just one proton and therefore just one electron. This leaves hydrogen with an unfilled shell (remember that the first shell takes two electrons). Oxygen, on the other hand, has six protons and electrons. As a consequence, the two hydrogens and oxygen "share" their electrons. The electrons in hydrogen spend some of their time in the hydrogen's shells and some of their time in the oxygen's shells. In return, some of oxygen's electrons also split their time between the two hydrogens. When electrons are not transferred outright but shared across a short distance, this is known as a **covalent bond.** Figure 2.6 shows how water is formed in a covalent bond.

One of the consequences of sharing electrons between the atoms of water is that the electrons are sometimes closer to one atom than another. Because

**FIGURE 2.6**
Water molecules are formed when two hydrogens and one oxygen share their electrons through covalent bonds.

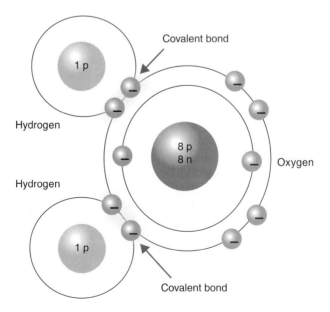

**Bohr Model of H₂O**

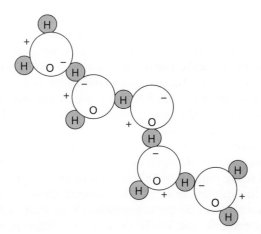

**FIGURE 2.7**
Because of the slight negative charge on the oxygen and the slight positive charge on the hydrogens, water molecules will assemble into structures that create hydrogen bonds. These are shaded in this image.

oxygen is a much larger atom than hydrogen, the electrons do tend to spend more time on the oxygen side of the molecule. As a result, the oxygen acquires a slight negative charge. For the same reason, the hydrogens each end up with a slight positive charge. This is known as a **dipole.** When several water molecules are present together, they arrange themselves so that the slightly positive hydrogens of neighboring molecules are oriented toward the slightly negative oxygens as shown in Figure 2.7.

The organization of molecules around a dipole creates weak bonds that hold the molecules in place, but which can be broken quite easily. The weak bonds that hold water molecules in strings (as shown in Figure 2.7) are known as **hydrogen bonds** because they are formed between hydrogens on one water molecule making weak connections to the oxygen on a different molecule. Hydrogen bonds are most common in water, but they can occur in any molecule that contains hydrogens and atoms that can take on a slightly negative charge (like oxygen).

### Energy and Chemical Bonds

When ionic or covalent bonds form, it is through a process known as a reaction. A certain amount of energy is required for the reaction to proceed and the bond to form. This energy is captured within the bond and released when the bond is broken. Some bonds require more energy to form than they release when broken, and these are known as **endothermic** reactions. In contrast, some bonds require very little energy to form, but can release large amounts of energy when broken. These are known as **exothermic** reactions. For example, the reaction where pure hydrogen and oxygen combine to form water is extremely exothermic: usually there is a tremendous release of energy that creates a small explosion.

Of course, for this reaction to occur, the hydrogen and oxygen have to be heated (i.e., energy is added to the system). The amount of energy required before a reaction can proceed is known as **activation energy.** When the activation energy is very high, as it is in the case of the formation of water from oxygen and hydrogen, then the reaction does not proceed spontaneously. In contrast, some reactions have a very low activation energy and can occur nearly spontaneously.

For example when table salt (NaCl) is dissolved (ionic bonds of NaCl are broken) in water, little energy is required for the bonds to break.

The strength of a bond is a measure of the activation energy of the reaction that would break those bonds. The strength of a bond can vary depending on the environment, however. Take the instance of table salt. The ionic bonds between Na and Cl seem to be very weak because you can dissolve (break the bonds) NaCl so quickly in water. However, if you were to try to break NaCl bonds by heating table salt, you would need to increase the temperature to 800°C before the bonds begin to break. In contrast, covalent bonds will break very easily when heated. However, in water, the covalent bonds are much stronger than the ionic bonds. As with many things, the context of a reaction matters as much as the components of the reaction. In a biological context, almost everything occurs in a water-based environment. So the strongest bonds we see in biological molecules are covalent ones. Many ionic bonds occur in this context as well, but they are weaker because of the water environment present in all living systems.

In living systems, some atoms and molecules are extremely common, whereas others are rare or never found. There are over 100 known types of atoms (elements), but only about 25 occur in living systems. The most common elements found in living systems are hydrogen, carbon, nitrogen, oxygen, and phosphorus. Together these atoms combine to form molecules. Some of these molecules can grow in size and complexity to the point where they incorporate many thousands of atoms. These are known as **macromolecules.** Some examples of macromolecules are DNA and large proteins.

Carbon is the most common element in living systems. Indeed, it was originally thought that any molecule containing carbon had to be associated with living organisms. Thus, molecules that contain carbon are known as **organic.** Although we now know there are ways to create carbon molecules that do not require living systems, the majority of all carbon compounds are still generated by living systems.

You will encounter carbon atoms in much of this chapter because they are at the heart of so many important structures within cells. Given the prevalence of carbon compounds, chemists and biochemists have developed notations that allow them to draw and represent them in a sort of shorthand. In the stick figures in Figure 2.8, the carbons are not shown at all. Rather, each of the vertices of the hexagonal pattern represents a carbon.

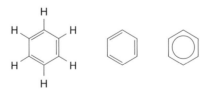

**FIGURE 2.8**    Many carbon structures are represented without specifically labeling the carbon atoms within the structure as shown here for the carbon-based molecule benzene. Rather, each of the vertices of the hexagon represents a carbon atom that is bound to a hydrogen (H).

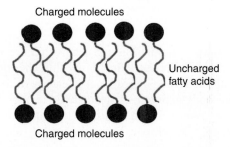

Charged molecules

Uncharged
fatty acids

Charged molecules

**FIGURE 2.9**    The cell membrane of all cells is made up of two layers of fatty acids, each of which has a charged molecule at its head. The membranes can "roll up" into small packages, known as micelles. When they enclose small amounts of water or other contents, they are known as liposomes. When they enclose the entire contents of a cell, we refer to them as cell membranes.

## 2.2.3  A Parts List for Life

### The Cellular Great Wall

The first feature that all cells share is a barrier that separates the cell's internal contents from its environment. In cells, this barrier is known as the **cell membrane.**

All cells have a cell membrane.[2] The cell membrane is actually made up of two kinds of materials. The internal portion contains fatty acids, which are **hydrophobic,** or "water-fearing." The ends of the fatty acids have charged molecules, however, that are **hydrophilic,** or "water-loving." The charged particles face outward from the cell and into the cell, and the fatty acid portion faces into the cell membrane as shown in Figure 2.9. Because there are two layers of molecules, the cell membrane is known as a **bilayer.** Because of the hydrophobic nature of the fatty acid tails, charged particles and large molecules cannot easily cross the membrane. This circumstance allows the membrane to act as a barrier, preventing the free movement of molecules.

Why would the cell membrane be so important for the cell's survival? Cells are essentially minuscule chemical factories. Every chemical reaction requires just the right environment in order to occur. The cell membrane creates the first of several isolated environments that can be used to run various chemical reactions.

Cells are largely made up of water, a charged molecule with some unique properties. Within this **aqueous** environment, cells must create and regulate the flow of energy and information. This is done through a series of chemical processes that create, maintain, and break bonds between molecules.

Chemical processes usually require specific conditions to be satisfied prior to the reactions occurring. For example, hydrogen and oxygen, the two components of water, will not spontaneously form water in any reasonable time.[3] For water to

---

[2] Some cells, such as plant cells and some bacteria, have an additional barrier known as the cell wall.

[3] It has been calculated that it would take on the order of several billion years for such a spontaneous reaction to produce even one molecule of water.

A key feature of the internal environment of the cell is its ability to maintain a steady state, or equilibrium among hundreds of chemical reactions. In biology, this is known as homeostasis. Systems that are at **homeostasis** are difficult to perturb. That is, you cannot easily shift the equilibrium that the cell maintains without adding a great deal of energy or force to the system. For example, your body maintains a steady body temperature around 37°C (98.6°F). It takes extreme shifts in the external temperature (about ± 40°C) before your body loses its ability to maintain a steady temperature.

form, the hydrogen and oxygen must be heated to very high temperatures. This causes an explosive reaction in which water is formed.

In the same manner, the many thousands of chemical reactions required for a cell to function depend on the creation of the right environment. The temperature must be correct, the physical and chemical properties of the molecules involved must be accommodated, and any energy required for the reaction to occur must be provided. These are just a few of the conditions required for certain reactions to occur. The cell membrane provides the best mechanism for creating appropriate environments for chemical reactions to occur within the cell.

A barrier is critical to ensuring that the cell's contents are protected from the environment, but the cell needs to know what is going on in its environment. "Input devices" embedded in the cell membrane communicate changes in the environment. These input devices, called **receptors,** are able to "perceive" input through a chemical interaction: a molecule from the environment chemically bonds to a portion of the receptor. This initiates changes in the receptor that result in the transfer of information into the cell. Unlike modern-day computers, cells do not "read in" data and information from the external environment. Rather, they usually respond to binary changes in the receptor state. Either the receptor is "off" and nothing is bound to it, or the receptor is "on" because something *is* bound to it.

### Cellular Innards

Inside the cell, the various cellular hardware components float in a jelly-like substance known as the **cytoplasm.** This is a water-rich environment in which most of the reactions of the cell are carried out. All the "hardware" of the cell are embedded in the cytoplasm. The cellular hardware is "welded" to the cell membrane by special proteins known collectively as the **cytoskeleton.** These proteins are able to reorganize their orientation, allowing some cells to move around their environment. The amoeba, for example, can inch along a surface by extending and contracting parts of its cellular surface, as shown in Figure 2.10.

In prokaryotic cells, the various hardware is distributed throughout the cell in a relatively unordered manner. However, in eukaryotic cells, the same hardware is distributed into smaller compartments separated by the same sort of

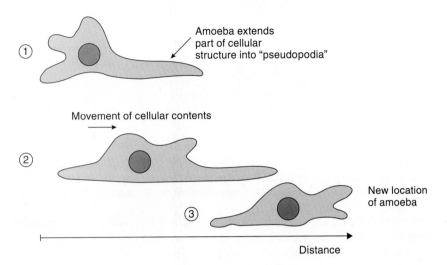

Amoeba extends
part of cellular
structure into "pseudopodia"

Movement of cellular contents

New location
of amoeba

Distance

**FIGURE 2.10**    The amoeba moves around in its environment by extending and
contracting parts of the cytoskeleton. As shown in this figure, it begins by extending a
small section of the cell outward in the direction it wishes to go. It then contracts the
"back" of the cell and scoots forward. The amoeba can inch along in this fashion for
extremely long distances, and the entire motion is coordinated by specialized proteins
within the cytoskeleton [1].

membrane that forms the cell membrane. That is, each organelle has its own
membrane.

At the heart of all eukaryotic cells is the **nucleus,** the main control center and
the place where the full set of cellular instructions known as the **genome** is stored.
It is also where most of the programs of the cell are first "compiled," and where
decisions about how to respond to changes in the cell's environment are made.
We will discuss the genome in much greater detail in the next section.

### Energy Sources and Uses

Every cell must have an internal power source or a mechanism for generating
the energy necessary to conduct its daily activities. For most cells, this is done
through a series of chemical reactions in which molecules with high-energy bonds
are created. When these bonds are broken, the energy released can be utilized to
run the various chemical reactions needed for survival, replication, and adaptation to the environment. In eukaryotes, the power sources are known as the
**mitochondria.** Oddly enough, the mitochondria are actually small cells in their
own right. The current theory is that they were prokaryotic microorganisms that
were "swallowed" by a precursor to the eukaryotic cell. The mitochondria now
depend on the larger, eukaryotic cell to provide them with nutrients and other
raw material. In return, they provide the eukaryotic cell with a steady supply of
energy.

Because the mitochondria used to be free-living organisms at some point
in the past, they have their own genomes (sets of programs and instructions for

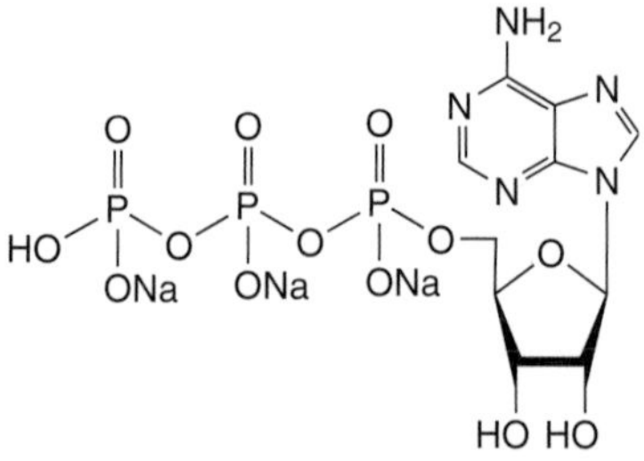

**FIGURE 2.11**    The energy molecule used in most cells is ATP, adenosine triphosphate. Each of the three phosphate bonds shown on the left can be broken, releasing 30 kJ of energy, which can be harnessed to run other chemical reactions within the cell.

running those programs). So every eukaryotic cell has at least two genomes: a large one stored in the nucleus, and a small one stored in the mitochondria.[4]

The energy that mitochondria produce is stored in a special molecule known as **adenosine triphosphate (ATP).** The energy is actually stored in phosphate bonds (covalent bonds of three oxygens around a phosphorus atom). This is shown in Figure 2.11. Each time a phosphate bond is broken, 30 kJ (kilojoules) of energy is released. Food you consume is eventually converted into these high-energy bonds in the phosphate groups of ATP. Your cells have a number of complex biochemical pathways dedicated to the chemical conversion of various food types into ATP.

Most eukaryotic cells have many more organelles, and each of these has a specific function. Just as a computer can have various components that provide added functionality, eukaryotic cells have acquired organelles to handle very sophisticated tasks. We will discuss some of these organelles as we explore the workings of the cell. For now, though, we turn to the challenge of getting all these pieces of hardware to work together. We turn to the "software" needed to run the cell.

## 2.3  THE LANGUAGES OF THE CELL

*"When a programming language is created that allows programmers to program in simple English, it will be discovered that programmers cannot speak English."*
—Anonymous

Just as with computers, cells have several "languages" that control the flow of information. In cells, the equivalent of assembly language is a set of chemical interactions, which do the "grunt work" of the cell. Although each such inter-action is crucial for the functioning of the cell and its continued survival, the language of interaction is rather limited. It is defined by the chemistry of the components involved and is restricted to those interactions that are physically

---

[4] Plant cells have a third genome stored in a special organelle called the chloroplast, which generates energy by converting sunlight into molecules with high-energy bonds.

and energetically favorable. In other words, proteins usually do not interact with one another spontaneously. The environment must be favorable for the interaction to occur. That interaction is bounded by the laws of physics and chemistry. To change the behavior of the cell, you have to change its chemical processes and interactions.

## 2.3.1  Operating Systems for Cells

Hardware is just the first step to assembling a functioning computer. For most users, a computer is not a functional piece of equipment until it has an operating system: a mediator between the hardware and the user. This is true for cells as well. Proteins interacting willy-nilly will not promote survival; they must work together at specific times and in specific ways. Without some kind of regulation, proteins would interact randomly, resulting in chaos. It would be like a computer in which the hard drive is accessed at random intervals in no particular order and for no purpose. The result would just be random bits of data. To make for a cohesive whole, the various components of a cell or a computer must be coordinated. This is one of the primary activities of the operating system.

Within cells, no specific component is directly analogous to the operating system. Rather, several components combine to perform the tasks similar to those an operating system would accomplish. For example, biological modules ensure that certain activities are accomplished on an hourly or daily basis. Some components monitor the current state of affairs, and others receive input and respond to it. The core of the activity is centered around the genome of the cell, but the activities themselves are distributed to relevant areas of the cell.

You may have heard the term *genome* before. Often referred to as the blueprint for the cell, the genome contains all the instructions for making a new cell. In this sense, it is the blueprint for designing the cell. In contrast to computer hardware, which is manufactured outside the individual unit and installed by others, cells manufacture their own "hardware." The instructions for building cellular hardware are contained in the cell's genome.

The genome is more than just the set of instructions on how to make the cellular hardware. It is also capable of copying itself and modifying itself. Cellular genomes are instances of self-editing code. In addition to specifying the parts of a cell, the genome is able to direct the manufacturing of those parts and to have those parts then interact with the genome to initiate the generation of other, possibly new, parts. So the genome is much more than just the blueprint for the cell. It is also the heart of the operating system; it creates the environment in which the cellular hardware can interact with a variety of software within the cell and from external sources. The genome commands, informs, and controls the cell. Paradoxically, the genome is itself commanded, informed, and controlled by the cell!

Let's consider an example. All cells must have ways to sense changes in their environment and adapt to those changes. Cells that cannot respond to the environment would be maladapted and would be selected against. Bacterial cells have especially sophisticated mechanisms for sensing chemical gradients in their environments. For example, the bacterium *Escherichia coli* lives in watery environments (including your gut) and needs to move toward food sources and away from toxic substances. It does this by checking its immediate environment for certain kinds of chemicals. "Food" chemicals will draw the *E. coli* toward the source, but "waste" chemicals will repel the bacterium.

*E. coli* is able to sense the presence of food or toxins through special proteins on the surface of the cell. These proteins are known as receptors (the input devices we spoke of earlier). When receptors bind a molecule of a chemical, they trigger a network of signals that leads to changes within the *E. coli* cell itself. The end result of these signaling networks is that the bacterium uses a specialized motor structure known as the flagellum to move toward the food [6].

Let's take a closer look at the signaling network involved when *E. coli* is in search of food. Just as it was said that all roads once led to Rome, all signaling networks in the cell lead to the genome. There is a very good reason for this: the genome is both the repository of instructions and the decision-making kernel of the cellular operating system. Therefore, most responses (or outputs) from a cell cannot be generated without consulting the genome.

For most cells the first step is to make a protein or group of proteins. The cell needs these pieces of hardware to generate its output. The instructions for making these proteins are contained in the genome, so it's not all that surprising that signaling networks generally culminate at the genome.

In the case of *E. coli*, moving toward food requires "running the motor." Essentially, the flagella have to be turned at high speed to propel the bacterium in a particular direction. The proteins that operate the flagella are generated, or **synthesized,** to use the biological term, from instructions in the genome. This occurs when the signals from the receptor indicate that food is in the vicinity of the bacterium. The decision to activate the flagellum is the result of the receptor signaling the genome, which makes the relevant proteins, which then turn the flagellum [6].

Not all decisions in the cell are as binary as this one. In the *E. coli* example, it's obvious that if there's food in a particular direction, the bacterium should go in that direction. This is a simple decision. Most decisions in cells, however, are much more complex and involve **integrating signals** from a variety of networks. Integration culminates at the level of the genome: signals converge, decisions are made, and proteins are generated. Whenever a protein is made, we say that its gene has been expressed. *Most signaling networks lead to changes in gene expression.*

In many such instances, the proteins that are made can also operate on the genome, perhaps to activate other proteins or to turn off the signaling network when a response has been generated. Biologists refer to these interconnected networks as **signaling cascades.** The combinatorial possibilities of multiple cascades converging on a region of the genome at the same time are unlimited, and this is the basis for much of the complexity of living cells.

In fact, even as you sit here reading this, your cells are engaging in hundreds if not thousands of minute modifications and adjustments. These are in response to signals from the exterior of the cell and involve manipulations of the genome. You have anywhere from a million cells as an infant to a billion cells in an adult body, and each is engaged in a complex dance, which is both beautiful and absolutely essential for your survival. This is all mediated by the genome, which as we'll discuss in the next section, is just a string of four kinds of molecules. It's fair to say that your cells are the most incredible computers you'll ever encounter.

## 2.3.2  Deciphering the Language of Cells

*"Twas brillig, and the slithy toves*
*Did gyre and gimble in the wabe;*
*All mimsy were the borogoves,*
*And the mome raths outgrabe."*
        —Lewis Caroll, *Jabberwocky*

### DNAStrings as a Human Language

So what is the genome, anyway? The genomes of all cells are made up of a molecule known as **deoxyribosenucleic acid (DNA),** which we introduced in Chapter 1.

It is the molecule that all cellular organisms use as the basis for their genomes. Like all "natural languages" or languages that humans use, it has an alphabet, a vocabulary, and a grammar. We do not fully understand all the aspects of this language, and one of the challenges of the new fields of bioinformatics and systems biology is to decipher it. Unlike natural languages such as English or Latvian, understanding DNA will not allow us to write poetry or read literature. Rather, like a computer programming language, it will allow us to understand and work with the cellular computer. So DNA has aspects of a human language and aspects of a computer programming language. When we refer to DNA as a language, we will call it DNAStrings to distinguish it from references to the molecule known as DNA.

Let's look at the human language parts of DNA first. DNAStrings has an alphabet of four letters. The English language has 26, so at first glance we might assume that English is a far more complex language than DNAStrings. However, there are human languages with as few as 18 letters, and others with thousands of characters. In the computer world, the basic language is one of binary digits. Its alphabet is the set {0,1}. Its words are sequences of letters like 0011001010 and 1111. If you wish, you may refer to the letters of this alphabet as bits. Even though BinaryStrings, the language of binary, has only two letters, it can be used in very sophisticated computation. So the size of the alphabet is not necessarily a reflection of the complexity of the language.

A better measure of complexity is the size and variety of the vocabulary. It has been estimated that the English language has between 50,000 and 70,000 words.[5] Most words in the English language are between 3 and 10 letters long. In computing a special importance is attached to groups of 8 bits. Indeed, the special

---

[5] You will find an active and very heated debate about this estimate if you search online. As it turns out, it all depends on how you define a *word.*

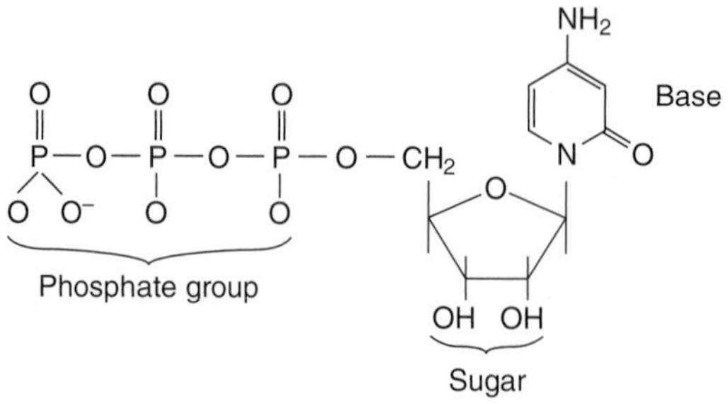

**FIGURE 2.12**   Nucleotides are made up of three key components. The sugar molecule binds to the phosphate group to create the backbone of a strand of DNA. The nitrogen base on each nucleotide determines the letter of the alphabet. There are four letters: A, C, G, and T, and each is the result of a specific nitrogen base.

term *byte* is used to refer to a group of 8 bits. In DNAStrings, each gene represents a "word," and there may be as many as 1 million words.[6] DNAStrings words can have word lengths of 10,000 or more letters each. So it is possible that DNAStrings is a language that is more complex than any human language.

English has an extremely complex and involved grammar, as anyone who has tried to learn it as a second language knows. Even with a relatively small vocabulary (small when compared with DNAStrings's vocabulary, that is), English has been able to facilitate communication on a multitude of levels: from the basic transfer of information to the high art of William Shakespeare. How does DNAStrings compare here? Since we are only just beginning to understand the grammar of this language, we do not yet know what the full extent of its sophistication might be. It is probably safe to say that high art is possible in DNAStrings if you are willing to consider yourself an example of high art!

### The Alphabet of DNAStrings

The alphabet of DNAStrings, as mentioned earlier, has four "letters." In fact, these letters are four kinds of molecules and each is known as a **nucleotide.** Each molecule has three basic components: a sugar molecule, a nitrogen ring, and a phosphate group (Figure 2.12). The phosphate group is negatively charged so DNA has an overall negative charge. This property can be utilized in experimental manipulation of DNA, as discussed in Chapter 3.

The phosphate group interacts chemically with the sugar group to form bonds. The result is a long, lanky chain of molecules that can twist and turn much like a section of bicycle chain. Like the bicycle chain, it can twist in some directions better than others, and it has a certain rigidity to it. This has to do with the physical and chemical properties of the phosphate group and the sugar. The chain of phosphates and interlinked sugars is known as the **sugar–phosphate backbone** of DNA (Figure 2.13).

---

[6] If each protein encoded in DNA is a "word," then it is reasonable to estimate that the total set of nonredundant proteins present in all organisms would be about 1 million [1].

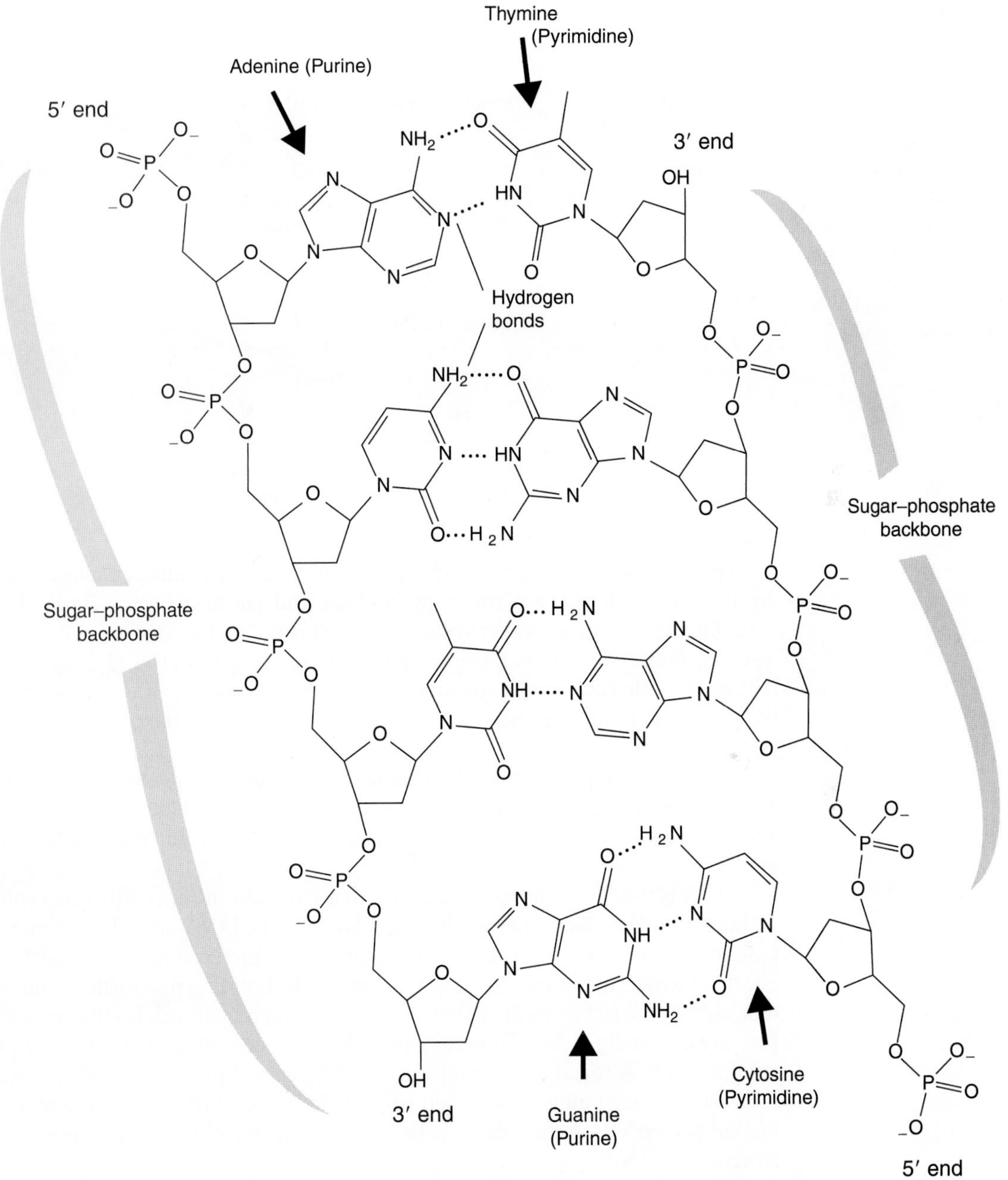

**FIGURE 2.13**    Covalent bonds that form between adjacent phosphate groups and sugar groups on neighboring nucleotides yield a DNA strand. Because the links occur between sugar and phosphate groups, this is known as the sugar–phosphate backbone of a DNA strand. Hydrogen bonds between the nitrogen bases allow for the formation of the DNA double helix.
(Image designed and generated by Madeleine Price Ball.)

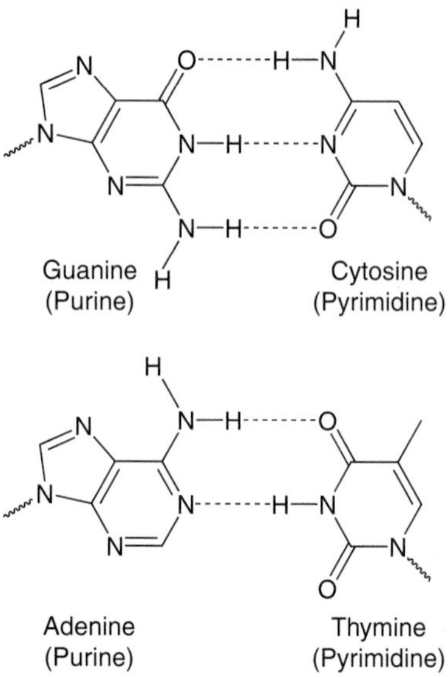

**FIGURE 2.14**
DNA has two
pyrimidines and two
purines. Purines
basepair with
pyrimidines as shown.
They have slightly
different chemical
structures, and these
variations allow them
to be utilized as
letters in the alphabet
of DNAStrings.

Guanine
(Purine)          Cytosine
(Pyrimidine)

Adenine
(Purine)          Thymine
(Pyrimidine)

Hanging off this sugar–phosphate backbone are the nitrogen rings. There are two kinds of nitrogen rings: **pyrimidines** and **purines** (Figure 2.14). They have different chemical properties and are used in distinct ways within the DNA. You can think of them as being roughly analogous to vowels and consonants. Although both vowels and consonants are letters, vowels can do some things that consonants cannot and vice versa. The same is true of the pyrimidines and purines.

There are two pyrimidines: **thymidine** and **cytosine.** These are abbreviated as T and C, respectively, and we will refer to them by these letters from now on. The two purines are **adenosine** and **guanine.** They are represented by the letters A and G.

DNA is usually found as two strands that wrap around each other in a spiral within a spiral, or **double helix.** The two strands of the DNA are held together by weak interactions known as hydrogen bonds. These interactions are "weak" in a chemical sense: that is, they are not as strong as the bonding that forms when two molecules trade electrons or share them. Even though hydrogen bonds are weak, they are extremely stable. To break apart the hydrogen bonds that hold the two strands of DNA together, the molecule must be heated to 96°C. In other words, the molecule must almost be boiled to get it to come apart. One of the reasons life has succeeded on this planet is the tremendous stability of the double-helix structure of DNA.

The stability of the structure also allows DNA to grow to extraordinary lengths. For example, the DNA in your cells is actually about 1 meter (m) in length. Yet it fits in cells that are about 100 nanometers (nm) in length! To squeeze all that DNA into your cells, the DNA is wrapped and twisted into a very tight bundle. Imagine taking a rubber band and twisting it over and over until you have a small, very tight bundle. This is what happens to the DNA in your cells. The

DNA is wrapped tightly around itself and several proteins until it can fit inside the tiny space of the cell.

DNA has certain requirements before hydrogen bonds can form between its two strands. The first requirement is that if a C (cytosine) occurs on one strand, then the other strand must have a G (guanine) and vice versa. The same applies for T (thymine) and A (adenosine): the hydrogen bonds form when there is a T on one strand and an A on the other. In practice, this means that if one strand has the sequence of letters AGGCAT, then the other strand would have the sequence TCCGTA to match up with the letters on the first strand. This is known as the **complement** of the letters on the first strand.

The chemical structure of DNA also forces a certain orientation to the strands. In Figure 2.13, the end containing a free phosphate group is called the 5′ (read as "five prime") end. This refers to the point on the sugar molecule where the phosphate group binds to the sugar. This is also the "top," or "head," of the DNA molecule. At the other end is a sugar molecule that represents the "end," or "bottom," of the DNA molecule. This is known as the 3′ (read as "three prime") end. Each DNA strands runs from a 5′ end to a 3′ end.

For the sequence of letters on one strand to match up with the letters on the other strand, the two strands have to run in opposite directions. That is, one strand is positioned with the 5′ end at the top right of Figure 2.13 and the other has the 5′ end at the bottom left of the figure. This is known as an **antiparallel** orientation.

To understand why this is necessary, let's go back to our string of letters: ACGT. If we read the letters on the first strand from the 5′ end to the 3′ end, it would be AGGCAT. If we now read the letters on the other strand from 5′ to 3′, the sequence would be ATGCCT. For these two strands to pair up and form the hydrogen bonds, the second strand "flips" orientation so that the 3′ end is at the top. So reading the sequence from 3′ to 5′ gives the correct sequence of letters to pair up with the first string:

5′ A G G C A T 3′   (first strand or forward strand)
 |  |  |  |  |  |
3′ T C C G T A 5′   (second strand or reverse strand)

In biology, we say that the second strand is a **reverse complement** of the first strand. Because we think of the strands as running from the 5′ end to the 3′ end, we also refer to the first strand as the **forward strand.** The second strand, running in the "opposite" direction is also known as the **reverse strand.** As we will see shortly, each strand plays an important role in storing and directing the execution of programs written in DNAStrings.

The problem of which direction to read information is not unique to cells. Back in the distant past of computers, when input and output were still performed via paper tape or punched cards, many sequences punched onto cards or tape could make sense if the card or tape were upside-down or reversed, as illustrated in Figure 2.15. Steps were necessary to ensure correct positioning, and cards were deliberately made to be nonsymmetrical to help this. It is conceivable that

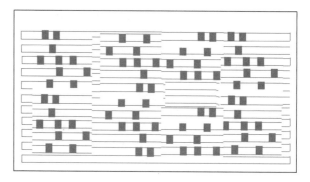

**FIGURE 2.15**    Paper tape and punched cards used for I/O in the early days of computing. These media must be read in the correct orientation and right-side up. Flipping them leads to legitimate but unintended reads, just as reading the "wrong" strand of DNA might produce unexpected results.
© Bettman/CORBIS

DNA can contain useful information simultaneously in both strands. Similarly, it is conceivable that a paper tape or even modern digital media may contain information that is meaningful both when read normally and when read "upside-down" or "inside-out." Try this fun exercise:

**Exercise 2.1**    Write a program that compiles and runs both when it is read normally *and* when you reverse the order of the characters. This task is much more easily accomplished in languages like C or Lisp rather than in more disciplined modern languages.

Our understanding of the structure of DNA is quite recent: 2003 was the 50th anniversary of the discovery of its structure. The two people most instrumental in that discovery are James Watson and the late Francis Crick. In their honor, the base pairing mechanism that lines up an A with a T and a G with a C is known as Watson–Crick base pairing.

Francis Crick went on to produce influential work about the ways in which the language of DNA could direct the formation of proteins, as we will discuss shortly. It is hard not to overstate the importance of the discovery of the structure of DNA or its "recentness." Biology has had just over 50 years to start piecing together the puzzle of how DNA directs the formation of proteins. We have a pretty good understanding of how this process occurs in bacteria, but we are still uncertain about some of the aspects in eukaryotes like our own cells. Before we look at the exact process that generates proteins from DNA, let us take a closer look at the language of DNA.

### Nouns in DNAStrings

Now that we know about the alphabet for DNAStrings, what sort of words can we form with it? For this, we have to define what a word is in DNAStrings. Let's say that the "nouns" of DNAStrings correspond to individual proteins. Sometimes these words are fairly short—just a few hundred letters long. Or they may be many thousands of letters in length.

The nouns of DNAStrings are the protein-coding genes. Many genes have the codes required to make proteins. Many hundreds of thousands of genes code for proteins across the spectrum of life. Some genes code for other kinds of molecules, and we will discuss these genes later.

Groups of genes share similarities. These similarities can be in the "spelling": they have the same or very similar sequences of letters. In English for example, the words *cat* and *rat* both refer to a furry creature with four legs. In the same fashion, some genes have similar spellings and meanings. They are considered to be members of the same **gene family.** In contrast, English also has many words that are similarly spelled but with vastly different meanings. For example, *read*, *lead*, and *tread* all include the same juxtaposition of letters—*ead*. Yet, they have very different meanings. This is not as common in DNAStrings. *In general, if a gene shares the same or very similar sequence of letters with another gene, then the two genes will make very similar proteins.* We will discuss why this is the case shortly.

### Programming Concepts for Cells

The "verbs" of DNAStrings are usually much shorter words that make decisions about when a protein should be made. At this point we must abandon the analogy with human languages and start thinking about DNAStrings as a computer language.

DNAStrings has many of the same elements as a programming language. We know there are words to define if–then–else relationships and loop control. It is possible that DNAStrings has data structures, too, but we do not yet understand how those might work. Let's look at some examples of if–then–else statements in DNAStrings.

The *E. coli* example provides us with an if–then–else decision. "If there is food, go toward it. Else do not move in that direction." In DNAStrings, an if–then–else statement is sometimes encoded as something called a **promoter.** When the promoter is on, the if–then part of the statement is executed. When the promoter is off, the else statement is in effect. What do we mean by a promoter being on or off? A promoter is on when a protein is bound to it. A promoter is frequently turned off by the removal of the protein that turned it on. Sometimes, however, a promoter can also be inactivated by a different protein binding to it. This allows for fine-tuning of the simple binary on–off mechanism.

Promoters are found in front of most genes. When the promoter is on the if–then statement is executed. In most cases, the if–then statement would read something like "If (some condition), then make this gene's protein." Loop control can be added in by regulating how long the promoter is on. For example, "while the promoter is on, if (some condition), make this gene's protein."

Sometimes a single protein can turn on many genes at the same time. This is the *for* loop of DNAStrings. Essentially, it would read something like this: "for all promoters this protein can bind, if (some condition), make the proteins from those genes." Usually, the if–then statement is implicit. That is, if a protein can bind the promoter, then that if–then statement's condition has already been fulfilled. So really, in DNAStrings, you would write "for all promoters this protein can bind, make the proteins from those genes."

We do not have many examples of data structures in DNAStrings. Those few are mostly from bacterial cells. Arrays of genes can be accessed at one time using just one promoter. These arrays are known as **operons.** In DNAStrings, the command might read something like this: "if (some condition), access each gene in array operon, make each gene's protein in sequence." Examples of linked lists, associative arrays, or more sophisticated data structures do exist, but they are beyond the level of our present discussion.

Accessing all the genes in an operon can have very powerful and subtle effects. Just as in programming languages, the more complex the data structure, the more sophisticated the possible operations. In the case of operons, the cell has the ability to fine-tune its responses based on a variety of inputs. A good example of this is the *lac* **operon.** Most bacterial cells can utilize the sugar lactose as an energy source. They have a set of enzymes that break down lactose and transfer the energy contained in the sugar bonds to other molecules. Five enzymes are needed for this process, and each is encoded by a gene. All five of the genes are part of an array with a common promoter. When lactose is not present, these enzymes are not needed. The promoter is bound by a special protein known as a **repressor** and is off by default. When lactose is present in the environment, it is transported into the cell. It binds to an **inducer** that can then bind to the promoter. Now the promoter is on, and the array of enzyme genes can be accessed. The enzymes are made, and the lactose is used up. When there is no longer any lactose to use, the promoter is turned off. This is because in the absence of lactose, the inducer protein can no longer stay on the promoter. It is replaced by the repressor protein. The array cannot be accessed any more, so no additional enzymes are made. The system is now off until lactose becomes available again. The process is summarized in Figure 2.16.

So what would the code for this operation look like in DNAStrings? It might read something like this:

```
if (lactose+inducer)
    bind lactose+inducer to promoter;
    while(lactose+inducer bound to promoter)
      make enzymes to use lactose as energy source;
else
    remove inducer from promoter;
    place repressor on promoter;
```

### 2.3.3 Compiling DNAStrings Programs

Now that we know something about DNAStrings as a computer language, we need to think about how the instructions are executed when a program is run.

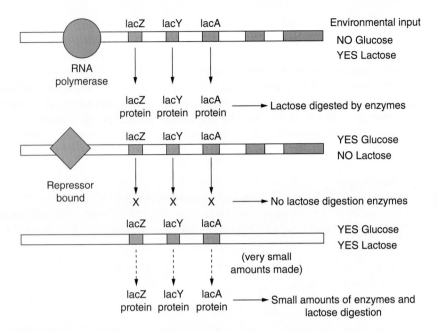

**FIGURE 2.16**    The *lac* operon and its operation under various conditions.

Let's look again at the *lac* operon program. The while loop we set up includes this statement:

```
while(lactose+inducer bound to promoter)
   make enzymes to use lactose as energy source;
```

How does the cell go about executing the statement make enzymes to use lactose as energy source;? These instructions require two steps to actually execute. The first step is to compile the code. The process in biology is known as **transcription** and is performed by a specialized protein known as ribonucleic acid (RNA) polymerase. **RNA polymerase** is essentially the compiler for all DNAStrings code; we share many of the components of RNA polymerase with every other form of life on this planet.

One difference between prokaryotes and eukaryotes is the number of RNA polymerases each includes. Prokaryotes have one, all-purpose RNA polymerase. Eukaryotes have three, each specialized for a specific class of genes. Another difference is that in prokaryotes, the process of transcription is straightforward: a copy of the DNA is made using ribonucleic acid, which is a temporary molecule. In eukaryotes, many other steps occur before the final RNA is made. So in prokaryotes, RNA polymerase is more of a copier than a compiler. In eukaryotes, it performs more of the functions we associate with computing language compilers.

Eukaryotic RNA polymerases are actually remarkable compilers. In most organisms, RNA polymerase "compiles," or reads the DNA sequence at the rate of 1000–2000 nucleotides per second. It generates the binary, or executable, version of the DNAStrings code at the rate of about 500–1000 characters per second. From a programming perspective, RNA polymerase appears to run as a linear process. Were it, instead, to be a quadratic $O(n^2)$ process or, even worse, an exponential $2^n$ process, then we would find that performance would severely degrade as the length of genes increases. Compilers that run in time $O(n)$, where $n$ is the length of the program source are acceptable. Doubling the length of your source doubles the compiling time, and nobody can complain about that.

---

**Exercise 2.2**

Company Macinsoft has developed a Java compiler javaA that can compile a program comprising $n$ characters in an average time of $750n + 1800$ microseconds ($\mu$s). Company Microtosh has a compiler javaB that takes $12n^2 + 3n + 2\,\mu$s.

1. How long does a 24-line program with an average of 12 characters per line take to compile
   **(a)** on compiler javaA
   **(b)** on compiler javaB
2. How long does a 240-line program with an average of 12 characters per line take to compile
   **(a)** on compiler javaA
   **(b)** on compiler javaB
3. How long does a 2400-line program with an average of 12 characters per line take to compile
   **(a)** on compiler javaA
   **(b)** on compiler javaB

A quadratic time compiler might be fine for short programs, but as program length increases so too does compiling time. Software developers could never accept this. Likewise evolution has produced a linear time compiler in our cells.

---

## Executable Files from DNAStrings

The result of transcription (compiling) is a temporary copy of the program in the equivalent of an executable file. For DNAStrings, the final executable file is a molecule called **messenger RNA (mRNA).**

The key feature of mRNA is that it is chemically similar to DNA. It has four letters in its alphabet as well. One major difference between the alphabets of DNA and mRNA is that in mRNA **uracil,** represented by the letter U, replaces the thymine (T) used in DNA. The chemical properties of U are very similar to those of T, at least for our purposes here. The chemical structure of uracil is shown in Figure 2.17. The letters of mRNA are also nucleotides because they have the same chemical and physical properties as the letters of DNA.

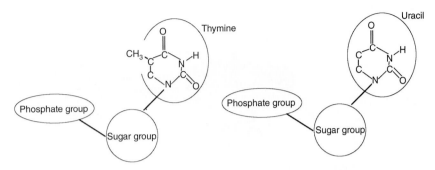

**FIGURE 2.17**   The nucleotide uracil is used in place of thymine in RNA. It is chemically related to thymine and, for our purposes, functions in essentially the same way as a thymine would in DNA.

Another difference between DNA and mRNA is that mRNA occurs as a single strand, running from a 5′ end to a 3′ end. As a result of these differences, mRNA is nowhere near as stable as DNA. It is very easily **degraded.** Cells have come up with a variety of ways to keep mRNA around long enough to use it.

## 2.3.4  Executing Code from DNAStrings

Just as with the executable file of a program, the mRNA can be used many times. Each time the mRNA "program" is run, a protein is produced. The process of making the protein is known in biology as **translation** because it involves converting the A, C, G, and U letters (remember that mRNA does not have T letters) of the mRNA into a string of **amino acids**—the chemical units that make up all proteins. Proteins are the output resulting from running DNAStrings code.

The actual process of running the executable file of code from DNAStrings involves two steps. The first step is to consult a lookup table that converts triplets of ACGU letters in the executable table into amino acids. The second step is to create the string of amino acids that make up the actual protein. Both steps occur as part of the "running" of the mRNA executable code and are carried out on a structure called the **ribosome** (Figure 2.18).

The ribosome is a processor that runs an "executable" mRNA. Each cell has hundreds if not thousands of ribosomes, so these processors constitute a vast "cluster" of computing nodes within the cell. Bacterial ribosomes, which are the best understood, are extremely fast processors. They can read and execute the mRNA executable code at the rate of about 60 mRNA letters per second. They are also extremely precise, with an error rate of less than 0.0001% in most cases. This may not seem very impressive, especially since computer processors today are even faster than this and even more accurate. The ribosome is such an astonishing processor because it evolved to its current level of complexity and sophistication without deliberate design.

After finding and attaching to the mRNA, the first thing the ribosome does is to start reading the string of ACGU letters that are encoded in the mRNA. The

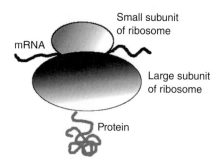

**FIGURE 2.18**  The ribosome is a large complex made up of two subunits that have four RNA strands and about 50 proteins. These RNA strands are not like the mRNAs; they do not code for proteins and are never translated. Rather, they have special functions within the ribosome—translating mRNAs.

**FIGURE 2.19**  The standard genetic code is a mapping of triplet nucleotides to amino acids. Notice that some amino acids have more than one triplet nucleotide code. Since multiple triplets can represent the same amino acid, we say that the genetic code is degenerate. In mathematical terms, the mapping from triplets to amino acids is onto but not one-to-one.

| AMINO ACID | CODONS |
|------------|--------|
| Ala | GCA,GCC,GCG,GCU |
| Arg | AGA,AGG,CGA,CGC,CGG,CGU |
| Asp | GAC,GAU |
| Asn | AAC,AAU |
| Cys | UGC,UGU |
| Glu | GAA,GAG |
| Gln | CAA,CAG |
| Gly | GGA,GGC,GGG,GGU |
| His | CAC,CAU |
| Ile | AUA,AUC,AUU |
| Leu | UUA,UUG,CUA,CUC,CUG,CUU |
| Lys | AAA,AAG |
| Met | AUG |
| Phe | UUC,UUU |
| Pro | CCA,CCC,CCG,CCU |
| Ser | AGC,AGU,UCA,UCC,UCG,UCU |
| Thr | ACA,ACC,ACG,ACU |
| Trp | UGG |
| Tyr | UAC,UAU |
| Val | GUA,GUC,GUG,GUU |
| stop | UAA,UAG,UGA |

ribosome parses the mRNA letters by reading groups of three letters at a time. In fact, that set is so important that it even has its own name—**codon.** Each three-letter codon indicates an amino acid. This mapping is referred to as the **genetic code** and is illustrated in Figure 2.19. The genetic code is a mapping between a set of triples of one type of chemical unit (nucleotides) to a set of completely different chemical units (amino acids).

Why use a triplet nucleotide code for the genetic code? The reason is quite simple. There are 20 amino acids commonly used in biological systems, and we can figure out the minimum number of nucleotides required to provide at least one unique code for each amino acid. What is the minimum number of nucleotides required?

## The Purpose of Codes

Any mapping from a set of words in one language to a set of words in another (possibly the same) language is a **code.** Codes that map fixed-width words to fixed-width words are the easiest to use. For example, the ASCII code provides a mapping between the set of eight[7]-letter words in BinaryStrings and some of the characters that we can type on our keyboards or print to our screens. More recently, Unicode provides a mapping from the set of 16-letter words in BinaryStrings. There are many valid ways to look at the mapping provided by codes such as ASCII or Unicode: The usual view is as a map between a set of numbers and a set of characters, many of which can be printed or specified via a keyboard. Figure 2.20 provides a key to the ASCII code.

Morse code shows some advantages to considering variable-width codes. Morse code provides a mapping between English and DotDashStrings. DotDashStrings is a language with the alphabet dot, dash. Figure 2.21 shows the mapping from the letters of English to words in DotDashStrings provided by the Morse code. The Morse code was developed for nonvoice communication using a single key switch. The dash was transmitted as a long pulse, the dot as a short pulse. Morse code tries to provide a certain economy in transmission time by using short sequences for common letters while allowing the codes for less common English letters to be relatively long. Similarly, compression algorithms typically replace commonly occurring patterns with short codes and use longer codes for rarer ones.

The key point is that codes allow for the efficient transmission of information from one format into another. The result is that some kind of action can be taken based on the information. For example, Morse code was used for radio communications to coordinate military activities during World War II. We use ASCII for binary representation of English words every day when we enter information into a computer and expect it to complete some processing task as a result.

The genetic code allows cells to transform information into an action. The code represents all 64 possible triplet combinations of the four letters of DNA-Strings. The point is again information transfer: to transfer the information contained within the mRNA into a protein that can actually do something within the cell.

You will note that Figure 2.20 displays some "sensible" features. A comes before B, which comes before C, ... which comes before Z. 0, 1, 2, ... , 9 occur in the "correct" order. But what is behind the ordering of the punc-

---

[7] Historically, ASCII was originally formulated as a 7-bit code. There is no harm in adopting modern usage and considering it an 8-bit code as we do in this text. In any case ASCII is gradually being replaced by the 16-bit Unicode.

## ASCII Character Codes Table & Cheat Sheet

| Special Chars | | Upper Case | | Lower Case | | Extended ASCII | | | Extended ASCII | | | Extended ASCII | | |
|---|---|---|---|---|---|---|---|---|---|---|---|---|---|---|
| 9 | \t (Tab) | 65 | A | 97 | a | 128 | € | &#128; | 174 | ® | &#174; | 220 | Ü | &#220; |
| 10 | \n (NL) | 66 | B | 98 | b | 129 | □ | &#129; | 175 | – | &#175; | 221 | Ý | &#221; |
| 13 | \r (CR) | 67 | C | 99 | c | 130 | ‚ | &#130; | 176 | º | &#176; | 222 | Þ | &#222; |
| 32 | Space | 68 | D | 100 | d | 131 | ƒ | &#131; | 177 | ± | &#177; | 223 | ß | &#223; |
| 33 | ! | 69 | E | 101 | e | 132 | „ | &#132; | 178 | ² | &#178; | 224 | à | &#224; |
| 34 | " | 70 | F | 102 | f | 133 | … | &#133; | 179 | ³ | &#179; | 225 | á | &#225; |
| 35 | # | 71 | G | 103 | g | 134 | † | &#134; | 180 | ´ | &#180; | 226 | â | &#226; |
| 36 | $ | 72 | H | 104 | h | 135 | ‡ | &#135; | 181 | µ | &#181; | 227 | ã | &#227; |
| 37 | % | 73 | I | 105 | i | 136 | ˆ | &#136; | 182 | ¶ | &#182; | 228 | ä | &#228; |
| 38 | & | 74 | J | 106 | j | 137 | ‰ | &#137; | 183 | · | &#183; | 229 | å | &#229; |
| 39 | ' | 75 | K | 107 | k | 138 | Š | &#138; | 184 | ¸ | &#184; | 230 | æ | &#230; |
| 40 | ( | 76 | L | 108 | l | 139 | ‹ | &#139; | 185 | ¹ | &#185; | 231 | ç | &#231; |
| 41 | ) | 77 | M | 109 | m | 140 | Œ | &#140; | 186 | º | &#186; | 232 | è | &#232; |
| 42 | * | 78 | N | 110 | n | 141 | □ | &#141; | 187 | » | &#187; | 233 | é | &#233; |
| 43 | + | 79 | O | 111 | o | 142 | Ž | &#142; | 188 | ¼ | &#188; | 234 | ê | &#234; |
| 44 | , | 80 | P | 112 | p | 143 | □ | &#143; | 189 | ½ | &#189; | 235 | ë | &#235; |
| 45 | - | 81 | Q | 113 | q | 144 | □ | &#144; | 190 | ¾ | &#190; | 236 | ì | &#236; |
| 46 | . | 82 | R | 114 | r | 145 | ' | &#145; | 191 | ¿ | &#191; | 237 | í | &#237; |
| 47 | / | 83 | S | 115 | s | 146 | ' | &#146; | 192 | À | &#192; | 238 | î | &#238; |
| 48 | 0 | 84 | T | 116 | t | 147 | " | &#147; | 193 | Á | &#193; | 239 | ï | &#239; |
| 49 | 1 | 85 | U | 117 | u | 148 | " | &#148; | 194 | Â | &#194; | 240 | ð | &#240; |
| 50 | 2 | 86 | V | 118 | v | 149 | • | &#149; | 195 | Ã | &#195; | 241 | ñ | &#241; |
| 51 | 3 | 87 | W | 119 | w | 150 | – | &#150; | 196 | Ä | &#196; | 242 | ò | &#242; |
| 52 | 4 | 88 | X | 120 | x | 151 | — | &#151; | 197 | Å | &#197; | 243 | ó | &#243; |
| 53 | 5 | 89 | Y | 121 | y | 152 | ˜ | &#152; | 198 | Æ | &#198; | 244 | ô | &#244; |
| 54 | 6 | 90 | Z | 122 | z | 153 | ™ | &#153; | 199 | Ç | &#199; | 245 | õ | &#245; |
| 55 | 7 | | | | | 154 | š | &#154; | 200 | È | &#200; | 246 | ö | &#246; |
| 56 | 8 | | | | | 155 | › | &#155; | 201 | É | &#201; | 247 | ÷ | &#247; |
| 57 | 9 | | | | | 156 | œ | &#156; | 202 | Ê | &#202; | 248 | ø | &#248; |
| 58 | : | | | | | 157 | □ | &#157; | 203 | Ë | &#203; | 249 | ù | &#249; |
| 59 | ; | | | | | 158 | ž | &#158; | 204 | Ì | &#204; | 250 | ú | &#250; |
| 60 | < | | | | | 159 | Ÿ | &#159; | 205 | Í | &#205; | 251 | û | &#251; |
| 61 | = | | | | | 160 | |   | 206 | Î | &#206; | 252 | ü | &#252; |
| 62 | > | | | | | 161 | ¡ | &#161; | 207 | Ï | &#207; | 253 | ý | &#253; |
| 63 | ? | | | | | 162 | ¢ | &#162; | 208 | Ð | &#208; | | | |
| 64 | @ | | | | | 163 | £ | &#163; | 209 | Ñ | &#209; | | | |
| 91 | [ | | | | | 164 | ¤ | &#164; | 210 | Ò | &#210; | | | |
| 92 | \ | | | | | 165 | ¥ | &#165; | 211 | Ó | &#211; | | | |
| 93 | ] | | | | | 166 | ¦ | &#166; | 212 | Ô | &#212; | | | |
| 94 | ^ | | | | | 167 | § | &#167; | 213 | Õ | &#213; | | | |
| 95 | _ | | | | | 168 | ¨ | &#168; | 214 | Ö | &#214; | | | |
| 96 | ` | | | | | 169 | © | &#169; | 215 | × | &#215; | | | |
| 123 | { | | | | | 170 | ª | &#170; | 216 | Ø | &#216; | | | |
| 124 | \| | | | | | 171 | « | &#171; | 217 | Ù | &#217; | | | |
| 125 | } | | | | | 172 | ¬ | &#172; | 218 | Ú | &#218; | | | |
| 126 | ~ | | | | | 173 | | &#173; | 219 | Û | &#219; | | | |

**FIGURE 2.20** The ASCII code as specified for use with Tektronics equipment.

tuation characters? The truth is that a good deal of arbitrariness is inherent in the selection of which numbers will be mapped to which characters by the ASCII code. Once you understand that the AS in ASCII stands for "American Standard," you can probably appreciate that a committee made a number of arbitrary decisions in setting up this code. Granted, the committee applied some common sense by making it fairly straightforward to use ASCII-encoded characters to correctly alphabetize sets of data; but many of the decisions were arbitrary. To correctly program a sorting algorithm that has some very stringent requirements for deciding whether "Clinton, William Jefferson" should precede "Clinton, William, Jefferson," or vice versa, you need to be able to consult the ASCII code table. Where is it? It's published in many places, including Figure 2.20.

Huffman codes [2] and other codes used for data compression follow a similar philosophy: Frequently occurring entities are given short encodings, and the rarer entities may have quite long encodings. Exercise 2.3 asks you to investigate this. Morse code suffers from potential ambiguity. Look at Figure 2.21 again and notice that the sequence $\cdot\_\_$ could represent the single letter *W*, or it might be the triplet *ETT*, or *EM* or *AT*. The key switch operator distinguishes between these possibilities by using a short pause between encodings of individual letters. Since the pause is thus incorporated as an integral and important feature of the language, the alphabet of DotDashStrings needs to be enhanced with a third

## Morse code
### The alphabet

| | | | | | | | | | | |
|---|---|---|---|---|---|---|---|---|---|---|
| .- | A | --. | G | -- | M | ... | S | -.-- | Y |
| -... | B | .... | H | -. | N | - | T | --.. | Z |
| -.-. | C | .. | I | --- | O | ..- | U | | |
| -.. | D | .--- | J | .--. | P | ...- | V | | |
| . | E | -.- | K | --.- | Q | .-- | W | | |
| ..-. | F | .-.. | L | .-. | R | -..- | X | | |

### Numbers

| | | | |
|---|---|---|---|
| .---- | 1 | -.... | 6 |
| ..--- | 2 | --... | 7 |
| ...-- | 3 | ---.. | 8 |
| ....- | 4 | ----. | 9 |
| ..... | 5 | ----- | 0 |

### Punctuation marks

| | | |
|---|---|---|
| Point (.) | .-.-.- | (AAA) |
| Comma (,) | --..-- | (MIM) |
| Comma (,) | --..-- | (MIM) |
| Question-mark (?) | ..--.. | (IMI) |
| Colon (:) | ---... | (OS) |
| Hyphen (-) | -....- | (BA) |
| At-sign (@) | .--.-. | (AC) |
| Error | ........ | |

**FIGURE 2.21**    The Morse code.

character –, the pause. Huffman codes have no need for such extensions. They are designed to have a prefix property so that no encoding is allowed to be a proper prefix of another encoding. In this way, the end of an encoding is uniquely determined, and when encountered the decoder can proceed to decoding a new entity [2].

**Exercise 2.3**

Following the directions in an algorithms textbook such as [2] write a program to generate a human code to produce binary strings for each character in your favorite Shakespeare play. Compare the length of the code for the letter *e* with the length of the code for the letter *x*. Repeat the exercise, but instead of using individual characters as the encoded unit, have your program develop an encoding for each individual word. Now compare the length of the code for the name of the leading character in your Shakespeare play with another word chosen by you at random from somewhere within the play.

Now let's turn our attention to the genetic code (see Figure 2.19). We can see some signs of sensible assignment of amino acid to codon. For example, there is some grouping so that minor errors in the nucleotides might still result in the same amino acid, or at least an amino acid that shares some important chemical property.

Whether the genetic code used is the best one possible is open to debate. Remember that evolution does not have the luxury of designing things ahead of time. Rather it must use what is already available and innovate from that. An interesting discussion of the extent to which the genetic code is arbitrary can be found in a chapter entitled "The Genetic Code: Arbitrary?"[8] in [3].

### Cellular Processors for DNAStrings

Translation according to the genetic code must be accomplished by ribosomes. Ribosomes "parse" the mRNA by introducing a subprocessing unit, called the **transfer RNA (tRNA).** The tRNA is represented by the cloverleaf-shaped piece of RNA shown in Figure 2.22. It is made up of the same four nucleotides,—A, C, G, and U—as in the mRNA. Unlike mRNA, however, the tRNA folds up into a complex shape by using hydrogen bonds.

Translation occurs when tRNAs are recruited by the ribosome and brought into close proximity to the mRNA. A tRNA has an **anticodon** end, which can bind to a complementary triplet of nucleotides (the codon) in the mRNA. The other end provides the correct amino acid for the ribosome to attach to its growing protein. In this sense, the different tRNA molecules within a cell provide the translation table for the genetic code. The tRNA is the mechanism that cells use to "look up" values in the genetic code. The tRNA is essentially an adapter that matches mRNA nucleotides to amino acids.

---

[8] Notice the capital letters in the title of Hofstadter's chapter.

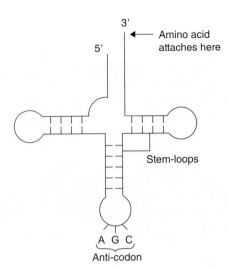

**FIGURE 2.22**   The tRNA is a specialized RNA molecule that matches codons in the mRNA to amino acids. Its structure is critical for its function.

The ribosome also provides the right chemical environment so that the amino acids held on the other end of the tRNA (see Figure 2.22) can form special bonds. More than one ribosome can be on an mRNA at any given time, so it is common to see long chains of proteins coming off the same mRNA strand. In this fashion, hundreds of copies of a protein can be made from a single mRNA. Each time the ribosome proceeds through the mRNA, it generates one copy of the protein.

As you'll see in the genetic code (see Figure 2.19), there are some triplet combinations that have special functions, one of which is to indicate where the protein synthesis should begin. This is known as the **start codon.** In most organisms, the start codon is an AUG. If you look at the genetic code, you'll see that AUG codes for the amino acid methionine. Almost all proteins begin with a methionine as the first amino acid in their sequence. In later stages of protein processing, this methionine is sometimes removed. But for protein synthesis to begin in the ribosome, the first tRNA into the ribosome has to carry a methionine.

There are three common **stop codons** that indicate where the ribosome should stop the synthesis of the protein: UAA, UAG, and UGA (see Figure 2.19). When the ribosome encounters one of these, it allows a special protein with the appropriate complementary codon sequence to enter the ribosome. This protein does not carry an amino acid. This absence of the amino acid on the protein carrying a match to a stop codon causes the ribosome to chemically terminate the protein chain. The ribosome then releases the finished protein. The protein can now fold into its correct shape and is ready for use by the cell.

### Executing DNAStrings: A Synopsis

Let's recap the events that lead to the execution of DNAStrings code. The primary objective of executing code in DNAStrings is to make a protein.[9] When signals

[9] We'll postpone a discussion of other kinds of code execution for the time being.

turn on the gene by activating a promoter (if–then–else statements in DNA-Strings), the equivalent of an executable copy of the code is made. This is stored in the molecule known as mRNA. Compiling to mRNA is accomplished by a protein called RNA polymerase. Once mRNA is made, the code is run by a processor known as the ribosome. The ribosome allows the protein to be made by creating the right environment for translation. The genetic code for triplet mRNA letters is used to convert mRNA sequences into strings of amino acids. This is done using a special adapter molecule known as the tRNA. Each tRNA matches up a triplet letter sequence known as a codon with an amino acid. The ribosome then makes special bonds between neighboring amino acids. These bonds are called peptide bonds. The long string of amino acids joined by these bonds will be the protein. Protein synthesis begins at a special signal, the start codon, and ends at a special signal, the stop codon. All proteins are synthesized with a methionine at the start, although sometimes the methionine is removed after synthesis.

The idea that information contained in the DNA passes into mRNA, which then transfers the information to protein is known as the **central dogma of molecular biology** and was formulated by the late Francis Crick, codiscoverer of the structure of DNA. Originally, the idea was that information flowed in just one direction: from DNA to mRNA to protein (Figure 2.23).

It turns out that the only rule in biology is that for every rule, there is an exception. We have since discovered that information can flow "backward" from mRNA into DNA in some viruses. This includes the human immunodeficiency virus (HIV), which causes acquired immunodeficiency syndrome (AIDS). These viruses store their genome as RNA rather than DNA and have a special enzyme, **reverse transcriptase,** which creates a DNA copy from the RNA genome. The DNA copy then makes more mRNA that can be translated into viral proteins. Some of the most potent anti-HIV drugs available today target this unusual enzyme in an effort to stop the virus from replicating and spreading.

In some instances proteins can also change the information content of the mRNA without changing the DNA. One such example is RNA editing in which some nucleotides of the mRNA are selectively changed. The result is that the

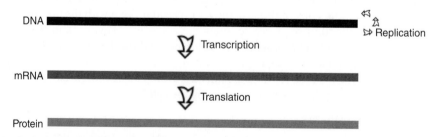

**FIGURE 2.23**    The central dogma of molecular biology states that information flows from DNA to RNA to protein. Since this original idea was stated in the 1950s, we have learned that information can flow "backward" from RNA to DNA and possibly from protein to RNA.

mRNA no longer exactly matches the DNA from which it was copied [7]. This is a bit like a computer in which some executable program files are occasionally edited "on the fly" to allow them to run in less time. Rather than edit the original code, the processor just makes adjustments to the executable file. If a computer actually did something like this, we would probably get pretty worried because we would have trouble understanding what was going on.[10] But it turns out cellular computers are constantly editing and modifying their code: at the source level (DNA), at the executable level (mRNA), and sometimes even after the protein has been made. Evolution has had 4 billion years to tinker with these processes, and it has come up with an extraordinary range of solutions.

## 2.4  FURTHER NUANCES IN DNASTRINGS

Now that we understand some of the process that executes DNAStrings code, we can look at more specific processes that occur during that execution. The description provided so far is actually the process as it occurs in bacteria or prokaryotes. These are the simpler cells in which all the components are jumbled together. The process is much more complicated in our own eukaryotic cells.

Prokaryotes are like computers using an old version of computing languages. In the early days of computing, programs were stand-alone sequences of instructions. These instructions might be punched onto cards and perhaps stored together in one box. To run a program, the cards had to be read, as a single continuous stream from the cards into contiguous locations in the computer's memory. When a few bells and whistles were correctly invoked, the program could then begin to execute. When it had finished its task, another program would be read into memory from another box of punched cards.

An analogy can be drawn with simple prokaryotic genes. Each is a set of cards unto itself, with perhaps some bells and whistles in the form of promoters and starts and stops. Groups of genes may be activated together, as in an operon, but each gene is essentially making its own protein.

In bacteria, each gene or box of cards is one contiguous sequence of DNA. These regions of the DNA sequence are called **open reading frames (ORFs)** (pronounced to rhyme with "morphs"). Genes in bacteria are relatively easy to find because you can search for the start codon and stop codon within the DNA sequence. Whenever you find a start codon followed by a minimum set of nonstop codons, you have an open reading frame. The ORF ends when you find a stop codon. Improved methods for finding a gene in bacteria that go beyond this

---

[10] It's interesting to note that in the early days of computing, before the development of modern conveniences like index registers, it was common for programmers to create self-modifying code to achieve what are today considered fairly mundane tasks such as operating on each member of an array. Nowadays we frown on the technique because it's hard for us to understand and verify the action of self-modifying code. On the other hand, we are not very good at simulating biological phenomena using our disciplined structured programming approach. Could it be that self-modifying code will be the key to successful computer simulation of life?

**FIGURE 2.24**
Overview of gene
structures in bacteria
and eukaryotes.

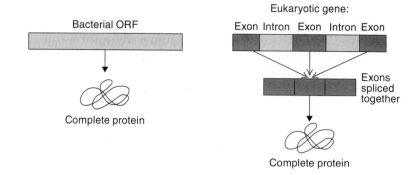

simple approach are discussed in Chapter 7. An example bacterial gene is shown in Figure 2.24.

Programmers soon came to realize that combining the effects of several program segments, albeit still sequentially, could enhance their abilities to achieve sophisticated computing. For example, one program segment might analyze some returns from exit polls after an election and leave its results (e.g., means, medians, or standard deviations) somewhere accessible to the next program segment. That program might look at the statistics generated by the first program and make some predictions about the expected winner. Although programs were still stand-alone sequences of instructions punched on cards, they could be made to act in groups and to communicate among one another to achieve the desired results.

Some prokaryotic genes find themselves grouped into operons. They may share bells and whistles and other signals. Their relative proximity makes it all possible. Just like the boxes of punched cards for coupled programs needed to be kept close together.

With the advent of secondary storage devices, ancestors of today's disk drives, it became possible to store portions of programs in such a way that other programs could invoke them as subprograms. Libraries of useful routines were accumulated. Sometimes copies of useful routines would be made and incorporated into the executables of the larger programs that called them. Sometimes, it was possible to arrange for "action at a distance," and program A could call up subroutine B without actually copying it into its own executable file.

We are far from understanding the mechanisms by which eukaryotic genes can work. This is because, much like modern-day, object-oriented programming, some of the "classes" and "methods" necessary to run these programs are fragmented and distributed at great distances from one another. We can see that the actions of a gene or group of genes can affect the actions of others. But it is not entirely clear how these effects occur. Science is only beginning to appreciate some of the interactions that characterize networks of genes.

The computing industry has not had the luxury of spending 4 billion years in the pursuit of effective regulation of program segments. But run a task manager program to see how different programs and groups of programs interact. See what happens when you randomly kill threads and obscurely named system routines. How can one program, such as Microsoft Word, within a suite like office conscript code from another program, say PowerPoint, to copy a graphic from a slide presentation into a typed document? Even outside of suites, programs are collaborating or interfering with one another all the time. Any modern multitasking operating system demonstrates a microcosm of collaborative network activity. If you were a visitor from another planet, you might be hard pressed to fathom the workings of the standard desktop computer from a sequential read of the bits on its hard drive. The same challenge faces us when we try to figure out what goes on as eukaryotic cells work with their genomes.

### Skipping Comments in DNAStrings Code

You can think of eukaryotic genes as being pieces of code held in multiple files, such as "header files," objects and classes from separate methods that need to be incorporated, and other subroutines, which must be distributed across several different "files." All the files are required for the code to generate a functional protein, but the files are interspersed with long stretches of DNA that do not contribute to the information content of the program. An example eukaryotic gene is shown in Figure 2.24 and the distribution of gene sizes is shown for human genes in Figure 2.25.

The portions of the code that do contribute to the generation of a protein are contained in regions of the gene called **exons.** These are like the individual files required for the code to execute properly. Interspersed within the gene sequence are also the long tracts of noncoding sequence known as **introns.** You can think of these as long sections of "comments" on the code. Although they don't contribute to the actual execution of the code, they do have some effect on the length of the code and on the way it is executed.

During transcription, the process of compiling the code into an executable file, the compiler (RNA polymerase) makes a copy of the entire stretch of the gene.

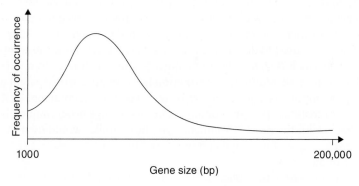

**FIGURE 2.25** Eukaryotic genes come in a range of sizes from as small as a few thousand bases to many hundreds of thousands of bases. Most genes are several thousand bases long, as shown here, but the distribution is extremely long-tailed. (Based on data from human genes in the RefSeq collection of GenBank).

**FIGURE 2.26**
The process of splicing involves looping the intronic sequence around and then cutting it at the 5′ and 3′ ends as shown here.

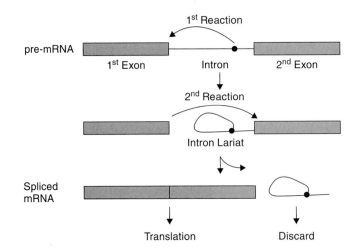

This includes both the exons (files that contribute to the final protein generation) and the introns (comments on the code). In a separate step, the introns are removed by a mechanism called **splicing.** Figure 2.26 shows how this would occur in an eukaryotic gene.

An amazing piece of machinery known as the **spliceosome** actually carries out the chemical reactions necessary. The spliceosome is itself made up of RNA as well as some proteins, and it reads the executable file of mRNA to find and remove the introns. It does this with remarkable accuracy: 98% of all mRNAs are correctly spliced in your cells. What makes this accuracy so impressive is that it appears that primarily two short signals specify the regions where the introns are. Introns are marked by a GU at the 5′ end of the intron and an AG at the 3′ end of the intron. When you think about it, this is a pretty small signal. At random a GU will occur once in every 16 bases ($4^2$) as would the AG. Yet, the spliceosome is able to find and splice out the introns with extraordinary accuracy!

To get a sense of how difficult this task actually is, consider a piece of computer code in which comments are marked with the # sign. Let's suppose that the # sign is also used to demarcate array data structures. Now the compiler has to figure out which # signs refer to comments and which refer to an array. The compiler has to have additional information because otherwise it might accidentally skip an important data structure or try to compile a comment as if it were an array. For instance, perhaps comments in this strange programming language always begin with the word "Comment." So the compiler would treat this string: #Comment ... as if it were a comment and this string: #my_files ... as the name of an array.

We would expect the spliceosome, which is a kind of compiler, to utilize additional signals in identifying the sites at which splicing should occur. There have been a number of tantalizing hints about what those signals should be, but no one yet knows what, how or where these signals are. We are still trying to figure out how the spliceosome finds the actual introns rather than splicing out every stretch of DNA between a GU and an AG. We will discuss some strategies for finding such signals in the introns in Chapter 7.

### *Setting Permissions*

Earlier, we mentioned that mRNA is relatively unstable and can be degraded rather quickly. This is like a system in which executable files are periodically deleted, perhaps as a protection against computer viruses. In fact, the same may be true of the cellular process of degrading mRNA. It turns out that many cellular viruses have RNA as their genome (rather than DNA). By deleting or degrading mRNA on a regular basis, the cell may be able to protect itself from infection by these RNA viruses. The caveat is that executable files that are important for the cell itself will also be subject to deletion. This is a big problem because the cell cannot make proteins if it does not have the executable files of mRNA.

Cells have worked out a solution to this problem. They chemically modify the mRNA at two places. At the beginning or 5′ end, the cell adds a chemically modified guanine (G). This is known as the **5′ cap.** At the endpoint or 3′ end of the mRNA, the cell adds a long string of adenines (A). This is known as **polyadenylation** (derived from the words *poly* [meaning "many"], *adenine*, and the suffix *-ation* [meaning to indicate an action]). Without these two protectors, the mRNA would be rapidly degraded and the nucleotides in the mRNA reused for some other mRNA.

The chemical modifications of mRNA may remind you of the use of a **dirty bit** in page-replacement schemes in a computer system. When code or data is being switched into and out of memory one page at a time during the execution of a program, it is possible to avoid rewriting some pages to disk if it is known that they did not change while they were paged in to memory. The dirty bit is set if any part of a page has been modified. Without the dirty bit, the system will allow the page to be overwritten without first copying its contents to disk. The page's bits in memory will simply "evaporate."

These modifications of mRNA are common to all eukaryotes but do not occur in bacterial or other prokaryotic cells. They are just one example of the increase in complexity as you move along the tree of life from prokaryotes to eukaryotes (see Figure 2.1).

## 2.5  PROTEINS: CELLULAR MACHINES

We have described at length the ways in which cells make proteins. But what are proteins themselves? Proteins are essentially the cellular hardware. They are the machines and processors that handle all the tasks the cell needs to survive.

Recall the example of the *E. coli* receptors that can sense the presence of food or toxic molecules in the environment. Receptors are proteins. DNA polymerase, which replicates DNA, is also a protein. So is RNA polymerase, the compiler that compiles DNAStrings code. When you hear people talking about "getting enough protein" in their diet, they are actually talking about the full set of proteins present in the cells we consume as food. Whether it is animal protein or plant protein, all proteins share some common features. We will consider these properties in this section.

## 2.5.1  Proteins as Molecules

Let us start by describing proteins chemically. As we mentioned earlier, proteins are long strings of chemical units known as amino acids. Twenty amino acids are used by all biological systems. Some of their chemical properties are shown in Figure 2.27.

Amino acids are made up of two parts: a carbon chain, sometimes known as the R chain, and a nitrogen group known as the amine group. One end of the carbon chain contains an acid structure, accounting for their designation as acids. The carbon chain provides each amino acid with its unique chemical properties. Amino acid structures are shown in Figure 2.27.

Amino acids bond to each other through a special kind of chemical connection called a **peptide bond.** Unlike the hydrogen bonds of DNA, peptide bonds are true covalent bonds. That is, they result from the electrons within the amine group being shared with the electrons of the acid group on the next amino acid. The result is an extremely strong, flexible bond. Amino acids can be strung together into long chains via these peptide bonds to form proteins.

Most proteins range between a few dozen to a few thousand amino acids in length; but we don't know of any specific upper limit to this length. So these 20 amino acids have a potentially infinite set of combinations, given the lengths of possible proteins. However, in practice, many of these combinations would be chemically or energetically unstable. A conservative estimate is that about a million distinct amino acid sequences exist among all the organisms on the planet.

Proteins are often complex three-dimensional structures because the amino acids can interact with one another through the carbon chain portions of the molecules. They can form hydrogen bonds and other weak interactions. They can also form bonds that involve sharing electrons or trading electrons. As a result, it is rare to find a protein that is just one long, straight chain of amino acids. Rather, proteins are folded up into complex 3-D structures (Figure 2.28).

### Protein Structure

Protein structure occurs on four levels, each of which contributes to the overall shape of the protein. The first level, or **primary structure,** is just the string of amino acids. This is the 2-D view of proteins. In cells, this string of amino acids rapidly folds up into a 3-D shape that is composed of two kinds of **secondary structures**—level two of protein structure. Secondary structures include the **alpha (α)-helix** and the **beta (β)-sheet.** The α-helix is a rigid corkscrew structure. It is often present to provide structural integrity within a protein. An example is shown in Figure 2.29. The β-sheet is a flat layer of strands that wrap back and forth as shown in Figure 2.30. This is also a rigid structure used

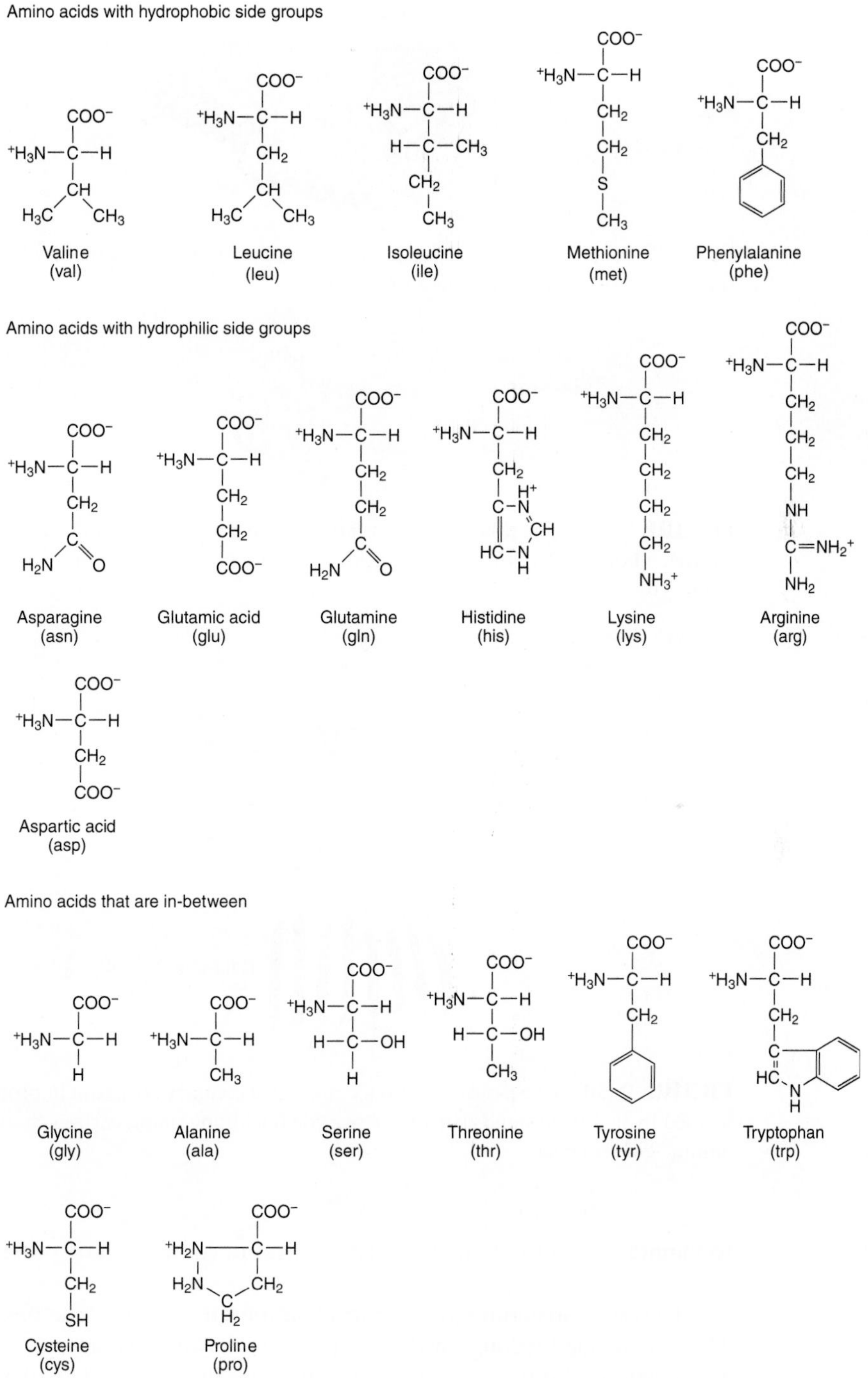

Amino acids with hydrophobic side groups

Valine
(val)

Leucine
(leu)

Isoleucine
(ile)

Methionine
(met)

Phenylalanine
(phe)

Amino acids with hydrophilic side groups

Asparagine
(asn)

Glutamic acid
(glu)

Glutamine
(gln)

Histidine
(his)

Lysine
(lys)

Arginine
(arg)

Aspartic acid
(asp)

Amino acids that are in-between

Glycine
(gly)

Alanine
(ala)

Serine
(ser)

Threonine
(thr)

Tyrosine
(tyr)

Tryptophan
(trp)

Cysteine
(cys)

Proline
(pro)

**FIGURE 2.27**   The 20 amino acids found in all biological systems. The chemical structure of an amino acid determines its properties and will influence the shape and function of the resulting protein.

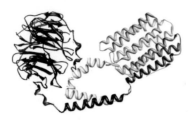

**FIGURE 2.28**    Proteins are made up of chains of amino acids that fold into complex three-dimensional structures as shown here.

**FIGURE 2.29**    The α-helix is a common secondary structure in proteins formed by hydrogen bonds along the peptide backbone (main carbon chain) of an amino acid sequence.

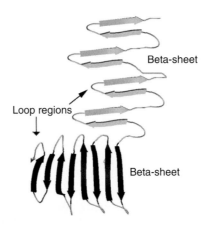

**FIGURE 2.30**    The β-sheet is also a common secondary structure in proteins. It is formed by hydrogen bonds across the peptide backbone (main carbon chain) of an amino acid sequence.

to maintain structural integrity. The central portion of many proteins contains a β-sheet.

These two structures are the most common secondary structures in proteins. They are formed through hydrogen bonding between the amine (nitrogen) and acid portions of different amino acids. Because these regions are the central part of the amino acid chain, they are also known as the **peptide backbone.** Many

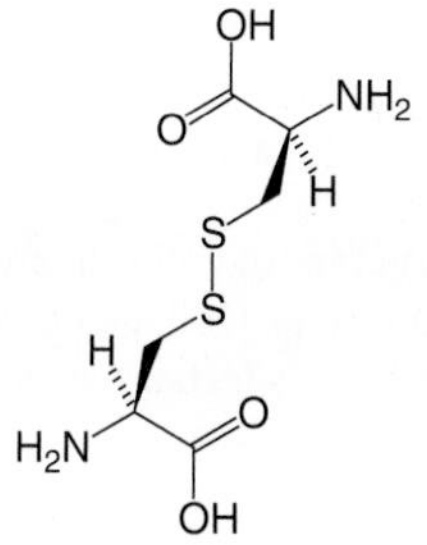

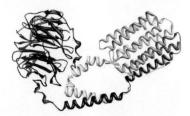

**FIGURE 2.31**   Disulfide bonds can form between two cysteines on different parts of a peptide chain to create a secondary structure. The bonds are true covalent bonds (not like hydrogen bonds) and are very stable even at high temperatures.

**FIGURE 2.32**   The full three-dimensional structure of a protein is known as its tertiary structure. Note the presence of the secondary structures such as β-sheets and α-helices. This is a good example of how secondary structure contribute to the final tertiary structure of a protein.

different kinds of amino acids can participate in the formation of α-helices and β-sheets because the bonds are formed along the main carbon chain rather than with specific side chains.

Specific interactions with side chains can also create secondary structures. For example, the amino acid cysteine contains a sulfur atom, which can bond to the sulfur in another cysteine to create a **disulfide bond** (Figure 2.31). Disulfide bonds are quite common in the proteins that make up hair. In fact, the curliness of hair is determined in part by the presence of these disulfide bonds. The more cysteine present in the hair protein, the more disulfide bonds formed, and the curlier the hair. This is a good example of how secondary structure alone can affect the resulting shape of a protein.

For most proteins, however, the real 3-D shape is formed when the secondary structures fold up into a complete protein. The **tertiary structure** of a protein is its final, three-dimensional shape as shown in Figure 2.32. The two most common tertiary structures are **globular** and **fibrous.**

Globular proteins are often involved in mediating chemical reactions. For example, the enzymes that break down food in your intestines are globular proteins. So are the "machines" that process code in DNAStrings: both DNA and

**FIGURE 2.33**    The tertiary structure of collagen creates a ropelike appearance, which is critical to its function in skin elasticity. Collagen is actually made up of three α-helices that twist around each other to create its tertiary structure.

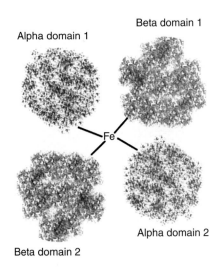

**FIGURE 2.34**    Hemoglobin, the protein that transports oxygen within the blood, is made up two kinds of proteins. Hemoglobin has a total of four protein molecules, two of each kind of protein, that together create its quarternary structure. Note the prevalence of helices in these structures.

RNA polymerases are globular proteins. An example globular protein is shown in Figure 2.32.

Fibrous proteins are most often part of structural units. For example, collagen is the protein that allows your skin to be smooth and elastic (Figure 2.33). Collagen fibers disintegrate over time, and as a result you develop wrinkles as you grow older. As a piece of trivia, the most common protein in your body is collagen: you have more collagen proteins in your skin than any other kind of protein in any other organ.

Several protein chains can assemble together to create a larger structure. The whole set of protein chains that constitute the protein is said to have **quaternary structure** (level four). A good example of such a structure is hemoglobin, the molecule that carries oxygen in your blood. As you can see in Figure 2.34, hemoglobin has four distinct protein chains, each with its own primary, secondary, and tertiary structure. The quarternary structure forms when the four units assemble around an iron atom. It is the iron that binds and holds on to the oxygen in your blood. The rest of the protein creates a stable chemical environment so that the oxygen is not lost during transport.

## 2.5.2  Proteins as Engineered Machines

From an engineering perspective, each protein in a cell is part of a module that will accomplish a given task. The way proteins perform their work is primarily through chemical interactions with other proteins or molecules.

### Protein Interactions

Recall the receptors on the surface of the *E. coli* cell that receives input about the presence of food or toxins in the environment. That receptor is a protein that changes its shape when a food molecule chemically binds to a part of it. The change in shape is communicated to an associated protein on the inside of the cell membrane. This protein then separates from the cell membrane and can interact with various proteins within the cell. Each of those proteins then interacts with others and so on until a protein binds the promoter (as described in our discussion of the biological equivalent of the if–then–else statement in DNAStrings). The result of all these proteins communicating with one another is that "decisions" are made and new proteins may be generated depending on circumstances.

**SIDEBAR**

## Viruses

Ligands are not limited to just small molecules. They can be large proteins in their own right. A good example of this is a special protein found on the surface of HIV. These proteins can bind to specific receptors on the cells that participate in the body's response to infections—the immune system. The receptors on these cells are actually specific for other molecules, but HIV has evolved mimics of the real ligands. Because the chemical structure of the virus coat proteins is very similar to that of the receptors' actual ligand, it can bind to the receptor. It then sets off a signaling cascade within the cell (just like the real ligand would). This allows the virus entry into the cell. Once inside the cell, the HIV viral genome takes over the cellular machinery for reading, compiling, and executing DNAStrings code. The result is that the cell simply becomes a factory for manufacturing virus rather than doing its actual job.

If you think about receptors as input devices into the cell, then biological viruses are exactly like computer viruses. They enter the cell by disguising their true contents and appearing to be a real, harmless ligand. Once inside the cell, they take over the cell's computing and processing abilities to duplicate themselves. When they leave the cell, the cell often dies through loss of resources or because its membranes have been ruptured.

So how does this communication between proteins occur? They are the result of chemical interactions. In the case of the *E. coli* receptor, the protein receptor is able to chemically bind to various molecules. Each molecule that can bind a receptor is known as a **ligand.** Every protein has **specificity,** that is, it can only bind to certain kinds of ligands. Because each protein interaction is a critical activity in the function of the cell and has to be closely regulated, very few proteins can bind to broad ranges of ligands. Proteins that can bind many different ligands are more difficult to control. So most cells have evolved multiple proteins to handle specific types of ligands rather than having one master protein capable of binding everything.

Within cells, groups of proteins often "band together" into complexes. For example, although DNA polymerase is the main protein involved in DNA replication (Section 2.6.1), it is part of a larger complex. This complex includes the proteins that unwind DNA, stitch the fragments of the strands together, and many other proteins with functions related to DNA replication. The whole set of proteins are required for DNA replication, and from a systems perspective, the complex as a whole is a module. The same is true for RNA polymerase, which "compiles" DNAStrings code into mRNA. It is also part of a complex of proteins, all of which are required. Protein complexes are probably the most basic modules present within cells.

### Types of Protein Machines

It is far beyond the scope of this text to detail the many thousands of types of proteins present in a cell. However, there are a few classes of proteins so common and so important for cellular function that you will need to know about them.

We have talked a great deal about receptors, the input devices for the cells. These proteins are known as **transmembrane proteins** because they usually traverse the two layers that form the cell membrane. Most transmembrane (or TM) proteins share certain common features. For example, to cross the membrane, they must have stretches of amino acids that are chemically stable within the membrane. The cell membrane is made up partly of fatty acids, and these molecules are very hydrophobic. That is, they repel water. Think of adding oil to a glass of water. The oil molecules tend to bunch up and exclude water from their interiors. This is exactly what happens in the interior of the cell membrane. The fatty acids assemble in a way that excludes water from the interior of the cell membrane.

To cross the cell membrane, all TM proteins have stretches of hydrophobic amino acids. These are usually assembled into a set of $\alpha$-helices so that the protein can span the entire width of the cell membrane. However, most TM proteins also have sections that will extend out past the cell membrane or extend into the cytoplasm. Both of these environments are very rich in water. So TM proteins also have regions that contain hydrophilic amino acids.

One of the key challenges with identifying proteins computationally is to determine if the sequence of amino acids alternates between very hydrophobic and very hydrophilic regions. If an amino acid sequence has such a characteristic, then it is likely to be a TM protein. We will discuss issues of identifying protein structure computationally in Section 9.3 of Chapter 9.

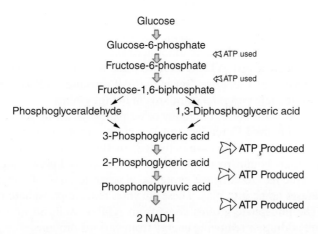

Glucose

⇩

Glucose-6-phosphate

⇩        ◁ ATP used

Fructose-6-phosphate

⇩        ◁ ATP used

Fructose-1,6-biphosphate

Phosphoglyceraldehyde            1,3-Diphosphoglyceric acid

3-Phosphoglyceric acid

⇩        ⇨ ATP Produced

2-Phosphoglyceric acid

⇩        ⇨ ATP Produced

Phosphonolpyruvic acid

⇩        ⇨ ATP Produced

2 NADH

**FIGURE 2.35**    Glycolysis—one of the best studied metabolic pathways is common to both bacteria and eukaryotes. The glycolytic pathway involves a series of biochemical reactions that break down glucose (a sugar) to obtain energy. The energy is stored in molecules of ATP.

Another class of extremely important proteins are **enzymes.** These are the chemical catalysts that allow reactions to occur. As we mentioned earlier, chemical reactions require very specific environments and conditions. Enzymes allow reactions to occur by creating a microenvironment within the enzyme that has the right conditions for the reaction. In biology, you can usually identify enzymes by their names. Most enzymes end in the suffix -*ase*. For example, DNA polymer*ase* is an enzyme that creates the right environment in which nucleotide letters can be strung together to form a DNA strand.

Many of the enzymes we know about are involved in **metabolic pathways**— processes that allow molecules to be chemically modified and converted to yield energy. Recall that in cells, energy is stored in a special molecule, ATP. All cells have sophisticated mechanisms for transferring the energy stored in various molecules into the high-energy bonds of ATP. Figure 2.35 shows one of the best studied pathways for generating ATP from sugar molecules.

Why would cells need to transfer the energy to ATP? Why not just use the energy inherent in any given molecule? The fact is that most molecules, especially from substances we think of as food, have very low energy bonds. Breaking each of these bonds would release just a small amount of energy. Sometimes, a process that occurs within the cell requires more energy than the breaking of such bonds can provide. For example, DNA replication requires about 60 kJ[11] for every nucleotide added to the new DNA strand. Rather than try and corral many different types of molecules to obtain the needed energy for a process, cells use one ATP molecule for each nucleotide added to the DNA strand. This simplifies the process of obtaining and using energy within the cell.

---

[11] This is exactly the amount of energy contained in two phosphate bonds of ATP.

ATP molecules in essence store the cumulative energy of many different kinds of molecules. It turns out that breaking each bond of the three high-energy phosphate bonds yields about the right amount of energy for the majority of reactions that occur within the cell. ATP is often referred to as the "currency" of the cell to conduct its energy-exchange "business." All cells use ATP as their currency, so it is one of the few universal standards in living systems.

Enzymes are also present in many other pathways within the cell. One class of enzymes is involved in regulating when certain proteins are turned "on" or turned "off." Many proteins are activated, or turned "on," when they have a phosphate group bound to them. Enzymes known as **kinases** add phosphate groups to proteins. To turn off proteins, a separate class of enzymes known as **phosphatases** come into play. These enzymes remove phosphate groups from proteins. The phosphate groups come from ATP as well. So in a sense, these enzymes are adding or removing energy from various proteins.

A signaling cascade, such as the one that communicates the presence of food to the *E. coli* is usually composed of multiple kinases and phosphatases. Essentially, information is transmitted around the cell when phosphate groups are added or removed from various proteins.

Recall that we described the machine language of cells as being the language of chemical interactions. We can refine that description now. In fact, for the vast majority of processes in the cell, the actual "machine language" is expressed in terms of the phosphate groups bound to or removed from various proteins. In this sense, the machine language of cells is a binary one just like that in computing systems. Unlike computing systems, however, the language is not expressed as 0's or 1's. Rather, it is determined by the presence or absence of a phosphate group.

## 2.6  DATA MAINTENANCE AND INTEGRITY TASKS

Now that we understand how cells make proteins, it should be clear that the DNA in the genome is central to the process. When we talk about mutations that lead to natural selection, we are talking about changes to the DNA—the genotypic changes we discussed earlier. Over time, these genotypic changes can lead to phenotypic (i.e., large, visible) changes.

Small mutations to the DNA can affect how the code is read or compiled. They can also directly influence the end product of the execution of the code: the sequence of amino acids within a protein. The reason evolution can proceed is that the DNA is open to mutation. On the other hand, too many mutations within one cell can lead to disaster. If too many mutations occur, the code will be so corrupted that the cell cannot read or execute it. Cells have to balance the need to evolve in the long-term with the more immediate need to preserve the integrity of their data and code.

### 2.6.1  Backing up DNA Data

The first and foremost concern of cells and computing systems is to maintain the integrity of the code and data required for operation. In many computing systems, this takes place in essentially three ways. The first is through "back-ups" of the data and source code at routine intervals. The second is through error detection mechanisms that can identify where the code is corrupted or modified at random. Having found an error, systems must also have mechanisms for correcting those errors to the best of their ability. We will see in this section how both computing systems and cellular systems have methods for maintaining data integrity.

The first step to ensuring that data integrity is maintained is to back up the data. In essence, a second copy of the data needs to be retained. This is important not only to ensure a replacement if the first copy is destroyed, but also that errors in one copy can be corrected by consulting the other copy. In computing systems, back-ups can be done in one of two ways. The first is to store a copy of the data on a separate, often different medium. For example, magnetic tapes can be used to store all the data normally found on a hard drive. This approach is advantageous because the tape archives can be stored in a separate location, thereby ensuring that disaster at one location does not wipe out all the instances of the data.

However, tape archives have a limited storage capacity. As hard drives have grown exponentially, backing up to a tape archive has become increasingly impractical. Therefore, the preferred method for data storage and back-ups has been to store to another hard drive. One solution is through a variety of RAID (redundant arrays of inexpensive drives) architectures which allow for replication and storage of data across hard drives. The data is synchronized at regular intervals across the RAID drives. The result is a mechanism for ensuring that replicates of the data and their organization are retained.

Cells tend to favor the second approach to data storage. In fact, cellular back-ups resemble a RAID array in that a duplicate of the data is stored in the same medium and in the same location as the first copy. Specifically, cells adopt the equivalent of a RAID1 configuration. In computers, RAID1 arrays essentially write the same data to two separate disk drives. The result is a perfect replica of the data. In terms of storage, this is an expensive operation. However, in terms of reliability, it is the best choice.

For cells, RAID1 architectures are implemented through DNA. The physical structure of DNA, the double helix, essentially provides two copies of the DNA code. DNAStrings code is read off of just one strand of DNA at any given time. The other strand therefore serves as the "back-up." Each strand of DNA is like a disk drive. The RAID1 configuration means that each strand is an exact replicate of the other. In practice, the DNA strands have complementary sequences. But the information content of each strand is identical.

## DNA: Duplicating RAID Arrays

When cells divide to produce new cells, the DNA information of the cell must be transferred as well. This is done by making a new copy of the DNA for each new cell. Most cells divide in a binary fashion: one cell becomes two, two become four, and so on. Each time, the cell must make two copies of double-helixed ("double-stranded" in biology parlance) DNA for the daughter cells. This is done through **DNA replication.** In essence, this process creates two new RAID1 arrays from the existing one.

The first step in DNA replication is to separate the two strands of DNA. Each strand of original DNA acts as a **template** for the generation of a new strand. In general, the DNA strands are not completely unwound. Instead, a small section of DNA is unwound at a specific location, known as the **origin of replication.** As replication proceeds, this small "bubble" where replication begins widens and spreads in both directions as shown in Figure 2.36. At no time in the process is the DNA left in a single-stranded state for very long because single-stranded DNA would be unstable and could be degraded just like single-stranded mRNA.

**DNA polymerase,** the machine that does DNA replication, is a quite remarkable parser of DNAStrings code. It reads each letter of DNA and then creates the complementary letter, stringing these new letters together to create an entirely new, complementary strand to the one it is reading. Like RNA polymerase, DNA polymerase is very fast: it can replicate all 3.2 billion letters of the human genome in about 1 hour.

The chemical structure of DNA forces DNA polymerase to move in the 5′-to-3′ direction, adding new letters to the 3′ end of the new strand. To get the correct complement to the existing strand, DNA polymerase reads off the template strand in the 3′-to-5′ direction. *That is, DNA polymerase synthesizes in the 5′-to-3′ direction and reads in the 3′ to 5′ direction.* Recall that the two strands of DNA run in opposite directions or are antiparallel. So for the reverse strand, the one running from 3′ to 5′, DNA polymerase can just move along the strand, adding the appropriate complement letter to the new strand (see Figure 2.36).

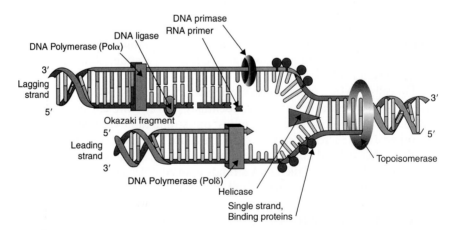

**FIGURE 2.36**  DNA replication involves a complex of several proteins that unwind the DNA from the helix and then duplicate the strands. Some of the components are shown here. The DNA polymerase on the leading strand can synthesize a continuous strand, whereas the DNA polymerase on the lagging strand synthesizes short fragments called Okazaki fragments. These are then stitched together to yield the complete strand. (Source: This image was generated by Mariana Ruiz Villanreal and has been released to the public domain.)

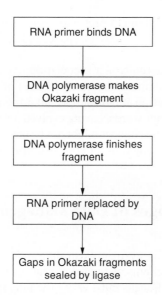

**FIGURE 2.37**    For the lagging strand, DNA replication must occur in short stretches that are then stitched together. The short segments that are initially synthesized are known as Okazaki fragments.

However, for the forward strand, running in the 5′-to-3′ direction, the mechanism is more complex. The DNA polymerase skips forward a little distance, reads about 50–100 letters and synthesizes the complement sequence. It then stops, moves forward a little more, and repeats the process. The result is that many little fragments of DNA need to be stitched together to get the complete strand of new DNA. These fragments, known as **Okazaki fragments,** and a set of special enzymes, known as ligases, stitch the fragments together (Figure 2.37).

When you view DNA replication under a microscope, it looks like one strand is being replicated at top speed, while the other seems to be trailing along. The strand that is synthesized continuously is known as the **leading strand.** The other strand, being synthesized in short segments with stitching together, is known as the **lagging strand.**

Why does DNA polymerase have to contort itself in this fashion? Why not have two DNA polymerases, each running along the original DNA template from the 3′-to-5′ direction? In other words, why not have two leading strands instead of just the one? There is not a clear answer to this, save that evolution is a "blind engineer," so design is not necessarily inherent to the process.

However, a simple chemical necessity may force the arrangement we observe in cells. If there were two DNA polymerase complexes, one running in each direction along the template, larger sections of DNA would have to be unwound to provide access for these very large proteins. As mentioned earlier, single-stranded DNA is not very stable. So by unwinding larger sections, the cell runs the risk that the DNA template will degrade before the DNA polymerase can read the template. Therefore, the cell might prefer to open a small section of DNA, allow one DNA polymerase complex into the space, and accept the lower efficiency of this arrangement.

This explanation is actually just speculation; we have no reason to believe that evolution "thought" about the consequences of the arrangement. Like a good programmer, evolution might simply take the approach that "if it ain't broke, don't fix it!" In other words, having evolved a functional system for DNA replication, any incremental changes might not be favorable enough to be selected. As a result, new solutions might never appear simply because the current system works well enough.

## 2.6.2  The Challenges of Data Management

### Verifying Data Integrity

Cells need more than just a way to duplicate data and distribute it to their daughter cells. They also need mechanisms to ensure that the current data have not been corrupted. In other words, cells must verify the integrity of the DNA at regular intervals. Cells use a variety of mechanisms to check the integrity of their data, some of which have direct corollaries to computing solutions. Computing systems must also ensure the integrity of their data, so we consider solutions from the realm of computing first.

One of the key challenges in computing is to store data in as efficient a way as possible. We just discussed the use of RAID arrays for backing up data and suggested that cells take the RAID1 approach to data back-up. This is the most expensive solution in terms of storage but is the best solution in terms of maintaining data integrity. To get around the cost of storing multiple duplicates of large amounts of data, computer scientists have developed a variety of solutions. Chief among these are methods for data compression.

### Data Compression

Data compression seeks to minimize the storage or bandwidth necessary to store or transmit information. This is true whether we are considering binary strings of information stored on a hard drive or DNAStrings code stored in a cell: it is often necessary to compress the data to maximize storage efficiency. The size of the hard drive, for instance, is a physical limitation that could determine the need for data compression. The size of the cell is also a physical limitation and an extreme one at that. Most eukaryotic cells are on the order of a few hundred micrometers ($\mu$m, $10^{-6}$m) in diameter. The DNA of most cells, however, is many times this length. For example, the DNA in any one of your cells if stretched out would be about 1 m in length [1]! Obviously, massive compression is necessary to fit the DNA into microscopic cells.

DNA is compressed, or "packaged," by twisting it tightly around and around until it is a tight ball. Think of a rubber band that you keep twisting and knotting until you have a small, tight ball. This is similar to what happens to most DNA. The actual packaging of DNA is handled by special proteins, chief of which are the **histones.** These proteins bind at regular intervals along bare DNA, and the DNA is wrapped around them, much as string would be wrapped around a yo-yo (Figure 2.38).

DNA compression takes place on many levels. The first level involves four types of histone proteins, which together form the core **nucleosome.** Each nucleosome covers about 250 nucleotides of DNA sequence. Between each nucleosome is a short stretch of DNA, known as **linker DNA.** A separate histone protein binds to the linker DNA. The nucleosomes and linker DNA are then wrapped around each other and packed tightly in a variety of ways, with increasing compression at each level (Figure 2.39).

DNA compression, like other forms of data compression, presents some practical problems. Although it is convenient to package the DNA in order to fit it inside a cell, the DNAStrings code cannot be read or executed while it is in a packaged (compressed) state. Just as with binary data, it must be uncompressed before it can be utilized. Specific regions of DNA are unpackaged when a particular gene's worth of code is required.

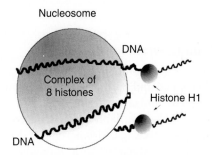

**FIGURE 2.38**   Depicted here are several histone proteins, each of which helps bind to and wrap the DNA. The nucleosome contains four types of histones and has two molecules of each of these four histones. In addition, another histone known as histone H1 binds the DNA between nucleosomes.

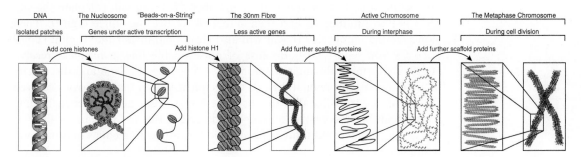

**FIGURE 2.39**   The many levels of DNA packaging are shown here. The first level involves the nucleosomes, made up of DNA and histone proteins. Further packaging allows the DNA to be compressed up to 10,000-fold so it can fit inside microscopic cells.
(Image designed and updated by Richard Wheeler.)

We do not fully understand how sections of DNA are unpackaged, but we do know that most cells have unpackaged regions of DNA as well as tightly packaged ones. The unpackaged regions, known as **euchromatin,** contain the DNAStrings code that the cell requires to function. Regions that are not required are kept tightly packaged and known as **heterochromatin.**

A multicellular organism such as yourself has many different cell types. Since every cell in your body has the same genomic content,[12] cells cannot just cut out the parts of the genome that are not needed for their particular function. Rather, they regulate which regions of the DNA are packaged or unpackaged. Only the unpackaged euchromatin regions of the DNA can be compiled and executed. For example, a liver cell's euchromatin will include those genes (containing the DNAStrings code) required for liver function. A brain cell, in contrast, would have euchromatin in other regions of the genome that are required for brain function. The regions of the DNA related to brain function are packaged as heterochromatin in the liver cell and vice versa. This allows cells to maintain their specialized functions even though each cell has the full genome. We refer to specialized cells that have packaged unnecessary regions of the genome as **differentiated** cells.

### Redundancy and Data Compression

As long as storage devices and communications channels are perfectly reliable, data compression is beneficial and problem-free. Unfortunately, reliability is not always one hundred percent, and errors occur in hardware and noise (unwanted, intrusive extra information) is invariably present on communication channels. Error-detecting and error-correcting codes have been developed that use redundancy to overcome problems associated with unreliable components and noisy channels.

A simple error-detecting scheme for the transmission of numerical data is sometimes referred to as a **checksum.** The idea is to repeatedly add up all the digits in a number that you wish to store or transmit until only a single digit remains. You then append that digital sum in a prearranged location. For example, before you store or transmit the number 5751 you will calculate the sum 5+7+5+1 to produce 18 and then sum 1+8 to give the single digit 9. Then, alongside the number 5751 you will also store or transmit that digital sum 9. Let's say you send 57519. Because of noise on the line, a recipient receives 56519. By forming the digital sum $5 + 6 + 5 + 1 \rightarrow 17 \rightarrow 8$ and discovering that 8 differs from the final digit 9, the recipient knows that an error occurred. Of course, it is possible that two or more errors occur and cancel each other, thereby causing the errors to escape undetected. But for very noisy lines we can develop similar but more sophisticated error-detecting codes that use more redundancy.

---

[12] With some exceptions, as always. Certain cells in your immune system actually cut out portions of DNA from their genomes as they become specialized to attack a specific infectious agent.

## Stem Cells and Differentiation

You may have heard about stem cells, special cells sometimes taken from embryos, which are able to become any kind of cell within an organism. These cells are unique in that they can access any part of the genome they need. In contrast, differentiated cells have so tightly packaged certain regions of the genome that they can never access them again. For example, a normal skin cell cannot spontaneously become a liver cell because it cannot unpack the DNA regions that contain the code to begin making liver cell proteins.[13] However, a stem cell from an embryo can do this: it can make skin cells and, presumably, liver cells, muscle cells, and brain cells.

How do stem cells retain the ability to become any kind of cell? Part of the answer lies in their source. Embryonic stem cells, which can generate the widest range of possible cell types, are derived from very early human embryos. During fertilization, the process that creates a human embryo, an egg and a sperm combine to create a single cell that will give rise to all the other cells in the body. This cell is said to be omnipotent, meaning it can make any kind of cell. Over the course of the first two weeks after fertilization, this cell divides over and over again to form a small ball of cells. Each of these cells is also capable of becoming any kind of cell within the body. It is these cells that are harvested and grown in the laboratory as embryonic stem cells.

If these cells are left to grow in the embryo, they start the process of specialization. Cells that are harvested in this stage are called pluripotent, meaning they can still become many types of cells, but the range is more limited than that for the original fertilized cell. Eventually, each of these stem cells will become even more specialized, resulting in a fully formed fetus and eventually a human baby.

Some stem cells remain, however, even in the adult human. The best known are the stem cells that reside in the bone marrow. These cells are pluripotent: that is, they can become any kind of blood cell (red blood cells, white blood cells, macrophages, and others). You may have heard of bone marrow transplants for treating leukemia or other cancers that damage blood cells. A bone marrow transplant essentially replaces the damaged stem cells with fresh ones that will be able to make healthy blood cells.

The hope is that one day we will be able to use stem cells to replace many different kinds of damaged cells from brain cells to skin cells. You can find out more about stem cells by visiting the National Institutes of Health Website at: http://stemcells.nih.gov/index.asp

---

[13] An interesting exception to this general fact has been manipulated in cloning organisms. It turns out if you place the nucleus of a fully differentiated cell such as a skin cell into an egg cell, then the nucleus resets itself and can produce a viable embryo with every kind of cell type again.

In any case, we hope you see how, by storing or sending more than the bare minimum of information necessary, it is possible to use that redundancy to detect errors in storage or transmission. Some codes even go beyond error-detection and provide reliable error correction. MacWilliams and Sloane describe many in [8].

### Cellular Approaches to Data Integrity

Cells have evolved error-detecting and error-correcting mechanisms to deal with genomic replication, which is fraught with dangers. Mutations can and do occur. Many mutations, however, are corrected. As usual, evolution has produced a mechanism that allows just enough mutation for successful evolution to occur! The previously mentioned discussion in [3] also considers the balances between the competing concepts of efficiency of data transmission and the need for redundancy to correct errors. Over 4 billion years, evolution has achieved an interesting compromise.

Cells back up their data by making another copy of it. Any time you begin a copying process, there is a small chance of an error occurring during the copying. It's hard to find information on error rates for copies to and from computer drives, but one in a trillion is probably an overestimate. In the case of DNA replication, the base rate for errors during copying is about 1 letter in 10,000 ($10^4$). This might not seem so terrible until you consider the size of genomes, including ours. The human genome has about 3.2 billion letters ($3.2 \times 10^9$). How many errors would you expect given the base error rate of DNA polymerase?

Obviously, this base error rate becomes dangerously high as the size of genomes increases. Therefore, the DNA polymerase includes a proofreading mechanism that checks each nucleotide that is added to the new strand against the letter that is present on the template strand. If the wrong nucleotide is added, the polymerase moves back one letter, removes the incorrect nucleotide, adds the right one, and moves forward again. With just this basic mechanism of checking the accuracy of duplication, DNA polymerase has an actual error rate of 1 error in a billion letters ($1 \times 10^9$). This means that across the entire human genome, only three mistakes are likely in each replication cycle. This level of fidelity in replication is quite extraordinary.

### Catching and Fixing Errors

The cells in your body have probably undergone well over a hundred thousand replication cycles already.[14] So even three mistakes on average in each replication cycle can be magnified over time. In addition, since conception, your cells have been exposed to a large number of "insults," or chemical and physical accidents that could potentially damage your DNA. These forms of damage must also be identified and fixed as quickly as possible.

Unlike computers, where technicians can find and repair errors on a hard drive, each cell is essentially independent in terms of the code and data it has

---

[14] Counting from the first cell division of the fertilized egg to adulthood.

available for use. Should an error occur in the DNA sequence and not be corrected, the consequences could be disastrous for the cell and the organism. Either the cell dies prematurely, or it begins to grow out of control—the disease known as cancer.

Most cancers are the result of errors in the DNA sequence of key sections of code that control when and how cells grow and replicate. Cancer is essentially like code with an infinite loop. A program with an infinite loop could run forever, using more and more computing resources until the system crashes. The same is true for cells: errors in the DNA code cause cells to keep growing and dividing until they use up all the system resources. So eventually the cell "crashes." Unfortunately for us, there is no way to "reboot" such a cell.

As a result cells have evolved powerful mechanisms to prevent cancer from developing in the first place. The first step to preventing cancer is to prevent errors in the DNA sequence during replication. We have already seen how DNA polymerase reduces the chances of errors, but three errors are likely in each replication cycle. So over time, that base error rate will cause random mutations to accumulate. Other mechanisms are needed to compensate for this base error rate.

The second line of defense is to regularly check the DNA sequence itself to see if there are any errors. This is a bit like evaluating the checksum from a transmission. In our example, we checked the last digit of the transmitted string with the sum of the remainder of the digits. If these differed, we knew an error had occurred. For DNA error checking, cells rely on the fact that DNA has two strands, each a complementary copy of the other.

Errors in DNA usually take the form of mismatches. That is, given a T on one strand, you would expect an A on the other strand. If DNA polymerase made a mistake, then it might have inserted a C instead at that position. **Mismatch repair enzymes** identify such mistakes and then make a "reasoned guess" about what the correct sequence should be. We do not yet know how these enzymes work, but they are able to tell which strand was the template during replication and which was the newly synthesized strand. They selectively correct the new strand rather than the template one. So in our example, if the template had a T and the new strand has a C, the mismatch repair enzymes will replace the C with the correct complementary letter, A. If the template strand had a C, they will correct the T on the other strand to a G.

This mechanism is also powerful because it can handle errors that occur as a result of exposure to chemical toxins and spontaneous degradation. Cells are constantly combating the forces of entropy, or, to put it another way, the forces of chaos. Chemical processes are the lifeblood of cells, but they are also the biggest hazard for cells. In fact, one theory for why we age is that cellular processes in our cells slowly degrade and damage our DNA and other components. Cells must find ways to maintain the integrity of their data given that chemical processes are necessary evils.

One of the most dangerous chemical processes at the DNA level is a spontaneous change: C's tend to become T's over time. This is a change in the chemical structure of the nitrogen base part of the C nucleotide, and it occurs at some relatively low rate. It also happens at random, so there is no reason why any particular C would be changed over any other C. The same mismatch repair enzymes that catch errors left by DNA polymerase can also catch these C-to-T changes. These enzymes note the mismatch that occurs: if there was a C at one point, the other strand should have a G. So if the enzymes spot a G-T combination, then either the G is wrong or the T is wrong. Somehow, the enzymes are able to tell which is the wrong nucleotide. Again, it is not clear how the enzymes know whether a C changed to a T at one point or whether the DNA polymerase made a mistake and added a G instead of a A at that point. Yet, it appears that they are able to reliably correct for most mistakes without introducing new ones.

For the most part, cells try to deal with errors in their data with the RAID1 array approach. They check the back-up copy and compare the two copies. Errors in the "new" copy are corrected based on the older one. The problem with this approach is what if the error was on the "old" copy? The error is then likely to be preserved and propagated in every generation. The good news is that most errors or mutations have no long-term consequences for the cell. In fact, biologists have speculated that large sections of the genome are composed of repetitive, nonfunctional DNA. Mutations in these regions have no negative effect on the cells, and so they are neither selected for or against. They are merely the flotsam and jetsam of evolution, and they continue to be propagated faithfully across the millenia.

## Data Integrity in Extremis

Sometimes, however, just having two copies of data is not enough to ensure data integrity. The bacterium, *Deinococcus radiodurans*, whose natural environment is the desert, has four complete copies of its genome. That is, it has eight strands of DNA. Why would *D. radiodurans* need so many backups of its DNA? It turns out *D. radiodurans* has an extraordinary ability to survive harsh environments.

Researchers first discovered this organism in food-canning factories. Certain bacteria can grow in canned foods and cause deadly forms of food poisoning (botulism, caused by *Clostridium botulinum*, is one such example). So canning factories have developed a number of ways to kill such bacteria. The standard approach is to irradiate the cans with UV (ultraviolet) light or sometimes with low doses of gamma radiation (from a radioactive source). Then, a random sample of cans is selected and tested to see if any bacteria are present. In one such experiment, a certain bacterial agent kept showing up regardless of how much radiation was used. Despite having been exposed to radiation equivalent to several atomic bombs (1.5 million megarads of

*(continued)*

radiation), this organism continued to grow and thrive. The organism was *D. radiodurans*.[15]

It turns out that *D. radiodurans* can resist extremely high levels of UV and other radiation because it is uniquely adapted to overcome the dangers of such exposure. Usually, when cells are exposed to UV or gamma radiation, the DNA within the cell breaks apart or fragments. If it breaks into very small pieces, the DNA cannot be reassembled into the complete genome again. The cell self-destructs (in biology this is known as apoptosis) rather than trying to salvage its fractured DNA strands.

*D. radiodurans* is not like most cells. It can reassemble at least one complete version of the genome even when radiation has fragmented all eight copies of the DNA into sections of a few hundred letters each. This is a grand biological version of the shortest superstring problem in computing; we will talk about this in much greater detail when we cover sequence fragment reassembly in Chapter 4.

It is not enough to simply reassemble one complete copy of the genome after DNA fragmentation occurs. Cells also have to correct for damage to the DNA letters themselves that occur because of exposure to the radiation. How does *D. radiodurans* have such an amazing tolerance for radiation-induced damage to its DNA sequence? Part of the answer may be that it has four times as many DNA repair enzymes as most other cells. In conjunction with having eight copies of the genome, this ensures that at least one copy can be reconstructed.

Why does *D. radiodurans* have all these adaptations in the first place? It is possible that these adaptations were selected because of the harsh living conditions of the bacterium's natural habitat. *D. radiodurans* lives on the surfaces of rocks in the desert and is exposed to much higher levels of UV radiation than most other organisms. So this might have been a necessary adaptation for survival in its particular environment.

Or, if you want to be more fanciful, you can subscribe to the view promoted by the late Francis Crick and the renowned astronomer Sir Fred Hoyle: *D. radiodurans* is an extraterrestrial bacterium sent to this planet by a superior intelligence from somewhere else in the galaxy. Its adaptations ensured it could make it here without being destroyed by the high levels of radiation present in outer space [5].

Regardless of which explanation you prefer, the case of *D. radiodurans* highlights the remarkable adaptability of life. It also emphasizes just how critical data integrity and maintenance are for cellular systems. In this sense, cells are no different from computing systems: their survival depends on the accurate retention of information.

---

[15] You can learn more about *D. radiodurans* by visiting a number of sites including: http://deinococcus.allbio.org/

# KEY TERMS

blueprints (2.1)

evolution (2.1)

species (2.1)

mutation (2.1)

natural selection (2.1)

selected (2.1)

speciation (2.1)

genes (2.1)

genotypic (2.1)

phenotypic (2.1)

stochastic process (2.1)

selection pressure (2.1)

prokaryotes (2.2)

eukaryotes (2.2)

organelle (2.2)

complexes (2.2)

ionic bond (2.2)

covalent bond (2.2)

dipole (2.2)

hydrogen bonds (2.2)

endothermic (2.2)

exothermic (2.2)

activation energy (2.2)

macromolecules (2.2)

organic (2.2)

cell membrane (2.2)

hydrophobic (2.2)

hydrophilic (2.2)

bilayer (2.2)

aqueous (2.2)

homeostasis (2.2)

receptors (2.2)

cytoplasm (2.2)

cytoskeleton (2.2)

nucleus (2.2)

genome (2.2)

mitochondria (2.2)

adenosine triphosphate

(ATP) (2.2)

synthesized (2.3)

integrating signals (2.3)

signaling cascades (2.3)

deoxyribosenucleic acid

(DNA) (2.3)

nucleotide (2.3)

sugar–phosphate backbone (2.3)

pyrimidines (2.3)

purines (2.3)

thymidine (2.3)

cytosine (2.3)

adenosine (2.3)

guanine (2.3)

double helix (2.3)

complement (2.3)

antiparallel (2.3)

reverse complement (2.3)

forward strand (2.3)

reverse strand (2.3)

gene family (2.3)

promoter (2.3)

operons (2.3)

*lac* operon (2.3)

repressor (2.3)

inducer (2.3)

transcription (2.3)

RNA polymerase (2.3)

messenger RNA (mRNA) (2.3)

uracil (2.3)

degraded (2.3)

translation (2.3)

amino acids (2.3)

ribosome (2.3)

codon (2.3)

genetic code (2.3)

code (2.3)

transfer RNA (tRNA) (2.3)

anticodon (2.3)

start codon (2.3)

stop codon (2.3)

central dogma of molecular

biology (2.3)

reverse transcriptase (2.3)

open reading frames (ORF) (2.4)

exon (2.4)

intron (2.4)

splicing (2.4)

spliceosome (2.4)

$5'$ cap (2.4)

polyadenylation (2.4)

dirty bit (2.4)

peptide bond (2.5)

primary structure (2.5)

secondary structure (2.5)

alpha ($\alpha$)-helix (2.5)

beta ($\beta$)-sheet (2.5)

peptide backbone (2.5)

disulfide bond (2.5)

tertiary structure (2.5)

globular (2.5)

fibrous (2.5)

quarternary structure (2.5)

ligand (2.5)

specificity (2.5)

transmembrane proteins (2.5)

enzyme (2.5)

metabolic pathways (2.5)

kinase (2.5)

phosphatase (2.5)

DNA replication (2.6)

template (2.6)

origin of replication (2.6)

DNA polymerase (2.6)

Okazaki fragments (2.6)

leading strand (2.6)

lagging strand (2.6)

histones (2.6)

nucleosome (2.6)

linker DNA (2.6)

euchromatin (2.6)

heterochromatin (2.6)

differentiated (2.6)

checksum (2.6)

mismatch repair enzyme (2.6)

# BIBLIOGRAPHY

1. Bruce Alberts, Dennis Bray, Karen Hopkin, et al. *Essential Cell Biology*. Garland Science Publishing, New York, 2004.

2. T. Cormen, C. Leiserson, and R. Rivest. *Introduction to Algorithms*. MIT Press, Cambridge, MA, 1990.

3. Douglas R. Hofstadter. *Metamagical Themas: Questing for the Essence of Mind and Pattern*. Basic Books, New York, 1985.

4. John L. Holland. *The Surprising Archaea: Discovering Another Domain of Life*. Oxford University Press, New York, 2000.

5. Fred Hoyle. *Evolution from Space: A Theory of Cosmic Creationism*. Simon & Schuster, New York, 1981.

6. S. Kalir, J. McClure, K. Pabbaraju, et al. Ordering genes in a flagella pathway by analysis of expression kinetics from living bacteria. *Science*, 292:2080–2083, 2001.

7. L. M. Keegan, A. Gallo, and M. A. O'Connell. The many roles of an RNA editor. *Nat Rev Genet*, 2:869–878, 2001.

8. N. J. A. MacWilliams, F. J. Sloane. *The Theory of Error-Correcting Codes*. North-Holland, Amsterdam, 1977.

9. Michael Majerus. *Melanism: Evolution in Action*. Oxford University Press, New York, 1998.

# 3

# Wet and Dry Lab Techniques

*"An idea which can be used once is a trick. If it can be used more than once it becomes a method."*
  —G. Polya in *How to Solve It: A New Aspect of Mathematical Method*

In Chapter 2 you learned some basics of biology and, it's to be hoped, gained an appreciation for the spectacular mechanisms by which cells manage the information of life. The discovery of DNA's structure and the unraveling of the genetic code truly revolutionized science, thereby explaining mysteries that had persisted for more than a century. An important offshoot of the ensuing increased understanding of the molecular biology of the cell has been another revolution of sorts—in biotechnology, which is the field of applied biology. The relationship between biology and biotechnology is akin to that between computer science, with its emphasis on theory, and the application of that theory in the fields of software engineering and information technology. In biotechnology many scientists have combined biological knowledge and theory with advances in engineering and technology to put molecules to work in the laboratory to enable further discovery. Here we will introduce you to some of the major "wet lab" techniques that biological scientists employ. Keep in mind that development of effective and appropriate computational approaches to working with and managing biological data ("dry lab" techniques, if you will) requires an understanding of the nature of those data, including their biological context and a myriad of technical issues.

Throughout this chapter, as in the rest of the book, we will use the human immunodeficiency virus (HIV) as an exemplar. HIV today remains one of the major public health threats worldwide. Although the virus genome has only nine genes and encodes only 15 proteins, which may seem on the surface a simple problem, the virus does not kill directly but rather disrupts the host's immune system. Major efforts in the fight against HIV require an understanding of how the virus interacts with human immune cells and how to block those interactions. Bioinformatics has played a major role in these endeavors, providing the means to store and manage laboratory data, as well as to share and mine those data.

We will explore many of the bioinformatics applications to HIV data throughout this book but will start here with a look at many general types of data and the technologies that generate them.

Consider the following scenario: A major research laboratory has the goal of developing drug therapies for preventing and treating infection with HIV. To do so, the scientists must understand how the proteins of the virus interact with the proteins of the host cell to allow the virus to make many copies of itself and eventually to disrupt the normal functioning of the immune cell leading to disease. This problem can be reduced to asking questions such as: What is the nature of the language of HIV? Which DNAStrings determine the important "words," and how is the expression of these words controlled? How does the language of the virus, in a sense, rewrite the book of the healthy, normal cell? To answer these questions, the scientist has an arsenal of tools at his or her disposal. Many have been around for some time, and others, especially the high-throughput techniques, are relatively new.

The study of any biological entity, whether it be mice, fish, fruit flies, worms, bacteria, cultured cells, or virus, requires that the scientist has a source of the organism on hand. It is relatively straightforward (although often expensive) to maintain mouse colonies, tanks of zebra fish, or jars of fruit flies. Maintaining stocks of a lethal human pathogen, like HIV, requires special precautions. These include not only extreme measures to prevent exposure when handling the virus or virus-infected materials but also biological interventions which cripple the virus by knocking out function in genes that are essential for the virus to replicate or infect cells. Here, we won't detail those measures but will assume that a stock of virus is available.

How might one go about studying the molecules that control the virus and its activities? In Chapter 2 you learned that HIV is a family of retroviruses. This means that their genomes consist of RNA rather than DNA. Recall also that RNA is difficult to work with because of its propensity to be degraded. So, one solution to this problem is to work with DNA copies of the viral genome rather than RNA. Interestingly, this involves the use of an enzyme, reverse transcriptase, an important tool for the molecular biologist, that was first discovered in retroviruses such as HIV. In order to see how DNA copies of the HIV genome can be made it is necessary to provide a little background information about some of the most basic techniques of molecular biology.

# 3.1  HYBRIDIZATION: PUTTING BASE PAIRS TO WORK

A fundamental technique with broad application is nucleic acid hybridization. Simply put, **hybridization** is the complementary (or Watson–Crick) base-pairing of two single strands of nucleotides to form a double-stranded nucleotide product. Since DNA is a double-stranded structure held together by chemical and

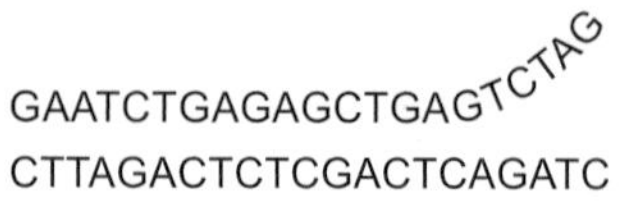

**FIGURE 3.1**
Hybridization occurs when two nucleotide sequences anneal by the pairing of complementary bases.

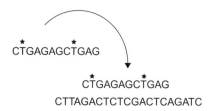

GAATCTGAGAGCTGAGTCTAG
CTTAGACTCTCGACTCAGATC

**FIGURE 3.2**
Labeling of nucleotides (*) allows the detection of hybridization.

CTGAGAGCTGAG

CTGAGAGCTGAG
CTTAGACTCTCGACTCAGATC

physical forces it can be separated by disrupting these forces. Two single-stranded nucleotide sequences are able to reanneal (or hybridize) if there is sufficient complementarity between the bases and if conditions are favorable (Figure 3.1).

Fortunately, for the sake of experimentation, many conditions can be leveraged to control hybridization. We might want to force double-stranded molecules to come apart, or "melt;" we might want to allow only the best matched sequences to anneal; or conversely, allow those that aren't perfectly matched to anneal. In addition to Watson–Crick base-pairing in the hybrid, another factor that affects the stability of the hybrid is the contribution of **CG** base pairs, which have three hydrogen bonds, relative to the less stable **AT** base pairs, which have only two. Characteristics of the solution in which hybridization occurs such as salt concentration, temperature, and presence of denaturants are also important, as is the length of time that hybridization is allowed to progress. The products of hybridization may be DNA:DNA, DNA:RNA, or RNA:RNA. In an experimental situation, we need a way to determine whether hybridization has occurred. In solutions we can take advantage of the fact that DNA absorbs electromagnetic energy in the ultraviolet range (maximum at 260 nm) and that single- and double-stranded nucleotides absorb differently. Thus, we can measure the quantity of nucleotides that exist in the reannealed double-stranded state. More often, detection of hybridization is accomplished by incorporating a label of some type in one sequence, often referred to as the "query" or "probe" sequence. The label is usually a radioactive, fluorescent, or enzymatic tag (Figure 3.2).

To sum up, at the end of a hybridization experiment, detection of the tag or double-stranded nucleotide strings in solution tells us that our specific sequence of interest is present and, depending on the experimental design, may tell us how much and where. A partial list of hybridization applications includes identification and quantification of specific sequences in solutions, in cells or on artificially created experimental substrata such as nylon membranes or glass slides, estimation of the relatedness of nucleotide sequences, localization of DNA and RNA sequences along chromosomes and elsewhere within cells (in situ hybridization), the establishment of effective transfer of nucleotides to another organism, high-throughput sequencing, and amplification of specific sequences (via polymerase chain reaction, PCR). Of course, hybridization has a more natural role too, as it is integral to many physiological processes including replication and recombination, to name but two.

## 3.2  MAKING COPIES OF NUCLEOTIDE SEQUENCES

Just as we are accustomed to easily generating copies of important or valuable information contained in written or digital documents, the lab scientist can make copies of the information contained in nucleotide sequence so as to generate enough material for experimentation and for "back-up" of the original sequence information. When working with RNA, one of the first steps is to make **cDNA,** which is short for complementary DNA or copy DNA (complementary is the more common term. Do a Google search to see for yourself). cDNA is produced from an RNA template, a synthesis reaction made possible by the enzyme reverse transcriptase (RT), an RNA-dependent DNA polymerase discovered in groups of viruses known as retroviruses, including HIV. Do you see any problem with "reverse transcription"? Recall that this is one of the prime examples of exceptions to the central dogma, that is, genetic information flows backward, from RNA to DNA.

To understand just how remarkable this is, think of a computing process that is usually a one-way street. For example, many programs can take a file of postscript commands and correctly render the corresponding image to a screen. Reverse transcription is as noteworthy as would be a program that converted a screen image into a postscript file. Reverse transcriptase is critical for the HIV life cycle, unfortunately allowing it to enter the human genome, but the discovery of RT also made possible the generation of cDNA in the laboratory, a basic technique that supports many advanced technologies.

Hybridization is an integral part of the techniques used to make cDNA. Like the other DNA polymerases, such as the enzyme responsible for DNA replication, RT requires a double-stranded sequence as a starting point. In the lab this is accomplished most often via the poly(A) tail, a naturally occurring string of A's which is added on to the $3'$ end of mRNA molecules as one of the posttranscriptional processing steps in eukaryotic cells. A synthetic poly(T) oligonucleotide is used to hybridize to the poly(A) tail of the mRNA template (makes a poly(A)/poly(T) hybrid) and provide a starting point or "prime" the reaction (Figure 3.3).

If a mixture of different mRNA sequences is present, then cDNAs complementary to all of them will be made, as long as they have a poly(A) tail. Sometimes primers are designed that are complementary to other sequences in the mRNA of interest. Applications of cDNA synthesis are many. cDNAs, made double-stranded, are used in cloning, which in this context means the insertion of the cDNA into another piece of DNA called a vector in order to copy it.

**FIGURE 3.3**
cDNA synthesis
begins with the
hybridization of a
poly d(T) primer to
the poly(A) region of
an mRNA or viral
RNA. Reverse
transcriptase
synthesizes a
cDNA/RNA hybrid.
After removal of the
RNA template, the
cDNA is made
double-stranded with
the enzyme DNA
polymerase I.

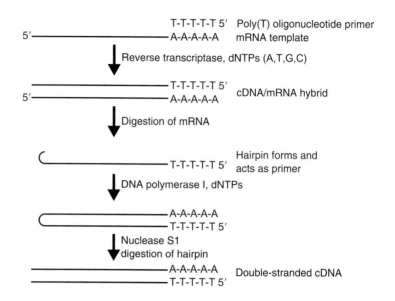

Although many, relatively stable copies of an individual RNA sequence can be made through cDNA synthesis, cloning the resultant cDNA into a vector will facilitate easy storage, copying, and manipulation of the sequence. Cloning vectors (Figure 3.4) are self-replicating, double-stranded DNA into which foreign DNA can be inserted in a process that produces recombinant DNA. It is recombinant because it is a combination of both vector DNA and foreign DNA. Vectors used today are highly engineered, and their components have been obtained from many different sources. Popular cloning vectors are plasmids, isolated from bacterial sources, viral vectors, and engineered artificial chromosomes derived from

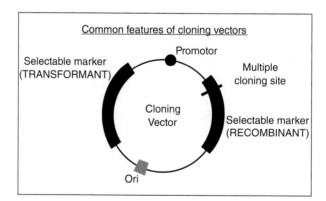

**FIGURE 3.4**   Cloning vectors contain sites that control the origin of replication (Ori) of the vector in the host cell, a multiple cloning site for opening the vector DNA and inserting foreign DNA, a promoter to control expression of the inserted DNA, and sites to detect whether the host cells carry the cloning vector (transformant) and whether the vector contains foreign DNA (recombinant).

chromosomal DNA of yeast and bacteria (YACs and BACs, respectively). Vectors have been engineered to have certain basic components: a multiple cloning site, to provide easy ways to insert the foreign DNA using restriction enzymes, genes that code for selectable characteristics of cells carrying foreign DNA, and, of course, regulatory elements that control replication of the vector and expression of the genes carried in the vector. One of the earliest and best known vectors is named PBR322.

At this point we need to step back and discuss the restriction enzymes in more depth. **Restriction enzymes** are commonly referred to as "molecular scissors," and their discovery provided one of the most useful tools to the molecular biologist. Many of these enzymes belong to a group of enzymes known as endonucleases. The prefix *endo-* means that they act on, and cut, nucleotide sequences at positions within the interior of the nucleotide string, rather than at the ends. The "restriction" component of the name derives from the history of their discovery and from their biological function. In the 1950s and 1960s it was observed that phage (virus particles) were restricted in their ability to infect different bacterial cells. A given phage may be able to infect one type of bacterium but not another, whereas a second phage could infect only the latter. Years of investigation led to the understanding that phage could successfully infect a bacterial cell if the phage DNA had been protected by a chemical modification known as methylation. As a defensive mechanism by the bacterium, phage DNA can be chopped into pieces by bacterial endonucleases (the restriction endonucleases) but only when certain nucleotides are unmethylated. The same nucleotide sequence, when methylated, is protected from the enzyme attack. Thus, infection in a given bacterial cell is restricted to only those phage whose DNA is protected from that bacterium's arsenal of enzymes.

A major breakthrough came in 1968 when H. O. Smith, K. W. Wilcox, and T. J. Kelley, working at Johns Hopkins University, isolated and characterized the first restriction endonuclease, *Hind* II, whose function depended on a specific DNA nucleotide sequence. Working with *Haemophilus influenzae* bacteria, this group isolated an enzyme, now called *Hind* II (the name is derived from the genus and species names of the bacteria). It was found that *Hind* II always cut DNA molecules at a particular point within a specific sequence of 6 base pairs (bp) but would not cut at any other sequences. The specific sequence became known as the recognition sequence [19]. Moreover, *Hind* II always cut the sequence between the third and fourth nucleotides on both strands, leaving two pieces with "blunt ends."

Many hundreds of known restriction nucleases are now known, both endo- and exonucleases, some of which have specific recognition sequences and others which don't. Another well known restriction endonuclease is *Eco*RI, discovered in *E. coli*. Like *Hind*II, this endonuclease has a recognition sequence of 6 bp, but unlike *Hind*II or small (Figure 3.5), it makes an asymmetrical cut leaving "sticky ends" due to an overhang of base pairs at both ends of the molecule. Notably, many of the recognition sequences of restriction endonucleases are palindromes, meaning that the sequences (on the two strands) read the same way forward as back. For example, the recognition sequence for *Eco*RI is GAATTC—reading

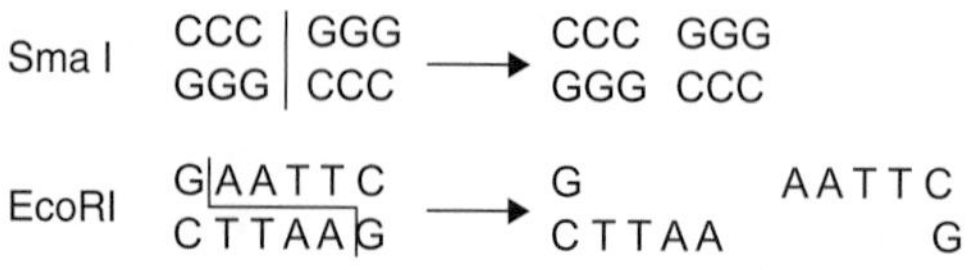

Sma I
```
CCC | GGG          CCC   GGG
GGG | CCC    ──►   GGG   CCC
```

EcoRI
```
G|AATTC           G           AATTC
CTTAA|G    ──►   CTTAA            G
```

**FIGURE 3.5**   Restriction endonuclease SmaI recognizes a specific 6-bp sequence and cuts both strands at the same site, leaving "blunt ends." *Eco*RI recognizes a different specific 6-bp sequence and makes an asymmetrical cut with "sticky ends."

from 5′ to 3′ on either strand will be the same. The palindrome sequence is important for recognition of the sequence by the endonuclease and also positioning of the cut. For *Eco*RI, the cut is made after the G on each strand, resulting in the overhangs (Figure 3.5). The discovery of the molecular scissors provided a means by which molecular biologists could "cut and paste" DNA molecules in a predictable, useful way. For example, a DNA molecule to be cloned can be cut with a restriction enzyme, like *Eco*RI, and vector DNA can be cut with *Eco*RI, as well. The sticky ends of the two can then be pasted together, or ligated, into one contiguous DNA molecule as their overhangs base-pair.

The vector, now carrying the foreign DNA, is then put into bacterial cells (affectionately known as bugs), in a process known as transformation. Under the proper conditions many copies of the vector and its inserted cDNA are produced by the bacterial cells. The bacterial cells are grown under conditions that allow the scientist to recognize which bacteria contain the recombinant DNA, and these can then be isolated (Figure 3.6). A culture of millions of bugs, each carrying self-replicating, recombinant vectors will efficiently generate many copies of the sequence (think gene) of interest, which can be used in hybridization experiments, sequenced, and then used to introduce foreign genes into cells, among other uses.

Often scientists will refer to cDNA libraries. A **cDNA library** is simply a collection of cDNAs, cloned into appropriate vectors, which, in theory, represent all of the mRNAs expressed in a given cell type or organism. Today it is a routine laboratory procedure to make cDNA libraries, and it is also possible to select from among myriad cDNA libraries available for purchase from biotech companies. For example, one can make (or buy) a human liver library, a *Drosophila* library or an HIV cDNA library. In our scenario, the laboratory studying HIV will likely generate HIV cDNA clones in order to have ready supplies of viral sequences for experimentation. You may think of creation of the cDNA library as a way for the scientist to "back up" the lab's data. In fact, it is common practice to freeze stores of cloned sequences as back-up in the case that mutation occurs in sequences currently in use in the lab. Although the specific methodologies vary, it is also fairly routine to make genomic libraries, which carry cloned segments of genomic DNA, rather than cDNA.

Let us continue our analogy comparing the "normal" central dogma direction to the generation of a screen image from a postscript file. A cDNA library can be compared to a set of premade small segments of postscript commands that can be used to generate a collection of graphical components that are likely to be of use in a given context. For example, if the context is

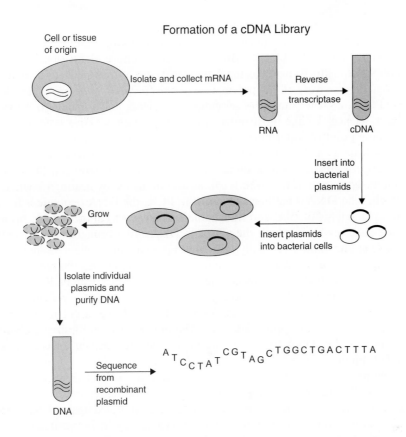

Formation of a cDNA Library

**FIGURE 3.6**
DNA can be cloned
into a plasmid or
other vector.
Recombinant
plasmids are then
inserted into bacteria
to generate many new
copies of the DNA.

"UML Diagrams" the set of premade graphical components might consist of rectangles, subdivided rectangles, vertical lines, horizontal lines, lines with arrows,
and so on.

Collections of cDNA have many uses, as we'll discuss later in this chapter
when we consider methods for studying gene expression.

## 3.3  AN EXPLOSION OF COPIES

Imagine now that you have very small amounts of a DNA of interest, almost
too small to detect, and certainly too small to work with. What can be done?
The **polymerase chain reaction (PCR)** to the rescue! PCR is another way to get
many copies of a sequence and it has become famous in the public eye for its use
in forensics. Known as amplification, PCR is a rapid process that can be automated and generates billions of copies of DNA within a matter of a few hours.
The PCR process [17], invented by Kerry Mullis in 1983 and for which he won
the 1993 Nobel Prize in chemistry, was a major scientific breakthrough and was
made possible by the discovery of heat-stable polymerases in bacteria living in
hot springs. Thomas Brock, the bacteriologist who discovered and learned how

to grow the ancient heat-tolerant bacterium, was interested, in studying bacteria in simple, real-world environments [3], he was not thinking about revolutionizing the world of molecular biology. Brock donated a culture of *Thermus aquaticus* to a public repository known as the American Type Culture Collection, enabling the eventual discovery of *Taq* polymerase (from *Thermus aquaticus*) and its later use in PCR—a great example of serendipity in science and a tribute to the value of basic science. Unlike most polymerases, *Taq* remains active even at 100°C the boiling point of water and a temperature that would unfold and inactivate other polymerases. That feature is critical because in order to make a copy, a polymerase needs access to a single strand of the double-stranded DNA. In a test tube, separation of the strands can be accomplished by heating to denature, or "melt," the DNA, breaking its bonds. In PCR, the DNA template is heated to approximately 90–95°C and then cooled somewhat to allow specific primers to base-pair, or anneal, with the template DNA. Two primers, which bind to opposite strands and are usually up to 400 bp apart along the template DNA, are added and where these primers bind effectively delineates the region of the DNA to be amplified and the place where replication starts. The PCR reaction is set up in vitro (in a small vial) and contains template DNA, *Taq* polymerase, all four nucleotides as building blocks, primers that flank the target sequence and other goodies such as appropriate ions. *Taq* polymerase synthesizes a complementary strand of DNA from each primer so that each sequence has now been doubled (Figure 3.7).

The novelty comes next when the entire solution is heated again (which is okay with *Taq*) to denature the strands and allow another round of replication. Each new strand can now act as a template and be doubled again. This process of denaturing, annealing, and extension, known as a cycle, is repeated over and over, typically for 30–40 cycles. After a few cycles, most of the newly synthesized DNA is of a discrete size (determined by the distance between the two primers; Figure 3.7), and this DNA will be doubled with each cycle (logarithmically). The number of copies at any given point, thus, is theoretically $2^N$ cycles (Figure 3.8).

Fortunately, a machine called a thermocycler can accomplish all of the necessary temperature changes efficiently so that each cycle completes in less than a minute. Once the reaction is started, human intervention is not needed until the end. Not only is this process convenient, but it reduces the possibility of contamination with trace amounts of DNA—a hallmark of the sensitivity of PCR. Computer scientists are accustomed to thinking about performance issues when writing code that requires the computer to perform many operations. It is not a good sign when complexity analysis shows that an algorithm is exponential. One way to enhance performance is to parallelize the algorithm so that multiple processors can be crunching the numbers simultaneously. This requires that the algorithmic operations can be separated into individual components and that the communication between processors is good when the data are interdependent. The PCR reaction rapidly generates new sequences exponentially and perhaps can be thought of as a biological form of parallel computing. Each molecule of *Taq* polymerase can be considered a processor that carries out many operations on the primed template, incorporating nucleotides one by one. These "processors"

PCR amplification of target sequence

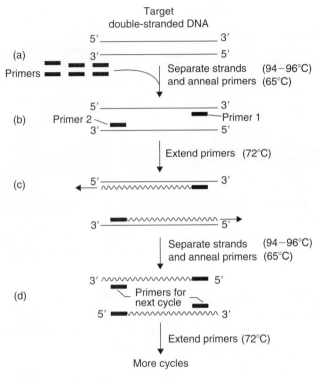

**FIGURE 3.7**   The target sequence, delineated between two primers, is amplified in a reaction that is repeated many times.

can function independently and only depend on prior reactions for synthesis of new template strands, which are easily "communicated" in the solution. The simplicity and formidable power of this technique can probably best be appreciated by considering Mullis' own words [16]:

> Beginning with a single molecule of the genetic material DNA, the PCR can generate 100 billion similar molecules in an afternoon. The reaction is easy to execute. It requires no more than a test tube, a few simple reagents and a source of heat. The DNA sample that one wishes to copy can be pure, or it can be a minute part of an extremely complex mixture of biological materials. The DNA may come from a hospital tissue specimen, from a single human hair, from a drop of dried blood at the scene of a crime, from the tissues of a mummified brain or from a 40,000-year-old wooly mammoth frozen in a glacier.

Another important consideration is that sometimes we need to start our amplification from RNA. To address that need a variation on PCR, RT-PCR, has been developed. RT-PCR starts with a reverse transcriptase step (remember cDNA synthesis?) because *Taq* polymerase cannot use RNA as a template. Experimental conditions keep traditional RT-PCR from being truly quantitative and

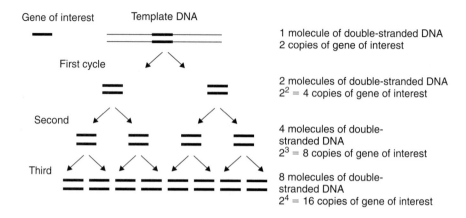

**FIGURE 3.8**   PCR reactions typically are carried out for 30–40 cycles. The number of copies of DNA increases exponentially. Although not shown in this simple example, early cycles produce DNA strands that are longer than the sequence of interest. After a few cycles, most of the DNA in the reaction is of one size, determined by the distance between the two primers.

limit its use for comparing amounts of RNA between samples. For example, the reaction eventually runs out of steam, causing a gradual leveling off. A solution to this problem is Real-time PCR, a technique in which each amplification reaction is measured only when it is in its early logarithmic phase.

**Exercise 3.1**   Write a program to simulate the PCR process. One approach is to define a PCR class that contains a collection of DoubleDNAStrand objects, a collection of Nucleotides, a collection of Primer objects, and an empty collection of SingleDNAStrand objects. DoubleDNAStrand objects have a denature( ) method that gives rise to two SingleDNAStrand objects. Primer objects have an extend( ) method that relies on the availability of Nucleotides to build a DoubleDNAStrand object containing the Primer's string of nucleotides together with the reverse-complement string of the SingleDNAStrand object. Add methods to the PCR class so that you can simulate the denaturing and annealing processes. Add a certain amount of randomness so that some SingleDNAStrand objects will fail to find the required Primers to extend. Find out more about why PCR is not, in practice, an exactly exponential process. How close does your simulation come to real-life experience?

## 3.4  SEQUENCING DNA STRINGS

Many applications in molecular biology and genetics require that we know the sequence of a nucleic acid. Ideally, this means that the sequence is free of errors and without breaks. In practice, we often settle for less, although the rapid, high-throughput generation of DNA sequence today can be done with greater than 99% accuracy. DNA sequencing plays an important role in the study of HIV pathogenesis and also in identifying viral variants, which is important for managing the disease. Although the genome of HIV has been fully sequenced (many, many times) and its nine genes and 15 proteins are known, the situation is not as simple as it may seem. The sequence of HIV genomes is actually extremely heterogeneous, primarily because the reverse transcriptase enzyme does not have "proofreading" ability. That means that errors introduced spontaneously during the viral reverse transcription process are not corrected and the sequence is not copied with fidelity. The heterogeneity of the viral genome is one of the major hurdles in developing effective vaccines and drugs to control HIV infection, and patients can develop drug resistance due to sequence variation over the course of their treatment. It is important that researchers can accurately read the sequence and identify variants of the virus. This process of genotyping and DNA sequencing is the gold standard for genotyping HIV from patient serum or typing laboratory stocks.

How is sequencing achieved? If we have only RNA, not surprisingly the usual strategy is first to convert the sequence to cDNA, since RNA is so much more difficult to handle. Of course, as previously mentioned, the intrinsic error rate associated with reverse transcriptase already introduces a potential for some inexactness in the sequence. In the case of genotyping HIV, it is common practice to start with an RT-PCR reaction to generate sufficient amounts of viral DNA. Assuming we have DNA, then, how can the nucleotide sequence be obtained?

Sequencing DNA on a large scale has been made possible by a breakthrough that predated PCR but similarly dramatically changed the research landscape—the development of new reagents and their use in new analytical methods. The central role and importance of rapid DNA sequencing to the genome projects (human and otherwise) cannot be overstated. As the term implies, DNA sequencing is the process of determining the precise sequence of nucleotides in a DNA sample. In the mid-1970s new sequencing techniques were developed in two competing research laboratories, and each method subsequently came to be known among scientists by the names of its architects. **Maxam and Gilbert sequencing** (named for Allan Maxam and Walter Gilbert) [15], determines the DNA sequence by selective chemical cleavage of radioactively labeled DNA, which produces a signature pattern. **Sanger sequencing** (named for Fred Sanger) [20], also called **dideoxy sequencing,** relies on DNA synthesis in the presence of chain-terminating dideoxy nucleotides to generate a set of fragments that can be resolved to reveal the DNA sequence (Figure 3.9). The Maxam and Gilbert method is considered to be outmoded and so will not be discussed in any detail here, whereas the Sanger dideoxy chain-termination technique is the cornerstone for much of the high-throughput automated sequencing used today. The Sanger method applies the theory of DNA replication to the sequencing problem. DNA polymerase is used to extend an oligonucleotide primer that is annealed to the template single-stranded DNA of interest. DNA synthesis occurs in the presence of natural precursor deoxynucleotide triphosphates (dNTPs) and synthetic dideoxynucleotide triphosphates (ddNTPs). The latter are human-made chemicals and their synthesis provided one of the breakthroughs leading to the development of the Sanger method. Dideoxynucleotide triphosphates are referred to as chain-terminating because once a ddNTP has been incorporated, synthesis cannot continue due to the lack of a 3'-OH group.

To accomplish sequencing, four separate reactions are run—one for each of the four ddNTPS (ddATP, ddCTP, ddGTP, ddTTP). The key is that all dNTPs are present in excess relative to the given ddNTP in a single sequencing reaction. As the replication machinery cranks out many, many DNA synthesis reactions, all starting at the same position in the template, a normal dNTP usually is incorporated at each position, but every so often a ddNTP is incorporated. The chain is terminated at that base and falls away from the enzyme. For example, in a given reaction containing a template DNA sequence of interest, dNTP precursors, and ddGTP, a nested set of all varying-length DNA products will be randomly generated starting at the first base after the oligonucleotide primer, each product representing termination at a different "G." So, all we have to do to find out where all the G's are in the sequence is to determine the length of each new DNA product (Figure 3.10).

Similarly, we can find the positions of all the C's, A's, and T's by analyzing the length of the DNA sequences generated in each respective reaction. If you think about it, it will make sense that the ratio of dNTP:ddNTP needs to be high enough to generate sequence data for sequences that are hundreds of nucleotides in length and also that it is more difficult to generate a sequence close to the primer.

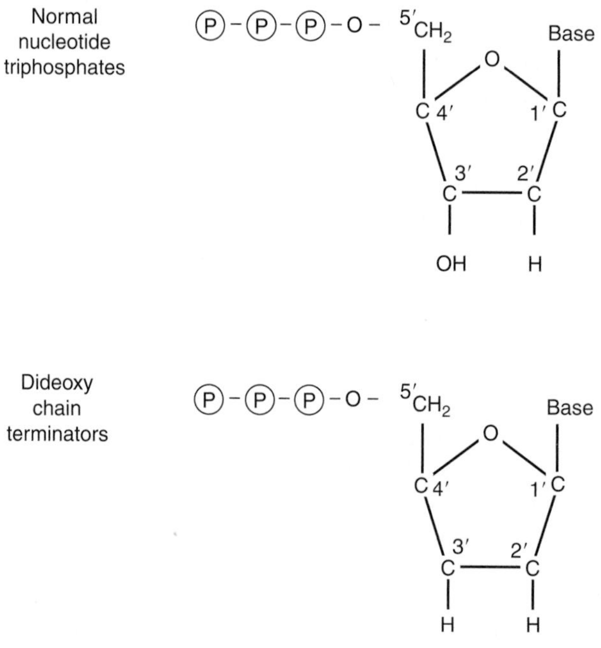

**FIGURE 3.9**

Dideoxy nucleotides are used as chain terminators in DNA sequencing. The dideoxy NTP lacks the 3' hydroxyl.

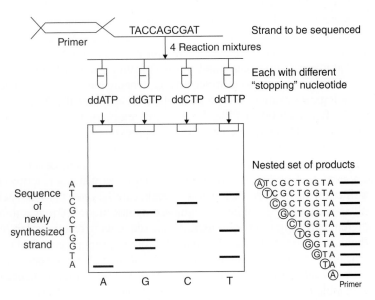

**FIGURE 3.10**   Individual sequencing reactions for each nucleotide are loaded into separate lanes of a slab sequencing gel (or onto a column) to separate the newly synthesized, and terminated, DNA sequences by size. The sequence may be read directly from the gel.

> **Exercise 3.2**
>
> Write a program to simulate Sanger sequencing. You will need a `Primer` class (containing a string of `Nucleotides`) and a `SingleDNAStrand` class. When you have objects of both classes, you can start the DNA synthesis process in the presence of a large number of nucleotides, a small proportion of which are ddNTPs and which, as soon as they are incorporated into the growing DNA, will terminate the process. Your simulation should enable you to adjust the ratio of ddNTPs to dNTPs and obtain statistics about how many DNA molecules of what length are produced. When your simulation is successfully running, try to answer the following question: Do you have "plenty" of molecules of all possible lengths? Or are there some lengths of molecule in short supply?

Prior to the advent and wide availability of automated sequencers, scientists would obtain the sequence by running each of the four samples in separate lanes of a large polyacrylamide gel in a process known as **electrophoresis.** This separates the DNA products by size and is done under conditions that can resolve differences in length of only 1 nucleotide. Since the synthesized DNA products contain some radioactive or chemically labeled precursors, we can detect them and distinguish them from starting, template DNA. When run on a gel, which is then dried and used to expose X-ray film, the products are visualized as bands, and the sequence is simply read by following the ladder of bands across the four lanes from the bottom to the top of the gel (see Figure 3.10).

In practice, to help ensure accurate sequencing and to produce contiguous sequence, double-stranded DNA is usually sequenced from both ends and the sequence is generated from at least six overlapping reads. You have probably guessed that manual sequencing can be time-consuming and tedious, and created a bottleneck for such ambitious projects as sequencing the entire human genome. The technological advances that came about with automated DNA sequencers, invented by Leroy Hood in 1986, broke down many of the barriers to rapid, high-throughput DNA sequencing. Varying degrees of automation are now available, ranging from automatic setup of the reactions to automatic readout of the sequence to a computer. Rather than radionucleotides, safer, easier to dispose of, fluorescent nucleotides are now used and all four sequencing reactions can be run together through the gel (often now a small, capillary gel) because each fluorescently labeled ddNTP can be distinguished by its unique color as it fluoresces at a different wavelength under a laser. As the sequencing reactions run past the laser, the fluorescence output is stored as a chromatogram (Figure 3.11).

Typically, the average read length of automated sequencers is about 600–700 bp of sequence/run but only about 500–550 bp of that sequence is considered reliable (see preceding discussion). A large number of errors resulting from poor resolution toward the end of the sequence is to be expected and will

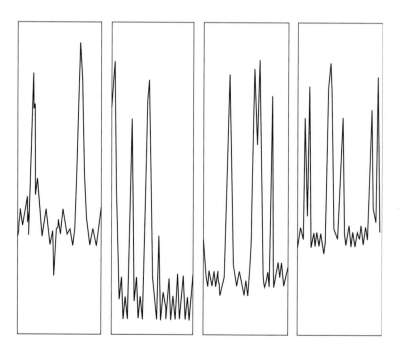

**FIGURE 3.11**    Automated sequencers produce a chromatogram showing individual peaks at each position in the sequence and the outcome of base-calling for each peak. Sequencing the relatively small HIV genome (<10,000 bp) seems like a fairly easy task with current technology. Indeed, the major challenges reside in the need to sequence many genomes, or specific portions of genomes, frequently because of the wild variation that occurs. What about the case of the human genome?

require the scientist to do some editing. Today, because most of the biotechnology of DNA sequencing has been standardized and automated, it is probably fair to say that the major challenges for the lab scientist lie in working with the computer and the software. Advances continue to be made in sequencing technologies, allowing more sequences to be obtained in a single run and facilitating a faster total process. There is also room for improvement in the image processing required for automatic reading of the sequence (known as "base-calling") from the laser scan. Typically, sequencing is carried out today in a DNA sequencing facility where proprietary software specific to individual sequencers is used, and the resultant sequence files are sent out to the investigator. Several free or relatively inexpensive software packages are available for individuals to use outside of the facility, which allows for viewing and manipulation of the electropherogram and the text files. One such program is Chromas, which allows import, viewing, base call editing, and export of sequence files.

In retrospect, perhaps the sequencing of the human genome seems a foregone conclusion once scientists had DNA sequencing technology in hand. However, the road to this achievement, although shorter than expected, was littered with controversy. First formally proposed in the mid-1980s, some parties hotly contested the feasibility and ethics, as well as the public versus private nature of such a venture and related copyright and patent issues surrounding the genomic sequence. A complete timeline of the major players and events that led up to the sequencing of the human genome has been published in a special issue of *Science* [22] that is free and open to the public, a situation that is telling of the importance of this information.

The sequencing of the human genome is often portrayed as a race between two competing entities: the government-sponsored Human Genome Project at the National Center for Human Genome Research (NCHGR, renamed the National Human Genome Research Institute, NHGRI, in 1997) led first by James Watson and then Francis Collins, and the private efforts by Craig Venter at The Institute for Genome Research (TIGR) and Celera Genomics. The perception of a race likely arose from the heated debates surrounding the different strategies adopted by these two projects. Which would be fastest? Which would be more effective at producing finished sequence? Although mired in ethical controversies and disagreements over the "best" genome sequencing strategies, both efforts published draft human sequences in the same week in 2001, one in the journal *Science* [27] and the other in the journal *Nature* [11]. Moreover, each strategy benefited from the other and, of note, current genome strategies are a hybrid of both approaches.

## 3.5 THE HUMAN GENOME PROJECT: COMPUTING TO THE RESCUE

For a moment, let us go back in time to late 1999. The human genome projects are hurtling to a conclusion. There are two projects: one funded by a consortium of international agencies, known as the "public" project, and the other funded by the private company Celera Genomics Corporation. By all accounts, the latter is nearly ready for publication, while the former is struggling to completion. The stakes are enormous, and the politics as heated as they can get in academia. Scientists in both camps are busy making exorbitant claims and ludicrous accusations. This is high drama as almost never happens in science. Then, suddenly, in June 2000, both projects release versions of the genome simultaneously. In a carefully scripted White House ceremony, then President Bill Clinton congratulates Dr. Francis Collins, head of the International Human Genome Sequencing Consortium, and Dr. J. Craig Venter, President of Celera, for their tremendous contributions to mankind and scientific knowledge [24]. Everyone shakes hands, takes pictures, and smiles. The story behind that happy little ceremony is an interesting tale, and one which could have ended very differently but for a small group of dedicated researchers who specialize in data visualization.

To understand the story of the Human Genome Project is to take a look at some of the challenges and successes of the nascent field of bioinformatics. This textbook has focused on introducing you to the methods and ideas that created this field. This project, however, will take you on a tour of a different kind: you will encounter both sophisticated computational solutions to extremely difficult data management problems and the people who participated in the innovations you will read about. The story of the human genome is as much about the people who sequenced almost all of the 3 billion base pairs of human DNA as it is about each base pair of that final, published sequence.

### 3.5.1  Mission Impossible: Sequencing the Human Genome

In the latter part of the 1980s, scientists at the National Institutes of Health (NIH) and its counterparts in Europe and Japan began proposing an ambitious new project. They argued that it was time to stop sequencing small sections of human genes and take the big plunge. It was time to sequence the entire human genome so that the full complexity of it would be laid bare and ready for investigation.

At the time this project was proposed, it was audacious in the extreme. Sequencing technology was in its infancy, and even sequencing a few megabases (millions of base pairs) of DNA required months if not years of effort. In Section 9.1, you will see how visualization aids the process of calling bases in DNA after a sequencer has completed its run. In the late 1980s, the process of deciding what each base of the sequence should be was still done by hand. That is, a human being would sit down with a picture of the sequencing electrophoresis gel and try to decide what each base of the sequence would be. An example sequencing gel is shown in Figure 3.12.

Given the state of technology, and the fact that reading even a few hundred bases from a gel in one day was considered fast, many scientists scoffed, "Sequencing the human genome," they said, "will be the graveyard of a thousand graduate students." Or words to that effect. Essentially, the argument against sequencing the human genome went like this: it will take too long and require too many people to dedicate so much of their time as to be impossible. In a sense, the naysayers

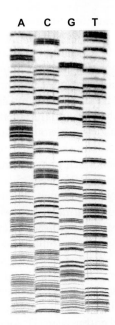

**FIGURE 3.12**   An example of a sequencing electrophoresis gel. Each column represents one of the four nucleotides. The position of the band in each column and row indicates the base at the position in the sequence. To read the sequence, you would start from the bottom of the gel and work your way up.
(© Scott Camazine/PhototakeUSA.com)

were right. It would take a long time. The initial estimate by the NIH was that it would take 20 years, but that was considered an optimistic timetable.[1] It would require a huge amount of staffing power and resources, and some argued that those resources should be dedicated to other, more pressing causes.

Yet, the romantic visionaries won out. They argued that sequencing the human genome would be like landing a person on the moon. It would be a singular accomplishment of the truly extraordinary, and that whatever quibbling might occur regarding its scientific merits, the opportunity was ripe to aim for something bigger and better than anything we had done before. Through the late 1980s, the debate wandered back and forth, until finally, a new voice weighed in. James Watson, the codiscoverer of the structure of DNA, appeared in public on numerous occasions championing the cause of the Human Genome Project. His tremendous stature within the biological community settled the debate once and for all; the NIH and a consortium of international research institutes would fund the sequencing of the human genome.

In the early 1990s, an ambitious young molecular biologist became excited about the idea of sequencing genomes. He had a new method for sequencing,

---

[1] In reality, it took just under a decade.

and he was convinced it was ready for use in sequencing genomes. That man was Dr. J. Craig Venter, and he would go on to play a central role in the human genome drama. But back in the early 1990s, Venter was more interested in a new sequencing technology known as whole-genome shotgun sequencing (see Chapter 4). Using this method, he and his colleagues sequenced one of the first complete genomes. It was the genome of a nasty bacterium, *Hemophilus influenzae*, that can cause fatal illnesses in young children and the elderly [6]. They did the sequencing in a record 9 months, a fact that Venter would tout often in the years to come.

Venter took the whole-genome sequencing technology with him when he founded a company, Celera Genomics, to sequence other genomes. The group at Celera sequenced several other bacterial genomes, and then in quick succession, portions of a variety of eukaryotic genomes. Then they tackled a real challenge: the genome of the fruit fly, *Drosophila melanogaster*. With the *Drosophila* genome, the group at Celera had many things to prove. They had to prove that the whole-genome shotgun sequencing approach could yield a reliable final assembly; that the assembly process could overcome obstacles such as repeat regions, transposons, and other oddities; and that it could yield a final assembly on a genome that was nearly a hundred times the size of the bacterial genomes they had completed before. In early 2000, the Celera group published the genome of the fruit fly to great fanfare and general enthusiasm [1]. Again, they managed to sequence the genome in record time, with relatively few major errors or inaccuracies. Venter was convinced that the human genome lay within his reach; indeed sequencing of the human genome had been going on apace with that of the *Drosophila* genome.

Even as the team at Celera celebrated the release of the fruit fly genome, they were preparing to assemble the human genome. It looked, for all the world, that a private company would surpass the public effort at NCHGR and that the human genome would be shrouded behind the proprietary walls of Celera's subscription-only database. Where was the public attempt? NCHGR, though it had started earlier than Venter and Celera, had initially committed to a slower, more conservative sequencing approach. Chunks of DNA about 100,000 bases long were sequenced at a time, and then carefully assembled along maps of the chromosomes that had been developed earlier. The process was slower, more painstaking, but NCHGR's lead scientists argued it would be more reliable than Celera's hurried approach to DNA sequencing. As the 1990s progressed, however, it became apparent that NCHGR's stepwise approach was cumbersome, difficult to automate, and did not really yield any better assembly than could be obtained with whole-genome shotgun sequencing. Eventually, as Venter's rhetoric became more inflammatory and the pace of sequencing at Celera picked up, NCHGR began incorporating whole-genome shotgun sequencing runs into its assembly as well.

So we came to 1999, the critical year in which Venter claimed to be just months from completing the human genome, and the public work could honestly say that only about 85% of the genome had been sequenced at a level sufficient for publication [25]. NCHGR had much in its favor, however, including the claim to the moral high ground: its version of the human genome would be freely available. While Celera laid out an ambitious plan to charge for access to its version, the

NCHGR touted the fact that its version would be free of charge and completely open to all.[2]

The biggest problem for NCHGR was not that it was behind in the sequencing. By the time the race between Celera and NCHGR had heated up, the international consortium had just as many if not more sequencers than Celera, and it had a huge collection of resources, staff power, and expertise at its disposal. In essence, the leaders of the public effort were confident they would complete the sequencing in time to publish with or even slightly ahead of Celera. The problem was both very simple and very challenging. There was no way to organize the genome data or allow users to access, explore, or utilize it. There was no central interface that would allow users to ask the interesting biological questions. Rather, vast collections of sequences, partial assemblies, and other segments of the genome were deposited onto the ftp servers of GenBank, EMBL (European Molecular Biology Laboratory), and DDBJ (DNA Data Bank of Japan). These three repositories of sequence data around the world together serve as central storage sites for most of the sequence data generated across the entire biological community. They were not the vehicles for presenting the human genome data to the world; they were simply storage sites for it.

The reason this was such a problem for the public effort was simple. Researchers need more than a way to access some portion of the 3 billion bases of DNA that constitute the human genome. They want to be able to find specific genes, identify regulatory elements, investigate gene expression, consider protein structure, and all the myriad things we have discussed so far in this textbook. The number of researchers who want to download the individual sequences of a genomic region pales in comparison to the number of biologists who want to use those data to ask questions about human biology. In essence, there was no point in sequencing the human genome if the consortium could not find a way to guide users through the morass of data.

Celera had the upper hand here. From the start, its business plan was predicated on users paying to access not only the raw sequence data but all the bioinformatics analysis that would result from those data. As a result, they had built a sophisticated interface that would allow users to explore the data in a million different ways with the touch of a mouse. At early demonstrations of their technology, the Celera team made a point of highlighting the ease of using their database in contrast to the apparently clunky organization of the NCHGR's data. As the millenium dawned and the two projects rushed to completion, it became apparent that NCHGR's greatest failing might not be its sequencing approach but its lack of thought regarding data visualization. With just months to go before the publication of both genomes, a small team of researchers at the

---

[2] A side argument that raged for months was whether Celera should be allowed to publish its version of the human genome in a peer-reviewed journal at all. One of the predications for publication in most journals is that the data on which the work is based must be made available to anyone in the research community who asks for it. Celera would not be making the data publicly available because they planned to charge for access to their version of the genome. Eventually *Science* magazine found a loophole in its policy that allowed it to go ahead with publication, but not before it had raised a very acrimonious debate among scientists.

University of California Santa Cruz (UCSC) took up the challenge. The public effort would have its interface, and it would not only be as sophisticated as Celera's, they promised it would be better.

The key player was a PhD student named Jim Kent working with a well-known bioinformatics scientist, David Haussler. Kent had already spent a lifetime in software design and development, but in the late 1990s, he went back to school to learn more about the new field of bioinformatics. Coming as he did from the world of software development and spectacular dotcom successes, Kent was an ardent devotee of the open-source movement. To his mind, the possibility that Celera might have the only usable version of the human genome trapped behind a subscription-only database was a travesty. If the only thing standing in NCHGR's way was a good interface, then that was a simple problem indeed. Jim Kent decided he would create that interface and populate it with an assembled version of the human genome.

There were two challenges. The first became apparent even before Kent began work on the interface. NCHGR's version of the human genome was not fully assembled. Some pieces had been pulled together, and several chromosomes were assembled. The majority, however, remained in long but disparate chunks. The first task, then, was to create an assembled version of the entire genome. With just 2 months to go before the proposed announcement of the release of the genome, Kent frantically pulled together an algorithm and the code needed to assemble the genome [13].

His next problem was to organize all the myriad analyses of the assembled genome so that researchers could explore the results of the assembly and the bioinformatics analysis that accompanied it. Working essentially nonstop for over a month, Kent designed and implemented the Human Genome Browser, a sophisticated interface for exploring the vast amount of data and analyses that NCHGR had contributed over the past decade [14]. It is available at: http://genome.ucsc.edu/cgi-bin/hgGateway

One of the hallmarks of the Human Genome Browser is that it can zoom in to the level of individual nucleotides or all the way out to the level of the entire genome. Another key point is that at each level along the way, it incorporates all the information available from any publicly available resource anywhere in the world. As a result, it is a one-stop shopping solution for researchers trying to understand any aspect of human biology that has been documented to date.

How you use the Human Genome Browser depends on what type of question you want to ask. If you are interested in a specific sequence region, you might enter its coordinates and zoom into the level of individual nucleotides. Or you might zoom out slightly to consider one or several genes in a chromosome region. For example, researchers suspect that a small section of chromosome 22 may be associated with certain kinds of schizophrenia. Using the genome browser, we can explore the genes in this region and ask which of those genes might be expressed in the brain. These might then be good candidates for further investigation.

In addition to tying information about genes and sequences together, the Human Genome Browser provides an interesting display of the sequence conservation with other genomes. As more genomes are sequenced, this last aspect of the genome browser has become quite powerful. You can now compare any region of the human genome with its corresponding region in the mouse, rat, dog, chicken, and even armadillo or elephant. Regions of high conservation likely indicate areas of critical genes, whereas those with little conservation might highlight genes unique to primates or even possibly to our species. These sorts of comparisons can provide the launching pad for many interesting research speculations and questions.

The final assembly of the genome, the browser, and the entire computing infrastructure were in place just 4 days before President Clinton congratulated Francis Collins and Craig Venter at the White House. With nearly superhuman effort, NCHGR had caught up to the Celera team. Together, the two teams made peace and electrified the world with the release of not just one but two nearly complete human genomes. But without Jim Kent and his assembly and interface, there might not have been very much to celebrate. In the end, as much as anything else, the story of the human genome sequencing projects is the story of why data organization and visualization are paramount if data is to be anything more than a string of letters or numbers.

## 3.6  HUMAN GENOME SEQUENCING STRATEGIES

The need for special strategies is related to several challenges posed by the nature of the human genome—not the least of which is its size of 3 billion base pairs. Factor in other characteristics such as its double-stranded, antiparallel nature, its distribution among 23 pairs of chromosomes, and the presence of a large proportion of repetitive sequence.

Where to start? A first step is to break the genome apart into smaller, more workable pieces, which is made possible by cloning fragments that are generated by mechanical shearing or restriction digestion. Many different cloning vectors are available, each able to accommodate different sizes of DNA insert, typically ranging from a few kilobases to about 1 Mb. This helps, but each cloned piece is still too big to sequence in a single sequencing run (recall 500–600 bp), and there are a lot of them! A technique that can "walk" along a piece of DNA in order to sequence it is called **directed sequencing.** Here, each sequencing run provides new sequence information that can then be used to custom design a new primer and to extend the sequence with a follow-up reaction. This sequential approach, although useful, is slow and expensive and so, by itself, was not considered a feasible solution to the human genome sequencing problem.

The two major sequencing efforts tackled the problem by designing new and different strategies. The method championed by Craig Venter, took advantage of rapid technological advances in automated sequencing and an approach known as **whole-genome shotgun sequencing (WGS).** In WGS the entire genome is broken into pieces and these varied-sized pieces are cloned into vectors. Three different-sized vectors were used. The cloned inserts are then sequenced from both sides—double-barreled sequencing—and the distance between the two sequenced portions is determined based on the size of the insert and the length of DNA that

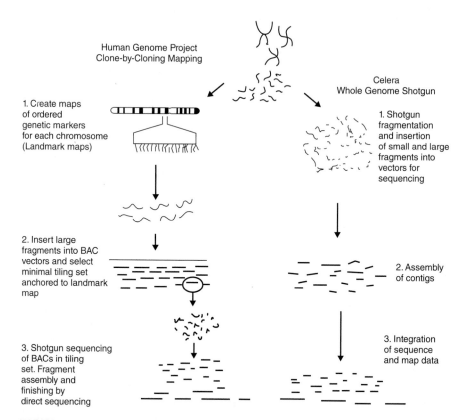

**FIGURE 3.13**  The two major human sequencing projects used different, but complementary, approaches to arrive at a draft sequence at approximately the same time.

was sequenced (Figure 3.13). This is done enough times to provide reasonable coverage of the entire genome.

The computational problem then is to reassemble the sequence from the many individual sequence reads, to create **contigs,** or contiguous sequences—and then to join them into **scaffolds,** keeping in mind the many challenges outlined earlier. The double-barreled sequencing, producing "mate-pairs," or two reads from the same cloned piece of DNA, was a plus. If mate-pairs occurred in two different contigs, they could be joined in the scaffolding process. What about the many repetitive sequences? In which orientation is the insert in the vector? Although WGS is fast and requires few cloning steps, the assembly poses a difficult computational problem. (See Chapter 4 for an in-depth look at this.)

The Human Genome Project attacked some of the challenges from the start to try to reduce the problem, rather than relying on the prowess of automated sequencing and the potential of computational fragment assembly. Instead, a time-consuming physical map-based strategy, known as the **clone-by-clone** approach was adopted. Initially, the genome was broken into relatively large fragments of about 100,000 bp, which could be cloned into **bacterial artificial chromosomes (BACs).** The ends of these clones were sequenced to allow them to be **mapped** to individual chromosomes (using many different experimental methods and markers that allow these sequences to be localized to particular regions). Through this physical mapping process a tiling set, the least number of BACs needed to provide coverage of the genome, was defined. Each of the BAC inserts was fragmented and then cloned into sequencing vectors for WGS using rapid DNA sequencing. A major disadvantage of this approach is the need to create many DNA libraries and the accompanying error that results from the instability of these libraries. The computational assembly problem is a smaller one than WGS since each BAC is sequenced separately and the mapping of the BAC to the chromosome is known, a trade-off with the slow initial mapping process.

## 3.7  FROM STRUCTURE TO FUNCTION

The sequencing of the human genome truly revolutionized science, and its effect on medicine is just beginning to emerge. It enabled a major shift in the mindset of the research biologist from consideration of one or a few genes to consideration of whole sets or even the entire genome. Emphasis has moved from genome sequencing and mapping, or **structural genomics,** to studying gene function. This new era of **functional genomics** has been described as the "development and application of global (genome-wide or system-wide) experimental approaches to assess gene function by making use of the information and reagents provided by structural genomics" [10]. Not only do modern-day biologists have the necessary tools to analyze many genes, it is expected by funding agencies that they will do so. As we will see, this has created a whole new set of associated computational challenges that has made the collaborative efforts between biologists and computational scientists even more critical.

Let's return to our HIV laboratory scenario. At this point we have considered some possible techniques for creating "reagents" for experimentation (e.g., viral cDNA and cDNA clones of individual viral genes) and have learned about DNA sequencing, one of the mainstays of understanding genome structure. Using techniques such as these, the large, international community of HIV researchers collectively have defined and characterized the genomes of many variants of HIV and these are publicly available to support ongoing studies aimed at understanding the function and pathology of HIV. One of the major repositories is at Division of AIDS of the National Institute of Allergy and Infectious Diseases (NIAID), a part of the NIH. Another is the Stanford University HIV Drug Resistance Database.

We'll now turn to some important laboratory techniques in functional genomics. Developing effective treatments for HIV requires an understanding of which genes or, using our book analogy, words, are expressed, and how they interact with components of the host cell to rewrite the book. Recall the central dogma, and the flow of genetic information from DNA to RNA and protein.

When scientists use the term *gene expression* they usually are referring to the production of messenger RNA (mRNA), although protein is usually the ultimate product of gene expression and usually the functional one. We'll stick to that convention and discuss the expression of mRNA first here. Although high-throughput, multiple-gene techniques have become state of the art, it is still worth discussing single-gene expression analysis techniques because they are still widely relied on in verification experiments and for gene localization studies. Earlier we described one technique—RT-PCR. An older technique, the Northern blot, another method for analyzing between one and a few genes, has been around longer and is a technique of high fidelity. Although RNA is difficult to work with, we sometimes choose to work with it in spite of its instability and the prevalence and stubbornness of enzymes—RNAses—that are everywhere and out to degrade RNA. Often, too, the RNA of interest is isolated from a tissue or sample that cannot be reproduced. This means that the biologist usually has only small amounts of RNA to work with and those samples are considered to be precious. This affects how many experiments can be run, which, in turn, affects later data analysis.

Gene expression analysis begins with the isolation of the RNA, either total RNA or only mRNA, from the sample. In the HIV research lab, viral and host cellular transcript RNAs will typically be isolated from patient serum or infected cells in culture (Figure 3.14). This extract will contain all of the RNAs that were "expressed" at the time of extraction and identifying them will create a transcriptional profile.

Remember from the discussions in Chapter 2 that the pathway from DNA to mature mRNA in eukaryotic cells is a complex one, with lots of processing steps as the RNA moves from the nucleus into the cytoplasm. So, we need to think of the profile of RNAs in the sample extract as just a "snapshot in time." Cells are very sensitive to their environments and can respond to changes at the level of gene expression. If we had taken that sample at a different time, or if the cells had been exposed to different conditions, the subset of RNAs in the sample would most likely be at least partly different.

Essentially, the Northern blot allows us to separate and identify individual mRNAs from within a sample extract (Figure 3.15). The mRNAs, which differ in

**FIGURE 3.14**
Total RNA or mRNA
can be isolated from
cells and tissues.

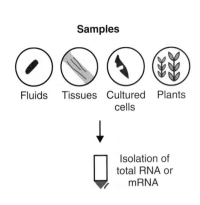

Samples

Fluids    Tissues    Cultured    Plants
                      cells

Isolation of
total RNA or
mRNA

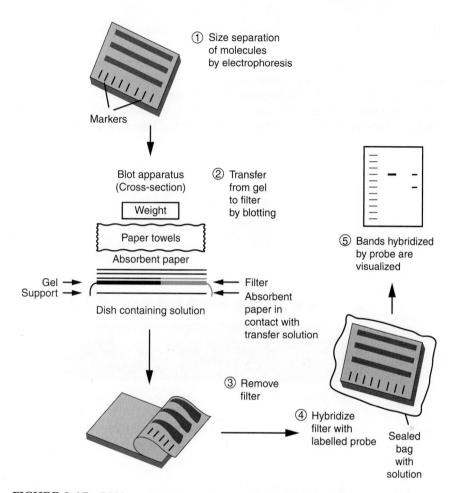

**FIGURE 3.15**    RNA extracts are analyzed by Northern Blot. RNA molecules are separated electrophoretically, transferred to nitrocellulose and hybridized to labeled specific probes for genes of interest.

size, are separated electrophoretically. That is, in an aqueous solution they move through a porous gel, composed of agarose, which is placed within an electrical field. Nucleic acids have a net negative charge and so will migrate through the gel toward the positive pole. The pores of the gel come into play as they cause the nucleic acids to migrate differentially according to size. Smaller molecules move more rapidly because larger ones spend more time moving in and out of the pores. The result of the separation can be visualized under ultraviolet (UV) light when stained with ethidium bromide. Normally, a ladder of DNA standards or markers is run in an adjoining lane to help determine the size of bands of interest.

Notice that individual bands cannot really be discerned in the sample, and moreover we still don't have any idea about the identity of mRNAs in the sample.

This is where hybridization comes in. Following transfer of the gel to a solid support such as nylon or nitrocellulose, we next incubate it with a labeled probe, which is complementary to our gene of interest. Often today, scientists are using enzyme-linked probes and chemiluminescence to detect the signal as a safer alternative to radioactivity. Under the proper conditions, the probe will hybridize only where complementary and will "find" the mRNA within the sample. We see the RNA as a band on the gel. The identity of the RNA of interest by its hybridization

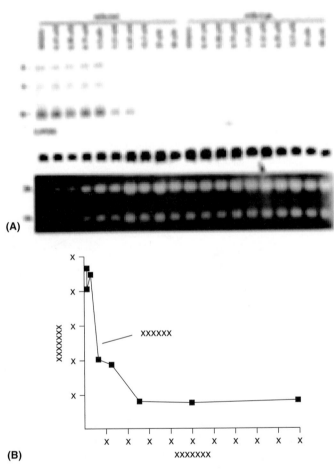

**FIGURE 3.16**    (A) Northern blot showing that full-length (f), singly spliced (s), and multiply spliced (m) transcripts are suppressed in infected cells with increasing dose of drug, roscovitine. The control transcript, GAPDH shows that RNA was present in all lanes. (B) shows a dose-response curve generated by determining the abundance of transcripts in each sample [18].
(Credit: *AMERICAN SOCIETY OF NEPHROLOGY JOURNAL* by Peter J. Nelson, Irwin H. Gelman, and Paul E. Klotman. © 2001 by American Society of Nephrology. Reproduced with permission of American Society of Nephrology in the format Textbook via Copyright Clearance Center.)

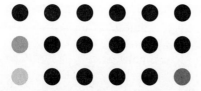

**FIGURE 3.17**  Dot blots can be used to measure mRNA expression in multiple samples simultaneously.

to a specific probe may be verified by its size, if known, determined by relative migration in the gel. We can determine the RNA's apparent size and compare with the expected size, by measuring its migration in the gel relative to the migration of standards of known size. We also get data about the relative amount of expression of the gene of interest from the darkness or intensity of the band on the gel when compared with controls (genes that are not expected to vary under the conditions of interest, such as the GAPDH "house-keeping" gene). For example, scientists studying HIV infection are interested in finding drugs that will suppress expression of viral genes. In a study by Nelson and colleagues [18], Northern blotting was used to show that a drug that inhibits cell division also inhibits HIV gene expression (Figure 3.16).

Variations on the Northern blot can be used to analyze mRNA. In one example, the dot blot, mRNA samples are applied by pipetting or vacuum onto the nylon membrane instead of being separated by electrophoresis (Figure 3.17). Information about size is lost but it is often a good rapid alternative when one has many samples to assay.

## 3.8  PROFILING THE TRANSCRIPTOME

The single-gene expression techniques are often used as an adjunct to the high-throughput, system-wide approaches made possible by the advent of **microarray** technology. As in programming, think of an array as an orderly arrangement of elements, in this case the elements are nucleotide sequences, which are present in small spots, and thus referred to as *micro*arrays. Arrays are known by many names including cDNA arrays, oligoarrays, gene chips, DNA arrays, and biochips, to name a few. The high-throughput array allows the researcher to assay the expression of tens of thousands of genes simultaneously and has dramatically changed the types of questions that can be asked. For example, the HIV researcher may be interested in profiling the expression of genes in a specific cell type at different stages of HIV infection in order to develop new targets for drug intervention. Large-scale transcriptional profiling may lead to discovery of genes that were not previously thought to be involved in infection.

Two major formats of arrays prevail today: the spotted cDNA micro-array and the Affymetrix oligonucleotide array. The cDNA array has been widely used and made popular through the work of Patrick Brown at Stanford

**FIGURE 3.18**
Representation of the
output of two-color
spotted array.
(Courtesy of the
Center for Array
Technologies at the
University of
Washington)

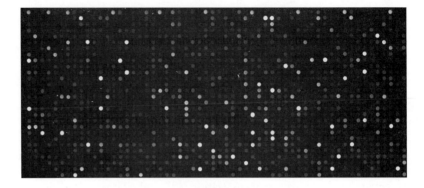

University [21]. Although they can be produced by hand, microarrays are usually fabricated by a high-speed robotic method, which spots cDNA "probes" onto solid supports, usually glass slides. Thousands of cDNAs are spotted onto an individual array, and these probes, of known identity, are used to "query" by complementarity, the RNAs in a sample of unknowns. The cDNA array uses a two-color, red/green, fluorescent assay, labeling the experimental sample with one color and a reference sample with the other. Both labeled samples are hybridized simultaneously to the probes on the array, and the array is viewed under both laser wavelengths. Reading in both the red and the green channels allows the determination of relative binding of experimental:reference for each probe, which is represented as an expression ratio (Figure 3.18).

The fact that expression levels are relative, not absolute, and the high degree of experimental variation in microarrays present great difficulty for the scientist in terms of comparing results from array to array and in terms of comparing results from one lab to the next. The cDNA microarray technique has more than 100 experimental steps and creates a huge potential for experimental variation.

The oligoarray, developed by Affymetrix Inc., contains oligonucleotide probes 25 nucleotides in length (25-mers), which are synthesized on the chip by a patented process of photolithography coupled with combinatorial chemistry (Figure 3.19).

These 25-mers are designed to be complementary to sequences within genes of interest, with a given gene being represented by many probes. For example, on a region of the chip an individual gene will be represented by 16 probe pairs, where each probe pair consists of a perfect-match 25-mer and a mismatch 25-mer, with a single-nucleotide mismatch at the thirteenth base in the 25-mer. The latter is designed to measure nonspecific binding of sample RNA to the probe. The Affymetrix technique employs a single fluorescent label, which is incorporated into the sample during a cRNA synthesis step, and internal controls within the array provide reference to determine relative expression levels (Figure 3.20).

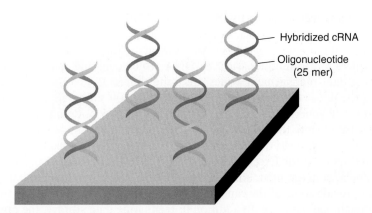

**FIGURE 3.19**   The design of the oligoarray by Affymetrix, Inc. Shown are 25-mer probes that have been hybridized to labeled cRNA.
(Courtesy of Affymetrix, Inc. and Louis M. Mansky)

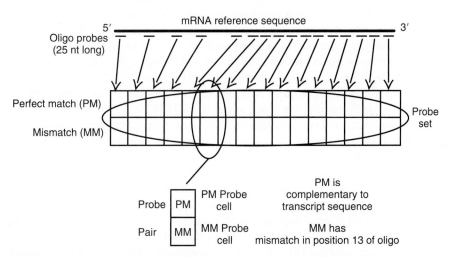

**FIGURE 3.20**   Probesets on oligoarrays consist of 16 perfect match (PM)/mismatch (MM) pairs of 25 nucleotide-long probes.

Although these array types differ in their technical aspects, cost, and ease of use, both allow scientists to perform massively parallel gene expression studies and to characterize the transcriptional profile, known as the **transcriptome.** This topic is explored in depth in Chapter 8. DNA array technology also is applied in large-scale assays of genetic variation (SNP-chips).

Up to this point, with the exception of DNA and genome sequencing, most of the molecular biology lab techniques we have discussed have probably not raised any data management "red flags." It is fairly straightforward to keep good lab records of individual experiments when measuring the expression of a few genes or the localization of genes and proteins within cells and tissues. Most biologists are accustomed to keeping detailed lab notebooks and comfortably turn to spreadsheet tools such as Excel for routine data management, statistical analysis, and graphing capabilities. When we are talking about high-throughput data generation techniques, such as DNA sequencing and microarrays, however, the data management issues are quite different. For one, consider the size of the datasets. Running 10 arrays with 25,000 probesets in a study, for example, will generate many, many datapoints when considering all of the various measurements that are taken for each probeset. Many scientists still use Excel to manage these datasets, and many of the analysis tools for microarray data are designed for Excel import/export. However, Excel began as a spreadsheet application (granted, it now has considerable additional functionality) and doesn't provide some of the capability that one may achieve by putting the data into a relational database. In addition to facilitating data storage, the organization of the data into tables in a relational database, rather than a flat file, and the ability to query the database using the structured query language (SQL), gives the scientist a more flexible access to the data. (Note: Microsoft Office 2007 now offers an SQL add-on for Excel). Individual laboratories may use a relatively small relational database management system such as Microsoft Access, but labs generating a lot of microarray data, for example, increasingly use larger, more robust systems such as the free MySQL or PostGres or the proprietary Oracle Database Management System. Taking data management to the next level, large laboratories and especially centers carrying out high-throughput DNA sequencing and microarray studies, are turning to the Laboratory Information Management Systems (LIMS). LIMS track, manage, and store all information associated with a laboratory. This includes customers, samples, protocols, parameters, results, operators, passwords, among other things. The system may be integrated with laboratory instruments and with relational databases such as MySQL and is designed to match laboratory workflow. Depending on the type of data being collected, a fully integrated LIMS may link to multiple resources, providing a wide variety of information related to the data. Some good examples are the SPINE LIMS system, a system that supports collaborative structural proteomics work [7] and LIMaS, an integrated system for microarray analysis [23]. The large, integrated systems known as knowledge environments (KE) are state-of-the-art systems designed to help biomedical researchers manage and interpret data as well as integrate information from the data with related knowledge. One example of a KE is the signal transduction knowledge environment (SDKE) developed by the American Association for the Advancement of Science and *Science* magazine [8]. Another example is caBIG (Cancer Biomedical Informatics Grid), which was launched by the National Cancer Institute. The goals of KE are to promote sharing of data among researchers in scientific communities and to support new insight and discovery leading to hypothesis generation and eventually understanding of biological processes. Major challenges remain in developing these systems, especially in creating effective standards and mechanisms for data sharing and integration. As is typical in bioinformatics there is a need for computing and domain experts to work together.

Another possible application of DNA arrays may be for sequencing genomes. "Sequencing by hybridization" is an attractive concept because it leads to a more tractable computing problem than does the sequencing approach described earlier. The basic idea is to use a DNA chip to determine which k-mers appear in a genome of interest, and which do not. In Chapter 4 we will see how this information may be of use in reconstructing a genomic sequence.

A method that addresses the lack of quantitative analysis offered by microarrays is **serial analysis of gene expression (SAGE).** SAGE uses DNA sequencing technology to generate a quantitative profile of cellular gene expression. Unlike microarrays, SAGE is quantitative because, rather than measuring relative levels of expression, it actually generates counts of the occurrences of specific sequence "tags." Each transcriptional product has a specific tag of 9–11 nucleotides, and counts of these tags are generated by DNA sequencing. The output of SAGE is a list of tags, each with their corresponding count values. The major computational challenge, then, lies in unambiguous identification of the gene from a given 9- to 11-bp tag. To learn more about the specific technical aspects of this technique, see the original paper by Velculescu and co-workers [26].

# 3.9  A FEW PROTEOMICS TECHNIQUES

In our HIV scenario, we would like to understand the physiological effects of viral infection on immune cells. Just as we profiled the transcriptome, we want to understand the proteome—those proteins that are expressed by the virus and the infected cells at different phases of infection. This is useful information for many reasons. As examples, we can gain an understanding of cellular pathways and processes that are involved in infection and we can also identify possible drug targets. Many of the laboratory techniques for protein analysis have significant similarities to those for RNA analysis. A major difference is that, whereas we detect and identify nucleic acids via hybridization, proteins are often detected and identified through the use of specific antibodies. **Antibodies** are themselves proteins, which recognize and bind to antigens in a highly specific manner (Figure 3.21).

These antigens often are sites on proteins that are recognized as foreign by the individual's immune system. Of course, the production of antibodies is a natural physiological process with which we are all familiar, but in the lab the scientist can engineer antibodies to recognize proteins of interest. Polyclonal antibodies are generated by injecting a protein, usually into a rabbit or goat, to cause the animal to produce antibodies against the protein. The antiserum, isolated from the blood, contains antibodies that are polyclonal in nature, because they are produced by more than one cell. Each antibody in the serum may recognize a different site on the protein. A **monoclonal antibody,** which is produced in a culture dish by a clone of a single cell, called a hybridoma cell, is more specific because it recognizes only one antigenic site.

In terms of the analysis of single to a few proteins the **Western blot** is the counterpart to the Northern blot, and its name was coined in a similar fashion.

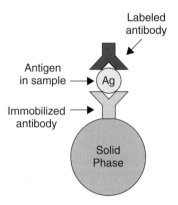

**FIGURE 3.21**    Proteins (antigens; Ag) can be localized and identified using specific antibodies.

Briefly, proteins are extracted from a given sample, the extract is electrophoresed, the separated proteins are transferred from the gel to a nitrocellulose membrane, and then put through the blotting procedure with specific antibodies. Rather than an agarose gel, the cross-linked polymer acrylamide is used, and the proteins are solubilized in a detergent solution. The detergent, usually sodium dodecyl-sulfate (SDS), wraps around the proteins, denaturing them and giving them a net negative charge. You will hear biologists refer to this technique as **SDS-PAGE,** the acronym for sodium dodecyl/sulfate polyacrylamide gel electrophoresis. After the blotting procedure, the bound **primary antibodies** can be detected using a **secondary antibody** that recognizes the primary. For example, if the primary is a polyclonal antibody made in goat, then the secondary antibody would be a generic antigoat antibody, linked with some type of agent to facilitate fluorescent or chemical detection.

Many more proteins can be analyzed simultaneously using a variation on SDS-PAGE known as **2-dimensional (2-D) electrophoresis.** This technique allows a much better separation of proteins and thus permits the scientist to resolve many more different proteins from a given extract. 2D-gel electrophoresis first employs a separation of proteins by charge. Recall that in SDS-PAGE the detergent gave all of the proteins a negative charge and the separation primarily depends on differences in size, commonly referred to as molecular weight. What appears to be a single band on SDS-PAGE is actually a collection of proteins of similar size. The first dimension of 2D-gel electrophoresis separates proteins according to their overall charge by running them through a pH gradient in a tiny tube gel. This gel is then placed across the top of an SDS-PAGE gel and further electrophoresed in the second dimension to separate proteins by size. Individual proteins can be visualized on the gel by staining although proteins present only at trace levels may require a more sensitive radioactive-labeling procedure. Like in SDS-PAGE, the proteins of the D-gel can be transferred and subjected to Western blotting. (Figure 3.22).

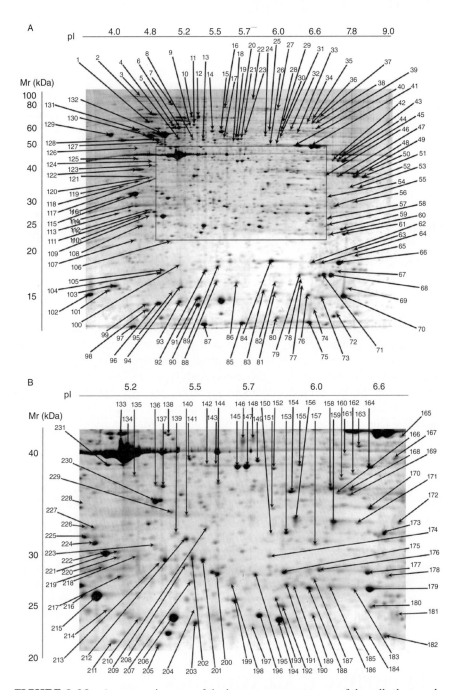

**FIGURE 3.22**    A proteomics map of the human monocyte, one of the cells that can be infected by HIV. The map has been created by 2D-gel electrophoresis followed by mass spectrometry of the most abundant proteins. Numbers indicate proteins that have been identified. This figure from a highly accessed, open access article by Jin et al., 2006 [12]. (Photos reprinted Courtesy of Ming Jin, et al, Two-dimensional gel proteome reference map of blood monocytes, *Proteome Science* 2006, 4:16; licensee Biomed Central Ltd)

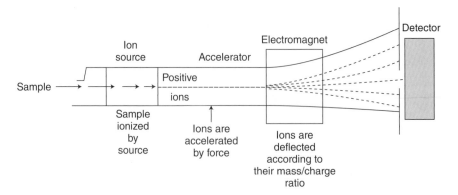

**FIGURE 3.23**    Separation of masses in a mass spectrometer.

The marriage of 2D-gel techniques to **mass spectrometry** has allowed this approach to develop into an effective high-throughput analysis for proteins. To identify individual proteins in the gel, spots can be excised, and proteins can be separated from the gel material and then subjected to further analysis.

For mass spectrometry (Figure 3.23), the proteins are first digested into peptide fragments using enzymes known as proteases. Some proteases, such as the enzyme trypsin, will cut proteins in a reproducible manner. Trypsin will make cuts in the peptide bonds next to the amino acids lysine and arginine. In the mass spectrometer the fragmented proteins are given charge (ionized) then the machine uses electric and magnetic fields to measure the mass ("weight") of the charged particles. This results in the generation of a "fingerprint," a particular pattern of behaviors by the protein fragments related to their mass. The computational challenge, then, is to match up that fingerprint with theoretical fingerprints derived from sequence data in the genomics databases.

The profile of proteins expressed in a given cell or tissue, the proteome, can be analyzed using high-throughput arrays, in a manner similar to the DNA microarrays used to analyze the transcriptome. Protein arrays use proteins (e.g., antibody) or other ligand-bonding reagents immobilized on a surface, such as glass, membranes mass spectrometer plates, or beads, among others. The immobilized protein can "capture" other proteins from a mixture in a specific manner. Like the DNA microarray, a major advantage is that many proteins can be assayed in parallel. Bioinformatics support is important because the data handling demands sophisticated software. Fortunately, some of the software, hardware, and detection systems can be adapted from that used for DNA arrays.

## 3.10  PUTTING IT ALL TOGETHER

The high-throughput assay techniques are considered to be best for generating new hypotheses (for discussion see Chapter 8), rather than finding answers, and results usually need to be verified through other lab techniques. Moreover, we would like to have a complete picture of where and when genes and their products are expressed and how each gene functions within networks of other genes and gene products. A major thrust of bioinformatics today is to build an understanding of how entire systems function, starting with data on biomolecules and integrating these data with biological "knowledge." The picture can be generated using both web lab techniques and computing approaches. For example, in the HIV scenario, microarray studies may suggest that a particular gene is up-regulated. To understand its possible role in infection we would like to know where within a tissue or even at the subcellular level the gene is expressed. An exciting new technology for the former is single-cell PCR, in which individual cells are harvested from within tissue sections by laser ablation, and their gene expression assayed by RT-PCR (see previous discussion). Another method is to perform in situ hybridization, literally doing the hybridization experiment at the site of origin. Individual cells or prepared sections of tissues are hybridized with labeled probes, processed to develop the signal, and viewed under a conventional light microscope or even an electron microscope (Figure 3.24 and Figure 3.25).

As in situ hybridization can help us relate gene expression patterns to known networks by localizing time and place of expression, "knockout" experiments can help identify downstream network components. The term *knockout* refers to the elimination of the function of specific genes by genetic ablation of the gene or by inactivating an intact gene. The knockout mouse is created using homologous recombination to remove specific genes in embryonic stem cells. Inactivation of genes in cell culture can be accomplished by expression of antisense RNA, which blocks the complementary expressed RNA, or more recently by the technique of RNA interference (see Chapter 9 for more details on this technique). Both approaches have been used for the study of gene networks involved in HIV infection (for examples, see [2,4]). Functional knockout often reveals interesting phenotypes but also may demonstrate the relationships between the inactivated gene and other genes in its functional network. In Chapter 9 we explore some of

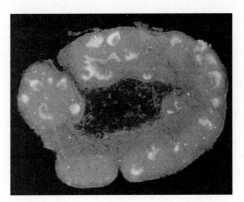

**FIGURE 3.24**   In situ hybridization has been used to localize HIV-1 (white areas) in infected lymph node tissue. Molecular Histology, Inc.
(Dr. Cecil H. Fox)

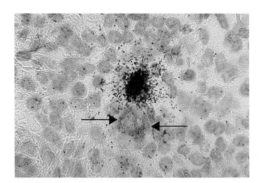

**FIGURE 3.25**  In situ hybridization of RNA used in conjunction with histochemical techniques to localize specific proteins allows the researcher to relate HIV infection to cellular phenotype. Here a cell expressing HIV-1 transcript (*dark grains*) is adjacent to a cell expressing a particular cellular gene product (*arrows*).
(Dr. Cecil H. Fox)

the ways that computers are used to reconstruct networks and to build models and simulations of biological systems. These approaches are at the forefront of bioinformatics today and have already been applied to the important problem of HIV infection (for example, see [9]).

## 3.11  A FEW SELECTED DRY LAB TECHNIQUES

So far in this chapter, we have discussed techniques developed primarily by biologists for use mainly in biological laboratory settings. Equally important in bioinformatics are algorithmic, programming, theoretical, mathematical, analytical, statistical, and empirical techniques developed primarily by computer scientists for use and study mainly in laboratories equipped with computing equipment. The term *wet lab* has been in vogue for some years to describe the former setting; let us coin the equally inadequate term *dry lab* to describe the second setting—the computing lab. We will assume you have some familiarity with the kinds of topics taught in elementary computing courses, and hope the descriptions here will kindle some (fond, we hope) memories of your days as neophytes in the dry labs.

### 3.11.1  Algorithms

An algorithm[3] is a procedure for solving a problem.

Bioinformatics presents us with plenty of problems. Some are variants on problems that have been well studied over the years by researchers in diverse

---

[3] The term *algorithm* is derived from the Latin form of the name of the ninth-century scholar Muhammad ibn Musa al-Khwarizmi who lived not far from modern-day Baghdad. Interestingly, he is also responsible for the name *algebra* which derives from the title of his book on mathematics, "Al-jabr wa'l muqabala."

fields. It is important for bioinformatics practitioners to maintain a healthy and inquiring interest in all fields of science and the humanities. Many of the problems arising in phylogenetics, for example, which we will study in Chapter 6, bear a striking resemblance to problems relating to the origins and evolution of human languages. Many of the problems relating to mining huge deposits of information for nuggets of scientific truth are shared among bioinformatics, astrophysics, and meteorology, as well as other fields. Some of the algorithms developed for sequence alignments are among the most intricate studied by mathematicians and theoretical computer scientists.

String algorithms will be useful when we turn to pattern matching for studying fragment reassembly in Chapter 4 and sequence alignment in Chapter 5. Familiarity with recursive programs will aid us in developing algorithms that reduce the difficulty of the main problem by subdividing it into smaller ones. Skillful use of recursion enables us to develop algorithms that are convincingly plausible. By this we mean that the algorithm is so closely related to the statement of the problem that we can be confident that it will lead to a correct[4] program.

Sometimes, we will know from our dry lab studies that certain problems are not amenable to correct and computationally feasible solutions. When that happens, we turn to the repertory of approximate algorithms that sacrifice a certain and, we hope, measurable amount of exactness in return for realistic running times. As an example, consider the problem of packing a container with the largest weight of items.

### Container Packing Problem

You are given the dimensions (length, breadth, and height) of a container together with a set of rectangular boxes. You are given the dimensions and the weight of each box. The problem is to pack some of the boxes into the container in such a way that you maximize the weight.

As a first example, your container is 50 cm by 80 cm by 20 cm high. Your boxes are:

- 40 by 60 by 20, weight 30 kg
- 40 by 40 by 17, weight 19 kg
- 20 by 20 by 20, weight 15 kg
- four boxes, each 25 by 20 by 10, each weighing 10 kg
- 20 boxes, each 5 by 5 by 5, each weighing 100 g

An obvious approach to this problem is to start by placing the heaviest box first, then the second heaviest, and so on. This approach is referred to by the not-too-technical name **greedy algorithm.** In general, a greedy algorithm is one that proceeds by steps, at each stage making the obviously optimal local choice in the hope that this process will lead to an optimal global solution when the steps are combined.

Some problems are amenable to the greedy approach. Consider the problem of trying to find, in a connected graph all of whose edges are labeled with a **weight**

---

[4] But we will note in Section 3.11.2 that plausibility and efficiency often do not go hand in hand.

or **cost,** a tree whose edges span the whole graph but whose total edge weight is as small as possible. This is often called the **minimum spanning tree problem.** The following (greedy) algorithm can be proved to produce an optimal solution:

```
input: a connected graph G on n vertices with a cost on each edge;
initialize result to an empty set of edges;
repeat {
 remove the lowest cost edge eMin from G;
 if eMin does not form a cycle when added to result then {
   add eMin to result;
 }
} until result contains n−1 edges
```

**Pseudocode describing an algorithm to find the minimum spanning tree of a graph.**

Other problems are not amenable to a greedy solution. Nevertheless, the greedy algorithm will, although not producing an optimal solution, produce a pretty good one. In Chapter 4 we will look at a greedy algorithm for reconstructing a genome sequence from examination of hundreds or thousands of fragments.

In the case of the fragment reconstruction problem, no known optimal algorithm runs in time better than exponential in the number of fragments. Fragment reconstruction is an example of an **NP complete** problem, a class of problems for which computer scientists strongly suspect there are no polynomial time algorithms. The container packing problem mentioned previously is another example of an NP complete problem.

Other problems, although not being amenable to a greedy solution, do, however, have optimal algorithms that run in acceptable polynomial time. In Chapter 5 we will meet algorithms that can align genomic sequences to demonstrate evolutionary relatedness. Alignment problems are generally solvable using dynamic programming techniques.

## 3.11.2 Analysis

*What do the public, the great unobservant public, who could hardly tell a weaver by his tooth or a compositor by his left thumb, care about the finer shades of analysis and deduction!*
—Sherlock Holmes: *The Adventure of The Copper Beeches,* Arthur Conan Doyle

Current usage of the word *analysis* is very broad. Sherlock Holmes would analyze a problem as a step towards its solution. That's the kind of analysis we did in the preceding section: **Problem analysis** is a cognitive skill involving finding basic principles underlying a problem statement, and the application of knowledge and experience to find an appropriate algorithmic solution. Chemical analysis is less a cognitive skill but involves techniques for breaking a complex whole into constituents that are amenable to methodical examination leading to a more thorough understanding of the whole. Psychiatric analysis is another realm. And literary and musical analyses seem to be a different pursuit altogether.

But all senses of the word indicate that analysis involves studying small parts in order to gain an understanding of the whole. This section looks at a very specialized kind of analysis:

- Carefully consider how often each step of a program is executed in order to estimate total running time, and
- Carefully consider each part of a program that may make demands on resources (such as memory) in order to estimate total resource needs.

Traditionally, program analysis of this kind has required fairly sophisticated mathematical knowledge. And we will use mathematical techniques like recurrence relations and series summation as tools for program analysis. Often, the variation in runtime and resource allocation for different instances is so great that we will need to develop **average-case** and **worst-case** scenarios. Average-case analysis is the pragmatic person's tool—most of the time predicted performance will be a fairly good match with actual performance; but, once in a while, things may turn out significantly worse. For this reason, it is wise to also perform worst-case analysis.

When analyzing programs, we tend to look at structured components, especially recursive procedures and loops. When we look at loops, we can often tell that its code will be executed a maximum of $n$ times, where $n$ is a number related to the size of the problem instance or the size of the input to the program. Because of conditionals and other factors, we often are unable to say exactly how many steps will be executed for each iteration of the loop, but we can often tell that there will be at most a constant number, such as 42 steps. No matter how large the constant, as long as it is a constant and in no way depends on $n$, computer scientists will say that such a loop that is executed at most $n$ times has running time of order $O(n)$ (pronounced "big oh of n").

Mathematicians, as is their wont, use somewhat more formal language, and define $O(n)$ in terms of limits and upper bounds. Good discussions of the concept are to be found in [5]. As an example of loop analysis, let us analyze the code in Figure 3.26.

The input to the program consists of two `ints`, `start`, and `finish`. With integer inputs, it is usual[5] to say that the size of the input to a program that works with `ints` is simply related to the input `ints`. In this particular case, we'd say: "Let $n = $ `finish` $-$ `start` be the size of the input." To continue with our analysis, we'd observe that the loop in Figure 3.26 is executed $n$ times (or is it $n + 1$? A neat thing about big Oh notation is that it doesn't matter if we're off by one or two in cases like this). And each time through the loop, an `int` is squared and the result accumulated in variable `result`. It's easy to see that each iteration

---

[5] It is usual but not universal. Sometimes, such as when analyzing programs dealing with large primes, we prefer to measure the input in terms of the length of the sequence of digits that represents that number. In this book, however, we'll adopt the simpler and commoner usage.

```
public int sumsquares(int start, int finish) {
  // Sum the squares of the integers from start to finish inclusive
  // Precondition: finish > start
  int value = 0;
  for (int i = start; i <= finish; i++) {
    value += (i * i);
  }
  return value;
}
```

**FIGURE 3.26**   A program to sum the squares of integers. Can you estimate its runtime?

```
int[ ] candidates;
public boolean find(int target, int lo, int hi) {
  int mid;
  if (lo >= hi) return (target == candidates[lo]);
  else {
    mid = (lo + hi) / 2;
    if (target == candidates[mid]) return true;
    else if (target < candidates[mid]) return find(target, lo, mid-1);
    else return find(target, mid+1, hi);
  }
}
```

**FIGURE 3.27**   Binary Search Program. Is the target contained in the sorted array candidates? Can you analyze it for expected runtime?

of the loop consists of a constant number[6] of integer operations. Since the loop is executed $n$ times, the expected runtime is $O(n)$. In this example, the worst-case runtime is also $O(n)$.

We will find that analysis of runtime performance of programs involving calls to recursive procedures often leads to the derivation of recurrence relations. A recurrence relation is like a mathematical equation that gives the runtime of a procedure when input is of size $n$ in terms of runtimes of the same procedure when input is smaller. Together with clear **base cases**, we may be able to solve the recurrence to obtain an estimate for the runtime.

The binary search procedure of Figure 3.27 looks in an array candidates between the indexes lo and hi for a target. By looking at the center element mid, midway below lo and hi, the procedure can decide whether to immediately return success or to continue searching in one half or the other of the array. When so much halving has taken place that lo >= hi, we reach our base case and can determine the answer very easily.

---

[6] (in this case 2) but it really doesn't matter. What's important is that the number of steps executed in any one iteration of the loop is in no way connected to $n$.

Let $T_n$ denote the expected runtime when the input size (`hi - lo`) is $n$. The most work required in the current incarnation of the procedure find is

- a comparison of `lo` to `hi`
- a computation of `mid = (lo + hi) / 2` for three arithmetic operations
- two comparisons of `target` to `candidates[mid]`
- a recursive call with input half the size of this incarnation's input

Thus, in the worst case, we have the recurrence:

$$T_n = T_{\frac{n}{2}} + 6$$

Together with the base case:

$$T_o = 2$$

We can now embark on solving this recurrence equation. By repeatedly applying the recurrence we get:

$$T_n = T_{\frac{n}{2}} + 6 = \left(T_{\frac{n}{4}} + 6\right) + 6 = \left(T_{\frac{n}{8}} + 6\right) + 6 + 6$$

It is clear that we can keep on halving, each time adding 6, until it is no longer possible to halve. So how often is that? How many times can you halve $n$ before you reach 0? Well, that's almost the definition of $\log(n)$ when log is taken to the base 2 (as it always is in computer science).

So the worst-case runtime of binary search is six operations $\log(n)$ times plus the two operations needed when we reach the base case. Since the exact values of 6 and 2 are disputable and irrelevant, we prefer to say that runtime is order $O(\log(n))$.

So far, we've looked in fairly informal terms at traditional mathematical techniques for runtime analysis. Less traditionally, we will encourage experimentation and empirical studies, not as a replacement for mathematics, but as a speedy indication of what is going on when we are developing algorithmic solutions to new and fascinating problems. We realize that simulation is only rarely an acceptable substitute for mathematical rigor, but we recognize that in experimental laboratory situations strict mathematical rigor is not always immediately called for.[7]

## KEY TERMS

| | | |
|---|---|---|
| hybridization (3.1) | cDNA library (3.2) | Maxam and Gilbert |
| cDNA (3.2) | polymerase chain | sequencing (3.4) |
| restriction enzyme (3.2) | reaction (3.3) | Sanger sequencing (3.4) |

---

[7] Just as, in grammatical rigor, ending sentences with prepositions is a sloppy habit up with which we will not put (W.L.S. Churchill, attrib.)

dideoxy sequencing (3.4)

electrophoresis (3.4)

directed sequencing (3.6)

whole-genome shotgun
   sequencing (WGS) (3.6)

contigs (3.6)

scaffolds (3.6)

clone-by-clone (3.6)

bacterial artificial chromosomes
   (BACs) (3.6)

mapped (3.6)

structural genomics (3.7)

functional genomics (3.7)

microarray (3.8)

transcriptome (3.8)

serial analysis of gene expression
   (SAGE) (3.8)

antibodies (3.9)

monoclonal antibody (3.9)

western Blot (3.9)

SDS-PAGE (3.9)

primary antibodies (3.9)

secondary antibody (3.9)

2-dimensional (2-D)
   electrophoresis (3.9)

greedy algorithm (3.11)

weight (3.11)

cost (3.11)

minimum spanning tree
   problem (3.11)

NP complete (3.11)

problem analysis (3.11)

average-case (3.11)

worst-case (3.11)

base cases (3.11)

# BIBLIOGRAPHY

1. Mark D. Adams, Susan E. Celniker, Robert A. Holt, et al. Galle. The Genome Sequence of *Drosophila melanogaster. Science*, 287: 2185–2195, 2000.

2. D. Boden, O. Pusch, R. Silbermann, et al. Enhanced gene silencing of HIV-1 specific sirna using microRNA designed hairpins. *Nucleic Acids Res,* 32(3):1154–1158, 2004.

3. T. D. Brock. *Life at High Temperatures.* Yellowstone Association for Natural Science, Yellowstone National Park, 1994.

4. E. Castigli, F. W. Alt, L. Davidson, et al. Cd40-deficient mice generated by recombination-activating gene-2-deficient blastocyst complementation. *Proc Nat Acad Sci,* 91:12135–12139, 1994.

5. T. Cormen, C. Leiserson, and R. Rivest. *Introduction to Algorithms.* MIT Press, Cambridge, MA, 1990.

6. R. D. Fleischmann, M. D. Adams, O. White, et al. Whole genome random sequencing and assembly of *Haemophilus influenzae* Rd. *Science*, 269:496–512, 1995.

7. Chern-Sing Goh, Ning Lan, Nathaniel Echols, et al. Spine 2: A system for collaborative structural proteomics within a federated database framework. *Nucl Acids Res,* 31(11):2833–2838, 2003.

8. Nancy R. Gough. Science's signal transduction knowledge environment. The connections maps database. *Ann N Y Acad Sci,* 971(1):585–587, 2002.

9. A. Grilo, A. Caetano, and A. Rosa. Immune system simulation through a complex adaptive system model. In Proceedings of the Third Workshop on Genetic Algorithms and Artificial Life (GAAL1999), 1999.

10. P. Hieter and M. Boguski. Functional genomics: It's all how you read it. *Science,* 278:601–602, 1997.

11. The International Human Genome Sequencing Consortium. Initial sequencing and analysis of the human genome. *Nature,* 409:860–921, 2001.

12. M. Jin, P. T. Diaz, T. Bourgeois, et al. Two-dimensional gel proteome reference map of blood monocytes. *Proteome Sci,* 4(16), 2006.

13. James W. Kent and David Haussler. Assembly of the working draft of the Human Genome with GigAssembler. *Genome Res,* 11: 1541–1548, 2001.

14. James W. Kent, Charles W. Sugnet, Terrence S. Furey, et al. The Human Genome Browser at UCSC. *Genome Res,* 12:996–1006, 2002.

15. A. M. Maxam and W. Gilbert. A new method for sequencing DNA. *Proc Natl Acad Sci USA,* 74:560–564, 1977.

16. K. B. Mullis. The unusual origin of the polymerase chain reaction. *Sci Am,* 262: 56–65, 1990.

17. K. B. Mullis, F. A. Faloona, S. Scharf, et al. Specific enzymatic amplification of DNA in vitro: The polymerase chain reaction. In Cold Spring Harb Symp Quant Biol, 51:263–273, 1986.

18. P. J. Nelson, I. H. Gelman, and P. E. Klotman. Suppression of HIV-1 expression by inhibitors of cyclin-dependent kinases promotes differentiation of infected podocytes. *J Am Soc Nephrol,* 12:2827–2831, 2001.

19. Richard J. Roberts. Perspective: How restriction enzymes became the workhorses of molecular biology. *PNAS,* 102(17):5905–5908, 2005.

20. F. Sanger, S. Nicklen, and A. R. Coulson. DNA sequencing with chain-terminating inhibitors. *Proc. Natl. Acad. Sci. USA,* 74:5463–5467, 1977.

21. M. Schena, D. Shalon, R. W. Davis, and P. O. Brown. Quantitative monitoring of gene expression patterns with a complementary DNA microarray. *Science,* 270(5235):467–470, 1995.

22. Special issue on "The Human Genome." *Science,* 291:1145–1434, February 2001.

23. S. C. Webb, A. Attwood A, T. Brooks T., et al. Limas: The java-based application and database for microarray experiment tracking. *Mamm Genome,* 15(9):740–747, 2004.

24. White House Press Release. Remarks by the president...on the completion of the first survey of the entire human genome project. http://clinton5.nara.gov/WH/New/html/genome-20000626.html

25. Wired News Story. Genome mappers to make amends. http://www.wired.com/news/technology/0,36815-0.html

26. V. E. Velculescu, L. Zhang, B. Vogelstein, and K. W. Kinzler. Serial analysis of gene expression. *Science,* 270:484–487, 1995.

27. J. Craig Venter, Mark D. Adams, Eugene W. Myers, et al. The sequence of the human genome. *Science,* 291:1304–1351, 2001.

# 4

# Fragment Assembly

*"Humpty Dumpty sat on the wall.*
*Humpty Dumpty had a great fall.*
*All the kings horses and all the kings men*
*couldn't put Humpty together again."*

The announcement of the sequencing of the human genome and accomplishments of the Human Genome Project and Celera Genomics have brought the attention of the world's media to the field of bioinformatics. This work was described in some detail in Chapter 3. Another good point from which to start exploring the history and achievements of the Human Genome Project is [8].

The Human Genome Project, initially headed by James Watson, was set up by the U.S. National Institutes of Health (specifically the National Human Genome Research Institute) and the Department of Energy in 1990. One of its many goals was the determination of the entire nucleotide sequence of the human genome by 2005.

A press release issued on April 14, 2003, by the International Human Genome Sequencing Consortium asserts that as of that date, all the goals of the Human Genome Project have been met or surpassed.

Recall from Chapter 3 that sequencing machines can reliably produce the nucleotide sequences of DNA segments of length up to about 500 bp. To determine the sequences of each of the chromosomes of the human genome, it is necessary to somehow "stitch together" lots of these 500-bp pieces and reconstruct unbroken stretches of hundreds of millions of base pairs. In this chapter, we will look at techniques and algorithms that can be used toward that end.

## 4.1 THE NATURE OF THE PROBLEM

### 4.1.1 Two Analogies

In Chapter 3 we described the laboratory techniques that result in reliable sequences of approximately 500 nucleotides (500-mers). If all we have are lots and lots of 500-mers, we don't really know much about the original genome from which these 500-mers were produced. It's as if somebody cut up several copies of *Great Expectations* into 5-cm square pieces of paper and gave you some of the pieces. Although you might thus accumulate a significant amount of Charles Dickens' novel, can you truly say that you have much insight into the story? Let's call this scenario the "book reconstruction" puzzle. As we shall see, the analogy will provide us with useful insights into our real target: the sequence reconstruction puzzle.

Jigsaw puzzles offer another analogy for the genome-sequencing problem. Just as jigsaw puzzles break up a complete picture into several pieces that need to be joined to re-create the original picture, laboratory sequencing techniques produce lots of relatively small (500-nucleotide) pieces that need to be joined together to reassemble the original large sequence. But there is a weakness with the jigsaw puzzle analogy: The pieces of a jigsaw puzzle are disjoint and fit together closely with no overlap. Each individual point in the completed picture of the jigsaw puzzle belongs to one, and only one, jigsaw piece. It is important to realize that the laboratory techniques in Chapter 3 produce pieces that will overlap; furthermore, each point in the genome will likely occur in several different pieces. A small jigsaw puzzle is shown in Figure 4.1.

A more accurate analogy with the fragment reassembly problem can be made if we imagine several companies producing jigsaw puzzles of the same scene. Each company cuts up the scene into pieces in its own independent way.

Now we can construct a different puzzle that is more akin to the sequence reconstruction puzzle. We are given a large number of jigsaw pieces with no way of telling which pieces came from which company's jigsaw puzzle. We are to reconstruct the original scene from which all the individual jigsaw puzzles were created.

Let's recap: Several companies have each produced a different jigsaw puzzle of the same scene. Each company cut up the scene in its own way. We are given a large number of jigsaw pieces taken from each of the different companies, and we

**FIGURE 4.1**   Jigsaw puzzles have disjoint pieces. Sequence reconstruction puzzles have overlapping pieces.

don't know which piece came from which company. We probably don't have all the pieces from all the companies. Our task is to generate a picture of the original scene. That's the **multiple jigsaw puzzle.**[1]

The **book reconstruction puzzle** presented us with lots of 5-cm squares cut by different people in different ways from several copies of a novel. We probably don't have all the pieces from all of the book vandals. Our task is to generate one copy of the original book.

The fragment reconstruction problem presents you with a large number of fragments, such as:

```
ACC   AC AT
AC       AT    GG      ACTTA  TC
  CGT   CGG   TG    TT   TT
  GG ACTTA TC A  GTCA        ACT AC  AAT
CAT     GA   GAC      ATTC
```

Your aim is to figure out what the original sequence might have been before the DNA strand was cut into tiny pieces. By laying out the preceding fragments in this tableau:

```
ACC   CAT     GA   GAC     ATTC
AC       AT    GG      ACTTA  TC
  CGT   CGG   TG    TT  TT
  A   GTCA        ACT AC  AAT
```

you might decide the original sequence was

```
ACCGTCATCGGGACTGACTTAATTC
```

Unlike in a jigsaw, we have overlaps, and this fragment reconstruction problem corresponds to approximately 2* coverage. Each nucleotide in the original sequence occurs about twice in the fragments.

On the other hand, jigsaw puzzles like the one in Figure 4.2 have exactly 1* coverage, and there is no overlap between the pieces.

The **sequence reassembly puzzle** presents us with several lengths of nucleotide string, each about 500 nucleotides in length and all taken from the same stretch of DNA. But several copies of that stretch of DNA were cut up in different ways. We probably don't have the entirety of any one copy of the original DNA stretch. Our task is to generate the sequence of that original stretch of DNA.

## 4.1.2 The Need for Multiple Coverage

For the book reconstruction puzzle we would like a guarantee that from among all the pieces of paper in our possession, we have at least one copy of every single occurrence of every single word in the book. For the multiple jigsaw puzzle we

---

[1] To make it more realistic, imagine that the number of ways the pieces of a jigsaw puzzle can be cut is more restricted than it really is; so that many pieces might fit with one another.

**FIGURE 4.2**    A puzzle more akin to fragment reassembly. Several copies of
*La Giocanda* (or the *Mona Lisa*) have been cut up. Your task is to put together one
perfect copy of the whole.

would like some assurance that every single pixel of the original scene appears in at
least one of the jigsaw pieces in our possession. And for the sequence reassembly
puzzle, we'd like to be certain that every occurrence of every nucleotide in the
original stretch is represented at least once somewhere among our collection of
500-mers.

It is too much to expect our somewhat random processes to provide an absolute guarantee of any of these conditions. However, it is possible to engineer the

circumstances of the puzzle in such a way that it is overwhelmingly likely that our puzzle is complete by our definition. The key is to ensure an adequate level of coverage. For the book reconstruction puzzle, we do this by starting with an adequate number of copies of the book and collecting a large number of 5-cm squares from those available. For the multiple jigsaw puzzle the more companies making different individual jigsaw puzzles of the same scene, and the more pieces we obtain from them, the more likely are we to have adequate representation. For the DNA sequence reassembly puzzle we need many copies of the genome, randomly sheared to generate many overlapping fragments of different size, and we need to sequence a large number of the resulting pieces to provide adequate input to our algorithms. The best we can do is to aim for an average coverage rate that is sufficient to make it statistically extremely unlikely that we have missed any section of the genome. Exercise 4.1 will investigate just how much of this type of overkill is necessary to guarantee a reasonable level of certainty that nothing has been missed.

Another important reason to use many copies of the human genome is that there is not *a* human genome sequence. Recall from Chapters 2 and 3 that the variation in our genomes is what makes us unique individuals and is a driving force in evolution. The human genome sequencing projects were based on agreement that the completed sequence should be a composite of several individuals representing both genders and diverse ethnic backgrounds.

## 4.2  PUTTING THE PIECES TOGETHER

Let's now suppose that we have some reasonable assurance that among all the small squares of paper in our possession we actually have full coverage of the novel. Or some assurance that we have full coverage of the scene for the jigsaw puzzle. Or some assurance that we have adequate coverage of our stretch of genome.

Now we need to fit the pieces together. It will be useful for us to continue in this section with our *Great Expectations* and with our multiple jigsaw puzzle analogies.

### 4.2.1  Location, Location, Location

Experience has taught us some "tricks" to help us put jigsaw puzzles together. For example:

- Corner pieces are easy to recognize because two straight edges meet in a right angle. These pieces are easy to locate correctly.
- Side pieces are recognizable because of their straight edge, but it's not quite so easy to place them precisely in their final positions.
- Some visual clues may help us. For example, we know that a piece containing an eye is likely to be close to and above a piece containing a mouth or a nose.

Similar clues pertain to the DNA-sequencing puzzle. Prior research has established some useful pointers for us. For example:

- A certain gene is known to be located on a particular chromosome.
- A certain sequence of a small number of nucleotides is known to occur only in one place. Such sequences are called sequence-tagged sites (or STS).
- The amount of separation between two identified locations is known.

## 4.2.2  Mapping

Over the years, scientists have built up a base of knowledge about certain locations on the genome. Careful study of this information can be used to construct a partial schematic map indicating relative locations of salient genomic features.

Imagine that some scholars of *Great Expectations* have published important facts about the book that can be used to help us locate our little 5-cm squares. As a rather fanciful example, suppose that a biblical scholar was seeking connections between the book of Jeremiah and Dickens' *Great Expectations*. This scholar read the novel very carefully, and among the conclusions, she remarks that the word *lamentation* appears exactly once in *Great Expectations* toward the end of Chapter 22.[2] So if the word *lamentation* appears on one of our 5-cm squares, we can place that square in its approximate location, correct to within a chapter.

Once we have the unique location of *lamentation* we can look around at the context. In the case of this word the context found at the Website of http://www.literature.org happens to be[3]

> We were waiting, I supposed, for Mr Pocket to come out to us; at any rate we waited there, and so I had an opportunity of observing the remarkable family phenomenon that whenever any of the children strayed near Mrs Pocket in their play, they always tripped themselves up and tumbled over her—always very much to her momentary astonishment, and their own more enduring lamenta-tion. I was at a loss to account for this surprising circumstance, and could not help giving my mind to speculations about it, until by-and-by Millers came down with the baby, which baby was handed to Flopson, which Flopson was handing it to Mrs Pocket, when she too went fairly head foremost over Mrs Pocket, baby and all, and was caught by Herbert and myself.

## 4.2.3  Using Overlaps

Let's say we find the preceding quote from *Great Expectations* on one of our 5-cm squares. Where do we go from here? One approach would be to look for other

---

[2] You may think we're going overboard with this analogy, but we're making the entirely serious point that published research conducted without specific thought for the use of its results for genome sequencing can, in fact, provide important mapping information to help us solve today's reassembly puzzles.

[3] A subtle complication occurs here: If we look at the quote carefully, we will see that *lamentation* has, in fact, been erroneously rendered as *lamenta- tion* at this Website. Most likely this transcription occurred at some stage of the scanning process. Similar errors occur often in the biological world. It is quite common for humans or programs to miscall or simply miss or duplicate a base. Robust algorithms need to take this into account, as we shall discuss later.

5-cm squares that have some words in common with this one. We can look for **overlap.** Suppose we find a square of paper containing

> about it, until by-and-by Millers came down with the baby, which baby was handed to Flopson, which Flopson was handing it to Mrs Pocket, when she too went fairly head foremost over Mrs Pocket, baby and all, and was caught by Herbert and myself. 'Gracious me, Flopson!' said Mrs Pocket, looking off her book for a moment, 'everybody's tumbling!' 'Gracious you, indeed, Mum!' returned Flopson, very red in the face; 'what have you got there?' 'I got here, Flopson?' asked Mrs Pocket.

What do we conclude? Did you notice the significant overlap between the two squares? The "suffix"

> about it, until by-and-by Millers came down with the baby, which baby was handed to Flopson, which Flopson was handing it to Mrs Pocket, when she too went fairly head foremost over Mrs Pocket, baby and all, and was caught by Herbert and myself.

of the first sequence is also a "prefix" of the second. This enables us to place the second immediately after the first. In sequence assembly this joining process using overlaps results in the formation of a longer sequence from the two sequences being joined. Once the fragments begin joining in this way, we refer to those longer sequences as **contigs.** More and larger contigs are then ordered and oriented relative to one another as they are assembled into a higher order structure known as a "scaffold." Can you also see that you're going to appreciate the assistance of a computer program that can seek out overlaps like this? Despite efforts at complete coverage of the genome, gaps inevitably exist between contigs and scaffolds. Some sections of DNA will simply not be covered by any of the fragments we sequenced. One approach to resolving these gaps relies on obtaining new sequence data. Primers can be designed to facilitate the generation of sequence segments that flank other existing ones. As each fragment is identified, a primer is derived from the "newly discovered" end, and used to discover the next new fragment. This technique has been given the evocative name **sequence walking.**

Reliance on and generation of mapping information was one of the differences in approach between the public and the private teams sequencing the human genome. The public project intended to rely heavily on mapping knowledge to ensure a high level of confidence in correct placement of sequenced fragments and to reduce the problem space of the sequence reassembly.

## 4.2.4  Whole-Genome Sequencing

More cavalierly, perhaps, Craig Venter and Celera advocated a whole-genome shotgun strategy that relied heavily on the power of the new automatic sequencers and computer algorithms that used overlap information to try to locate the sequenced segments relative to each other.

As usual in biological science, nothing is quite that simple. The public project emphasized mapping but needed reassembly programs to fill in the frame provided by mapping information. The private enterprise made use of the mapping information gathered by the public project and employed derived scaffolds to assist the whole-genome shotgun reassembly programs.

## 4.2.5  The Problem of Repeats

Some short sequences (such as *lamentation* in *Great Expectations*) are rare, and when found, the information derived is very valuable. Other sequences are more common. For example, if we were to find the sequence *Magwitch* on one of our 5-cm squares, and if we were fortunate enough that prior scholars had investigated the appearances of *Magwitch* very carefully, it would not enable an exact placement of our square of paper; only that it belongs in one of Chapters 40, 42, 46, 53, 54, 55, or 56. This information is not definitive, but it does help a little in our reconstruction problem. More extremely, the value of finding a common string like *Pip* on one of our squares of paper is very small. (Pip is the main character of the novel, and his name appears at least once in most of the chapters.) Frequently occurring words like *the, and* and *is* provide essentially no useful information. In fact, using an overlap as short or as commonly repeated as *the* would be most unlikely to help us correctly reconstruct the novel.

The same phenomenon occurs in biology. Some sequences are very commonly repeated throughout the genome. It is important to identify them so we do *not* rely on their occurrences to compute likely overlaps between sequence segments. Repeated subsequences can cause reassembly algorithms to miss sections of genome in between the repeats. Consider the following simple, unrealistically small example to illustrate how this can happen:

## 4.2.6  A Worked Example

Suppose our original sequence is

ACGATTGAGAATTCCGA

and suppose our wet lab sequencers presented us with fragments

(a) GAGA
(b) ATTC
(c) AC
(d) GATT
(e) CGA
(f) ACGAT
(g) TGAGAA
(h) TTCCGA

(If you are patient enough, you will note that we have exactly 2* coverage of the original sequence, but that is just a fortuitous accident.)

Most reconstruction algorithms will immediately throw out fragments (a), (c), and (e) on account of their being entirely contained in other fragments, and thus providing no useful information. We are left with

(b) ATTC
(d) GATT

**(f)** ACGAT

**(g)** TGAGAA

**(h)** TTCCGA

As we know from Section 4.2.3, information about the ovelaps between fragments is one of the most important clues in any reassembly process. The huge overlaps between **(b)** and **(h)**, between **(f)** and **(d)**, and then between **(d)** and **(b)** makes it almost a certainty that any reassembly algorithm would place **(f)(d)(b)(h)** all in a row to form ACGAT GATT ATTC TTCCGA. Compressing the overlaps results in a predicted reassembly of ACGATTCCGA. If you go back and compare this result with the original sequence ACGATTGAGAATTCCGA, you see that the repetition of ATT within the sequence has caused the reassembly algorithm to short-circuit by collapsing the underlined section ACGATTGAGAATTCCGA. It takes a very sophisticated reassembly algorithm to resist the temptations provided by all those large overlaps.

## 4.3  THE SIZE OF THE PROBLEM

As we have seen, mapping information can be used to subdivide the main reassembly problem and to provide clues as to location of some fragments. Taken literally, whole-genome shotgun sequencing would use no localization, mapping, or subdivision and would attempt to reconstruct a genome of 3.5 billion nucleotides, using segments of approximate length 500. With a 10-fold coverage we should have $\frac{3,500,000,000*10}{500}$ or 70,000,000 fragments. Each of these would be a sequence of 500 nucleotides, and our program would need to investigate all possible pairwise overlaps.

More modestly, suppose we did a reasonable amount of mapping. To start with, we should divide the genome into 25 chromosomes for instance. And then let's say our mapping techniques are good enough that we can subdivide each chromosome into about 100 pieces that we know how to place relative to one another. Now the average reassembly problem is to correctly combine a sequence of length, $\frac{3,500,000,000}{25*100}$ or 1,400,000. Again assuming 10-fold coverage by 500-mers, we would expect a more reasonable 28,000 inputs. Of course, we would have 2500 problems, each with 28,000 fragments; but, as we shall see, this should be more manageable than a single problem with 70,000,000 inputs.

Think what it takes to create programs that input $n$ sequences of length $k$, find overlaps, and arrange the pieces in the likely complete order from which they were disintegrated. Such programs cannot afford to be inefficient. Just reading and storing the inputs will require time and memory proportional to the $kn$ bytes. Investigating pairwise overlaps requires us to look at all possible pairs, and compare up to $k$ bytes within each. A straightforward approach would take time proportional to $kn^2$ since there are about $n^2$ ways to find pairs among $n$ objects.[4]

We're not even finished yet: We still need to reconstruct the sequence from the overlap information. We'll study the algorithm further, so we leave the complexity

---

[4] You may recall that the exact number here is $\frac{n(n-1)}{2}$ which is certainly of the same magnitude as $n^2$.

SIDEBAR

# Where Do Repeats Come From?

The problem of repeated sequences within genomes has been a major stumbling block for any reassembly algorithm. Oddly enough, the larger the genome, the more regions are repeated sections that do not appear to carry any relevant information. These regions are called **repeat regions** in biology, and genomes acquire these stretches of sequence in a number of ways. We do not yet know if these repeat regions serve a specific biological purpose, but they are faithfully copied from generation to generation. As one example, the human Y chromosome, which is carried by all males, is composed almost exclusively of repeat regions. The few genes on the Y chromosome are critical for our species (without them we would have no males and hence no reproduction! Or, at the very least, reproduction would contrast greatly with our current method.), but they are buried in endless stretches of apparently nonsense DNA.

The puzzle about repeat regions extends in many different directions. Aside from the puzzle of their purpose, if any, the second most interesting puzzle is how they arose in the first place. Some repeat regions are the result of mistakes in replication in which a section of DNA is accidentally copied several times. Another possible resaon for repeat regions is that a section of DNA is transferred from one chromosome to another, creating a second copy of a DNA sequence. An interesting class of repeat regions appears to be capable of facilitating their own transport and replication: they will cut themselves out of one part of a genome and paste themselves elsewhere. These regions are collectively known as transposons [9].

One relatively common way a genome acquires a transposon is through a retrovirus such as HIV. Retroviruses use an unusual strategy to ensure their replication and persistence in cells. Once they enter a cell, they generate a DNA copy of their RNA genomes using a special enzyme called a **reverse transcriptase.** The DNA copy of the viral genome is then sometimes integrated into the host cell's genome. From there, it will be faithfully recopied along with the entire genome every time the cell replicates. At certain times, the viral sequence can be activated in such a way that it "jumps out" of the cellular genome and reintegrates elsewhere. This can allow a genome to acquire many hundreds of copies of the viral genome. The really astonishing feature of these viral transposons is that they can direct the synthesis of viral proteins under certain circumstances, triggering reinfection of the cell or its neighbors. These remarkable bits of DNA, known collectively as **retrotransposons,** are a major constituent of our genomes. Indeed, some estimates suggest that nearly half of our genomic sequences are the result of retrotransposon activity by past viral infections [2]. So one could almost speculate that half of who we are is foreign DNA from some very ambitious viruses.

TABLE 4.1    Minimum Time and Memory Requirements
for a Fragment-Reassembly Program
Assuming $n$ Fragments of Size $k$

| Task | Time | Memory |
|------|------|--------|
| Read the sequences | $O(nk)$ | $O(nk)$ |
| Measure and store all potential overlaps | $O(kn^2)$ | $O(n)$ |
| Determine full sequence | ? | ? |

of that final part of our algorithm undefined in the summary information in Table 4.1.

Table 4.1 shows the absolute minimum "Big $O$" requirements of time and space for any reassembly program. With $n$ at our original 70,000,000 and $k$ at 500, $kn^2$ is 2,450,000,000,000,000,000, or about 2.45 quintillion operations. Even with a computer capable of 10 billion operations per second, this would take 245,000,000 seconds, or almost 3000 years.

By subdividing our problem into 2500 problems, each with $n = 28,000$, we will find $kn^2$ is a more reasonable 392,000,000,000. On currently available personal computers, a billion operations per second is standard, and each $kn^2$ is achievable in a matter of minutes. Of course, we will have 2500 separate problems, but even so we are back in the realm of the realistic. In practice, fragments of about 2,000,000 nucleotides are cloned into plasmids. With coverage at 10 times and sequenced pieces of length about 500 nucleotides, this would lead to a value for $n$ of about, $\frac{2,000,000*10}{500}$ or about 40,000. More details of sequence reconstruction strategy are described in [7].

We are acutely aware that we are working at the limits of current computer technology and barely within the limits of human patience. And that only gets us to the first stage, the identification of pairwise overlaps between the fragments, an operation that is of magnitude $O(kn^2)$. If the expected runtime of any other part of our reassembly algorithm significantly exceeds the $O(kn^2)$ required for overlap investigation, then the entire algorithm ceases to be workable for problems of currently expected size on contemporary computing equipment (See Exercise 4.2). In Exercise 4.3 you will consider the effects on expected running time of various schemes for subdividing the fragment-reassembly problem.

## 4.4 A PURELY COMBINATORIAL PROBLEM

In this section, we will describe an idealized[5] problem that will enable us to tackle the essential elements of our problem in a setting amenable to straightforward analysis techniques. We postpone consideration of the real biological sequence

---

[5] An **idealized** problem is a mathematical simplification that is used for preliminary investigations, analyses, and algorithm development without the complicating and often distracting "clutter" often associated with real-life problems.

reassembly problem until we have a firm understanding of the underlying combinatorial principles.

## 4.4.1  Problem Statement

Several (let us say $c$) copies of an original sequence of length $l$ over an alphabet of $a$ symbols have been cut into subsequences of average length $k$. We call those subsequences **fragments,** and suppose there are a total of $n$ fragments. Our input is the set of $n$ fragments of average length $k$. We do not know $c$ or $l$. There is no particular advantage to be had from dealing with generalized alphabets, so let us simply state that $a$ is 4, corresponding to the number of nucleotides. Our goal is to find a minimum length sequence $s$ with the property that each and every one of our input fragments appears as a subsequence of $s$.

Computer scientists more often speak of **strings** and **substrings** rather than **sequences** and **subsequences,** so the problem we have just described is commonly referred to as the **shortest common superstring** problem.

The shortest common superstring problem is not the same as the biological fragment-reassembly problem. In particular, it does not take into account difficulties associated with:

- repeated sections of sequence (Exercise 4.4)
- inexact recording of some nucleotides within fragments (Exercise 4.5)
- the bidirectional nature of DNA (Exercise 4.6)

Nevertheless, study of the shortest common superstring problem will provide us with valuable insights into the nature of the biological sequence reassembly problem and will indicate how to proceed to solve it and to understand solutions proposed by others.

It turns out that the shortest common superstring problem is NP-complete [4]. This means that the only completely reliable solutions are likely to be about as slow as an exhaustive search program. Such programs are not practical for problems even a fraction of the size of those in which we are interested. With the numerous and large instances associated with fragment reassembly, we must make compromises and seek quick algorithms that are likely to produce solutions that are acceptable and useful, even if they are not necessarily optimal.

## 4.5  SOLVING THE COMBINATORIAL PROBLEM

### 4.5.1  Overlaps

Given $n$ strings (fragments) of average length $k$, find the shortest superstring that contains each and every one of the $n$ strings as a substring.

The first step toward solving this problem is to obtain all the information we need about overlaps between the fragments and to place that information into a data structure that enables quick access.

An **overlap** occurs if a suffix of one fragment is a prefix of another. For example CG, is both a suffix of $S =$ ATCGATCCG and a prefix of $T$ = CGATCCGATTAT.

Is CG the only overlap between ATCGATCCG and CGATCCGATTAT? Well, no, it isn't. Did you notice that CGATCCG is both a suffix of $S$ and a prefix of $T$? Because CGATCCG is longer than CG it is preferred. Intuitively, since a sequence within overlaps is involved in accounting for more of the fragments within the eventual superstring, we expect that longer overlaps recorded between pairs of fragments will lead to shorter superstrings. Computer scientists would say that seeking long overlaps is a useful **heuristic.** Other folks might prefer to say that we have a **hunch** that the longer overlap is correct. Exercise 4.7 will investigate this question further.

For now, let's accept the fact that CGATCCG is the overlap between $S$ = ATCGATCCG and $T$ = CGATCCGATTAT. That's because CGATCCG is the longest suffix of $S$ that is also a prefix of $T$. That's our definition:

> **Definition 4.1** The overlap between string $S$ and string $T$ is the longest suffix of $S$ that is also a prefix of $T$.

Notice that our definition of overlap is order-dependent. The overlap between $S$ and $T$ is not the same as the overlap between $T$ and $S$. For our example strings $S$ = ATCGATCCG and $T$ = CGATCCGATTAT, the overlap between $T$ and $S$ is AT.

Figure 4.3 shows pseudocode for a simple algorithm to find the best overlap between two fragments. Notice that it contains one loop that will be executed an average of $k$ times. (Recall that $k$ is an average length for our fragments.) Within that loop is a comparison of each suffix of the first string with the equal-length prefix of the second string. The average length of each suffix (and prefix) will be $\frac{k}{2}$. This naïve algorithm will thus run in time $O(k^2)$. Exercise 4.8 asks you to develop a $O(k)$ algorithm.

## 4.5.2 Fragments Within Fragments

What would the program in Figure 4.3 return as the overlap between $S$ = ATTACCTACT and $T$ = TCGATTACCTACTTTAG? The given code would

```
String overlap(String s, String t) {
    int best = 0;
    int slen = s.length();
    int tlen = t.length();
    int shorter;
    if (slen < tlen) shorter = slen;
    else shorter = tlen;
    for (int i = 1; i < shorter; i++)
        if (s.substring(slen-i,slen).equals(t.substring(0,i))) best = i;
    return(t.substring(0,best));
}
```

**FIGURE 4.3** Naïve algorithm to find overlap between two strings.

```
frags is a collection of fragments;
if any fragment is entirely contained in another fragment {
    remove the shorter fragment;
}
for each pair (x,y) of fragments {
    record the overlap between x and y;
    record the overlap between y and x;
}
```

**FIGURE 4.4**   Pseudocode for the beginning stages of our Shortest Common Superstring solver. Java code is to be found in package alg:greedy.

return the single-nucleotide string T, and that would be correct. But it's not what we really want.

Did you notice that ATTACCTACT is a substring entirely contained within TCGATTACCTACTTTAG? In terms of solving the shortest superstring problem, the fragment ATTACCTACT provides us with no useful information beyond what we already have knowing that TCGATTACCTACTTTAG is a fragment.

To obtain truly useful overlap information for our set of fragments, we first need to remove any fragments that are entirely contained within another fragment. One way to do this is to preprocess the set of fragments through a filter that removes any fragment entirely contained in another. A naïve approach to this would add a procedure taking $O(nk)$ steps to our developing program. It might be better if containment detection were incorporated into the overlap detection code. This will also be discussed in Exercise 4.8.

To recap, Figure 4.4 summarizes the first few steps in our solution to the shortest common superstring problem:

## 4.5.3  A Graph Model

A good data structure for storing information about fragments and about overlaps between pairs of fragments is a directed graph. The nodes will be labeled with the strings corresponding to each fragment. The directed edge (arc) from the node labeled with fragment $x$ to the node labeled with fragment $y$ will be labeled with the overlap between $x$ and $y$. A small example of an **overlap graph** for the fragment set ATCC CCTA AAA is shown in Figure 4.5.

Some of the Java classes defined in package alg.greedy (source code available on the website http://mhhe.com/gopal) are used to represent this kind of data structure. Look especially at classes GraphNode and GraphArc.

A path in an overlap graph corresponds to a superstring of all the labels of the nodes encountered in the path. The labels of the arcs encountered in the path indicate how that superstring can be contracted by not repeating the suffix of the label at the tail of the arc (which, by definition, is the same as the prefix of the label at the head of the arc). For example, in Figure 4.5 the path from ATCC to CCTA to AAA corresponds to the common superstring ATCCTAAA and avoids repetition of the arc labels CC and A. The path from AAA to CCTA to ATCC

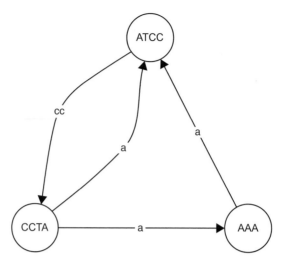

**FIGURE 4.5**    Overlap graph for ATCC CCTA AAA. Arcs with empty labels are omitted.

corresponds to the much longer superstring AAACCTATCC because the edge labels on this path provide so little opportunity to reuse sections of overlap.

In order that its corresponding string should include all of the fragments in an instance of the shortest common superstring problem, a path must visit each and every node of the overlap graph. Paths that visit every node of a graph are called **Hamilton paths** after the Irish mathematician William Rowan Hamilton, the Astronomer Royal of Ireland, who in 1857 invented "The Traveller's Dodecahedron—A Voyage Round the World" (also called the "Icosian Game"), a boardgame involving finding a Hamilton path on a dodecahedron [6, 10]. In order that its corresponding string be short, it helps if the arcs along a path have labels as long as possible. This is because long labels correspond to large overlaps, which in turn lead to more reuse of genome sequence and hence a shorter overall string. We will refer to the length of an arc label as the arc's **weight.** These observations motivate the following lemma:

**Lemma 4.1**    The shortest superstring containing all the fragments is given by a Hamilton path with maximal sum of arc weights.

Solving the shortest common superstring problem can thus be done by finding an optimally weighted Hamilton path in the overlap graph. Sadly, the Hamilton problem is NP-complete [4], and therefore we cannot expect an efficient accurate algorithm to develop from this approach.

## 4.5.4  A Nonoptimal Greedy Algorithm

When a problem is NP-complete, computer scientists seek compromise solutions. It is not possible to program a solution that is guaranteed to be optimal in any but the smallest problem instances. Instead, we look for a plausible program that might feasibly produce fairly reliable results. Of course, we'll also need analytical or statistical techniques to test the accuracy of our admittedly imperfect solution. We proceed to develop a program that we can reasonably expect to produce a good reassembly of fragments, and we'll develop some experiments to measure how good the reassemblies are.

Greedy algorithms are often quite successful at solving optimization problems. Optimization problems may often be posed in terms of trying to make a succession of choices. For example, the problem of trying to find an optimal Hamiltonian path in a graph can be posed in terms of successively making choices for the first node, then the second node, then the third, and so on. A greedy algorithm works by measuring a simple quantity and successively making the best looking choice in terms of that simple quantity at every stage. A greedy algorithm for finding an optimal Hamiltonian path starts by selecting the heaviest weighted arc in the graph and removing that arc from further consideration. The greedy algorithm continues through several stages by selecting the heaviest weighted arc, subject only to the condition that it should not close a cycle when added to the already chosen arcs. Java code implementing this algorithm can be found in the package `alg.greedy`. The ideas to look for in the code are the use of a priority queue to store the arcs, so that the arc with the longest label is always readily available, and the need to detect possible cycles in the emerging contigs. Most of this code is in the class `GreedyAlg.java` in the package `alg.greedy`.

The program produces a list of contigs. If we are very lucky, it will be a single contig corresponding to a list of `GraphArcs` that form a single path that visits each and every node in the overlap graph. It's not guaranteed to be a maximum-weight Hamilton path, but we have reason to believe it may not be too bad. Sometimes, however, the list of arcs produced by `greedyHamiltonian` will not give rise to a single path; rather it will be a set of two or more disjoint paths. Each of these corresponds to a sequence of nucleotides spanned by a subset of the input fragments. The contig may, or may not, be a subsequence of the original sequence that we are trying to reassemble. There are at least two reasons why the greedy algorithm might produce multiple contigs instead of a single path:

- It may be that the fragments do not cover the entire target sequence; because of inadequate coverage, pieces are missing.
- It may be that the greedy algorithm erroneously placed a fragment where it doesn't belong, and, as a result, it is no longer possible to correctly continue to build up a correct solution.

If the first eventuality has arisen, then even a correct reassembly program would fail to produce a single correct contig. If the second is the case, we cannot be sure: We know the greedy algorithm has failed, but we don't know for sure that a correct program would succeed.

Exercise 4.9 asks you to construct sets of fragments that will lead to both scenarios.

## Programming Project 4.1

Write a program to empirically test the credibility of the results of the greedy fragment-reassembly algorithm. You will need to:

1. Write a program to input a nucleotide string, a desired average coverage, a desired range of fragment sizes, and output a set of fragments.
2. Run the greedy program on sets of fragments generated by your program.
3. Collect and analyze your results.
   (a) How often did the greedy program produce a single correct config?
   (b) How often did the greedy program produce a single incorrect config?
   (c) How often did the greedy program produce several configs?
      i. How many of these would have been correctly handled by a perfect program?
      ii. Of the others, why would the perfect program fail?
      iii. Would the greedy program fail in the same way?

This project asks you to combine your programming skills, your skills for simulation experiments, and your skills for analyzing empirically derived data. As such, it's an ideal bioinformatics project!

### 4.5.5  Improving on Greed

Because the problem is NP-complete, a correct algorithm for the shortest common superstring problem must in all probability require time exponential in the length of the input. The greedy algorithm we have described is fast, but its reliability is poor. Is there a compromise program, slower than greedy, but not exponential, and more likely to produce better solutions?

Think of our problem as a series of choices. Our first choice is any of the arcs of the overlap graph. The greedy algorithm considers only one choice: the heaviest arc, whereas the exponential algorithm needs to consider all the possible choices. Now comes the second choice: choose one of the remaining arcs. The greedy algorithm knows exactly which one it will choose, whereas the exponential algorithm needs to consider all possible choices.

The selection process is therefore a treelike phenomenon (Figure 4.6). The tree is as deep as the number of nodes in the overlap graph. X denotes a path that fails on account of prematurely forming a cycle. Such a path need not be considered further. Y denotes a path that has a node with in-degree 2 or out-degree 2. Again, such paths deserve no further consideration. Paths marked Z can be eliminated from consideration because they are rearrangements of others already considered. A perfect, correct algorithm will search all the remaining paths in the tree. Even though it can perform a great deal of pruning by terminating paths as soon as an X, Y, or Z condition is detected, it still requires examination of a

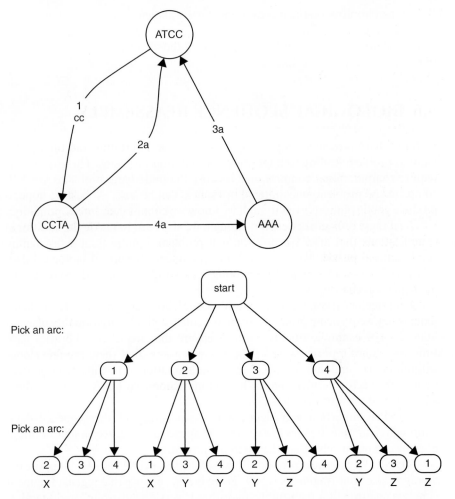

**FIGURE 4.6**    The tree of choices for solving the Hamiltonian path problem for the overlap graph of fragments in Figure 4.5.

number of paths exponential in the height of the tree. The greedy algorithm, by contrast, heads unidirectionally down a single path and hopes for the best.

A significant portion of the early study of artificial intelligence [11] was, fundamentally, tree search of this kind. A correct solution requires exhaustive backtracking, and its runtime is exponential in the size of the input. Many applications of artificial intelligence involved the development of heuristics, or hunches, that could be incorporated into the search code to reduce the search space. Other applications, particularly game playing, sought numerical bound approaches to allow large-scale pruning of the search tree. The ultimate in pruning, of course, is to be found in greedy algorithms—they prune the entire search space down to a single twig!

We can improve on the greedy algorithm by allowing some branching in the effective search space. To keep runtimes manageable, we must place limits on the number of nodes to be expanded at each level of the search tree. Some approaches to this will be explored in Exercise 4.10.

## 4.6 BIOLOGICAL SEQUENCE REASSEMBLY

So far we have presented sequence reassembly as an interesting and fun combinatorial problem leading to interesting computation problems. These questions require computational compromises because the underlying problems are NP-complete and problems encountered in the field will be large. At best we hope to produce good solutions even though we know we cannot guarantee optimality.

As if these difficulties were not enough, we still need to tackle the additional complications that arise because the real problem is more than a fascinating combinatorial puzzle. They derive from experimentally derived biological data that present us with new and fascinating real-world dilemmas that add to the mathematical challenges.

Many technical issues arise as a result of the laboratory processes required for sequencing. Sequencing projects require the construction of high-quality plasmid libraries. For example, quality controls ensure that sequencing libraries have sufficient clones representative of the entire genome, that there are few clones without inserts, and that there is as little contamination as possible from sources such as the vector itself, *E.coli*, or human mitochondrial DNA. Even so, these all occur and must be detected.

Another important consideration is the accuracy of the sequence data. Although error rates are very low with automatic sequencers, even a small amount of error can negatively affect the assembly process.

Suppose we have an error rate of 1 miscalled base per 10,000. And suppose the average size of our fragments is 500. There is a 5% chance that a given fragment contains an error. If a reassembly algorithm is very "headstrong" and literal, it will insist that a section of genome containing an error must be disjoint from the same section sequenced and reported without the error. For example, suppose two overlapping segments were sequenced and that one of the sequencers missed a base within the overlap portion. Thus within the overlap, one sequencing machine reported

    ---***CGAGGCA***

where as another sequencing machine reported

    ***CGAGCA***---

The *** indicates nucleotide sequence where both machines agreed 100%, and the --- indicates parts of the two fragments that extend beyond the overlapping section. A highly "literal-minded" reassembly algorithm will fail to recognize the overlap on account of the one-nucleotide difference. A reassembly algorithm that relies on exact pattern matching[6] to detect overlaps will fail to recognize any overlaps in which even one of the overlapping fragments contains a base-calling error. As a result, reassembly programs that use exact pattern matching for overlap detection will predict reassembled sequences that are far too long.

Ironically, increasing the level of coverage exacerbates this problem. As the coverage increases, the number of overlapping sections increases, as will the number of overlapping sections in which at least one of the fragments contains a base-calling error. Each such error causes the program to place the fragment containing it elsewhere in the reconstruction rather than recognize the fragment as a participant in the overlap. Inflexibility of pattern matching and insistence on exact matching will lead to predicted reassemblages that are too long. The greater the level of coverage, the greater the general overage in the predicted sequence length.

On the other hand, multiple coverage makes it possible to detect and even to correct most base-calling errors. If a program can look at a large number of fragments that all contain a certain section, and if one of those fragments contains a miscall within the section, then it is not difficult for the programmer to include code so that a consensus is formed of what the section *should* be, and even to compute the correction necessary for the rogue fragment. Sadly, such error detection and correction is possible only if we know just where each fragment belongs. Herein lies our conundrum: We need the reassembly to determine where each fragment belongs, and we need to determine where each fragment belongs to gather evidence to arbitrate and correct sequence errors so that we can produce a correct reassembly!

The logic circle can be broken by compromise. The pattern matching necessary for overlap detection needs to be less literal-minded. The overlap detection aspect of the reassembly algorithm can be made more flexible so that overlaps can be recorded even if a base is miscalled within the overlapping section. Of course, if the overlap detection becomes too flexible, the algorithm will begin to report nonexistent overlaps as possible overlaps, and this will lead to predictions of reassemblage that will be too short.

**Phrap** and **Phred** (http://www.phrap.org) are programs developed at the University of Washington that deal with these types of technical issues. For example, Phred trims the vector by comparing the generated sequence with a known vector sequence. Phred also has algorithms to assess the quality of base-calling at the ends of segments, where sequence quality is known to degrade. Phrap constructs a consensus based on a mosaic of the highest quality base-calling reads generated by Phred at each position. Phrap's algorithms avoid the complex problems associated with multiple alignment algorithms (see Chapter 5).

The biological issues in sequence reassembly are due to the nature of DNA, chromosome structure, and composition. One factor we have yet to consider is sequence orientation. Recall that the two strands of DNA are antiparallel. When randomly sheared DNA fragments are inserted into plasmid vectors for cloning, we don't know the orientation of that insert. For each fragment retrieved from

---

[6] The topic of exact pattern matching is described more fully in Chapter 5.

sequencing machines, we have no idea if it belongs to the forward or to the reverse strand. We don't know which strand we have sequenced and so don't know how a given fragment should be oriented relative to others. We need to realize that what we have is effectively two linked puzzles. It's almost as if we had two jigsaw puzzles printed on opposite sides of the same piece of wood. One aspect of this makes our solving process harder: We don't know which side of the puzzle piece should be up. On the other hand, having two problems to solve in parallel, makes our task easier. Especially if we are solving the puzzles on a glass table and are able to see the emerging reassemblage on the bottom as well as on the top. In short, the presence of the two DNA strands requires us to add some logical complexity to the (combinatorial) fragment reassembly algorithm in order to make it applicable for (two antiparallel strand) fragment reassembly. But the heart of the algorithm is unchanged.

A more problematic issue is the occurrence of a large proportion of repetitive sequence in the human genome. Some sequences, such as the 2- to 6-bp sequences known as microsatellites, are present in millions of copies in the genome. Longer repetitive sequences, including Alu and long interspersed elements (LINE), as well as tRNAs and rRNAs, occur hundreds of thousands of times, throughout the genome. These sequences confound the overlap process as well as the ability to generate unambiguous order and orientation when creating scaffolds. Consequently, reassembly pipelines generally find and mask repeats so that these sequences don't adversely affect the overlap process as described in Section 4.2.5. Resolving repeats in order to construct a finished sequence has been one of the most challenging aspects of the genome projects.

## 4.7  SEQUENCING BY HYBRIDIZATION

Some of the inventors[7] of DNA microarrays envisaged their use for sequencing. Recall from Chapter 3 that a microarray has on its surface many different oligos (short sequences of nucleotides). When a sample is washed over the array, hybridization occurs at those oligos on the array that are the reverse complements of sequences present in the sample.

Imagine now that our DNA array has on its surface all the possible oligos of length $k$. This requires that the array have $4^k$ different oligos. So, realistically, $k$ is likely to be in the range 5 to 10 (corresponding to arrays of about a thousand to about a million spots). After hybridizing with our sample we know precisely which $k$-tuples are present and which are not present in our sample. After such an experiment we have a set of, say $m$ $k$-tuples, that we know will occur in the target sequence we wish to identify.

Is that enough information to determine the target sequence? The general combinatorial problem is: Given a set of $m$ $k$-tuples that are known to be precisely those $k$-tuples that occur within a target sequence, find that target sequence. Let's

[7] DNA-chip technologies were simultaneously and independently invented in the late 1980s in England, Russia, and Yugoslavia. Later claims are made for inventors in other countries.

consider a simplified example in which the value of $k$ is an unrealistically low 3, and $m$ is 14.

## 4.7.1 A Worked Example

Let's say a hybridization experiment assures us that the following 3-tuples occur in our sample:

ACC AGC ATG CAG CAT CCA CCG CGT CTT GCA GCC GCT GTG TGC

Our task is to construct a target sequence whose length-3 subsequences are exactly those given.

First note that any sequence of length $n$ has exactly $n - 2$ length-3 subsequences. Since we have a set of 14 triples, this suggests a target sequence of length 16. Interestingly, it turns out that this particular set of triples is going to require at least 17 nucleotides in any solution sequence. This will become apparent as we develop the algorithm.

We develop the algorithm for the general problem where we are given $m$ $k$-tuples. As with many combinatorial problems, the first step in the solution is the construction of a graph. The graph we make has $4^{k-1}$ nodes, corresponding to the possible $(k - 1)$-tuples of nucleotides. Each node is labeled with one of the possible $(k - 1)$-tuples. Our illustrative example has 16 nodes, as shown in Figure 4.7. Our graph is actually a directed graph, or **digraph,** with $m$ arcs, each of which corresponds to one of the $k$-tuples. Specifically, the arc corresponding to the $k$-tuple $a_1, a_2, \ldots, a_k$ joins the node labeled $a_1, a_2, \ldots, a_{k-1}$ to the node labeled $a_2, \ldots, a_{k-1}, a_k$.

Note that some of the nodes in the digraph of Figure 4.7 are not connected to anything. They can safely be discarded. The remaining nodes and arcs have been repositioned in Figure 4.8 to help us visualize the rest of the algorithm.

Our intention is to find a sequence of nucleotides that contains each of the $m$ given $k$-tuples (and no others). As is true for the greedy algorithm for reassembly, it is desirable that the target sequence be as short as possible. Notice that any path within the graph of Figure 4.8 corresponds in a natural way to a sequence of nucleotides. For example, the path through the nodes labeled CA, AT, TG, and GC, using the arcs labeled CAT, ATG, and TGC, corresponds to the sequence CATGC. In an equally natural way, that path "consumes" the triples CAT, ATG, and TGC that appear as labels along its arcs.

Notice that we are seeking a path through the digraph that consumes, in this sense, each and every one of the arc labels. For economy, and to ensure the shortest target sequence possible, we would like to use each and every arc exactly once. As we shall see, this is not quite possible for our illustrative example. In the mathematical literature, paths that traverse each arc of a digraph exactly once are called **Eulerian paths.** Many theorems and algorithms are known concerning such paths. In particular, the following is a theorem due to the Swiss mathematician for whom the paths were named (Leonhard Euler,[8] 1707–1783). Before we state the

---

[8] Euler has long been considered the founder in 1736 [1] of the field of mathematics called graph theory. His theorem can be used to solve a famous puzzle concerning the bridges of Königsberg.

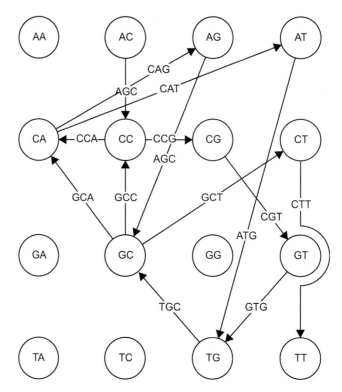

**FIGURE 4.7**    The digraph corresponding to our illustrative example of sequencing by hybridization. Nodes are the possible $(k-1)$-tuples of nucleotides. Arcs correspond to the $m$ given $k$-tuples.

theorem, we should define the **in-degree** of a node to be the number of arcs entering that node, and the **out-degree** of a node to be the number of arcs that exit it.

> **Theorem (Euler):**    A connected digraph will have an Eulerian path if and only if each of its nodes, except perhaps two, has in-degree equal to its out-degree. Of the exceptional nodes, one will have in-degree = out-degree − 1 and will be called the **start** node, and the other will have in-degree = out-degree + 1 and will be called the **end** node. If no exceptional nodes occur, the digraph will contain a closed Eulerian cycle.

We will not prove the theorem here, but will observe that, except for its start and its end, an Eulerian path enters each node exactly the same number of times as it leaves. That observation is key to the proof of the theorem and helps us understand the rest of the algorithm.

We mark each node with a pair of integers: the in-degree and the out-degree as shown in Figure 4.8. Notice that the digraph does not meet the conditions of Euler's theorem, and so there is no Eulerian path. In the interest of keeping our

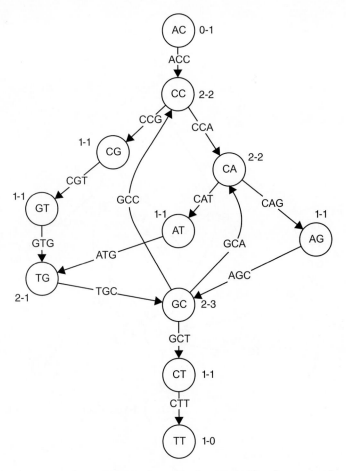

**FIGURE 4.8**   The digraph of Figure 4.7 with disconnected nodes removed and the remainder repositioned for ease of viewing. The nodes have been annotated with their in-degree and out-degree.

eventual solution as short as possible, we need to add as few arcs as possible to ensure that the digraph *does* meet the conditions of Euler's theorem. One way to do this is shown in Figure 4.9. In the general problem you need to add as few arcs as possible in order to ensure the conditions of Euler's theorem. It is important, however, only to add duplicates of existing arcs. Otherwise you would be adding arcs whose labels would need to correspond to $k$-tuples that did not hybridize with your sample. You would thus be solving for data from a different hybridization experiment. In any case, it is not a difficult exercise to design an algorithm to add as few duplicates of existing arcs as possible to ensure the existence of an Eulerian path. See Exercise 4.11.

Now all that remains is to find an Eulerian path in the digraph. For this you can use an algorithm due to a rather obscure mathematician, André-Hercule de Fleury (the Abbot of Fleury) in 1883 [3].

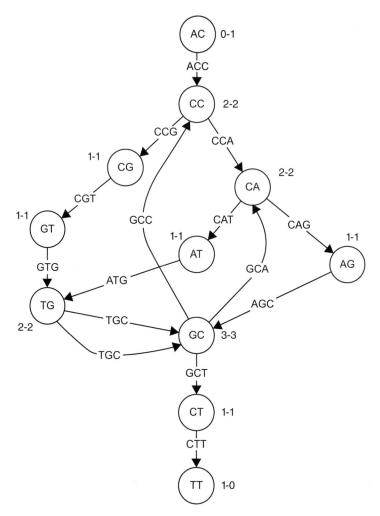

**FIGURE 4.9** The digraph of Figure 4.8 with one additional arc used to ensure the resulting digraph contains an Eulerian path. Note that the added arc must duplicate an existing arc to ensure that we do not introduce any extraneous $k$-tuples.

**Algorithm (Fleury):** Find an Eulerian path in a digraph satisfying the conditions of Euler's theorem. Start with a node whose out-degree exceeds its in-degree. If the digraph has no such node, start with any node. At each step select an arc whose removal does not disconnect the digraph, unless you have no choice, in which case select an arc whose removal could disconnect the digraph. Add that arc to your growing Eulerian path and remove it from the digraph. Repeat these steps until no arcs are left, at which point you will have an Eulerian path.

Following this algorithm in our illustrative case in Figure 4.9 we must

1. start at AC,
2. proceed to CC,
3. at which point we have a choice: let's choose CA;
4. at which point we again have a choice: let's choose AT;
5. now we must proceed to TG,
6. then to GC. Choosing CT now would disconnect the digraph, so we
7. proceed to CA.
8. There is no choice as we have already consumed the arc to AT, so we
9. proceed to AG,
10. then to GC. Again, we must not choose CT and have already used the arc to CA, so this time we must
11. proceed to CC, where there remains only the arc to
12. CG, from which we must
13. proceed to GT,
14. then to TG, and use the second available arc to
15. GC, where this time we have no choice but to
16. proceed to CT and
17. end at TT.

Our travels have traced the path AC CC CA AT TG GC CA AG GC CC CG GT TG GC CT TT, corresponding to a target sequence ACCATGCAGCCGTGCTT. You can verify that this 17-nucleotide sequence has exactly 14 different 3-tuples that exactly match the tuples we were initially given. The 3-tuple TGC occurs twice because we duplicated the arc labeled TGC.

We did, during our execution of Fleury's algorithm, encounter a number of choices. The choices we made resulted in our solution ACCATGCAGCCGT-GCTT. Different, but equally valid, choices can predict different solutions, such as ACCGTGCATGCCAGCTT.

There is no way to distinguish which of the possible solutions is "the correct solution." The technique of sequencing by hybridization can lead to multiple solutions, and another technique must be used to distinguish the likely true sequence.

Furthermore, the technique may be vulnerable to inaccuracies from a number of causes, such as:

- imprecise readings of the microarrays,
- repeats within the target sequence

An enormous saving grace of the technique of sequencing by hybridization, however, comes from the fact that Fleury's algorithm is easily coded to run in time polynomial in the number of nodes. Despite the superficial similarity of the Hamilton path problem (which needs to be solved for reassembly by overlap computation) to the Eulerian path problem (which is the workhorse of sequencing by hybridization), the first is NP-complete but the second is easily tractable.

Although vastly interesting to the algorithm specialist, this distinction may not be enough to persuade the general biological community to vigorously pursue sequencing by hybridization, especially since sequencing machines have been developed to produce very accurate sequences very quickly. Reassembly as described earlier in this chapter is likely to remain the predominant technique for the sequencing of large genomes.

However, sequencing by hybridization has been eagerly adopted by some researchers who work with HIV. One of the biggest problems with treating HIV infection is that the virus mutates very rapidly. Often, patients receiving one form of drug treatment will develop a drug-resistant strain of the virus within months of beginning the regimen. It is also generally the case that an individual will be infected with multiple strains of the virus, some of which will evince resistance to the next drug that is tried or the one after that. As a result, controlling the development of the illness into full-blown AIDS requires knowing ahead of time which strains are present and anticipating what treatments would be best for a given individual with a given complement of virus strains. In this specific context, sequencing by hybridization seems to be the best answer [5] because this method can report even small changes in the target sequence, helping researchers detect the sometimes tiny differences in strains of HIV. Using sequencing by hybridization, it is possible that every HIV-infected individual could be screened to identify those drugs that are most likely to control the virus. In a clinical setting such as this, sequencing by other methods would be expensive and time-consuming. Sequencing by hybridization, in contrast, could be very cost-effective. So sequencing by hybridization may become more widely used in applications in which rapid, accurate results are needed.

## Programming Project 4.2

Write programs to:

1. Generate long sequences of "random" nucleotides to be regarded as target sequences.
2. Simulate the biological cutting of a target sequence into fragments of average size 500 nucleotides with varying levels of coverage of the target.
3. Simulate a hybridization experiment for a target with variable values of $k$.
4. Attempt to reconstruct the sequence from the "biologically cut" fragments using the greedy algorithm (using code like that in package `alg.greedy`).
5. Attempt to reconstruct the sequence by building a digraph from the hybridization results and finding an Eulerian path with Fleury's algorithm.

Use these programs to evaluate the time taken to reconstruct the targets. Develop your own methods for evaluating the quality of the reconstructions.

# 4.8  EXERCISES FOR CHAPTER 4

Suppose you have a sequence of length $n$ symbols and you write a program to randomly generate $m$ subsequences of average length $k$. For any one of the symbols in the original sequence, what is the expected number of subsequences in which it will appear? Obviously, you will have to make some assumptions about what happens near each end of the original sequence, and you should answer the question for symbols away from the ends. This exercise may be solved statistically if you enjoy mathematics or by simulation if you enjoy programming.

**Exercise 4.1**

Investigate the greedy algorithm for fragment reassembly given in this chapter and estimate (in big-oh notation) its runtime for $n$ fragments of average length $k$. What would happen to this estimated runtime if you decided to use an exhaustive search for the optimal sequence instead of the greedy algorithm?

**Exercise 4.2**

Compare expected running times for a single reassembly problem with $n$ pieces of size $k$ and a pair of reassembly problems, each involving $\frac{n}{2}$ fragments of size $k$. Does this say anything about the advisability of subdividing a large sequencing project into smaller separate problems?

**Exercise 4.3**

Design an experiment to investigate how repeats affect the fragment reassembly problem. If you completed Programming Project 4.2 you can adapt your random sequence generator to produce various levels of repetition of various expected lengths. How do these changes affect the accuracy of your reassembly programs? Although it is conceivable that you can apply mathematical analysis to this exercise, we strongly recommend that you approach it through simulation.

**Exercise 4.4**

Similar to Exercise 4.4, design an experiment to investigate how sequence read errors affect the problem and its solution.

**Exercise 4.5**

Discuss which changes are necessary in your reassembly programs for Programming Project 4.2 if the fragments input could come from both a forward and a reverse strand of DNA.

**Exercise 4.6**

**Exercise 4.7**
For the fragments CAGCA, ACCA, CACA, CACAG, CCAC, ACC, and CAG from the target sequence ACCACAGCA you will observe that the greedy algorithm leads to a correct prediction. Construct a small simple example of a fragment reassembly problem in which the greedy algorithm leads to an incorrect solution.

**Exercise 4.8**
Design an algorithm for finding the overlap between two fragments of average size $k$ whose runtime is $O(k)$. Your algorithm should also detect if one fragment is entirely contained in the other.
    Hint: Read ahead about suffix trees in Chapter 5.

**Exercise 4.9**
Construct two sets of fragments that will lead to both scenarios described in the text.

- fragments that fail to ensure coverage,
- fragments that lead the greedy algorithm to yield two or more contigs instead of the correct path.

**Exercise 4.10**
One way to limit the time spent on exhaustive search for the optimal Hamiltonian path through a graph is to perform a breadth-first search that allows only the best $b$ nodes at each level to be investigated. Determining the "best" nodes at any level requires an estimating function to try to predict which $b$ of the possible nodes will result in good solutions. Such estimators are often referred to as heuristics. A good heuristic is rather like a good hunch. Because the number of nodes investigated at each level of the search tree is constant, the process resembles a parallel beam of light aimed through the tree. For this reason, the technique is sometimes referred to as **beam search.** Analyze the expected runtime of beam search for fragment reassembly. You can do this by implementing the algorithm and running simulations, or you can do the mathematics. For your heuristic, choose something simple like "how much overlap has been used so far?" If you choose the simulation method, see if you can measure any improvement in accuracy of beam search compared with the greedy algorithm. If you chose the mathematical route, try to concoct data that will lead to a successful prediction with beam search while failing to predict correctly with the greedy algorithm.

**Exercise 4.11**
Write a program to input a connected digraph and output a supergraph that satisfies the conditions of Euler's theorem and thus contains an Eulerian path. One caveat: You may only add duplicates of existing arcs; you may not add arcs that connect two nodes that are not already connected by an arc. Is this always possible? If not, what should your program do?

# KEY TERMS

multiple jigsaw puzzle (4.1)

book reconstruction puzzle (4.1)

sequence reassembly puzzle (4.1)

overlap (4.2)

contigs (4.2)

sequence walking (4.2)

repeat regions (4.2)

reverse transcriptase (4.2)

retrotransposons (4.2)

idealized (4.4)

fragments (4.4)

strings (4.4)

substrings (4.4)

sequences (4.4)

subsequences (4.4)

shortest common superstring (4.4)

overlap (4.5)

heuristic (4.5)

hunch (4.5)

overlap graph (4.5)

Hamilton paths (4.5)

weight (4.5)

Phrap (4.6)

Phred (4.6)

digraph (4.7)

Eulerian paths (4.7)

in-degree (4.7)

out-degree (4.7)

start (4.7)

end (4.7)

beam search (4.8)

# BIBLIOGRAPHY

1. E. Biggs, K. Lloyd, and R. Wilson. *Graph Theory 1736–1936*. Oxford University Press, London, 1986.

2. N. de Parseval and T. Heidmann. Human endogenous retroviruses: From infectious elements to human genes. *Cytogenet Genome Res*, 110:318–332, 2005.

3. André-Hercule de Fleury. Deux problemes de geometrie de situation. *J. Math Element,* 257–261, 1883.

4. Michael R. Garey and David S. Johnson. *Computers and Intractability: A Guide to the Theory of NP-Completeness.* W. H. Freeman, 1979.

5. George J. Hanna, Victoria A. Johnson, Daniel R. Kuritzkes, et al. Comparison of sequencing by hybridization and cycle sequencing for genotyping of human immunodeficiency virus type 1 reverse transcriptase. *J. Clin. Microbiol,* 38:2715–2721, 2000.

6. Puzzle Museum. http://www.puzzlemuseum .com/month/picm02/200207icosian.htm

7. J. Craig Venter, Mark D. Adams, Eugene W. Myers, et al. The sequence of the human genome. *Science,* 291:1304–1351, 2001.

8. Web author. http://www.genomics.energy.gov/

9. H. A. Wichman, R. A. Van den Bussche, M. J. Hamilton, and R. J. Baker. Transposable elements and the evolution of genome organization in mammals. *Genetica,* 86:287–293, 1992.

10. R. J. Wilson. *Introduction to Graph Theory.* Academic Press, New York, 1972.

11. Patrick Henry Winston. *Artificial Intelligence.* Addison-Wesley, Reading, MA, 1981.

# 5

# Sequence Alignment

*"If I could get to the top of that hill: and here's a path that leads straight to it—
at least, no, it doesn't do that—' (after going a few yards along the path, and turning
several sharp corners), 'but I suppose it will at last. But how curiously it twists! It's
more like a corkscrew than a path! Well, THIS turn goes to the hill, I suppose—no,
it doesn't! This goes straight back to the house!"*

—Alice in *Through the Looking Glass* by Lewis Carroll

**A**lignment refers to the process of placing two things next to each other in
such a manner as to make their similarities and their differences stand
out clearly. We say *thing* because we want to be as general as possible in
this introduction; however, when we get down to specifics in the following sections,
our *thing*s will generally be strings or nucleotide sequences. But the same ideas
have many interesting applications where the aim is to align two images, or two
sound files, or two fingerprints.

Before we proceed to examine alignment in a biological context, we need to
refresh our ideas about pattern matching. Computer scientists speak of searching
for a **pattern** within a **target text.** The pattern is a string, and the target is typically
a single string or a collection of strings. For the concept to make sense, target
strings are typically much longer than the pattern.

At their most fundamental levels computers and general-purpose computer
programs are well suited to tasks involving exact pattern matching. The goal in
pattern matching is to find each and every occurrence of a pattern (usually a
string) in a set of objects within which the pattern might occur. For example,
we might be searching a movie database and want to find every occurrence of
*Bogart* within an entry in the *actor* category. Database programs provide powerful tools for efficiently searching for exact matches for this type of application.
Most programming languages provide excellent support for programmers in the
area of pattern matching and substring search. The programming language Perl
sometimes appears to be dedicated to the proposition that pattern matching is
the be-all and end-all of the art of programming. Data structures both simple
and intricate have been invented to facilitate and expedite the pattern-matching
process. Internet search engines apply much of the expertise developed by generations of users and designers to quickly search the gigantic distributed collection
of data called the World Wide Web. On June 15 of 2005, Google reported over

5 million hits when asked to search the Web for **pattern matching.** That means that an awful lot of references to pattern matching have found their ways to pages on various Websites. Doubtless, many of these are copies of other posted pages, but the fact remains that today's computing facilities enable extremely fast and efficient searching of a huge target to find all occurrences of a given pattern.

Unfortunately, exact pattern matching is too inflexible for many important applications. Searching a database for an exact match with a newly sequenced portion of some genome is very unlikely to succeed (unless the portion is not, in fact, newly sequenced!). BLAST (basic local alignment search tool) is a very popular engine for detecting biologically meaningful similarities between a new sequence and previously entered data. BLAST is a kind of inexact pattern matcher, which can tell the user that the newly sequenced segment is similar to some number of existing sequences within the database.

Not only biological applications can benefit from inexact pattern-matching techniques. Popular search engines fail to perform well when their users mistype a word. Who among us can honestly claim to have never mistyped a word? The previously noted 5 million hits from a Google search for *pattern matching* shrank to a mere 112 when Google was asked for the mistyped *patturn matching*. And on a particularly bad day, the user might commit two typos and get no hits whatsoever for *patturn matchong* (until, of course, somebody posts the text of this textbook!). But sometimes errors can compound and compensate for each other. Due no doubt to contributors' typos, a search for *Bogarte* in the cast lists of movies may well produce some successes, but nothing like the correct information we seek for Humphrey Bogart. Some of the hits may even come from yet another's typos while entering Dirk Bogarde's name!

Without specialized programming, similarity detection is not in the repertoire of most computers. It is difficult to write correct programs that can tell that two photographs taken from slightly different angles are of the same person or object. It is difficult to write programs that can identify when two different performances are of the same symphony. But humans are, in general, pretty good at such approximate pattern matching. You can recognize friends even if they change their hairstyles and wear a Groucho disguise. You would know what I wanted if I asked for a list of movies featuring Humphrey Bogarte. Many people can identify both the theme and the composer being mimicked when they listen to Joshua Rifkin's *Baroque Beatles Book* (a 1965 record featuring Baroque-like arrangements of early works by the Beatles). Many people can tell a genuine Picasso from a good forgery. However, a computer program to perform such human feats of approximate matching would require major breakthroughs in several fields, including cognition and artificial intelligence.

Bioinformatics has more need for similarity detection than for exact pattern matching. To compare genomic sequences it is important to align them in such a way that similarities are apparent and differences can be quantified. In this way, it may be possible to infer degrees of relatedness, or even to estimate propensities for disease. Variation in genetic sequences distinguishes individuals and drives evolution. The ability to detect and measure degrees of relatedness is crucial to our endeavors in investigating life processes.

Nevertheless, techniques used in exact pattern matching can help us properly understand issues involved in alignment and inexact pattern matching. On some occasions we may also need to search exactly for patterns even in bioinformatics. This chapter begins, therefore, with an overview of exact pattern matching.

## 5.1  EXACT PATTERN MATCHING

Computers can do exact pattern matching extremely well and much faster than humans. Google searches of the Web take mere seconds, dictionary lookups occur in times so short we don't even notice any delay. And that's because exact search is straightforward, well adapted to computer architectures, and supported by some very clever data structures and algorithms. We'll look at some of those aspects in this section mostly because they will help us understand and develop inexact pattern matching ideas later on. But also because they are very interesting in their own right.

### 5.1.1  The Naïve Algorithm

Because of the excellent support for string searching provided by most programming languages, we must resort to working with arrays of characters in order to emphasize the inner workings of pattern-matching algorithms. If we instead worked with strings, you would quite rightly chastise us for not using the built-in features of Java's `String` class. So, let's pose:

**Problem:** Pattern match

**Input:** An array `pattern[]` of $m$ chars

An array `target[]` of $n$ chars

**Output:** A list of `int`s $i$ such that for each $i$

`target[i] = pattern[0]`

`target[i+1] = pattern[1]`

$\vdots$

`target[i+m−1] = pattern[m−1]`

To visualize the naïve algorithm's working, think of a small template `pattern` sliding along a large string `target` one letter at a time. If we were looking for gcca in agcagccatgc we would start with:

```
gcca
agcagccatgc
```

We immediately fail with the mismatch of g above the a, and so move on to the next stop:

```
 gcca
agcagccatgc
```

At each stop, characters in `pattern` and the portion of `target` under the template are compared one at a time until either

- a mismatch is found, or
- we run out of `pattern`

In this case, a mismatch is found at the third letter, so we move the template forward and start comparing again:

```
 gcca
agcagccatgc
```

Immediate failure leads to another shift:

```
  gcca
agcagccatgc
```

and another immediate failure causes one more shift:

```
   gcca
agcagccatgc
```

This time we reach the end of the pattern, and we need to report the finding of this occurrence of `pattern` within `target` before we move the template forward and continue.

Figure 5.1 has Java code implementing the naïve algorithm. Exercise 5.1 asks you to modify the program so that the `target` string is read from a file. In this way, you can run the program to count the occurrences of the word *varlet* within the complete works of Shakespeare. With a few more adjustments you can answer questions such as "How often do four consecutive STOP codons appear in the genome of rice?" Before we embark on too many searches of large data files, it is worth pausing to consider how long we expect to have to wait for our results. A simple approach to this is to note that most modern computers are capable of about a billion comparisons per second; so a rough count of expected number of comparisons would be useful.

## 5.1.2  Algorithm Analysis

The naïve pattern matcher takes at least one and at most $m$ comparisons in its inner loop to find a mismatch or to discover that the match needs to be reported, where $m$ is the length of `pattern`. Since the template needs to move forward $n - m$ times, where $n$ is the length of `target`, it is clear that the running of the naïve pattern matcher requires at least $n - m$ and at most $(n - m)m$ comparisons. Because of the upper bound, we are able to note that this algorithm exhibits $O(nm)$ time requirements. However, to achieve anything approaching this upper bound, the naïve algorithm needs to make significant progress through its inner loop each time. For this to happen requires that a lot of `pattern` matches occur many times within `target`. In searching English text, this is not likely to happen very often.

```java
import java.util.*;
public class Naive {
    // Naive algorithm for finding occurrences of pattern in target
    // Uses char arrays to demonstrate action
    public Vector <Integer> find(char[] pattern, char[] target) {
        boolean failed;
        Vector <Integer> matches = new Vector <Integer> ();
        for (int i=0; i<target.length - pattern.length; i++) {
            failed = false;
            for (int j=0; j<pattern.length && !failed; j++) {
                if (pattern[j] != target[i+j]) failed = true;
            }
            if (!failed) matches.add(i);
        }
        return matches;
    }
    public static void main(String[] args) {
        // For testing Naive.
        Naive test = new Naive();
        System.out.println(args[0] + " appears in " + args[1] + " at ");
        System.out.println(test.find(args[0].toCharArray(),
                                     args[1].toCharArray()));
    }
}
```

**FIGURE 5.1**   Naïve algorithm to find all occurrences of pattern within target. Call it with two string command line arguments. The code uses arrays of char rather than Strings to emphasize the nitty-gritty details of each individual comparison the algorithm requires.

The **best case** analysis of Naïve occurs when a mismatch is immediately detected as soon as the inner loop is invoked. This would occur if no character in target matched the first character in pattern. The best case, then, is extremely unlikely, but would result in exactly $n - m$ comparisons.

The **worst case** occurs when the inner loop is exited as late as possible. This requires the first $m - 1$ characters of pattern to match the first $m - 1$ characters of that part of target that's currently under the template. For this to occur at every position is also extremely unlikely, but if it did our program would make $m(n - m)$ comparisons.

Calculating the **expected case** requires us to do a little elementary probability and statistics. So let's suppose that pattern is a random string of length $m$ characters taken from an alphabet of $k$ letters. Similarly target is a random string of $n$ characters from the same $k$-letter alphabet.

Whenever we position the template, there is a 1 in $k$ chance that the first character of target under the template matches the first character of pattern. The probability that the first two characters under the template match the first two characters of pattern is $\frac{1}{k^2}$. The probability of $i$ consecutive matches is $\frac{1}{k^i}$.

**TABLE 5.1**    The number of comparisons we can expect will occur if the naïve algorithm searches for a random pattern of length $m$ within a target string of length $n$. $k$ is the size of the alphabet

| Event | Number of comparisons needed | Probability of this event | Expected number of occurrences | Total number of comparisons |
|---|---|---|---|---|
| 0 matches | 1 | $\frac{k-1}{k}$ | $\frac{(n-m)(k-1)}{k}$ | $\frac{(n-m)(k-1)}{k}$ |
| 1 match | 2 | $\frac{k-1}{k^2}$ | $\frac{(n-m)(k-1)}{k^2}$ | $2\frac{(n-m)(k-1)}{k^2}$ |
| 2 matches | 3 | $\frac{k-1}{k^3}$ | $\frac{(n-m)(k-1)}{k^3}$ | $3\frac{(n-m)(k-1)}{k^3}$ |
| .. | .. | .. | .. | .. |
| $i$ matches | $i+1$ | $\frac{k-1}{k^{i+1}}$ | $\frac{(n-m)(k-1)}{k^{i+1}}$ | $(i+1)\frac{(n-m)(k-1)}{k^{i+1}}$ |
| .. | .. | .. | .. | .. |
| $m$ matches | $m$ | $\frac{1}{k^m}$ | $\frac{(n-m)}{k^m}$ | $m\frac{(n-m)}{k^m}$ |

We are interested in a slightly different probability. What is the probability that *exactly* $i$ consecutive characters in the target match the first $i$ characters of the pattern. For this, we need $i$ matches (probability $\frac{1}{k^i}$) followed by a mismatch (probability $\frac{k-1}{k}$). The combined probability $\frac{(k-1)}{(k^{i+1})}$ is the probability of exactly $i$ matches.

Table 5.1 summarizes some of our analysis. The inner loop of the naïve algorithm will be executed $i+1$ times whenever the first $i$ characters (and no more) of the pattern appear consecutively in the target. This can be expected to happen $(i+1) \times \frac{(n-m)(k-1)}{k^{i+1}}$ times, and $i$ can take any value from 0 to $m-1$. Additionally, there is a probability of $\frac{1}{k^m}$ that $m$ comparisons are needed because a match is found. So the expected number of comparisons is:

$$\sum_{i=0}^{m-1} \frac{(i+1)(n-m)(k-1)}{k^{i+1}} + m\frac{(n-m)}{k^m} \tag{5.1}$$

That formula may look complicated, but it's easy to write a dozen lines of code to input three values for $n$, $m$ and $k$ and calculate the result. If you write the program suggested in Exercise 5.3 you will be able to satisfy yourself that the expected behavior of the naïve algorithm is much closer to the best case than to the worst case in all but the most degenerate cases.

## 5.1.3  Other Pattern-Matching Algorithms

Pattern matching is a very well-studied area of algorithmics. Richard M. Karp and Michael O. Rabin [10] proposed an algorithm that uses hashing. A 1977 algorithm due to J. Strother Moore and Robert Boyer [2] preprocesses the pattern so that a scan can be made of the target string in such a way that a template makes long leaps rather than just the single position shift of the naïve algorithm.

Similarly, the Knuth-Morris-Pratt [11] algorithm also achieves **sublinear** performance. (The term *sublinear* is applied to these algorithms because some characters in the target string need never be consulted. In many cases, the pattern matching can be done with fewer than $n$ comparisons.)

We have noted that the naïve algorithm performs well for many purposes. Exercise 5.5 asks you to research faster algorithms. If you find your program being held up too much by your use of the naïve algorithm, then you should consider incorporating a faster method. While you are developing code for new explorations (of which there are many in the field of bioinformatics) it is not a bad strategy to keep it quick and simple and leave the incorporation of more sophisticated pattern matchers until the consistent need for speed is apparent. That is because the context of the search is important for the selection of the best algorithm. The next two sections will look at DFAs and suffix trees: DFAs are good for searching for the same pattern in many targets, whereas a suffix tree developed for one target string provides fast searches for many different patterns.

### 5.1.4  DFAs for Search

**Deterministic finite-state automata (DFAs)** derive from theoretical considerations and, like most of the theoretical concepts in computer science, have tremendous practical applicability. There are different views of DFAs and different ways to represent them.

Our first view is as a picture. Look at Figure 5.2. The DFA shown has five states, each represented by a labeled circle. We refer to a state by its label. The DFA in Figure 5.2 has a set of five states: $\{0, 1, 2, 3, 4\}$. In general, we can say that a DFA has a finite number of **states.** In the picture view of a DFA each state will be represented by a labeled circle. The label can be thought of as the name of the state.

A DFA also has a number of **transitions,** shown in Figure 5.2 as labeled arcs. An arc labeled $c$ from state $x$ to state $y$ indicates that if the DFA is in state $x$

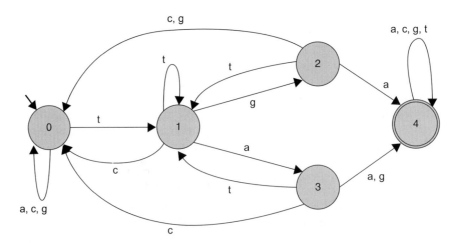

**FIGURE 5.2**   A DFA to recognize sequences containing a stop codon (TAG or TAA or TGA).

and reads the symbol $c$ then it will change to state $y$. For instance, looking at Figure 5.2 you can see that if the DFA is in state 1 and reads a g then it will enter state 2. Likewise, if the DFA is in state 0 and it reads g then it will stay in state 0. Thus loops indicate transitions that leave the state unchanged.

To properly understand the workings of a DFA, you need to consider sequences of transitions. Look again at Figure 5.2 and follow what happens when it starts in state 0 and reads the sequence acctgtga. It eats the first a and stays in state 0; then reads c again staying in state 0; and another c leaves it still in state 0. Now a t takes it to state 1 and a g takes it to state 2. But a t takes it back to state 1. Then a g takes it to state 2 and the final a takes it to state 4. To recap, the DFA started in state 0 and eating the string acctgtga proceeds through states 0, 0, 0, 1, 2, 1, 2, and 4.

Study the DFA of Figure 5.2. Try to follow its sequence of states for various strings. Satisfy yourself that if it ever enters state 4 then it will stop because it has nowhere to go. Satisfy yourself that the only way to enter state 4 is by reading one of the sequences taa, tag, or tga. Satisfy yourself further that if started in state 0, the DFA will always enter state 4 if it reads one of those three sequences anywhere. Since it is well known that taa, tag, and tga are the stop codons, we see that the DFA of Figure 5.2 is a machine to detect **stop codons.**

The last few details of the general picture definition of a DFA are:

- You need to specify a **start state.** In Figure 5.2 we intend to use state 0 as the start state. We use a thick arrow in to denote the start state.
- Create a list of final states at which some action will be performed. In the case of Figure 5.2, 4 is a final state and the picture indicates this by using a double circle. The action is to declare that a stop codon has been found. DFAs may contain several **final states,** some with different actions; but can only contain one start state. In our picture, once the DFA enters state 4 then it stays there forever. But be warned that in general, such behavior is not required and DFAs can enter and leave final states just like any other state. In this sense, it is confusing that computer scientists still use the terminology *final state*.

Another way to specify a DFA is by providing a table of its transitions. The DFA of Figure 5.2 has the transitions listed in Table 5.2.

Table 5.2 indicates, as does Figure 5.2, how the DFA changes states on reading a symbol. To be sure you understand the picture, satisfy yourself that our DFA in state 2 reading a t goes into state 1, and our DFA in state 1 reading an a goes into state 3.

Again, to complete the specification of a DFA it is necessary to designate one of the states as the start state and some states as final states with specified actions.

You may wonder where DFAs come from. Given a regular expression (which will be formally defined on pages 171 & 172), it is an interesting puzzle to create a DFA to recognize exactly those strings that contain a match to the regular expression. Exercise 5.17 asks you to design some DFAs.

TABLE 5.2    The transition matrix for a
DFA to detect stop codons

| In state* | Reading | | | |
|---|---|---|---|---|
| | A | C | G | T |
| 0 | 0 | 0 | 0 | 1 |
| 1 | 3 | 0 | 2 | 1 |
| 2 | 4 | 0 | 0 | 1 |
| 3 | 4 | 0 | 4 | 1 |
| 4 | 4 | 4 | 4 | 4 |

*From the state named in the first column of row $i$ reading the character listed at the head of column $j$, a transition occurs that causes the DFA to enter the state at the $j$th entry of row $i$. For instance, the DFA in state 3 reading a G will change to state 4.

Finally, we need to dot some "i'"s and cross some "t'"s. It is traditional to denote inputs to DFAs using lower case letters; that is why Figure 5.2 labels arcs with acgt even though we have usually used uppercase ACGT to denote nucleotides. A DFA is considered **deterministic** if from any one state only one transition is possible when reading one particular symbol. Machines without this property are called **nondeterministic** finite automata, or NFAs. You can read about them in any textbook on computer theory such as [9]. Lastly, we don't like DFAs to get stuck, meaning that in any state reading any potential input, a transition must be specified. Some authors make an exception to this rule for final states. In such cases we can restore sanity by simply adding loops back to the final state labeled with each possible input. Such modified DFAs will always consume all their input and end up in the first final state they enter.

## 5.1.5  DFAs as Programs

Another view of DFAs is as programs. It is not difficult[1] to look at the picture of a DFA and write a Java program to simulate its action. A program equivalent to Figure 5.2 is given in Figure 5.3.[2]

Each state of the DFA gives rise to a section of code that consumes one character of the input string and causes a transfer of control to the section of code corresponding to the next state. This can effectively be managed by a series of labels and switch statements or by (less efficiently) using the method-calling mechanisms of Java as we have done in Figure 5.3.

---

[1] Exercise 5.11 asks you to automate this process by writing a program to write programs equivalent to descriptions of DFAs that are input.

[2] You will probably realize that representing states by individual methods in a Java program as this program does is not very efficient. For greater efficiency, we should replace method calling by a more direct transfer of control without the overhead of procedure calling. The Java program, although inefficient, does, however, map directly to the transition matrix of the DFA (Table 5.2) and clarifies the connection between the concepts.

```java
public class StopDetector {
    // Rhys Price Jones, July 11, 2005
    // Implements DFA of Chapter 5 to detect stop codons
    String target;
    int pointer;
    public StopDetector(String s) {
        target = s;
        pointer = 0;
    }
    void state0() throws TerminateException {
        if (pointer >= target.length())
            throw new TerminateException("Reject -- not found");
        else {
            System.out.println("State 0");
            char myChar = target.charAt(pointer++);
            if (myChar == 'a') state0();
            if (myChar == 'c') state0();
            if (myChar == 'g') state0();
            if (myChar == 't') state1();
            throw new TerminateException("Bad character in target");
        }
    }
    void state1() throws TerminateException {
        if (pointer >= target.length())
            throw new TerminateException("Reject -- not found");
        else {
            System.out.println("State 1");
            char myChar = target.charAt(pointer++);
            if (myChar == 'a') state3();
            if (myChar == 'c') state0();
            if (myChar == 'g') state2();
            if (myChar == 't') state1();
            throw new TerminateException("Bad character in target");
        }
    }
    void state2() throws TerminateException {
        if (pointer >= target.length())
            throw new TerminateException("Reject -- not found");
        else {
            System.out.println("State 2");
            char myChar = target.charAt(pointer++);
            if (myChar == 'a') state4();
            if (myChar == 'c') state0();
            if (myChar == 'g') state0();
            if (myChar == 't') state1();
            throw new TerminateException("Bad character in target");
        }
    }
}
```

**FIGURE 5.3**   A program equivalent to the DFA in Figure 5.2.                    (*continued*)

```
    void state3() throws TerminateException {
        if (pointer >= target.length())
            throw new TerminateException("Reject -- not found");
        else {
            System.out.println("State 3");
            char myChar = target.charAt(pointer++);
            if (myChar == 'a') state4();
            if (myChar == 'c') state0();
            if (myChar == 'g') state4();
            if (myChar == 't') state1();
            throw new TerminateException("Bad character in target");
        }
    }
    void state4() throws TerminateException {
        System.out.println("State 4");
        throw new TerminateException("Accept -- stop codon found at location"
                                     + (pointer-3));
    }
    public static void main(String[] args) {
        if (args.length != 1)
            System.out.println("Usage: java StopDetector string");
        else {
            StopDetector sd = new StopDetector(args[0]);
            try {
                sd.state0();
            }
            catch(TerminateException e) {
                // end the execution
            }
        }
    }
}
class TerminateException extends Exception {
    public TerminateException(String message) {
        System.out.println(message);
    }
}
```

**FIGURE 5.3** (*continued*)

We have shown how a DFA can find occurrences of any member of the set {TAG, TAA, TGA} by making a single scan of the target string. Furthermore, there is a straightforward way, given a description of the DFA, to produce a program efficiently implementing the action of the DFA. What we have not yet discussed is how to devise the required DFA in the first place.

Let us begin by defining what we mean by a **regular expression** and by a **regular set**.[3] First of all, any single character such as a from our alphabet is a regular

---

[3] Most computer science theory books use the term *language* to refer to a set of strings.

expression and it denotes the regular set consisting of the single one-character string {a}. Next, if $r_1$ and $r_2$ are regular expressions denoting the regular sets $R_1$ and $R_2$, respectively, then $(r_1 + r_2)$ is also a regular expression and denotes the regular set $R_1 \cup R_2$, which is the **union** of $R_1$ and $R_2$. Also $(r_1 r_2)$ is a regular expression and denotes the **concatenation** $R_1 R_2 = \{xy | x \in R_1, y \in R_2\}$. Another way to obtain a new regular set from an old regular set $R$ is to form its **Kleene closure** $R^*$: Informally, the Kleene closure $R^*$ is the set of strings each of which is the concatenation of zero or more strings from $R$.

This brings us to a tricky point. As Martin Gardner has pointed out in the first two chapters (originally columns in *Scientific American*) of [7], nothingness is a difficult concept. What exactly is the **concatenation of zero strings**? We'll use the symbol $\epsilon$ to denote the **empty string,** or the string of length 0. And that's what we get if we concatenate zero strings, we get $\epsilon$. Let us use $R^i$ to denote the set of all strings that are formed by concatenating $i$ strings from the set $R$. Then $R^0$ denotes the set $\{\epsilon\}$ consisting of the single string $\epsilon$. Notice that this is *not* the same as the empty set $\emptyset = \{\}$, which is a set consisting of *no* strings. $R^0$ consists of exactly one, albeit empty, string; so it is not the same as the empty set $\emptyset$.

With this clarification, we are now ready to proceed with the third formula for getting new regular sets from old. We already saw union and concatenation. Now for Kleene closure. If $r$ is a regular expression denoting the regular set $R$, then $(r)^*$ is a regular expression denoting the (infinite) union

$$R^0 \cup R^1 \cup R^2 \cup \ldots \cup R^i \cup \ldots$$

more conveniently denoted $R^*$.

Before we write the full formal definition, we need base cases. All recursive definitions require base cases, something to start from. We already noted that for any character $x$ in the alphabet, $x$ is a regular expression denoting the set $\{x\}$. We also need to introduce the regular expression $\epsilon$ denoting the regular set $\{\epsilon\}$ and the regular expression $\emptyset$ denoting the regular set $\emptyset$ or $\{\}$.

In summary, here is our definition of regular expressions and regular sets: For any character a in our alphabet and any regular expressions $r, r_1, r_2$ denoting the regular sets $R, R_1, R_2$, respectively

- $\emptyset, \epsilon,$ a are regular expressions denoting $\{\}, \{\epsilon\}, \{a\}$ respectively;
- $(r_1 + r_2)$ is a regular expression denoting the regular set $R_1 \cup R_2$;
- $(r_1 r_2)$ is a regular expression denoting the regular set $R_1 R_2$;
- $(r)^*$ is a regular expression denoting the regular set $R^*$;
- parentheses may be omitted if meaning is clear.

For example TAA + TAG + TGA is a regular expression denoting the set {TAA, TAG, TGA} of stop codons. (ATG)* denotes the infinite set of repetitions of a triple coding for methionine {$\epsilon$, ATG, ATGATG, ATGATGATG, ...}. AT*G denotes the infinite set of strings starting with A, ending with G and having any number (including 0) of Ts in between.

It is a remarkable fact that there is a procedure for obtaining a DFA to recognize exactly the regular set associated with *any* regular expression. Exercise 5.15 leads you through the first few steps toward a proof of this fact. To deal with unions and Kleene closures, however, requires the use of nondeterministic finite-state automata. This is beyond the scope of this book, and the interested reader is referred to [9].

If you are familiar with the Perl programming language, or if you have used the `grep` command in Unix, you are already familiar with the notion of regular expression. Both Perl and Unix can automatically generate efficient search programs specific to any regular expression following the principles already discussed. Furthermore, they both extend the syntax of regular expressions to make it easier and more friendly for the user. In essence, however, the principles and theory are as we have described in our minimal setting. We have established that, given any pattern that can be stated as a regular expression, automatically generating an efficient program that can search any target string for that pattern is a straightforward matter. Exercise 5.16 asks you to manually generate a program to search sequences for possible introns based solely on the observation that the 5' end of an intron is marked by **GT** and the 3' end by an **AG** pair.

## 5.1.6 Suffix Trees

If frequent searches are made within the same target for different patterns, then it becomes worthwhile to consider preprocessing the target string to enable faster searches for many patterns. One way to do this is by using suffix trees [14] as proposed by Edward McCreight in 1976. They are described in a very readable 1996 article by Mark Nelson [16]. Once a suffix tree has been constructed for a target string of length $n$, then all locations of a substring pattern of length $m$ can be found with just $m$ comparisons.

In Java code provided for Chapter 4 at http://mhhe.com/gopal, we used suffix trees in our development of a program to implement the greedy algorithm for fragment reassembly. Recall that in the code and in Exercise 4.8, we built a suffix tree. Then, in order to find the overlap between $f_1$ and $f_2$ we would use successive characters from $f_2$ to index our way through the suffix tree for $f_1$. If we reach a leaf, we know that we have traced a prefix of $f_2$ that is also a suffix of $f_1$, giving us the longest overlap between $f_1$ and $f_2$. If we fail to proceed, then the overlap is empty.

## 5.1.7 A Worked Example: abracadabara

Look at Figure 5.4. If you use successive characters from the word **arabian** to index your way through the tree, you will reach the leaf labeled 9 as soon as you have consumed the initial **ara**. This indicates that **ara** is the overlap between **abracadabara** and **arabian**. The significance of the 9 is that the overlapping suffix begins at the ninth character of **abracadabara** (remember computer scientists always start counting at 0). If, on the other hand, you were to use the suffix tree of Figure 5.4 to find the overlap between **abracadabara** and **barbarian**, you would start by following the b arc from the root, and proceed into the ar.. arc, where you would get stuck. This indicates there is no overlap between **abracadabara** and **barbarian**.

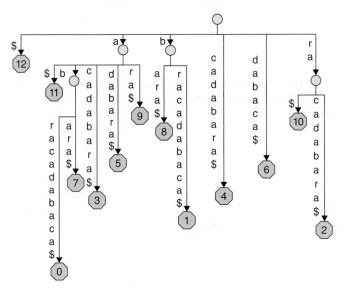

**FIGURE 5.4**   A suffix tree for abracadabara$. The $ is added to ensure that no suffix is also a prefix—a condition that makes the suffix tree be potentially ill-defined.

That's a reminder of how we used suffix trees in Chapter 4. Now we will discuss the use of suffix trees to find different patterns within a single target. Once we have built a suffix tree for the target [which can be done in time $O(n \log(n))$, where $n$ is the length of the target], then for any pattern, we can start to trace its characters and index through the tree. If we fail to proceed, then the pattern appears nowhere in the target, and we will have discovered this fact in at most $m$ comparisons, where $m$ is the length of the pattern. If we consume the entire pattern within the trace of our tree, then all the leaves below the point at which we ran out of pattern will correspond to starting points for the pattern within the target.

For example, suppose our target is abracadabara so that we can again use the suffix tree of Figure 5.4. If we search for the pattern ab we will trace down the highest a arc, then to the b arc that leads us to an internal node from which grows a subtree with two leaves: the leaf labeled 0 and the leaf labeled 7. We deduce that the pattern ab appears twice in our target: once at location 0 and again at location 7.

## 5.1.8  Recap of Exact Pattern Matching

In summary then we note:

- Exact pattern matching is well understood.
- For many purposes the $O(mn)$ naïve algorithm is quick, easy to code, and adequate in performance.
- But when called for, there are faster, more efficient algorithms.

- When the same pattern is being sought in many different targets, it may be a good investment to generate a specialized program (such as a DFA) to search for the pattern. Such a search program will have $O(n)$ time complexity.
- When seeking many different patterns is necessary in a single fixed target, it may be a good investment to build a specialized structure (e.g., a suffix tree) that can be used to find all occurrences of a pattern of length $m$ in time $O(m)$.

The field of pattern matching is well studied and can provide us with some superb and well-aimed armaments for attacking our search problems. When designing algorithmic solutions to bioinformatics problems it is important to know how to apply some of these big guns. It is equally important to know when the sophisticated fast tool is not really warranted so that short, simple, reliable code can be used without penalty.

## 5.2 THINGS PEOPLE DO WELL: SIMILARITY DETECTION

Have you ever found yourself waiting for a friend or a relative to emerge from an airport terminal. You scan hundreds or thousands of faces in a period of minutes. But when your party appears, you "immediately" recognize him. And you'll recognize him even though he may have aged many years since you last met, or even if he's cut his hair dramatically shorter, or grown a beard, or put on lots of weight. You'll recognize him whether he's looking straight at you or looking left or right.

We hear much about the need for quickly recognizing people, for example those on the FBI's most wanted terrorist list [4]. Despite significant investment for developing programs to perform these tasks, security services still distribute photographs, knowing that agents and normal citizens can often outperform machines.

Certainly, progress is being made in the fields of motion tracking and interpretation, and in face detection and recognition. In particular, clearly defined problems in feature-based facial recognition have seen significant progress. Programs picking out faces with specified ratios between the lengths of various features have met with success. Nevertheless, the human brain currently excels in detecting **unanticipated patterns** and discovering **unexpected coincidences.** Humans do not have to be told precisely what to look out for in minute and precise detail. It's conceivable that a computer program could see past a false mustache and still recognize a wanted person *as long as the programmer had anticipated and coded for this.* And the programmer won't think of everything: The program that succeeded in recognizing a villain even through a false mustache might well be fooled by a nose job or a wig.

Evolution has rewarded those of our ancestors who were adaptable, innovative and creative in dealing with the unexpected. As a result, these are human traits. Unfortunately, we do not understand these skills well enough yet to confer the same abilities on our computer programs.

In a young science like bioinformatics, it is important for researchers to be ready for anything. They must expect the unexpected. They must adapt in the face of unanticipated changes and new discoveries. In essence, bright researchers need to be as different as possible from the inflexible programs of today's computers. But we also need to know when we need to write programs to help us acquire or analyze the signals that we detect.

# 5.3 COMPUTERS HELPING PEOPLE: PRESENTING DOTPLOTS

DotPlots are easily generated by computer and can present a lot of information in a compact format that helps humans scrutinize the data. The programs presented here will generate primitive **ASCII**-graphics. More sophisticated programs can easily be constructed that can take advantage of much finer resolutions available on today's screens and printouts. We refrain from presenting such sophisticated graphics programs here because we do not want to distract from the underlying theory. So we will use * for a dot and a space for a lack of a dot. Our graphs are low resolution, but will illustrate our points well. Interested readers are encouraged to pursue higher resolution graphics programs and animations.

We begin with a straightforward search for substrings that match exactly. We'll modify that exact matcher to produce an inexact matcher that is more suited to finding evolutionarily linked substrings. That will raise issues affecting selectivity and sensitivity. A highly selective program will filter out all but the best candidates, whereas a highly sensitive program will present the user with all the candidates, even the weak ones. **Selectivity** is the ability to reject all but the best candidates, and **sensitivity** is the ability to accept even the weakest candidates. Clearly there is a tradeoff between selectivity and sensitivity. With selectivity too high, the user can miss interesting links; but with sensitivity too high, the user can be swamped by a tsunami of false-positives.

When in later sections we look at heuristic alignment programs, you may notice how these simple dotplot programs may well have provided the original inspiration for the programs that are in such common use in bioinformatics today.

## 5.3.1 Straight DotPlot: Searching for Areas of Exact Matching

Consider the rather clumsy program presented in Figure 5.5. When two strings are input, the program lays one out along a horizontal axis and the other along a vertical axis. A $*$ is placed in the $(i,j)$ position if the $i$th character of the first string matches the $j$th character of the second.

```
// DotPlot.java
// Simple dot plot of two strings entered on command line
// Example usage:
// java DotPlot CANYOUDANCETHECANCAN YESICANDANCETHECANCAN

public class DotPlot {
  public static void main(String[] args) {
    StringBuffer x = new StringBuffer(args[0]);
    StringBuffer y = new StringBuffer(args[1]);
    // Print header:
    System.out.print("    ");
    for (int j=0; j<x.length(); j++) System.out.print(x.charAt(j)+" ");
    // and separator
    System.out.println();
    System.out.println();
    // For each character of second string
    for (int i=0; i<y.length(); i++) {
        // print it at left edge of table
        System.out.print("  "+y.charAt(i)+" ");
        // and compare it with each member of the first string
        for (int j=0; j<x.length(); j++) {
            // print a * if they match; otherwise a space
            if (x.charAt(j)==y.charAt(i)) System.out.print("* ");
            else System.out.print("  ");
        }
      System.out.println();
    }
  }
}
```

**FIGURE 5.5**   Program DotPlot.java plots two strings against each other, placing a * at $(i, j)$ locations where the strings match.

## 5.3.2  A Worked Example:
## Can You Dance the Can-Can?

When we run the program DotPlot with inputs CANYOUDANCETHE-CANCAN and YESICANDANCETHECANCAN we obtain the output shown in Figure 5.6.

Do you notice the many diagonal lines that go in the direction top-left to bottom-right? You should satisfy yourself that they correspond to substrings within the two input strings that match each other. The longest such diagonal line, of course, corresponds to the common substring DANCETHECANCAN. But there are other shorter diagonals corresponding to shorter matches within the two input strings. And what do you make of the short bottom-left to top-right diagonals? (*Hint:* Look for short substrings of one string that appear backwards in the other.)

```
          C A N Y O U D A N C E T H E C A N C A N

    Y           *
    E                       *           *
    S
    I
    C   *               *           *       *
    A       *           *               *       *
    N           *           *               *       *
    D                   *
    A       *           *               *       *
    N           *           *               *       *
    C   *               *           *       *
    E                   *       *
    T                       *
    H                           *
    E                   *       *
    C   *               *           *       *
    A       *           *               *       *
    N           *           *               *       *
    C   *               *           *       *
    A       *           *               *       *
    N           *           *               *       *
```

**FIGURE 5.6**   Output of `java DotPlot CANYOUDANCETHECANCAN` YESICANDANCETHECANCAN showing the asterisks where the strings match. The diagonal patterns indicate matching subsequences.

`DotPlot.java` is an example of a program that produces output that helps humans find patterns. Some of the patterns are wholly expected, but others might be a surprise.

Certainly the long top-left to bottom-right diagonals were no surprise to anybody; and it would be an easy matter to extend the program so that it could "discover" such long stretches of perfect match and identify them to the user. But the perpendicular diagonals corresponding to "reverse partial matches" are the kind of unanticipated pattern that humans are so good at discerning.

Exercise 5.18 asks you to examine some outputs from the `DotPlot` program and interpret them.

## 5.3.3  Controlling Sensitivity and Selectivity

Run the previous `DotPlot` program with the command

```
java DotPlot 1000011010101000  101011100000001010001010
```

You will see patterns, but there are so many that it's difficult to assign any meaning to them. Because there are only two symbols (0 and 1) in the strings many spurious matches occur, which contribute to a veritable surfeit of asterisks.

The program is too sensitive, or equivalently, not sufficiently selective, to give us the feedback we really want.

One way to make the program less sensitive, and thereby more selective, is to refrain from inserting an asterisk unless two consecutive characters from the first string match the two corresponding consecutive characters in the second string. A program that would require three consecutive matches before allowing an asterisk is even less sensitive.

Exercise 5.19 asks you to modify the `DotPlot.java` program to make it more selective by insisting on more than just one character match before inserting an asterisk.

English speakers would agree that the words *culler* (one who culls or gathers) and *color* sound pretty similar. Run the `DotPlot` program with the command

```
java DotPlot culler color
```

to see a relative paucity of asterisks that indicate next to nothing.

This time, the `DotPlot` program just isn't sensitive enough. Sure it catches the matches between the consonants. But it regards the vowel o as completely distinct from the vowel u even though, in the words culler and color they can be pronounced the same. Similarly, the e of culler is pronounced the same as the second o of color.

A similar phenomenon arises when comparing biological sequences. Often small mutations can replace one amino acid with another whose properties are very similar to the original. We would like sensitive dotplot programs to indicate when two characters, although not identical, represent similar functionality.

We will return to this topic when we look at PAM and BLOSUM matrices. In the meantime look at Exercise 5.20.

## 5.4  PEOPLE HELPING COMPUTERS: ALGORITHMS

In the previous section, graphics programs helped us investigate patterns that arise when we compare two sequences. In particular, they helped us to understand what features we need to measure in order to discover biologically meaningful comparisons of pairs of sequences. Computer programs drew pictures that helped us humans to evaluate connections between sequences.

In this section, our aim is to have the computer programs evaluate the connections between sequences. We must somehow convert our experience and intuition into computer code that produces desirable results.

### 5.4.1  Alignment

In 1967 an amusing book was published under the title *Mots d'Heures: Gousses, Rames* with the subtitle *The d'Antin Manuscript* [19]. It consists of fragmented bits of French syntax put together, not to make any particular meaningful statement in French, but to sound rather like familiar English nursery rhymes even while being intoned in French. If you have any knowledge of French try to read aloud the first part of the first of these rhymes:

Un petit d'un petit

S'étonne aux Halles

Familiar? No? Try again! We will shortly see an alignment of this verse with another that you probably recognize.

Even the title of *The d'Antin Manuscript* is intended to invoke thoughts of *Mother Goose Rhymes*. Instinctively, we feel that **mothergooserhymes** and **motsdheuresgoussesrames** are similar. Note that we've now removed punctuation and capitalization to make our example a more appropriate analog of the similarity problem for sequences of amino acids.

Let us place the two strings **mothergooserhymes** and **motsdheuresgoussesrames** one above the other and try to position them to enhance any similarity. We'll try to place identical symbols together and introduce spacers "-" in order to facilitate this. We'll also try to put letters or combinations of letters that fulfill similar tasks (e.g., ER and EURE or OO and OU) in close proximity.

```
MOT--HE-R--GOOS-E-RHYMES
MOTSDHEURESGOUSSESR-AMES
```

This is an alignment of the two strings: In each column we have either

- two identical letters, or
- two letters of similar function (whatever that means!), or
- a letter and a -

For one more *alignment* let's return to the two lines given earlier:

Un petit d'un petit

S'étonne aux Halles

and perform the promised "alignment":

```
-UNPETITDUNPETITSETONNEAUXHALLES
HUMP-TY-DUMP-TY-SATON--THEWALL
```

This "alignment" of letters is far from perfect. But if we look at the **functionality** of the letters; that is if we consider the sounds produced by a native speaker reading those letters, we note that we have a great match. So it is also with biological sequence comparisons: When two sequences are very distantly related, it is often the case that exact nucleotide matches have all but disappeared. Nevertheless, when we compare the functionality (perhaps the amino acids corresponding to groupings of nucleotides into triplets), we often find the similarity between the sequences still persists even though exact letter matches have long since eroded through nonlethal mutation.

Returning to the more orthodox alignments of biological sequences, it is intuitively clear that the fewer - symbols used and the more often we find identical ones aligned, the more similar are the strings. It is important to quantify this notion of similarity.

## 5.4.2 Quality of Alignments: Scoring Schemes

Consider two sequences CAAACCGTCGT and AACCCGCCGTA. If we run our simple `DotPlot` program to compare them, we obtain:

```
    C A A A C C G T C G T

A     * * *
A     * * *
C   *         * *       *
C   *         * *       *
C   *         * *       *
G                   *     *
C   *         * *       *
C   *         * *       *
G                   *     *
T                     *     *
A     * * *
```

We can see significant evidence of substring matching between the two sequences. A human might select a long promising diagonal from the following dotplot. We've changed the asterisks into periods except for those matches that we want to select. With this approach we're trying to find a good alignment between the sequences by eyeballing a good long diagonal. An * in our diagonal "indicates" an exact match between the corresponding characters. Skipping both downward and across without an asterisk indicates a mismatch, and moving horizontally or vertically introduces a gap. Let's say we pick this diagonal:

```
    C A A A C C G T C G T

A     .  *  .
A     .  .  *
C   .        *   .       .
C   .          .  *      .
C   .          .  .      .
G                  *       .
C   .          .  .       .
C   .          .  .     *
G                 .       *
T                    .      *
A     .  .  .
```

This selected near-diagonal indicates that we have lined up the sequences as

```
C A A A C C – G T C G T –
– – | | | | – | X | | | –
– – A A C C C G C C G T A
```

Our convention is to use | for a match, X for a mismatch and – for an insertion or deletion. Whether it's an insertion or a deletion depends on which sequence you consider primary. Since we are, at this stage, utterly unbiased, we'll use the single term **indel** to refer to either.

Look at the aligned sequences carefully, and be sure that you understand the relationship between the alignment and the selection of the near-diagonal in the dotplot.

We might just as reasonably have selected the following near-diagonal:

```
        C A A A C C G T C G T

  A     *  .  .
  A     .  *  .
  C  .           .  .           .
  C  .        *     .           .
  C  .           .  *           .
  G  .              *        .
  C  .           .  .           .
  C  .           .  .        *
  G  .              .        *
  T  .                 .        *
  A     .  .  .
```

corresponding to the alignment

```
C A A A C C G T C G T –
– | | X | | | X | | | –
– A A C C C G C C G T A
```

How likely is it that the two sequences CAAACCGTCGT and AACCCGC-CGTA are "related"? Of the two alignments

```
C A A A C C – G T C G T –          C A A A C C G T C G T –
– – | | | | – | X | | | –   and    – | | X | | | X | | | –
– – A A C C C G C C G T A          – A A C C C G C C G T A
```

which is more likely to be biologically meaningful?

The truth is, of course, that we cannot really know. But we would like to propose a criterion for which we can write a computer program that can select the "best" alignment of two sequences.

A simple criterion involves a scoring system. Let's score $+5$ for each match, $-10$ for each mismatch, and $-3$ for each indel. Under this scoring system, the first alignment scores 40 for eight matches, $-10$ for its mismatch and $-12$ for its four indels. That's a total of 18. The second alignment scores $40 - 20 - 6$ for a total of 14. So, under the 5, $-10$, $-3$ scoring scheme, the first alignment is better.

Now let's try a different scoring scheme. This time, let's make it $+2$ for each match, $-1$ for each mismatch and $-2$ for each indel. This time the alignments score 7 and 10, respectively, making the second alignment the preferred one.

Another scoring scheme for an alignment is to calculate what is sometimes called the distance measure or the edit distance corresponding to the alignment. This scores 0 for a match and 1 for a mismatch or an indel. Unlike our other schemes, in this one the alignment with the smaller score is preferred. For our two alignments we get distance measures of 5 and 4, respectively, again inclining us to choose the second alignment over the first.

Therefore, to be able to quantify the quality of an alignment, we must first specify a scoring scheme.

### 5.4.3  Global Alignments: The Needleman–Wunsch Algorithms

In 1970, Saul Needleman and Christian Wunsch [15] proposed a general method for finding similarity between two amino acid sequences based on principles of dynamic programming.

### 5.4.4  A Worked Example

Let's begin with a small example illustrating how their algorithm works.

Suppose we want to align CACGA and CATTGA and we want to score $+2$ for matches, 0 for mismatches, and $-1$ for indels. We're going to write the first sequence along a horizontal axis and the second along a vertical axis like this:

```
          C   A   C   G   A

      C
      A
      T
      T
      G
      A
```

We're going to fill in a matrix of values where the $(i, j)$ entry is the score of the best alignment between the first $i$ characters of the second sequence and the first $j$ characters of the first sequence. When $i$ is 0, we are looking at the best alignment between the first $j$ characters of CACGA and the empty string. Clearly, the best such alignment consists of as many indels as are required to match the lengths. For example to get the $(0, 3)$ entry, we need to look at

```
CAC
– – –
```

with a score of $-3$. Thus we can fill in the top row:

```
        C   A   C   G   A
    0  -1  -2  -3  -4  -5
C
A
T
T
G
A
```

By a similar argument, we can fill in the first column:

```
        C   A   C   G   A
    0  -1  -2  -3  -4  -5
C  -1
A  -2
T  -3
T  -4
G  -5
A  -6
```

Notice that the $(0, 0)$ entry comes from aligning the empty sequence with the empty sequence. There are no matches, no mismatches, and no indels, so the score must be 0. Now let's consider the $(1, 1)$ entry. It comes about by extending the $(0, 0)$ entry with a match between C and C, resulting in a score of $0 + 2$ (extending from the northwest), or from extending the $(0, 1)$ entry with an indel for a score of $(-1) + (-1)$ giving a total of $-2$ (extending from the north), or from extending the $(1, 0)$ entry with an indel for a score of $-2$ (extending from the west). Clearly the first alternative is to be preferred. So now we have:

```
        C   A   C   G   A
    0  -1  -2  -3  -4  -5
C  -1   2
A  -2
T  -3
T  -4
G  -5
A  -6
```

Now consider the $(1, 2)$ position. We can either extend the $(0, 1)$ alignment from the northwest with a mismatch of A and C, giving a total score of $-1$, or we can extend the $(0, 2)$ alignment from the north with an indel, for a score of $-3$, or we can extend the $(1, 1)$ alignment from the west with an indel for a score of 1 (2 in the $(1, 1)$ position plus $-1$ for the indel). This time we choose to extend from the west. By a similar process we can fill in the whole of row 1:

```
        C   A   C   G   A
    0  -1  -2  -3  -4  -5
C  -1   2   1   0  -1  -2
A  -2
T  -3
T  -4
G  -5
A  -6
```

Notice that the 0 in position $(1, 3)$ can come either from the west, corresponding to the alignment

```
C A C
C - -
```

or from the northwest, corresponding to the equally good alignment

```
C A C
- - C
```

By a symmetrical process, we can fill in column 1:

```
        C   A   C   G   A
    0  -1  -2  -3  -4  -5
C  -1   2   1   0  -1  -2
A  -2   1
T  -3   0
T  -4  -1
G  -5  -2
A  -6  -3
```

Exactly the same reasoning can be used for the next row and column. Satisfy yourself that the following are correct:

```
        C   A   C   G   A
    0  -1  -2  -3  -4  -5
C  -1   2   1   0  -1  -2
A  -2   1   4   3   2   1
T  -3   0   3
T  -4  -1   2
G  -5  -2   1
A  -6  -3   0
```

Continuing in this mode, we complete the table:

```
        C   A   C   G   A
    0  -1  -2  -3  -4  -5
C  -1   2   1   0  -1  -2
A  -2   1   4   3   2   1
T  -3   0   3   4   3   2
T  -4  -1   2   3   4   3
G  -5  -2   1   2   5   4
A  -6  -3   0   1   4   7
```

That bottom right entry, 7, gives the score for the best alignment. To recreate the alignment, we must backtrack through our process. Where did the 7 come from? It came from the northwest, so the alignment must end with

A

A

tacked on to the alignment that led to the 5 that is to the northwest.

Similarly, that 5 came from the northwest indicating that our optimal alignment proceeds from the alignment that led to the 3 at $(4, 3)$ and ends with

GA

GA

Now the 3 at $(4, 3)$ could have come from the north, extending the alignment at $(3, 3)$ with

−GA

TGA

or it could have come from the northwest, extending the alignment at $(3, 2)$ with

CGA

TGA

It is not unusual, especially with simple scoring schemes like this one, for there to be several optimal alignments, each with the same score.

By completing the process, one of the alignments with a score of 7 for our example is

CAC−GA

CATTGA

Exercise 5.21 asks you to find another.

With this specific example in mind, let us proceed to develop the general algorithm. In developing our version of the Needleman–Wunsch algorithm, we'll follow a method popularized by Udi Manber [13]. Manber encourages the design of algorithms by induction. We will develop a recurrence relation for the score of the best alignment between two sequences $a_1, a_2, \ldots, a_n$ and $b_1, b_2, \ldots, b_m$ using the principle of mathematical induction. Translation of that recurrence relation into a program in your favorite programming language will complete the process. This is a common, useful, and reliable way to develop algorithms.

We write $A(k,l)$ to denote the best alignment score between the prefix sequences $a_1, a_2, \ldots, a_k$ and $b_1, b_2, \ldots, b_l$. So, assume that we know $A(k,l)$ for every pair $(k,l)$ that precedes pair $(i,j)$. For our purposes, we say that $(k,l)$ precedes $(i,j)$ if either

- $k < i$ and $l \leq j$, or
- $l < j$ and $k \leq i$.

Roughly speaking, points to the left and high in the grid occur earlier in the ordering.

With the ordering established, we can proceed to derive a recursive equation for $A(i,j)$.

How does the best alignment for $a_1, a_2, \ldots, a_i$ and $b_1, b_2, \ldots, b_j$ relate to its predecessors? There are three possible scenarios:

- Alignment for $a_1, a_2, \ldots, a_{i-1}$ and $b_1, b_2, \ldots, b_{j-1}$ followed by $a_i$ matched or mismatched with $b_j$
- Alignment for $a_1, a_2, \ldots, a_i$ and $b_1, b_2, \ldots, b_{j-1}$ followed by a gap with $b_j$
- Alignment for $a_1, a_2, \ldots, a_{i-1}$ and $b_1, b_2, \ldots, b_j$ followed by a gap with $a_i$

Pictorially, these three cases look like:

- $\begin{pmatrix} previous \\ alignment \end{pmatrix} \begin{matrix} a_i \\ b_j \end{matrix}$

- $\begin{pmatrix} previous \\ alignment \end{pmatrix} \begin{matrix} - \\ b_j \end{matrix}$

- $\begin{pmatrix} previous \\ alignment \end{pmatrix} \begin{matrix} a_i \\ - \end{matrix}$

Now let's do some analysis for each of these cases:

- $\begin{pmatrix} previous \\ alignment \end{pmatrix} \begin{matrix} a_i \\ b_j \end{matrix}$

In this case, the best previous alignment is (using our inductive hypothesis) $A(i-1, j-1)$. We add to that either the match score (if $a_i = b_j$) or the mismatch score (otherwise). Let's denote that additional amount by $s(a_i, b_j)$. In this case the calculated new alignment score would be $A(i-1, j-1) + s(a_i, b_j)$.

- $\begin{pmatrix} previous \\ alignment \end{pmatrix} \begin{matrix} - \\ b_j \end{matrix}$

In this case, the best previous alignment is (again using the induction hypothesis) $A(i, j-1)$. We need to add on the gap penalty. Let's denote the gap penalty by $g$. In this case therefore the calculated new alignment score is $A(i-1, j) + g$.

- $\begin{pmatrix} previous \\ alignment \end{pmatrix} \begin{matrix} a_i \\ - \end{matrix}$

By a similar argument, the calculated new alignment score in this case is $A(i,j-1)+g$

Since we want the highest possible score, we must choose the case that leads to the largest value for the calculated new alignment. $A(i,j)$ is thus the maximum of

- $A(i-1,j-1)+s(a_i,b_j)$
- $A(i,j-1)+g$
- $A(i-1,j)+g$

We have derived the recurrence

$$A(i,j) = \max \begin{cases} A(i-1,j-1)+s(a_i,b_j) \\ A(i,j-1)+g \\ A(i-1,j)+g \end{cases}$$

This immediately suggests the program portion:

```
int A(int i, int j) {
    if ...            // ... denotes our yet to be determined base cases
    then return .../// to be determined
    else return max(A(i-1,j-1)+s(a[i],b[j]), A(i,j-1)+g, A(i-1,j)+g);
}
```

As usual, the recursive case of our program is easy to derive. To ensure proper termination of the recursion we must correctly specify the base cases. These occur as each of the subscripts $i$ and $j$ get to 0 in the top row and left column of our tableau. The $A(0,j)$ entry corresponds to matching the first $j$ characters of one sequence with a collection of "$j$ indels" characters. It incurs a penalty score of $jg$. Similarly, the other base cases $A(i,0)$ can be dealt with.

In view of what we've just seen, look carefully at program NW.java in Figure 5.7. It is a simple implementation of the Needleman–Wunsch algorithm. In the exercises you will be modifying and extending it. For now use it to check your hand-derived arrays.

The program in Figure 5.7 outputs a dynamic programming matrix that can be used to produce a corresponding alignment. You will construct the corresponding alignment by hand in the exercises. Exercise 5.6 expects you to generate small **dynamic programming matrices** by hand and check them by program.

Exercise 5.7 is similar, but you'll use a distance measure for scoring purposes. This makes for significant differences in the program. You will need to **minimize** the northwest-, north-, and west-derived scores. You will need to change more than just three lines of NW.java.

The program in Figure 5.7 produces the scoring matrix showing at every position $(i,j)$ the score of the best alignment to that point. It is possible to backtrack from the bottom-right entry to the top-left entry and reconstruct the corresponding alignment. The backtracking process involves working backwards, figuring out which of the choices (from the north, from the west, from the northwest) occurred to create the current entry. In this way, we know whether to insert a gap in the first sequence or in the second sequence, or to match or mismatch a

```java
// NW.java
//
// Simple Needleman-Wunsch global alignment of
//    two strings entered on command line
// Example usage:
// java NW IamAGoodString IamAnotherString

public class NW {
    // Using simple linear gap score (-2 per indel)
    // and 4 for a match, -1 for a mismatch
    // Feel free to change this
  public static final int gapscore = -2;
  public static final int matchscore = 4;
  public static final int mismatchscore = -1;

  private String x;   // First string
  private String y;   // Second string
  private int xlen, ylen; // their lengths
  private int[][] scoreArray;

  public NW(String a, String b) {
    x = a;
    y = b;
    xlen = x.length();
    ylen = y.length();
    scoreArray = new int[ylen+1][xlen+1];
  }

  public void fillScoreArray() {
    int row, col;      // for indexing through array
    int northwest, north, west;  // (row, col) entry will be max of these
    int best;    // will be the max
    // Fill the top row and left column:
    for (col=0; col less than or equal xlen; col++) scoreArray[0][col] = gapscore*col;
    for (row=0; row less than or equal ylen; row++) scoreArray[row][0] = gapscore*row;
    // Now fill in the rest of the array:
    for (row=1; row less than or equal ylen; row++) {
      for (col=1; col less than or equal xlen; col++) {
        if (x.charAt(col-1)==y.charAt(row-1))
          northwest = scoreArray[row-1][col-1] + matchscore;
        else northwest = scoreArray[row-1][col-1] + mismatchscore;
        west = scoreArray[row][col-1] + gapscore;
        north = scoreArray[row-1][col] + gapscore;
        best = northwest;
        if (north>best) best = north;
        if (west>best) best = west;
        scoreArray[row][col] = best;
      }
    }
  }
}
```

**FIGURE 5.7**  A simple implementation of the Needleman–Wunsch algorithm.

```
public void print3(int x) {
  // Print x in 3 spaces
  String s = ""+x;
  if (s.length() == 1) System.out.print("  "+s);
  else if (s.length() == 2) System.out.print(" "+s);
  else if (s.length() == 3) System.out.print(s);
  else System.out.print("***");
}

public void printArray() {
  for (int row=0; row less than scoreArray.length; row++) {
    for (int col=0; col less than scoreArray[row].length; col++)
      print3(scoreArray[row][col]);
    System.out.println();
  }
}

public static void main(String[] args) {
  NW nw = new NW(args[0], args[1]);
  nw.fillScoreArray();
  nw.printArray();
}
}
```

**FIGURE 5.7**   (*continued*)

character from both sequences. Working back from the bottom right to the top left, we create the alignment whose score we have recorded.

Exercise 5.8 asks you to write a program to perform the backtracking so you won't have to do it by hand. The program in Figure 5.8 achieves that by simulating the process you probably used to do the backtracking by hand. A better approach is to have your program build another array that contains in the $(i, j)$ entry the direction from which the value in the $(i, j)$ entry of the scoring matrix was calculated. Exercise 5.8 asks you to write your own program that takes this more elegant (and efficient) approach.

## 5.4.5 Local Alignments: The Smith–Waterman Algorithm

So far, we have looked at programs for performing **global alignment** between two sequences. This means that we have looked for the best alignment between the whole of the first sequence $X$ and the whole of the second sequence $Y$. Such comparisons are done, for example, when determining the evolutionary relatedness of a given gene sequence among different species.

Perhaps it is more "biologically useful" to find a subsequence of $X$ and a subsequence of $Y$ such that the *global alignment score between the two subsequences* is as large as possible. That's what we mean by a **local alignment** between $X$ and $Y$. We throw away parts of both sequences from the left and the right ends in

```
// NW1.java
//
// Goes beyond NW.java by analysing array to produce alignment
// Simple Needleman-Wunch global alignment of
//    two strings entered on command line
// Example usage:
// java NW1 IamAGoodString IamAnotherString

public class NW1 {
    // Using simple linear gap score (-2 per indel)
    // and 4 for a match, -1 for a mismatch
    // Feel free to change this
  public static final int gapscore = -2;
  public static final int matchscore = 4;
  public static final int mismatchscore = -1;

  private String x;  // First string
  private String y;  // Second string
  private int xlen, ylen; // their lengths
  private int[][] scoreArray;

  private String xalig, yalig;  // for the alignments

  public NW1(String a, String b) {
    x = a;
    y = b;
    xlen = x.length();
    ylen = y.length();
    scoreArray = new int[ylen+1][xlen+1];
  }

  public void fillScoreArray() {
    int col,row;      // for indexing through array
    int northwest, north, west;  // (row,col) entry will be max of these
    int best;    // will be the max
    // Fill the top row and left column:
    for (col=0; col<=xlen; col++) scoreArray[0][col] = gapscore*col;
    for (row=0; row<=ylen; row++) scoreArray[row][0] = gapscore*row;
    // Now fill in the rest of the array:
    for (row=1; row<=ylen; row++) {
      for (col=1; col<=xlen; col++) {
        if (x.charAt(col-1)==y.charAt(row-1))
          northwest = scoreArray[row-1][col-1] + matchscore;
        else northwest = scoreArray[row-1][col-1] + mismatchscore;
        west = scoreArray[row][col-1] + gapscore;
```

**FIGURE 5.8**   An extension of the NW.java program that backtracks through the array to reproduce the "winning" alignment.

```
                north = scoreArray[row-1][col] + gapscore;
                best = northwest;
                if (north>best) best = north;
                if (west>best) best = west;
                scoreArray[row][col] = best;
        }
    }
}

public void print3(int x) {
    // Print x in 3 spaces
    String s = ""+x;
    if (s.length() == 1) System.out.print("  "+s);
    else if (s.length() == 2) System.out.print(" "+s);
    else if (s.length() == 3) System.out.print(s);
    else System.out.print("***");
}

public void printArray() {
    for (int row=0; row<scoreArray.length; row++) {
        for (int col=0; col<scoreArray[row].length; col++)
            print3(scoreArray[row][col]);
        System.out.println();
    }
}

public void setAlignment() {
    int row = ylen;        // start at end of sequence 2
    int col = xlen;        // and at end of sequence 1
    xalig = "";            // start with empty alignment
    yalig = "";            // ditto for sequence 2
    while ((col>0) || (row>0)) {
        // work your way from bottom right to top left
        if ((row>0) &&
            (scoreArray[row][col] == scoreArray[row-1][col] + gapscore)) {
            // came from north
            xalig = "-" + xalig;                  // gap in sequence 1
            yalig = y.charAt(row-1) + yalig; // consume char from sequence 2
            row--;                                // move up in array
        }
        else if ((col>0) &&
                (scoreArray[row][col] == scoreArray[row][col-1] + gapscore)) {
            // came from west
            xalig = x.charAt(col-1) + xalig; // consume char from sequence 1
            yalig = "-" + yalig;              // gap in sequence 2
            col--;                            // move left
        }
```

**FIGURE 5.8**   *(continued)*

```
      else {
        // came from northwest
        xalig = x.charAt(col-1) + xalig; // consume char from sequence 1
        yalig = y.charAt(row-1) + yalig; // and from sequence 2
        col--;                           // move left
        row--;                           // and up
      }
      // Uncomment these if you want to see the buildup:
      // System.out.println(xalig);
      // System.out.println(yalig);
    }
  }

  public void printAlignment() {
    System.out.println(xalig);
    System.out.println(yalig);
  }

  public static void main(String[] args) {
    NW1 nw = new NW1(args[0], args[1]);
    nw.fillScoreArray();
    nw.printArray();
    nw.setAlignment();
    nw.printAlignment();
  }
}
```

**FIGURE 5.8**   *(continued)*

```
          C-G--A-A
          CTGCGAGA
```

a global alignment scoring 0 (+4 for the matches and −4 for the indels).

```
            CGAA
          CTGCGAGA
```

a local alignment scoring 3 (+3 for the matches and 0 for the mismatch).
Leading or trailing indels do not score against a local alignment, but do
count against in global alignments.

**FIGURE 5.9**   The best global (upper) and the best local (lower) alignment between
CGAA and CTGCGAGA, scoring by +1 for a match, 0 for a mismatch, −1 for an indel.

such a way that the remaining pieces have as large as possible an alignment
score. Peripheral pieces of both sequences that do nothing but hurt the score are
discarded. Figure 5.9 shows the best global and the best local alignment between
CGAA and CTGCGAGA with a scoring system that applies +1 for a match, 0
for a mismatch, and −1 for an indel.

In 1981, Michael Smith and Temple Waterman [18] proposed an adaptation to the Needleman–Wunsch algorithm that would identify the longest stretch of high-scoring alignment within two sequences.

It takes very little to modify our alignment program to give the best local alignment between two sequences. As long as your alignment scoring method is such that

- two empty strings align with score 0 and
- mismatches and indels both contribute negative scores and
- matches contribute positive scores,

all you need do is ensure that you never insert a negative number into your matrix. After generating the matrix, search it for the largest score. From that, you can deduce the best local alignment within your sequences.

## 5.4.6  A Worked Example

For example with match +2, mismatch −1, indel −2, a global alignment of ACTACT and GTAC can be obtained from the scoring matrix:

```
    -   A   C   T   A    C    T
-   0  -2  -4  -6  -8  -10  -12
G  -2  -1  -3  -5  -7   -9  -11
T  -4  -3  -2  -1  -3   -5   -7
A  -6  -2  -4  -3   1   -1   -3
C  -8  -4   0  -2  -1    3    1
```

You can derive corresponding global alignments by backtracking to get either

```
A C T A C T
- X | | | -
- G T A C -
```

with global score 1, or, just as good:

```
A C T A C T
X - | | | -
G - T A C -
```

With the same scoring, an optimal local alignment can be deduced from the Smith–Waterman scoring matrix:

```
    -  A  C  T  A  C  T
-   0  0  0  0  0  0  0
G   0  0  0  0  0  0  0
T   0  0  0  2  0  0  2
A   0  2  0  0  4  2  0
C   0  0  4  2  2  6  4
```

Notice that the only modification is that we never allow negative scores to enter the tableau. Where the old algorithm would generate a negative entry, the new algorithm simply inserts a 0. Otherwise, the entries are computed in exactly the same way as in the Needleman–Wunsch program. This Smith–Waterman matrix indicates the alignment

```
a c T A C t
  g T A C
```

where lowercase letters indicate nucleotides not involved in the alignment. It is obtained by backtracking *from the largest score location in the matrix.*

Exercise 5.9 asks you to modify your previous Needleman–Wunsch program to find local alignments. That produces a basic implementation of the Smith–Waterman algorithm.

## 5.5 AFFINE GAP PENALTIES

The version of the Needleman–Wunsch algorithm presented earlier scores each occurrence of an indel exactly the same. This is a gross oversimplification of the original algorithm, which accommodated more general gap penalties in which the cost of a gap depends on its length. It recognized that gaps should be scored in terms of **block indels** rather than as individual, independent single indels. Biologists have found that a long consecutive sequence of $n$ gaps is much more likely to have occurred than $n$ separate gaps of length 1. When we make the cost of a gap to be a function $g(x)$ that depends on the length $X$ of the gap, adjustments need to be made in the derivation of the algorithm. Instead of the single recurrence:

$$A(i,j) = \max \begin{cases} A(i-1,j-1) + s(a_i, b_j) \\ A(i,j-1) + g \\ A(i-1,j) + g \end{cases}$$

we now deal with a system of recurrences:

$$\begin{aligned} N(i,j) &= \min_{k \in \{0 \ldots i-1\}} A(k,j) + g(i-k) \\ W(i,j) &= \min_{k \in \{0 \ldots j-1\}} A(i,k) + g(j-k) \end{aligned}$$

$$A(i,j) = \min \begin{cases} A(i-1,j-1) + s(a_i, b_j) \\ N(i,j) \\ W(i,j) \end{cases}$$

where $N(i,j)$ is the best alignment that ends with a gap in the second sequence (we call it $N$ because it's from the north), and $W(i,j)$ is the best alignment ending with a gap in the first sequence (from the west), and $g(x)$ is the penalty assigned to a gap of length $x$.

These recursions, together with base cases for instances when $i$ or $j$ are 0, lead to the original Needleman–Wunsch algorithm. It deals in a more satisfactory way with gaps by allowing appropriate scoring for block indels. But this approach slows performance (see Exercise 5.12).

Nevertheless, as pointed out by Fitch and Smith [5], some kind of block indel scoring appears to be essential for finding alignments that are biologically relevant. A way to achieve this, without the performance hit of general gap penalties, is to use **affine gap penalties.** Instead of a general $g(x)$ an affine gap penalty takes the form $g(x) = s + cx$, where $s$ can be thought of as the **gap start,** or **initiation, penalty** and $c$ as the **gap continuation penalty.** It remains true that a single long gap will be more heavily penalized than a single short gap, but the important (and significant for biological applicability) point is that a single long gap will be preferred to several shorter gaps that add up to the same total length. For example, with an initialization penalty of 10 and a continuation penalty of 1, a single gap of length 8 will be penalized 17 points (one initialization and seven continuations), whereas four gaps each of length 2 would be penalized 44 points (four initialization penalties plus four continuation penalties).

The previous recurrences become:

$$N(i,j) = \min \begin{cases} A(i-1,j) + s \\ N(i-1,j) + c \end{cases}$$

$$W(i,j) = \min \begin{cases} A(i,j-1) + s \\ W(i,j-1) + c \end{cases}$$

$$A(i,j) = \min \begin{cases} A(i-1,j-1) + s(a_i, b_j) \\ N(i,j) \\ W(i,j) \end{cases}$$

Exercise 5.13 asks you to implement this version of the Needleman–Wunsch algorithm with affine penalties, and to verify that the performance hit is acceptable.

## 5.6 EVOLUTIONARY CONSIDERATIONS

### 5.6.1 PAM and BLOSUM

During the 1960s, Margaret Dayhoff [3] and her colleagues produced a set of substitution matrices based on global alignments of closely related protein sequences.

Dayhoff's *Atlas of Protein Structure* represented a monumental amount of work, much of which compared protein sequences. The notion of **point accepted mutation (PAM)** was proposed—a measure of divergence between sequences. 1 PAM is the amount of divergence that occurs when 1% of amino acids have changed. By extensive study, it is possible to devise Table 5.3, where the $(i,j)$ entry indicates the observed frequency with which the $i$th amino acid has been replaced by the $j$th. For example, since the A-A entry is .9867, experiment indicated that 98.67% of the alanines would have been conserved between the entire available set for which 1% of amino acids were observed to have changed. The A-S entry is .0028 and indicates that 0.28% of the alanines were replaced by serines in the same set.

The table was obtained by considering a large set of very similar sequences. They were pairwise-aligned (using a simple scoring method that worked well because the sequences were very similar) and then the occurrences of each amino

# TABLE 5.3  Observed frequencies of amino acid replacement during 1 PAM of divergence

|   | A | R | N | D | C | Q | E | G | H | I | L | K | M | F | P | S | T | W | Y | V |
|---|---|---|---|---|---|---|---|---|---|---|---|---|---|---|---|---|---|---|---|---|
| A | .9867 | .0002 | .0009 | .0010 | .0003 | .0008 | .0017 | .0021 | .0002 | .0006 | .0004 | .0002 | .0006 | .0002 | .0022 | .0035 | .0032 | .0000 | .0002 | .0018 |
| R | .0001 | .9913 | .0001 | .0000 | .0001 | .0010 | .0000 | .0000 | .0010 | .0003 | .0001 | .0019 | .0004 | .0001 | .0004 | .0006 | .0001 | .0008 | .0000 | .0001 |
| N | .0004 | .0001 | .9822 | .0036 | .0000 | .0004 | .0006 | .0006 | .0021 | .0003 | .0003 | .0025 | .0000 | .0001 | .0002 | .0020 | .0009 | .0001 | .0004 | .0001 |
| D | .0006 | .0000 | .0042 | .9859 | .0000 | .0006 | .0053 | .0006 | .0004 | .0001 | .0000 | .0003 | .0000 | .0000 | .0001 | .0005 | .0003 | .0000 | .0000 | .0001 |
| C | .0001 | .0001 | .0000 | .0000 | .9973 | .0000 | .0000 | .0000 | .0001 | .0001 | .0000 | .0000 | .0000 | .0000 | .0001 | .0005 | .0001 | .0000 | .0003 | .0002 |
| Q | .0003 | .0009 | .0004 | .0005 | .0000 | .9876 | .0027 | .0001 | .0023 | .0001 | .0003 | .0006 | .0004 | .0000 | .0006 | .0002 | .0002 | .0000 | .0000 | .0001 |
| E | .0010 | .0000 | .0007 | .0056 | .0000 | .0035 | .9865 | .0004 | .0002 | .0003 | .0001 | .0004 | .0001 | .0000 | .0003 | .0004 | .0002 | .0000 | .0001 | .0002 |
| G | .0021 | .0001 | .0012 | .0011 | .0000 | .0004 | .0007 | .9935 | .0001 | .0000 | .0001 | .0002 | .0001 | .0001 | .0003 | .0021 | .0003 | .0000 | .0000 | .0005 |
| H | .0001 | .0008 | .0018 | .0003 | .0001 | .0020 | .0001 | .0000 | .9912 | .0000 | .0001 | .0001 | .0000 | .0002 | .0003 | .0001 | .0001 | .0001 | .0004 | .0001 |
| I | .0002 | .0002 | .0003 | .0001 | .0002 | .0001 | .0003 | .0000 | .0000 | .9872 | .0009 | .0002 | .0012 | .0007 | .0000 | .0001 | .0007 | .0000 | .0001 | .0033 |
| L | .0003 | .0001 | .0003 | .0000 | .0000 | .0003 | .0001 | .0001 | .0004 | .0022 | .9947 | .0002 | .0045 | .0013 | .0003 | .0001 | .0003 | .0004 | .0002 | .0015 |
| K | .0002 | .0037 | .0025 | .0006 | .0000 | .0006 | .0004 | .0002 | .0002 | .0004 | .0001 | .9926 | .0020 | .0000 | .0003 | .0008 | .0011 | .0000 | .0001 | .0001 |
| M | .0001 | .0001 | .0000 | .0000 | .0000 | .0002 | .0000 | .0000 | .0000 | .0012 | .0045 | .0020 | .9874 | .0001 | .0000 | .0001 | .0002 | .0000 | .0000 | .0004 |
| F | .0001 | .0001 | .0001 | .0000 | .0000 | .0000 | .0000 | .0001 | .0002 | .0007 | .0013 | .0000 | .0004 | .9946 | .0000 | .0002 | .0001 | .0003 | .0028 | .0000 |
| P | .0013 | .0005 | .0002 | .0001 | .0001 | .0008 | .0003 | .0016 | .0001 | .0000 | .0003 | .0003 | .0000 | .0001 | .9926 | .0012 | .0004 | .0000 | .0000 | .0002 |
| S | .0028 | .0011 | .0034 | .0007 | .0011 | .0004 | .0006 | .0021 | .0001 | .0001 | .0001 | .0008 | .0001 | .0003 | .0017 | .9840 | .0038 | .0005 | .0002 | .0002 |
| T | .0022 | .0002 | .0013 | .0004 | .0001 | .0003 | .0002 | .0003 | .0001 | .0011 | .0002 | .0011 | .0004 | .0001 | .0005 | .0032 | .9871 | .0000 | .0002 | .0009 |
| W | .0000 | .0002 | .0000 | .0000 | .0001 | .0000 | .0000 | .0000 | .0000 | .0000 | .0004 | .0000 | .0000 | .0003 | .0000 | .0001 | .0000 | .9976 | .0002 | .0000 |
| Y | .0001 | .0000 | .0003 | .0000 | .0003 | .0000 | .0001 | .0000 | .0004 | .0001 | .0002 | .0001 | .0000 | .0021 | .0000 | .0001 | .0001 | .0002 | .9945 | .0001 |
| V | .0013 | .0002 | .0001 | .0001 | .0003 | .0002 | .0002 | .0003 | .0003 | .0057 | .0011 | .0001 | .0017 | .0001 | .0003 | .0002 | .0010 | .0000 | .0002 | .9901 |

W.J. Wilbur, "On the PAM matrix model of protein evolution," *Molecular Biology and Evolution*, 1985, Vol 2, 434–447, by permission of The Society for Molecular Biology and Evolution.

acid and how often it aligned with a different amino acid were counted. The counts were then converted into probabilities by scaling. Scaling is necessary because the definition of the PAM unit requires one accepted mutation per 100. It is necessary to weight the sum of all mutations by the frequency of occurrence of the mutating amino acid to ensure conformation with this standard.

Notice how the numbers in each column sum (within the accuracy of our table) to 1. This is because something must happen to each amino acid $i$: either it stays the same (probability given by the $i, i$ entry) or it is replaced by some other amino acid $j$ (probability given by the $j, i$ entry). Scaling has ensured that the sum of each diagonal element weighted by the frequency of occurrence of its corresponding amino acid amounts to 0.99. To the 1 accepted point mutation, this 0.99 represents the 99 "accepted nonmutations."

A key aspect of the use of PAM matrices in evolutionary studies is that successive powers of the original PAM-1 transition matrix provide expected transition probabilities for successive degrees of PAM divergence. If you multiply the PAM-1 matrix of Table 5.3 by itself, you obtain the PAM-2 matrix, whose entries indicate the frequencies with which one amino acid can be expected to be replaced by another over a period of divergence of 2 PAM units. By the time we take the 250th power of the PAM-1 matrix we will have measures of likelihoods of mutation of one amino acid to another over a period for which the PAM divergence measure[4] is 250.

Margaret Dayhoff used the PAM-$n$ matrices to derive a scoring scheme that has been used extensively for aligning sequences of amino acids. The key idea is that some matches are more frequently observed in nature than others. The same is true for some mismatches. The scoring method we have used since Section 5.4.2 assumes that all matches are equal and deserve the same reward. Also all mismatches are equally bad and deserve the same punishment. This is not so in real life. The PAM matrices offer some guidance on how to develop a scoring system that is relevant to biological observations. From a given PAM-$n$ transition matrix with entries $m_{i,j}$, Margaret Dayhoff derived a scoring matrix by forming

$$ s_{i,j} = \left\lceil 10 \log_{10} \frac{m_{i,j}}{p_j} \right\rceil $$

where $p_j$ is the frequency of occurrence of the amino acid $j$. The $\lceil$ and $\rceil$ notation indicates the "ceiling" function: one should round the enclosed quantity up, thereby guaranteeing an integer scoring matrix.

Exercise 5.22 asks you to modify your DotPlot program to make use of a scoring matrix. All that is necessary is to enter the scoring matrix into a two-dimensional array `score[20][20]`. The simple existing DotPlot program decides if an asterisk is placed in position $(i, j)$ depending on how many matches of corresponding characters from the substrings starting at $i$ and $j$ in each string

---

[4] We defined a PAM of divergence to be the amount of divergence that has occurred in order that 1% of amino acids have changed. You may be curious as to how 250% of the amino acids can be expected to have mutated! In truth, the definition does not generalize as-is; the definition itself needs to mutate. By the time we get to PAM-250 we should be clear that 250 PAM units is the amount of divergence needed so that each amino acid has, on average, undergone 2.5 mutations.

are contained in the window. Instead of counting 1 for a match and 0 for a mismatch, your new program will sum the values

```
score [string1.charAt[i+k], string2.charAt[j+k]]
```

for values of $k$ from 0 to w (i.e., within the window).

Similarly, your Needleman–Wunsch and Smith–Waterman programs can easily be adapted to use a scoring matrix like PAM250. All you have to do to modify your Needleman–Wunsch or Smith–Waterman programs to use a PAM scoring matrix is to enter the matrix into a two-dimensional array `score[20][20]`. Then, instead of adding `matchscore` or `mismatchscore` to compute a value for the variable `northwest`, you will do a lookup in the array `score` for the PAM score corresponding to the two amino acids being compared. You will encounter this task in slightly modified form in Exercise 5.24.

Another family of scoring matrices is based on the work of Jorja and Steven Heniko [8]. BLOSUM (a contraction of *blocks* *substitution* *matrix*) matrices are based on the frequencies with which pairs of amino acids are aligned with each other in multiple alignments of well-conserved portions within protein families. We will discuss multiple alignments in Section 5.9.

The number following BLOSUM (e.g., 62 in BLOSUM 62) indicates that a weighting has been applied normalizing for pairs of sequences that are 62% or more identical. Whereas higher numbered PAM matrices are more appropriate for comparing more distantly related sequences, the reverse is true for the BLOSUM family. More distant relatedness calls for *lower numbered* BLOSUM matrices.

Most programs for alignment of protein sequences allow the user to choose from a menu of PAM and BLOSUM matrices. The algorithmic aspect of alignment is fixed. Choices in scoring schemes for matches, mismatches, and indels should be made with an understanding of biological and evolutionary considerations. Whereas computer scientists would like precise definitions of quality of alignment, biology requires versatile programs that can use different criteria depending on evolutionary distance and other considerations.

Computer scientists can learn from this. Although a mundane program like the Unix utility `diff` might seem straightforward, the truly curious will appreciate the ability to customize the comparison of two files. For example, the differences of interest between version 7.1 and 7.2 of an established program are probably minor, and a `diff` program needs to be very sensitive and point out all the differences no matter how minor. But if you're comparing version 4.0 and 7.8 you will be overwhelmed by trivial differences and won't see the big picture unless you can tune the utility so it emphasizes the major changes and downplays the trivial.

## 5.7   SPACE/TIME ANALYSIS OF DYNAMIC PROGRAMMING ALGORITHMS

The Needleman–Wunsch and Smith–Waterman algorithms both work by filling in $n \times m$ arrays of numbers in a systematic and progressive manner. It is not difficult to deduce that both algorithms require $O(nm)$ runtime and $O(nm)$ memory. For gene sequences, $m$ and $n$ are likely to be hundreds to tens of thousands in magnitude. Even in the tens of thousands, *mn* is still only hundreds of millions, so the algorithms will have runtimes of the order of seconds and storage requirements well within the range of modern computers.

For focused comparisons of sequences of lengths in the hundreds or tens of thousands, therefore, the dynamic programming algorithms are eminently practical. Time and memory problems, however, may arise when it is necessary to compare one sequence of interest with a very large selection of the sequences within some large collection. Millions of sequences are possible in the collection, and the dynamic programming programs would then need runtimes of perhaps millions of seconds. A million seconds is almost 2 weeks. Runtimes of this length mean problems.

# 5.8  HEURISTIC APPROACHES: FastA AND BLAST

A heuristic approach uses past experience to select portions of the inputs to guide decision making when it is not possible to explore all the possibilities. It is a way of reducing the search space using "hunches." Aligning a newly discovered sequence with a collection of known sequences in a large data bank is a case in point. We saw earlier that the dynamic programming approaches of the Needleman–Wunsch and Smith–Waterman programs may be too slow.

## 5.8.1  A Worked Example: Bill Gates at Ballgames

As we know, the alignment problem consists of searching a two dimensional-space as constructed by a DotPlot program for the longest more-or-less diagonal line of dots. To align **BILLGATES** with **ATBALLGAMES** requires exploring a $11 \times 9$ grid looking for a largely diagonal line.

```
   B I L L G A T E S
A            *
T              *
B  *
A            *
L    * *
L    * *
G      *
A        *
M
E                *
S                  *
```

In general, the dynamic programming methods will visit every one of *mn* locations in an $m \times n$ field. Can we impart any insights, intuitions, or pieces of wisdom to the program so as to eliminate vast tracts of this field?

In 1980, William Pearson described the FastA suite of programs. FastA does exactly what we have been describing: It uses an insight (technically we speak of a heuristic) to eliminate vast tracts of the search space. The cost is that we may as a result miss the best alignment. But with a good heuristic, that risk should be minimal.

FastA begins by selecting a tuple size $k$. Let's say we pick a tuple size of 2 for our BILLGATES–ATBALLGAMES alignment problem. Then our 2-tuples are:

- in BILLGATES — BI IL LL LG GA AT TE and ES
- in ATBALLGAMES — AT TB BA AL LL LG GA AM ME and ES

We'll consider BILLGATES to be our **specimen** string and ATBALLGAMES to be our **database string**. FastA calculates a numerical value for each $k$-tuple in the specimen. Exercise 5.25 asks you to do this for amino acids. For the purposes of our BILLGATES–ATBALLGAMES example, we'll calculate a number for each single letter that is its position in the alphabet: A is 0, B is 1, etc. For a 2-tuple $xy$ we'll take 26 times the number for $x$ added to the number for $y$. So the numerical values for BILLGATES in our example are:

- in BILLGATES — 34 219 297 292 156 19 498 and 122

FastA associates with each $k$-tuple a number indicating its position in the string. Now for our BILLGATES example, the values and positions are:

- in BILLGATES — 34:0 219:1 297:2 292:3 156:4 19:5 498:6 and 122:7

FastA proceeds to investigate the database string (ATBALLGAMES in our example). For each 2-tuple, it computes the numerical value and figures out a set of offsets indicating how far off the main diagonal it is from any k-tuple in the specimen string.

The first 2-tuple AT has value 19, occurs at position 0 in the database string and at position 5 in the specimen for an offset of $-5$. Looking at the 2-tuple TB, we calculate its numerical value is $26 \times 19 + 1$ or 495. It happens there is no 495 value in the specimen string, so the set of offsets for TB is empty. Similarly BA and AL contribute no offset. But LL (position 4 in the database string) has the numerical value of 297, which does exist with position 2 in the specimen string. This gives an offset of 2.

In this way, FastA counts how many times each possible offset occurs.

A diagonal of asterisks in the dotplot corresponds to a large number of identical offsets. A near-diagonal in the dotplot corresponds to a large number of offsets fairly close to each other. The heuristic behind FastA is to begin a dynamic programming search in areas corresponding to offsets that occur very frequently. Exercise 5.26 takes you through the first few steps of the FastA process.

When you've done that, you'll appreciate that this $O(n)$ algorithm identifies the diagonals with the highest numbers of matches along them. The rest of the program will join up some of the diagonals, allowing for gaps and rescoring according to some scoring matrix. Except in the most pathological and extremely unlikely contrived cases, the entire stitching process is easily bound above by $O(n)$.

In 1990, the original paper [1] on the basic local alignment search tool (BLAST), authored by Stephen Altschul and colleagues, appeared in the *Journal of Molecular Biology.* ScienceWatch [17] reports that it is the third most cited paper in the two decades from 1983 through 2003.

Similar to FastA, BLAST applies a heuristic to reduce the search space. Instead of seeking exact matches of $k$-tuples BLAST preprocesses the $k$-tuples to extend the specimen's set of $k$-tuples to include more $k$-tuples that are within a certain threshold of scoring of occurring in the specimen. For example, if the user chooses to use the PAM250 scoring matrix, and if the 2-tuple MM occurs in the specimen, then BLAST would add to the 2-tuple set any 2-tuple whose PAM250 score with MM is at least some threshold value. If the threshold value is, say 9, then the 2-tuples ML and LM would be added because their PAM250 score with MM is 10 according to this small extract from the PAM250 table:

|   | I | L | K | M |
|---|---|---|---|---|
| I | 5 | 2 | −2 | 2 |
| L | 2 | 6 | −3 | 4 |
| K | −2 | −3 | 5 | 0 |
| M | 2 | 4 | 0 | 6 |

Like FastA, BLAST begins by applying its heuristic so that its subsequent action works only with a segment of size $O(n)$ of the original search space (size $O(mn)$). There is a very small possibility of missing the best alignment. In practice that possibility is negligible.

Both FastA and BLAST are now capable of estimating the statistical relevance of the alignments they find. The computations involved are straightforward and if you are interested in developing your own programs, you should study the statistics involved.


## 5.9 MULTIPLE ALIGNMENTS

A traveler in Scotland once remarked "It's just like Wales but there's more of it." Both of these Celtic countries have extensive difficult mountainous terrain that for centuries enabled them to maintain their identities apart from the English invaders. Scotland is that much larger than Wales, its mountains are a tad higher, and its features are somewhat more extensive.

So it is with multiple alignment. It's just like pairwise alignment, but there's more of it. To align two sequences, you try to find a way to write them one above the other, perhaps admitting some gaps, so that you can see their connectedness. For example

```
ACC-GGCA--TTAC
-CCAG--ATTTT-C
```

is a fairly decent alignment of the sequences ACCGGCATTAC and CCA-GATTTTC.

Multiple alignment is a similar concept, only there are more than two sequences that need to be simultaneously compared. What do you think of

```
ACCGTTA-CCATAC
A--GTTTA-CAT-C
TCCGATT--CAGAC
AC-GTATACCCG-G
```

as an alignment between the four sequences ACCGTTACCATAC, AGTTTACATC, TCCGATTCAGAC, ACGTATACCCGG? How would you measure the goodness of the alignment? Just as in the pairwise alignment case, one way to do this is to add up the total agreement/disagreement in each column. You need to decide a score for a match, a score for a mismatch, and a score for an indel. It's just like pairwise alignment, but there's more of it! If you have sequences of amino acids to multiply align, the ideas are similar. But you may want to take into account an evolutionarily based scoring matrix such as PAM or BLOSUM. There are many ways to count up the scores in each column. Probably the simplest and most believable is to add up all the scores for all the pairs that occur in a column. For the first column of the previous alignment, you need a score for each of the pairs AA, AT, AA, AT, AA, and TA. In general, if $k$ sequences are being aligned, there will be $\binom{k}{2}$ pairs that need to be considered.

We've dealt with how to score a multiple alignment. It's just like scoring a pairwise alignment, but there are several pairs to score and sum in each column instead of just one. Next we need to consider how to find good alignments.

In the case of two sequences DotPlots presented a useful visual technique. We wrote one sequence along the $x$-axis, the other along the $y$-axis. We draw a dot at any point $(x_0, y_0)$ where the $x_0$th member of the first sequence matches the $y_0$th member of the second. Or we can ask for many matches or a threshold of numbers of matches within a window just as we did in Section 5.3.

When we have several sequences we need to progress to higher dimensions. Not too bad for a multiple alignment of three sequences: We just write each of the sequences along the $x$-axis, the $y$-axis, and the $z$-axis. We'll place dots at any point $(x_0, y_0, z_0)$ where the corresponding members of the sequences match. Then we look for linear clusters in the three-dimensional space.

Beyond three sequences, it's harder for us humans to visualize the multi-dimensional dotplots that arise in the obvious way. But we can write computer programs either to help us with the visualization or to locate likely looking linear clusters. If you think about it, such programs would just be fairly easy extensions of the part of the FastA algorithm that looked for frequently occurring offsets.

DotPlots, FastA, and BLAST all generalize to the multiple-alignment scenario in fairly straightforward ways. They just become bigger! The Smith–Waterman dynamic programming algorithm also generalizes. Recall that the

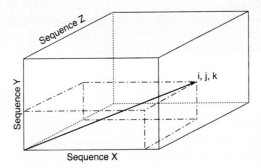

**FIGURE 5.10**   The dynamic programming approach to alignment of two sequences requires a two-dimensional array to be filled with values. A multiple alignment of three sequences X, Y, Z will fill a three-dimensional array. The entry at (i, j, k) will be the score of the best multiple alignment of the subsequences X.substring(0,i), Y.substring(0,j) and Z.substring(0,k).

pairwise alignment version of the Smith–Waterman program keeps track of partial alignments from three directions: north, west, and northwest. The relevant part of the code is:

```
if (x.charAt(col-1)==y.charAt(row-1))
   northwest = scoreArray[row-1][col-1] + matchscore;
else northwest = scoreArray[row-1][col-1] + mismatchscore;
west = scoreArray[row][col-1] + gapscore;
north = scoreArray[row-1][col] + gapscore;
best = northwest;
if (north>best) best = north;
if (west>best) best = west;
scoreArray[row][col] = best;
```

For aligning two sequences, you needed to keep track of alignment scores in the 2-dimensional array scoreArray. For $k$ sequences you will need a $k$-dimensional scoreArray. In two dimensions, you picked the best of three calculated scores west, north, and northwest. To align $k$ sequences you will need to pick the best of $2^k - 1$ calculated scores. Same algorithmic idea, it's just that there's more of it! Figure 5.10 indicates this idea when $k = 3$.

Notice that the running time of the generalized Smith–Waterman algorithm posited earlier increases exponentially with the number of sequences being multiply aligned. That's because to fill each entry of an increasingly dimensioned array takes $O(2^k)$ computations. In each sequence of length $n$, there are $n^k$ entries to be computed. Overall, therefore, the generalization of the two-dimensional pairwise alignment programs to work with $k$ sequences, although fairly straightforward, will have running time bounded by $O(2^k n^k)$. The dynamic programming approach to multiple alignment quickly becomes infeasible for realistic sequences.

Because of this, most practical multiple-alignment programs adopt a pragmatic approach. It can be summed up in the following gross approximation to an algorithm:

```
begin with a set of k objects
    -- the k sequences you want to multiply align;
repeat {
  pick the 2 most similar objects;
  replace them with a consensus object;
} until there is only one object
```

### 5.9.1 A Worked Example

Let's apply that algorithm to form a multiple alignment of the four sequences $S_1$ = ACCGTTACCATAC, $S_2$ = AGTTTACATC, $S_3$ = TCCGATTCAGAC, and $S_4$ = ACGTATACCCGG.

First we need to decide which are the two most similar objects. For this purpose we compute an alignment score for each of the possible pairs.

Using a scoring system of 0 for a match and 1 for a mismatch or indel, we can form the pairwise scores for each possible pairwise matching:

|       | $S_1$ | $S_2$ | $S_3$ | $S_4$ |
|-------|-------|-------|-------|-------|
| $S_1$ |       | 5     | 5     | 6     |
| $S_2$ |       |       | 7     | 6     |
| $S_3$ |       |       |       | 8     |
| $S_4$ |       |       |       |       |

With this scoring of course, less is better, so the best alignment occurs between $S_1$ and $S_2$ with a score of 5. Actually, the score between $S_1$ and $S_3$ is equally good, but we are allowed to decide ties arbitrarily. An alignment between $S_1$ and $S_2$ that scores 5 is:

```
ACCGTT-ACCATAC
A--GTTTAC-AT-C
```

and a resulting consensus sequence is ACCGTTTACCATAC. We have simply replaced gaps by the corresponding nucleotide in the other sequence. This is by no means the only way to proceed; it's one of many plausible interpretations of "consensus."

Now we're reduced to the problem of multiply aligning the consensus object ACCGTTTACCATAC with the original $S_3$ and $S_4$. We seek the best pairwise alignment among these three objects:

|                | $consensus_{12}$ | $S_3$ | $S_4$ |
|----------------|------------------|-------|-------|
| $consensus_{12}$ |                |       | 5     | 6 |
| $S_3$          |                  |       | 8     |
| $S_4$          |                  |       |       |

The best alignment is between the consensus object and $S_3$.

```
ACCGTTTACCATAC
TCCGATT--CAGAC
```

The new consensus is XCCGXTTACCAYAC, where X is a symbol meaning half A and half T, Y is a symbol meaning half G and half T. Gaps have just been filled as before. Now we're down to just two objects: the new consensus and the original $S_4$. We have to modify the global alignment procedure so it can take care of hybrid symbols like X and Y. Basically the score for X and another nucleotide will be the average of the score that A would fetch and that T would fetch. So here's an alignment of XCCGXTTACCAYAC and ACGTATACCCGG:

```
XCCGXTTACCAYAC
AC-GTATACCCGG-
```

It scores

- 0.5 for the X and A mismatch
- 1 for the C and − for the gap
- 0.5 for the second X and T mismatch
- 1 for the following T and A mismatch
- 1 for the A and C mismatch
- 0.5 for the Y and G mismatch
- 2 more for the final two positions (a mismatch and a gap)

for a total of 6.5. We obtain the corresponding multiple alignment by "undoing" the consensus building:

```
                                            ACCGTT-ACCATAC
                       ACCGTTTACCATAC       A--GTTTAC-AT-C
XCCGXTTACCAYAC         TCCGATT--CAGAC       TCCGATT--CAGAC
AC-GTATACCCGG-         AC-GTATACCCGG-       AC-GTATACCCGG-
```

At the beginning of this section, we postulated

```
ACCGTT-ACCATAC
A--GTTTAC-AT-C
TCCGATT--CAGAC
AC-GTATACCCGG-
```

as a multiple alignment between these four sequences. The algorithm we just described led us to:

```
ACCGTTA-CCATAC
A--GTTTA-CAT-C
TCCGATT--CAGAC
AC-GTATACCCG-G
```

Which do you like better? Technically, we don't know which is better. So much depends on your choice of scoring method.

Most practical algorithms for multiple alignment work roughly like this: They perform lots of pairwise alignments, and from those they create a larger multiple alignment using some form of consensus-building to extend pairwise alignments to ever-increasing numbers of sequences. The choice of which pairs of original sequences to start with is often directed by a guide tree. The **guide tree** for the rough algorithm we described is built up as the algorithm executes. It starts by conjoining nodes corresponding to the two nearest neighbors among the original sequences into a new fork consisting of a consensus and its two children. It proceeds to conjoin pairs of near objects (be they original sequences or consensuses) into new forks until only one object remains. That object's structure is the guide tree associated with our process. Its leaves are the original sequences, and its internal nodes are consensus-formed at different stages of the process. The root of the tree corresponds to the final "grand consensus" of all the original sequences.

Different multiple-alignment algorithms differ mainly in their generation of guide tree and in their notions of consensus. Exercise 5.27 asks you to investigate this idea further.

## 5.9.2 Analysis of Multiple-Alignment Algorithms

The natural generalization of dynamic programming pairwise alignment to deal with $k$ sequences, as we noted earlier, requires $O(2^k n^k)$. Some improvements have been proposed over the years, but essentially we observe that exact alignment of large numbers of sequences is not feasible.

The practical algorithms essentially start with a pairwise alignment of two sequences and then continue to add to the alignment by repeatedly performing pairwise alignments, sometimes between sequences but often involving intermediate consensus objects. They start with $k$ objects and continue performing pairwise alignments until only one object remains. Each pairwise alignment reduces the number of objects by 1. Thus $k - 1$ pairwise alignments are required. Additionally, the practical algorithms need to construct a guide tree or otherwise decide an order for performing the individual pairwise alignments. Typically, this requires evaluating about $\binom{k}{2}$ pairwise alignments. Since this is bounded by $k^2$, we conclude that the inexact but practical algorithms for multiple alignment will have running times approximately $k^2$ times the running times of the pairwise alignment methods they employ.

Since both BLAST and FastA are close to $O(n)$ in their running times for sequences of length $n$, we conclude that algorithms such as T-Coffee and ClustalW are likely to run in time proportional to $k^2 n$.

### Multiple Sequence Alignments and HIV

Why might you want to build a multiple-sequence alignment? We ask for pairwise alignments to learn whether a newly sequenced portion of a genome resembles anything we have already sequenced. In multiple sequence alignments, we are asking if a given sequence resembles a family of other sequences, all of which share some similarity.

A key idea here is the notion of "relationship": we assume that sequences that share similarity are related in evolutionary history. We will explore this in much greater detail in Chapter 6. For now, let us take it for granted that if two or more sequences are similar, then they share an evolutionary history. With this assumption, we can use multiple sequence alignments to try and understand the origins of HIV.

HIV is a virus specific to humans, but it appears to be closely related to several viruses that infect other primates, and monkeys. The most similar virus to HIV is known as simian immunodeficiency virus, or SIV. SIV infects a wide range of primates, including chimpanzees, which are thought to be our closest nonhuman relatives. So it makes sense to expect that SIV in chimpanzees (known as SIVcpz) might be related to HIV. Can we prove that this is the case, however?

The actual details of the experiment that demonstrated the relationship between HIV and SIVcpz are quite involved, and you can read the full account here [6]. In brief, however, researchers identified a chimpanzee that appeared to have an immune response to HIV, even though this animal had never been exposed to HIV. When they analyzed viral sequences extracted from some of the chimp's tissues, they discovered that the animal had been infected with a strain of SIVcpz. To determine whether this strain of SIVcpz was similar to HIV, the researchers sequenced the strain of SIVcpz and, using a multiple-alignment program known as ClustalX (a more recent version of ClustalW mentioned earlier), attempted to align it to known sequences of HIV. Although there were some differences, the similarities were striking, suggesting that this strain of SIVcpz could be the ancestral origin of HIV in humans. A small portion of the sequence alignment between SIVcpz strains and HIV strains is shown in Figure 5.11 derived from [12].

The researchers used this sequence alignment to build an evolutionary tree of how SIVcpz could have given rise to HIV, but that will be discussed in more detail in the next chapter. As you will see in the ensuing chapters, sequence alignments are the foundation for much of the analysis of genomes.

```
A1.TZ.01.A341_AY253314     1 MAGRSGS--S-D-EE--LLR-AIRTIKILYESNP-YP----KPRG
B.AU.x.1181_AF538302       1 MAGRSGG--S-D-ED--LLK-TVRLIKQLYQSNP-PP----SPEG
O.SN.99.SEMP1300_AJ302647  1 MAGRS-D--G-D-QP--LLR-AIQIIKILYQSNP-HPX--XPTTG
CPZ.CD.x.ANT_U42720        1 MAGREEL--E-G-TDXXQLLKAVKIIKILYQSNP-YP----KPAG
CPZ.CM.x.CAM3_AF115393     1 MAGRSEG--D-D-DAXXLLQ-AVRIIKVLYS-NP-YP----DNKG
CPZ.CM.98.CAM5_AJ271369    1 MAGRSEG--D-E-DTXXLLQ-AVRIIKILYD-NP-YP----DNKG
CPZ.GA.x.CPZGAB_X52154     1 MAGRSEP--Q-D-DAXXLLQ-AVKIIKILYQSNP-YP----SPEG
```

**FIGURE 5.11**   A multiple sequence alignment of some strains of SIVcpz and HIV show enough sequence conservation to suggest that SIVcpz and HIV share a common ancestral viral genome. The human strains begin with the letters A1, B, and O. The chimp SIV strains begin with CPZ in the first column. From http://www.hiv.lanl.gov/content/hiv-db/ALIGN_CURRENT/ALIGN-INDEX.html. (Courtesy of data derived from http://www.hiv.lanl.gov/cgi-bin/NEWALIGN/align.cgi)

## 5.10 EXERCISES FOR CHAPTER 5

**Exercise 5.1** Modify the naïve pattern-matcher program so that it reads the target string from a file whose name can be entered on the command line.

**Exercise 5.2** Extend your program from Exercise 5.1 so that it can print out data about its own working and operation. In particular, have it count the number of comparisons it performs between characters. See if you can figure out any relationship between the number of compares and the lengths of the strings and the size of the underlying alphabet. This exercise asks you to empirically analyze your program by means of **instrumenting.** It is a valid and worthwhile technique for evaluating an algorithm and deciding if devising a more efficient program is worthwhile. Exercises 5.3 and 5.4 will guide you through more traditional methods of algorithm performance analysis.

**Exercise 5.3** Write a program to input three numbers and evaluate formula 5.1 (page 163).

1. Use your program to analyze the growth of the number of comparisons with the length of the pattern when the alphabet consists of just one letter. In other words, run your program with the $n$ input set to 10,000, the $k$ input set to 1, and let the $m$ input range from 1 to 10. How does the number of comparisons vary with $m$? How does this compare with the worst-case analysis of the naïve algorithm?

2. Use your program to analyze the growth of the number of comparisons with the length of the pattern when the alphabet consists of two letters. In other words, run your program with the $n$ input set to 10,000, the $k$ input set to 2, and let the $m$ input range from 1 to 10. How does the number of comparisons vary with $m$? How does this compare with the worst-case analysis of the naïve algorithm? How does it compare with the best-case analysis?

3. The nucleotide alphabet consists of four symbols. Repeat the preceding experiments with the $k$ input set to 4.

4. Repeat your experiments with the amino acid alphabet (20 symbols) and the English alphabet (26 letters, upper- and lowercase, together with punctuation).

**Exercise 5.4** Instead of using a program to evaluate formula 5.1, see if you can create a closed form expression for the sum. (*Hint:* You can use your calculus knowledge to differentiate the formula for the sum of a geometric series. If you have not studied calculus, skip this exercise!)

Perform an online search for fast pattern-matching algorithms. Look in particular for animations that can help you understand their method of working. Decide which is your favorite. Find an implementation of your favorite, and then devise an experiment to compare its performance with that of the naïve algorithm. Place your experiment within a practical context that appeals to you. For example, if you are interested in stop codons within the worm's genome, design an experiment to compare the pattern matchers' ability to help you locate them.

**Exercise 5.5**

Produce dynamic programming matrices for ACCTGCTAC and TCCAGCTTC using the scoring scheme 4 for a match, −1 for a mismatch, −2 for an indel. Check your calculations by running NW.java.

Now repeat using 5 for a match, 0 for a mismatch, −4 for an indel. Check your calculations by modifying NW.java (three small changes is all you need) and running it.

**Exercise 5.6**

Produce a dynamic programming matrix for ACCTGCTAC and TCCAGCTTC, using the distance measure (0 for a match, +1 for either a mismatch or an indel). Check your answer by modifying NW.java and running it.

**Exercise 5.7**

Write your own NW1 using the auxiliary array fromWhere so that you print out an optimal alignment of your command line arguments. It should behave thus:

**Exercise 5.8**

```
>java NW1 ACGTCGT GCACGTA
java NW1 ACGTCGT GCACGTA
   0  -2  -4  -6  -8 -10 -12 -14
  -2  -1  -3   0  -2  -4  -6  -8
  -4  -3   3   1  -1   2   0  -2
  -6   0   1   2   0   0   1  -1
  -8  -2   4   2   1   4   2   0
 -10  -4   2   8   6   4   8   6
 -12  -6   0   6  12  10   8  12
 -14  -8  -2   4  10  11   9  10
ACGTCGT-
GCA-CGTA
```

Here are some suggestions:

1. 
```
// define some constants:
public static final int NOTDEF = 0;
public static final int FROMNW = 1;
public static final int FROMN = 2;
public static final int FROMW = 3;

// define the score array:
private int[][] scoreArray;
// and the direction array:
private int[][] fromWhere;
// will hold values
NOTDEF, FROMNW, FROMN or FROMW
```

2. Then find the portion of code where the `scoreArray` entries are made. At the same time you make those entries, it should be possible to make the correct entry in the `fromWhere` array.

3. Finally, here is code to generate the alignments. Fill in the gaps. Assume you have instance variables `xalig` and `yalig` that have been declared as `Strings`

```
int row = _____; // Start row and col
int col = _____; // in the bottom right corner
xalig = "";            // Initialize the alignments
yalig = "";
while (_____) { // condition for continuing in loop
        if (fromWhere[row][col] == FROMN) {
            // came from north
            xalig = "-" + xalig;
            yalig = y.charAt(row-1) + yalig;
            row--;
        }
        else if (fromWhere[row][col] == FROMW) {
            // came from west
            xalig = x.charAt(col-1) + xalig;
            yalig = "-" + yalig;
            col--;
        }
        else {
            if(fromWhere[row][col]!=FROMNW) // ERROR -- just print warning
                System.out.println("Goofy row col "+ row+" "+col);
            xalig = x.charAt(col-1) + xalig;
            yalig = y.charAt(row-1) + yalig;
            col--;
            row--;
        }
    }
}
```

Rewrite your previous program so it finds the best local alignment between the two sequences. You will need to ensure that you never create a negative score (that's the essential difference between local alignment and global). Following is a list of some code hints that you may use if you wish. When you have completed this exercise, you will have programmed the Smith–Waterman algorithm for local sequence alignment. Your output should match (or be better than):

**Exercise 5.9**

```
> java SW ACTACT GTAC
   0  0  0  0  0  0  0
   0  0  0  0  0  0  0
   0  0  0  2  0  0  2
   0  2  0  0  4  2  0
   0  0  4  2  2  6  4
Best (row,col) is (4,5)
Match ACTACT from 2 to 4
with GTAC from 1 to 3
TAC
|||
TAC
```

*Hints:*

```
// Instance variables
   private int bestrow, bestcol;   // for location of best entry
   private int bestval;            // for best entry
   private int startrow, startcol; // for location of start of alignment
...
// As you're filling the score-array:
if (best > bestval) {
   bestval = best;
   bestrow = row;
   bestcol = col;
// Your alignment will end at (bestrow, bestcol)
// which is where your backtracking will start
```

Modify your program to accept its sequences from files whose names are entered on the command line. For example, to align the sequences in file1.txt and file2.txt you will type

**Exercise 5.10**

```
java SWFile file1.txt file2.txt
```

Because you are now able to handle large inputs, you will want to modify the way you print out the alignments. I would suggest printing out

*(continued)*

BASESPERLINE characters from the first sequence (or -'s), followed by BASESPERLINE alignment symbols

```
X | -
```

followed by BASESPERLINE characters from the second sequence (or -'s), all on separate lines, followed by a blank line before the next cluster. For example, with BASESPERLINE set to 60, some of your output might look like:

```
ABCDEFJASDLKFJKLDAJFKLJELAHRJKRHJTHZHGJKDFHKJ--------HKLHKJR
|||||||||--------||||||||||||||X|||||||||||--------X||||||
ABCDEFJAS--------AJFKLJELAHRJKRHKTHZHGJKDFHKJAIOEWREFDKLHKJR

EHTKLWEHTLKHKLJHKFSDHKGLJHASDJFJASJHDFLH--------------ASDHFJ
||||||||||||||||||X|||||||||||||||||||||--------------X|||||
EHTKLWEHTLKHKLJHKFSCHKGLJHASDJFJASJHDFLHAADSFLDJFLJASDJSDHFJ

KSDHFKJHDSAHFKJDHHFSKDHFKJHDSKJFHDKSHFKJHSADHKJ--ERIOTRBKJSB
|||X||||||||||||||||||||||||||||||----------------||--||||X||||||
KSDAFKJHDSAHFKJDHHFSKDHFKJHDS---------------KJFHERIOSRBKJSB

ADKFDKEIIREITREWRTVNMNVHCNBEYFDHDUYJDFHUASDBHFKJADFHALJDHFAD
|||||||---||||||||||||||||||X|||||||||||XXX||||||||||||||||||||
ADKFDKE---EITREWRTVNMNVHCNBFYFDHDUYJDFHUUUNBHFKJADFHALJDHFAD

---AFJDALKHKDHALHDKHKAJHAHDKFHKJADHKLAHFKJHADHFJOIEO--------
---X|||||||||X|||||||||||||||||||||||||||||X|||||--------
AALLFJDALKHKDHBLHDKHKAJHAHDKFHKJADHKLAHFKJHADIFJOIEOANKLDALL

------JRKLWEIFLLDSIJLASNDLNFAKHDKJANJDNFKLANKDNFKADNK
------||||||||||||||||||--------------||||||||||X||||||
DJDLFKJRKLWEIFLLDSIJLA--------------JDNFKLANKDMFKADNK
```

---

**Exercise 5.11**    Write a program to input:

- A list of names of states,
- A list of characters in an alphabet,
- The name of one of the states to serve as the start state
- The names of some of the states to serve as final states
- A transition matrix

The output should consist of two things:

- A picture of the DFA that has just been input (like Figure 5.2), and
- a Java program that is equivalent to that DFA

Show that the Needleman–Wunsch algorithm with the general gap penalty $g(x)$ depending on length $x$ of gap takes time $O(mn(m + n))$, where $m$ and $n$ are the lengths of the two sequences. *Hint:* Show that the $N$ and $W$ entries take time $O(m + n)$ to compute.

**Exercise 5.12**

Implement the Needleman–Wunsch algorithm with affine gap penalties. Perform experiments to compare its performance with the program of Figure 5.7. Run both programs on several pairs of inputs with different lengths and see if there is a simple correlation between the running times of both programs.

**Exercise 5.13**

What values for gap initiation penalty ($s$) and gap continuation penalty ($c$) would make the Needleman–Wunsch program with affine gap penalties equivalent to the original Needleman–Wunsch program of Figure 5.7?

**Exercise 5.14**

Construct a DFA to accept no strings. (*Hint:* Any DFA that can continue regardless of result but which has no final states will do. But then so will any DFA that makes no transitions. All DFAs need a start state, but an empty transition matrix is acceptable.) Next construct a DFA to accept just the empty string $\epsilon$ and nothing else. (*Hint:* It's very similar to, but not quite the same as, the first DFA. What's the difference?) For each character x of the alphabet, construct a DFA to accept the set $\{x\}$. Finally, given two DFAs, the first accepting set $R_1$ and the second accepting set $R_2$, how would you connect them to form a new DFA that accepts the concatenation $R_1 R_2$?

**Exercise 5.15**

In Chapter 7 we will study ways to discover genes in genomes. A feature of eukaryotic genes is introns, segments within genes that are not themselves translated. The 5′ end of an intron is marked by a GT pair and the 3′ end by an AG pair. A regular expression representing this oversimplified notion of intron is easily seen to be GT (A + C + G + T )* AG. See if you can build a DFA to recognize such an intron. The action of your DFA should be to terminate in a final state after the first occurrence of such an intron. Once you have drawn your DFA, write a program based on it (as described in the text) to be a single-scan search program for an intron.

**Exercise 5.16**

**Exercise 5.17**  Construct DFAs to accept each of the following sets:

1. The set of strings of symbols acgt that start with three as.
2. The set of strings of symbols acgt that end in three as.
3. The set of strings of symbols acgt that contain three consecutive as.
4. The set of strings of symbols acgt that do not contain three consecutive as.

**Exercise 5.18**  Run the DotPlot program with the following inputs. Explain the visual features you observe in the output in terms of sequence features in the input strings.

1. aaaaaaaaaaaaabbbbbbbbb and aaaaaaaabbbbbbbbbbbbbb
2. abcdefghijkpqrstuvwxyz and abcdefghijklmnopqrstuvwxyz
3. forwards and sdrawrof

**Exercise 5.19**  Modify the code in DotPlot.java so that the resulting program, let's call it DotPlotWindow, will accept an extra integer on the command line. The command

```
java DotPlot 1000011010101000 1010111000000001010001010 3
```

should produce a grid of blanks and asterisks, with asterisks only appearing at positions where three consecutive characters of each string match.

**Exercise 5.20**  Modify the code in DotPlot.java to produce a more sensitive program. It should place an asterisk in any position corresponding to a vowel in each string, even though the vowels may not be the same. Call the new program SensitiveDotPlot. It should perform like this:

```
java SensitiveDotPlot culler color
   c u l l e r
c  *
o     *       *
l        *  *
o     *       *
r              *
```

In the text we found an optimal alignment for CACGA and CATTGA using a scoring scheme of +2 for a match, 0 for a mismatch, and −1 for an indel. We found

```
CAC-GA
||| ||
CATTGA
```

Find another alignment with the same global score.

Modify your existing dotplot program to use a PAM scoring matrix for comparing two sequences of amino acids. You should be able to set a window size and a threshold so that, whenever the summed PAM scores of corresponding amino acids within a window exceed the threshold, an asterisk is output for the top left point of the windows; otherwise leave it blank. A portion of the PAM250 scoring matrix is:

|   | I | L | K | M |
|---|---|---|---|---|
| I | 5 | 2 | −2 | 2 |
| L | 2 | 6 | −3 | 4 |
| K | −2 | −3 | 5 | 0 |
| M | 2 | 4 | 0 | 6 |

Use Google or any search engine to help you find a complete listing of PAM250. When plotting MMMM against MILK with a window size of 1 and a threshold of 3, we obtain

```
 MMMM
M****
I
L****
K
```

because M against M and L against M both score more than the threshold 3. Likewise with a window of 2 and a threshold of 5, we obtain

```
 MMMM
M***
I***
L
K
```

because MI against MM and IL against MM both score more than the threshold 5, whereas LK against MM scores a total of 4 which is below the threshold.

When you have completed your program, use it on sections of HIV 1 and 2, and find values for window and threshold that give good diagonal dotplots for similar sections.

**Exercise 5.23**    The PAM250 scoring matrix is appropriate for comparing sequences where approximately 250 point-accepted mutations may have occurred for every 100 positions.

1. Is PAM250 a good scoring matrix for HIV 1 and 2? Why or why not?
2. Would you obtain a better diagonal dotplot in Exercise 5.22 by using a smaller numbered PAM like PAM2? Why?
3. Would you obtain a better diagonal dotplot in Exercise 5.22 by using a larger numbered PAM like PAM500? Why?

**Exercise 5.24**    Modify your Needleman–Wunsch or Smith–Waterman program to use BLOSUM 62. Compare sections of HIV 1 and 2. Would another BLOSUM matrix be more appropriate for comparing these sequences? Why?

**Exercise 5.25**    Write a program to give a numerical value to a $k$-tuple of amino acids. Each single amino acid $a$ should be associated with a number $n(a)$ in the range 0 to 19. The tuple $a_1 a_2 \ldots a_k$ should have the value $20^{k-1} n(a_1) + 20^{k-2} n(a_2) + \ldots + n(a_k)$.

**Exercise 5.26**    In this exercise, you will code the early stages of the FastA algorithm in Java, mainly to persuade you that the whole program ends up running in $O(n)$ time.

```
import java.util.*;
public class FastA {
    //The beginnings of FastA on a specimen protein
    //and a database member dbaseString
    private String specimen;
    private String dbaseString;
```

We're importing `java.util.*` because we need Vectors in which to store the list of suffixes at which each $k$-tuple begins. Think of the two strings that FastA is going to align as a `specimen` that you have just sequenced, and a string `dbaseString` that is stored in a database. We'll further assume that the $k$-tuple size is 2.

You'll need a way to convert amino acids to `int`s. Use the following code if you like (but if you're smart you'll write your own and use the `indexOf(char c)` method of the `String` class):

```java
private int aaToN(char c) {
    if (c=='A') return(0);
    else if (c=='R') return(1);
    else if (c=='N') return(2);
    else if (c=='D') return(3);
    else if (c=='C') return(4);
    else if (c=='Q') return(5);
    else if (c=='E') return(6);
    else if (c=='G') return(7);
    else if (c=='H') return(8);
    else if (c=='I') return(9);
    else if (c=='L') return(10);
    else if (c=='K') return(11);
    else if (c=='M') return(12);
    else if (c=='F') return(13);
    else if (c=='P') return(14);
    else if (c=='S') return(15);
    else if (c=='T') return(16);
    else if (c=='W') return(17);
    else if (c=='Y') return(18);
    else if (c=='V') return(19);
    else {
        System.out.println("BAD Amino Acid");
        return(-1);
    }
}
```

Since we're assuming $k$-tuples of size 2, we'll need to convert pairs of amino acids to `int`. A convenient way to do this that gives a unique `int` to each possible pair is `20*aaToN(first) + aaToN(second)`, where `first` and `second` are the amino acids. For example, since D converts to 3 and C converts to 4, CD will convert to 20*3+4 or 64.

Verify that DC converts to 83.

For each possible pair of amino acids, we'll need to keep track of all the locations in `specimen` where that pair appear. So let's declare:

```java
private Vector[] spec;
 // for storing the indexes in specimen where each
 // pair appears spec(x) will store the list of all indexes
 // where pairs that code to x begin in specimen
```

*(continued)*

You'll need code to fill up that array of `Vectors`. Here's mine:

```
for (int i=0; i < 400; i++) spec[i] = new Vector();
for (i=0; i < specimen.length()-1; i++)
    (spec[20*aaToN(specimen.charAt(i)) +
          aaToN(specimen.charAt(i+1))]).add(new Integer(i));
```

If you use my code, be sure you understand it.

Now that we've filled the `spec` array of `Vectors`, let's look at the other string `dbaseString`. We'll look at each consecutive pair of amino acids, and determine the offsets at which the same pair appears in the first string `specimen`. Suppose we're looking at the pair beginning at index i. Now let's convert the pair to an int: `(20*aaToN(dbaseString.charAt(i))` `+ aaToN(dbaseString.charAt(i+1)))`. Let's name that value j. We can look up `spec[j]` to find all the indexes in `specimen` at which the same pair occurs. For each of those indexes, you'll want to compute the offset:

```
for (i=0; i < dbaseString.length()-1; i++) {
    j = 20*aaToN(dbaseString.charAt(i)) +
        aaToN(dbaseString.charAt(i+1));
    Enumeration e = (spec[j]).elements();
    while (e.hasMoreElements())
        (offsets[dbaseString.length()+
                ((Integer)(e.nextElement())).intValue()
                - i])++;
```

Notice that the program counts the number of times each possible offset occurs by incrementing the entry in an array of possible offsets. It previously declared that as:

```
private int[] offsets;
```

and initialize all entries to 0:

```
offsets = new int[specimen.length()+dbaseString.length()];
for {int i=0; i < offsets.length; i++)offsets[i] = 0;
```

Finally, let's print the offsets, and have a main program to drive the whole operation:

```
public void printOffsets() {
    for (int i=-dbaseString.length(); i < specimen.length(); i++)
        System.out.println("Offsets at "+i+" : "+
                           offsets[dbaseString.length() + i]);
}
public static void main(String[] args) {
    FastA fa = new FastA(args[0], args[1]);
    fa.printOffsets();
}
```

Write the program FastA to calculate and print the offsets corresponding to args[0] and args[1] on the command_line.

```
>java FastA ACACAC CACACACC
java FastA ACACAC CACACACC
Offsets at -8 : 0
Offsets at -7 : 0
Offsets at -6 : 0
Offsets at -5 : 1
Offsets at -4 : 0
Offsets at -3 : 3
Offsets at -2 : 0
Offsets at -1 : 5
Offsets at 0 : 0
Offsets at 1 : 4
Offsets at 2 : 0
Offsets at 3 : 2
Offsets at 4 : 0
Offsets at 5 : 0
```

Now you've written a major component of the FastA program. Now we ask you to perform a simple analysis of your code.

Argue informally that the running time of the program you wrote for the previous exercise is $O(n)$, where both the inputs have length $O(n)$.

Find out what you can about some common multiple-alignment programs including T-Coffee and ClustalW. Can you discern their guide tree and their concept of consensus?

**Exercise 5.27**

## KEY TERMS

alignment (Intro)
pattern (Intro)
target text (Intro)
pattern matching (Intro)
best case (5.1)
worst case (5.1)
expected case (5.1)
sublinear (5.1)
deterministic finite-state automata
    (DFAs) (5.1)
state (5.1)

transition (5.1)
stop codon (5.1)
start state (5.1)
final state (5.1)
deterministic (5.1)
nondeterministic (5.1)
regular expression (5.1)
regular set (5.1)
union (5.1)
concatenation (5.1)
Kleene closure (5.1)

concatenation of zero
    strings (5.1)
empty string (5.1)
unanticipated patterns (5.2)
unexpected coincidences (5.2)
ASCII (5.3)
selectivity (5.3)
sensitivity (5.3)
functionality (5.4)
indel (5.4)

dynamic programming
    matrix (5.4)
minimize (5.4)
global alignment (5.4)
local alignment (5.4)
block indel (5.5)

affine gap penalty (5.5)
gap start penalty (5.5)
initiation penalty (5.5)
gap continuation penalty (5.5)
point accepted mutation
    (PAM) (5.6)

specimen (5.8)
database string (5.8)
guide tree (5.9)
instrumenting (5.10)

# BIBLIOGRAPHY

1. S. F. Altschul, W. Gish, W. Miller, et al. Basic local alignment search tool. *J Mol Biol*, 215:403–410, 1990.

2. Robert S. Boyer and J. Strother Moore. A fast string searching algorithm. *Communications of the ACM*, 20:762–772, October 1977.

3. M. O. Dayhoff, R. M. Schwartz, and B. C. Orcutt. A model of evolutionary change in proteins. In M. O. Dayhoff, editor, *Atlas of Protein Structure*, volume 5(Suppl. 3), pp. 345–352. National Biomedical Research Foundation, Silver Spring, MD., 1979.

4. FBI. http://www.fbi.gov/wanted.htm

5. W. S. Fitch and T. F. Smith. Optimal sequence alignments. *Proc Natl Acad Sci USA*, 80:1382–1386, 1983.

6. Feng Gao, Elizabeth Bailes, David L. Robertson, et al. Origin of HIV-1 in the chimpanzee *Pan troglodytes*. *Nature*, 397:436–441, 1999.

7. Martin Gardner. *Mathematical Magic Show*. Alfred A. Knopf, New York, 1977.

8. S. Heniko and J. G. Heniko. Amino acid substitution matrices from protein blocks. *Proc Natl Acad Sci USA*, 89:10915–10919, 1992.

9. John E. Hopcroft and Jeffrey D. Ullman. *Introduction to Automata Theory, Languages, and Computation*. Addison-Wesley, New York, 1979.

10. Richard M. Karp and Michael O. Rabin. Efficient randomized pattern-matching algorithms. *IBM J Res Dev*, 31:249–260, March 1987.

11. D. E. Knuth, J. H. Morris, and V. R. Pratt. Fast pattern matching in strings. *SIAM J Comput*, 6:323–350, 1977.

12. Los Alamos National Lab. HIV Sequence Database. http://www.hiv.lanl.gov/content/hiv-db/HTML/outline.html

13. U. Manber. *Introduction to Algorithms : A Creative Approach*. Addison-Wesley, New York, 1989.

14. Edward M. McCreight. A space-economical suffix tree construction algorithm. *J ACM*, 23:262–272, April 1976.

15. Saul B. Needleman and Christian D. Wunsch. A general method applicable to the search for similarity in the amino acid sequences of two proteins. *J Mol Biol*, 48:443–453, 1970.

16. M. Nelson. Fast string searching with suffix trees. *Dr. Dobbs Journal*, August 1996.

17. Science Watch. Twenty Years of Citation Superstars, September 2003. http://www.sciencewatch.com

18. T. F. Smith and M. S. Waterman. Identification of common molecular sequences. *J Mol Biol*, 147:195–197, 1981.

19. Luis d'Antin van Rooten. *Mots d'Heures: Gousses, Rames*. Grossman Publishers, New York, 1967.

# Simulating and Modeling Evolution

*"Biologically the species is the accumulation of the experiments of all its successful individuals since the beginning."*

—H. G. Wells, *A Modern Utopia*

## 6.1 THE BIOLOGICAL TIME MACHINE

Since the dawn of life on Earth many species have arisen, developed, and died out. Imagine that you could build a time machine that could take you back over those billions of years. As you traveled back in time, you would see today's many species go through a reverse development process. At various points in the journey you would see species merging into their common ancestor. Richard Dawkins describes just such a journey in [2], where he uses the term *concestor* to mean the common ancestor of multiple species. Eventually we would arrive at a concestor for all of the forms of life on Earth. Perhaps surprisingly, almost all of the descendant species of that concestor are now extinct. We, together with the apes, hippos, fish, insects, bacteria, and other living species, are the exceptions. We are the rare survivors.

In Chapter 2, we introduced the tree of life (Figure 6.1) as one way of representing the relationships among species. The tree of life depends on some very important assumptions:

1. All life on Earth is related;
2. All life shares a common, universal ancestor (known as LUCA for last universal common ancestor) lost in the mists of time, and
3. The position of a given species within the tree of life allows us to understand some of the fundamental aspects of the biology of a group or family of species.

This last point needs some explanation. Many features of a biological species point (often unreliably) to its position within the tree of life. It's like a biological

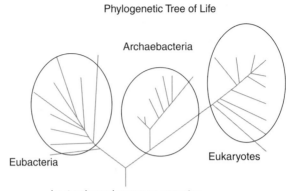

Phylogenetic Tree of Life

**FIGURE 6.1**    A tree of life showing the three main groups of organisms alive today and postulating a universal common ancestor.

Web address, if you will. The Web address of a server can indicate all sorts of information (none of which is reliable!):

- Is the server affiliated with an academic institution (indicated by .edu) or a commercial establishment (.com)?
- Is the server in the United Kingdom (indicated by .uk) or the United States (indicated by the lack of a country designation)?
- Does the server use the hypertext transfer protocol (http) or the file transfer protocol (ftp)?

Why do we say that Web addresses are unreliable? As noted, an address ending in .edu typically denotes an educational institution. But nothing prevents profit-driven diploma mills from masquerading under the .edu flag (http://www.rushmore.edu). United Kingdom companies often use the .co.uk ending, but archetypically British companies can choose not to (http://www.marksandspencer.com).

So it is with nature. Many species conspire to confuse our efforts at accurate classification. Mammals are characterized by live birth, and yet the duck-billed platypus defies this rule. Birds fly don't they? What then of the ostrich? Accurate classification of Websites and of species require much more than a quick inspection of simple features like Web addresses and obvious physical traits.

Nevertheless, just as each server on the Web has a precise physical location (at least instantaneously) and a definite purpose, so each species has a unique position within the tree of life. Biologists use a series of names to describe the location of the species. We start with the broadest category, such as prokaryote (bacteria or archaebacteria) or eukaryote (cells like ours). Within eukaryotes, there are several **kingdoms** of organisms: plants, animals (including us), fungi, and so on. Each kingdom has several **phyla;** for example we are classified as being in the kingdom Animalia (animals) and the phylum Chordata (organisms with a spinal cord). We are also further classified as being in **class** Mammalia (mammals), **order**

Primates (including all the other apes), **family** Hominidae (includes the many extinct precursors to modern humans), **genus** *Homo,* and, finally, **species** *sapiens.*

Our position within the tree of life is uniquely defined by these terms. This helps us to identify and categorize the species that are alive at present. Most of the species that have lived on this planet, however, are already extinct. Over the course of the evolution of life, many more species have gone extinct than are currently alive. So for most of our studies, we have to reconstruct the past. Because of the vast timescale over which evolution has occurred, the reconstruction of its history must be mostly a process of inference. Fossil evidence and carbon dating offer some clues to guide us in this process. It is possible thus to construct a chronological sequence dating some species relative to others. The collected body of evidence overwhelmingly supports evolutionary theory, and the evolutionary relationships between species is one of the strongest tenets of modern science.

## 6.1.1  Evolutionary Processes

In Chapter 2, we introduced the concept of evolution and the primary force that drives it: **mutation.** What is mutation? Any change to the information content of a genome, even if it is very slight, constitutes a mutation. This is a very broad definition of a mutation, so if we are to understand mutations, we need to consider the different ways in which they can occur.

Mutations are of three kinds: **point mutations, insertions,** and **deletions.** The most common type are the point mutations. These mutations change a single letter of the DNA sequence of an organism's genome. We also refer to such mutations as substitutions because one nucleotide is substituted for another. Substitution mutations can have dramatic effects when they occur within the protein-coding regions of genes (see Chapter 2) because even a single-letter change can affect the amino acid encoded by a DNA sequence. Insertions represent mutations in which a nucleotide or set of nucleotides is introduced into the existing DNA sequence. Not surprisingly, insertions can garble the overall coding message by introducing new codons into a coding region or by affecting promoters or other signals. Deletions are the opposite of insertions; they are instances in which one or more nucleotides are excised from the DNA, thereby removing information that might be critical. Insertions and deletions are much rarer than substitutions, so the majority of this discussion will focus on substitutions.

Because of the random nature of mutations, a mutation's location is largely the result of chance. When a mutation occurs, its effect is also a consequence of its location. Sometimes the mutation occurs in a coding region of a gene. These mutations are most likely to have a dramatic influence on the organism. However, most mutations do not occur in coding regions. This is partly because, in the larger genomes, there is usually much more noncoding DNA than coding DNA. As a result, the probability of a mutation occurring at random is higher in a noncoding region than a coding region.

In a population, a mutation can have one of three effects: it can damage the organism, it can aid the organism, or it can be entirely neutral with no effect at all. An example of detrimental mutations are those that lead to cancer; in cancer, the accumulation of mutations eventually results in uncontrolled cell growth and the death of the organism. Most mutations are deleterious. Like those that cause cancer, they tend to disadvantage the organism rather than help it. Occasionally however, a mutation will afford a specific advantage to an organism, allowing it to flourish in a particular environment. Such an organism will have more opportunities to reproduce, and its success will translate into more members of the population sharing its advantages. This is where natural selection comes into play: organisms with advantageous mutations tend to dominate the population, but those with deleterious mutations are eliminated. We say that the advantageous mutation has been selected in the population because it comes to dominate the population.

Mutations are believed to occur at a relatively steady background rate, but the assumption of a regularly ticking "molecular clock" is not strictly necessary for our understanding of evolutionary history. Organisms and species must constantly adapt to their changing environments. Mutations provide the basis for these adaptations, since each organism in a population will have a slightly different set of mutations. Natural selection causes some organisms to succeed where others die off, and we say that the successful organisms are "well adapted" to their environments.

The original basis for the theory of evolution, as formulated by Charles Darwin, was derived from just such a situation in which organisms had become well adapted to the specific demands of their environment. Darwin visited the Galapagos Islands, each of which has a specific microenvironment. Darwin noticed that finches, a type of bird, were common to all the islands, but the shape of the finches' beaks varied a bit from island to island. It turns out that the shape of the finch's beak is adapted for particular food types. Some finches feed on seeds and have large, rounded beaks; others feed on fruit or insects and have narrow, sharp beaks. Although the finches all descended from one common finch species many thousands of years ago, they have since evolved and adapted to the food available on each of the islands. The changes in beak shape were the result of mutations that were selected because they provided a specific advantage in a particular environment. This is the classic example of evolution in action. An interesting modern-day study of watching bacterial evolution in action is described in the next section.

## 6.2 *E. COLI* EVOLUTION

Ordinarily, we think of evolution as occurring on a large time scale, on the order of many thousands or millions of years. However, the rate of evolution is actually tied more directly to the rate at which an organism reproduces. The reason for this should be obvious: natural selection can only operate on the existing set of mutations present in a population. Each new generation is likely to have some slightly different mutations or combinations of mutations, and these variations are the playground for natural selection. So evolution operates at different time scales depending on the generation time, defined as the time it takes for a generation to produce offspring. If you look at humans, for example, it takes on average between 20 and 30 years to produce a new generation of human beings (i.e., you grow up and have children who are now the new generation). So evolution in humans is limited to selection about once every 25 years. For finches, the generation time is about 2 years, so natural selection can operate much faster in finches. If we now consider bacteria, which produce a new generation on average every 20 minutes, we are talking about evolution occurring at a much more accelerated pace than in humans. So if we want to ask questions about the ways in which natural selection and mutation operate on a population, and we want to have answers to those questions in a reasonable amount of time, we have to look at organisms with very rapid generation times.

One of the best documented instances of watching evolution in action is based on the work of two researchers: Richard E. Lenski and Albert F. Bennett. In 1988, Lenski and some graduate students set up a series of bacterial cultures of *E. coli.* They started with a set of genetically identical *E. coli,* but placed them into separate flasks. Each flask represented an independent environment, and each population evolved in isolation from its compatriots in the other flasks. The isolation of these populations was complete: at no time did any of the bacteria in one flask mix with their neighbors. So in some ways, this was an even better set up than the case with Darwin's finches on the relatively isolated islands of the Galápagos. Unlike the finches, which could fly from one island to the next occasionally, the isolation of Lenski's bacterial populations was absolute.

After allowing the bacterial populations to evolve for 2000 generations, Lenski and his colleagues decided to see how different the populations had become. To do this, they introduced what are known as "stresses" to the populations of bacteria. The idea was to make the environment just a little less comfortable for the bacteria and then see how each population would respond to the shift in environmental conditions. One of the most common stresses for a bacterium is a change in the temperature of its environment. Ordinarily, *E. coli* grow best at a temperature of 37°C, although they can accommodate some shifts in temperature, tolerating temperatures up to 40°C. Above that temperature, a normal *E. coli* (also known as wild type) will die because the higher temperature damages critical cellular components. The question Lenski and Bennett wanted to ask was this: If the *E. coli* in the flasks were exposed to a higher temperature, would they adapt to this new temperature and flourish or would they all die just like their original, wild-type counterparts?

Based on the behavior of the wild-type strain, Lenski and Bennett decided to test the populations at a temperature of 41.5°C. At this temperature, the ancestral (i.e., original) *E. coli* were severely stressed. Rather than reproducing every 20 minutes, they did so sporadically or not at all, and their overall growth was reduced. However, in some of the flasks where the *E. coli* had been evolving on their own, a few bacteria survived and seemed to thrive. They were able to reproduce and their offspring proved to be robust in the higher temperature. In other words, some members of the population had a beneficial mutation that allowed them to tolerate the higher temperature. Over time, these organisms came to dominate the flask populations, so that all the organisms in the flasks were able to tolerate the new, higher temperature.

The researchers next decided to ask what specific changes had occurred to allow the bacteria to tolerate this higher temperature. They decided to look at a set of genes that are known to be involved in the normal response to higher environmental temperatures. These genes, known as heat shock genes, are present in almost all organisms studied to date, including humans. The proteins made by these genes protect critical parts of the cellular machinery from the damage caused by higher temperatures. When Lenski and Bennett looked at the heat shock genes in their flask populations, they discovered some very interesting variations. First, they noticed that the activity level of many of the heat shock genes was higher than in the original strain. This is not surprising since any adaptation to higher temperatures must involve making more heat shock proteins to protect cellular components. Interestingly, all the flasks tested seemed to have the same shifts in gene activity, specifically an increase in the activity of 5 of the 27 known heat shock proteins. Although each flask had evolved independently, only five of the genes seemed to be critical for survival at the new temperature. It was these changes in gene expression that contributed to the success of the flask populations at the higher temperature [15].

A number of lessons were learned from this innovative set of experiments. The first is that evolution in isolated populations can accumulate mutations that will be beneficial to the population at some future point. Remember that as far as natural selection is concerned, the key point is survival of the species, not of individuals. As long as some individuals survive long enough to reproduce, evolution can proceed. When the flask populations of *E. coli* were first introduced to the higher temperature, most of the organisms died just as in the ancestral strain. The few individuals who did survive were able to reproduce and repopulate the flasks with *E. coli* that were robust in the new temperature.

A second interesting observation from the work by Lenski and Bennett is that the advantageous mutations seem to have clustered in specific genes rather than across all the possible genes that could be influenced. That is, rather than randomly affecting all 27 known heat shock genes, the flask populations all seem to have focused on changes to just 5 of them. This suggests that although mutation itself may be a random process, evolution can occur in a more targeted fashion. That is, it is possible to have a very large pallet of possible combinations to choose from, but the most successful combinations will be from a more limited set.

Why might this be the case? Consider for a moment that *E. coli* has over 4000 genes, and that mutations to many of them will kill the bacterium well before it has a chance to deal with shifts in the environmental temperature. In other words, even bacteria are very complex webs of interacting genes, and most changes perturb the system so dramatically that they kill the organism before it has a chance to adapt to its environment. Because of these constraints, advantageous mutations must occur in such a way that they do not jeopardize any other part of the system. It should be obvious now why advantageous mutations are so rare: they occur at random, but they have to be changes that will not in any way perturb the system even while they afford some selective advantage.

This is also why the random process of mutation can give rise to the perception that a process has been designed rather than evolved. The problem is not in the process but in our observation of it. We usually observe the endpoint of the process, when an advantageous mutation has come to dominate a population, as in the case with the heat-resistant *E. coli*. At this point, it is easy to look at the population and say, "The *E. coli knew* that it had to modify its heat shock genes. That's proof of a creator, or at least, of intelligence!" In reality, however, we tend to forget that the vast majority of *E. coli* in the flasks died. They either missed the memo from the creator informing them to mutate their heat shock genes, or, more realistically, they simply were not lucky enough to have a mutation in one of the necessary heat shock genes. What we see are the rare, but extremely successful, mutations. The history of this planet is replete with species and organisms that failed to survive. So although it might appear that the myriad species today had to be designed to achieve the level of complexity we see, if we could see all the intermediates who failed to make it, we would see the jerky forward–backward motion of random mutations alternately aiding and interfering with species' survival.

## 6.3  SIMULATING EVOLUTION IN SILICO

Another way to study and think about evolution is to mimic its processes on the computer. The term *in silico* is very much in vogue because it refers to the idea of studying biological processes computationally rather than in the organism (in vivo) or in the laboratory (in vitro). By simulating the process of evolution through a program, we can speed up evolution times significantly. In theory, we could compress a million or even a billion years into a few seconds of processor time. So from the perspective of studying evolution, a program that mimics the process is a very exciting alternative.

The other side of the coin is that evolution is demonstrably a very effective way for entities to emerge that are highly robust and capable of adapting to, and even flourishing in, novel and unexpected surroundings. In contrast, today's software engineers tend to produce entities that are almost the antithesis of the robustness and adaptability we see in nature. Programmers would, of course, be very pleased to be able to produce programs that could adapt to every vagary of the user's whim, every new development or change in the program's operating environment, every new desideratum that arises among the computing community. A program that could satisfactorily adapt to succeed even when unanticipated changes occur in its environment without any intervention by its creator would truly be a wonder. If you are willing to think of organisms as programs, then this is in fact what we have in the biological world.

Programmers try to anticipate every eventuality; but, by the very definition of the word, *unanticipated* eventualities are beyond the capabilities of standard software engineering. The intelligent design that pervades most software development is incapable of producing robustness and adaptability to unforeseen events. A program compiled for the PowerPC architecture running Mac OS will fail catastrophically tomorrow if loaded onto an Intel machine running Windows. But a domesticated overindulged pedigree Siberian husky in New York City could be released into the wilds of Snowdonia and might flourish. The differences between computer platforms are trivial compared with the chasm that separates the centrally heated home of the New York pampered pooch and the rugged terrain of the North Wales mountains. The products of intelligent design (programs) are utterly pathetic and unadaptable compared with the robust achievements of evolution (life). If only we could evolve programs instead of creating them we would have a chance to find suitable solutions to the problems at hand and the ability to achieve new solutions as the environment subtly changes the specifications of the problems. The day when computer programs evolve instead of being created is a long way off. But it may be time for the first few cautious steps.

The study of evolutionary programming and genetic algorithms is relatively new. The basic idea is to mimic the process of evolution. Instead of designing specific programs to achieve specific tasks in carefully prescribed ways (standard programming), we allow pools of programs to mutate and evolve in order to achieve desired goals. To achieve results within acceptable time frames, we must make massive compromises that detract from the purity of true evolution. The biggest departure is that nature does not have any particular goal in mind for evolution; we, however, will be trying to evolve programs that achieve specific purposes. Nature's fitness function is simple: "Whatever is fit to survive will survive." We will subvert that simplicity by substituting our own fitness rule: "Whatever gets closest to doing what we want will survive." It's a perversion, but, as we shall see, we can have fun and amaze ourselves with the results even in our artificial settings.

## 6.3.1  Genetic Algorithms: A First Pass

Let us take a minute to think about what sort of things we would need to evolve programs instead of organisms. When we look at how organisms evolve, we can reduce the many complexities to three critical features. We need a "genome," or information stored in a specific structure. This information will be passed on from generation to generation, with **mutation** changing bits of the information from time to time. Since mutations act on genomes, the two are necessarily intertwined. We also need a way to "**select**" individuals who are well adapted to a given situation and eliminate those that are poorly adapted. So if we want to evolve something, at a minimum we need an entity that has a genome that mutation and selection can act on.

Now let us turn to the idea of a program that evolves as new challenges appear. What is a program? For simplicity's sake, let's say it's something that converts input to output. In general, input can be arbitrarily complicated and output can require many components, but in essence we can represent input as a single string and output as a single string. Though this oversimplification may chafe, it is, in theory, perfectly sound. A program is a function that takes a string as input and produces a string as output.

How can we represent a program? We know we can write programs in our favorite language and store them in files. Those files are just a convenient way to store strings. So we can represent a program as a string. Since a program converts a string to a string, and since a program can itself be represented by a string, is it reasonable to consider programs that input and output programs? Certainly it is. You've already met the Java compiler, a program that inputs programs written in Java and outputs programs written in Byte code.

Just as the information necessary for the production of an individual life form is encoded in its DNA, so our program that creates programs needs to encode information. Specifically, we need to encode the information necessary for the generation of a program in some kind of data structure. We can think of this data structure as similar to the genome of an organism; it serves the purpose of holding all the relevant information. We have one constraint on the data structure: it must be flexible enough to allow us to easily mutate or alter bits of information in a random fashion. In the simplest example, a program would be stored as a binary string, and then we can flip bits at random to imitate mutation.

We now have two of the requisite items: a genome structure and a way to enact mutations. This leaves us to address the final element for evolution: a mechanism for selection of entities, be they organisms or programs. How do we determine what criteria are appropriate for selection of programs? What is a "good" machine-generated program? If there is some way to measure how good a program is, then we can select among the large number of machine-generated programs and choose one that suits our needs. For organisms, the measure of a "good" individual is one who can reproduce. So that is a pretty straightforward measure, but it is not going to help us find a "good program" when we define it as a program that does what we need it to do.

We therefore have to introduce a numerical value of "fitness," where we define fitness in terms of parameters and standards that describe the desired goal of our optimal program. Then we allow our programs to mutate and evolve, and in each "generation" of programs, we ask what the fitness of each program is. If "unfit" programs are removed from the pool and "fit" programs retain their place and even multiply or merge (i.e., cross breed) with each other, the hope is that the pool of programs will improve over time. By maintaining a diversity of successful programs, one can even hope that the pool will be able to cope with environmental changes and adapt new and better programs as operating conditions change.

Suppose we start with a diverse population of 100 programs. If we can measure how good each is, then we can keep the best 90, kill the worst 10, and replace them with programs similar to the best performing programs. By "similar to," we mean that the new programs are produced from old programs by processes like mutation and cross-breeding. The initial population of 100 programs thus is replaced by a new population consisting of the best 90 of the original programs together with 10 new programs derived from the best of the original population. We hope that the programs of this second generation are, on average, a little better than the programs of our initial population. These hopes will become reality if and only if we have identified an appropriate measure of fitness because this is what drives the decision to keep a program or terminate it.

In practice, what we need is some kind of **fitness function** for programs. The programs that achieve high fitness scores will survive; the others will perish. The term **genetic algorithm** is applied to program generation schemes that follow this roughly Darwinian scenario. The essential features are:

- A way to represent programs such that mutation and other processes can lead to runnable descendant programs
- A fitness function that can be used to measure the quality of a program
- An initial population of programs
- A driver loop to create new generations from old, allowing the high-quality programs to survive and the others to disappear

## 6.3.2 Monkey Shakespeare: An Extended Example

What is the probability that a monkey provided with a typewriter and a lot of paper will produce the complete works of William Shakespeare? What is the probability that a tornado moving through a junkyard will assemble a Boeing 747 aircraft?

Both these ridiculous questions have been posed in the context of asserting the unlikelihood that an enzyme made up of, say 200 amino acids, can come into being without some kind of divine intervention. If all three processes, monkey typing, tornado assembly, and enzyme assembly, are essentially random processes, then of course each probability is as close to zero as makes no difference.

But evolution is not a random process. Individual mutations may be random, but Darwinian natural selection is what makes the eventual products so fit for their environments. Let's follow Richard Dawkins [1] and show how a simple simulation of natural selection can encourage Shakespearean traits in simulated simian outputs. We'll present the argument as a sequence of exercises that will lead you to a simple evolutionary (but guided) program.

Let's simplify the typewriter to have only 27 keys, one for each letter *a-z* and one space bar. Rather than the complete works of Shakespeare, let's adopt the more modest target of the phrase "*Methinks it is like a weasel.*"

**Exercise 6.1** In which work of Shakespeare does the phrase "methinks it is like a weasel" occur? This is an exercise to remind you of the tools you have at your disposal to find target phrases in large files and to locate large files on and download them from the Internet.

The next exercise asks you to write a simulation of a fixated monkey. This monkey will always generate exactly the same (almost certainly nonsense) phrase.

**Exercise 6.2**

Create a random sequence of 28 characters, each of which is a lowercase letter or a space. Write a program MyMonkey that returns that precise sequence every time it is called. *Hint:* You can use whatever technique you like to generate a random phrase, store that phrase in a String variable, and have your method simply return that String whenever it is called.

Example usage:

```
java MyMonkey
ldncjfd djshskfj htwoxd sjyx
java MyMonkey
ldncjfd djshskfj htwoxd sjyx
java MyMonkey
ldncjfd djshskfj htwoxd sjyx
```

The random 28-character phrase is irrelevant, but the same gibberish should appear each time you run the program.

What is the probability that your monkey will produce the phrase "methinks it is like a weasel"? Since each of precisely 28 character positions needs to be exactly 1 among 27 characters, the chances are just 1 in $27^{28}$. This is about 1 in $10^{40}$. The universe is estimated to be at most 20 billion years old. That's about $6 \times 10^{17}$ seconds. Even if you did Exercise 6.2 once per second for 20 billion years, it is virtually impossible that you will have a monkey whose phrase is "methinks it is like a weasel."

Exercise 6.2 cries out for automation.

**Exercise 6.3**

Write a class Monkey to do Exercise 6.2. Each time you call the constructor of this class, it will create a new simulated fixated monkey. Each simulated monkey so produced will have its own randomly generated 28-character phrase, which it will print each time it is run. If you add the following main method,

```
public static void main(String[] args) {
    Monkey anne = new Monkey();
    Monkey paul = new Monkey();
    anne.print();
    paul.print();
    anne.print();
}
```

then your output should consist of a random-looking, 28-character phrase, followed by another, followed by a repeat of the first phrase.

Now you have a program that can generate monkeys for you. In a little while you'll call it to produce an initial population of many hundreds of monkeys.

**Exercise 6.4**    Write a method to mutate a monkey. Here's a skeleton:

```
Monkey mutateMonkey(Monkey inMonkey) {
    // return a new monkey whose output phrase is different from
    // inMonkey's by replacing one character with another
}
```

Now you can see how useful mutation in a population can be. Instead of having to generate entirely new strings each time, you can get many variations on existing phrases. The problem is that even with mutation, your monkeys are very unlikely to produce the desired phrase because we are still relying on pure chance to get all the positions right.

However, given enough time, some of your monkeys might in fact get parts of the phrase right. For example, perhaps after generating many thousands of monkeys, you have monkey A that produces the phrase "methinks ip lak ea pavmaiva" and monkey B that has come up with "apvoamvpai vakv a weasel." This is pure conjecture, but bear with us for a moment. Ideally, what you want to have happen next is that monkey A and monkey B combine their phrases, because then you might get "methinks ip lak ea a weasel" which is almost what you want. Mutating this new string could get you much closer to the desired final result "methinks it is like a weasel." To do this, we have to allow monkey sex. That is, we have to allow monkeys to **cross breed** so that we can evaluate their offspring. Monkey sex in this context is very prosaic. We take monkey A and monkey B and recombine the phrases by splitting the strings at a randomly selected point. We glue a piece of A to a piece of B to generate an "offspring" monkey that is now a legitimate member of the population. The following exercise outlines how you can do this for your monkeys.

**Exercise 6.5**    Write a method to cross breed two monkeys and produce an offspring that combines portions of each parent's phrases. For example, if you cross a monkey whose phrase is aaaaaaaaaaaaaaaaaaaaaaaaaaaa with a monkey whose phrase is bbbbbbbbbbbbbbbbbbbbbbbbbbbb the output should be a monkey whose phrase consists of some a's followed by some b's followed by enough a's to make a phrase of length 28. The precise location of the boundaries should be random. A possible output for the inputs is a monkey whose phrase is aaabbbbbbbbbbbbbbbbbbbaaaaaaa.

Finally, we come to the critical engine of our monkey evolution program. To drive the evolution, we need a fitness function. This is crucial to our goal. The better the fitness function, the more likely we'll succeed in evolving a monkey that can type Shakespeare!

HIGHLIGHT

# Why Sex?

The question, "Why sex?" tends to haunt those who spend their careers looking closely at evolution. This is not because evolutionary biologists are by nature a tedious, hidebound lot who don't appreciate the finer things of life (although this may also be true). Biologists spend a lot of time thinking about why species choose sexual reproduction because, on the face of it, there does not seem to be enough biological reward for the amount of energy it requires. To solve this enigma, let's consider an example.

Consider one of North America's native finches, the cardinal. The male spends most of the Spring singing, instead of eating or sleeping, in order to attract a mate. This cardinal has put its own survival in jeopardy in many ways: aside from not eating and sleeping, it is also doing a great deal to attract the attention of predators. The cardinal has made life very easy for a predator because it is making so much noise and its bright red plumage makes it easy to spot in a tree. Why does the cardinal risk its own survival to find a mate? What could possibly be so important as to put individual survival, a trait that we have already said is selected for, at risk?

We hope you can begin to see the outlines of the problem that intrigues biologists. The problem is this: sexual reproduction in any species requires individuals to devote a significant amount of their time and energy to finding potential mates, attracting a mate, and maintaining a relationship with that mate, however briefly. These activities take up precious resources, require individuals to expose themselves to much greater risks, and to generally endanger their own survival in ways that we would think would ensure their extinction. Yet, when we look across the natural world, most multicellular organisms reproduce sexually. As we know, multicellular organisms are more complex and presumably are evolutionarily more advanced than single-celled organisms. So the fact that they nearly all reproduce sexually suggests that sex has some significant advantage to offer.

In contrast, most single-celled organisms are perfectly happy to just clone themselves. When a bacterium decides to make descendents, it usually just splits in half, generating two daughter cells from the one parent cell. Each daughter cell is genetically identical to the other daugher cell and to the parent cell. Since there are more bacteria in the period at the end of this sentence than there are people on the planet, it would seem that bacteria have the competitive advantage. However, think back to Lenski and colleagues' experiment. When they raised the temperature of the flasks, most of the organisms in each flask died. Only the rare individual survived. This was because almost all the organisms in each flask were identical, so when conditions changed, none of them could adapt in new ways. The rare individual with an advantageous mutation survived, but the population as a whole did not make it.

*(continued)*

Now consider a sexually reproducing population of individuals such as human beings. During the Middle Ages, repeated epidemics of bubonic plague (the Black Death) swept across Europe, often killing as much as a third to a half of the population of a town. In some towns nearly 80% of the population was wiped out. However, humans survived in Europe despite this terrible catastrophe. Had we been asexually reproducing organisms like bacteria, then likely all of the European population would have gone extinct. Luckily for us, though, we reproduce sexually.

Sexual reproduction offers one critical advantage over asexual reproduction: the genetic information of two individuals is combined in a new and entirely novel way in each offspring. So if two individuals have moderate resistance to the plague, their children might be even more resistant because they get the protection of beneficial mutations from each parent. Indeed, this is the strongest argument in favor of sexual reproduction: your offspring might get new combinations of genes that will give them a significant advantage when conditions change. With sexual reproduction, organisms no longer have to wait for the chance mutation to help them survive disaster. They can take any mutations already present in the population and mix and match. This increases the likelihood that at least some offspring will make it, even if no individual in the original population does.

The advantage of mixing and matching existing mutations in a population is so powerful that species choose sexual reproduction whenever they can. Even bacteria will have "sex," if we define sex as trading bits of genetic information. Bacteria are known to pass along small circles of DNA called plasmids when they meet other bacteria. These plasmids often have handy genes that allow the receiving bacterium to gain some advantage, such as resistance to an antibiotic. Sexual reproduction is favored in multicellular organisms precisely because they are so complex: too many things could go wrong if you just waited for a random mutation to confer advantageous adaptations. Rather, you combine two individuals who already have reasonably good adaptations and hope that the offspring are even better suited to their environment.

So, why sex? The tremendous risk to personal survival is worth it because the reward is equally tremendous: your offspring might survive, thrive, and therefore reproduce at a faster rate. This means that at least some of your genetic information will persist in the population. That chance at immortality, at least for your genes, is worth the myriad risks of sex. So, in some basic sense, this is why the cardinal sings and why you make an extra effort to look good for that next party you plan to attend.

**Exercise 6.6**

Write a fitness function that assigns a numeric value to a monkey. Your aim is to give high ratings to monkeys according to how Shakespeare-like their phrases are. Here are some suggestions:

- Reward a good proportion of spaces. No spaces at all is bad because English doesn't usually run for 28 characters without a break. But a dozen spaces is also bad, because that gives too many short words, or sequences of two or more spaces in a row.
- Reward a good ratio of consonants to vowels. (What is a good ratio? You can either guess, or you can write a program to figure out what the ratio is in, say, one of Mr. Shakespeare's plays.)
- Punish long sequences of consonants without vowel or long sequences of vowels without consonants.
- Highly reward an exact hit with the sequence "methinks it is like a weasel." For example, if the fifth letter in your monkey's phrase is an *i*, then give the monkey lots of points.

This last suggestion is, perhaps, too brazen for the kind of evolution we're trying to simulate, but it may be necessary for you to get results that are satisfying.

**Exercise 6.7**

Now you're ready to evolve a monkey that can type Shakespeare! Here's the outline:

```
create a pool of, say, 100 monkeys;
repeat {
    use the fitness function to assign a score to each monkey;
    remove the bottom, say 4, monkeys from the pool;
    add a mutation of each of two good monkeys to the pool;
    add two offspring from cross-breeding good monkeys;
} until your best monkey phrase is sufficiently Shakespearian
```

By the time you've completed Exercise 6.7 you will have had a lot of fun, and you will have programmed a very simple genetic algorithm. It shows how a combination of reproduction, mutation, cross-breeding, and, most importantly, natural selection can gradually build up objects that initially might seem impossibly complicated. It's not really a fair illustration of how real evolution works, because the fitness function is so artificial and so clearly designed to produce a particular outcome. True evolution in nature proceeds with no particular goal, but it produces even more spectacular results: creatures that *appear* perfectly designed to survive in their environments. They are not, of course, designed by anybody or anything. It's just that their fitness function is precisely "do well and succeed in your environment."

### 6.3.3  Monkey Evolution: Making Whales from Weasels

If you run your monkey evolution for many thousands of generations, you might find that after a while, certain monkeys dominate the population. This dominance is partly because they are very fit, but also because we start with a limited pool of original monkeys. Eventually, all the monkeys that differ substantially from the dominant monkey will have died out. The driving force of evolutionary programming is to keep the successful and lose the unsuccessful. An unfortunate, and undesirable, side effect is that diversity within the gene pool suffers. All the surviving monkeys will be very similar, and cross-breeding will no longer produce sufficient change.

In the artificial evolution of genetic algorithms, this stagnation of the population is actually quite common. Indeed, one way that researchers decide that the evolution has gone on long enough is to look for this plateau in fitness improvement. That is, when no significant improvement takes place in fitness after many hundreds of generations, we say that the genetic algorithm has found the best possible answers with this particular population. Continued evolution in this case is pointless because it would produce only minor variations on the same answer. This can be a good thing, in that you may have found the right answer and be done with your work. Or it might be a very bad thing, in that the genetic algorithm has gotten "stuck" in some solution that is not optimal.

### Exercise 6.8

1. Apply your fitness function from Exercise 6.6 to each of the monkeys whose outputs are listed here:

   - `methings ip is ghrusitb`
   - `meghings ip is ghrusitb`
   - `methings in is ghrusitb`
   - `methings ip it ghrusitb`
   - `methings ip is ghvusitb`
   - `methings ip is ghrusjtb`
   - `methings ip iskghrusitb`
   - `messings ip is ghrusitb`
   - `methingstip is ghrusitb`
   - `methingstip is ghrusity`
   - `methingstip iskghrusitb`

**2.** Apply your fitness function from Exercise 6.6 to each of the monkeys whose outputs are listed here:

- `dsafas adufejlsei kasle`
- `iertmre erkgsiemasa dke`
- `menalejgiouoa nlkaejkal`
- `jklpdasekljeksljke asel`
- `dsklgpelg pejjka wesitb`
- `methings ip is ghrusjtb`
- `melkp emlkr jleksejgilp`
- `messi rlkwj ijal ndkjeq`
- `methink tip is ghrusitb`
- `polkjauggekgke htazzity`
- `dsfsdin slkjgleas lfogh`

**3.** When you add the individual scores of each monkey in the preceding sets, which is the higher scoring set?

**4.** What do you conclude about the desirability of diversity in a population?

In the natural world, this kind of stagnation of a population is very rare. Indeed, a population in which the individuals are very similar usually presages imminent extinction. That is, we rarely see a situation in which a population has become so perfectly attuned to its environment that it can no longer evolve, which would be the natural corollary to the genetic algorithm of finding the "right" solution. More often we see a population that has become so inbred that it can no longer find new solutions to the perennial problem of adapting to an environment. This is the natural corollary of the genetic algorithm getting stuck in a less than optimal solution with no way out.

So what do we do when our genetic algorithm is working well yet is unable to move beyond some locally optimal solution to find the best solution possible? We simulate what happens from time to time in the natural world: catastrophe. In the natural world, species are forever in a race to adapt to a current environment before something changes. Change can be subtle, such as the change of seasons. Or change can be dramatic, such as hurricanes, volcanic eruptions, earthquakes, or meteoric impacts. These dramatic changes force species to adapt very quickly to new conditions or die. The dinosaurs were so well adapted to their environments that they dominated the planet for 300 million years. But one catastrophic event, a comet or meteor crashing into the planet, wiped them out in the space of a few million years. But that disastrous event was not all bad news. Small shrew-like creatures with fur and relatively bigger brains survived by adapting to the new conditions, and we, their mammalian descendants, are here to tell the tale.

When running a genetic algorithm program, we might simulate such disasters by randomly wiping out 90% of the population and starting fresh with whatever is left together with a lot of random "new blood." For example, suppose your monkey evolution was stuck in a rut, unable to get past some variation on "methavao it issss ali a wesel." What could you do? Well, one option would be to increase the number of cross-breedings between the very fittest of your monkeys in the hope that one of them would have some variation to get you past this obstacle in the evolutionary path. This tactic might solve your problem, or it might make it much worse because the best monkeys in your population are all so similar that recombination just reinforces the status quo. In that case, you might have to go with the brute force of catastrophe, randomly killing most of your monkeys and introducing a whole lot of new ones.

**Exercise 6.9**     Modify your program from Exercise 6.7. Occasionally[1] you will depart from the normal sequence of code by arbitrarily deleting some large (perhaps 90% or more) proportion of your population. The deleted individuals can be replaced by new random monkeys.

Let us say that after creating your catastrophe, you begin re-evolving your monkeys. After a few hundred generations, you look to see what the best performing monkeys are producing. To your surprise, they have come up with "methinks it is like a whale." Now, on the one hand, this is not the phrase you wanted. On the other hand, this is still a genuine English phrase, and the fact that this evolved from a bunch of random monkeys is still striking. What do we do with these new monkeys? For the specific context of the genetic algorithm, it depends on what you wanted the answer to be. But in the context of the natural world, this is a perfectly common occurrence — called **speciation.** In speciation, new species emerge from existing ones as the result of some kind of selection pressure. The selection pressure might be slight or it might be dramatic, but the new species that evolves now has its own place in the environment.

So how did we get a bunch of monkeys talking about whales when the original population were working toward weasels? Recall that each monkey in the population has a specific string, and that this string is mutated and interbred with other strings over the course of the evolution. As long as the resulting strings in each generation pass our fitness function, they continue to mutate, mix, and match. The same happens in natural populations. Organisms in a population have specific adaptations for their particular environment. When the environment changes, or new challenges are presented, some organisms in the population will adapt faster than others. This is because each organism has its own unique set of mutations. Many of those mutations may have had little or no effect in the old environment, but they might be of use in the new one. Organisms lucky enough to have advantageous mutations in the new environment adapt more quickly, are able to reproduce faster, and therefore come to dominate the new population. Over time,

---

[1] One way to do this is to select a random number, and if it exceeds some threshold, it should trigger the catastrophe code; otherwise you should just continue.

the new population may alter enough from the old one that it no longer bears any resemblance to the original population. At this point, we usually designate the new population as being a new species, separate from the ancestor population from which it arose.

Sometimes the old population dies out altogether or is entirely replaced by the new, better adapted population. At other times, however, the two populations and eventually two species may live side by side. The finches on the Galápagos Islands are a good example of this. Darwin's finches all descended from a single common ancestor, but they evolved into 14 species. These new species were produced by two pressures: isolation of populations on each island and the need to find a reliable food source. On some islands, only one population of finches existed. Here, the competition to find food was minimal, and these finches could afford to be generalists, eating whatever was available. Other populations did not have this luxury. If more than one population was present on an island, the competition for food would be quite intense. Generalist finches might have to compete with many other generalists for any one food source. However, if a finch or a population of finches is able to specialize, it might stand a better chance of getting enough food without having to constantly fight off competitors. This is why some of the finches adapted to eating seeds, and others became fruit or insect eaters. That way, each population was able to identify an appropriate niche, or specialized environment, that reduced the overall competition for food. Eventually, the finch populations got to be different enough that they were identified as separate species.

How do we define a population as a new species? This is a tricky business, and biologists do not always agree. In the past, it was generally accepted that we delineate a population as a species when it can no longer interbreed with other populations. So if we were to mix our whale monkeys with our weasel monkeys and found that they could not cross breed, then we would say we had two species of monkeys. In our artificial scenario, though, there would not be much to prevent the weasel and whale monkeys from cross-breeding because we are simply mixing and matching strings of letters. In the natural world, however, the changes that accompany speciation are usually so extensive that they inhibit successful interbreeding.

There are plenty of examples of populations that we have designated as species, but we do not actually know if they could produce viable offspring if interbred. For example, we think of Neanderthals as being a different species from us, but we do not know if we could interbreed with them because there aren't any around to check. So biologists now say that a population has become a new species when enough has changed between the new and original species that we can make a clear distinction. For example, we could observe that "methinks it is like a weasel" and "methinks it is like a whale" have a total of four letter changes and the loss of one character. We could argue that this is sufficient to say that they are two independent species. This distinction is less clear than the one about interbreeding, but like much of biology, it better describes the murky state of reality.

Designers of genetic algorithms take pains to create environments and fitness functions that ensure their goals will be met. Rather than allowing for new species to develop or letting the genetic algorithm get stuck, the goal is to get the right answer. A real-life example is described in Section 6.3.4.

Evolutionary programming is in its infancy. From our discussion, we can derive the following broad conclusions:

- Robustness and adaptability are a natural consequence of evolutionary processes; robustness and adaptability are extremely difficult to achieve through traditional software design.
- Diversity is essential to avoid unproductive plateaus.
- Current computer limitations necessitate compromises that make evolutionary programming distinct from real evolution:

  - Encoding schemes are developed to ensure that most mutated offspring are viable and allowed to compete. In life, almost all mutations are deleterious and lead to death.
  - The "fitness function" used to determine what programs survive into the next generation is goal-oriented. In life, survival happens through a combination of factors: the measure of fitness has no goal—it just happens.
  - Most evolutionary programming concentrates on the evolution of one "species." In nature, fitness derives from complicated interactions and relationships among many.

Just because it's complicated is no reason for us not to study and learn from life and apply some of what we observe to our own ends.

## 6.3.4  A Worked Example: A Genetic Algorithm for Gene Finding

In many areas of bioinformatics, including the design of drugs, it is important to be able to identify the DNA sequence corresponding to an individual gene. We will see in Chapter 7 that a number of clues can indicate the starting and ending locations of genes within a chromosome or genome. Some of the gene clue features can be detected easily by a simple program:

- Stretches of DNA between potential start codons and in-frame[2] stop codons are easy to identify using straightforward pattern matching. Such stretches are open reading frames (ORFs) that are candidates for being genes.
- Variations in local densities of nucleotides are easy to detect, again via a simple program. Some variations, such as high concentrations of C and G nucleotides, have been noted as indicative of the start of genes.
- Many bacterial species exhibit a Shine–Dalgarno region [17], a short sequence of nucleotides that seems to provide a grip for the ribosome to attach to the mRNA transcript and begin translation. Many genes will be preceded in

---

[2] *In-frame* means that an integral number of triples of nucleotides occurs between the start and the stop, none of which is itself a stop codon.

their sequence by a close approximation (not necessarily an exact match) to the Shine–Dalgarno sequence. This approximate match occurs a short-ish distance, perhaps 12 to 30 nucleotides, before the start codon of the gene. Approximate pattern-matching techniques allow us to locate Shine–Dalgarno candidates and measure the closeness of the fit.

- There are other signals and features, all of which can be straightforwardly detected programmatically.

A gene-finding program can certainly find lots of clues, but the challenging question is to determine which of the features and signals, and in what combination, are truly indicative of a functioning gene. The entire community of scientists has yet to come up with a definitive answer. And yet, the cellular machinery seems to have little difficulty locating the genes it is going to transcribe and translate. If we want to write a program that performs even approximately as well as the cell, we could wait until the academic community understands the science well enough to precisely define how a nucleotide sequence operates as a functioning gene, and then translate that specification into a program. Unfortunately, we might have a very long wait. In the meantime, we can write the best possible program based on the current state of science.

The current state of the art microbial gene finder used at the Institute for Genomic Research (TIGR) is called Glimmer (gene locator and interpolated Markov modeler), which uses Markov models to locate genes in bacterial genomes [3]. **Markov models** are used to study systems that at any one time can be in any one of a finite number of states. Imagine a hypothetical device that is making its way along a strand of DNA. Let's suppose it can be in any one of two states: coding or noncoding. As it proceeds along the strand, it observes the current nucleotide and may change state. In a first-order Markov model, the next state is effectively determined knowing just the current state and the current nucleotide. In a second-order Markov model, the next state depends on two previous states and so on. Glimmer currently uses a combination of Markov models from first to eighth order. To determine the transition matrices for each of the orders, we need information about known genes in the organism under study. Those known genes are the **training set.** Once the parameters of the models have been determined, Glimmer can go into predictive mode and attempt to predict genes in the rest of the genome.

Glimmer is a sophisticated program incorporating the best of scientific investigation, statistical and mathematical understanding, and skillful program development. Glimmer is reported to be able to identify the start sites of known genes in *E. coli* with an accuracy of 87.4% [3]. Ribosomes, the cellular machines that translate mRNA into proteins and have never spent even a minute studying in a university, do significantly better!

Ribosomes were never programmed. There is no designer or programmer responsible for life. They evolved. Ribosomes that are good at translation contribute to the success of their hosts, who will therefore be more likely to produce offspring, who will in turn have similar ribosomes that are good at their job. Unsuccessful ribosomes let down their hosts and are less likely to persist.

In [14] the authors simulate the process of evolution to develop programs that predict the start sites of bacterial genes. They begin with a pool of programs, each of which has the code necessary to identify and quantify many features associated with gene start sites. Each program implements its own formula to combine the measurements made for every potential start site and come up with a single numerical value. In this way, each program produces its own assessment of each potential start site in the genome.

We can compute a score for several features that contribute to an overall evaluation of a potential start site for a gene. Let us call these feature scores $f_1$, $f_2, \ldots, f_k$. Each $f_i$ is an easily evaluated feature, such as:

- the resulting length of the gene
- the percentage CG content in the neighborhood of the start
- the quality of the potential binding sites preceding the start

In [14] each program is encoded by a parameter value set (PVS) $[\alpha_1, \alpha_2, \ldots, \alpha_k]$. The program uses these parameters to form a linear combination of the feature scores at every potential start site: $\alpha_1 f_1 + \alpha_2 f_2 + \cdots \alpha_k f_k$. Therefore, a program parameterized by $[\alpha_1, \alpha_2, \ldots, \alpha_k]$, is effectively a start site evaluation function. Because some functions perform better than others in predicting the known start sites of the genes in the training set, they provide the fitness function to drive the genetic algorithm.

An initial population of random vectors, each of the form $[\alpha_1, \alpha_2, \ldots, \alpha_k]$ is created. In each generation:

1. A subset $S$ of the training set is selected.
2. Each of the vectors is used to evaluate all of the potential start sites for genes in $S$. The highest scoring potential start site is noted as that vector's prediction.
3. The total number of correct predictions is calculated for each of the vectors. The vectors are ranked by these scores.
4. The highest scoring vectors are cross bred (intermingled) with other vectors; the lowest scoring vectors are deleted; the remaining vectors are subjected to random mutation.
5. This results in a new population of vectors ready for the next generation.

After hundreds or thousands of generations this program will develop a good set of $\alpha$ parameters resulting in a good start site predictor. The success of this genetic algorithm can be measured by seeing how well the resulting predictor performs on the remainder of the verified set.

The genome of *E. coli* has been very well studied in the EcoGene [16] project, and a large number of verified start sites are reported. In [14] the genes with verified starts are divided into a **training set** and a **testing set.** That pool of programs mentioned earlier is let loose on the training set. Whenever a program produces a high assessment for the verified start site, it is rewarded with survival points; any time it produces a high assessment for other sites or a low assessment for the verified site, it is punished by losing survival points.

The pool of programs undergoes several generations. In each generation, a subset of the training set is selected. Each program in the pool assesses a value for each of the potential start sites for each of the genes in the training set and receives or loses survival points according to the quality of its predictions. Some programs will do better than others.

The essence of a genetic algorithm is that the programs that do well should persist into the next generation, perhaps with minor modifications, and the unsuccessful programs should disappear. Ideally, it should be possible to perform mutations on the surviving programs, and it should be possible to produce "offspring" programs from two or more "parent" programs. By thus simulating the process of evolution, the authors of [14] report a program evolved that correctly predicted the verified start sites of the genes outside of the training set with a success rate of 95%.

# 6.4 MODELING EVOLUTIONARY RELATIONSHIPS

When we design a genetic algorithm we have the advantage of simulating evolution at a pace at which we can observe the changes relatively rapidly. In reality, of course, most evolutionary change occurs over such a long time span that we simply cannot see the steps in the process. All we usually have is the endpoint of those evolutions. Therefore, the second, and more fundamental task for evolutionary biologists is to model evolution given an observed endpoint and a presumed start point.

Suppose we have a population of creatures whom we shall designate as being of species A. At some point in the history of this species an event occurred that physically separated one group of A from the rest. Perhaps a river changed direction or some volcanic activity separated this group. As time went on, mutations occurred in the separated group as well as in the rest. It is statistically implausible that exactly the same mutations occurred in both populations, so over time, the two populations undergo speciation. The exact moment at which the speciation event occurred is not determinable. There may have been a longish period when the populations were not entirely incompatible: For example it may be that for a time some, but not all, individuals of the breakoff population were capable of breeding with some individuals of the other group. Although we cannot determine an exact moment at which a new species arose from a population, we can often determine a time interval during which it happened.

So we start with population A, which after splitting and mutation, becomes species B and C. We say that population A was the **common ancestor** or concestor. Species B and C are the new species. Notice that individuals of A and B or of A and C can never coexist: They belong to distinct eras; they will never meet; so the question of whether an A can produce offspring with a B is moot. Accordingly, we generally represent evolutionary separations of species as bifurcation events: One concestor species gives rise to two new species. (Figure 6.2).

The choice of B or C to be the continuation of species A is arbitrary. The creatures of the C community being considered the same species as A is depicted

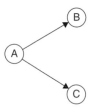

**FIGURE 6.2**    Species A bifurcates and gives rise to species B and species C.

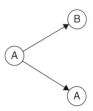

**FIGURE 6.3**    Species A continues, but a new species B splits off.

in Figure 6.3. It is important to realize, however, that significant mutation will have occurred, and the genomes of the two communities both labeled A will be very different. It can never, of course, be known if it is possible for parents, one from each of the two groups labeled A, to produce viable offspring.

As an example, consider humans and chimpanzees. Humans and chimpanzees likely share a concestor. Declaring that concestor a chimpanzee is another arbitrary call. Some physiological evidence may exist to support or to refute the claim; but one thing is for sure: Much mutation has occurred between the two groups named "chimpanzee." It can never be verified if the two groups labeled "chimpanzee" are, in fact, the same species. If somebody chooses to claim that they are, we will not contradict them. The naming of the groups is irrelevant to the computational study of phylogeny. Nevertheless, such distinctions do severely vex many worthy scientists. Phylogeny can be very controversial.

Let us list the properties that we believe underlie the speciation process:

1. Speciation occurs by bifurcation: One concestor gives rise to two new species (one of which may, accidentally and largely meaninglessly, share the name of the concestor species).
2. It is not generally possible to identify the exact moment when bifurcation occurs. Nevertheless, it does occur, and we can put limits on that event.
3. Every pair of species has exactly one nearest concestor.

This means that there exists a "tree of life." At its root is the concestor of all the species extant on Earth today or that ever existed at any point in the past. Species living today occur as leaves of the tree (they may or may not be the same species as the species corresponding to an internal "parent" node, but that is irrelevant and untestable). Extinct species occur as leaves of the tree (and again, they may or may not be the same as a parent species at an internal node). If you

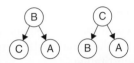

**FIGURE 6.4**    Other possible ancestral relationships between the species of Figure 6.2.

wish, you may claim all species at internal nodes are effectively extinct; or you may say that they continue by being the same as a child species. Figure 6.1 shows one version of a tree of life.

Ideally, the tree of life is a directed, rooted binary tree. One more factor further complicates our process. Sometimes we have no way of telling the direction of the arrows. Consider the relationships shown in Figure 6.2: Species A bifurcated to produce species B and species C. How do we know that? We don't. If all we possess is unreliably dated fossil evidence for the existence at one time of all three species, how can we know that the relationship is not, in fact, one of those depicted in Figure 6.4? Answering this question is the central challenge of the field of **phylogenetics,** the study of evolution as it has occurred. The output from a phylogenetic reconstruction is a **phylogenetic tree**—a visual representation of the postulated evolutionary history of a species. We say "postulated evolutionary history" because we cannot be certain that a given path was the actual path of evolution. We simply make our best guess based on the evidence available from molecular as well as fossil records.

## 6.4.1 Models of Mutation

To decide which of several possibilities represents the correct history of the evolution of a set of species, evolutionary biologists usually examine the history of mutations within each species. The idea is that the differences in the genomic sequences of species A, B, and C will help us organize them hierarchically so that we can more confidently say that A gave rise to B and C. In essence, we argue that if B and C share certain sequences with A, then they probably inherited those sequences from A. Therefore, A is the concestor of B and C. Any changes from A that we observe in B and C are mutations that accrued after speciation. By tracking the number of changes between concestor A and its descendants B and C, we can estimate a time interval during which A gave rise to species B and C. This is what we meant in the previous section when we said we could determine the interval during which speciation might have occurred but that we cannot pinpoint the specific moment of speciation. We use mutations to guess the time points at which speciation events occur, so to model evolution, we have to first model mutations.

When considering a mutation we need to know if it alters the information content of a given DNA sequence. A mutation that occurs in a coding region results in two possibilities: either it alters the information content, or it does not and is silent. Recall from Chapter 2 that triplets of nucleotides compose codons. More than one codon can code for an amino acid, so it is possible to alter a codon without altering the corresponding amino acid. When a mutation in a coding region results in a change that does not affect the downstream product, we say it is a **synonymous substitution.** Synonymous mutations are essentially silent mutations that occur in coding regions. If the mutation changes the amino acid, it is a **nonsynonymous substitution.**

Consider a family of proteins known as the histones. These proteins play a critical role in the cell: they are used to package and compress DNA so it can be stored within the nucleus of the cell. Because correct DNA packaging is essential for the cell to be able to store and protect its genetic content, any changes to the histones will result in cell death. As a result, the histone proteins in your cells look nearly identical to the histone proteins of every other eukaryote. In fact, our histone proteins have just three amino acid changes from the ones used in yeast. Several hundred million years ago humans and yeast diverged from a common ancestor. So the relative lack of change is striking. To give you a sense of how well conserved these proteins are, consider that up to 70% of the amino acids have changed between the average human protein and its yeast counterpart.

If three amino acid changes have occurred between the human histone and the yeast histones, we can say that three nonsynonymous substitutions have taken place. Finding these substitutions is easy. We simply align the protein sequences and note where the amino acids do not match exactly. In contrast, to find the synonymous substitutions, we must look at the DNA sequences. When we line up the DNA sequences of human and yeast histones, as many as 57 changes are evident. Of these, 54 are synonymous substitutions (remember that there were three nonsynonymous substitutions too). So you can see how synonymous mutations can be much more frequent without ever affecting the fitness of a given individual.

The mutation rate is not evenly distributed across a genome. Some regions of the genome have more mutations over time than other regions. In general, mutations tend to accrue in regions of the genome where changes to the DNA have little or no effect on the organism's survival. The reason for this should be obvious: silent mutations do not confer any advantages, but they are also not deleterious. There is no selective pressure on these mutations, so they simply accumulate over time. For example, the noncoding regions of genes (introns), have many more changes than the coding regions (exons). In fact, one way to find the exons in a genome is to compare it with a related species. The conserved regions are most likely to be the exons, and the unconserved regions are the introns or other noncoding regions of the genome.

Because the well-conserved regions of the genome are likely to be functional, we say these regions are **functionally constrained.** That is, there is strong pressure for these regions to be unchanged. What does this mean? It means that organisms that sustain a mutation in these regions are likely to be eliminated from the population. This is true for two reasons. First, the majority of mutations will be deleterious because random modification of nucleotides will more often disrupt the information content of the genome than enhance it. Second, if the region in question is critical for the organism's survival, then any mutation, however small, is likely to upset the organism's overall functioning. Again, this leads to death.

Functionally constrained regions can have variable rates of mutation, however. Remember that synonymous substitutions are well tolerated because they have a minimal effect on the downstream products. They do not alter the overall information content of the region. Nonsynonymous substitutions alter the information content and they are therefore likely to be deleterious. Since mutations are random by nature, we expect that a given genomic region will have about equal numbers of synonymous and nonsynonymous substitutions. In reality, however, the ratio of synonymous to nonsynonymous can vary dramatically across a genome, a genomic region, and even within a gene. The variability results from whether a functional constraint exists in that region.

When estimating the background rate of mutation, therefore, we must consider whether our genomic region is under a functional constraint. If it is, then any estimates of the mutation rate will be skewed. Given this consideration, where should we look for the best estimate of the background rate? Obviously, we want those regions of the genome that have little or no functional constraints. Repeat regions are a good bet because they do not usually serve a vital function within the organism's genome, but they do accrue mutations just like the rest of the genome.

## A Worked Example: Modeling Mutation Rates in HIV

Let us say we want to determine the rate of mutation in the HIV genome. As with any genome, rates vary across the genome because of functional and other constraints. The background mutation rate, or the average across the entire genome, is likely to be very different from the rates within specific regions of the genome. So when we consider the mutation rate for HIV we have to ask ourselves which rate we are most interested in determining.

Considering the mutation rates in a viral genome such as HIV adds another twist. In Chapter 2, we mentioned that HIV is a member of a family of viruses known as retroviruses. Recall that the HIV genome is actually RNA that is reverse-transcribed to DNA before being transcribed and translated into the proteins that are required for the virus to infect and replicate in host cells. The reverse transcription process is more prone to error than DNA to DNA replication. This is because unlike in DNA to DNA replication, no proofreading of the newly synthesized strand takes place during reverse transcription. This is somewhat like copying a program's code without spell-checking the code during the copying process. Every now and then, a spelling mistake or typo might be introduced, and no attempt is made to check the new copy to see if such an error has occurred. As a result, although the error rate for DNA to DNA replication is barely 1 error per 1 billion bases, ($1 \times 10^{-9}$) the error rate with reverse transcription is closer to 5 to 7 errors in every 10,000 bases ($5 \times 10^{-4}$). Since the HIV genome is 9749 nucleotides long, we can reasonably expect about five to seven errors with each round of reverse transcription. The end result is that each viral particle is likely to have five to seven mutations compared with its parent. Each "generation" of virus particles is likely to be much more diverse as a population than in a species with high-fidelity replication. In essence, a population of HIV virus particles will be much more diverse than a similar population of bacteria or humans.

This brings up a key point. The background mutation rate in HIV will be several-fold higher than it is for organisms that use DNA as their genomic material. However, even if the rate of mutation is higher, the types and effects of these mutations will be the same as they would be in an organism such as *E. coli*. In other words, we can still look at HIV as a means for understanding how mutations occur and how they influence the survival of a population.

We have already discussed the types of mutations that can occur. As with DNA replication, reverse transcription errors most often result in substitution mutations. That is, one nucleotide is accidentally replaced by another. The frequency with which any particular nucleotide is replaced is not evenly distributed, however. Certain nucleotide replacements are more common than others. In Chapter 2, we explained that nucleotides come in two forms: pyrimidines and purines (Figure 6.5). In DNA, the nucleotides A and G are purines and the nucleotides C and T are pyrimidines. In RNA as in the HIV genome, T is replaced by U, which is also a pyrimidine. It is much more common for an A to be replaced by a G or vice versa than it is for an A to be replaced by a C. That is, it is more common to accidentally replace one purine with another than to replace a purine with a pyrimidine. When a mutation results in a change between two purines (A to G, for example), we say that a **transition** mutation has occurred. The rarer case of a purine to pyrimidine change (A to C for example) is known as a **transversion.** We can build a table (known as a transition–transversion matrix) of the probabilities of transitions versus transversions for a given species. Table 6.1 is an example of how we might construct such a table.

In the HIV genome as with other genomes, transitions are much more frequent than transversions. In addition, certain transitions are particularly common. For example, a recent study found that the most common mutation between generations of HIV particles was a G to A transition. The set of mutations identified in this study are reproduced in Table 6.2. As you can see, substitution mutations and especially transitions are very common. Some transversions never occurred, at least in this sample, but that might reflect the nature of the study and the data rather than some unusual frequency distribution. In any case, the general principle holds: substitution mutations are most common, with transition substitutions being the most frequent type of substitution. As you can see from Table 6.2, insertions and deletions are very rare.

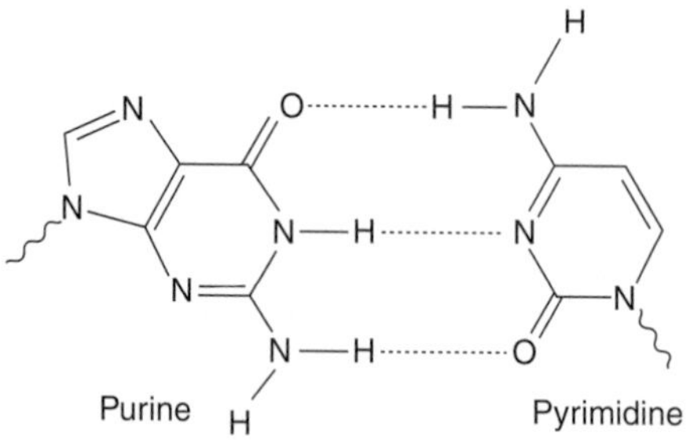

**FIGURE 6.5**    Purine and pyrimidine structures.

**TABLE 6.1   Transition–Transversion matrix***

|   | A | G | C | T |
|---|---|---|---|---|
| A | $1-a-2b$ | a | b | b |
| G | a | $1-a-2b$ | b | b |
| C | b | b | $1-a-2b$ | a |
| T | b | b | a | $1-a-2b$ |

*This table is an example of a transition–transversion matrix. We estimate the rate of transitions (a) and transversions (b) from a set of representative sequences. The table then allows us to plug in the estimated values. For the identity transitions (i.e., A → A or G → G), we estimate the probability that no change occurred as what remains if neither a transition nor a transversion takes place. Hence, we say it is $(1-a-2b)$. We have to include both possible transversions (2b) because an A could have become either a C or a T, whereas the only transition possible for an A would be to G.

**TABLE 6.2   Types and frequency of mutations in HIV**

| Nucleotide change(s) | Number of recovered mutants |
|---|---|
| G to A | 15 |
| C to T | 6 |
| T to C | 2 |
| T to G | 1 |
| T to A | 1 |
| deletion of 8 nucleotides | 1 |
| deletion of 21 | 1 |
| deletion of 33 | 1 |
| deletion of 4, insertion of 15 | 1 |
| Total | 38 |

L. M. Mansky and H. M. Temin. Lower in vivo mutation rate of human immunodeficiency virus type 1 than that predicted from the fidelity of purified reverse transcriptase. *J Virol,* 69:5087–5094, 1995, by permission of the American Society for Microbiology.

Tallying the number and type of mutations in a genome is known as estimating the rate of mutation. Because substitutions are the most common mutations, we frequently estimate only the rate of substitution and use this to extrapolate the overall rate of mutation in a genome. To estimate the rate of substitution, we have to compare the genomes of the population after every generation with the original or parent strain. In this study, for example, HIV particles were compared with those of the parent strain after just one generation. Because of the high error rate of reverse transcriptase, we can get a reasonably good sense of the mutation rate after just one generation of HIV particles. In other organisms, we would need to wait many more generations before estimating the rate of substitution because of the higher fidelity of DNA replication. In any case, estimating the rate of substitution is a simple process: we count up the number of substitutions in the progeny generation's genome and compare it with the number in the parent generation's genome. The key point is that we can use sequence comparisons and some knowledge of the nature of mutations to estimate the rates of mutation in a specific organism or virus such as HIV.

### Modeling Mutation Rates in General

Although substitution rates for individual species and organisms can be valuable, we need a more general sense of the rates of mutation across a variety of species and conditions. That way, we can begin to understand how evolution operates across a broad spectrum. We therefore want to use individual estimates of substitution rates from various species to create a general model of substitution. A model of substitution is a fairly straightforward concept. We want to capture the idea that some substitutions are more common than others (e.g., transitions versus transversions), and we want to quantify these observations so that they can be applied across a variety of species.

With a generalized model of substitution, we can ask how genomes and organisms are related to each other. We do this by considering how many changes exist between two organisms or their genomes. The more changes in the genomes, the farther apart the two are on the tree of life. This is because we expect substitutions and mutations in general to accrue over time, so the more differences that occur, the longer the two genomes have been apart as separate species. If we want to create a tree of relationships amongst organisms, we must have a way of modeling the substitutions we see between their genomes. So the model of substitution becomes a key prerequisite for building phylogenetic trees.

There are three commonly used models of substitution. The simplest is known as Jukes–Cantor, after Thomas H. Jukes and Charles R. Cantor who first proposed the model in 1969. In this model, we weight all substitutions the same. At first glance, this seems hardly worth the effort; we already know that some kinds of substitutions seem to be more common than others. Oddly enough, however, the Jukes–Cantor model remains surprisingly robust. In other words, many times, just using the simple, unweighted measure of substitutions generates as good a phylogenetic tree as one with a more complex model. This suggests that despite the fact that some differences occur in the types of substitutions, the differences may not be as important over long evolutionary periods of time. This is actually the key reason for using the Jukes–Cantor model: when we look across millions of years of evolution, the number of substitutions is sufficiently large that slight differences in the transition versus the transversion rate are smoothed out. In other words, the preference for transitions over transversions gets averaged out over time and has little influence on the overall evolutionary history between two species.

Despite the success of the Jukes-Cantor method, in some situations we need a more nuanced model of substitution. For example, when we compare two closely related species, such as chimpanzees and bonobos (*Pan paniscus*), the number of substitutions is likely to be small. In this case, we want to be able to weight each transition and transversion a little differently so that we can maximize the importance of every substitution we can identify. For these situations, we use a model of substitution known as the Kimura 2 parameter. Named after the mathematical biologist Motoo Kimura, the "2 parameter" part of the model name refers to the idea of having two weights: one for transitions and one for transversions. We do not worry too much about whether the transition is from A to G or T to C or some other combination. In the Kimura 2 parameter model, all transitions and all transversions are equally probable events. The difference in frequency is between transitions and transversions, not between specific instances of either.

Between the Jukes–Cantor model and the Kimura 2 parameter, almost all phylogenetic problems can be adequately modeled. In addition, because these are relatively simple models with few parameters (variables), we can use them even when we have limited data available about the substitutions between two species. However, in some rare instances we need even more detail than either model can provide. For example, if we were trying to understand the evolutionary divergence of strains of HIV, we may need to model not just transitions and transversions but the specific frequency of substitutions that transform an A to a G or vice versa. Since there are four nucleotides, a total of 12 transformations are possible (excluding the 4 identity transformations of A to A, C to C, G to G, and T to T). We can weight each of these separately and then model the rate of substitution. This is known as the full-parameter model. To use this model, however, you would need a very large amount of reliable data on substitutions so that you could accurately estimate the frequency of each transformation. The full-parameter model is used very rarely, in part because the need for large, reliable data sets limits its use. Generally, the results from the Jukes–Cantor model or the Kimura 2 parameter give a good enough approximation so using a more complex model is unnecessary.

# 6.5 DISCOVERING EVOLUTIONARY RELATIONSHIPS

We now have all the pieces in place to build a phylogenetic tree. We have some data from species, an understanding of how evolution works, and a likely model of mutations. What next? Here is where things start to get murky. Phylogenetic reconstruction is almost as much an art as a science.

The art of phylogenetic analysis is the plausible reproduction of the most likely tree of relationships between species based on a study of observed changes. But what do we mean by "most likely tree of relationships"? Since we do not *know* the exact trajectory of a species' evolutionary history, we have to rely on conjecture. Is it possible to discern this trajectory working from first principles? How can we transfer our reasoning process to an algorithm that can generate the most plausible trees? There are no easy answers. That's what makes phylogeny such an interesting challenge.

Before we look at techniques that have been used in bioinformatics, let us note that the problem of how best to build phylogenies is not unique to our discipline. For example, linguists have tried to establish ancestral relationships between languages. They might begin with the observation that Italian and Spanish share much vocabulary and syntax, indicating that both may be "descended" from a common ancestor. Then German and English are fairly similar and likely share a recent common ancestor. Then one might seek common ancestry between those ancestors ... It's a very similar problem to ours. Indeed, in a recent paper, some linguists used a phylogenetic technique called **maximum parsimony** (Section 6.5.1) to try and figure out the "evolution" of language in the peoples who colonized the Pacific islands and Australia [8].

Because of the uncertainty inherent in any reconstruction of the past, each of the methods we describe in this section can only yield a "best guess" phylogenetic tree. This is one of those areas where there may be no single right answer or even any right answer. This is part of what makes phylogenetics so difficult: sometimes all the hard work of reconstruction yields a solution that we then have to abandon as completely incorrect. The following example demonstrates this in some detail.

Figure 6.6 presents three options for the possible phylogeny of snakes, chickens, and humans. We concentrate on one physiological feature: In humans, its arms; in chickens its wings; and in snakes its nothing. Which of "snake first," "chicken first," "human first" presents the most plausible scenario?

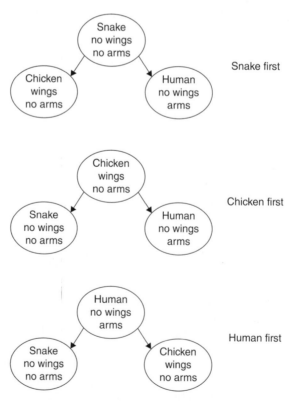

**FIGURE 6.6**   Three plausible phylogenies for snakes, chickens, and humans.

"Chicken first," in which chickens beget humans and snakes, requires chickens to lose their wings in one branch and to lose wings and gain arms in the other branch. That's a total of three major mutations. Humans beget snakes and chickens in "human first": One branch loses arms, the other loses arms and gains wings. Again "human first" requires three major mutations. The left branch of "snake first" shows snakes begetting chickens and gaining wings (one major mutation), and the right branch depicts snakes begetting humans by gaining arms (one more major mutation). So the scenario in "snake first" requires fewer major mutations than the other scenarios, and on that basis we consider it to be the most plausible of the three. It's a simpler, more economical explanation of the relationships between the three species, and therefore to be preferred. In phylogenetic analysis, we say this is the most **parsimonious** explanation. In general, scientists prefer parsimonious, or simple, explanations over more complex ones. This idea derives from Occam's razor, a central tenet to most scientific enterprises formulated by William of Occam in the fourteenth century. William of Occam suggested that "entities should not be needlessly multiplied," or in modern-day parlance, "keep it simple, stupid!"

Nevertheless, the analysis is wrong! There is much evidence that snakes and birds are descended from a reptilian ancestor who shares a common ancestor with humans. The more plausible phylogeny is shown in Figure 6.7. Three changes occur along arcs of this new tree: protoarms to wings, protoarms disappearing to vestigial arms, and protoarms becoming human arms. In a sense, these changes are not as drastic as those along any of the arcs in Figure 6.6. The approach we used in generating our trees is fundamentally flawed and leads to the wrong tree. We will return to why our approach produced the wrong tree in Section 6.5.3.

In the meantime, here's the problem: *Given a set of species, each with its own set of characteristics (be they physiological or molecular), place the species as vertices in a tree, possibly adding new intermediate ancestral nodes, in such a way that it represents the plausible evolutionary history of the species.* The next sections describe different ways we can solve this problem algorithmically.

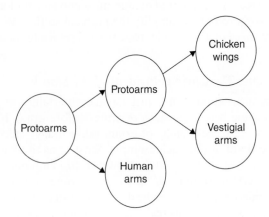

**FIGURE 6.7**   Another phylogenetic tree linking snakes, chickens, and humans.

## 6.5.1  Parsimony

As we discussed earlier in the context of ancestral relationships between birds, snakes, and humans, parsimony seeks the evolutionarily most economical ancestral relationship among species of interest. That is that the one that requires the fewest evolutionary events to explain itself. In principle, seeking the maximally parsimonious tree is an excellent way to reconstruct the likely progress of evolution in producing a diversity of species. In practice, however, parsimony is limited because of the intractably large number of potential trees. Exercise 6.10 helps you explore this for yourself.

---

**Exercise 6.10**    How many binary trees are there on $n$ nodes? (*Hint:* A good way to answer this question is to observe that every binary tree on $n$ nodes has a left child on $k$ nodes (for some $k$) and a right child on $(n - k - 1)$ nodes. There is one binary tree on one node. This gives a recursive formula for the number of trees on $n$ nodes. You'll need to sum over all the possible $k$ values. So you'll have a recursive function implementing the recurrence $T_n = \sum T_k T_{n-k-1}$ with appropriate ranges for $k$ and appropriate base cases. Your program should predict that the number of trees on 1, 2, 3, 4, 5, and 6 nodes, respectively are 1, 2, 5, 14, 42, and 132. It's a very fast growing sequence, and if you want to know more about it, do an Internet search for "catalan numbers.")

---

Technically in Exercise 6.10 we are counting rooted binary trees, and the case can be made that evolutionary trees should be unrooted. Either way, it doesn't make much difference to the observation that for significant $n$ (more than just a few species) the number of possible evolutionary trees is so large as to prevent a thorough examination of every single possibility. Beyond the difficulty that the number of trees on $n$ nodes is so large, consider also the fact that there are about $n!$ ways to place each species at a node. And beyond that, we have not even considered the additional complexity of adding new common ancestral nodes! To get an answer in a reasonable amount of time, most implementations of maximum parsimony use workarounds to simplify the problem so that we do not have to search the entire space of all possible trees. We will return to these workarounds shortly.

### A worked example: The Curious Incident of the Skunk

Phylogenetic reconstruction is not just an idle entertainment in speculating whether snakes came before chickens or wings before arms. It provides very important insights into the biology of extant (alive today) species. The mysterious case of the skunk is one such example. Most of us think of skunks, if we think of them at all, as stinky roadkill. However, from a biologist's perspective they represent a very interesting puzzle. The mysterious case of the skunk is an example of how misclassification can lead to all sorts of confusion; much like the diploma mills can masquerade as real educational institutions by using the .edu Web address suffix.

For many decades it was thought that skunks were a member of the weasel family. Before the advent of rapid genome-sequencing technologies, biologists classified organisms based on their physical characteristics, known as **morphological characters.** When we were trying to decide if wings or arms came first earlier in this section, we were looking at morphological characters. Today, most phylogenetic analyses use genetic data, but morphological characters remain important in some areas, especially when genetic data is lacking.

Sometimes the appearances of a species are deceptive. For example, both the leopard moth and the leopard cat have dark spots against a pale yellow background. Does this make the moth and the cat closely related species? Hardly! Both the moth and the cat have these markings because spots help camouflage them in the dappled shade of wooded areas. The fact that they each independently developed the same solution is an example of **convergent evolution.** Sometimes, natural selection strikes on the same solution, even though the starting points were entirely different. One of the difficulties with using morphological characters to classify species is that convergent evolution gets in the way. Indeed, one of the reasons that our parsimonious solution to the "arms first" versus "wings first" analysis was incorrect was because we were focusing on large-scale, morphological characters instead of the underlying subtle changes that would drive protoarms to wings (in chickens), arms (in humans), and no arms (in snakes).

Which brings us to the case of the skunk. In appearance, skunks, look a great deal like weasels. The mystery arose because although skunks certainly look like weasels, their genomic organization and composition are very different. How could they share a common ancestor with weasels if there is so little similarity in their genetic makeup? This might not seem like an important problem. So what if skunks were badly misunderstood? Unfortunately, the wrong classification of skunks has led to all sorts of confusion, not only about skunks but also about weasels [4].

To build a family tree of weasels, skunks, and other species, two researchers decided to look at DNA sequences from mitochondria of these species. The mitochondria are unique in that they contain their own DNA (see Chapter 2), and they are passed exclusively through the maternal (mother's) line. In other words, all the mitochondria in your body are genetically identical to those in your mother. This is a great asset because any changes that occur in the mitochondrial genome are entirely the result of mutations and random forces, rather than the result of combining with genetic information from other sources. This contrasts with the DNA in the nucleus of cells, where one copy comes from each of the two parents.

To compare the mitochondrial sequences of these species and determine their relationships to one another, the researchers followed the standard procedure in phylogenetics [19]. They started by lining up the sequences using a multiple sequence alignment algorithm (see Chapter 5). Each point where some of the sequences differed would be noted. For example, Table 6.3 shows a segment of the alignment among four sequences from different species.

To build a tree of relationships among species, we look at the columns of the alignment. We want to determine the likely ancestral relationships among

**TABLE 6.3**    **An example of a multiple sequence alignment that can be used in phylogenetic analyses***

| Species | Nucleotide Sequence | | | | | |
|---|---|---|---|---|---|---|
| | 1 | 2 | 3 | 4 | 5 | 6 |
| Species I | C | T | G | A | A | C |
| Species II | C | T | G | A | A | T |
| Species III | C | A | A | A | G | C |
| Species IV | C | A | G | A | G | C |

*An example of a multiple sequence alignment that can be used in phylogenetic analyses. The objective is to identify those nucleotide positions that are informative, or that would allow you to distinguish between two or more possible phylogenetic trees.

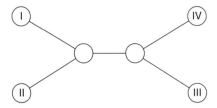

**FIGURE 6.8**    Is this the ancestral relationship between the species aligned in Table 6.3?

species I, II, III, and IV. Is it likely to be as shown in Figure 6.8? Or do the labels at the leaves need to be permuted? We will apply the principle of maximum parsimony to help us decide. First of all, we need to identify those columns of the alignment that will help us to build a tree of the relationships among the species. In Table 6.3, columns 1 and 4 contain the same nucleotide in all four species. We therefore assume that any ancestral sequence probably had a C in position 1 and an A at position 4. Any other assumption would make us less parsimonious! But the column gives us no information at all as to whether the positioning of the species as shown in Figure 6.8 is correct. Columns 1 and 4 are termed **uninformative.**

In each of the other columns the sequence changes from one species to another. These are the columns we care about. But not all of these columns can help us identify a parsimonious tree. If two species have one nucleotide and two others have a different one, then we can say that the change occurred after the first two species had evolved but before the other two species became distinct. Consider column 2: species I and II have a T in that position, but species III and IV have an A. This suggests that species I and II are more closely related than species I and III. In other words, the information in column 2 helps us make a decision about relationships. We consider such a position to be **informative.** It supports the top labeling we have shown in Figure 6.9 over the second labeling, because the sum of letter-changes over all edges of the top diagram is only one, whereas in the lower diagram, there is no way to label the inner nodes to produce a total of fewer than two letter changes.

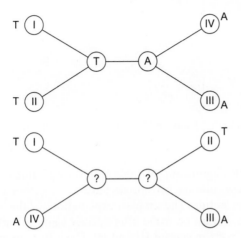

**FIGURE 6.9**   Column 2 of Table 6.3 is informative. It enables us to recognize the upper tree as more parsimonious than the lower.

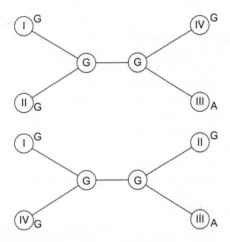

**FIGURE 6.10**   Column 3 of Table 6.3 is uninformative. It does not enable us to distinguish between these two trees.

Sometimes a column contains the same nucleotide in three positions (see column 3). What can we deduce from this column? We can conclude that species III had a mutation that differentiates it from the other three species. However, we cannot directly draw any further conclusions about the relationship of species III to the other species. This is because we can draw several different trees from this one column of information, but they all look the same (Figure 6.10), and the total number of letter changes on edges of all possible trees is just one (the single change from G to A on the edge leading to species III). So column 3 is also uninformative.

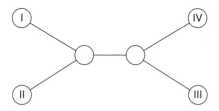

**FIGURE 6.11**    Columns 2 and 5 of Table 6.3 are the informative sites. Both sites support the same tree.

In our example alignment (see Table 6.3), only columns 2 and 5 have informative sites. In these columns two species have one nucleotide and the other two have a different nucleotide. The simplest explanation for the information in column 2, is that a mutation occurred after species I and II had evolved and that this mutation is carried in species III and IV. The information in column 5 also supports this tree as the more parsimonious solution. Figure 6.11 shows the final version of a putative tree of the four species.

So what was the final result of the maximum parsimony analysis of skunk mitochondrial DNA? The results were surprising. It turns out that skunk sequences are much more ancient than any other members of the weasel family. Skunks evolved well before the common ancestor of weasels, minks, and badgers. In fact, the phylogenetic analysis elevated skunks to a new, prestigious position: oldest extant carnivore [4]. In other words, skunks are now believed to be the only living members of Earth's first family of carnivorous mammals. The phylogenetic analysis using genetic data also resolved the mystery of the skunks within the weasel family; they are not members of that family at all. Instead, skunks are now classified in their own family (Mephitidae), which is derived from the Latin root for "noxious odor." So the mystery of the skunk turns out to be a case of mistaken identity; it is also an example of how computational and molecular techniques can help further our understanding of biology.

### The Parsimony Approach

In general, algorithms employing maximum parsimony use the following steps to identify the most parsimonious tree from a set of sequence data.

1. Generate an unrooted tree with nodes that represent each of the species (or *taxa*, a more general term often used in this context).
2. Evaluate the number of changes required to generate this tree.
3. Compare this value with the values from other trees.
4. Select the tree that has the lowest value (least number of changes).

Most algorithms iterate this procedure across each column of the multiple sequence alignment, summing the number of changes required for each informative site. The algorithm then identifies the tree that best explains each informative site in the alignment. When we say a tree "best explains" an informative site, we mean that it represents an organization of the taxa in a way that requires the fewest possible changes to go from one taxa to the next. Exercise 6.11 allows you to try your hand at the maximum parsimony approach using a simplified version of the required input data.

**Exercise 6.11**

Write a program to determine which of the sites in the multiple-sequence alignment are informative. Then, draw the trees derived from each of these informative sites and identify the most parsimonious tree. How many changes in total does this tree require to explain the informative changes observed?

| Taxa | 1 | 2 | 3 | 4 | 5 | 6 |
|---|---|---|---|---|---|---|
| Species I | C | G | T | T | A | C |
| Species II | C | T | A | A | T | G |
| Species III | C | G | A | T | C | C |
| Species IV | G | T | A | A | G | G |

So far, we have taken straightforward examples of four species and a few informative sites per alignment. Obviously, these simple examples are not representative of the full complexity of a problem such as figuring out the evolutionary history of skunks. In the specific case of the skunk analysis, the researchers compared sequences from 26 different species. Each DNA sequence analyzed was over 1100 base pairs long. So you can see how this would require a good deal more work than the simple examples we have presented here. If you go back to Exercise 6.10, you can estimate the number of rooted trees possible for 26 taxa. The number of unrooted trees and the kind of trees generated by maximum parsimony, would be several orders of magnitude higher.

### Workarounds to Exhaustive Searching

This illustrates the first problem with maximum parsimony: The search space for the maximum parsimony algorithm includes a potentially enormous number of candidate trees. To evaluate every possible tree in this huge search space is an NP-hard problem. As with other problems in the biological realm that are either NP-complete or NP-hard (think of global pairwise sequence alignment from Chapter 5), however, we can find a way around this apparent obstacle.

A common approach is to start by building a candidate tree using a different tree-building method, such as neighbor joining or UPGMA (see Section 6.5.2). These methods are faster computationally, and they help provide a sense of the right "neighborhood" of trees. That is, given the set of all possible trees, which would be impossible to search completely, we narrow our search to those trees most likely to be "right." You can probably see the inherent problems with this approach immediately: how do we know that we are looking at the trees that are most likely to be "right?" And if we know what the right tree is, why are we even bothering to build a tree in the first place? The danger with this approach, also known as **branch and bound,** is that we end up like the proverbial drunk searching for his car keys under the lamppost because "there's more light here," even though we lost the key somewhere else.

Having said that, our situation is better than the drunk's because, unlike locating a lost object in the dark, phylogenetic reconstruction is contingent on several, related factors. Remember that the evolutionary history of an organism is captured in its genomic record through the mutations and changes that accrue over time. Phylogenetic reconstruction focuses on these changes, and any tree-building method will derive a tree based in some fashion on the mutation records of the species of interest. Therefore, using a quick method to find the right neighborhood and then an iterative, intensive method such as maximum parsimony can help solve an otherwise intractable problem.

To better understand why this might be the case, imagine you are trying to locate your friend's house in a new city. Your friend has just moved there, so you cannot remember the exact street address of his new home. What he can tell you is that his home is "the yellow house down the street from the gas station." With only this bit of information, locating his home in any sizable city might prove impossible. Certainly if his home were the only yellow house in the entire city, or near the only gas station in the city, you would have a good chance. But otherwise, you are left with a bewildering set of options: many yellow houses, some coincidentally near gas stations, and no idea of which is your friend's. This scenario is similar to an exhaustive maximum parsimony search, in which every possible tree must be evaluated to identify the best tree. Sometimes this method works: in those cases where the best tree is so distinctive (like the only yellow house or the only gas station) that it pops up. Usually, this is not the case. Instead, days, weeks, months later, the algorithm is still considering possible trees, and you would have likely moved on to other pursuits that do not require phylogenetics at all.

Now suppose that just as you are despairing of ever finding your friend's new home, you suddenly remember the zip code for his new address. Things are suddenly much more promising: with a zip code, you can now hunt around a relatively small area for the yellow house by the gas station. The chances are greater that within any given zip code, there will only be one or maybe a handful of yellow houses near gas stations.[3] Searching for your friend's home among this limited area is more likely to yield success.

The same logic applies to branch and bound. You use another tree-building method to get to the right "zip code" of the tree space, and then you hunt for the best (i.e., most parsimonious) tree among the trees in this area. If it turns out that none of these trees are particularly parsimonious, you can iterate the procedure: try a different tree-building method, locate a different part of the tree space, reevaluate the trees there with maximum parsimony and see if the best tree exists in that region. So branch and bound approaches are not nearly as foolish as they might appear at first glance. More on branch and bound and other workarounds to exhaustive searching can be found by following some of these references [9,18].

---

[3] Unless of course you are in some bizarre wonderland where every house is yellow and every block has a gas station!

### Workarounds to Multiple Most Parsimonious Trees

Maximum parsimony creates some other roadblocks on the path to successful phylogenetic reconstruction. One of the biggest problems is illustrated in Exercise 6.12.

**Exercise 6.12**

Identify the informative sites from the following multiple-sequence alignment and identify the most parsimonious tree from these data.

| Taxa | 1 | 2 | 3 | 4 | 5 | 6 |
|------|---|---|---|---|---|---|
| Species I | G | A | T | A | T | C |
| Species II | G | C | T | A | T | A |
| Species III | T | C | T | A | G | A |
| Species IV | T | A | T | G | G | C |

Can you identify just one tree that yields the best explanation for the changes you see in the table? As it turns out, there are actually two trees, both of them equally parsimonious, that can explain the data we see here. This leads to one of the biggest disadvantages of maximum parsimony: more than one tree can yield the same or a very similar level of parsimony. The problem is that each tree postulates a different evolutionary history, so you are then left to decide which of the trees is the most likely. Sometimes, you can use other evidence, such as the fossil record, to discard some of the trees as unlikely. Unfortunately, all too often you have to pick a tree based on relatively arbitrary criteria.

For example, in the past the phylogenetic analysis of humans, chimps, organutans, and gorillas came up with two equally parsimonious trees. In the one tree (Figure 6.12) humans share a common ancestor with chimps; gorillas and orangutans are presumed to have diverged at an earlier point. The equally likely alternative, however, was that humans shared a common ancestor with gorillas, and chimps and orangutans had diverged earlier (Figure 6.13). Which is the true evolutionary history of our species? At the time, no one knew for sure. Since then, additional genetic analyses have swayed opinion toward the first tree (see Figure 6.12).

The larger the number of taxa analyzed, the more likely that maximum parsimony will yield multiple, equally parsimonious trees. This is such a prevalent problem in the field, it has its own acronym: multiple MPTs (most parsimonious trees). The problem of multiple MPTs arises in part because we often do not have enough data to reliably pick the one best tree. This is certainly the case in Exercise 6.12, where we are looking at just six columns of an alignment. If we looked at more of the alignment, one of the two trees might become more encumbered with changes, thereby helping us to pick the other as the more parsimonious. Unfortunately, in most phylogenetic analyses, the data we have is all the data we will ever have. So asking for more data to help refine MPTs is usually unfeasible.

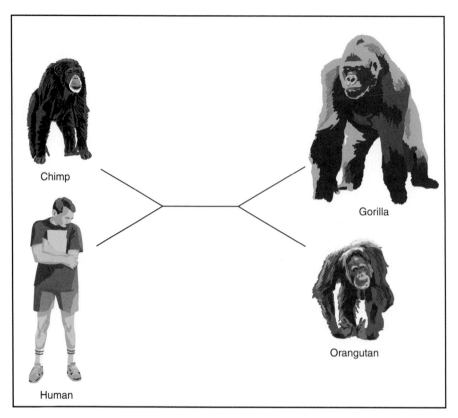

**FIGURE 6.12** One version of a phylogenetic tree of extant (living) species of primates. Here, humans share a common ancestor with chimps and are more diverged from gorillas and orangutans.

Instead, researchers in the field have devised some very clever statistical manipulations that can give us a good estimate of what trees are likely to be among the best. The chief method here is called **bootstrapping,** and at first glance, the approach will seem counterintuitive. We have just said that the multiple MPT problem arises because of a lack of data. In bootstrapping, you actually throw away parts of the data and ask how well you do with an even smaller dataset. So how can this possibly work? Here's a brief overview of the steps in bootstrapping:

1. Start by randomly picking informative sites from the overall dataset.
   Selection is not exclusive: you might pick the same site several times or not at all. The key here is that the selection of sites is *random.*
2. Use maximum parsimony to build trees.
3. Identify and save the set of MPTs.
4. Repeat steps 1 through 3 many times.
5. Note any trees that always show up in step 3.
6. Combine these trees using **consensus tree techniques.**

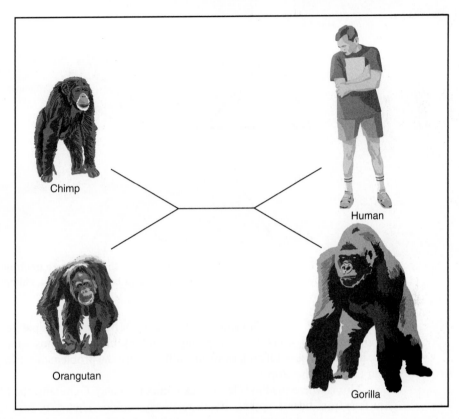

**FIGURE 6.13**   Another version of a phylogenetic tree for the same four species as Figure 6.13. Here, humans and gorillas share a common ancestor, and chimps and orangutans are more diverged.

The idea behind bootstrapping is that some of the data in your set may actually be adding noise instead of information. This is especially true of biological data: Some mutations may have no effect on the fitness of the population, and we might as well not look at those changes because they add nothing to the history of the species. So if you resample the data, randomly picking enough sites to fill your dataset, and then check the trees, you might overcome the noise in the data. In other words, by randomly sampling the data in different ways, you might be able to see through the distractions that the full dataset introduces in the analysis. In [10], the full algorithmic and implementation details for bootstrapping are provided in exhaustive detail.

You might still wonder what is so great about a technique that first eliminates data and then, over multiple iterations, generates even more MPTs than you started with (presumably each iteration of bootstrapping will yield several more MPTs)! Why would anyone ask for more confusion? The point is that if the data are consistent, then some of the trees will show up again and again. We will not delve into the details here, but it can be demonstrated statistically

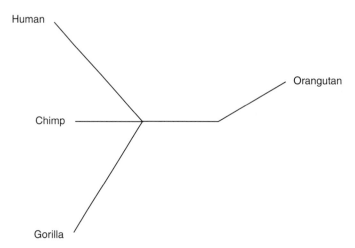

**FIGURE 6.14**    A consensus tree for primate species that contains a multifurcating node to accomodate uncertainties in the relationships between humans, chimps and gorillas.

that consistent data[4] will yield the same set of MPTs over multiple iterations of bootstrapping [10,11]. Bootstrapping, therefore, highlights those trees that are the best of the best. Of course, we are still left with the problem of picking among our cream of the crop.

This is where the final clever trick comes into play. Generally, the MPTs that surface from bootstrapping are all relatively similar. They may vary slightly in some branches, but the overall shapes are likely to be nearly identical. So rather than picking among entirely different trees, we now have to choose between trees that have only slight differences. Consider again the differences between the trees in Figures 6.12 and 6.13. In both trees, orangutans are on a different branch than humans. So we have to make a decision about just two species: chimps and gorillas. Which one goes with humans? This is at least a narrower problem than the question, "Which of humans, chimps, gorillas, and orangutans are most closely related?"

At this point, many phylogeneticists will simply start to combine trees using consensus tree techniques. Basically, wherever all the trees agree, such as that orangutans are always farther away from humans, that branch is transferred as is to the "master" tree. For places where trees are in dispute, the branches are merged into a multifurcating node rather than a bifurcating node. This approach essentially "passes the buck," in that it defers making a decision about whether one tree or another is right by equitably offering the possibility that all of them are right. Figure 6.14 shows the consensus tree that might derive from the analysis of humans, chimps, gorillas, and orangutans.

---

[4] Note the emphasis on *consistent* data; if you have conflicting data, you will never get any closer to solving the problem. However, with bootstrapping, you will at least know that you have conflicting data, which is a step toward fixing the problem.

## 6.5.2  Other Ways to Build Trees

Maximum parsimony is not a perfect solution to the phylogeny problem. Despite Occam's exhortations, the fact remains that the most parsimonious tree may not be the true tree. This is probably as much a consequence of the random nature of mutation as it is a reflection of the method itself. However, maximum parsimony is among the best methods for phylogenetic reconstruction available today. As a result, it tends to dominate the field.

Although maximum parsimony can yield a tree or set of trees that are likely to represent the evolutionary history of a group of species, the end result can be intellectually rather dissatisfying. For example, as we've already discussed, the multiple MPTs and the difficulty in trying to determine which (if any) is best is a problem.

This does not mean that there are not other ways to build trees. Indeed, we have already alluded to two other methods: neighbor joining and UPGMA. We turn next to these two methods. Both have several attractive advantages over maximum parsimony: they are computationally fast and they can often yield good estimates of the true tree. By "true tree" we mean the tree that represents the real evolutionary history of a group of species.

Furthermore, neighbor joining and UPGMA can give us something that maximum parsimony cannot: they can estimate the time since two species diverged. From an evolutionary perspective this is the real advantage. Imagine reading an entire history of World War II, but without ever knowing that it happened in the twentieth century. If you didn't know that, you might just as easily assume it happened during the time of the Egyptian pharaohs. You would then marvel at their technological prowess. With a sense of timescale, however, we gain both a perspective on what was impressive (the rapid development of technologies such as radar and the atom bomb) and what was more prosaic (the use of tanks and artillery to bombard the front lines). The same is true for phylogenetic reconstruction. It is all well and good to know that humans probably share a common ancestor with chimps, but how much better if we can say we think that chimps diverged from humans about the time that the savannahs began to expand in Africa. Now we can not only postulate the evolutionary history of humans and chimps, we can place them in an ecosystem and a context. Essentially, if we want to gain a sense of life at a point in the past, we need more than the narration of events, we need time as well.

So let's turn our attention to the problem of figuring out a numerical measure for the difference between two adjacent nodes in a phylogenetic tree. If the nodes contain purely sequence information, be it protein sequence or nucleotide sequence, we have seen enough examples when we studied alignment in Chapter 5 to know several ways to assign a measure to the distance between the two sequences. If the data at the nodes are morphological, then the methods for measuring the difference along the arc are far more arbitrary. For example, how would you assign a numerical value to the difference between a simple eye and a compound eye? Although biologists in the past have certainly attempted to assign distances based on morphological characteristics, we will focus here on sequence data.

### A worked example: Tree building with UPGMA

One technique that has been used with some success is known by the unfortunate and almost unpronounceable acronym UPGMA (unweighted pair group method with arithmetic mean). This fairly straightforward clustering technique depends on the assignment of numeric values to the differences between each pair of original nodes. Let's illustrate the technique with some invented data.

Suppose we have seven species: armadillo, beaver, cat, dog, elephant, flatfish, and gnu. And suppose we have a friendly biologist who assigns numeric values indicating how different each pair are from each other pair. Perhaps our biologist reckons cats and dogs are fairly similar (difference value 2), whereas armadilloes and flatfish are very different (value 23). In summary, after much persuasion, our friendly biologist fills in the matrix given in Figure 6.15.

The first step in the UPGMA process is to identify the closest neighbors, indicated by the lowest nonzero entry in the matrix. In our case, it is the dog and the cat, and their evolutionary distance is 2. So we create a new node, combining the dog and the cat, labeled CD. Think of it as the common ancestor of dog and cat, and it divided into the species 2 arbitrary time units ago. We now remove C and D from consideration, but replace them by the new node CD. The distance of CD from any other species X is the arithmetic mean of the distance of C from X and the distance of D from X. We obtain a new matrix shown in Figure 6.16.

Again we seek the lowest nonzero entry and combine them as in Figure 6.17. It is traditional to use a longer vertical line from AB to indicate the greater evolutionary distance between the common ancestor of A and B and its children. The next few steps are indicated in Figure 6.18. The common ancestor of ABEGCD and F is finally seen to be the root of our tree, and the last merge can take place, resulting in the tree shown in Figure 6.19.

In summary, UPGMA is a fairly simple clustering technique that relies on a measure of differences between the original nodes. It gradually pairs nearest neighbors, replacing a pair by a "common ancestor" that is at the arithmetic mean

|   | A | B | C | D | E | F | G |
|---|---|---|---|---|---|---|---|
| A | 0 | 7 | 12 | 13 | 9 | 23 | 11 |
| B |   | 0 | 7 | 9 | 10 | 19 | 10 |
| C |   |   | 0 | 2 | 11 | 24 | 13 |
| D |   |   |   | 0 | 12 | 22 | 12 |
| E |   |   |   |   | 0 | 18 | 9 |
| F |   |   |   |   |   | 0 | 24 |
| G |   |   |   |   |   |   | 0 |

**FIGURE 6.15**    Numerical values to pairwise species differences.

|    | A | B | CD | E | F | G |
|----|---|---|----|---|---|---|
| A  | 0 | 7 | 12.5 | 9 | 23 | 11 |
| B  |   | 0 | 8 | 10 | 19 | 10 |
| CD |   |   | 0 | 11.5 | 23 | 12.5 |
| E  |   |   |   | 0 | 18 | 9 |
| F  |   |   |   |   | 0 | 24 |
| G  |   |   |   |   |   | 0 |

```
        CD
        | distance 2
     ___|___
     |      |
     C      D
```

**FIGURE 6.16**   Step 1, C and D are merged.

|    | AB | CD | E | F | G |
|----|----|----|---|---|---|
| AB | 0 | 10.25 | 9.5 | 21 | 10.5 |
| CD |   | 0 | 11.5 | 23 | 12.5 |
| E  |   |   | 0 | 18 | 9 |
| F  |   |   |   | 0 | 24 |
| G  |   |   |   |   | 0 |

```
        AB
        | distance 7
     ___|___
     |      |
     A      B
```

**FIGURE 6.17**   Step 2, A and B are merged.

distance from its progeny. The process repeats, on each iteration, substituting a postulated common ancestor node for the lowest differing pair of nodes until only one node remains. That is the root, and the rest of the phylogeny can be inferred by going through the merging process in reverse, separating out pairs of children from each common ancestor.

Much criticism can be directed at the resulting phylogeny. The scaled distances don't make a lot of sense. They show the cat and the dog significantly closer to the common ancestor than the elephant and the gnu. Is that a necessary consequence of the algorithm? Can you think of a modification to the given algorithm that would correct for this anomaly?

In fact, most implementations of UPGMA are a bit more sophisticated about the distances. Instead of always using the smallest number that was picked from

|    | AB | CD | EG | F |
|----|----|----|----|---|
| AB | 0 | 10.25 | 10 | 21 |
| CD |   | 0 | 12 | 23 |
| EG |   |   | 0 | 21 |
| F  |   |   |   | 0 |

E and G merge ancestral distance 9

|      | ABEG | CD | F |
|------|------|----|---|
| ABEG | 0 | 11.125 | 21 |
| CD   |   | 0 | 23 |
| F    |   |   | 0 |

AB and EG merge ancestral distance 10

|        | ABEGCD | F |
|--------|--------|---|
| ABEGCD | 0 | 22 |
| F      |   | 0 |

ABEG and CD merge ancestral distance 11.125

**FIGURE 6.18**   Steps 3, 4, and 5.

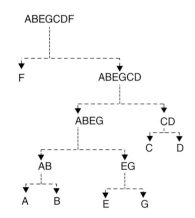

**FIGURE 6.19** The resulting phylogenetic tree.

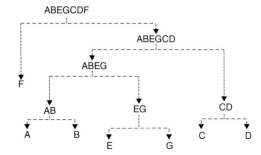

**FIGURE 6.20** The resulting phylogenetic tree when better distance calculations are used.

the array, it is possible to go back to the original data and calculate a more reliable distance for, say CD from ABEGCD if we know that F is a completely unrelated species. This is certainly the case for this dataset: We would expect that a fish like the flatfish would have diverged from the other species, which are all mammals, many millions of years before the mammals diverged from one another. So we can have UPGMA adjust the distances by using the very long distance to F as a way of determining which branch lengths should be shorter among the remaining species. This is known as using an **outgroup**—a species unrelated to the ones we are interested in. Such an approach can yield a tree similar to Figure 6.20, which is actually a better representation of the evolutionary history of these species than Figure 6.19. Exercise 6.13 asks you to learn more about the methods available for adjusting distances appropriately. One place to start is [7].

One of the reasons we get the somewhat strangely organized branch lengths in Figure 6.19 is that UPGMA makes one assumption that simplifies the tree-building process. It assumes that all species and all regions of a genome acquire mutations at a steady rate. This is known as the **molecular clock hypothesis.** Based on what we discussed about functional constraints in Section 6.4.1, you can probably already say why this assumption is incorrect. Recall the histones, a class of proteins that appear to have changed very little over extremely large stretches of time. Other proteins, however, have changed dramatically in that time. The reason for this is that functional constraints vary for different genes, and the rates of mutation will therefore also vary. Using an outgroup can compensate for some of the problems of the molecular clock hypothesis, but it remains a problem for any tree generated by UPGMA. As a result, UPGMA is used only rarely for phylogenetic reconstructions. Nevertheless, it is the simplest and easiest way to implement many of the tree-building methods available, and when the molecular clock hypothesis is justified, it can provide a rapid method to use in a branch and bound analysis in maximum parsimony. That is why we ask you to explore your own implementation of UPGMA in Exercise 6.13.

**Exercise 6.13**

Implement a better way to calculate distances between hypothetical common ancestors and each of their children after doing a library or Internet search to identify resources for adjusting UPGMA tree distances. One place to start would be [7]. Test your program on the following data from Fitch and Margoliash [5]. You will note that these data provide the lower half of a symmetric matrix, whereas the earlier example used the upper half.

|         | Turtle | Man | Tuna | Chicken | Moth | Monkey | Dog |
|---------|--------|-----|------|---------|------|--------|-----|
| Man     | 19     |     |      |         |      |        |     |
| Tuna    | 27     | 31  |      |         |      |        |     |
| Chicken | 8      | 18  | 26   |         |      |        |     |
| Moth    | 33     | 36  | 41   | 31      |      |        |     |
| Monkey  | 18     | 1   | 32   | 17      | 35   |        |     |
| Dog     | 13     | 13  | 29   | 14      | 28   | 12     |     |

## Neighbor Joining

A more reliable way of building a tree based on a distance matrix such as the one shown in Figure 6.15 is to use neighbor relations methods. **Neighbor relations** is a broad category of methods that try to build unrooted phylogenetic trees by grouping those taxa that are most similar together as "neighbors." The idea is that you build the tree from the bottom up, asking at each step, "What is the closest pair of taxa to my current branch?"

Of these methods, **neighbor joining** is the most frequently used. Here is an overview of the steps in neighbor joining:

1. Start by assuming all taxa are on the ends of their own, equal-length branches. This creates a star pattern as shown in Figure 6.21.
2. Now calculate the sum of distances between each pair of taxa.
3. Identify the pair of taxa that has the shortest distance between them and all other pairs.

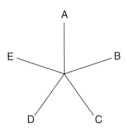

**FIGURE 6.21**    In the initial step of neighbor joining, all species are assumed to be equidistant from each other. This results in a star shape as shown here.

4. Group these into a consensus node.
5. Compare this consensus node with the remaining taxa to identify the next closest neighbor.
6. Iterate steps 1 through 4 until all taxa have been placed in a tree.

Let us walk through the UPGMA data in Figure 6.15 and use neighbor joining to generate the tree instead. The first step of neighbor joining is to create a list of the sums of distances between each node and every other node. To simplify the process, neighbor joining generally compares four species at a time, progressively mixing and matching until all the distances among all the species have been calculated. For any four species, there will be three sums of distances if comparing pairs (e.g., AB vs. CD, AC vs. BD, and AD vs. BC). Using the sum of distances for each pair, neighbor joining then picks the pair with the lowest sum of distances. After the initial analysis, neighbor joining picks the pair that appears most frequently. In other words, neighbor joining picks the pair of species that most often end up together because the sum of distances from this pair to any other pair is the smallest possible. Table 6.4 shows a partial calculation of sums of distances for a few of the nodes in the full dataset shown in Figure 6.15.

Based on just this preliminary analysis, it would appear that the pair CD is the first neighbor pair. This is because in Table 6.4, the (CD) pair appears three times and is therefore the one with the smallest sum of distances among the five species compared here. Exercise 6.14 asks you to complete the table for all of the species in the distance matrix of Figure 6.15.

**Exercise 6.14**    Write a program to compute the pairwise distances among all the species using distance data from Figure 6.15. Confirm that CD is in fact the first neighbor pair.

After this initial analysis, the next step resembles UPGMA. The distances are recalculated based on the arithmetic mean between each remaining species and the CD pair. So you next obtain the matrix shown in Figure 6.16. Then the process iterates, comparing each pair of remaining species with the CD pair to identify the next pair of closest neighbors, and so on through the set of species.

**TABLE 6.4**   **Partial calculation of sums of distances for a few of the nodes in the full dataset shown in Figure 6.16\***

| Species | Sum of pairwise distances | Neighbor pairs chosen |
|---------|---------------------------|-----------------------|
| A, B, C, D | $d_{AB} + d_{CD} = 7 + 2 = 9$ <br> $d_{AC} + d_{BD} = 13 + 7 = 20$ <br> $d_{AD} + d_{BC} = 12 + 9 = 21$ | (AB),(CD) |
| A, B, C, E | $d_{AB} + d_{CE} = 7 + 11 = 18$ <br> $d_{AC} + d_{BE} = 12 + 10 = 22$ <br> $d_{AD} + d_{BC} = 13 + 7 = 20$ | (AB),(CE) |
| A, B, D, E | $d_{AB} + d_{DE} = 7 + 12 = 19$ <br> $d_{AD} + d_{BE} = 13 + 10 = 23$ <br> $d_{AE} + d_{BD} = 9 + 9 = 18$ | (AE),(BD) |
| A, C, D, E | $d_{AC} + d_{DE} = 12 + 12 = 24$ <br> $d_{AD} + d_{CE} = 13 + 11 = 24$ <br> $d_{AE} + d_{CD} = 9 + 2 = 11$ | (AE),(CD) |
| B, C, D, E | $d_{BC} + d_{DE} = 7 + 12 = 19$ <br> $d_{BD} + d_{CE} = 9 + 11 = 20$ <br> $d_{BE} + d_{CD} = 10 + 2 = 12$ | (BE),(CD) |

\*The first column (Species) lists the four species currently being considered by neighbor joining. The second column (Sum of pairwise distances) shows the sum of distances for pairing up these species in the three possible ways. Distance values are drawn from the original distance matrix shown in Figure 6.15. After each set of four species are compared, neighbor joining picks the two pairs most likely to be neighbors based on the smallest sum of distances. This is shown in the final column of the table (Neighbor pairs chosen). Pairs are shown within parentheses [e.g., (AB) is a pair]. After [7].

Exercise 6.15 asks you to implement a version of neighbor joining based on the steps outlined earlier.

> **Exercise 6.15**
>
> Implement a version of neighbor joining based on the data in Exercise 6.13. You can use the code from Exercise 6.14 to calculate the pairwise distances for each distance matrix. Your code from Exercise 6.13 can be adapted to calculate the new distance matrix at each iteration so you will only need a method for selecting the neighbor pair after each iteration.

The end result of neighbor joining will often look a great deal like a tree from UPGMA. Like UPGMA, neighbor joining tries to find the shortest branch lengths, but unlike UPGMA, neighbor joining groups taxa into pairs first and then tries to organize the pairs with respect to one another. As a result, neighbor joining will produce an unrooted tree. By working on pairs of taxa at a time, neighbor joining does not need to assume an equal rate of mutation (the molecular clock) across all taxa. So it will more likely yield a tree similar to Figure 6.20 rather than the version that UPGMA prefers (in Figure 6.19). Of course, the tree will be unrooted, so it will look more like Figure 6.22.

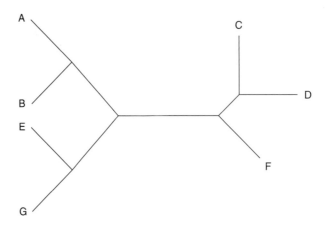

**FIGURE 6.22**    This tree illustrates the most likely tree as generated by neighbor joining. Note that it is very similar to the UPGMA tree in Figure 6.20 in this instance, although that is not always the case.

Neighbor joining and UPGMA have one critical advantage over maximum parsimony and other methods—they are computationally fast. As a result, you can get a quick answer to any pressing phylogenetics question. However, they are less rigorous approaches and are more or less limited to those datasets with sequence data. Maximum parsimony, in contrast, can work on either sequence data or physiological characteristics. For these reasons, you will most often see neighbor joining or UPGMA used as subsidiary methods to maximum parsimony rather than being employed as stand-alone methods.

One example of neighbor joining is the attempt to identify the ancestral virus that gave rise to HIV in humans. We know that HIV is related to a number of viruses in other primates, collectively known as SIV (simian immunodeficiency virus). In Chapter 5, we discussed some recent work that helped identify a strain of SIV in chimpanzees (SIVcpz) as the possible ancestral strain of HIV in humans [6]. This work began with a multiple sequence alignment (see Chapter 5), but the main thrust of the work built a phylogenetic tree of the sequences from SIVcpz and various strains of HIV. The first step of this work used a neighbor-joining approach to develop a quick assessment of the likelihood that SIVcpz might be an ancestral sequence to one of the various strains of HIV.

The initial analysis with neighbor joining was so positive, the researchers then went on to do a much more rigorous analysis of the sequences to estimate the date of divergence and the early evolution of HIV from SIVcpz [6]. For that, the researchers used a powerful new method for tree building—maximum likelihood. We discuss maximum likelihood and its uses in the following section.

## 6.5.3  Maximum Likelihood

We have now covered three methods of building trees, each of which has advantages and disadvantages for particular situations. The final approach is a relatively new introduction to the phylogenetics realm. However, it shows great promise and has such significant advantages over the other three methods that many researchers expect it to become dominant in the field in the next few years. This method, **maximum likelihood** (abbreviated ML), involves building a statistical model of the most probable evolutionary history of a set of species and generating a tree from that model. The central advantage of ML methods is that all the power and sophistication of statistical analysis can be brought to bear on the problem of phylogenetic trees.

One of the interesting features of the ML approach is that we start by developing a model of evolution. If this sounds grandiose, it is. In reality, we cannot fully model evolution because we cannot yet predict what random changes will happen in the future. Rather, we build our model based on our observation of changes that have already occurred in our taxa. As we discussed in Section 6.4, although we cannot model the overall process of evolution, we can build models of how and when mutations will occur.

In Section 6.4.1, we discussed models for rates of mutation. The Jukes–Cantor and Kimura 2-parameter models have relatively few parameters: one in the case of Jukes–Cantor and two in the latter instance. In ML, we develop a much more complex model with many more parameters. Each parameter in the ML model assigns a specific likelihood estimate to different transitions, transversions, and other mutations.

The resulting models resemble the PAM or BLOSUM matrices you encountered in Chapter 5, except that the values in the rows and columns represent the likelihood of such transformations as a T becoming an A and vice versa. Essentially, we need to assign a likelihood (akin to a probability) for each possible modification of a nucleotide or amino acid. Usually, we obtain the likelihood values as simple estimates of the relative frequency of a given mutation within a large dataset.

Look back at Table 6.2 to see the first step of this process. There, we counted up the number of occurrences of different mutations in HIV. To generate a likelihood, we simply transform these raw counts into relative frequencies. For example, T to C mutations occurred twice, and mutations of T to G and T to A occurred once each. Therefore, the likelihood of a T to C mutation is 2/4, or 0.5. This is because there were a total of four occurrences of T mutating to something else. If we continued in this fashion we would develop a set of likelihood values for HIV mutations. This might help us in generating a phylogenetic tree of HIV strains. To generalize this procedure for use with any species, we sample mutations across many different species to determine general likelihood values, which are most often used in ML analyses.

Once we have the likelihood values, we can then try to decide which changes are more likely and assign these to branches of a tree. We multiply the likelihoods for each change in each branch of the tree to obtain the overall likelihood for the tree.[5] Then we compare the likelihood values of the various trees and decide

---

[5] In practice, multiplying very small likelihoods rapidly leads to vanishingly small numbers. In most implementations, the negative log transformed values of likelihoods are used instead. These are

which is the best tree. The best tree in this approach is the one that is most likely given our starting model.

Simulations of phylogenetic data and statistical analyses have demonstrated that of all the methods for tree building, ML is the only one statistically guaranteed to find the true tree [20]. Of course, how you define "true" tree depends on what you already know about the evolutionary history of the species of interest. When we say that ML is guaranteed to find the true tree, we are using the results of many simulated experiments in which the correct tree is known in advance. In these circumstances, maximum parsimony will sometimes find the right tree and sometimes not, for reasons we will cover in the next section. ML, however, will always find the correct tree. This is what makes ML so promising for phylogenetic reconstruction.

| Exercise 6.16 | Use the description of how to estimate mutation rates to develop a program that builds an ML model for mutations in HIV. You can use the data provided in Table 6.2 on page 250. To build a complete model, you will need to obtain the full data-set from the original reference [13]. Can you generalize your program so that it is applicable for any species? |
| --- | --- |

### *Maximum Likelihood versus Maximum Parsimony*

ML is an approach that's similar in spirit to maximum parsimony, but it substitutes probabilities where parsimony makes a more qualitative distinction about informative and uninformative sites. The difference in ML is that rather than identifying the tree with the simplest explanation for the observations, the ML approach purports to find the tree that is most likely to represent the evolutionary history of the organisms. This assumes, of course, that our selected model for mutations is the correct one and that it represents the true model for the observed mutations. So the choice of mutation model greatly influences the end result of ML analysis. A full discussion of the models used in ML analysis is beyond our scope here, but the literature in this area abounds. A good place to start is [20].

Interestingly, when relatively few closely related taxa are used, the ML tree and the tree(s) generated by maximum parsimony tend to be very similar. Furthermore, ML is computationally so intensive that it can take days or weeks to run an analysis. So why not just use maximum parsimony and forget about ML altogether? There are several reasons to favor ML. Chief among them is that ML rests on a solid statistical foundation. Many powerful statistical methods can be applied to the evaluation of trees when using ML, and we can generate results that are highly reliable and reproducible [12].

The solid statistical foundation for ML is in sharp contrast to that for maximum parsimony, a method that is by nature a qualitative assessment of trees.

---

summed to generate the likelihood value for the tree (remember that to multiply logs you sum them). Thus, the most likely tree is the one with the lowest negative log likelihood value.

The most severe criticism of maximum parsimony is that under certain conditions maximum parsimony will reliably return the wrong tree. This tends to occur when the species being analyzed diverge significantly—a problem referred to as *long-branch attraction*. Briefly, long-branch attraction refers to the tendency for maximum parsimony to place taxa that are equally distant from each other next to each other, thereby implying that they are more closely related than, in fact, they are.

This might seem an obscure problem, but you have already encountered it! If you think back to the example in Section 6.5 with snakes, chickens, and humans, you will see a version of this problem. The most parsimonious tree was the one in which snakes with no arms give rise to chickens with wings and humans with arms (see Figure 6.6). But we know this is the wrong tree. The problem is that we are comparing species that diverged many hundreds of millions of years ago, and the actual history of their evolution suggests that snakes lost protoarms and chickens transformed arms into wings. Remember that species can change in many ways:

- Gain a feature after speciation
- Inherit a feature from an ancestor species
- Lose a feature after speciation
- Gain a feature through some other process such as convergent evolution

"Feature" in this instance could be anything: arms or wings or, more commonly, a nucleotide substitution mutation of some kind. The reason maximum parsimony is susceptible to long-branch attraction is that maximum parsimony assumes that features in a species are acquired by either the first or second process we described earlier. This is usually true but not always. And when that assumption fails, maximum parsimony yields the wrong tree. ML makes no such assumption about the mechanism by which a feature was acquired, and it has been shown statistically with simulated data that ML is very resistant to the long-branch attraction problem [12].

### Stumbling Blocks to Maximum Likelihood

All this may suggest that the method of choice for phylogenetic reconstruction should be maximum likelihood. You would be right to assume this is the case. Yet, most of the actual reconstructions of species are done with maximum parsimony or some other method. Why? Until recently ML could not be implemented at all for any analysis that compared more than a handful of species. This is because ML is incredibly computationally intensive, since it must evaluate every tree before it can identify the most likely one. If you remember the results of Exercise 6.10, you know that for even a dozen species the number of trees to be evaluated can be astronomical. The same workarounds we discussed for maximum parsimony (see Section 6.5.1) can be applied here, but then we also lose the statistical guarantee of finding the true tree. As computing power has increased in the last decade, however, ML has become more popular [20].

The other stumbling block to using ML is that large datasets are required to estimate the likelihoods in the underlying model of mutation. The large datasets are necessary because the likelihood values are essentially estimated from the frequency of occurrences observed. If you start with too small a dataset, you run the risk of overestimating some mutation frequencies and underestimating others. Indeed, this is one reason why BLOSUM has become more popular as a sequence alignment matrix than PAM (see Chapter 5). BLOSUM is based on a much larger dataset than PAM and therefore is more reliable when comparing sequences that have greater divergence times. As the size of the sequence databases has increased over time, the models needed by ML have become more reliable as well. We can now estimate the frequencies of mutations for a wide range of species using the data from GenBank and other sequence repositories.

So in essence, ML represents the best path forward for phylogenetic reconstruction. As computing power and sequence data have increased exponentially, ML has become more and more feasible. It remains to be seen if it will be widely adopted by the phylogenetic community, but the early trends suggest that ML will soon come to dominate the field.

In general, phylogenetic reconstruction is as much an art as a science. As you've seen in this chapter, there are many methods for studying evolution, building trees, and analyzing the results. We can simulate evolution to understand more about the larger questions of how evolution might occur or what its consequences might be. We can model evolution to some extent, and this allows us to ask specific questions about evolution. For example, we can ask, "Where did HIV come from?" and obtain a clear answer: HIV arose from a strain of chimpanzee SIV. But as we have discussed in this chapter, each of the methods available to us for reconstructing phylogenies has advantages and disadvantages. The biological time machine that is the genome can only take us so far in reconstructing the history of life. Some aspects will probably always be left to conjecture. But for many problems, we now have a way to at least investigate the process of evolution and to evaluate the answers in a meaningful way. That, at least, is a step in the right direction.

# KEY TERMS

| | | |
|---|---|---|
| kingdom (6.1) | speciation (6.3) | morphological characters (6.5) |
| phyla (6.1) | Markov models (6.3) | convergent evolution (6.5) |
| class (6.1) | training set (6.3) | uninformative (6.5) |
| order (6.1) | testing set (6.3) | informative (6.5) |
| family (6.1) | common ancestor (6.4) | branch and bound (6.5) |
| genus (6.1) | phylogenetics (6.4) | bootstrapping (6.5) |
| species (6.1) | phylogenetic tree (6.4) | consensus tree techniques (6.5) |
| mutation (6.1) | synonymous substitution (6.4) | outgroup (6.5) |
| point mutation (6.1) | nonsynonymous substitution (6.4) | molecular clock hypothesis (6.5) |
| insertion (6.1) | functionally constrained (6.4) | neighbor relations (6.5) |
| deletion (6.1) | transition (6.4) | neighbor joining (6.5) |
| fitness function (6.3) | transversion (6.4) | maximum likelihood (6.5) |
| genetic algorithm (6.3) | maximum parsimony (6.5) | |
| cross breed (6.3) | parsimonious (6.5) | |

# BIBLIOGRAPHY

1. Richard Dawkins. *The Blind Watchmaker: Why the Evidence of Evolution Reveals a Universe Without Design.* Norton, London, 1986.

2. Richard Dawkins. *The Ancestor's Tale: A Pilgrimage to the Dawn of Evolution.* Houghton Mifflin, Boston, 2004.

3. A. L. Delcher, D. Harmon, S. Kasif, et al. Improved microbial gene identification with GLIMMER. *Nucl Acids Res,* 27:4636–4641, 1999.

4. Jerry W. Dragoo and Rodney L. Honeycutt. Systematics of mustelid-like carnivores. *J Mammol,* 78:426–443, 1997.

5. W. M. Fitch and E. Margoliash. Construction of phylogenetic trees. *Science,* 155:279–284, 1967.

6. Feng Gao, Elizabeth Bailes, David L. Robertson, et al. Origin of HIV-1 in the chimpanzee *Pan troglodytes troglodytes. Nature,* 397:436–441, 1999.

7. Dan Graur and Wen-Hsiung Li. *Fundamentals of Molecular Evolution,* 2nd edition. Sinauer Associates, Sunderland, MA, 2000.

8. Russell D. Gray and Fiona M. Jordan. Language trees support the express-train sequence of Austronesian expansion. *Nature,* 405:1052–1055, 2000.

9. M. D. Hendy and D. Penny. Branch and bound algorithms to determine minimal evolutionary trees. *Math. Biosci,* 60:133–142, 1982.

10. D. M. Hillis and J. J. Bull. An empirical test of bootstrapping as a method for assessing confidence in phylogenetic systems. *Syst Biol,* 42:182–192, 1993.

11. D. M. Hillis, J. P. Huelsenbeck, and C. W. Cunningham. Application and accuracy of molecular phylogenies. *Science,* 264:671–677, 1994.

12. Carolin Kosiol, Lee Bofkin, and Simon Whelan. Phylogenetics by likelihood: Evolutionary modeling as a tool for understanding the genome. *J Biomed Inform,* 39:51–61, 2006.

13. L. M. Mansky and H. M. Temin. Lower in vivo mutation rate of human immunodeficiency virus type 1 than that predicted from the fidelity of purified reverse transcriptase. *J Virol,* 69:5087–5094, 1995.

14. Rhys Price Jones, David P. Russell, James Thompson, and Robert J. Zagursky. Bacterial protein start prediction program using a genetic algorithm. Unpublished work.

15. M. M. Riehle, A. F. Bennett, R. E. Lenski, and A. D. Long. Evolutionary changes in heat-inducible gene expression in *Escherichia coli* lines evolved at high temperature. *Physiol Genomics,* 14:47–58, 2003.

16. K. E. Rudd. Ecogene: A genome sequence database for *Escherichia coli* k-12. *Nucleic Acids Res,* 28(1):60–64, 2000.

17. J. Shine and L. Dalgarno. The 3′-terminal sequence of *Escherichia coli* 16S ribosomal RNA: Complementarity to nonsense triplets and ribosome binding sites. *Proc Nat Acad Sci U S A,* 74:1342–1346, 1974.

18. K. Takahashi and M. Nei. Efficiencies of fast algorithms of phylogenetic inference under the criteria of maximum parsimony, minimum evolution, and maximum likelihood when a large number of sequences are used. *Mol Biol Evol,* 17:1251–1258, 2000.

19. Mikael Thollesson. Phylogenetic inference. http://artedi.ebc.uu.se/course/X3-2004/Phylogeny/

20. Simon Whelan, Pietro Lio, and Nick Goldman. Molecular phylogenetics: State-of-the-art methods for looking into the past. *Trends Genet,* 17:262–272, 2001.

# 7

# Gene Finding

*"In all cases of secret writing, the first question regards the language of the cipher; for the principles of solution . . . depend upon and are varied by the genius of the particular idiom. In general, there is no alternative but experiment (directed by probabilities) of every [possible solution] . . . until the true one be attained."*
—William Legrand, in *The Gold Bug* by Edgar Allan Poe.

## 7.1 A MODERN CRYPTOGRAPHIC PUZZLE

Imagine for a moment that you have access to a powerful radio telescope. Every day you pick up many "transmissions," most of which are dismissed as random background noise from outer space. Every now and then, however, you receive a signal that does not look quite like random noise. Rather, you think it may be a coded message from some extraterrestrial intelligent being. How might you go about proving that your new transmission is actually a coded message and not just random noise?

Now suppose that instead of a message from outer space, the "transmission" you have is genomic sequence. You have just discovered a new species of bacteria with the ability to convert household waste into a usable product; perhaps your miracle bug can convert waste into gas for your car. Using the methods described in Chapters 3 and 4, you have isolated and sequenced the genome of your miracle bug. How do you figure out which parts of the genome enable your miracle bug to do its magic? Which parts of the genome are actually functional?

These two examples may seem completely unrelated, but they, in fact, share a common puzzle. Both involve coded messages, and the challenge is to crack the code so you can understand the message. In computer science, solving puzzles of this nature comes under the purview of the field of cryptography. Whether you are trying to decipher a message from outer space or the genome of a new organism, the challenges and solutions are very similar.

Richard Dawkins [4] has noted how DNA "carries information in a very computer-like way." Genomes are rather like hard disks. Some of the information is in current use and constantly being accessed for purposes related to the workings of the organism. Active genes are like the files on a hard drive we are constantly accessing. Other areas of the disk contain older versions of current files, or perhaps back-ups of some kind. Likewise, genomes contain repeats, some exact, others perhaps an echo of an older version of a gene. Yet other areas of the hard drive have been written and rewritten many times, fragmented and defragmented over and over—so much so that their contents would appear to be nearly random. Perhaps some areas of our genomes are so far removed from a time when they were in use and subject to evolutionary pressure to conserve pattern and function that by now those regions are essentially indistinguishable from random.

In this chapter, we will try to crack the genome code. What does it mean to decipher a genome? In essence, it means we have found and documented all the instructions for making the parts of an organism. Each of those instructions is a **gene,** so to crack the genome code is essentially to find all the genes.

Finding genes is actually an interesting variation on the standard cryptographic puzzle: given a string, how do you decide if it has any meaningful content? You can see how this is actually a similar problem to monitoring radio transmissions from outer space. How would you decide whether these transmissions (or genomic sequences) were meaningful bits of a message rather than random noise?

In the 1940s, a young mathematician at Bell Laboratories formulated a powerful set of ideas for distinguishing between truly random noise and encoded messages. Claude Shannon proposed that you could identify messages by several features. Shannon's theory distinguishes

- meaningful information
- redundancy
- noise

Genes and regulatory signals correspond to meaningful information. Modified "old" genes and repeats provide redundancy. And currently the term "junk DNA" is sometimes applied to what may be genomic "noise."

Meaningful information tends to go hand in hand with redundancy. We are able to detect meaningful transmissions in a cacophony of radio noise by identifying patterns. True noise is completely random, and any patterns detected are fleeting. Meaningful transmissions show themselves by presenting detectable features that persist. Redundancy helps preserve meaningful data. All data is subject to mutation: DNA replication errors occur, wire or wireless transmissions suffer from vagaries due to sunspots or thunderstorms. Human communication is notoriously uncertain. By adding redundancy, the information is more robust. With multiple copies of genetic material and with predicable patterns in expected places, DNA can repair many mutations before any lasting damage occurs. As another example, accountants add checksum digits to columns of numbers. These checksums are designed to cause all columns to add to a known total (often 9 when the addition is modulo 10). If a received transmission contains a column with a different total, then the receiver knows that an error occurred. Checksums are an example of **error-detecting codes:** they add enough redundancy that most errors can be detected. Somewhat more sophisticated are the **error-correcting codes** described by Richard Hamming [9].

### 7.1.1 Detecting Encryption

In this chapter we focus on ways of analyzing sequences to find patterns and identify their biologically meaningful aspects. How do we identify meaningful patterns? We look for redundancy. Let us start with an example from English. The word *the* is one of the most common words in English. It occurs far more often than would be expected at random, even given the frequency with which the letters *t*, *h*, and *e* occur in the language. Someone trying to decode an encrypted message originally written in English might notice that a particular pattern of three characters was repeated at a frequency much greater than expected at random. This redundancy would be a hint that such a pattern might represent the word *the*.

The frequency with which a meaningful pattern is repeated within a longer string is related to the Shannon entropy. **Shannon entropy** measures the average minimum number of bits required to encode the information in the string. The more repetition in the string, the more compression is possible, and so fewer bits are needed to encode the information. The likelihood that a pattern is meaningful (contains information) is derived as a measure of how often we might expect to see that pattern at random. To estimate the likelihood of occurrence at random, Shannon proposed that we measure the *complexity* of the string.

In this context, complexity is shorthand for how easy it is to compress a string. The more meaningful a string is, the more easily it is compressed. In other words, a meaningful string is less complex (more compressible) than a meaningless string (less compressible). Interestingly, what Shannon proposed is that a completely random string cannot be compressed at all.[1] It is infinitely complex. This concept is the key finding of **Shannon's theory of information** [15].

Let us consider an example from DNA. One of the key patterns used in finding genes is the **TATA box.** This short string, usually TATAA, is found at the start of many genes in eukaryotes. Let's suppose we want to encode the information contained in the string TATAA using a bitstring. If we establish a table associating T with 0 and A with 1, the encoding can be done in 5 bits: `01011`. We achieve even more compression by associating TA with 0 and A with 1. Now it's down to 3 bits: `001`. To be fair, the latter encoding is somewhat too specialized to be part of a generally useful encoding scheme. Nevertheless, the pattern TATAA is highly compressible and is therefore likely to be a meaningful pattern.

On the other hand, consider a more random pattern such as ACCGT. No plausible scheme is going to encode this string in fewer than 10 bits. ACCGT is therefore less compressible and consequently more complex. It is more likely to be a random string than is TATAA.

---

[1] Much information today is subject to compression. For example .jpeg files can represent the same information as much larger bit pattern files. Typically, compression programs work by identifying oft-repeated components and using short identifiers for each occurrence. In principle, you might think you could keep compressing until there was no more repetition. The resulting file would then be indistinguishable from random noise. In practice, that degree of compression is not possible.

So what does all this have to do with finding genes? Simply put, given a string of DNA nucleotides in a genome, is there any meaningful content (i.e., are there any genes)? If so, where is it? This is the classic cryptographic puzzle, and we can use Shannon's information theory to help us crack the code.

Any cryptographic puzzle presents challenges. First, you have to know that the message is encoded in some way. Shannon's information theory can help in this respect by determining the probability that meaningful information exists in a given string. Then, you need to know something about the language of the original, unencoded message. As we discussed, if you know the original language was English, then you might look for patterns of three characters that always occur together as a way to identify the characters for the letters *t-h-e*. Finally, you need to know where to look. For example, the encryptors might have embedded the meaningful parts of the message in a longer, random string. Again, Shannon's information theory can be of help.

## 7.1.2  Encoding Information

The most used encoding system for characters is called ASCII (for American Standard Code for Information Interchange). ASCII is pronounced "ask-ee" and has been in use since the late 1960s. It may eventually be supplanted by a standard (such as Unicode) that is more friendly to languages other than English. ASCII contains 33 nonprinting characters (largely obsolete control characters from earlier days of computing) and 95 characters that can be typed from a normal American keyboard and printed to a normal printer. Throughout the world, regional variations make for some amusing or annoying difficulties in reading documents. Table 7.1 lists all the ASCII codes for the printable characters.

Notice that ASCII uses exactly 7 bits to represent each and every one of its printable characters. Accordingly, any text consisting of $n$ characters can be encoded using ASCII into $7n$ bits. In practice, all computers will add a leading 0 to all the 7-bit codes so that characters are stored in 8-bit byte locations. Thus a file consisting of $n$ characters will require $8n$ bits of storage in a real computer. It is possible to extend the ASCII code by using some of the 8-bit patterns that begin with 1 for special characters.

The word *Code* is represented in 7-bit ASCII as

```
1000011110111111001001100101
```

but in the 8-bit code used in computers, *Code* would be:

```
01000011011011110110010001100101
```

It is possible to use ASCII to encode sequences of nucleotides. For example, you would use `1000001` for A, `1000011` for C, `1000111` for G, and `1010100` for T. In a computer you would need `01000001` for A, `01000011` for C, `01000111` for G, and `01010100` for T. Using ASCII encoding, a genome with $n$ base pairs would require a computer file of size $8n$ bytes. In the exercises, you will investigate ways to improve on this and discover what some of the popular Websites do to encode genomes.

**TABLE 7.1    The ASCII codes for printable characters**

| Binary | Decimal | Hexadecimal | Character | Binary | Decimal | Hexadecimal | Character |
|---|---|---|---|---|---|---|---|
| 0100000 | 32 | 20 | space | 1010000 | 80 | 50 | P |
| 0100001 | 33 | 21 | ! | 1010001 | 81 | 51 | Q |
| 0100010 | 34 | 22 | " | 1010010 | 82 | 52 | R |
| 0100011 | 35 | 23 | # | 1010011 | 83 | 53 | S |
| 0100100 | 36 | 24 | $ | 1010100 | 84 | 54 | T |
| 0100101 | 37 | 25 | % | 1010101 | 85 | 55 | U |
| 0100110 | 38 | 26 | & | 1010110 | 86 | 56 | V |
| 0100111 | 39 | 27 | ' | 1010111 | 87 | 57 | W |
| 0101000 | 40 | 28 | ( | 1011000 | 88 | 58 | X |
| 0101001 | 41 | 29 | ) | 1011001 | 89 | 59 | Y |
| 0101010 | 42 | 2A | * | 1011010 | 90 | 5A | Z |
| 0101011 | 43 | 2B | + | 1011011 | 91 | 5B | [ |
| 0101100 | 44 | 2C | , | 1011100 | 92 | 5C | \ |
| 0101101 | 45 | 2D | − | 1011101 | 93 | 5D | ] |
| 0101110 | 46 | 2E | . | 1011110 | 94 | 5E | ^ |
| 0101111 | 47 | 2F | / | 1011111 | 95 | 5F | _ |
| 0110000 | 48 | 30 | 0 | 1100000 | 96 | 60 | ' |
| 0110001 | 49 | 31 | 1 | 1100001 | 97 | 61 | a |
| 0110010 | 50 | 32 | 2 | 1100010 | 98 | 62 | b |
| 0110011 | 51 | 33 | 3 | 1100011 | 99 | 63 | c |
| 0110100 | 52 | 34 | 4 | 1100100 | 100 | 64 | d |
| 0110101 | 53 | 35 | 5 | 1100101 | 101 | 65 | e |
| 0110110 | 54 | 36 | 6 | 1100110 | 102 | 66 | f |
| 0110111 | 55 | 37 | 7 | 1100111 | 103 | 67 | g |
| 0111000 | 56 | 38 | 8 | 1101000 | 104 | 68 | h |
| 0111001 | 57 | 39 | 9 | 1101001 | 105 | 69 | i |
| 0111010 | 58 | 3A | : | 1101010 | 106 | 6A | j |
| 0111011 | 59 | 3B | ; | 1101011 | 107 | 6B | k |
| 0111100 | 60 | 3C | < | 1101100 | 108 | 6C | l |
| 0111101 | 61 | 3D | = | 1101101 | 109 | 6D | m |
| 0111110 | 62 | 3E | > | 1101110 | 110 | 6E | n |
| 0111111 | 63 | 3F | ? | 1101111 | 111 | 6F | o |
| 1000000 | 64 | 40 | @ | 1110000 | 112 | 70 | p |
| 1000001 | 65 | 41 | A | 1110001 | 113 | 71 | q |
| 1000010 | 66 | 42 | B | 1110010 | 114 | 72 | r |
| 1000011 | 67 | 43 | C | 1110011 | 115 | 73 | s |
| 1000100 | 68 | 44 | D | 1110100 | 116 | 74 | t |
| 1000101 | 69 | 45 | E | 1110101 | 117 | 75 | u |
| 1000110 | 70 | 46 | F | 1110110 | 118 | 76 | v |
| 1000111 | 71 | 47 | G | 1110111 | 119 | 77 | w |
| 1001000 | 72 | 48 | H | 1111000 | 120 | 78 | x |
| 1001001 | 73 | 49 | I | 1111001 | 121 | 79 | y |
| 1001010 | 74 | 4A | J | 1111010 | 122 | 7A | z |
| 1001011 | 75 | 4B | K | 1111011 | 123 | 7B | { |
| 1001100 | 76 | 4C | L | 1111100 | 124 | 7C | | |
| 1001101 | 77 | 4D | M | 1111101 | 125 | 7D | } |
| 1001110 | 78 | 4E | N | 1111110 | 126 | 7E | ~ |
| 1001111 | 79 | 4F | O | 1111111 | 127 | 7F | DEL |

# 7.2  CRACKING THE GENOME: A FIRST PASS

When we apply the principles of decoding messages in a biological context, we must grapple with the same challenges of any cryptographic puzzle. We gain some advantages in this particular context, but face some interesting twists as well. Unlike the problem of detecting meaningful extracts from signals received from outer space, we can safely assume that at least some part of a complete genome sequence contains information. So we are already one step ahead of the cryptologist faced with the transmission from outer space. However, we still have the daunting task of trying to decide which of the more than 3 billion base pairs of DNA in the human genome, as one example, carry information and which are just random noise.

One of the biggest challenges faced by the cryptologist in the biological context is not always knowing the language of the message. Recall that if you know the language of the encoded message, it is relatively easy to look for common words. For example, if we knew that a message must have been written in English, we might look for sets of three symbols that always occurred together. These would most likely be the word *the* or *and*. However, in the context of genomic sequence, we do not always know the exact language of the original message. As we discussed in Chapter 2, the language we call DNAStrings has many thousands if not millions of words. We do not have a complete dictionary of terms in the genomic language, making it more difficult for us to find and utilize its vocabulary.

A further complication is that time and evolution have altered and occasionally degraded the meaningful parts of the genome. As discussed in Chapter 5, genes from different species often differ in their nucleotide sequences. The end result may be very similar proteins, but at the genomic level, there can be a great deal of variation. Because the processes of evolution are based on random mutation, we cannot predict in advance how a gene sequence will change from one species to another. Rather, for each new genome, we have to come to a fresh understanding of its particular use of the language.

Finding genes in a genomic sequence presents one more challenge. Just like the clever encryptor who hides his message in a longer stream of gibberish, only some parts of the genomic sequence contain genes. The rest is made up of regions that control genes, regions of repeats, and some areas that have no apparent function. When we assemble genomic sequence, as described in Chapter 4, we have to account for all the pieces of the genome. But having assembled the sequence, the challenge is to find the parts that are meaningful. In other words, we must find the genes and their regulatory regions within a much longer string of potentially random gibberish.

Of course, genes and genomes possess features that are common across the spectrum of species. We can use these common patterns to help us locate the genes. We begin by considering some of the shorter signals in the genome. These signals can regulate genes, help maintain chromosome structure, assist in replication of the genome, and myriad other tasks necessary for the survival of the cell. Each of these signals modifies the behavior of the cell under certain circumstances, so decoding the genome requires us to identify as many of these signals as possible.

Finding the genes themselves is of course the biggest part of decoding a genome, but it is in essence a special subset of the larger problem of finding any meaningful sequence within the genome. We will return to gene finding in particular in Section 7.3.

From here onward, we use the term *signal* to mean a pattern or string that helps with some aspect of biological processing. This definition is deliberately vague because, as you will see, many different kinds of signals perform a variety of functions within the genomes of cells.

## 7.2.1  A Worked Example: HIV Integration Sites

To start our investigation of signals within genomes, let's look at one signal that is actually not of much use to the cell, but is of critical importance to an invader: HIV. Among its many activities within an infected cell, HIV sometimes integrates its genome into the cell's genomic sequence. The integration of the viral genome into the cell's genome gives the virus certain distinct advantages. For one, the virus' genome will now be faithfully copied and passed on to all the cell's descendants. This means that at some future point the virus can reactivate in one of these daughter cells and reinfect a new population of neighboring cells. A second advantage is that integration allows the virus to remain dormant inside an infected cell, helping to escape detection by the immune system. Because of these distinct advantages, viruses will often seek to "immortalize" their genomes by adding them to the cellular genome. As we noted in the sidebar following Section 4.2, cells carry around large chunks of such integrated viral sequences as repeat regions within their genomes.

The choice of where to integrate the viral genome is somewhat loose. The virus cares mostly about getting into the cell's genome and not very much about where it integrates. So at first glance it might appear that integration occurs in an essentially random fashion. On the other hand, biologists tell us that cutting and pasting DNA is a complex process that requires several enzymes, and that cutting generally occurs at very specific sequences of DNA. So this suggests that the virus will seek to integrate where it finds a particular sequence of DNA. We can consider this sequence of DNA to be a "signal" of sorts. It is a signal to the virus that integration might be possible here.

Before we consider such a signal in more detail, let us consider why the virus cares about inserting itself in a way that makes cutting and pasting of DNA easy. You can probably answer this question yourself. If the virus has to use the cellular machinery to cut and paste DNA, then it is in the "best interests" of the virus to make that cutting and pasting easy. This ensures that the virus gets into the genome without mangling the genome so badly that the cell dies, which would defeat the entire purpose of integrating into the genome. So viruses are obviously at some pains, one might say, to keep the cell alive if they are going to integrate into the cellular genome.

Given the requirement that the virus must keep the cell alive, which requires minimal damage to the genome, we can see why the virus might wish to integrate at specific sites or at least near sequences that are amenable to cutting and pasting DNA. So now we must try to find if any signals occur immediately before or after the site of integration. Our hypothesis is that such signals exist; the null hypothesis is that there are no such preferences and the virus is simply inserting itself willy-nilly.

How do we go about finding this signal, if it exists, if we have no idea what it should be? The answer is to turn to information theory. Essentially, we can use the Shannon entropy to measure the likelihood that a given pattern of nucleotides is meaningful in the context of integration signals.

Here is how we might go about doing this. We start by collecting a set of sequences that we know contain HIV integrated into the genome. For example, we can collect DNA samples from AIDS patients and use polymerase chain reaction (PCR, see Chapter 3) to get out those regions that contain HIV sequences. We can then map those regions back to the human genome to get the surrounding sequences that would originally have been the site of HIV integration. The specific details of this work are reported in [19].

With this dataset of possible integration regions, we can begin looking for patterns. What sort of patterns are we most interested in finding? From Shannon's theory, we know that patterns that occur with very high or very low frequencies compared with random sequence are most likely to be informative. So the first step might be to try and find short patterns that occur at unexpected frequency.

Many such patterns may occur, and sifting through them all could be difficult in the absence of any other criteria. We can use biology to narrow our search a bit. We know from other systems[2] that cutting and pasting of DNA works best when the sequences at either end of the cut site are identical. In fact, we usually look for *palindromes*, sequences that read the same backward and forward. For example, the word *noon* is a palindrome in English. In DNA, we can have two kinds of palindromes. A sequence such as:

GAATAAG

is a palindrome of nucleotides in the same way that *noon* is a palindrome in English. You can read this word from beginning to end or end to beginning and get the same sequence.

However, recall that DNA is made up of two strands, each running anti-parallel to the other (Chapter 2). As a result, it is possible to have a sequence on one strand that reads the same on the other strand. In biology, the most common type of palindromes are these. Let us consider an example. The string:

ACGT

does not appear to be a palindrome at the moment. But now consider that its complement sequence would be:

TGCA

---

[2] Specifically, in bacteria, a number of enzymes specialize in cutting sequences at specific sites. These enzymes, known as restriction endonucleases, are utilized in a wide array of applications in experimental biology for cutting and manipulating DNA. See Chapter 3 for more.

Again, not the same sequence. However, remember that one strand of DNA is the **reverse complement** of the other. In other words, we need to both complement and reverse the order of the string to get the sequence on the other strand. What happens if you reverse the complement sequence? You get:

ACGT

So, in fact, ACGT is a DNA palindrome.

Let's consider a longer example. In English, the sentence "Able was I ere I saw Elba," attributed to Napoleon, is a palindrome. If you were to read it backward, you would get the same sentence. Now take a look at the following sequence:

GAATTC

Its complement sequence is

CTTAAG

and its reverse complement sequence is:

GAATTC

So this string is also a DNA palindrome.

The advantage of cutting DNA at sites such as GAATTC is that it is easy to glue everything back together again because the cut points will base pair nicely with each other (Figure 7.1). We can speculate that the virus will also prefer to integrate at a palindromic sequence and look at those patterns that also happen to be palindromes. This will help us to narrow the search to the most likely set of patterns that might be part of the signal for integration.

### Finding Patterns in Sequence Data

The first step in determining whether a signal exists at the HIV integration sites is to build a multiple sequence alignment (Chapter 5). Table 7.2 shows some sample sequences that might represent HIV integration regions. In this and all the further discussion, we denote the nucleotides that are upstream (5′) of the integration site as negative values (−1, −2, etc.) and those nucleotides downstream (3′) of the integration site as positive values (1, 2, etc.). The virus will integrate between the −1 and +1 positions. This nomenclature will help us keep track of the orientation of the signal within a given strand of DNA.

As you look at this alignment, you might be concerned that at no position do all of these sequences share the same nucleotide. That is, we cannot develop an exact pattern that represents the signal for integration. This is often the case in biology. As discussed in Chapter 5, exact pattern matching rarely yields informative signals in a biological context. Instead, we need to rely on inexact pattern matching or matching that allows for some fuzziness.

So, do any inexact patterns occur among these sequences? To check for this, we need to tally up the relative frequency of a nucleotide occurring in any given position within our alignment. Based on just the six sequences in Table 7.2, we have calculated the relative frequencies for the four nucleotides in each position (see Table 7.3).

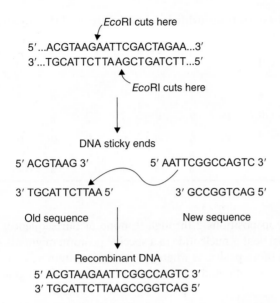

**FIGURE 7.1**   Cutting at palindromic sequences makes it easy to splice in a new piece of DNA because the ends will base pair with each other. This is shown for the specific case of an enzyme known as *Eco*RI, which cuts at the palindromic sequence GAATTC.

**TABLE 7.2   Sample alignment of putative sites of integration for HIV***

|      | −5 | −4 | −3 | −2 | −1 | 1 | 2 | 3 | 4 | 5 | 6 | 7 | 8 | 9 | 10 |
|------|----|----|----|----|----|---|---|---|---|---|---|---|---|---|----|
| Seq1 | C | G | T | A | G | A | T | T | A | C | A | C | A | T | G |
| Seq2 | A | T | G | T | G | G | A | A | T | C | C | T | A | A | T |
| Seq3 | C | T | T | G | A | G | T | A | A | C | A | T | A | C | C |
| Seq4 | G | A | T | T | G | G | T | A | A | T | C | A | T | C | T |
| Seq5 | T | C | A | G | G | G | T | T | A | C | C | A | C | T | C |
| Seq6 | C | C | T | A | A | A | T | T | A | T | C | C | A | T | T |

*The virus will integrate between the nucleotides at −1 and +1 positions in this scale. Adapted from [19].

At first glance, it is obvious that at some positions a particular nucleotide tends to dominate. As one example, consider position 4. All but one sequence has an A at this position. Similarly, position 2 is dominated by T (five out of six sequences). Less striking, but perhaps just as important, are those positions where one nucleotide is predominant: positions −1 and 1 favor G (four of six sequences), positions 5 and 6 favor C, position 8 favors A and position −3 favors T. These may all be part of an inexact pattern that constitutes the signal for integration.

Note also that at some positions certain nucleotides are never present. Take, for example, positions −3 to +4. In these positions, none of our sequences had

**TABLE 7.3** **Relative frequencies of each nucleotide in each position of the putative integration sites shown in Table 7.2***

|   | −5 | −4 | −3 | −2 | −1 | 1 | 2 | 3 | 4 | 5 | 6 | 7 | 8 | 9 | 10 |
|---|---|---|---|---|---|---|---|---|---|---|---|---|---|---|---|
| A | $\frac{1}{6}$ | $\frac{1}{6}$ | $\frac{1}{6}$ | $\frac{2}{6}$ | $\frac{2}{6}$ | $\frac{2}{6}$ | $\frac{1}{6}$ | $\frac{3}{6}$ | $\frac{5}{6}$ | 0 | $\frac{2}{6}$ | $\frac{2}{6}$ | $\frac{4}{6}$ | $\frac{1}{6}$ | 0 |
| C | $\frac{3}{6}$ | $\frac{2}{6}$ | 0 | 0 | 0 | 0 | 0 | 0 | 0 | $\frac{4}{6}$ | $\frac{4}{6}$ | $\frac{2}{6}$ | $\frac{1}{6}$ | $\frac{2}{6}$ | $\frac{2}{6}$ |
| G | $\frac{1}{6}$ | $\frac{1}{6}$ | $\frac{1}{6}$ | $\frac{2}{6}$ | $\frac{4}{6}$ | $\frac{4}{6}$ | 0 | 0 | 0 | 0 | 0 | 0 | 0 | 0 | $\frac{1}{6}$ |
| T | $\frac{1}{6}$ | $\frac{2}{6}$ | $\frac{4}{6}$ | $\frac{2}{6}$ | 0 | 0 | $\frac{5}{6}$ | $\frac{3}{6}$ | $\frac{1}{6}$ | $\frac{2}{6}$ | 0 | $\frac{2}{6}$ | $\frac{1}{6}$ | $\frac{3}{6}$ | $\frac{3}{6}$ |

a C. Similarly in positions 2 through 9, none of our sequences had a G. The absence of a particular nucleotide in a specific position might also be important. So taken with those positions where a nucleotide dominates, we may be able to develop a pattern that could represent the HIV integration signal.

### Measuring the Shannon Entropy of Sequences

The question then becomes: Of these positions, which deviate enough from random to be significant? This is where information theory provides some elegant solutions. We are not able in this text to explore the statistical basis of many of the metrics used in an information theory analysis, but you can learn more about the specific application of information theory to biological sequence analysis here [6]. Instead, we look at just two relatively simple measures derived from information theory.

Recall from Section 7.1.1 that Shannon's theory includes a concept termed entropy. If you are familiar with thermodynamics, then you know that a system with high entropy is very disordered. For instance, a liquid, where the molecules can slide around more freely, has higher entropy than a solid, where all the molecules are rigidly held in place. Shannon wanted to convey the same idea for information. When the Shannon entropy of a given string is high, the string is more disordered and therefore likely to have been generated by a random process. When the Shannon entropy of a string is low, it is more ordered and therefore more likely to have arisen from a specific process. That is, it is more likely to be meaningful. In the biological context, we would say that a string with low entropy is one that is likely to be part of a specific signal.

To measure the entropy of a string, we have to ask how likely it is that each individual nucleotide within the string could have occurred in that position. Formally, we will need to know the probability of each nucleotide occurring in each position of the string. In practice, we can roughly estimate the probability by looking at a set of sequences, such as the HIV integration regions, to develop a sense of the probability for each nucleotide in each position. That is, we can use the relative frequencies shown in Table 7.3 as a rough measure of the overall probabilities of nucleotide occurrence in each position.

Let's take an example. Suppose we want to know the probability of an A occurring in the +4 position. From Table 7.3, the relative frequency of A in this position is 5/6, or 0.83. Assuming our small sample here is representative of the entire dataset of HIV integration regions, we would say that the probability of A in the +4 position, $p(A_4)$, is 0.83.

How unusual is it that A seems to occur 83% of the time in our dataset at this position? It might be very unusual, thereby suggesting that it is part of a signal, or it might be very common. To determine how unusual the occurrence of A is in this position, we need to consider the overall frequency of A and the length of the string in which the A might occur. For the case of A occurring in position +4, our "string" has a length of one because we are interested in just this one position. The overall frequency of A in this position is 5/6, and of T is 1/6 times.

Let us now suppose that we have a machine that spits out a nucleotide each time we request one. The machine generates nucleotides at random, but with the same frequency as we observed in column +4 of Table 7.3. What is the probability it will produce an A? We already know the answer: 0.83. But what is the probability that it will spit out one A, then a second A, and a third A? That is, what is the probability over time that this random generator will keep on producing an A? Shannon entropy captures the answer to this question. In essence, the Shannon entropy tells you the likelihood of getting an A at random in a given position based on the overall observed frequencies for that position.

Here is how we calculate the Shannon entropy for position +4. We know that our machine can generate one of four symbols: A, C, G, or T. We also know the probabilities (in our case, relative frequencies) of getting each of these four symbols. We could just multiply the relative frequencies of the four symbols and get an overall probability for a nucleotide occurring in this position. However, it would be a very small value since multiplying fractions yields smaller and smaller values. To work around this, we take the logarithm. Basic algebra tells us that the log of a product is equal to the sum of the logs, so we will simply sum up the logarithms of the relative frequencies. Taking the logarithm also allows us to interpret the results more meaningfully. If we take the $\log_2$, our answer will be the number of bits of information contained in position +4. That is, we will know how many bits are required to encode the information contained in this position.

The Shannon entropy is calculated as

$$H(X) = -\sum_{i}^{n} p(x_i) \log_2 p(x_i) \tag{7.1}$$

where $H(X)$ is the entropy of position $X$, $p(x_i)$ is the probability of the $i$th nucleotide in position $X$ and $i \ldots n$ is the set of all possible nucleotides in that position (A, C, G, or T). We will not be deriving this equation as it is beyond our scope here, but you can read about how to arrive at this formulation in [14,15].

TABLE 7.4    The values for calculating the Shannon entropy in
position +4 from our dataset of HIV integration sites

| $p(x_i)$ | $\log_2 p(x_i)$ | $p(x_i) \times \log_2 p(x_i)$ |
|---|---|---|
| $p(A) = 5/6$ | $\log_2(p(A)) = -0.26$ | $5/6 \times -0.26 = -0.22$ |
| $p(C) = 0$ | $\log_2(p(C)) = -\infty$ | $0$ |
| $p(G) = 0$ | $\log_2(p(G)) = -\infty$ | $0$ |
| $p(T) = 1/6$ | $\log_2(p(T)) = -2.58$ | $1/6 \times -2.58 = -0.43$ |
| | $H(X) = -(-0.22 + 0 + 0 - 0.43) = 0.65$ | |

TABLE 7.5    The same entropy calculation for
purely random sequence with equal
probabilities for all four nucleotides

| $p(x_i)$ | $\log_2 p(x_i)$ | $p(x_i) \times \log_2 p(x_i)$ |
|---|---|---|
| $p(A) = 1/4$ | $\log_2(p(A)) = -2$ | $1/4 \times -2 = -0.5$ |
| $p(C) = 1/4$ | $\log_2(p(C)) = -2$ | $1/4 \times -2 = -0.5$ |
| $p(G) = 1/4$ | $\log_2(p(G)) = -2$ | $1/4 \times -2 = -0.5$ |
| $p(T) = 1/4$ | $\log_2(p(T)) = -2$ | $1/4 \times -2 = -0.5$ |
| | $H(X) = -(-0.5 - 0.5 - 0.5 - 0.5) = 2$ | |

For position +4, the values required to calculate the Shannon entropy are shown in Table 7.4. The entropy or $H(X)$ would be the sum of the values in the third column, 0.65. We lose the negative sign because in Equation 7.1 there is a minus outside the sum, and the two minuses cancel each other. This value means that we require 0.65 bits to encode the information contained in this position.

What if the sequence were entirely random? Then each nucleotide would have an equal chance of occurring in this position, the entropy for this is calculated in Table 7.5. In random sequence $H(X)$ would be 2. That is, a random sequence comprises 2 bits of information, whereas our position requires only 0.65 bits. Recall from Shannon's theory that a random sequence is more complex than a meaningful sequence, and as a result, a random sequence has a much higher entropy. Exercise 7.1 asks you to calculate the entropy for each position in Table 7.3. Based on your findings, do you think a signal for HIV integration exists in this region?

### Assessing the Likelihood of Occurrence

Entropy can tell us that a meaningful signal exists in a given sequence, but it cannot tell us the likelihood of finding a specific nucleotide in a given position. For that, we will use a different measure, the log odds ratio. The **log odds ratio** is a measure of how much a set of observed frequencies deviates from the expected (i.e., at random) frequencies. In some ways, it is like entropy, but we can use the log odds ratio to determine whether a particular position of an alignment is more or less important. The ratio reflects the likelihood that the given nucleotide in a specific position is not simply the consequence of random fluctuations in nucleotide composition. In other words, the log odds ratio can tell us how unusual the combination of nucleotides within the string is given the background frequencies for nucleotides in that genome.

The challenge now is to decide what constitutes an unusual frequency distribution for sequence patterns. For this, we need to find a comparable dataset in which we know the signal cannot exist. One way to do this is simply to generate a large amount of random data and count up the frequencies with which any particular nucleotide or pattern occurs. If we choose to go the route of generating a random sequence, we need to ensure that we are comparing apples to apples. In other words, our random sequence has to be as closely representative of the actual sequences in our dataset as possible, while retaining a random element. The most common way to generate a random sequence is to match the randomly generated sequences to the frequencies observed in known sequences. For example, if you were looking for a six-nucleotide pattern, you would want your random sequence to have the same frequency of six-nucleotide combinations as your known sequences. In our case, we simply match the random sequence to the known dataset at the single-nucleotide composition level. In other words, if the frequency of A in the known sequences is 20%, then 20% of the nucleotides generated by our random sequence generator should also be As.

We now have two datasets: a set of sequences from known sites of HIV integration and a set of comparable, randomly generated sequences. Just as we generated a set of nucleotide frequencies for the HIV integration data in Table 7.3, Table 7.6 shows the frequencies in randomly generated sequences that are matched at the single-nucleotide composition level with sequences in the HIV dataset.

Now we can calculate a log odds ratio between the observed frequencies in the HIV dataset and the random dataset for each position. We calculate the log odds ratio in Equation 7.2:

$$L(X) = \log_2 \frac{F_{obs}}{F_{exp}} \qquad (7.2)$$

**TABLE 7.6    Relative frequencies of random sequences generated to have the same single-nucleotide frequencies as known HIV integration sites**

|   | −5 | −4 | −3 | −2 | −1 | 1 | 2 | 3 | 4 | 5 | 6 | 7 | 8 | 9 | 10 |
|---|----|----|----|----|----|---|---|---|---|---|---|---|---|---|----|
| A | $\frac{1}{6}$ | $\frac{1}{6}$ | $\frac{1}{6}$ | $\frac{2}{6}$ | $\frac{2}{6}$ | $\frac{2}{6}$ | $\frac{2}{6}$ | $\frac{2}{6}$ | $\frac{2}{6}$ | $\frac{1}{6}$ | $\frac{2}{6}$ | $\frac{1}{6}$ | $\frac{1}{6}$ | $\frac{1}{6}$ | 0 |
| C | $\frac{3}{6}$ | $\frac{2}{6}$ | $\frac{2}{6}$ | $\frac{1}{6}$ | $\frac{1}{6}$ | $\frac{2}{6}$ | $\frac{2}{6}$ | $\frac{1}{6}$ | $\frac{1}{6}$ | $\frac{2}{6}$ | $\frac{1}{6}$ | $\frac{1}{6}$ | $\frac{2}{6}$ | $\frac{2}{6}$ | $\frac{2}{6}$ |
| G | $\frac{1}{6}$ | $\frac{1}{6}$ | $\frac{1}{6}$ | $\frac{2}{6}$ | $\frac{2}{6}$ | $\frac{1}{6}$ | $\frac{1}{6}$ | $\frac{2}{6}$ | $\frac{2}{6}$ | $\frac{1}{6}$ | $\frac{2}{6}$ | $\frac{2}{6}$ | $\frac{2}{6}$ | 0 | $\frac{1}{6}$ |
| T | $\frac{1}{6}$ | $\frac{2}{6}$ | $\frac{2}{6}$ | $\frac{1}{6}$ | $\frac{1}{6}$ | $\frac{1}{6}$ | $\frac{1}{6}$ | $\frac{1}{6}$ | $\frac{1}{6}$ | $\frac{2}{6}$ | $\frac{1}{6}$ | $\frac{2}{6}$ | $\frac{1}{6}$ | $\frac{3}{6}$ | $\frac{3}{6}$ |

where $L(X)$ is the log odds ratio for position $X$ of an alignment, $F_{obs}$ is the observed frequency for a given nucleotide in position $X$ (from the HIV dataset in this case), and $F_{exp}$ is the expected frequency for that nucleotide in position $X$ (determined from the random dataset). You can consult [6] for more on how this equation is derived.

Let's look at a specific position and see what the log odds ratio can tell us. In position $-5$, the frequency of C in the HIV dataset from Table 7.3 is 3/6. It is the same in the random dataset (see Table 7.6). So for this position, the log odds ratio is 0 ($\log_2$ of 1 will be 0). This suggests that position $-5$ in our alignment does not actually have any meaningful information regarding the signal, even though the entropy of the sequence region suggests it contains a signal. So already the log odds ratio has helped us understand that some parts of our alignment might be superfluous.

Let us now consider a different position within the alignment. Let us suppose that we have a candidate integration site with a G in the $-1$ position. From Table 7.3, the frequency of G in this position is 4/6. The frequency in random data is 2/6 (see Table 7.6). Plugging in these values into Equation 7.2, the log odds ratio for position $-1$ will be 1.02. The positive value of this ratio indicates that a G in this position is likely part of a signal. This is because it is more frequent in the HIV dataset than in the random dataset. A negative value from the log odds ratio would indicate that the nucleotide in that position is less frequently observed in the HIV dataset than in the random dataset.[3] Information theory tells us that both over- (higher than random frequency) and under-representation (lower than random frequency) are important and can be part of a signal. Exercise 7.2 asks you to write a program to calculate the log odds ratios for a given sequence alignment such as the one shown in Table 7.2. We can use the log odds ratio to score a putative integration site and use the score as a way of identifying candidate sites for HIV integration. This is described in much greater detail in [6].

### Generating a Consensus Sequence

So far, we have used the entropy to determine whether a given region might harbor a signal, and then used log odds ratios to identify which positions within that region are particularly important for the signal. The next question is whether a specific pattern exists in these positions that could be used to search other sequences for similar signals. The nucleotide pattern for this signal can be derived in a number of ways, and we will start with the simplest method. The method involves using the relative frequencies of nucleotides in each position to generate a **consensus pattern,** or sequence. The consensus pattern describes what is most commonly found at each position in our alignment. For example, in position 4, five of our sequences had an A. This is an overwhelming preponderance, so we will

---

[3] This is one of the conveniences of using a log scale: values less than 1 become negative, and values greater than 1 are positive. As a result, the sign of the log odds ratio can immediately tell us whether a given nucleotide or string is more or less likely to occur in our known dataset than in the random dataset.

say that in position 4, we should usually expect an A. Starting from the beginning of the alignment, here are our possible conclusions:

| −5 | −4 | −3 | −2 | −1 | 1 | 2 | 3 | 4 | 5 | 6 | 7 | 8 | 9 | 10 |
|----|----|----|----|----|---|---|----|---|---|---|-----|---|---|----|
| C | [CT] | T | [AGT] | G | G | T | [AT] | A | C | C | [ACT] | A | T | T |

At some positions, one of the nucleotides clearly dominates, and we can select this nucleotide to be the primary one in our consensus sequence. In position 4, for example, A is predominant, so we simply put an A in that position in our consensus sequence. But in positions −4, −2, 3, and 7, more than one nucleotide seems to be possible. We can try to force a choice here, but we do not have enough information to justify picking one over the other. For example, can we justify picking A in position −2, given that G and T have equal frequencies? Rather than try to make tough choices, we can more equitably say that any of the three nucleotides are possible there. To denote this, we put the three nucleotides in brackets: [AGT]. So our consensus sequence is

C[CT]T[AGT]GGT[AT]ACC[ACT]ATT

From the earlier log odds ratio analysis, we know that positions −5, −4, 9, and 10 are uninformative (see Exercise 7.2), so the actual pattern we would want to use is:

T[AGT]GGT[AT]ACC[ACT]A

When we originally began this exploration, we said that the integration signal might be a palindrome because this enables easy cutting and pasting of DNA after viral integration into the cellular genome. Is this sequence a palindrome? The overall consensus sequence is not, but the portion based on the log odds ratio is: T[AGT]GGT.ACC[ACT]A.[4] Note that we do not count the central nucleotide (represented here as . the dot between T and A) because the palindrome will read both ways regardless of what nucleotide occupies that position. So, in fact, it does appear that HIV prefers to integrate at a palindromic sequence [19].

### Searching for Instances of a Signal

Now that we have a sense of what the integration signal might be, how can we find places in the genome where such integration might occur? If we had an exact pattern, we could use any of a number of excellent computational methods to search for a substring (the signal) within a longer string (the genome). In some ways, our consensus sequence gives us a near exact pattern, with the exception of the two positions where more than one nucleotide seems acceptable. So we could simply search the genome for all the places where this occurs. Exercise 7.3 asks you to search a chromosome of the human genome and identify all the putative sites of HIV integration.

---

[4] This sequence renders a palindrome some of the time, depending on what nucleotides occupy the two optional positions. For example, TAGGT.ACCTA is a palindrome, but TAGGT.ACCCA would not be.

A more sophisticated approach to finding these locations is to look for any region of the genome that shares the nucleotide frequency distributions we observed in our set of known HIV integration sites. That is, we can search sequences and score them based on their compositional similarity by using the values we determined in Table 7.3. Table 7.3 is actually known as a **position-specific weight matrix (PSWM).** Each column represents a position within the consensus sequence; hence the term *position-specific* weight matrix. The weight of each nucleotide in a given position is simply the frequency with which it appears. We can use this matrix to score sequences based on the frequencies of the nucleotides in each position.

Look again at a sample sequence that might be an integration signal:

| −5 | −4 | −3 | −2 | −1 | 1 | 2 | 3 | 4 | 5 | 6 | 7 | 8 | 9 | 10 |
|----|----|----|----|----|---|---|---|---|---|---|---|---|---|----|
| C  | C  | T  | A  | G  | G | T | A | A | C | C | A | A | T | T  |

Would this sequence be a possible candidate for HIV integration? This is an artificial situation; just looking at this sequence you can probably see that it satisfies the consensus sequence we just developed. But let's say you were trying to search the entire genome for such strings and you have hundreds of instances. You probably do not want to devote several hours to examining each putative site and deciding the likelihood that it qualifies as an HIV integration site. To help automate the procedure, you would want to assign a quantitative score to it.

This is where the PSWM comes into play. With a PSWM, we can score the sequence based on the frequencies we have observed in Table 7.3. We will assume independence among the nucleotide positions; that is, each nucleotide occurs in its position independent of its neighbors' frequencies of occurrence. We will see later in Section 7.4 how to account for interdependencies among nucleotides. For now, assuming independence among the positions allows us to use basic probability theory to determine the overall likelihood that this string might occur. We will simply multiply the frequencies of the nucleotides in each position based on the values in Table 7.3. The number is vanishingly small: 0.00014, but we can take the $-\log_2$ of the value to get a positive integer value. In this case, the score now becomes 12.8.

Now let's consider a string that looks very similar:

| −5 | −4 | −3 | −2 | −1 | 1 | 2 | 3 | 4 | 5 | 6 | 7 | 8 | 9 | 10 |
|----|----|----|----|----|---|---|---|---|---|---|---|---|---|----|
| C  | C  | T  | A  | G  | C | T | A | A | T | C | G | A | T | T  |

This string also contains a palindrome, so might it also qualify as an integration site? Again, we use our PSWM to score this sequence, which yields a score of 0. This is because a C in position 1 has a frequency of 0 in Table 7.3 as does having a G in position 7. The power of the PSWM is in detecting these relatively small changes: just two nucleotides differ between this sequence and the first one we considered, yet the scores are dramatically different.

The advantage of the PSWM is that it is relatively easy to build the matrix and to score instances of a sequence. Some assumptions inherent to PSWM do need to be kept in mind, however. The PSWM is best when the signal is made up of a well-conserved nucleotide pattern and is of a constant length, such as the HIV integration signal we used here. In the next section, we will explore some ways to find signals that are not well conserved either in sequence composition or in length.

## 7.2.2  Regulating Genes: Transcription Factor-Binding Sites

The signal used by HIV to identify sites for integration is useful for the virus but incidental to the cell's behavior. However, many of the methods we developed in trying to find the HIV integration signal can come to our aid as we try to find those signals most important for the cell.

Recall from Chapter 2 that the control of when genes are turned on and off is critical for the survival of the cell. The careful control of gene expression is necessary for the cell to modulate its behavior as things within the cell and its environment change. We will explore how to measure and model changes in gene expression in Chapter 8. The regulation of gene expression is carried out at many different levels within the cell, but by far the most important level of control is in the decision to transcribe a gene into mRNA. Biologists refer to this level of control as **transcriptional control,** and the regulation of transcription is largely controlled by short sequences upstream of the gene in the **promoter** region.

The promoter region may be a very small region of DNA immediately upstream of the gene, but its role in regulating the gene is crucial. In prokaryotes such as bacteria, the promoter region is usually very close to the start of the gene, and many promoter sequences in bacteria are short (six to eight nucleotides long) strings. In eukaryotes such as our cells, promoter sequences can be located at variable distances from the start of the gene, and they can be quite complex in composition. Regardless of where a promoter sequence is located, the way in which it functions is common to all organisms. Special proteins known as **transcription factors** bind to the specific DNA sequences in a promoter region, allowing the rest of the transcriptional machinery to assemble at the start of a gene and transcribe the mRNA. If we can identify the sites where transcription factors bind, we gain some insight into the regulation of genes. As a result, identifying **transcription factor-binding sites (TFBSs)** is a very important task for decoding a genome.

We can use many of the methods we have already discussed to identify TFBSs in a genome. The TFBSs are sometimes close to the start of genes, so we can take the regions immediately upstream of the genes, align them as we did the sequences in Table 7.2, and build a PSWM. This has been done for many bacterial genes and some eukaryotic genes [7]. The short string TATAA, known as the TATA box (discussed in Section 7.1.1), is an example of a promoter sequence that was identified using a consensus sequence and PSWM approach.

Unfortunately, different genes are regulated by different transcription factors and therefore have different sequences in the promoter region. Often, the length of the signal varies for different regions. Consider these sequences, which could all be promoter sequences:

Sequence #1    CACACGC
Sequence #2    AGCACGCTC
Sequence #3    GCACGT
Sequence #4    CGCACGT
Sequence #5    CACGTGTT
Sequence #6    CCACGTATT

We could try to use multiple sequence alignment with gaps to develop a common set of patterns and then a PSWM. But our consensus sequence would also have gaps then, making it harder to search and retrieve other instances that might belong to this family of promoter sequences.[5]

Myriad statistical sampling techniques are available, some derived from information theory, that can come to our rescue in this situation. Essentially, we can scan the entire genome looking for "words," combinations of nucleotides that always occur together. Their frequency distributions can be compared with what we would expect at random using entropy and log odds ratios, for example, to determine whether their presence indicates a signal. In this case, the signal we are looking for is a putative TFBS that regulates a gene or set of genes. Statistical sampling techniques are quite sophisticated and beyond the scope of what we can cover here. You can read more about methods that rely on statistical sampling in these references [11,12].

One method that has proven very effective compares the upstream regions of genes from related species. From Chapter 6, you know that related species tend to have similar sequences, and these sequences accrue mutations more rapidly in the nonfunctional regions of the genome than in the functional regions. As long as the species we are comparing diverged relatively recently in evolutionary history, we can draw on sequence conservation to guide us in finding TFBSs. Because regulation of genes is critical for survival, mutations in these regions tend to be selected out. As a result, there should be good sequence conservation in those regions that regulate genes. It may not be as good a level of conservation as we would see in the protein-coding region of a gene, but nevertheless it should be sufficient to help us identify candidate sites. Recent work that ties phylogenetic analysis with statistical sampling methods has had very good results in this area [16].

Finally, many TFBSs are actually clusters of short sequences that together act as a regulatory module. Different TFBSs might incorporate different short sequences, but the cluster overall retains a certain organization. We can use this organizational pattern as a guide in identifying some of the signals that make up the cluster. Such approaches marry statistical sampling, phylogenetic analysis,

---

[5] You might note that all these sequences share a four-nucleotide sequence: CACG. So you could just search the genome with this four-letter string. However, given 3 billion nucleotides and a short string like this, how many occurrences would you expect at random?

gene expression patterns, and PSWMs into complex algorithms that can yield very accurate predictions of likely TFBSs [2,17]. This is an area of active research, so it is likely that newer methods will continually improve our ability to find these critical but often elusive signals within the genome.

# 7.3  A BIOLOGICAL DECODER RING

We now turn our attention to one of the most obvious problems encountered when trying to decode a genome: how to locate the precise positions of the genes within the genome. Before we begin, we need to emphasize that no method for finding genes is perfect. That is, no single gene prediction algorithm finds 100% of the genes in a genome while eliminating all the things that look like genes but are not biologically functional. As we discuss the different approaches to finding genes and predicting their presence in genomes, we will highlight the advantages and disadvantages of each approach. Although many people consider the problem of gene finding to have been solved, no gene prediction algorithm has proved more than about 85% accurate. So there is still room for investigation and improvement in this area.

Gene finding, or gene prediction, requires us to identify signals such as genes within longer strings of potential nonsense or misleading information. As we saw in earlier sections, we can use some of the ideas from information theory to locate those regions of the genome that are more likely to contain meaningful information. This approach helped us identify the signal that appears to be associated with HIV integration sites. Shannon's theory can help establish the presence of meaningful information, but it cannot on its own tell us what that meaningful information is. To determine what the potential signals are, we need to draw on biology.

One of the most important aspects of genes is that they must be regulated. We discussed in Section 7.2.2 how to locate promoters. We expect that downstream of a promoter or set of promoter sequences will be a functional gene. So locating promoters can also help us identify the location of genes. Similarly, signals at the end of genes indicate where the transcript should end. Collectively these signals are known as **terminators.** One signal found at the end of genes that is common to many eukaryotes (cells like ours) is known as the **polyadenylation** signal. It is a short string, usually AATAAA, used to demarcate the end of a transcript.

Signals such as promoters and terminators are very useful in helping us locate the regions of genomes that are likely to contain genes. To find the actual genes, we need to consider other biological features. Before we begin, recall that most genes code for proteins. A smaller subset of genes code for RNA molecules, many of which serve critical functions within the cell. Finding RNA genes is much more challenging, so we will leave that aside for now. The rest of this chapter focuses on finding protein-coding genes.

The best hint that a genomic region contains a gene is that the DNA in that area can generate an mRNA (messenger RNA) that could be translated into a

**FIGURE 7.2**    Diagrammatic representation of a typical gene. The gene region includes more than just the portion that codes for protein. In addition to this coding region, regulatory regions occur that include the promoter and termination signals. Transcription (the process of copying DNA sequence into mRNA) starts downstream of the promoter region and ends at the termination signals.

meaningful amino acid sequence. The challenge is deciding what is a *meaningful* amino acid sequence. Luckily, we can use what we know of the biology of organisms to lay out some ground rules.

The first is quite simple. Every protein we know of is synthesized beginning with a specific amino acid: methionine (Met or M). This methionine may be removed in later stages of processing, but every protein-coding gene must contain the nucleotide codon for Met at the start of the protein-coding region. The special codon that encodes Met is known as the **start codon** (see also Chapter 2).

Similarly, the end of the protein-coding region is marked by one of three specific nucleotide codons—the **stop codons.** So locating start and stop codons are the first hints to finding genes within a genome. In the DNA, the start codon would be ATG,[6] and the stop codons are TAA, TAG, and TGA. Recall, however, that in the mRNA, the T is replaced by U. So in the mRNA, we would look for AUG and UAA, UAG, and UGA. Exercise 7.4 asks you to find start and stop codons within the HIV genome.

For a gene to be able to code for a protein, it requires more than a start and stop codon. Between these two goal posts, as it were, the gene needs codons that encode the amino acid sequence of the protein. So in addition to looking for start and stop codons, we need to check that a translatable set of intervening codons exists. In any given gene region, several AUGs and stop codons can occur, but only one pair brackets a region of translatable codons. That region is known as an **open reading frame (ORF).**

The ORF is really more of a computational concept than a biological one. It is defined as being a region of the genome defined by a start codon, a set of translatable codons, and a stop codon. Not all ORFs actually code for proteins, but all genes must in some way yield an ORF. So at first glance, the challenge of finding a gene boils down to finding an ORF, which, in turn, encapsulates something called the **coding region** of a gene. Most biologists think of a gene region as including the promoter region, a coding region, and signals for ending the transcript (Figure 7.2). So the coding region is the subset of the gene region that actually codes for the protein. During gene finding, our primary focus is on finding the coding region.

---

[6] For most organisms, ATG is the only start codon, although a few bacteria also use GTG and TTG as start codons.

The coding region of a gene can be continuous, meaning that it begins with a start codon, extends through a series of translatable codons, and ends with a stop codon. Genes with this organization are most often found in viruses and prokaryotes such as bacteria. So in these organisms, ORFs are equivalent to coding regions. In eukaryotes, however, the situation is more complex. Recall from Chapter 2 that genes in eukaryotes are composed of both coding and noncoding regions. The coding regions are known as **exons,** and together all the exons of a gene compose an ORF. However, in the genomic sequence, the exons are interspersed with noncoding regions known as **introns.** The introns are removed (spliced) so that the exons can be assembled into a continuous coding region. To find genes in eukaryotes, therefore, we cannot look just for ORFs in the genomic sequence. Rather, we also need to look for bits of coding regions, the exons, and assemble them into an ORF. Some signals present in exons and introns can help us find the boundaries, and we will discuss them in more detail in the next section.

## 7.3.1  A First Try at Decryption: ORF Finding

As mentioned earlier, the idea of an ORF is more of a computational concept than a biological one. It is important to remember that not all ORFs are genes, but all genes generate ORFs (eukaryotes splice their exons together to create the ORF). To help keep this distinction in mind, we use the term *ORF* to refer to any putative region of the genome that could code for a gene. We use the term *coding region* when we refer to an ORF that is part of a functional gene.

Before we consider ORF finding as a means for gene finding, we need to consider some aspects of ORFs. Recall that each codon has three nucleotides and that each triplet combination encodes one amino acid. Since the nucleotide-to-amino-acid correspondence is 3:1, each codon has three positions. We can begin reading a set of codons from position 1, from position 2, or from position 3 of the first codon (Table 7.7).

**TABLE 7.7   Reading frames for a short segment of DNA sequence translated into amino acids***

| **Frame 1:** | | | | | | |
|------|------|------|------|------|------|------|
| AUG | GCC | CUU | GAC | CUU | UGA | |
| Met | Ala | Leu | Asp | Leu | Stop | |
| **Frame 2:** | | | | | | |
| A | UGG | CCC | UUG | ACC | UUU | GA |
| | Trp | Pro | Leu | Thr | Phe | |
| **Frame 3:** | | | | | | |
| AU | GGC | CCU | UGA | CCU | UUG | A |
| | Gly | Pro | Stop | Pro | Leu | |

*Note how the amino acid sequence changes dramatically from frame to frame as a result of shifting the start point for each codon.

Each of these three positions is known as a **reading frame.** Since there are two strands of DNA (DNA forms a double helix with two strands), a total of six reading frames are possible for a genomic sequence. That is, three frames each are present on the forward and reverse strands. The challenge is to figure out which of the six frames contains a gene in any given location. One way to simplify the search is to draw on what we know of the biology of gene organization within genomes. It is extremely rare to find a coding region on one strand that overlaps extensively with a coding region on the other strand. That is, if a gene is present on the forward strand, then it is highly unlikely that a gene exists in the same region on the reverse strand. There are exceptions, of course, mostly among viruses and other organisms with extremely small genomes. Nevertheless, it is usually safe to assume that if a coding region is present on one strand, then there cannot be a functional coding region in the exact region on the other strand. Generally, if you find two ORFs, one on each strand, that overlap significantly, then one of the two is nonfunctional (Figure 7.3).

Another feature of coding regions that we can use to our advantage is that they tend to be fairly long. Short ORFs are less likely to code for functional genes than longer ORFs. The reason is obvious: proteins tend to be fairly large molecules composed of many amino acids. The coding regions that generate these proteins must, because of the 3:1 relationship of nucleotides to amino acids, be three times longer. As a result, most gene-finding tools set a lower limit on how short an ORF can be if it is to be considered a likely coding region. For example, many gene-finding programs eliminate ORFs that are less than 100 amino acids (300 nucleotides) in length. The length restriction is somewhat arbitrary, and it can lead to problems. Some well-known regulatory proteins have very short amino acid sequences, which are often missed by traditional gene-finding programs. Sometimes the only way to find them is through experimental work in the laboratory.

Why not just find all ORFs regardless of their length? The problem is one of **false positives.** Basically, including every possible ORF of any length results in thousands if not hundreds of thousands of ORFs that are six or nine nucleotides long. Do all of these code for proteins? Which ones do? Which ones do not? It is difficult to tell from a computational perspective, and a human being cannot possibly be expected to look at a hundred thousand ORFs to decide which are relevant. We must therefore filter out the least likely candidates in some way. As we proceed through this chapter, we return again to this problem of false positives, or

**FIGURE 7.3**    When an ORF is found on each of the two strands of DNA, we need to decide which ORF to select. Generally, the longer ORF is taken to be the more likely of the two. In this instance, the ORF 2 on the reverse strand is selected, and the ORF 1 on the forward strand is eliminated during gene finding.

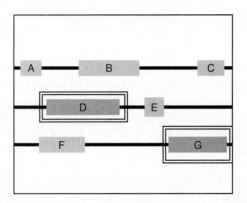

**FIGURE 7.4**   When finding open reading frames (ORFs), any segment of DNA can have putative ORFs on each of the three frames within a strand of DNA. ORFs are eliminated as unlikely to code based on a handful of criteria. In this example, ORFs **A**, **C**, and **E** are very short and unlikely to code for true proteins. ORFs **B** and **F** overlap with the longer ORF **D**. Similarly, **C** overlaps with the longer ORF **G**. After eliminating the unlikely ORFs, we are left with **D** and **G** in the set of genes predicted by ORF finding.

the problem of overpredicting ORFs for a genome. Most methods that find ORFs use criteria such as length and overlaps to eliminate unlikely candidates from the set of predictions for a genome. Figure 7.4 shows how this might work in a given region of a genome.

In Exercise 7.5 you will write programs to identify gene candidates within segments of genome.

## NCBI's ORF Finder

Finding ORFs in a genomic sequence is a relatively straightforward computational task. A number of such ORF-finding programs are publicly available, and you will be designing your own such program in Exercise 7.5. As an example of one such program, the National Center for Biotechnology Information (NCBI) offers a Web-based version called ORF Finder. ORF Finder essentially takes two inputs: a sequence file in a standard format known as the FASTA format and information about the codon usage profile.

Why might we need to know the codon usage of an organism before predicting ORFs? It turns out some organisms have relatively unusual codons for starts and stops as well as for the regular amino acids. For example, some bacteria use several different start codons. So rather than just AUG, they also use GUG and UUG. Similarly, a few bacteria use only one of the three stop codons. The other two codons usually reserved for stops are instead used to code for amino acids. An ORF-finding program has to take these details into account if it is to find the ORFs appropriate to a given organism's biology.

You can find out more about NCBI's ORF finder and try it out at: http://www.ncbi.nlm.nih.gov/gorf/gorf.html

SIDEBAR

### Codon Usage: Additional Clues for Decryption

One of the problems with using ORFs as a basis for finding genes is that we must decide which ORFs are most likely to be coding regions. The simple constraints we discussed, such as length of the ORF or the presence of overlaps, can only get us so far. Even after eliminating many ORFs as unlikely candidates, we are still likely to have several thousand ORFs from which to chose. Is there a way to distinguish amongst them to find those most likely to be coding regions?

Once again, we draw on biology to help identify likely coding regions. In Chapter 2, we discussed the process of translation, in which the mRNA copy of a coding region is used to create a string of amino acids that will become the protein. A key part of the translation process are the tRNAs, specialized RNA molecules that match up codons with amino acids. Although 61 possible codon combinations encode amino acids (the three remaining codons are stop codons and do not encode amino acids), only about 20 to 40 unique tRNAs usually occur in any cell. Why might this be the case? One reason for the smaller number of possible tRNAs is that many genes in an organism preferentially use one of several possible codons to encode any given amino acid. Because there are many more codons than possible amino acids (61 codons to 20 amino acids), organisms can favor the use of one codon over another without affecting the final amino acid output from the translation process. Preferential use of codons is very common, and biologists use the term **codon usage** to refer to this phenomenon.

Let us consider an example. The amino acid valine can be encoded by one of four codon combinations: GUA, GUC, GUG, GUU. [7] So species have a choice of four possible combinations of nucleotides, each of which codes for the valine amino acid. However, in most species, these four codons do not occur with equal frequency within genes. Rather, a strong preference exists for the GUG codon to encode valine. Nearly half of all the valine amino acids in proteins are encoded by the GUG codon. Although the other codon combinations are present, they are found at much lower frequencies. The frequencies of different codons across a spectrum of species is shown in Table 7.8.

Can we use this phenomenon to our advantage in gene finding? Indeed we can. Given an ORF that has passed our length and overlap constraints, we still need to decide if it is likely to be a real coding region. One clue is whether the codon usage of the ORF matches what we know to be the codon usage pattern for that genome. For example, if an ORF has many GUG codons but not many GUC codons, then it is likely to be a real coding region because we know GUG codons are preferentially used over the other codons for valine in many species. In contrast, if an ORF is composed largely of rarely used codon combinations, then it is less likely to be a real coding region.

Why might rare codon usage be an important clue that an ORF is not a coding region? The answer lies in efficiency: more copies of the tRNAs for frequently used codons occur than for rarely used codons. If a coding region utilizes many

---

[7] Recall that at the mRNA level, thymidine (T) nucleotides are replaced by uridine (U). So the codons at the DNA level would be GTA, GTC, GTG, and GTT.

TABLE 7.8    The standard genetic code reflects the codon usage of most species used as models of biology*

| AminoAcid | Codon | Number | /1000 | Fraction |
|-----------|-------|--------|-------|----------|
| Gly | GGG | 566992.00 | 16.55 | 0.25 |
| Gly | GGA | 562361.00 | 16.42 | 0.25 |
| Gly | GGT | 369863.00 | 10.80 | 0.16 |
| Gly | GGC | 770084.00 | 22.48 | 0.34 |
| Glu | GAG | 1360828.00 | 39.73 | 0.58 |
| Glu | GAA | 979887.00 | 28.61 | 0.42 |
| Asp | GAT | 743866.00 | 21.72 | 0.46 |
| Asp | GAC | 863505.00 | 25.21 | 0.54 |
| Val | GTG | 970825.00 | 28.34 | 0.47 |
| Val | GTA | 242244.00 | 7.07 | 0.12 |
| Val | GTT | 375620.00 | 10.97 | 0.18 |
| Val | GTC | 498469.00 | 14.55 | 0.24 |

*Individual species may vary somewhat from the standard genetic code, and some species may have dramatically different codon usage. A sample from the standard code is shown here.

rare codon combinations, then translation of that transcript will be very slow as the machinery awaits the arrival of the rare tRNA encoding the appropriate match to that codon. Over time, species have tried to optimize their coding regions for fast and efficient translation of transcripts. So an ORF with many rare codons is unlikely to be a real coding region because its translation would be very inefficient.

To apply the idea of codon usage to gene finding, we can simply compare the codons in a given ORF with a table like the one in Table 7.8. If we find an ORF with many frequently used codons, then it is more likely to be a coding region than an ORF with many rare codons. Of course, real biology is never this cut and dried. So we need to use more sophisticated techniques to assess the likelihood that a given ORF has a codon usage pattern consistent with what we know of the species' codon preferences.

## 7.3.2  Accounting for Discontinuous Coding Regions

Finding ORFs in genomes is a relatively straightforward computational problem, and as we have discussed, some strategies can help pick out those ORFs most likely to be coding regions. However, not all coding regions are continuous ORFs. Recall that in eukaryotes the coding regions are discontinuous. In other words, the ORF is assembled after transcription by piecing together the bits of the coding region, the exons (Figure 7.5). In Chapter 2, we compared the noncoding portions, the introns, to comments in a piece of code. The introns must be removed before the transcript is ready for translation, just as comments are ignored or removed during compilation of a program.

The process of removing introns is known in biology as **splicing.** Before an intron can be removed from a segment of mRNA, it has to be identified

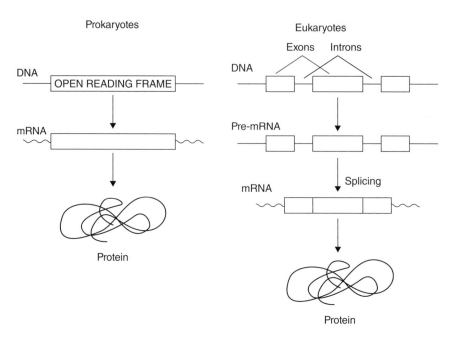

**FIGURE 7.5**  Prokaryotic genes usually have one continuous coding region. In contrast, eukaryotic genes may have discontinuous coding regions, with exons coding for the protein and introns removed prior to translation.

as an intron. You can imagine what a disaster would ensue if parts of exons were accidentally removed because the spliceosome erroneously decided they were introns instead. So the process of splicing has to be carefully regulated and orchestrated. A complex piece of machinery, the **spliceosome,** actually removes the introns through a series of chemical steps. The spliceosome is composed of RNA molecules and proteins known as the small nuclear ribonucleoprotein particles (snRNPs, pronounced as "snurps" to rhyme with "smurfs"). At least five components of the spliceosome participate directly in splicing. We focus primarily on the U1 and U2 snRNPs because these two molecules are the critical parts for recognizing the ends of introns within a transcript.

The first step in splicing is the recognition of a short signal at the 5′ or beginning of an intron. The signal is a two nucleotide pattern: GU (GT in the DNA). Obviously, this is a very small signal and could be expected to occur at random once every 16 nucleotides. In addition to the GU, the first four or five nucleotides of the intron tend to be well conserved in some species, and we can use this slightly longer signal in finding the 5′ end of each intron.

At the other end of the intron, the 3′ end, a second signal exists. This is also a two-nucleotide signal: AG. However, in many species, the sequences just before the AG are reasonably well conserved. The region tends to be pyrimidine-rich (many Cs and Us), and some of the nucleotides immediately upstream of the AG are very well conserved in groups of species such as mammals.

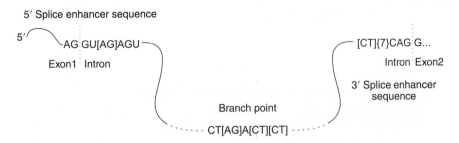

**FIGURE 7.6**   Some of the signals associated with intron removal. These signals tend to be the best conserved patterns in known introns, but even within a single species, different introns can have widely different versions of these signals [1].

Somewhere in the middle of the intron is a third signal of critical importance for splicing. This signal is known as the **branch-point adenine** (A). It is a single A located in the last third of the intron and is required for the chemical reaction that allows the intron to be removed from the transcript. All three of the signals associated with splicing are shown in Figure 7.6.

Although the signals associated with the intron appear to be well conserved in Figure 7.6, these signals, in fact apply to only a limited subset of all introns. Even in well-studied organisms such as mammals, a great deal of variation exists in the composition and juxtaposition of these signals. It is important to remember that we probably do not yet know all the signals associated with splicing and that the signals described here apply only to some portion of all possible intronic sequences in various genomes.

Regardless of what we know about the signals for splicing, we need a way to model these signals. After all, the key to finding coding regions in eukaryotes is to find the boundaries between introns and exons. Once we find the boundaries we can skip over the intronic sequences and assemble the ORF from the exonic sequences. We will describe several strategies for finding the ends of the introns, regions known as the **intron–exon boundaries.** Once we know where those boundaries are, in theory it is a trivial step to assemble the ORF and identify likely coding regions. As always with biology, though, the devil is in the details.

### Finding Introns Through Conserved Signals

In developing algorithms for finding eukaryotic genes, methods often focus on a particular species. This is partly because enough variation in intronic signals exists between species and especially across classes of species that a generic solution is unlikely to be reliable. So, for example, several methods focus primarily on mammals or just on humans. We restrict the discussion of methods to a more general level here, but it is important to keep in mind that many methods must be adapted to allow species-specific differences in signals and composition.

As you saw in Figure 7.6, some signals in the 5′ and 3′ regions of the introns are relatively well conserved. We can use these conserved regions to try and identify potential intron–exon boundaries. Note that the signals are well conserved and of a consistent length. We can use PSWMs (see Section 7.2.1) to build a consensus sequence of these regions of the intron. You will develop a PSWM based on intron–exon boundary sequences in Exercise 7.6.

### Finding Introns Through Spliceosomal Signals

The signals we have discussed so far are derived from sets of known introns. We know that these signals are used by the spliceosome to find the boundaries between introns and exons prior to splicing. However, these signals vary somewhat in the composition from intron to intron. Although we can use PSWMs to capture some of this variability and quantify it, the matrices are not a foolproof way of accounting for every variation present in known introns. Indeed, one of the difficulties with PSWMs is that they tend to blur subtle differences in composition by favoring the most common nucleotide(s) in each position of an alignment. As a result, it is possible to miss signals that might affect the efficiency of the splicing of a given intron.

This is a particular problem when considering **alternative splicing,** the process in which some exons are selectively skipped (treated like introns) to yield a variant protein from the same gene region. Many researchers believe that alternative splicing occurs quite frequently in higher eukaryotes, and any method for finding genes in these species must be able to account for this phenomenon. PSWMs derived from sets of intronic sequences are not very reliable in this realm because they tend to gloss over the subtle variation that might mean the difference between retaining or excluding an exon during alternative splicing.

An alternative is to look instead to the spliceosomal components. For example, the U1 and U2 snRNPs each have a section of RNA that must base pair with the relevant sequence on the intron before splicing can occur. So rather than model the variability of sequences on the intron, we can derive a PSWM from looking at the U1 and U2 sequences directly. PSWMs derived from U1 and U2 snRNPs of a variety of species can give us a more generalized model and account for a wider range of sequence variability than just looking at sets of known introns. This approach is utilized by the most successful eukaryotic gene prediction algorithm, Genscan [3].

### Finding Introns Through Sequence Homology

Each of the methods for finding introns we have discussed so far has a critical stumbling block: the problem of false positives. With any predictive method, some predictions are false. In this case, each method will generate some fraction of predictions that are a figment of the methodology rather than true introns. Obviously, we want to find a method that completely eliminates, or at least minimizes, false positives.

The problem of false positives arises because each of the methods discussed attempts to find the intron–exon boundaries in a given sequence without any prior knowledge about the location of a gene. In other words, given a sequence of some length, PSWMs and hidden Markov model (HMMs Section 7.4.3) will attempt a bests guess at the presence or absence of introns and exons. This is critical when we are trying to find genes in a newly sequenced genome.

However, this is not always the case. For example, even before the completion of the Human Genome Project, many hundreds of human genes had been identified and characterized experimentally. So one approach is to take advantage of previously characterized genes to resolve intron–exon boundaries.

The key to this approach, sometimes known as gene prediction through sequence homology, or **reverse mapping,** is that the final translated transcript is, in essence, an ORF. That is, it is a continuous coding region with a clearly demarcated start and stop. The clever solution to the problem of how to find the intron–exon boundaries is to take this continuous coding region and map it back to the original genome sequence. Sequences where the coding region exactly matches the genomic sequence must be exons. Any intervening, unmatched sequences represent introns. Figure 7.7 shows how this might work.

There are two ways to go about the reverse mapping. The simplest is to take the final mRNA transcript, after it has been spliced, and reverse-map it to the genome. However, the more common, albeit difficult, approach is to start from the protein sequence. Given a known protein sequence, the idea is to *reverse-translate* it into all the possible mRNA transcripts, and then map each one back to the genome.

The first challenge with reverse translation is that the amino-acid-to-nucleotide-codon correspondence is not 1:1 for most amino acids. Recall that the genetic code is degenerate, meaning several codons exist for most amino acids. The challenge is to figure out the correct codon present in the mRNA

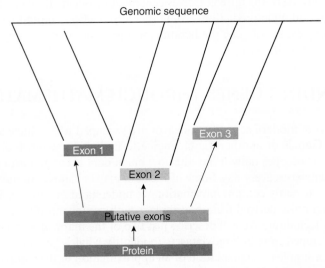

**FIGURE 7.7**   This example shows how reverse mapping of a protein can provide exact boundaries between exons and introns. The protein sequence is reverse-translated into DNA, and the putative exons are then mapped to the genomic sequence. The end result is a set of genomic exons that should yield the correct protein [8].

transcript. You can see how this could easily become a complex, combinatorial problem. Codon usage patterns can help guide the selection of which codon we use for each amino acid, but this is only a partial simplification of the problem.

The second challenge is how we map the reverse-translated sequences to the genome. We need an efficient algorithm to find regions of exact or near exact matches, a problem that is distinct from the sequence alignment problem described in Chapter 5.

The advantage with reverse-mapping approaches is that they produce no false positives. In essence, we can only map back proteins we already know exist in that particular species, so we avoid the problem of false positives altogether. So at first glance, this seems the way to go for gene prediction. Can you think of a reason why this might not be a suitable approach?

The problem lies with the other kind of error inherent to predictive methods. That is, a method can fail to find a known intron–exon boundary because it did not have sufficient information to determine the boundary. We call such errors false negatives because the method wrongly skips a known instance of an intron or other signal. Reverse-mapping methods present a very great possibility of false negatives because we do not have a protein sequence for every possible protein in most genomes. So, some novel genes, for which we have not yet identified the protein, will be missed by the reverse-mapping approaches. If we only use reverse-mapping techniques, we will never find new genes; we will simply confirm the presence of known genes.

How do we work around these problems? One solution is to combine approaches, so that the false positives generated by one method are corrected by another. Conversely, the false negatives generated by one method can be accommodated by adding in predictions from other approaches. The end result will be a more complete set of gene predictions for a genome than any single method could produce on its own.

## 7.4 FINDING GENES THROUGH MATHEMATICS

Many fields of modern scientific endeavor are swamped with a huge amount of data. Use Google or another search engine to find out how much data arrives from radio telescopes daily. Find out how much data is entered into biological sequence databases every day. Some of the data may be "noise" in the sense that it does not currently contain information we understand or can use. Some may just be plain noise derived from interference with equipment or inaccuracies in laboratory technique. We will describe just two of the many mathematical techniques developed to scan large datasets to identify what is "meaningful." First, we look at a simple implementation of an approximation to the complexity measure associated with Shannon entropy. Then we examine a straightforward way in which Markov models can be used to construct a discriminator for differently featured sequences.

## 7.4.1 Linguistic Complexity

A fast method for determining the complexity of strings was described by Troyanskaya [18]. For each length $k$ it is possible to determine how many different words of length $k$ *might* exist in a string and how many different words of that length *actually* occur in the string. In Exercise 7.7 you will write code to do this. Linguistic complexity is computed by summing over a range of reasonable values of $k$ the ratio of actual to possible numbers of different $k$-tuples.

Take a look at the following two nucleotide sequences:

- ATTAGTGATTAGTGATTAGTGATTAGTGATTAGTGATTAGTGATTAGTGATTAGTGA
  TTAGTGATTAGTGATTAGTGATTAGTGATTAGTGATTATAGCATCATTTTTTAAATT
- AAGAAAAAAAGATTAAAAACAACCAACTCGCTTTCGCTTTAAGCCTTTTT
  AATGGCGTGTTAGAAAAAATCAATGAAATTGACGCCCTCATCGAGCCGCA

Both are highly repetitive. When we apply the method described in [18] to the first sequence, we find its linguistic complexity is .286, whereas for the second sequence the linguistic complexity value is .917.

In the paper [18], the authors measure the changing linguistic complexity of various prokaryotic genomes within a sliding window. They note peaks and troughs and areas of increasing and decreasing complexity. With windows of size 40 they note complexity measurements ranging from 0.2 to 0.999. In Exercise 7.8 you are invited to follow their steps. We emphasize that this is an area where you may make significant discoveries. The connections between complexity and biological meaning are not well understood. Exercise 7.8 is a research exercise. It will help you understand the ways in which we can search for the meaningful components, primarily genes, within the longer stretches of genomic sequence that may or may not contain relevant information.

## 7.4.2 Looks Like a . . .

Once we find the meaningful regions of a genomic string, we are faced with a much more difficult task. We must assume that these meaningful regions contain genes. But how do we know what a gene looks like? RNA polymerase, which generates the mRNA transcripts in a cell, is capable of recognizing those portions of a genome that can be transcribed and eventually translated. So why can't we?

An old adage assures us that if it looks like a duck, walks like a duck, and quacks like a duck, then it probably is a duck. But to someone who has never seen nor heard a duck, the adage seems self-referential and useless for identification purposes. Buried in the adage is a fundamental truth: Experience is an important factor in recognizing objects. Later in the chapter, we'll look at other factors based on scientific knowledge and reasoning. For now, however, we examine ways to formalize the method of developing a familiarity with a class of objects and then using that familiarity to classify new objects not previously encountered. This is how a lot of classification gets done. For example:

- Experienced classical musicians have heard a lot of Mozart's music, and they've heard a lot of Beethoven's music. When they hear a previously unheard work by one of these masters, they are able to tell, from experience, that it "sounds like Mozart" or "sounds like Beethoven."
- Experienced art curators know that something "looks like a Vermeer" or "looks like a fake."

Does some mysterious "intuition" develop as you gain experience? Or is it something more tangible?

Look at the following sequences:

```
1110110011010011110110110100111000010101110000110 1
0001010101001110010011010010010000010000011001110 1
```

and

```
0000110001011100011010011101010101100111110011100 0
1100101101100011001101111001001011011000010001101 1
```

You may be interested to know that one of these strings is a short extract from an ASCII representation of Shakespeare's *Twelfth Night*, and the other is a randomly generated binary sequence that uses 0 and 1 in the same proportions as they occur in the ASCII *Twelfth Night*. Exercise 7.17 asks you to figure out which is which.

If you were able to distinguish between the sequences, you were most likely considerably helped by knowing the ASCII encoding scheme. Without that key, the task would have been much harder. For some biological problems, scientists have effectively obtained the key. We know a relationship between triplets of nucleotides and amino acids. This key lets us solve some related biological problems. Unfortunately, for many other biological "code-breaking" problems, we are very far from understanding the encoding scheme. In such cases, statistical techniques may come to our aid.

### 7.4.3 Markov Models

Consider the task of the Shakespearian scholar who is confronted with a new discovery, a play that purports to be by the Bard of Avon, but that has lain hidden for centuries. How can the scholar verify, or refute, the authenticity of the new play?

One method is to form a frequency count of how often each word in the play occurs, and compare that with a frequency count obtained from already authenticated Shakespearian works. For example, of the 21,172 words in *Twelfth Night*, the word *to* appears 395 times, the word *and* appears 521 times, but the word *foul* appears only twice. If in the new play the word *and* appears only half as often as the word *to*, the scholar has pretty strong evidence that this play is not by Shakespeare. Similarly, if the scholar finds widespread use of the word *foul,* she needs to look closely at the text to decide if this were dictated by the needs of conveying meaning (and therefore potentially Shakespeare) or just random (indicating a forgery).

The unit of counting need not be the individual word. The scholar might count the relative frequencies of each of the letters in the alphabet. Unfortunately she will not be able to discern much from this approach because the relative frequencies of the letters do not vary much between one author and another if both write in English.

On the other hand, relative frequencies of individual letters might be used by somebody with no knowledge of Earthly languages to discern that a play written in English is very different from a play written in Italian. Or if a certain text contains about the same number of $q$'s as it does $t$'s, it is most likely not written by Shakespeare because it is unlikely to be written in English. This presupposes, of course, that the un-Earthly researcher already knows that $q$ is a rarely used letter in the English language, but $t$ is a very common letter. In short, consideration of relative frequencies of individual units can give us some insight into authorship or origin. But the insight is limited.

Can we expect to get better information if we look at consecutive pairs of units? That is the thinking behind Markov models. If a system is currently in one state, what is the probability that it will enter into each of the possible other states? For example, suppose the questionable manuscript contains the word *to.* What is the probability that the next word will be *be?* Is that probability similar to the probability that Shakespeare would have transitioned from writing a *to* to writing a *be?* In the world of genomes, suppose we're tracing a sequence of nucleotides. We just saw a G. What's the probability that the next base is a C? Does that conditional probability differ if we're within a coding region as opposed to, say, within a promoter?

The kind of analysis we're proposing is this: For each possible pair of units $i$ and $j$ count up how often $i$ is followed by $j$ and call this total $n_{ij}$. Now count up how often $i$ appears, call it $n_i$. Then figure $p_{ij} = \frac{n_{ij}}{n_i}$. This is the **transition probability** from $i$ to $j$. You can form a matrix of all the $p_{ij}$ to summarize your findings.

If the process you are studying is a true Markov process, the transition matrix of the $p_{ij}$ you just created will be very informative. This is because a *Markov process is one in which the next state is a probabilistic function of nothing more than the current state.*

Is Shakespeare a Markov process? Certainly not. Is the formation of a genome a Markov process? Almost certainly not. Nevertheless, the assumption that they approximate Markov processes turns out to have useful predictive consequences.

Suppose we have two Markov processes either of which can give rise to a sequence of characters. Suppose one has a transition matrix with entries $p_{ij}$, and the other has entries $q_{ij}$. If we obtain a sequence $S$ of characters it is possible to perform some analysis and decide if $p_{ij}$ is a more or less likely explanation for $S$ than the other.

Basically, the idea is to look at every consecutive pair in $S$. Using an obvious notation, such a pair can be denoted by $S_k$ and $S_{k+1}$. If $p_{S_k S_{k+1}}$ is more than $q_{S_k S_{k+1}}$ then the presence of the pair $S_k S_{k+1}$ tends to corroborate $p_{ij}$ as the explanation for $S_k S_{k+1}$ rather than $q_{ij}$. Now we need to form a grand aggregate of all the indications we obtain by looking at all the consecutive pairs in $S$. Let's form the log of the ratio of each pair $r_{ij} = \log\left(\frac{p_{ij}}{q_{ij}}\right)$. If $r_{xy}$ is positive, it indicates that the $p_{ij}$ matrix is the better explanation for $x$ followed by $y$. If $r_{xy}$ is negative, it indicates that the $q_{ij}$ matrix is the better explanation for $x$ followed by $y$.

Mathematically we form the sum:

$$\sum_{k=0}^{\text{S.length()}-2} r_{S_k S_{k+1}} \tag{7.3}$$

This is our predictor. It has summed the $r_{xy}$ values for all the successive pairs $x, y$ in string $S$. If the total is positive, the $p_{ij}$ matrix is the better explanation for string $S$. If it's negative, $q_{ij}$ is a better predictor explaining $S$.

### A Worked Example: Was Twelfth Night Written by a Markov Process?

You'll need to use your imagination here. Imagine that you are an archaeologist of the future. You have just unearthed a large number of compact disks that, remarkably, have survived in a readable form so that you can discern the sequence of 0's and 1's on each disk. Further imagine that a museum has preserved a single copy of a compact disk on which was stored an encoded version of Shakespeare's *Twelfth Night*. Time has erased all human memory of ASCII, and this is all you have:

- A CD that the museum certifies contains a meaningful string of 0's and 1's attributed to somebody called "William Shakespeare," and
- A bunch of CDs whose content is unknown.
- Furthermore, you have the technology to read the sequences of 0's and 1's on each of the CDs.

Perhaps now you can see the parallels with today's large bioinformatics problems:

- We have some DNA that laboratory scientists have identified as something called "coding," and
- We have a bunch of DNA about which we know nothing.
- Furthermore, we have the technology to read the sequences of nucleotides in each of our samples.

Lab scientists take the place of the museum and attach some attribution to some test data. We have other unclassified data and want to know if it is likely to have come about by the same process as the designated test data.

On the Website http://www.mhhe.com/gopal you will find a file `master`. It's not crucial for you to know this, but it was generated by converting the text of Shakespeare's *Twelfth Night* into 7-bit ASCII. Think of this file as the CD attributed by the museum as a genuine "Shakespeare." Also at the same Website, you will find files `mystery1`, `mystery2`, and `mystery3`. These three files also contain binary data and take the place of the CDs the future archaeologist has unearthed.

You can do some preliminary analysis of your data by writing a program to:

- Count the number $n_0$ of 0,
- Count the number $n_1$ of 1,
- Calculate the frequency, $\frac{n_0}{n_0+n_1}$ of 0,
- Calculate the frequency, $\frac{n_1}{n_0+n_1}$ of 1.

For the *Twelfth Night* file, you find that the frequencies are about .4946 and .5054. When you do the same for `mystery1` you get .5258 and .4742; for file `mystery2` you obtain .4652 and .5348; and for file `mystery3` you obtain .5280 and .4720.

All we can deduce from these results is that `mystery1` and `mystery3` have somewhat similar frequencies of bits, but that `master` and `mystery2` are different. Not particularly illuminating.

Now let's go one level deeper and make the assumption that `master` was generated by a Markov process. This may seem like an arrogant assumption given that we know that the pattern of 0's and 1's ultimately derived from the creative genius of the Bard; but it's no less reasonable than the assumption made by thousands of scientists every day who use assumptions of hidden Markov models to enable them to compare biological sequences. The justification is that the assumption of a Markov process behind complicated phenomena leads to valuable results and insights. The entire scholarly endeavor behind the genius of Shakespeare or the wonders of evolution are far beyond our humble abilities. But we obtain valuable insights and make progress in our understanding by beginning with a simplifying assumption that lets us use our data.

Assuming a Markov process behind our `master` data, we write a program to analyze the data. Our program will:

- Count the number $n_{00}$ of times that 0 follows 0
- Count the number $n_{01}$ of times that 1 follows 0
- Count the number $n_{10}$ of times that 0 follows 1
- Count the number $n_{11}$ of times that 1 follows 1

We're assuming a Markov process that has two states:

- In the first state called A, the process will write a 0,
- In the second state called B, the process will write a 1

After each write, the process may advance to the other state, or it may stay in the same state. The probabilities:

- $p_{00}$ of staying in state A,
- $p_{01}$ of changing from state A to state B,
- $p_{10}$ of changing from state B to state A,
- $p_{11}$ of staying in state B

form the transition matrix for the Markov process.

We can compute the transition matrix $p_{ij}$ for the Markov process behind the data contained in `master`. The probability $p_{ij}$ that the system next goes to state $j$ given it is currently in state $i$ is the quotient of the number of times $j$ follows $i$ divided by the number of times that $i$ occurs.

$$p_{ij} = \frac{n_{ij}}{n_i} \tag{7.4}$$

When you write a program to find the transition matrix for the data in `master` you will find the matrix is approximately:

$$\begin{bmatrix} .49947 & .50053 \\ .48984 & .51016 \end{bmatrix}$$

To build a statistical classifier for sequences, we also need a transition matrix for the null hypothesis. The null hypothesis is that a sequence is generated, not by a Markov process, but by a random process. One way to do this is to generate a random file of the same size that contains 0's and 1's in the same ratio as the test file `master`. You can find such a file at the Website `randomsamelentwelthnightbin.txt`. Analyze that file with the same program you used to analyze the test data in `master`, and you will obtain the null hypothesis transition matrix $q_{ij}$:

$$\begin{bmatrix} .49536 & .50464 \\ .49430 & .50570 \end{bmatrix}$$

Now we're ready for the classification program shown in Figure 7.8. When you run `java TwelfthNight mystery1` you will obtain a large positive result. That should not be surprising because we can now reveal that `mystery1` is the 7-bit ASCII encoding of *Hamlet: Prince of Denmark*. `mystery3` produces a negative output, and again it's not surprising because we can now reveal that `mystery3` contains the 7-bit ASCII encoding of a Java program (that we don't think was written by William Shakespeare). `mystery2` also produces a positive output. This may be surprising because it's the 7-bit ASCII encoding of a text written in Latin: *De Bello Gallico,* or Julius Caesar's *Gallic Wars*.

In the exercises, we will pursue possibilities that use the same techniques to pursue more sophisticated classifiers. Had we worked with groups of, say 4 bits, as our basic unit, so that the transition matrices were 16 by 16 instead of 2 by 2, we might have ended up with a more accurate discrimination of Shakespeare works. Or we could even use characters, or, better still, individual words. Further sophisticated discrimination becomes possible as we learn more about the underlying "genomic puzzle." For our discussion we asked you to pretend you were completely in the dark. As we learn more about the underlying science, our Markov assumptions can become more sophisticated and produce more accurate discriminators.

```
import java.io.*;
public class TwelfthNight{
    /* A simple statistical classifier for binary sequences.
       Rhys Price Jones: January 2006.
       Array p is the transition matrix for the 7-bit ASCII Twelfth Night
       Array q is for the null hypothesis, a random sequence of equal
       length with the same bit frequencies
       Array s contains the log of the ratio of the transition probabilities
       If r[i][j] is positive, p is a better predictor
       If r[i][j] is negative, q is a better predictor
       We'll sum all the contributions for every pair in the input

       Usage: java TwelfthNight filename
       filename contains a sequence of 0s and 1s (nothing else)
       Positive output indicates similarity to Twelfth Night!
    */

    private static int NR_STATES = 2;
    private static double[][] s= new double[NR_STATES][NR_STATES];
    private static double[][] q= // transition probs for random
    {{0.49536, 0.50464},
     {0.49430, 0.50570}};
    private static double[][] p=  // transition probs for twelfth night
    {{0.49947, 0.50053},
     {0.48984, 0.51016}};

    public TwelfthNight() {
        // Instantiate the Log Odds Matrix r[][]:
        for (int i=0; i<NR_STATES; i++)
            for (int j=0; j<NR_STATES; j++)
                r[i][j] = Math.log(p[i][j]/q[i][j]);
    }
    public double tprob(char c, char d) {
        //  Get log likelihood to move from c to d
        return (r[c-'0'][d-'0']);
    }
    public static void main(String[] args) {
      int i;
      StringBuffer sb = new StringBuffer();
      try {
          FileReader fr = new FileReader(args[0]);
          i = fr.read();
          while (i>0) {
              sb.append((char) i);
              i = fr.read();
          }
      }
}
```

**FIGURE 7.8**   Program TwelfthNight, a discriminator showing similarity to the Markov process behind the ASCII encoding of the play.

*(continued)*

```
    catch (IOException ioe) {
    }
    TwelfthNight tn = new TwelfthNight();
    String x = new String(sb);
    double tot = 0.0;
    char[] a = x.toCharArray();
    for (int j=0; j<a.length-2; j++) {
        tot += tn.tprob(a[j], a[j+1]);
    }
    System.out.println("Total Estimator for "+args[0]+" evaluates to "+tot);
    System.out.println("Normalized it's "+100000*tot/x.length());
  }
}
```

**FIGURE 7.8**    (*continued*)

### 7.4.4  Genes as Markov Processes

We can also adapt the program in Figure 7.8 to distinguish between coding and noncoding sequences of DNA. The principles are the same. Known stretches of coding DNA serve as our `master`. Known stretches of noncoding DNA serve as our null hypothesis. We obtain a 4 by 4 transition matrix $p_{ij}$ for the coding segments, and a 4 by 4 transition matrix $q_{ij}$ for the noncoding segments. We form an $s_{ij}$ matrix via

```
    for (int i=0; i<4; i++)
      for (int j=0; j<4; j++)
        r[i][j] = Math.log(p[i][j]/q[i][j]);
```

and by summing the *r* values that occur in a mystery sequence, we can tell by obtaining a positive sum that the mystery sequence is likely coding or by a negative sum that the sequence is likely noncoding. We don't need to know everything about the science of the cell and its biological processes; we can work with what we have, and hope to learn more.

A certain beauty and meaning lies behind the seemingly random strings of 0's and 1's that constitute an ASCII encoding of Shakespeare. We know that because essentially we understand the plays and the process of encoding. That's what creates and explains the language of binary-encoded Shakespeare, something that future archaeologists may dig up and try to interpret, not having the benefit of our literary education.

Similarly, we conjecture that there is a beauty and a meaning behind the seemingly random strings of nucleotides we obtain from the DNA of nature. We don't understand the science behind most of the processes governed by the DNA. But, as we've seen in this section, we are making some progress in understanding the science that explains the language of those seemingly random sequences. Markov models have been used extensively in many areas of biological sequence analysis. In the following discussion, we explore the use of Markov models to distinguish between introns (noncoding regions) and exons (coding regions).

Recall in Section 7.3.1 we noted that ORFs that are functional coding regions tend to have distinctive biases in codon composition. That is, coding regions favor some codons over others. We can use this to our advantage in building a Markov model to identify putative coding regions. Just as with ORFs, we expect that true exons will have preferential codon usage, and so we can use nucleotide composition to better identify exons and introns. The exons are constrained, of course, in that they must code for amino acids using the nucleotide triplets or codons. The introns, on the other hand, can be more or less randomly organized, save for the short signals needed for splicing at the 5′, 3′, and branch points. We can use this shift between carefully ordered nucleotide composition to relatively random distributions of nucleotides to better pinpoint the regions that contain exons and introns, respectively.

The idea is quite simple. We expect exons to contain ordered sets of three nucleotides that abide by the codon usage patterns of the species in question. It turns out that the best way to evaluate nucleotide composition in exons is actually to consider two codons at once [3,5]. When we look at six nucleotides worth of information, we are more likely to see the sort of codon trends that might occur when an exon is actually part of a functional gene. That is, certain amino acids that never occur right next to each other, and others almost always occur in conjunction. By looking across six nucleotides of sequence, we are essentially asking if at least two amino acids are juxtaposed in a way that would suggest a functional gene, given the trends seen in that species.

If the hexamers of nucleotides correspond to known codon usage, then we are likely looking at an exonic sequence. When the hexamers shift in composition and no longer correspond well with known codon usage, we may be in an intron. If the hexameric composition shifts back to correlate with codon usage, then we have once again transitioned into an exon. So the shifts in nucleotide composition can be a very powerful way of determining whether we are in an exonic or intronic sequence.

The advantages of this approach are numerous. First, we can focus on known exons and introns and build a statistical model of what hexameric composition patterns are relevant for exons versus introns. Second, we can do this in a species-specific fashion, which enables us to account for species-specific variations in composition. Finally, we can use a powerful method known as the hidden Markov model (HMM) to scan long genomic sequences to identify likely exons and introns based on their composition. HMMs have become the mainstay of nearly every gene prediction algorithm available today [3,5,10].

## Genscan

One very popular tool used for finding genes in the human genome is Genscan. Developed by Chris Burge and Sam Karlin in 1997, Genscan remains one of the most accurate gene-finding tools available for the human genome and a few other genomes [13]. We present a brief description of the Genscan algorithm here, but interested students should consider reading the original Genscan paper to get a sense of the full scale of this algorithm [3].

(*continued*)

Genscan combines several of the approaches we have discussed here. It starts by looking for patterns that might indicate promoters or terminators immediately upstream and downstream of a putative gene region. Promoter finding is mediated through a PSWM in much the manner that we discussed in Section 7.2.2. Genscan looks specifically for the TATA box, the short sequence of TATAA or variants thereof found at the start of most human genes.

After identifying a putative promoter region, Genscan utilizes a fairly standard HMM (see Section 7.4) to identify putative exons. As with other programs, it considers hexameric nucleotide composition and employs a fifth-order Markov model to evaluate the likelihood that a given sequence region has the right composition to be an exon.

PSWMs are again brought into play to find the intron–exon boundaries. Using information from the spliceosome components, Burge and Karlin developed a PSWM to identify the sequences that must exist at the 5' and 3' ends of the intron for splicing to occur. The PSWM is used to check for these conserved signals whenever the HMM indicates that the codon composition no longer matches the pattern expected for a coding exon.

In addition to these methods, Genscan incorporates a length constraint. In human genes, introns tend to have a very distinctive length distribution, and Genscan takes advantage of this to check that any predicted intron falls within the known distribution. So, as the algorithm proceeds along the sequence, assembling exons and looking for intron boundaries, it also checks that the length of any putative introns fit the known distribution. An intron that looks too short, for example, might indicate an instance where Genscan has overextended an exon into the intron boundary. In these cases, Genscan can "back up" and revise the intron boundary so that the intron is more in keeping with the known distribution. Similarly, if an intron is unusually long, then Genscan may try to find an earlier splice site that would adjust the intron length and perhaps lead to the prediction of an additional exon for that gene.

The other reason to check the intron length is to determine if we are still inside a gene or if we have moved into an intergenic region. For example, a very long intron may actually be two separate genes. In this instance the "intron" is actually just intergenic sequence. Thus, Genscan avoids concatenating genes by checking that the introns between coding segments fit the known distribution for intron length. A very long intron is a good indication that Genscan should split the "gene" in two and find a promoter sequence at the start of each gene.

By combining all of these techniques, Genscan is remarkably accurate on human genomic sequences. However, it is worth noting that "remarkably accurate" is a relative term: the average accuracy of Genscan is about 80%, although it does perform better when presented with smaller sequence segments or with regions where shorter genes (i.e., fewer exons) prevail [3,13].

Nevertheless, 80% accuracy is possibly the best that any gene prediction program can achieve in the human genome. This is because there are so many alternative possibilities for gene structures within the length of the human genome that any prediction method is likely to generate some false positives and false negatives.

Genscan is valuable both as a reliable predictor of genes in genomic sequence and as an example of an algorithm that combines both statistical information and models (e.g., the HMMs for exon finding) with empirical information and experimental knowledge (e.g., the PSWMs to find promoters and intron boundaries). Genscan represents one of the best examples of how computational approaches can benefit from experimental results and vice versa during the design and implementation of an algorithm.

## 7.5  GENE FINDING BY LEARNING: LETTING A COMPUTER DO IT

At this point, we have looked at a number of individual strategies for identifying the components of a gene. We can look for ORFs, as described in Section 7.3.1, we can try to find likely coding regions by looking at codon usage statistics (see Section 7.3), and we can try to identify splice signals if needed (see Section 7.3.2). We can also try to find the promoters and terminator signals as described in Section 7.2. Each of these signals constitutes a part of a gene. But can we combine the different methods and signals to create one cohesive gene-finding system?

A number of algorithms are available for gene finding, but most of them select a subset of gene features, such as finding ORFs, or splice signals, or promoters, or some combination thereof. These methods each have their strengths, but they also have their weaknesses. In a given genome, it might be easy to find ORFs, but then difficult to decide which ORFs are functional and which are false positives. It helps in this instance to also check if codon usage is appropriate in each predicted ORF. Similarly, in another genome we might have a dependable way to find splice site boundaries so that we have a large collection of reliably predicted exons. But then we must determine which exons go with which genes. So, even though we have many methods for finding the individual components of a gene, we sometimes have difficulty figuring out which methods to use to reliably locate genes in a given genome.

We have two options in this situation. We can turn to the experimental biologists and ask them to help us identify those features of a gene that can be used to reliably identify genes in that genome. For example, a biologist might tell you that all functional ORFs in a single-celled organism are preceded by a particular signal sequence that is 5′ of the start codon. This handy piece of information can be used to validate ORFs predicted by other methods. Thus we might tailor our gene-finding program in this organism to only report ORFs that also have the

5′ signal sequence. Similarly, we can build up a repertoire of other signals and evidence to support our primary gene-finding method.

The advantage of this approach is that we use only the information we need, as suggested by experimental evidence. This ensures that we minimize false positives (predicting genes where none exist). The disadvantage of this method is that we also generate more false negatives, that is, skipping real genes because they do not match our criteria. These might be new genes that have not yet been characterized or that have some novel mechanism of regulation. So if we take this approach, we risk missing out on something new and interesting that might appear if we were less restrictive in our searching.

Given this concern, what are some alternatives? One option is to try out lots of different combinations of gene features until we hit upon one that reliably finds all the known genes and can find new genes with some reasonable confidence that the latter are likely to be functional. If we do this by hand, we could easily be at it for the rest of our lives. In this chapter, we have come up with eight key features for genes: ORFs, start and stop codons, codon usage and bias, splice signals, promoters, and terminators. In theory, therefore, we can combine these features in eight factorial (8!) ways. Again in theory, we have to test all of those combinations to figure out what works for a particular genome.

In reality, we can rule out some of the combinations. For instance, we generally know that if a gene is usually present as a continuous ORF, then we do not have to search for splice signals. Alternatively, if we know that a gene is discontinuous, we will not search for ORFs, and we place less emphasis on a start codon right at the start of the coding region. Rather, we need to determine that a start codon occurs somewhere within the overall gene structure. Even with these shortcuts, the challenge remains: Which of the various features of a gene are most indicative of a truly functional gene in a given genome?

One way to decide this is to turn over the reins to an algorithm that can try out many different combinations of features and determine which combination works best. In Chapter 6, we introduced the concept of the genetic algorithm (GA), a computational method that mimics the biological process of evolution. We can use GAs to "evolve" a solution to the gene-finding challenge. In essence, we provide the GA with all the known features of functional genes and a set of candidate genes. We then ask to weight each feature based on that feature's ability to reliably identify known genes. After many rounds of evolution, the GA returns a set of optimized weights, each of which tells us the relative importance of a given feature.

Another method that has shown some promise is a neural network in which each node represents the relative importance of a given feature. By altering the nodes and optimizing the path through the neural net, we can identify those features most important for genes in a given genome. Other machine learning methods also offer promise in this regard, and we may yet see the next generation of gene prediction algorithms moving away from the very deterministic approaches used so far toward more open-ended methods that can yield interesting and possibly unexpected solutions. As we said at the start of this chapter, algorithms for finding signals in a genome are far from perfect, and there is plenty of room for new approaches and ideas.

# 7.6  EXERCISES FOR CHAPTER 7

Calculate the Shannon entropy for each of the positions in the Table 7.3. Which positions are most likely to be part of a signal for HIV integration?

**Exercise 7.1**

Write a program that can calculate the log odds ratios for positions in an alignment. The input to your program will be a multiple-sequence alignment such as the one shown in Table 7.2. You will need to calculate the nucleotide frequencies in each position. You will also need an equivalent set of random sequence data. You can generate random sequences by determining the overall nucleotide frequencies from your input data and then randomly generating strings of the same length as your input alignment. After building the two position-specific matrices (similar to those shown in Tables 7.3 and 7.6), calculate the log odds ratio for each position. Using the data from the HIV integration example, can you determine which positions are important for the integration signal?

**Exercise 7.2**

Use the resources at the National Center for Biotechnology Information (NCBI) (http://ncbi.nlm.nih.gov) or the University of California at Santa Cruz Human Genome Browser (http://genome.ucsc.edu/) to search one of the chromosomes of the human genome for the consensus pattern we have identified for HIV integration. How many such sites exist on your selected chromosome? Can you determine whether any of these sites occur within a known gene? What might be the effect of HIV integrating in the midst of a gene?

**Exercise 7.3**

Download the HIV genome sequence from NCBI and identify all the instances of ATG and TAG. Do any of the intervening sequences match known HIV genes? How could you discover this?

**Exercise 7.4**

Pick a prokaryote and download its genome. A Web search will give you plenty of choices.

   While developing your programs, you might want to have a "minigenome" consisting of, perhaps, the first 10,000 nucleotides. You might find the following code helpful. It prints out the locations of the first

**Exercise 7.5**

(*continued*)

STOP codon in a genome whose filename is passed in on the command line:

```java
import java.io.*;
class Orf1 {
    String genome;
    String[] stops = {"TAG","TAA","TGA"};
    String[] starts = {"ATG","GTG","TTG"};

    public Orf1(String filename) throws Exception {
        BufferedReader br =
            new BufferedReader
            (new InputStreamReader
             (new FileInputStream(filename)));
        StringBuffer myString = new StringBuffer();
        String line = br.readLine();
        while (line != null) {
            myString.append(line);
            line = br.readLine();
        }
        genome = new String(myString);
    }

    public boolean isStart(int n) {
        // return true if a start-codon begins at n
        String myThree = genome.substring(n,n+3);
        int i = 0;
        while (i<3) {
            if (myThree.equals(starts[i])) break;
            else i++;
        }
        return(i<3);
    }

    public boolean isStop(int n) {
        // return true if a stop-codon begins at n
        String myThree = genome.substring(n,n+3);
        int i = 0;
        while (i<3) {
            if (myThree.equals(stops[i])) break;
            else i++;
        }
        return(i<3);
    }
```

```
    public int nextStop(int n) {
      // return location of next stop in genome at n or later
      if (n>genome.length()-2) return(-1); // no more stops
      if (isStop(n)) return(n);
      return nextStop(n+1);
    }
    public static void main(String [] args) {
      Orf1 foo = null;
      try {
        foo = new Orf1(args[0]);
      }
      catch(Exception e) {
        System.out.println("Bad file");
        System.exit(-1);
      }
    System.out.println("First stop "+foo.nextStop(0));
   }
 }
```

Assuming this code is in a file called Orf1.java, you compile with

```
    javac Orf1.java
```

And you run it via, say,

```
    java Orf1 ecoli.txt
```

or whatever organism you have the sequence for. Notice that the file Orf1.java has a few other utilities you may find useful for the rest of this exercise.

1. Write a program to locate the first stop codon after some number *n* in your sequence. For example:

   ```
   java Orf2 ecoli.txt 777777
   First stop after 777777 occurs at 777809
   ```

2. Write a program to locate the first *in-frame* stop codon after some number *n* in your sequence. For example:

   ```
   java Orf3 ecoli.txt 777777
   First stop after 777777 occurs at 777813
   ```

3. Now let's combine the two searches from Orf2 and Orf3. Write a program that accepts a genome, a location loc, and a minimum size min. It should search through the genome, starting at loc going one    *(continued)*

nucleotide at a time until it finds a stop, say at location `first`. Then it searches IN-FRAME for the next IN-FRAME stop at location, say, `second`. If the distance from first to second is at least `min`, then your program prints out its solution and halts: It has found the first stop–stop frame after `loc` that has length at least `min`. Otherwise your program continues its search at `first+1`, looking for an IN-FRAME stop that gives a stop–stop length of at least `min`.

Write a program to find the first stop–stop frame in the genome stored in `args[0]` after location `args[1]` that has length at least `args[2]` nucleotides. For example:

```
java Orf4 ecoli.txt 777777 500
First stop-stop of size at least 500 after 777777
occurs from 778262 to 778808
```

Incidentally, don't worry too much about what happens if your program *runs off the end of the genome*. Let it crash or try to terminate elegantly, it doesn't matter for the purposes of this exercise. Of course, we assume you know how to terminate elegantly.

4. Write a program that prints a list of possible start codons within the stop–stops generated by `Orf4`. For example

```
java Orf5 ecoli.txt 777777 500
First stop-stop of size at least 500 after 777777
occurs from 778262 to 778808
Possible in-frame starts occur at
    778265
    778289
    778304
    778319
    778337
    778394
    778415
    778442
    778472
    778547
    778679
```

---

**Exercise 7.6**  Given the following intronic sequences, can you construct a relevant PSWM for each of the three signals at the 5′, branch point, and 3′ sites within an intron? The sequences associated with each signal are included separated by ...

```
>ACU08131_1 641, 1065
GTGAGCCCAG...AATCCAGCTGCAAG...TAACTTTTCCCTTCTCTGGCAG
```

```
>ACU08131_2 1362, 1859
GTAAGAGACA...AATCAATTGCTGGG...CTTGTGCTCCTCTTCTCCATAG
>ACU08131_3 2028, 2636
GTGAGTGTGA...AATCAGTATAAGGG...CCTTTTTCAACTTTTTCTCTAG
>ACU08131_4 2802, 3557
GTAGGTACTA...AATCTCTTTCCTCA...TCCTTACCTTTCTCATACACAG
>ACU08131_5 3797, 4130
GTAATTTTCT...AATCCAAACACAGT...TCTTCCTTTTTCTTCTGGCAG
>AGGGLINE_6 3157, 3280
GTAGGCTCTG...AATCT...CACAG
```

---

**Exercise 7.7**

Write a program to measure the linguistic complexity of a string of nucleotides. Following [18] you can:

- For each $k$ calculate how many different sequences of nucleotides of length $k$ can exist in a string of length $m$. Write a method `maxNumWords(int m, int k)` to do this, observing that the returned value should be the smaller of $4^k$ and $k - m - 1$.
- For each $k$ calculate how many different sequences of nucleotides of length $k$ actually occur in your string $s$. Write a method `actualNumWords(String s, int k)` to do this. Your task will be facilitated by adroit use of data structures in Sun Microsystem's Java Collections.
- The linguistic complexity of a string can now be computed by forming the sum over a reasonable range of values of $k$ of the ratio of the actual to the maximum numbers of words of length $k$. Write the method `lingComplexity(String s)` to return

$$\sum_{k=1}^{10} \frac{\texttt{actualNumWords(s,k)}}{\texttt{maxNumWords(s.length(),k)}}$$

Test your program on some coding and noncoding prokaryotic genome.

---

**Exercise 7.8**

Adapt the code you wrote for Exercise 7.7 to investigate changes in linguistic complexity within a sliding window of various sizes along a genome. See if the troughs and peaks you detect correspond to any features noted in the published annotations for the genomes.

**Exercise 7.9**

Encode the string *"To be or not to be"* as a binary string using the 7-bit ASCII code of Table 7.1.

**Exercise 7.10**

Decode the binary string

```
0111010 0100000 1110100 1101000 1100001 1110100
0100000 1101001 1110011 0100000 1110100 1101000
1100101 1110001 1110101 1100101 1110011 1110100
1101001 1101111 1101110 0101110
```

using the 7-bit ASCII code of Table 7.1.

**Exercise 7.11**

In the text we noted that using ASCII, an $n$-base pair genome requires $8n$ bits to store on modern computer systems. Find out if the popular sites use ASCII encoding for genomes. Find and download some genome files. Use the Unix wc utility, or whatever tools you have available, to find the size of the file and the actual length of the genome. What do you conclude about the encoding in use at that Website?

**Exercise 7.12**

Invent another encoding for genome data. Since all you need to encode are the four symbols A C G T, you should be able to invent a 2-bit encoding scheme.

**Exercise 7.13**

If you did adopt a 2-bit encoding scheme as described in Exercise 7.12 then you would need to create an encoding program (to convert a genome *to* your 2-bit encoding scheme) and a decoding program (to recover standard genomic notation from your 2-bit code). Either of these is a trivial challenge in a programming language like Perl. Discuss the pros and cons of adopting a 2-bit binary code for storing and exchanging genomic data on the Internet.

**Exercise 7.14**

Morse code came into use in the mid-1830s to ensure rapid communication on channels that did not have the capacity for voice transmission. Instead, it employed short and long "beeps" in various combinations to relay characters. For example, transmitting a $D$ involved sending a long followed immediately by two short beeps. This was often referred to as "dash-dot-dot" or "—..". Today, we might use 1 for a dash and 0 for a dot, rendering $D$ as 100. With this notation, Table 7.9 gives the Morse code for the English alphabet.

**TABLE 7.9   Part of the Morse Code**

| A | B | C | D | E | F | G | H | I | J | K | L | M |
|---|---|---|---|---|---|---|---|---|---|---|---|---|
| 01 | 1000 | 1010 | 100 | 0 | 0010 | 110 | 0000 | 00 | 0111 | 101 | 0100 | 11 |

| N | O | P | Q | R | S | T | U | V | W | X | Y | Z |
|---|---|---|---|---|---|---|---|---|---|---|---|---|
| 10 | 111 | 0110 | 1101 | 010 | 000 | 1 | 001 | 0001 | 011 | 1001 | 1011 | 1100 |

Notice that commonly occurring letters such as *E* and *T* are given short encodings, whereas the rarer letters like *Q* and *Z* get longer encodings.

Encode the string *"All the world"* using our binary version of the Morse code. How many bits are necessary?

**Exercise 7.15**

Decode the "binary Morse code" message:

00 000 01 000 1 01 110 0

**Exercise 7.16**

Something is fraudulent about our use of the "binary" Morse code. We used another character – the pause, denoted in Exercise 7.15 by a space, and it is necessary. How else could you tell the difference between *MORSE* (11 111 010 000 0) and *TONDS* (1 111 10 100 000). In pure binary they are both 111110100000 and indistinguishable.

It is therefore misleading to say that the Morse code enables us to encode *MORSE* as a 12-bit string. In practice, something must be used to separate the individual letters. Nevertheless, Morse code gives some indication that savings can be obtained by using variable-length encodings. Some variable-length encodings have a highly desirable **prefix property.** No encoding is a prefix of any other encoding. This means that as your read an encoded message from left to right you will know exactly when one character ends and another begins. Find out what you can about variable-length codes and Huffman coding.

**Exercise 7.17**

Look at the following sequences:

11101100110100111011011010011100001010111000011010
00010101010011100100110100100100000100000110011101

and

00001100010111000110100111010101011001111100111000
11001011011000110011011110010010110110000100011011

*(continued)*

One of these strings is a short extract from an ASCII representation of Shakespeare's *Twelfth Night,* and the other is a randomly generated binary sequence that uses 0 and 1 in the same proportions as they occur in the ASCII Twelfth Night. Your task is to tell which is which. Remember:

- ASCII is a 7-bit code as given in Table 7.1.
- You are not guaranteed that either of the sequences actually begins at a boundary between two 7-bit codes.

**Exercise 7.18**    Write a program, similar to the one given in Figure 7.8 but that looks at transitions from a pair of bits to a pair of bits. Your arrays will need to be 4 by 4 instead of 2 by 2. You must also determine which entries should be for the $p_{ij}$ and $q_{ij}$ arrays. This requires analysis of files by counting how often one binary pair (say, 01) is followed by another binary pair (say, 11). Does this improve on the discrimination obtained by the program in Figure 7.8?

**Exercise 7.19**    Write a program, similar to the one given in Figure 7.8 but that looks at transitions from one character to another. Your arrays will need to be 95 by 95 instead of 2 by 2 to account for all the possible printing ASCII characters you may encounter. You need to determine the entries for the $p_{ij}$ and $q_{ij}$ arrays. This will require analysis of files, counting how often one character (say, ') is followed by another character (say, s). You will need to analyze text files to obtain these values. You can obtain many literature files from Project Gutenberg. Does the resulting discriminator improve on the discrimination obtained by the program in Figure 7.8?

**Exercise 7.20**    Write a program, similar to the one given in Figure 7.8 but that looks at transitions from one nucleotide to another. Your arrays will need to be 4 by 4 instead of 2 by 2 to account for the four nucleotides A, C, G, and T. You must figure out which entries should be included in the $p_{ij}$ and $q_{ij}$ arrays. This will require analysis of files, counting how often one nucleotide (say, C) is followed by another nucleotide (say, G). You will need to analyze genomic data files to obtain these values. In particular, you need to identify some coding sequence from which to derive the $p_{ij}$ matrix and some noncoding sequence from which to compute the $q_{ij}$ matrix. Note that our null hypothesis now corresponds to known noncoding data rather than randomly generated data. Can you devise convincing ways to test your discriminator?

# KEY TERMS

gene (7.1)
error-detecting code (7.1)
error-correcting code (7.1)
Shannon entropy (7.1)
Shannon's theory of
  information (7.1)
TATA box (7.1)
reverse complement (7.2)
log odds ratio (7.2)
consensus pattern (7.2)
position-specific weight matrix
  (PSWM) (7.2)
transcriptional control (7.2)

promoter (7.2)
transcription factor (7.2)
transcription factor-binding site
  (TFBS) (7.2)
terminator (7.3)
polyadenylation (7.3)
start codon (7.3)
stop codon (7.3)
open reading frame (ORF) (7.3)
coding region (7.3)
exon (7.3)
intron (7.3)
reading frame (7.3)

codon usage (7.3)
splicing (7.3)
spliceosome (7.3)
branch-point adenine (7.3)
intron–exon boundaries (7.3)
alternative splicing (7.3)
reverse mapping (7.3)
false negatives (7.3)
false positives (7.3)
transition probability (7.4)
prefix property (7.6)

# BIBLIOGRAPHY

1. B. Alberts, D. Bray, A. Johnson, et al. *Essential Cell Biology,* 2nd ed. Garland Publishing, New York, 2003.

2. A. Ambesi-Impiombato, M. Bansal, P. Lio, and D. di Bernardo. Computational framework for the prediction of transcription factor binding sites by multiple data integration. *BMC Neurosci,* 7:Suppl 1:S8, 2006.

3. C. Burge and S. Karlin. Prediction of complete gene structures in human genomic DNA. *J Mol Biol,* 268:78–94, 1997.

4. Richard Dawkins. The Information Challenge, *The Skeptic,* 18(4), Dec 1998.

5. A. L. Delcher, D. Harmon, S. Kasif, et al. Improved microbial gene identification with GLIMMER. *Nucl Acids Res,* 27:4636–4641, 1999.

6. R. Durbin, S. Eddy, A. Krogh, and G. Mitchison. *Biological Sequence Analysis.* Cambridge University Press, Cambridge, UK, 1998.

7. J. W. Fickett and A. G. Hatzigeorgiou. Eukaryotic promoter recognition. *Genome Res,* 7:861–878, 1997.

8. Mikhail S. Gelfland, Andrey A. Mironov, and Pavel A. Pevzner. Gene recognition via spliced sequence alignment. *Proc Natl Acad Sci USA,* 93:9061–9066, 1996.

9. R. W. Hamming. Error detecting and error correcting codes. *Bell Sys Tech J,* 29(2):147–160, April 1950. Reprinted in E. E. Swartzlander, *Computer Arithmetic,* Vol. 2, IEEE Computer Society Press Tutorial, Los Alamitos, CA, 1990.

10. A. Krogh. Two methods for improving performance of an HMM and their application for gene finding. In D. J. State, P. J. Agarwal, T. Gaasterland, et al (eds.), In *Proceedings of the Fifth International Conference on Intelligent Systems for Molecular Biology,* pages 179–186, Menlo Park, CA, 1997. AAAI Press.

11. C. E. Lawrence, S. F. Altschul, M. S. Bogouski, et al. Detecting subtle sequence signals: A Gibbs sampling strategy for multiple alignment. *Science,* 262:208–214, 1993.

12. H Li, V. Rhodius, C. Gross, and E. D. Siggia. Identification of the binding sites of regulatory proteins in bacterial genomes. *Proc Natl Acad Sci USA,* 99:11772–11777, 2002.

13. Sanja Rogic, Alan K. Mackworth, and B. F. Francis Ouellette. Evaluation of gene-finding programs on mammalian sequences. *Genome Res,* 11:817–832, 2001.

14. Thomas D. Schneider. Information theory primer with an appendix on logarithms. Web-based primer, 2007. http://www.ccrnp.ncifcrf.gov/toms/suggested-reading.html

15. C. E. Shannon and W. Weaver. *The Mathematical Theory of Information.* University Press, Urbana, IL, 1949.

16. R. Siddharthan, E. D. Siggia, and E. van Nimwegen. PhyloGibbs: A Gibbs sampling motif finder that incorporates phylogeny. *PLoS Comput Biol,* 1:e67, 2005.

17. S. Sinha, E. van Nimwegen, and E. D. Siggia. A probabilistic method to detect regulatory modules. *Bioinformatics,* 19:Suppl 1:i292–301, 2003.

18. O. G. Troyanskaya, O. Arbell, Y. Koren, et al. Sequence complexity profiles of prokaryotic genomic sequences: A fast algorithm for calculating linguistic complexity. *Bioinformatics,* 18:679–688, 2002.

19. Xiaolin Wu, Yuan Li, Bruce Crise, et al. Weak palindromic consensus sequences are a common feature found at the integration target sites of many retroviruses. *J Virol,* 79:5211–5214, 2005.

# Gene Expression

*"Life is a relationship among molecules and not a property of any molecule."*

—Linus Pauling

## 8.1 INTRODUCTION

The nucleus of a cell has much in common with a modern digital library. Both are repositories for vast amounts of information, and accessing information in the cell parallels the process of using a digital library. Imagine you have a programming assignment requiring you to incorporate some new database and Web technologies. Your university library has a database of computing textbooks that you can access online but that can't be "checked out" in the traditional sense. Rather, you are able to read them online and print out pages of interest. So, you look through several books and select and print the pages best suited to your needs. Think of the individual books as resembling DNA organized into genes (pages or sections of the book) that can be selectively transcribed (printed) to address a specific context or problem. The books themselves can't be "checked out," just like DNA does not leave the nucleus, but the information stored there can be accessed by changing it into another form (the printed page), similar to what occurs in RNA transcription. Consider further that the database is provided to the university library as a paid service, so its use must be tracked and controlled. To that end, the online service needs to know which pages are printed, how many copies of each are printed, which topics generate a lot of interest and activity, and which appear to be related in terms of interest to the user (think of Amazon's "customers who bought this book also bought ..." function). Similarly, the cell biologist wants to know which genes are expressed (transcribed) and at what levels. Discovering relationships between genes' expression patterns is important for reconstructing genetic networks and pathways, and can take the biologist closer to understanding the context or "topics" to which the expressed genes belong.

## 8.2 GENES IN CONTEXT

The concept of the gene has changed dramatically over time. Prior to the discovery of the chemical and physical structure of chromosomes, the gene was primarily a mental construct used to explain patterns of heredity in plants and animals.

The existence of some type of hereditary material was appreciated, but neither its physical basis nor any mechanisms for its activity were known. Although today we still think of the gene as a unit of heredity, aided by a good understanding of the chemical basis of gene structure, our view of the gene has changed and expanded. Scientists today recognize that understanding gene function is central to understanding how cellular processes are controlled. Moreover, the experimentalist view has changed from *a* gene to *many* genes. Very few physical states or diseases are controlled by a single gene. How then can we decipher which of the 30,000 or so genes in the human genome control each of the myriad of cellular processes, states, and diseases?

When exploring this question, first consider the idea of context. Although all cells in an organism have the same genes, not all of them are active in a given cell. Which genes are active (i.e., expressed) depends on the cellular context. Context is important in information systems also. When an author creates a new work, he or she must make many choices, including determining the language, words and sentence structure, format, and layout. The set of elements from which to choose is available to all, but the selection and use of specific elements, influenced by the context of the work, sets the style. For example, the style of Dickens is different from that of Dumas [24]. Similarly, the style of an e-commerce Website is different from that of an academic one. They share elements but the final works vary according to their intended context of use. Because context influences gene expression, we must monitor all of the conditions surrounding a gene expression experiment. We will return to this topic later in the chapter when we discuss data management.

## 8.3  GENOTYPE TO PHENOTYPE

How are gene expression and cellular context related?

To address the complexity inherent in this seemingly simple question we must revisit the central dogma of molecular biology. Along the way, we also will review many of the concepts and laboratory techniques that were covered in detail in Chapters 2 and 3. Recall that the usual flow of genomic information in the cell is from DNA to RNA to protein. RNA is the first information transfer step between gene and protein. To measure a gene's expression or activity, a scientist often collects, measures, and analyzes mRNA, which carries the information from the nucleus to the cytoplasm, where it may be translated into protein. Until now, our primary focus has been on the genome itself; that is, on the DNA component. We have explored sequencing of the genomic DNA; reassembly of the fragmented genome; and identification of open-reading frames, exons, introns, and regulatory regions to delineate genes. All these activities define the structure, or anatomy, of the genome. To date, the major effect of the Human Genome Project and of genomics in general has been that of defining the genomic structures of not only the human but also of many other organisms. Hundreds of complete genomes have been sequenced, ranging from Archaea, to Bacteria, to Eukaryota, and major inroads have been made into identifying their coding genes. Defining this underlying structure is absolutely essential to understanding how the components work together to direct the myriad complex biological processes at work in any living organism. This genome-centric view of biology is evolving towards a more functional view and ultimately to a systems view. The study of how genes regulate life processes from embryology, to control of metabolism, to cancer has often been called "physiological genetics," which now falls within the realm of functional genomics. To achieve the long-term goal of understanding normal cell physiology and disease and to enable drug discovery, it will be necessary to relate gene identity to gene function and, even more challenging, to decipher the intricate networks of interactions between genes and their products.

This takes us back to the flow of information but now with an emphasis on RNA and protein, the major players in the functional genomics story. When we say "gene expression" we are usually referring to the formation of RNA, (i.e., the transcript or mRNA), through the process of transcription. However, keep in mind that proteins are the major workhorses of the cell and the true players in functional genomics. Why then, do we study RNA expression? Are there limitations to this approach? These questions, and many others, will be addressed in this chapter as we explore the many challenges presented by the biology itself, by RNA expression data, and by the computational approaches being developed for gene expression analysis. As you read this chapter, also consider that the methods used to generate, manage, and analyze data are much better established for structural than they are for functional genomics. Computational approaches to analyzing gene expression data are undergoing continual change as talented individuals from a variety of fields focus on the problem. Consequently, there is no "one correct way." Indeed, entire courses and textbooks are devoted to in-depth discussions of the many biological, biotechnical, and computational issues of microarrays and gene expression analysis. This chapter is intended to introduce you to many of these topics, with some illustrative examples, and cannot provide full coverage of each. We encourage you to do some further reading of the references provided throughout this chapter.

## 8.4  THE EXPECTED (BY NOW) COMPLICATIONS OF BIOLOGY

Before delving into the data analysis issues we need to review some of the fundamental properties of gene expression in cells. Understanding the basics of gene expression will enable us to appreciate the nature and complexity of the currently available technologies and to approach data analysis and interpretation from an informed, biologically relevant perspective. First, consider again the central dogma in the context of the following questions: What is the relationship between an organism's DNA and its RNA? Does all DNA give rise to RNA? The answer to the latter, of course, is no. Not all DNA is transcribed to RNA (even when considering all types of RNA). In prokaryotes most of the DNA codes for proteins (through mRNA), but in eukaryotes, such as humans, only a small percentage of total DNA codes for proteins.

Do all cells in an organism have the same mRNA? This is the critical question for functional studies! As we already discussed, although all cells of an organism carry the same genes (i.e., the **genotype**), not all genes are active. The cellular context determines which genes are active. The subset of active genes (expressed) varies with context: from cell type to cell type; between normal and diseased states of the cell; between different developmental stages of a given cell; and in response to environmental stimuli such as exposure to chemicals, pathogens, heat, and ultraviolet light, among others. The expression of a subset of genes and their complex and orchestrated interactions and networks confer specific properties on the cell, thereby establishing its **phenotype.** Gene expression is dynamic and, as a result, the cellular phenotype is rather fluid. We say that genes are "differentially expressed," meaning that two samples may differ in which genes are expressed or in how much any given gene is expressed (or in both). Figure 8.1 illustrates some examples: muscle cells differ from epithelial cells in the outer layer of the skin. A muscle cell expresses a high level of the mRNA transcribed from genes that code for the muscle fiber proteins, actin and myosin, whereas a skin cell makes a lot

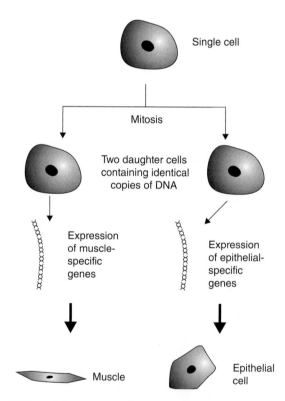

**FIGURE 8.1**    Differential gene expression is responsible for the phenotype of different cells. All cells within an organism have the same DNA, but not all genes are expressed in every cell. A skin epithelial cell expresses only genes specific to skin, whereas a muscle cell expresses genes necessary for its development.

of keratins, which are fibrous proteins that make the cell tough and able to resist the wear and tear of exposure to the external environment. In genetic diseases that result from defects in crucial muscle genes, breakdown occurs in the muscle tissue but not the skin. Conversely, in some genetic skin diseases, inheritance of defective keratin genes results in skin that blisters extremely easily, but muscle (where these genes are not expressed) is unaffected. Cells are highly influenced, at the level of gene expression, by their external environments. When we expose our skin to excessive UV light from the sun, our skin cells respond by changing expression of genes whose products enable recovery from the DNA damage and inflammation associated with sunburn. When cells of the immune system are infected by HIV, gene expression in the infected cell changes dramatically—a change that continues over time. These examples show that to understand a phenotype we must identify the genes constituting the expression subset. We may also want to determine when a gene is expressed in the context of an event that is expected to cause a change in gene expression.

Remember that, from a functional point of view, we ultimately want to know which proteins are present in a given cell or under a given condition. So, is it fair to measure RNA expression as a true representation of "gene expression"? Usually, yes, but biology is full of exceptions. For example, the correspondence, in time or space, between RNA and protein is not strictly one-to-one.

This complication must be recognized and considered during the design and interpretation of studies of RNA expression. As usual, the story is far simpler for prokaryotes than eukaryotes. As described in Chapter 2, bacterial genes are organized into operons. The expression of these functionally related genes is regulated primarily by a simple "on/off" mechanism of transcriptional control. Because prokaryotes have no discrete nucleus, transcription and translation are usually coupled, meaning that the protein is made from the RNA template even while the RNA template is still being transcribed on the DNA. That is, as soon as one end of the new strand of RNA emerges from the transcriptional machine on the bacterial chromosome, the translational machines of the ribosomes get to work making protein. In most cases the delay between synthesis of RNA and protein is short. This supports the notion that by measuring RNA expression in prokaryotes we generate a fairly complete picture of gene expression.

Let us turn now to the more complicated situation in eukaryotes, in which regulation of related genes located at disparate sites in the genome is coordinated, as opposed to the operon organization seen in prokaryotes. Eukaryotes require more intricate mechanisms than the operon. Gene expression is not only controlled by an on/off switch but also a "volume control," or rheostat-like, mechanism so that more refined patterns of **differential gene expression** are possible. Additionally, transcription is spatially separated from translation in eukaryotes due to the presence of the nucleus. Much evidence suggests that the concentration of mRNA within a eukaryotic cell is poorly correlated with the actual abundance of that protein [1]. Why? In the eukaryotic cell mRNAs must be processed and transported out of the nucleus in order to be available to the ribosome. As a result, at least six different levels of regulation determine the functional activity of a gene: transcription, RNA processing, mRNA transport from the nucleus to the cytoplasm, mRNA degradation, mRNA translation, and post-translational modifications of protein. In spite of this complexity, the good news is that the structural relationship between mRNA and protein is closer than that between gene and protein (due to splicing), and experimentally we can select and study cytoplasmic mRNAs, which are a pretty good indicator of active genes. Inaccuracies in data interpretation can still arise because some mRNAs present in a given sample may be prevented from being translated. As a result, an experiment could show high copy numbers of the transcript but these transcripts might result in only a small amount of protein. Another concern in interpretation of data is post-translational chemical modifications, which occur in both prokaryotes and eukaryotes. These can affect the folding of the protein, its stability, and the protein's location in the cell—all of which are important to protein function. So, we ask, if a particular mRNA occurs in a sample, is its protein necessarily present and functional? Moreover, when we carry out multigene analyses, can we make inferences about which genes may function together? Although these questions have no straightforward, simple answers, keep in mind that the RNA measured from any single sample represents only a snapshot of that cell's or tissue's dynamic transcriptional profile. Even with all of the caveats, studying the RNA component of cells is a highly informative approach to understanding the cellular phenotype. All involved in such study, whether designing experiments in the lab or analyzing the data, should keep in mind the complexities of gene regulation and be wary of overinterpreting their results.

## 8.5  A FLOOD OF DATA

Current gene expression analysis is exemplified by the use of high-throughput techniques such as the DNA microarray or serial analysis of gene expression (SAGE) that have effectively moved transcript analysis from one or a few genes at a time to whole-genome global approaches. (For the details on these gene expression analysis platforms and technologies, refer to Chapter 3.) The ability to capture information about the activity of most or even all of the genome has ushered in the era of functional genomics on the heels of structural genomics. Phil Hieter and Mark Boguski aptly described functional genomics as:

> "The development and application of global (genome-wide or system-wide) experimental approaches to assess gene function by making use of the information and reagents provided by structural genomics . . . . It is characterized by high throughput or large-scale experimental methodologies combined with statistical and computational analysis of the results. The fundamental strategy is to expand the scope of biological investigation from studying single genes or proteins to studying all genes or proteins at once in a systematic fashion" [15].

With the sequencing of the human genome it rapidly became apparent that new technologies were needed for large-scale analyses rather than the typical one-gene approach. Everything fell into place—gene sequence information became available to enable measurement of protein-coding genes (whether the gene identity was known or still a mystery), hybridization and cloning techniques were refined, and advanced molecular chemistry was developed that allowed scientists to label gene sequences for experimental detection. Through the imagination of scientists such as Patrick Brown, the cDNA spotted microarray first became available, and the oligonucleotide array was soon to follow. (See Chapter 3 for a detailed description of the methods and technologies.) These technologies enabled scientists to carry out the simultaneous measurement of the expression levels of thousands of genes. The new terms **transcriptional profiling** and **transcriptome** became part of the scientist's lexicon for describing the process and output of this high-throughput approach. Think of the transcriptome as the complete set of transcripts present within a cell. A profile is generated experimentally that can be considered characteristic of a given cell or cell state. In practice, it is hoped that gene expression profiling will define signature patterns that will support future molecular characterization of disease.

Today many array-based technologies are used, and not only for analysis of RNA expression. Gene expression analysis, one of the first and best developed, has received the most attention, and the major use of microarrays today remains the investigation of genetic mechanisms, such as comparative transcriptional profiling between tumors and normal cells. These applications have already shown great promise. Other uses of arrays include high-throughput genotyping with single-nucleotide polymorphisms (SNPs) [9, 25], protein expression [20], DNA sequencing [10], and even DNA computing [11].

In general, high-throughput approaches produce vast amounts of data never before encountered by the biologist. Unfortunately, just because one can generate the data does not mean that one can effectively analyze or interpret those data. Consider that, in a typical study, thousands to tens of thousands of individual genes may be assayed simultaneously, in several different samples, and often in replicate, producing on the order of millions of data points. New and better computational approaches are needed for image processing and analysis, data preprocessing, data analysis, data mining and interpretation, data storage, retrieval, and integration. Currently, each of these areas has borrowed tried and true techniques from mathematics, statistics, and computing, but all have required considerable modification to meet the unusual needs imposed by biological systems. Interestingly, gene expression analysis is clearly a two-way street. Not only are computing approaches being modified to meet gene expression analysis needs but also, as these analytical approaches evolve, the feedback affects how biologists conduct their experiments.

The development of computational approaches to the analysis of gene expression data is a dynamic, exciting area ripe for the intellectual input of interdisciplinary teams.

A case in which the computing specialist may be called in at the pre-analysis stage is for custom design of a microarray. Although a wide selection of commercial arrays is available, it is not unusual for an experiment to focus on a particular set of genes for which an array does not exist. Perhaps prior research has generated an interest in genes belonging to a particular molecular pathway or to a cellular process. It then makes sense, from both a technical and data analysis standpoint, to focus the analysis on a specific set of genes rather than adopt a genome-wide approach.

Selection and design of probes for a custom array can be fairly complicated. Desired attributes of the array are that it has sufficient specificity and sensitivity and its quality should guarantee that the results are reproducible. Consideration must be given to the types of the probes. Should they be full-length cDNAs, expressed sequence tags (ESTs), or oligonucleotides? If the last, then what length? Here, we focus on the design of oligonucleotide probes and discover how a "pipeline" of analysis techniques can be used to generate a solution. It is not uncommon in bioinformatics that a series of computing programs can be stitched together and used in sequence to generate a desired result. In fact, just such an integrated pipeline is available in the Microarray Oligonucleotide Design and Integrative Tool (MODIT), available from the University of North Carolina, Charlotte (http://gaia.uncc.edu/modit/index.html).

The terms **sensitivity** and **selectivity** were introduced in earlier discussions of sequence alignment in Chapter 5. In the context of oligonucleotide probes, a sensitive probe is one that generates a strong signal for its complementary target sequence when it is present in the sample. Factors that negatively affect sensitivity are secondary structure in the probe or target sequence or binding to other identical probes on the array. Specificity means that the probe sequence generates at most a weak signal when the target is absent from the sample. This means that it does not hybridize to other targets. Cross-hybridization is primarily a consequence of base-pairing, and nonspecific hybridization can be caused by the presence of G-quarters, which are hydrogen-bonded G-tetraplexes, in the sequences [19, 30]. Another desired attribute of probes selected for the custom array is that they be isothermal so that all probes behave similarly under the changing conditions of the hybridization. Such changes include changes in temperature and the concentrations of salt and other agents in the hybridization solution. Choosing probes that have similar melting temperatures (the temperature at which 50% of a double-stranded DNA species becomes single-stranded) is a usual strategy [30].

What follows is a series of analysis steps that may be taken in oligonucleotide design as proposed by Stekel [30] (see also [19, 32]). First, choose genes to be used as probes for the array. This, of course, depends on the purpose of the experiment but likely involves exploration of resources such as GenBank (for sequence and annotation data), UniGene (which has clusters of mRNAs and ESTs for genes in GenBank), and the Gene Ontology (which can provide information regarding cellular component, biological process, and molecular function). It is advantageous to select well-annotated genes, where possible. Next, for each gene, select a sequence within a few hundred nucleotides of the 3′end of the target sequence (because labeled target molecules are usually prepared with a 3′ primer giving them a 3′ bias). Eliminate low-complexity regions in the sequence (using a program such as RepeatMasker), and then select oligonucleotides from nonrepetitive regions. We are interested in short oligonucleotides (e.g., 25 nucleotides long), so many oligonucleotide sequences are possible. Now check these for homology, and discard any that are strong candidates for cross-hybridization. To do this effectively, you may need to refresh your understanding of BLAST and the various bioinformatics databases. Determining the melting temperature $T_m$ of remaining candidate probes is a more complicated process. The $T_m$ depends on both the length of the oligonucleotide and the nucleotide makeup. DNA–DNA duplexes will have different properties from DNA–RNA duplexes (the type that occur in Affymetrix arrays). The theory and methodology for determining melting temperature is detailed in [30], if you wish to learn more about it, and several of the commercial oligonucleotide design pipelines have implemented an algorithm to calculate $T_m$. The final step in determining probe secondary structure relies on some of the same thermodynamic measures as the melting temperature. In this case we are concerned with a probe forming structures such as a hairpin due to complementarity within the sequence itself. The most commonly used program for measuring this property is MFold, a Web-based application that predicts secondary structure in RNA or DNA [38]. With any luck, after rejecting those probes with significant secondary structure, enough candidates will remain so that a few probes can be selected for each gene on the custom array.

## 8.6  NOISY DATA

Before setting off down any road to data analysis, consider the quality of your data. First note that DNA microarray data are typically very "noisy." We need to separate genuine experimental variation (i.e., differential gene expression) from noise—a process akin to tuning into a radio station with a lot of static. The signal to noise ratio can be increased using a variety of established techniques. In the biological sense, noise is systematic variability resulting from the experimental techniques themselves rather than the biological system under study. Variability in DNA microarray data comes from many sources. Suppose we're trying to compare the expression pattern of immune cells infected with HIV to those not infected, so as to characterize the cellular response to infection. First, consider the source—the living, biological system. Cells are living objects with great built-in environmental sensors. We would like the only differences in the genes expressed to be due to the viral infection. This means we must control everything else that might affect the living state of the cell, such as how crowded the cells are in the culture dish, how many nutrients are available, and how warm they are. Unfortunately, it is difficult, if not impossible, to precisely control all the elements of the cells' environment, so variation between our samples is likely. Consider another common scenario, in which the transcriptional profiles of tumors from many different people are compared. Tumors are inherently heterogeneous. Many tumors are composed of more than one cell type, and each tumor in a study usually comes from a different patient. So, again, the potential for variability in gene expression data is great right from the start.

Next, we must extract RNA and label the expressed sequences from each of the cell conditions or samples, in other words we must prepare the microarray target. RNA is extremely sensitive to degradation, and its extraction involves several complicated steps and painstaking laboratory technique. It's possible that in one sample the test tube was not properly sterilized and RNase enzymes might have chewed up some of the RNA. Or perhaps the chemicals were not entirely mixed. The possibilities for error are numerous, and any one could affect the quality of RNA in one or more of the samples—yet another source of variability. Recall from Chapter 3 that analysis using a spotted two-color microarray requires that each RNA in the sample be copied to cDNA and given a fluorescent label. This process creates more room for error and hence more possibility for experimental variability. For example, in a two-color cDNA array, the experimental and control samples are labeled with different fluorescent dyes. If one labeling reaction works better than the other, a situation known as dye bias occurs that can lead to misinterpretation of the data.

The microarray itself provides yet another major source of variation. In either a spotted cDNA or synthesized oligonucleotide array, inconsistencies in placement or quality of the probe DNA across the array can occur. If some probes are applied less efficiently or if some regions of the array are faulty, the data will be unreliable. A microarray experiment includes a total of more than a hundred experimental steps. Fortunately, major advancements in the laboratory techniques and production of commercial microarrays make them more reliable. In fact, one study involving eight universities showed that with 2005 technologies, the variance in lab procedures is far greater than in the arrays themselves [16]. The Microarray Array Quality Consortium (MAQC) recently showed a high degree of intra- and interplatform consistency in microarrays [18]. These studies help relieve some of the doubts about microarray reliability and the research that uses them. The task now is for scientists to establish and maintain good experimental technique. The bad news is that laboratory and data analysis methods are continually changing for microarrays, and experiments are still relatively expensive. According to one study [31] the cost to analyze one gene is down to pennies when using a microarray. This still adds up when considering that an array typically has tens of thousands of genes. A typical microarray experiment (one array per experiment) cost in the range of $1000 to $2000 in 2006.

## 8.6.1 Turning down the Noise

Noise in the data is common enough in computer science as well as in statistics. Much unwanted variability in statistics can be limited through good experimental design—an axiom that also applies for the DNA microarray. For example, we can apply the principle of randomization in our design. Several copies of a given probe sequence may be placed randomly at different locations on the array to control for inconsistencies across the array. Replication is another desirable feature of experimental practice. Replication simply means the ability to repeat an experiment. In addition to confirming observations, replication can help diminish the corrupting contributions of uncontrollable factors. Another purpose of the replicate is to estimate the experimental error. The extent of replication, in terms of how many of the individual steps are repeated, should be considered when creating the experimental design. Unfortunately, because the microarray experiment requires so many experimental steps, it is financiallly and logistically impractical to undertake the entire process more than once. True replication (repeating every step individually) of a microarray experiment is therefore infeasible. One array does not make a study since each is just a snapshot of the genes expressed in that particular sample. More often, the scientist is comparing a series of transcriptional profiles over time or among multiple samples (e.g., comparing tumors from several patients). Even with very limited replication, a study can likely involve 10 to 20 individual microarray experiments. Rather than strive for true replication, only certain elements of the design are typically repeated. For example, to control for position on the array, the probe may be repeated elsewhere. To replicate the RNA extraction process, each sample can be divided and extracted more than once. To control for a potential difference in dye-labeling efficiencies, it is common to divide the samples and conduct a separate labeling reaction with each fluorescent dye. Even when the extraction steps and labeling are replicated, it may not be possible to replicate the hybridization on the array. Often, the amount of starting sample is sufficient for only a single array, as in the case of small tumor specimens.

Ultimately, data analysis requires that we be discriminating when doing comparisons between and among DNA microarray experiments. Determine precisely how the experiment was conducted. Decide how you can conclude whether differences observed are real and meaningful or a reflection of "noise" in the system. We will return to these issues later when we discuss statistical methods designed to remove unwanted variation from the data.

## 8.7  THE MANY MODES OF GENE EXPRESSION DATA

What do gene expression data look like?

Return to the example in which we compare the transcriptional profile of HIV-infected cells with noninfected ones. The initial output from the experiment is image data generated in the following way (This example is developed for the two-color array. It would differ in some aspects for the oligonucleotide array.):

- The experimental and control (reference) RNA samples are separately prepared as targets by labeling with spectrally distinct dyes. For example, the infected, experimental sample may be labeled with Cy5 (red), and the noninfected control sample labeled with Cy3 (green). Note the choice of fluorescent label for the experimental and reference samples is arbitrary.
- The labeled targets are then queried simultaneously by washing them over the spotted probe sequences that are immobilized on the solid support of the microarray. This allows them to hybridize.
- After hybridization is complete fluorescence intensities are measured for each spot on the array with a confocal laser scanner, which can excite and detect each dye individually.

- The intensities in the red and green channels are measured and stored in a computer file for each spot, which is identified on the basis of its position on the array.
- These data may be used to create an image using synthetic colors that enable the scientist to visualize the results.

Computers are good at dealing with the predictable, but human scientists may see something unexpected in the visualization. There is always the chance that they will observe a key feature that explains important principles. Good computer programs that effectively present visualizations of data to skilled scientists are of immense value. Typically, such visualizations show a composite of red- and green-labeled spots, representing the relative levels of the mRNA from each target sample and thus each gene's activity in both the experimental and control samples. For example, if the gene is more active in the infected cells, the probe spot will fluoresce more strongly in the red channel, whereas if the gene is more highly expressed in the control cells, fluorescence is stronger in the green range. Although these dyes are measured individually with a laser, the final output of synthetic color for each spot may be red, green, or a mixture (yellow) as the fluorescence in each channel is overlaid.

It's difficult to extract meaning from a very large, complex pattern like that of the DNA microarray image in Figure 8.2. Nevertheless, examining the raw image is valuable for quality control purposes. It's relatively easy to determine if the experiment was successful by evaluating the color intensities and searching for any anomalies such as smearing or drying. Images of the raw data, like that in Figure 8.2, are typically stored in a database (if the database design can accommodate images) and made available to anyone using the data. Computer programs have been developed to assist the scientist in identifying spot locations and in evaluating the quality and usefulness of the data.

Image analysis software performs three fundamental functions: gridding, segmentation, and information extraction. **Gridding** locates each spot on the slide.

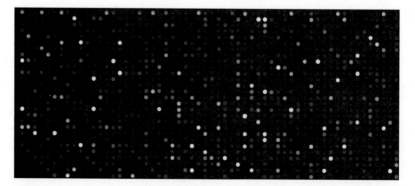

**FIGURE 8.2**    Courtesy of the Center for Array Technologies at the University of Washington. This picture shows part of the composite image obtained by scanning a microarray to detect fluorescence from Cy3- and Cy5-labelled cDNAs. The experiment was a study of T-cell gene expression following infection with HIV-1.

This process is also referred to as "spot finding" in some of the available software packages. **Segmentation** differentiates the pixels within a spot-containing region into foreground (true signal) and background. **Information extraction** includes two parts: spot intensity extraction and background intensity extraction. **Spot intensity extraction** refers to the calculation of fluorescence signal from the foreground determined from the segmentation process. **Background intensity extraction** employs different algorithms to estimate the background signal due to the nonspecific hybridization on the glass. Many algorithms have been developed to achieve these ends. The method selected can affect the final intensity measurement, which subsequently influences downstream data analysis methods. Therefore, it is important to choose the image analysis process best suited to the experiments and to use methods consistently when comparing results across experiments [37].

A wide assortment of software packages is available for microarray image processing and analysis—some free and open source, others commercial and proprietary. For example, ScanAnalyze is free software that can be downloaded from Stanford University. It provides an interactive graphical environment for semiautomated gridding and information extraction (including fluorescence intensities, background intensities, fluorescence ratios, and several quality control measures). SpotFinder has similar functionality and is offered free and open source from The Institute of Genomic Research (TIGR). Spot, which is commercially available, supports automatic grid location; flexible spot segmentation, and morphological background estimation.

The output of each program differs, but some typical values of interest to the scientist are shown in Figure 8.3.

Recall that to find instances of differential gene expression, we must:

- run the microarray experiments
- scan the arrays
- extract data from the images.

This provides us with measurements of fluorescence intensities (channel 1, CH1 red, and channel 2, CH2 green), background intensities, and fluorescence

| ID-Ref | VALUE | PRE_VALUE | CH1_MEDIAN | CH1_BKD_MED | CH2_MEDIAN | CH2_BKD_MED |
|---|---|---|---|---|---|---|
| 159769_1 | −0.392 | 0.762 | 3195 | 600 | 2502 | 861 |
| 160345_1 | −0.121 | 0.919 | 3544 | 565 | 3077 | 804 |
| 160921_1 | −0.941 | 0.521 | 3036 | 567 | 1899 | 832 |
| 161497_1 | −0.571 | 0.673 | 3020 | 552 | 2194 | 815 |
| 162073_1 | 0.658 | 1.578 | 3135 | 520 | 4237 | 813 |

**FIGURE 8.3**   Partial data from one microarray in a time course series of gene expression analyses of HIV-infected and uninfected lymphocytes using the two-color cDNA spotted array. The ID-Ref identifies the probe (gene) and the replicate number. For each probe, intensity and background values are given for both the red and green channels. The Value column shows the usual number of interest as the $log_2$-transformed ratio of experimental (channel 2, CH2) to reference (channel 1, CH1). Data retrieved from the Gene Expression Omnibus (GEO, Accession GSE 1441).

ratios. In the two-color system, where both experimental and reference samples are hybridized simultaneously, the value of primary interest is the ratio of experimental: control or red (Cy5) channel to green (Cy3) channel. This ratio represents the expression of any given gene in the experimental situation relative to that in the control situation and can be an indicator of differential gene expression. For example, if a gene is activated in response to HIV expression, we expect to see a higher measurement of fluorescence intensity in the experimental sample (because more of the mRNA was available in that sample to hybridize to the array) than in the control, thus producing a ratio greater than 1. If the gene's activity is suppressed, the ratio would be less than 1. Remember that these ratios represent relative rather than absolute measurements of gene expression. Thus, we can say that a gene's expression is increased twofold *relative* to the reference sample, but we cannot say, for example, that 1000 copies of the mRNA are expressed for that gene based on microarray data.

# 8.8 A WORKED EXAMPLE: GENE EXPRESSION IN HIV-INFECTED CELLS

## 8.8.1 Data Preprocessing

### Cleaning up the Noisy Data

At this point we have produced potentially noisy data that were generated by the use of several microarrays (different experiments) and even possibly by several different laboratories. The experimental variability (which exists even despite heroic efforts to prevent it) does not stop the biologist from looking for interesting patterns in the data. After all, the goals of microarray analysis are to discover genes whose expression changes with different conditions or to find gene signatures that are characteristic of given samples. These goals require that data be analyzed across many array experiments. Remember that the fundamental quest is to identify differences in gene expression that are due to biological forces rather than to experimental variability. Ideally, in order to make comparisons, the data should be independent of the particular experiment and the particular technology used. Most computational methods for analyzing gene expression data rely heavily on statistical approaches. What can be done to reduce the uncertainty in the data and to make the data more manageable? Prior to mining the data for patterns of gene expression several data preprocessing steps are typically carried out, including gene filtering, scaling, normalization, and transformation. These steps have a significant influence on the process of data analysis. Many different methods are available, and these are continuously evolving. In many cases the methods available are platform-dependent. Along with reliability of the array itself, variation in data preprocessing has been somewhat of a stumbling block for the adoption of microarray data in clinical and regulatory settings.

## Gene Filtering

Most microarray software packages include functionality for **gene filtering,** a process for removing some genes from the final analysis. What types of genes should be filtered out? Some "control" genes may be from a different species than the one being studied and so are not useful outside of the particular microarray. For example, a known amount of *E. coli* cDNA may be spiked into the target mixture before it is applied to the microarray for hybridization. The extent of hybridization (determined by measuring the intensity of that spot) serves as an important control for the experimental process, but its value is otherwise irrelevant to the biological question at hand. Through the filtering function the spot can be identified and removed from the data before analysis. Outliers and replicates can also be identified and removed, if desired. Another type of filtering is possible through software designed to be used with the Affymetrix oligonucleotide arrays. The proprietary software makes a "call" for each probeset on the area, based on the intensity values of the **perfect match (PM)** and **mismatch (MM)** sequences for each probeset. (See Chapter 3 for some technical details of the Affymetrix array design.) The calls of "present," "marginal," and "absent" are indicators of relative amounts of RNAs in the target. When choosing data for analysis, the end user may filter to select only those that meet a certain criterion. For example, when comparing HIV-infected versus noninfected cells, one may choose only to look at genes that are labeled as "present" in the infected and "absent" in the noninfected sample. This strategy may enable the discovery of genes that are activated on viral infection.

## Transformation of the Data

Another means of interpreting the data is via $log_2$ **transformation.** This method makes sense for two reasons. One is historical and related to the ease of some types of calculations with logarithmic data. The other is easier to understand from a biological perspective. If we consider a gene that is up-regulated twofold (often the minimum considered significant by many biologists), then its ratio (experimental to reference) is 2. If the same gene is down-regulated twofold, then its ratio is 0.5. In fact, the values of all down-regulated genes are compressed between 0 and 1. And the values for up-regulated genes vary from 1 to infinity. Figure 8.4 is a histogram showing the gene expression ratios for HIV-infected versus uninfected cells. These values have not been transformed.

By taking the log transformation, we obtain values for down-regulation that range from 0 to negative infinity, and for up-regulation values that range from 0 to positive infinity (Figure 8.5). Genes whose expression levels don't change are associated with a value of 0. We also restore a sensible correspondence between the values: Fourfold up-regulation has a log value of $+2$, and fourfold down-regulation results in a log value of $-2$. In general, down-regulation by a factor of $n$ results in a log value that is the negative of the log value of up-regulation by the same factor. It just makes more sense from the biological perspective, because

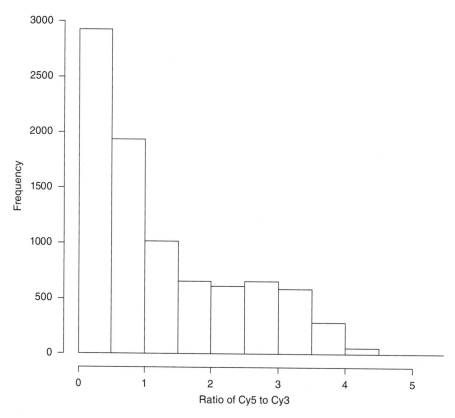

**FIGURE 8.4**   Histogram of gene expression ratios of experimental (HIV-infected lymphocytes; Cy5) and reference (noninfected lymphocytes; Cy3). Note that the distribution of ratios is compressed in the 0 to 1 range. Based on partial data from study available from Gene Expression Omnibus (GE0, Accession GSE 1441).

of the relative nature of measurements from DNA microarrays, to take logarithms. Why do we use base 2? The base really doesn't matter. Mathematicians like natural logs; in the days when logs were used to facilitate computation, base 10 logs were favored; computer scientists like base 2 for many reasons, not least of which is the binary nature of raw computer data. Taking logs in base 2 has the property that doubling expression corresponds to $log_2(2)$, or a value of $+1$, and halving of expression gives rise to $-1$ because $log_2(0.5) = -1$. For graphing purposes log transformation makes the data more symmetrical and more normal.

### Normalization Within and Across Arrays

**Scaling** may be done to control for dynamic range across experiments. For example, intensities may differ from array to array simply due to the settings of the scanner. Scaling is a type of per array normalization that may correct for these

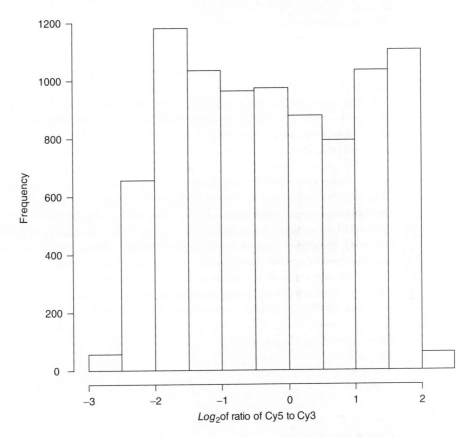

**FIGURE 8.5**  *Log₂* transformation of the gene expression ratios shown in Figure 8.4. It is more apparent that the distribution is normal and centered around zero. Note, that this is not a perfect normal distribution, but perfection is rare in real data.
Based on data available from Gene Expression Omnibus (GEO, Accession GSE 1441).

differences across arrays. Scaling helps eliminate minor variations in fluorescent dye labeling or hybridization. It is analogous to turning the brightness up or down on the monitor. It may, however, obscure more significant differences that could indicate a failed experiment. Scaling up the intensity on a very dim array may cover up the fact that the labeling reaction was bad and cause the user to spend time analyzing bad data. One way to scale is to subtract the mean log ratio of all data on the array from each log ratio on the array, thus ensuring that the means of all the distributions (each array) are equal and equal to 0 [30].

Other types of normalization are done within arrays to enable comparisons. Quackenbush [26] describes three major techniques for data normalization within a single microarray experiment (i.e., within an array). All of these assume that some subset of genes within the array will have an expression ratio equal to 1. That is, we expect certain genes to be expressed at some steady-state level so that equal amounts occur in both the experimental and control sample. For example, these may be cDNAs that have been spiked into each sample, or they may be "housekeeping" genes (more on this later). The normalization factor corrects for any experimental variability by adjusting to this ratio across the array.

The first method, total intensity normalization, is based on the rationale that across a given sample, some genes will be induced and some suppressed, but most genes will remain unchanged and so the average log ratio will be 0. This is reasonable because biological comparisons made on microarrays are often quite specific and do not affect all genes. If we assume that a symmetry exists between the up- and down-regulated genes, then differences should average out. The total amount of red dye integrated into one sample should be about the same as the total amount of green dye in the other, and so the intensities are adjusted. (This is also based on the underlying assumption that the quality of RNA in each sample is the same.) We can check the the validity of this assumption by swapping the dyes and repeating the experiment. Consider, for example, Figures 8.6–8.10, which show a series of scatterplots illustrating the effects of dye swap and total intensity normalization on gene expression data from experimental (HIV-infected lymphocytes) and reference (noninfected lymphocytes).

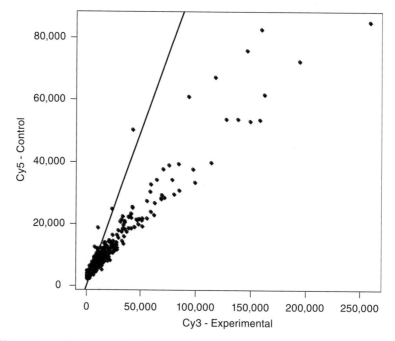

**FIGURE 8.6**    Plot of the data with Cy5 as the control and Cy3 as the experimental. Figure 8.7 shows the dye swap with Cy5 as the experimental. Based data from GEO (Assession GSE 1441).

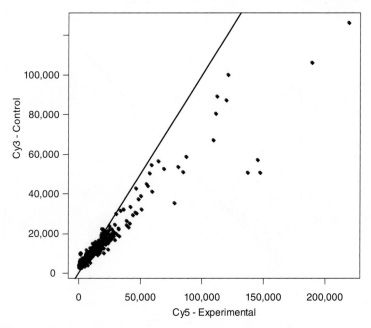

**FIGURE 8.7**   Plot of the same data as in Figure 8.6 with Cy3 as control. Both plots with multiple points below the reference line $(x = y)$ show that many genes in the HIV-infected cells are down-regulated.
Based on data from GEO (Accession GSE 1441).

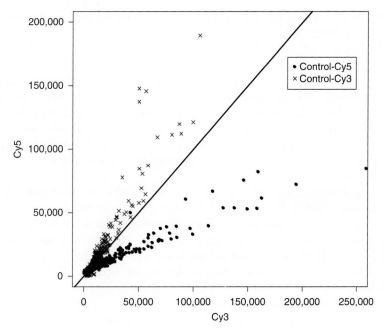

**FIGURE 8.8**   Plot of both dye-swap datasets on the same scatterplot.
Based on data from GEO (Accession GSE 1441).

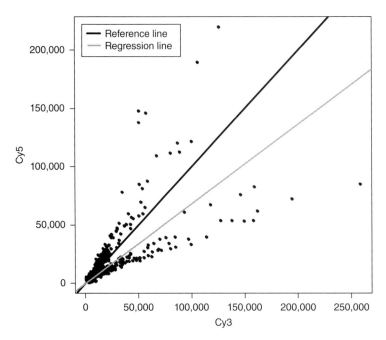

**FIGURE 8.9** A regression line is plotted and can be used to adjust gene expression values in datasets based on differences in labeling efficiencies between the dyes. Based on data from GEO (Accession GSE (1441).

When we combine the results of the dye-swap experiments, we can see where biases exist (Figure 8.8).

The second method is normalization by regression techniques. Here again, the rationale is that when comparing two closely related samples (e.g., experimental vs. control), some genes are induced and some suppressed, but most are unchanged. A scatterplot of red versus green intensities shows that most points fall along a line with a slope of 1. Regression techniques are used to calculate the best fit and to adjust the distribution to a line with slope of 1. More often, a localized regression approach is used to smooth the data (Figure 8.9). The data can then be scaled using the slope of the regression line, as shown in Figure 8.10.

A third method uses statistical analysis of the ratio of the so-called housekeeping genes, which, by definition, are involved in basic cellular functions and are assumed to be always turned on at relatively constant levels. The ratio of housekeeping genes in experimental and control samples is assumed to be 1 (or $log_2$ ratio of 0) and is used to normalize ratios of other genes across the array. This topic deserves some further explanation because the value in using housekeeping genes has been somewhat controversial. One of the problems with all normalization techniques, including this one, is that they are based on several assumptions that may not hold up. For example, some genes that have long been identified as housekeeping genes (i.e., are constitutively expressed;

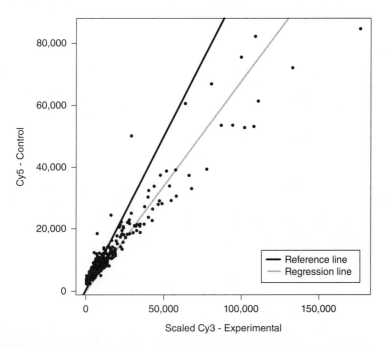

**FIGURE 8.10**   Effect of scaling gene expression data. Cy3 values were adjusted according to the slope of the regression line (slope = 0.680968). Based on data from GEO (Accession GSE (1441).

not differentially expressed even under varied conditions), were in fact, later found to be differentially expressed under some conditions and thus not suitable for use in normalization. One example is the beta-actin gene. This gene has been one of the most widely used internal controls for RNA experiments based on the assumption (now known to be faulty) that its expression levels remain constant under all conditions [27]. The bottom line is that faulty biological assumptions can corrupt the data even when the intention is to do the opposite!

Another classical method of data normalization, $Z$ score transformation, is often used for microarray data analysis. This also provides a way of standardizing data across a wide range of experiments and allows the comparison of microarray data independent of the original hybridization intensities. The $Z$ score transformation approach for microarrays corrects data internally within a single hybridization. The transformation is achieved by subtracting the mean and dividing by the standard deviation. Correction is done before sample-to-sample comparison and is therefore comparison-independent. Comparisons across samples or across experiments are then performed on equivalently transformed data, and changes in gene expression are expressed as differences between $Z$ ratios. Figure 8.11 shows how data from Figure 8.4 would be transformed with this approach. This approach is implemented in many available software packages

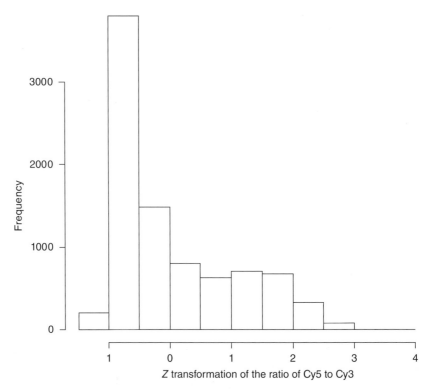

**FIGURE 8.11**   *Z* score transformation of the same data as in Figure 8.4. In this case, *Z* score transformation has not been as effective as $log_2$ transformation. Based on data from GEO (Accession GSE 1441).

such as the open-source Java-based MicroarrayExplorer (MAExplorer) and the TM4 application.

## 8.9  PROGRAMS TO WORK WITH GENES AND EXPRESSION VECTORS

Programs to analyze genes and gene expression data first require an object that corresponds to a gene and its expression levels over a set of experiments. Use a `String` for the name and an array of `doubles` for the expression levels. Figure 8.12 defines a `Gene` class.

Exercise 8.3 asks you to write a program to test the `Gene` class. In most cases you will be working with real data, but it is useful to generate some random data for the purposes of program development. As already discussed, much work is needed to preprocess the data. A normalizing step is needed to eliminate some of the experimental biases inherent in the process. After normalizing the data, logs must be taken. A random-number generator approach can be employed to create data with the required characteristics. Figure 8.13 is code to generate *N* genes

```
class Gene {
    private String name;
    private double[] expressionLevels;
    public Gene(String n, double[] es) {
        name = n;
        expressionLevels = new double[es.length];
        for (int i=0; i < es.length; i++) expressionLevels[i] = es[i];
    }
    public String toString() {
        String retVal = "Gene "+name+" has expression levels ";
        for (int i=0; i < expressionLevels.length; i++) {
          retVal += expressionLevels[i]+" ";
        }
        return retVal;
    }
    public double[] getExpressionLevels() {
        return expressionLevels;
    }
    public String getName() {
        return name;
    }
}
```

**FIGURE 8.12**   An implementation of a gene object and its expression levels.

```
double[] expressionLevels = new double[M];
for (int i=0; i < N; i++) {
    expressionLevels[0] = 0.0;
    expressionLevels[1] = 6.0*Math.random()-3.0;
    for (int j=2; j < M; j++) {
        // Create data :
        // 0, randomly -3->3, then successive values incremental
        // mimicking log transformed microarray data
        expressionLevels[j] = expressionLevels[j-1]+Math.random()-0.5;
    }
    genes[i] = new Gene("+i, expressionLevels);
}
```

**FIGURE 8.13**   Code to create random gene expression data.

with $M$ expression values each. This might correspond to $M$ microarray experiments involving expression measurements for $N$ genes. To make the data look like normalized, log-transformed data, the first expression level value should be 0.0. The next expression level for each gene is a uniformly distributed random value between $-3.0$ and 3.0. After that, each next expression value is obtained from the current expression value by adding a uniformly distributed random number

```
public String round2(double x) {
    double rax = Math.abs(x) + 0.005;
    String srax;
    if (x < 0.0) srax = "-"+rax;
    else srax = " "+rax;
    int i = 0;
    while (srax.charAt(i) != '.') i++;
    return(srax.substring(0,i+3));
}
public double distance(double[] x, double[] y) {
    double d = 0.0;
    for (int i=0; i < x.length; i++) {
        d += (x[i]-y[i]) * (x[i]-y[i]);
    }
    return d;   // True euclidean distance would take a square root here
}
public void printData () {
    for (int i=0; i < N; i++) {
        System.out.print(genes[i].getName()+": ");
        for (int j=0; j < M; j++) {
            System.out.print(round2(genes[i].expressionLevels[j])+ " ");
        }
        System.out.println();
    }
}
```

**FIGURE 8.14**   Implementation of some utilities for random gene expression data.

between −0.5 and 0.5. Figure 8.13 shows the code. This could be placed within the constructor for an ExpressionExperiment class. But you can make your own choices.

Figure 8.14 shows some handy utilities that will allow you to round the data to two decimal places, to calculate Euclidean distances, and to print out the data.

The utilities from Figure 8.14 will be necessary in Exercises 8.4, 8.6, and 8.7.

## 8.10  MINING THE GENE EXPRESSION DATA

### What Does It All Mean?

To draw inferences about the biological principles underlying development, disease, and other phenotypic changes it is necessary to analyze large-scale spatial and temporal gene expression patterns. The DNA microarray platforms and other high-throughput technologies such as SAGE [35] can certainly provide huge volumes of data but leave the biologist with the daunting task of trying to extract relevant information and interpret it. Many different approaches have been developed, ranging from analysis of individual genes to examination of the entire set.

## 8.10.1  A Worked Example: Looking for Differentially Expressed Genes

### Some Simple Approaches

Typically, in a gene expression experiment the scientist is interested in finding differences between two or more conditions (e.g., HIV-infected vs. uninfected; young mice vs. middle-aged mice vs. old mice, or across a time course of treatments). A series of samples is often chosen because the researcher is interested in the process, not just the endpoint of differential gene expression. The search for differentially expressed genes by a simplefold change approach may initially be chosen. That is, one may decide (somewhat arbitrarily) that a threshold of twofold change, either up or down, is of interest. In the simplest case, such genes may be identified on a scatterplot of $log_2$-transformed data plotted as experimental versus control values or on histograms of these ratios. These are good first approaches because they support easy visualization of the data. In the scatterplot, the genes that are up-regulated or down-regulated are easily identified by looking for points that fall above or below the diagonal, respectively (see Figure 8.10). The scatterplot is implemented in an R package, Standardization and NOrmalization of MicroArray Data (SNOMAD), which is available on the Web at www.snomad.org.

This approach is not without its limitations, however. First, the scatterplot allows comparison of a given gene only among two or three experiments. When plotted in two dimensions, those two are usually experimental versus control values, where the $y$-coordinate is the Cy5 intensity and the $x$-coordinate is the Cy3 intensity. We could add another experimental condition if we plot in three dimensions, but what do we do in the case that we have 10 or 20 conditions or samples? This interesting problem arises because of the high dimensionality of the data. With so many conditions or samples, which do we choose to look at? In Chapter 9 we will consider one solution to this problem. A group at the University of Maryland, College Park, implemented an interactive discovery tool for high-dimensional data like the microarray, in the Hierarchical Clustering Explorer [28]. Also, from the biological perspective, looking at simplefold changes is not always meaningful, considering the wide spectrum of expression levels in a given cell or condition. A twofold increase in a gene that is normally expressed at a low level may have quite different biological significance than a twofold increase in a highly expressed gene. Finally, from a statistical perspective the fold increase approach is unsound. It does not take into account the variability in expression levels of each gene between individual subjects in the experiment, and it doesn't account for sample size. If we are interested in generalizing from our results then we need to be more careful about how we draw inferences. Statisticians use methods known as hypothesis testing that test observed data against a null hypothesis using probabilistic models.

## 8.10.2 Testing Biological Hypotheses with Statistical Hypotheses

### *Applying Prior Biological Knowledge*

In samples that seem to belong to two different groups or conditions (e.g., control cells vs. infected cells, or different times of treatment, or different tumors), we may ask which genes change with the condition. We may have paired data, for example, an immune cell before and after infection with HIV-1, or unpaired data, such as different patients with one of two types of tumor. Often, based on biological knowledge, we already have particular genes of interest in mind and we want to focus on possible changes in those genes. Or perhaps, we would like to analyze each gene in the set individually. Here, we can apply some classical statistical approaches to data analysis. In this case, we employ a statistical technique called **hypothesis testing.** We decide on a null and an alternative hypothesis. The null hypothesis is a statement of no difference. The alternative hypothesis is a statement which we wish to prove true. It is sometimes referred to as the researcher's hypothesis. In the case of gene expression, the hypothesis could be:

$H_0$: Gene expression level is unchanged

$H_A$: Gene expression level is changed

We make our decision about whether to reject the null hypothesis based on a test statistic. Note here that we never actually accept the null hypothesis, we just conclude that there is not enough evidence to reject it.

Since a decision is made based on sample data, there is always a chance for a wrong choice. Hypothesis testing comes with two types of errors. Type I, denoted by A, is the probability that the null hypothesis is rejected although it is true. It is considered the significance level of the test. A type II error is the probability that the null hypothesis is *not* rejected although it is, in fact, false. Usually after data are collected, a test statistic is determined and a $p$-value is calculated. A ***p*-value** is the lowest value at which we would reject the null hypothesis. The majority of statistics packages will calculate $p$-values for hypothesis tests. The decision is made typically by comparing the $p$-value with the $\alpha$ risk. If the $p$-value is less that or equal to $\alpha$, then we reject the null hypothesis. Otherwise, we fail to reject the null hypothesis.

If the two groups we are testing come from independent normal distributions, then we can base our decision on a $t$-test, which is the test statistic in this case. Assume that $\bar{x}_i$, $s_i^2$, and $n_i$ are the means, variances, and sample sizes for the two groups, assuming that the two-sample $t$-test becomes

$$t_{stat} = \frac{(\bar{x}_1 - \bar{x}_2)}{\sqrt{\frac{s_1^2}{n_1} + \frac{s_2^2}{n_2}}} \tag{8.1}$$

Traditionally, statisticians have used the $t$-test to tell if the averages of two groups in a study are statistically different. For example, in Figure 8.15, a $t$-test is done to determine if a difference exists over two time points in HIV-infected cells

$$H_0 : \mu_{24hr} = \mu_{0hr}$$
$$H_A : \mu_{24hr} \neq \mu_{0hr}$$

| | $n_i$ | $\bar{x}_i$ | $s_i$ |
|---|---|---|---|
| 0 hr | 5 | 0.191 | 0.852 |
| 24 hr | 4 | −0.246 | 0.601 |

$$t_{stat} = \frac{(0.191 + 0.246)}{\sqrt{\frac{0.852^2}{5} + \frac{0.601^2}{4}}} = 0.90$$

$$p = 2[P(t_6 > |0.90|)] = 0.403$$

**FIGURE 8.15**   This example is based on a time-course study of HIV-infected lymphocytes treated with a drug to activate the virus compared with noninfected lymphocytes. Cells were treated with the drug and sampled at different times after treatment. Shown is a $t$-test for the difference between 0 hr and 24 hr for GeneID: 411811. Assume that $\alpha = 0.05$. Since the $p$-value is larger than 0.05, we fail to reject the null hypothesis.
Deta retrieved from Gene Expression Omninus (GEO, Accession GSE 1441).

that have been treated with a drug. The $t$-test is the instrument of choice in such circumstances. It takes into account, not only the averages (means) of the two groups, but also a measurement called the standard error of the differences of the means. As usual, the derivation and explanations for the statistical formulae are quite involved, but once you see the formulae writing programs to perform the analysis is relatively straightforward.

Paired $t$-tests are implemented in many software packages, both for general statistics and those developed for bioinformatics. In addition to MIDAS and R packages mentioned earlier, packages include SAS, Excel, and GeneSpring, to name a few. Recall that we assume that the two datasets come from independent populations that follow normal distributions. If these assumptions are invalid, then other methods for testing hypotheses should be employed. Bootstrap and permutation tests are examples of computer-intensive techniques that can be used. Also, some nonparametric techniques, such as the Mann–Whitney test and many of the nonparametric statistics, are also supported in available software packages.

The importance of applying careful statistical analyses, rather than just fold-change calculations, is apparent in a review of microarray data on gene modulation by HIV-1. This review of more than 6 years of studies considered only those studies that were validated using statistical significance based on $p$-values and an estimate of the false discovery rate, along with a few other considerations [12].

Often, we want to extend the analysis to more than two groups. For example, we have run experiments over a range of times following infection and have replicates at each time point. In this case, the analysis of variance (ANOVA) test, which is an extension of the $t$-test, or variations of the ANOVA [23] can be applied. This is a technique by which the equality of the means is assessed through comparing variances. The between-group variation is compared with

$$H_0 : \mu_{0hr} = \mu_{0.5hr} = \mu_{3hr} = \cdots = \mu_{72hr}$$
$$H_A : \mu_i \neq \mu_j \text{ for at least one } (i, j) \text{ pair}$$

| Source | DF | SS | MS | $F$ | $p$ |
|--------|----|----|----|-----|-----|
| Hours | 10 | 85.43 | 8.54 | 1.33 | 0.273 |
| Error | 24 | 154.66 | 6.44 | | |
| Total | 34 | 240.09 | | | |

**FIGURE 8.16**   The following example is based on a time-course study of HIV-infected lymphocytes treated with a drug to activate the virus compared with noninfected lymphocytes. Cells were treated with the drug and sampled at different times after treatment. Shown is an ANOVA analysis for difference in all of the means (all time points) for GeneID: 411881. Since the $p$-value, 0.273, is greater than 0.05, the null hypothesis is not rejected.
Data retrieved from Gene Expression Omnibus (GEO, Accession GSE 1441).

the within-group variation. Any statistical package can calculate these summary statistics and create an ANOVA table from which one can extract the $p$-value and make a decision on the null hypothesis. (Figure 8.16). Again, it's possible to scan through the derivations of the statistical formulae and then write programs to perform the required analysis. Many good sources are available on the Internet to help you select appropriate statistical tools in addition to the ones that we have already mentioned. Google or any other search engine is, as always, your friend in finding these. In addition we mention www.socialresearchmethods.net as an effective source for many useful formulae and their explanations.

Study of fold change and use of the simple statistical approaches seem appropriate when you already have a good idea of which genes are of greatest interest and you can form some hypotheses about a few genes. However, it can be argued that such gene-by-gene approaches fail to take advantage of the strength of microarray data—the ability to examine more global, system-wide changes. We want to be able to explore the data more fully. What we need are some methods to discover new patterns in the very large datasets typical of microarray studies.

## 8.11  A WORKED EXAMPLE: FORMING NEW HYPOTHESES

### 8.11.1  Organizing the Data

Regardless of the number of genes that enter the final analysis, the first step is usually to organize the data from multiple gene expression experiments into a **gene expression matrix** (Figure 8.17). We have already discussed some of the steps leading to creation of the matrix:

- Raw data, consisting of the microarray image produced after confocal scanning of the multiple arrays in a study is quantified through image processing.

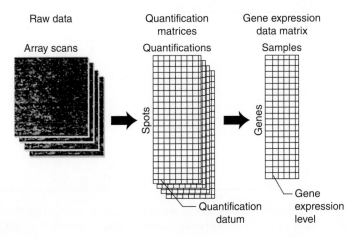

Raw data   Quantification matrices   Gene expression data matrix

Array scans   Quantifications   Samples

Spots   Genes

Quantification datum   Gene expression level

**FIGURE 8.17**   Steps involved in the construction of a gene expression data matrix. From Quakenbush [26].

- A quantification matrix is generated for each array experiment that relates fluorescence intensity measurements to individual spots on the array. Typically, each spot has multiple measurements, the exact nature of which depends on the particular array platform and software used.
- Quantification matrices are combined into a single gene expression matrix for visualizing expression values across array experiments (individual samples) and for preparing the data as proper input to many analysis programs. Generally, genes (ranging in the thousands) constitute the individual rows of the gene expression data matrix, and samples (on the order of 10's) make up the columns. To build the gene expression data matrix, data from several quantification matrices (representing a single experiment) are combined. A single value is selected for each "spot" (probe or gene), and that value is entered into a cell in the gene expression data matrix for the appropriate gene. For example, the value chosen is often the background-corrected ratio of experimental to reference data.
- Data preprocessing steps (filtering, scaling, $log_2$ transformation, normalization) may be performed along the way.

The gene expression data matrix then represents the combined data from a set of individual, related, microarray experiments. A row of the gene expression matrix is created for each gene, and a column for each microarray experiment (Figure 8.18).

Now we can do some operations on the combined data. By grouping rows that go up and down together like synchronized swimmers we can identify genes with similar transcriptional patterns that are perhaps also functionally related. For example, finding genes that go up or down (or both) together across a set of samples taken at different times, after a viral infection perhaps, indicates that they may participate in the same biological process such as cell division or cell death. They may belong to the same gene network or pathway. Grouping columns that are similar can provide information about samples that behave similarly. These

| | | no PMA | no PMA | 0.5 hr | 0.5 hr | 3 hr | 3 hr | 6 hr |
|---|---|---|---|---|---|---|---|---|
| ID_REF | UNIGENE | GSM24324 | GSM24325 | GSM24331 | GSM24333 | GSM24334 | GSM24336 | GSM24341 |
| 159762_1 | 411881 | 1.67 | −0.523 | 1.255 | −0.878 | −0.595 | −3.149 | −1.5 |
| 159763_1 | 25155 | 0.502 | 0.119 | 0.958 | 0.081 | −0.255 | 0.625 | 0.105 |
| 159764_1 | 386741 | −0.424 | 0.048 | 0.458 | 0.521 | 0.078 | 0.228 | 0.029 |
| 159765_1 | | 0.467 | −0.3 | −1.554 | −1.115 | −0.933 | −1.264 | −1.423 |
| 159766_1 | 446393 | −0.186 | −0.006 | 3.048 | 0.163 | 0.327 | 3.262 | −0.236 |
| 159767_1 | 338207 | −0.082 | −0.715 | 1.067 | 0.44 | 0.034 | 0.965 | 0.086 |
| 159768_1 | 435789 | −0.568 | −0.434 | 0.384 | 0.732 | 0.158 | 0.307 | 0.337 |
| 159769_1 | 256278 | **−0.392** | −0.667 | −1.285 | −0.31 | 0.076 | 0.001 | −0.403 |
| 159770_1 | 440896 | 1.345 | −0.233 | −0.497 | 0.322 | −0.582 | 9.149 | 0.983 |
| 159771_1 | | 0.233 | −0.456 | 0.582 | 0.319 | −0.335 | 0.216 | −0.074 |

**FIGURE 8.18** A gene expression matrix constructed from several individual microarray experiments of chronically HIV-infected lymphocytes treated with phorbol myristate acetate (PMA) to activate the virus and control compared with uninfected lymphocytes.*

*Shown are two replicate arrays (no PMA) representing the untreated condition, two replicate arrays of samples treated for 0.5 hr with PMA, two for 3 hr and one array for a sample treated for 6 hr. ID_REF, which identifies the probe, and UNIGENE ID are given, where known. For each probe, a value representing the $log_2$-transformed intensity ratio of HIV-infected versus uninfected is given for each array. For example, the value −0.392 (in bold) was taken from the array shown in Figure 8.3. Data retrieved from the Gene Expression Omnibus (GEO), GSE 1441.

might correspond to similarly endowed individuals or to conditions that have similar effects on many genes. For example, two patients' tumors may be of the same type, indicated by similar expression levels of many genes. Similarly, an HIV-infected cell culture treated with a drug may return to pretreatment gene expression levels several hours after treatment. Simply looking across the rows of the gene expression matrix to identify functionally related genes or down the columns to find similar samples may be possible. More likely, however, the matrix will be too large to analyze the data and reach conclusions efficiently by eye. Statistical approaches and computational power are required.

## 8.11.2 Clustering

Cluster analysis is one of the most popular approaches to looking for relationships in gene expression data. **Clustering** is the process of grouping together similar things—in our case, similar genes or similar samples. Those genes that end up in a cluster will be more similar to one another than to genes in another cluster. This multivariate technique has the characteristic that no a priori biological knowledge about the data is required. That is, it is an uninformed approach. Patterns and relationships may be discovered on the basis of the data alone (i.e., only the expression measurements). This may be an advantage or disadvantage, depending on the point of view. From one perspective, it means that developing effective clustering algorithms does not necessarily require a complete understanding of the biological problem. In fact, excluding biological information about the particular genes or samples may even limit or eliminate bias imposed by faulty or incomplete knowledge. Nevertheless, a plethora of valuable data and knowledge stemming from decades of research has been accumulated for many of genes on the microarray. Can it be incorporated in to the process? The short answer here, is yes. In the machine-learning realm, techniques known as supervised learning can take various parameters as input to the process. We will return to this topic later.

To group similar entities together requires some measurement of "similarity." Remember that in a microarray study we typically carry out multiple micro-array experiments and, thus, generate multiple measurements for each gene in the matrix. Each gene can be thought of as a point in $n$-dimensional space, with $n$, for example being the number of microarray experiments. From the perspective of samples or experiments, $n$ represents the number of genes measured for each experiment. Consider then the measurements across a given gene as a vector pointing somewhere in $n$-dimensional space (Figure 8.19).

Of the many similarity measurements employed in gene expression studies, we consider the **Pearson correlation** here.

Its popularity may stem from the fact that correlation between two entities is fairly easy to understand and also because this method can detect inverse relationships. That is, we can easily see when one gene generally goes up when the other gene goes down or vice versa across each experiment in the microarray dataset. The formula for the Pearson correlation can be expressed in many ways including:

$$r = \frac{1}{n-1} \sum_{i=1}^{n} \left( \frac{x_i - \overline{x}}{s_x} \right) \left( \frac{y_i - \overline{y}}{s_y} \right)$$

where:  $n$   is the number of conditions
  $\overline{x}$   is the average expression of gene $x$ in all $n$ conditions
  $\overline{y}$   is the average expression of gene $y$ in all $n$ conditions
  $s_x$   is the standard deviation of the $x_i$
  $s_y$   is the standard deviation of the $y_i$

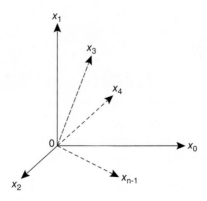

**FIGURE 8.19**   $n$-dimensional space.

A positive correlation between gene $x$ and gene $y$ means that they change in the same way across experiments. In which cases do we find positive correlation values? Suppose that an $x$ value is above the average, as is the associated $y$ value. Then the product $(x_i - \bar{x})(y_i - \bar{y})$ is the product of two positive numbers, which is therefore positive. If the $x$ value and the $y$ value are both below average, their product would be of two negative numbers and would therefore also be positive.

Therefore, a positive correlation is evidence of a general tendency that relatively large positive values of $x$ are associated with relatively large values of $y$ and large negative values of $x$ are associated with large negative values of $y$.

Conversely, consider the case where an $x$ value is above average, and the associated $y$ value is below average. Then the product $(x_i - \bar{x})(y_i - \bar{y})$ is the product of a positive and a negative number, which makes it negative. Similarly, if the $x$ value is below average and the $y$ value is above average, their product is also negative.

It follows that a negative correlation is evidence of a general tendency that relatively large values of $x$ are associated with relatively small values of $y$ and relatively small values of $x$ are associated with relatively large values of $y$. An analysis of data from the HIV-infected cells data using Pearson correlation is shown in Figure 8.20.

|  |  | Gene ID |  |  |  |  |  |  |
|---|---|---|---|---|---|---|---|---|
|  |  | 411881 | 25155 | 386741 | 435789 | 256278 | 440896 | 287721 |
| Gene ID | 411881 | 1.000 | 0.191 | 0.247 | 0.130 | −0.251 | 0.036 | −0.009 |
|  | 25155 | 0.191 | 1.000 | 0.237 | 0.243 | 0.374 | 0.408 | 0.080 |
|  | 386741 | 0.247 | 0.237 | 1.000 | 0.798 | 0.080 | 0.140 | −0.276 |
|  | 435789 | 0.130 | 0.243 | **0.798** | 1.000 | 0.185 | 0.084 | −0.212 |
|  | 256278 | −0.251 | 0.374 | 0.080 | 0.185 | 1.000 | 0.320 | 0.327 |
|  | 440896 | 0.036 | 0.408 | 0.140 | 0.084 | 0.320 | 1.000 | 0.049 |
|  | 287721 | **−0.009** | 0.080 | **−0.276** | −0.212 | 0.327 | 0.049 | 1.000 |

Pairwise correlation between genes 435789 and 386741 across treatment time course:

$$r = \frac{1}{(n-1)} \sum_{i=1}^{n} \left(\frac{x_i - \bar{x}}{s_x}\right)\left(\frac{y_i - \bar{y}}{s_y}\right)$$

$\bar{x} = 0.1795 \quad s_x = 0.354$

$\bar{y} = 0.2498 \quad s_y = 0.4097$

$$r = \frac{1}{(35-1)} \left[ \left(\frac{(-0.424-0.1795)}{0.354} \frac{(-0.568-0.2498)}{0.4097}\right) + \cdots + \left(\frac{(0.505-0.1795)}{0.354} \frac{(0.425-0.2498)}{0.4097}\right) \right]$$

$= 0.798$

**FIGURE 8.20** Pearson correlation table for seven genes from the time-course dataset (35 samples) of HIV-infected and noninfected lymphocytes.*

*Pairwise correlations are shown in the table. Genes 435789 and 386741 show strong correlation (positive value relatively close to 1) in expression over the time course sampled. Genes 287721 and 411881 show almost no correlation as the value is close to 0. Genes 287721 and 386741 show low correlation but in the opposite direction (small, negative value). Sample calculation is shown for Genes 435789 and 386741 below the table.

Another popular distance measure is the **Euclidean distance,** which is based on the Pythagorean theorem. The distance between two points can be expressed by the hypotenuse of a right triangle according to the formula: $a^2 + b^2 = c^2$.

For gene $X = (x_1, x_2, \ldots x_n)$ and gene $Y = (y_1, y_2, \ldots y_n)$

$$d(X, Y) = \sqrt{(x_1 - y_1)^2 + (x_2 - y_2)^2 + \cdots + (x_n - y_n)^2}$$

The Euclidean distance measures the absolute distance between two points in space, which in this case are defined by two expression vectors. Each of these similarity measures comes with its own set of advantages and disadvantages, and which is chosen affect downstream analyses. The Euclidean distance, for example takes into account both the direction and magnitude of the vectors, whereas the Pearson correlation accounts for shape but not magnitude of a series of gene expression measurements. Two genes may be close in Euclidean distance but dissimilar in terms of their correlation, especially if they are outliers within the gene expression measurements. Figures 8.21 and 8.22 show two different clustering results using Euclidean distance.

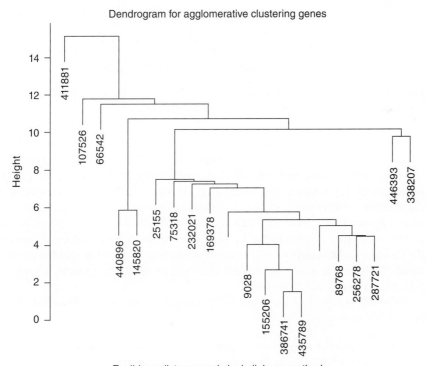

Dendrogram for agglomerative clustering genes

Euclidean distance and single linkage method

**FIGURE 8.21** Hierarchical clustering of gene expression data from a time-course study of activation of HIV in lymphocytes. Here, we show the result of clustering using the Euclidean distance metric and a clustering method known as single linkage. Data retrieved from GEO (GSE 1441)

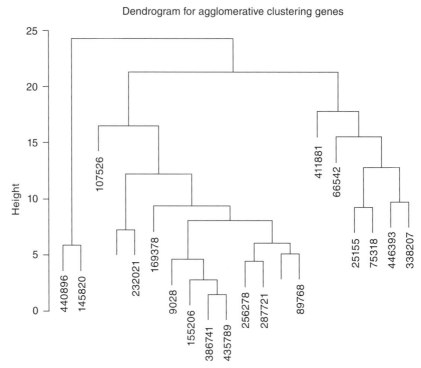

**FIGURE 8.22**    Hierarchical clustering of the same data as Figure 8.21 but with complete linkage clustering instead of single linkage clustering.

Clustering usually begins with the matrix of the pairwise similarity/distance measurements among the genes or samples analyzed. There are many different clustering algorithms, and, like similarity measures, each comes with its own assumptions, capabilities, and limitations. As a result, the same dataset can be clustered in various ways, and even the same distance metric can yield different results as seen in Figures 8.21 and 8.22. Add in the choices of similarity/distance metric, clustering algorithm, and a host of other possible initial conditions on the input, and the variety of results can be daunting. Remember that the primary value of cluster analysis is to look for trends in the data and to form hypotheses rather than to provide "answers."

The following quote from the NCBI Gene Expression Omnibus (GEO) site appears there in red!

"Cluster analyses help provide insight into the relationships between data. It is recommended that care is taken with biological interpretation using cluster results; classifications are based on basic clustering algorithms over a variety of dataset types, making no prior assumptions on original data distribution and range. Alternative algorithms, normalization procedures and distance metrics will generate different cluster outputs." [22]

## Hierarchical Clustering

Hierarchical clustering has been used since the inception of microarrays and also has found its way into sequence analysis and phylogenetic trees. Starting from the correlation or distance/similarity matrix, the algorithm recursively assembles all of the elements (genes) into a tree. This may be by a bottom-up (agglomerative) or top-down approach (divisive). In the bottom-up approach the process starts by assigning a leaf of the tree to each gene. Then, the two most similar genes (from the matrix) are joined. The two vectors representing the two genes are then averaged to create a new vector for the node. Next, a new matrix is computed, with the newly created vector replacing the two joined elements, and the process is repeated until a single node remains. There are multiple ways to compute the distances between clusters, as well. Some examples are single linkage, which is the distance between the two closest neighbors in the clusters (shown with Euclidean distance in Figure 8.21), and complete linkage, which is the average distance between all pairs of vectors, one from each cluster (see Figure 8.22). The latter method obviously requires more computation. The output of the process is a tree, rather than a set of clusters. This tree represents the hierarchy of categories, based on similarities and is known as a dendrogram.

An upper bound for the complexity of the bottom-up clustering approach can vary between $O(N^2)$ and $O(N^3)$, depending on which linkage method is chosen. Consider that for $N$ starting points (e.g., genes) the process is repeated at most $N - 1$ times until a single node remains.

The divisive approach works by splitting large clusters into smaller ones and requires that another clustering approach first be used to partition the dataset into two major clusters. These tend to be faster than agglomerative techniques but are sensitive to the partitioning algorithm chosen to initiate the process. Figures 8.23 and 8.24 show the results of divisive clustering using Euclidean and Pearson distances, respectively.

## k-Means Clustering

One of the most widely used algorithms is the $k$-means clustering algorithm. It is both simple and fast. In a typical implementation, the number of clusters, $k$, is given as a user input value, based on the expected number of clusters. The algorithm begins by randomly assigning $k$ points as the centers of the clusters. Then, each gene in the set is assigned to a cluster based on its distance from the cluster center. New centers are then computed and genes are then reassigned to clusters. This continues until no genes continue to move among clusters (Figure 8.25). One pitfall is that random selection of centers may provide values not close to any of the data and result in empty clusters. To prevent this, randomly selected data are commonly used to initiate the cluster centers. Obviously, this algorithm is sensitive to the value chosen for $k$ as well as the method used to select the initial cluster centers. It is not uncommon, therefore, to find that different clusters can be achieved each time the program is run. Techniques have been devised to assess the quality of such clusters [8].

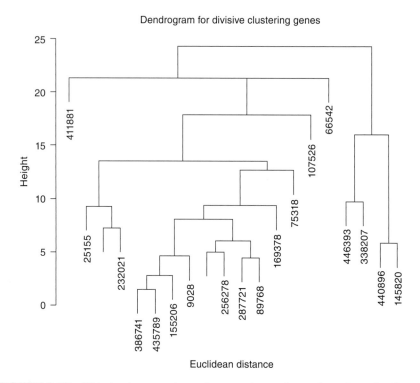

**FIGURE 8.23** This dendrogram shows the same data as in previous clustering figures, but with a method that subdivides groups into smaller clusters. Note differences in the relationships between genes, depending on which methods are used. This clustering used Euclidean distances.

### A Program for k-Means Clustering

Implementing a `Cluster` class is made easier by naming each cluster, so that we can observe the progress of our clustering algorithms. Since our clusters will be generated ad hoc, a good strategy is to use an `int` as the name. Each cluster will thus have an identifier (`int name`). The cluster must also record the dimension of the space in which it resides, because we'll need to calculate the centroid[1] of the cluster for some algorithms. For others, we need to figure the distance between two points in the cluster. In either case, the code to calculate that quantity—centroid or distance—requires the dimension of the space.

Figure 8.26 gives a possible implementation for the `Cluster` class:

Exercise 8.4 asks you to create a program to test the `Cluster` class.

For k-means clustering, you'll need an array of `Clusters`: `Cluster[] clusters;` and you'll need to specify your integer k for the number of clusters.

---

[1] The centroid of a set of points is the point whose coordinates are the arithmetic mean of the coordinates of all the points. In physics, if equal weights were placed at each of the points, the centroid would be their center of mass.

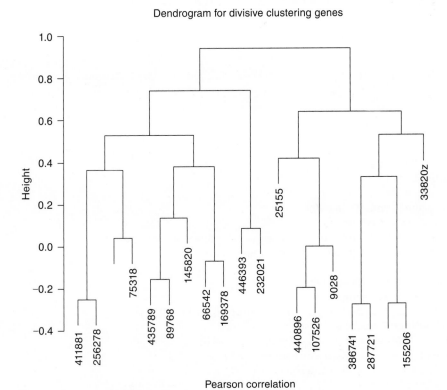

**FIGURE 8.24**   The dendrogram shows the same divisive approach as in Figure 8.23 but with Pearson correlation.

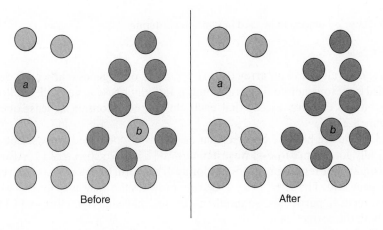

**FIGURE 8.25**   One pass of the *k*-means algorithm. On noting that point *a* is closer to the median of the black points than it is to the median of the gray, we move it to the black cluster. Similarly the gray *b* switches its allegiance to the blacks.

```
class Cluster extends Vector{   // Note to self: import java.util.* !!!
    public int name;
    public int dimension;
    double[] centroid;

    public Cluster(int n, int d) {   // Cluster called n, in d-dimensional space
        super();
        name = n;
        dimension = d;
        centroid = new double[d];
    }
    public void add(Gene gene) {
        addElement(gene);
    }
    public void remove(Gene gene) {
        if (!removeElement(gene))
            System.out.println("Oops - removing nonexistent gene");
            // Print a warning in case of bad usage
    }
    public void calculateCentroid() {
        Enumeration e = elements();
        for (int i=0; i < dimension; i++) centroid[i] = 0.0;
        while (e.hasMoreElements()) {
            Gene g = (Gene) e.nextElement();
            double[] c = g.getExpressionLevels();
            for (int i=0; i < dimension; i++) {
                centroid[i] += c[i];
            }
        }
        for (int i=0; i < dimension; i++) centroid[i] /= size();
    }
}
```

**FIGURE 8.26**   Program for Cluster objects to be used in $k$-means clustering.

You should also have an array Gene[] genes of $N$ genes (earlier, we demonstrated how to generate these randomly). Initially, these genes will be allocated to arbitrary clusters, except that each cluster must contain at least one gene (Figure 8.27).

Do you see how we ensured that each cluster contained at least one gene? Basically, for $i$ from 0 to $k-1$ we just put gene[i] into cluster[i]. After that, we assigned the remaining genes randomly. It's helpful to determine which cluster each gene is in. The int[] myCluster provides the answer as long as we keep updating it. In particular, we should make sure that each myCluster[i] starts out with the correct value.

Exercise 8.6 asks you to write a program to test the methods you have so far included in your public class ExpressionExperiment (or whatever you want to call your class).

```
public void makeClusters(int k) {
    numClusters = k;
    clusters = new Cluster[numClusters];
    // ensure each cluster has at least one datapoint:
    for (int i=0; i < numClusters; i++) {
        clusters[i] = new Cluster(i,M);
        clusters[i].add(genes[i]);
        myCluster[i] = i;
    }
    // Now assign the rest of the genes to clusters at random:
    for (int i=numClusters; i < N; i++) {
        int c = (int)(Math.random()*numClusters);
        clusters[c].add(genes[i]);
        myCluster[i] = c;
    }
}
```

**FIGURE 8.27**   Program to create initial cluster for $k$-means clustering.

The main workhorse of $k$-means analysis is the code that looks at each gene, figures out which of the clusters it's closest to, and then if needed, moves the gene to that cluster. We need to do that for each gene. We put the code in a Boolean method `reconsider()`.

Figure 8.28 is code to indicate how `reconsider()` works:

Why Boolean? Because, in order to determine when we're done, we need to know if any genes changed cluster during this particular pass. A Boolean method to scan all the genes can return `true` if somebody moved, `false` otherwise.

Now, after all this is done, the essence of $k$-means clustering is:

```
public void kMeans () {
    makeClusters(k);
    boolean somethingChanged = true;
    while (somethingChanged) {
        printClusters();
        somethingChanged = reconsider();
    }
}
```

Finally, Let's put the $k$-means analysis into a class `ExpressionExperiment` (Exercise 8.7). Figure 8.29 shows some of the necessary instance variables and initializations.

Figure 8.30. provides a main method to drive the whole process.

### Self-Organizing Maps

Another type of clustering algorithm is the **SOM (self-organizing map)**. SOMs were devised by Teuvo Kohonen, and first used by [31] to analyze gene expression

```
public boolean reconsider() {
    int jMinDist;
    boolean change = false;
    double[] dists = new double[k];
    for (int i = 0; i < N; i++) {
        jMinDist = 0;
        for (int j = 0; j < k; j++) {
            dists[j] = distance(clusters[j].centroid,
                                    genes[i].expressionLevels);
            if (dists[j]  <  dists[jMinDist]) jMinDist = j;
        }
        if (jMinDist != myCluster[i]) {
            // Next line provides running commentary
            System.out.println("Moving "+i+" from "+myCluster[i]+
                                " to "+jMinDist);
            clusters[myCluster[i]].remove(genes[i]);
            clusters[jMinDist].add(genes[i]);
            myCluster[i] = jMinDist;
            change = true;
        }
    }
    return(change);
}
```

**FIGURE 8.28**    Implementation of a method to move genes within clusters in *k*-means clustering.

```
public class ExpressionExperiment {
    int N;     // Number of datapoints
    int M;     // Number of experiments, dimension of
               // cluster space
    int numClusters;    // How many clusters
    Gene[] genes;
    Cluster[] clusters;
    int[] myCluster;
    public ExpressionExperiment(int numgenes, int numexperiments, int k) {
        N = numgenes;
        M = numexperiments;
        numClusters = k;
        genes = new Gene[N];
        myCluster = new int[N];
        double[] expressionLevels = new double[M];
    }
}
```

**FIGURE 8.29**    Implementation of the ExpressionExperiment class.

```
public static void main(String[] args) {
    ExpressionExperiment ee = new ExpressionExperiment(
                            Integer.parseInt(args[0]),
                            Integer.parseInt(args[1]),
                            Integer.parseInt(args[2]));
    ee.printData();
    ee.kMeans();
}
```

**FIGURE 8.30**   Implementation of the main method for the *k*-means clustering program.

data. The SOM is a type of neural network that reduces the dimensionality of the gene expression data by mapping it to one or two dimensions so that relationships can be visualized more easily. To initiate the SOM the user defines a geometric configuration for the partitions by specifying the $x$ and $y$ dimensions of the map. For example, if $3 \times 3$ is chosen, nine partitions occur. Then, nine random vectors are initialized, one for each partition. These vectors are of the same dimensionality as in the gene expression dataset. For instance if you have 10 experiments, then the vectors will be 10-dimensional; that is they will have 10 coordinates. An important concept is that the partitions have a physical relationship to one another, in that they sit in a two-dimensional grid. Thus, one partition can be considered to be physically closer to another partition than it is to a third. At the beginning, the map is unorganized. That is, the relationship of the partitions in physical space has no bearing on the relationships between the vectors that associate with them. Next, the SOM is refined. A gene from the list is picked at random, and its expression pattern is compared (using some selected distance measure) to each of the vectors that were initialized randomly in the first step. The vector to which the expression vector of the picked gene is most similar is then modified, so that it more closely resembles the expression vector of that gene. In addition, the vectors that belong to the partitions that are physically closest (in the two-dimensional grid) to the partition whose vector was just modified are also modified, so that they too resemble the gene's expression vector a little more closely. This process is repeated many times. Essentially a circle is drawn on the two-dimensional grid, with its center being in the center of the partition whose vector was most similar to the picked gene's expression pattern. Any partitions that fall within that circle are considered "close," and so their vectors are modified. The radius of this circle decreases with each iteration. With each iteration fewer vectors are modified by smaller amounts, so that the map eventually stops changing. In the end, the vectors of neighboring partitions are somewhat similar to each other, and vectors of partitions that are physically distant are dissimilar to each other. Thus the map has become organized. After all iterations have occurred, the genes are then partitioned. Usually, the contents of each partition are then clustered by hierarchical clustering.

### 8.11.3 Classification

In contrast to the unsupervised approaches of clustering, **classification** is a **machine-learning technique** that uses a **supervised approach** to organize the data into meaningful groups. The main goal of classification is the ability to assign a new sample to a previously specified class, based on sample features and a trained classifier. Building the classifier involves the identification of features (genes) that discriminate between classes.

One of the first applications of classification to microarray data was by Todd Golub and collaborators in what has now become a "classical" study [13] serving as a model for many to follow. The research team tackled the challenging problem of diagnosing two related, but different types of leukemia: acute myeloid leukemia (AML) and acute lymphoblastic leukemia (ALL). At that time no single reliable test was available that could distinguish AML from ALL yet it remained critically important to do so because both the clinical course and response to treatment differed greatly depending on the type of leukemia.

They reasoned that global gene expression profiles could be used to distinguish among these cancer types if genes could be identified that strongly correlated with one type or the other. The study design was to first perform microarray experiments on tumors known to be either AML or ALL. Over 6000 genes were assayed in 27 ALL samples and 11 AML samples. The statistical technique of neighborhood analysis was then used to assess all genes in terms of their correlation to an "idealized" pattern of expression for a gene that discriminates between the two types. For example, an ideal gene would be expressed at a uniformly high level across the ALL tumors and low level in AML, or vice versa. Figure 8.31 shows an example of an expression vector, $c$, for such a hypothetical ideal gene. Gene 1 shows a strong correlation with $c$, whereas gene 2 does not.

Eleven hundred of the approximately 6000 genes followed the class distinction, many more than would be expected purely by chance. Of these an arbitrary number of genes (50) were chosen to build the class predictor. Next, the predictor was tested by cross-validation (one sample was withheld and the predictor built

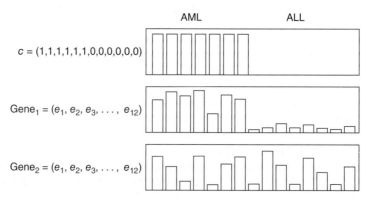

$c = (1,1,1,1,1,1,0,0,0,0,0,0)$

$Gene_1 = (e_1, e_2, e_3, \ldots, e_{12})$

$Gene_2 = (e_1, e_2, e_3, \ldots, e_{12})$

**FIGURE 8.31**  Discrimination between AML and ALL.
Source: Golub et al

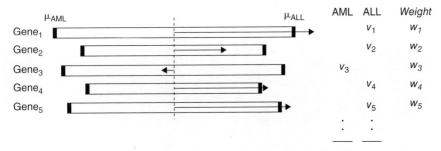

**FIGURE 8.32**   Expression levels of genes "vote" for inclusion of sample in AML or ALL class.
Source: Golub et al

from the remaining 37 samples; this was repeated for each sample). The predictor was then tested on an independent dataset from unknown tumor types. The method of prediction was one of weighted votes. That is, the gene expression measurement for each gene in the unknown sample was compared with that in the known sample. If the level was similar to the mean value for that gene in AML, the gene "voted" for AML (Figure 8.32). The vote weight was calculated based on how well the gene correlated with the class distinction and also on how well the unknown sample matched the known sample.

Importantly, this classifier was able to make strong predictions for 29 of 34 unknown samples and did so with 100% accuracy, and predictors based on as few as 10 genes or as many as 200 genes performed similarly. The patterns in Figure 8.33 demonstrate that no single gene would serve as a reliable classifier by itself. In contrast, the power of the predictor comes from the collective measurements of the 50 genes.

In addition to its power in classification, another important feature of this type of analysis is the identification of discriminating genes. This provides a window into the biology underlying these tumors. Figure 8.33 shows the identifications of the 50 genes in the classifier. Further exploration of these genes may be used to clarify misdiagnoses, to understand which biological processes are perturbed, to predict clinical outcomes, and to plan therapeutic treatments.

### 8.11.4  Using Visualization Techniques to Aid Interpretation

Figure 8.33 exemplifies one of the important aspects of any data-mining approach in gene expression: visualization of the output. Although not always consistently done, even simple techniques such as color coding are helpful in supporting the easy recognition of interesting patterns in the data. Another valuable feature of many types of program output and their visualization tools is the ability to explore relationships and make discoveries interactively. Many such applications provide "clickable" elements that allow biologists to access additional detailed information about a selected gene, such as its name, aliases, function, and the location of the gene product within the cell, to name a few. This is accomplished by linking

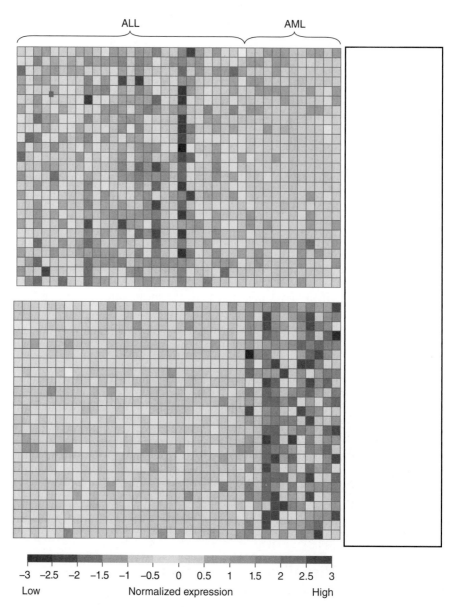

**FIGURE 8.33**    Expression levels of the 50 genes used in the classifier for ALL and AML.
Source: Golub et al

to a major database at a public site such as the NCBI or a custom database associated with the application. The knowledgeable biologist armed with effective visualization tools is thereby enabled in the discovery of meaningful biological relationships in the data. The Hierarchical Clustering Explorer (HCE) developed at the University of Maryland is one such tool that combines a powerful clustering algorithm with a visualization tool to enable interactive exploration by a domain expert [30]. GenMAPP is another free computer application designed to visualize gene expression and other genomic data. We will meet GenMAPP again in Chapter 9. In this application gene expression data can be visualized on maps representing biological pathways and groupings of genes. GenMAPP supports interpretation of expression data in the context of hundreds of pathways and thousands of gene ontology terms [6]. Recognizing the value of visualization, Heer and colleagues [14] have produced Prefuse, a user interface toolkit for building interactive visualizations of structured and unstructured data. Using the toolkit, developers can create responsive, animated graphical interfaces for visualizing, exploring, and manipulating data. This software could be used to visualize hierarchies of gene expression data as well as gene networks and will also be revisited in Chapter 9. Prefuse is written in Java using the Java2D graphics library and is designed to integrate with any application written using the Java Swing user interface library.

## 8.11.5  Advanced Classification Algorithms

### Genetic Algorithms

Classification is another problem that may be suited to attack by a genetic algorithm (GA). As noted in Chapters 6 and 7, GAs are suitable when we have lots of measurable data but are uncertain how to combine them usefully, and when we have a fitness function that can be used to drive the evolutionary GA.

In the case of the classification problem enormous quantities of data are provided by the microarrays. The parameters subject to slippage and convergence via a GA include:

1. parameters pertaining to how we normalize the data,
2. the number of clusters we aim for,
3. parameters determining how we measure distance between samples,
4. parameters for thresholds determining when we switch clusters,
5. and many other potential parameters.

The fitness function depends on the utility of the clusters produced by the parameters. As a simple first approximation, the fitness function can even be determined as the opinion of a human evaluator. References [7, 17, 33] provide a sample of research in this area.

### Support Vector Machines

The support vector machine (SVM) is a supervised learning approach that exploits prior knowledge of gene function to find genes with similar function. Used first by Brown and coworkers [4] to analyze gene expression data, this technique is rapidly gaining in popularity and breadth of application. This study showed the SVM outperformed several other machine-learning classification algorithms when used on a large dataset (2467 genes from 79 microarrays) from budding yeast. SVMs have many mathematical features that make them particularly appropriate for gene expression data. These include flexibility when choosing a similarity function, the ability to handle large feature spaces, the ability to deal with outliers, and, finally, the capacity to create a few solutions from large datasets [4]. The algorithm proceeds through two main stages. First is a training stage in which an initial presumptive classification (from supplied knowledge) and the expression data serve as inputs. The output of the training stage is a set of weights that will be used during the second, classification, stage. The weights and the expression data are used to assign a score to each element, which then places that element into or out of a class. The SVM is implemented in the TM4 suite of microarray analysis tools available from TIGR.

## 8.12  DATA MANAGEMENT

As the cost of microarrays has decreased and exciting findings have been published, more and more laboratories and individual scientists have been drawn to the power and promise genome-wide studies offer. This has had a huge impact on science, as evidenced by the tens of thousands of publications reporting the results of microarray data [34]. The unfortunate repercussion of the onslaught of data generated using the wide variety of technologies and platforms available for high-throughput gene expression analysis is the rather difficult problem of data management. Perhaps analogous to the state of DNA sequence databases more than a decade ago, today a large number of distributed databases exist containing gene expression data. Moreover, these data may come not only from microarrays but also SAGE or other analysis techniques. They may be scattered among many independent sites (accessible via Internet) or not publicly available at all. According to a 2006 review, about 3% of the more than 400 biological databases store microarray data [34].

The types of data management tools used for microarray data have evolved along with techniques for the generation and use of the data. In the infancy of the microarray when individual labs were creating arrays and running rather small studies, the data were typically kept on local computers in flat files or in a spreadsheet application. Even then, however, it was necessary to share data with other scientists because some labs could not afford to run their own arrays. Sharing data has a real advantage . Not only does it help to promote reproducibility of study results, but when the datasets are large it also promotes discovery. That is, different data analysis approaches or different algorithms used to explore the same microarray dataset are known to result in different discoveries. Both flat files and spreadsheets are limited when it comes to storing and exchange data. First, there is the problem with the *metadata,* or data about the data, a familiar term to those versed in database technologies. Whether using flat files or spreadsheets the metadata is not likely to be stored along with the data, but rather resides in another file or files. For any automated process (other than the scientist simply reading the file) the files must be parsed, using a language such as Perl, to extract the information in the metadata. In terms of the gene expression data, the spreadsheet offers some advantages over the flat file such as the ability to sort, do some data analysis, and produce graphs and charts. In fact, many addsons avaliable for Excel, particularly for statistical analysis, have been developed for microarray data. However, the spreadsheet has severe limitations in terms of updating, sharing, and exploring the data.

Relational database management systems have generally been the preferred solution for microarray data, although that is changing. In the relational database model, data are represented in two-dimensional tables. The table, or relation, has rows and columns, and tables are related through primary or foreign keys. The relational model supports several algebraic operations that can be used to manipulate the data. For example, the user can retrieve data elements of interest, such as gene expression ratios, from all tables containing the values of interest, using the SELECT command. Most commonly, the **structured query language (SQL)** is used to formulate and perform database queries. SQL is supported by many database management systems commonly used for gene expression data, including MS-Access, MySQL, PostgreSQL, and Oracle. A database schema is often provided as a graphical representation of the design of the relational database tables.

Microarray databases tend to be pretty big. Even the relational model is not totally suited to microarray data. For example, certain types of data such as images and documents are not handled well by the relational model, especially when scalability of the database is considered. For that reason, researchers are turning to object-oriented databases or object-relational databases for larger scale systems. The main advantage of such systems is that data can be encapsulated into objects so that some of the complexity is hidden and data can be accessed more easily through methods that operate on objects. In addition the object model is more extensible and reusable than the relational model.

Extraction of information from these large datasets and integration of biological knowledge are key to finding biological meaning in the data. This means that scientists not only need to be able to share data, but must also understand the nature of the shared data and relate gene expression data to other biological information stored in a variety of formats. Data management, integration, and annotation problems highlight a need for standardization that enables sharing. Clearly, there is far too much variability in gene expression data to easily share and use the data because of the need to document experimental details. Furthermore, many current databases differ in annotation, database structure, and availability.

## 8.12.1 Controlled Vocabularies and Standardization of Microarray Data

Microarray experiments are not only high-throughput, they are complex. Recall the large number of experimental steps required to carry a microarray experiment through to completion. The precise experimental conditions must be known in order to use or reproduce the data. For example, the type of experiment must be known, as well as the nature of the samples, how they were labeled, the conditions of hybridization, what controls were present on the array, if and how the data normalization was done . . . and on and on. Naming conventions must be adhered to consistently; for example, the word **probe** refers to the immobilized DNA on an array and not the labeled sample (the more traditional use of the word prior to the microarray) used to hybridize the array. This poses a major challenge because biologists have had a long tradition of personally naming cell types, organelles, genes, and proteins at the time of their discovery. Often the same gene or protein has been given a different name by a different researcher who may have studied it in a different context. Textual information used to describe biological molecules, processes, and experiments has generally been free-form. The lack of consistency and standards causes real problems for data exchange and integration and has led to widespread recognition that vocabularies need to be controlled throughout the different domains of biomedical research as well as in clinical and regulatory practice.

Controlled vocabularies are used to capture and formalize knowledge in a given domain, such as the microarray. The vocabulary consists of a list of terms and their relationships, which have been explicitly specified in an *ontology*. The use of terms belonging to a controlled vocabulary solves the computing problems that arise when writing parsers to search for terms and phrases in free text. This has been a common problem in the sharing of microarray data, especially when researchers provided the microarray data in flat files or when the metadata accompanying a relational database was written in a free-form manner. Probably the best known, and also most mature, ontology used in bioinformatics today is the Gene Ontology (GO). This project began in 1998 as a collaboration between three model organism databases, FlyBase, the Saccharomyces Genome Database, and the Mouse Genome Database, and grew to what is now the Gene Ontology Consortium (GOC). The GO project was proposed in response to the proliferation of disparate biological databases containing gene and genome data, and the GOC has spearheaded its implementation. The GOC noted the inconsistencies in annotation, arbitrary classifications, and multiple spellings and uses of terms and proposed three ontologies based on molecular function, biological process, and cellular component [2]. Today, the GO is widely adopted by the biological community. Used by at least 30 major bioinformatics databases it has become the de facto standard for biological database ontologies [5, 34]. New tools for data analysis using the GO are continually springing up. For example, ADGO is a Web application that supports analysis of differentially expressed gene sets with composite GO annotations. It is based on the principal that coordinated expression changes of specific gene sets, or modular expression, is most typical of biological processes. Gene annotation can be used to specify such gene sets. This tool, however, rather than relying on a single category to look for patterns, uses intersecting categories. When for example, some genes categorized by a particular molecular function are unaffected by an experimental condition, it may be that only those genes that also share a certain cellular component are affected. The ADGO can then find significant associations at the intersection of genesets that are revealed with unary annotations. Interestingly, the exemplary analysis used for ADGO is for gene expression in the HIV-1 immune response [21].

Fortunately, today a concerted effort is underway to standardize microarray data, along with the other types of "omics" data. For microarray data this work is being carried out at the U.S. National Center for Biotechnology Information

(Gene Expression Omnibus), at the European Bioinformatics Institute (Array-Express), and also at Stanford University where much of the first microarray analysis was done.

The Microarray Gene Expression Database (MGED) group, www.mged.org, is the primary force behind standardization of gene expression data and databases. The MGED working group is a multidisciplinary group collaborating to define and standardize the terminology required to publish a microarray experiment. Initially, four main projects were underway. The MGED has recently expanded to also address standardization issues in other "omics" such as toxicogenomics, environmental genomics, and nutrigenomics. One major microarray project [3], known as minimum information about a microarray experiment (MIAME), has worked toward defining the information required to interpret and verify microarray results. The MIAME group has published guidelines (see the MGED Website) that strictly define what information should be reported so that someone outside of the reporting lab can interpret the data. Many, if not most, databases today are required to be MIAME-compliant. Another group, Microarray and Gene Expression (MAGE), is concerned with the establishment of an XML-based data exchange format (MAGE-ML) and data exchange model (MAGE-OM), modeled using the Unified Modeling Language (UML), for microarray experiments. MAGE-ML is a type of eXtensible Markup Language (XML)—the international standard for defining descriptions of the structure and content of electronic documents. The document type definition (DTD) of MAGE-ML specifies all of the rules or declarations, allowable tags, and the content of tags for microarray data. XML allows information in different representations to be exchanged in a generic format and also provides a software- and hardware-independent mechanism for data sharing.

In addition to the definition of the information needed to describe a microarray experiment (provided by MIAME) and a mechanism to standardize data for exchange (provided by MAGE-OM and MAGE-ML), a controlled terminology for data annotation was also needed. Therefore, another major MGED project developed ontologies for microarray experiment description and biological material (biomaterial) annotation in particular. The MGED Ontology (MO) was developed as a resource for semantics-based descriptions of microarray experiments. It provides terms for annotation that comply with MIAME guidelines, and it supports the MAGE-OM. A detailed example of use can be found in the recently released, original paper describing the MO [38]. The MO is used primarily in three ways, depending on the needs of the user. It may be used by a biologist who has little knowledge of MO structure itself, when it is embedded within applications, to annotate, or to query data. The MO may be used directly by annotators and may be used by software developers for producing applications that use the MO [36]. The Transformation and Normalization working group has undertaken the development of recommendations on experimental controls and data normalization methods.

Another major effort toward microarray standardization is the MicroArray Quality Control (MAQC) Project [18]. In this project microarray specialists from almost 30 organizations are working with the U.S. Food and Drug Administration to provide quality control tools and develop data analysis guidelines. Another important collaboration is the External RNA Controls Consortium (ERCC). It involves more than 110 participants from approximately 70 organizations, who are collaborating to develop a set of external RNA control transcripts. These controls can be "spiked" into RNA preparations before cDNA synthesis and used to assess the technical performance of gene expression assays. These controls will also be qualified by the National Institutes of Standards and Technology (NIST)—the same group that qualifies universal standards such as atomic time, temperature, and mass. Eventually, with a better understanding of the variability and comparability among different arrays and methods and by developing standardized data representations, scientists and clinicians will be able to use appropriate procedures to ensure accurate results and will be able to combine their transcriptional profiling efforts.

## 8.13  EXERCISES FOR CHAPTER 8

**Exercise 8.1**

Choose one of the HIV-1 genes. Write a program that uses this sequence as input and provide a list of candidate oligonucleotide probes that fit the following criteria:

- 25 nucleotides in length
- within 300 bp of the 3′ end of the coding sequence

Next, using some publicly available tools, test any candidate oligonucleotides for the following:

- repetitive elements
- significant homology to other known sequence

For extra credit, suggest ways that you could link your program to the others so that it could run with less user intervention.

**Exercise 8.2**

Locate some gene expression data from one of the public repositories. Examine the data to understand its format. Depending on the data selected, perform some *t-tests* or ANOVA analyses using available tools. Report on your findings.

**Exercise 8.3**

Write a program to test the Gene class. Your main method should create a Gene with name and expression levels from the command line, and then output the values from the gene.

```
> java GeneTest fred 0.0 1.0 2.0
Gene fred has expression levels 0.0 1.0 2.0
```

Write a program to test the `Cluster` class provided in this chapter.

**Exercise 8.4**

Write a program to perform a Pearson correlation. Test your program on an appropriate data set.

**Exercise 8.5**

Write a program to test the methods created in this chapter for *k*-means clustering.

**Exercise 8.6**

Create a program to generate random expression data and cluster it using *k*-means analysis. All the code is included in this chapter, in various places. Running the code with java ExpressionExperiment 20 5 3 will set up random data for an experiment involving five measurements of expression levels of 20 genes and clustering into three clusters. Your program might behave like the following:

**Exercise 8.7**

```
java ExpressionExperiment 20 5 3
0:  0.00   0.92   0.87   1.12   1.50
1:  0.00   1.44   1.30   1.75   1.31
2:  0.00   1.98   1.70   1.48   1.56
3:  0.00  -2.02  -2.15  -1.81  -1.49
4:  0.00   1.94   2.38   2.78   3.23
5:  0.00  -2.90  -3.11  -3.35  -3.69
6:  0.00  -1.19  -0.73  -0.61  -0.21
7:  0.00   1.12   1.46   1.01   0.78
8:  0.00   0.49   0.44   0.07   0.49
9:  0.00   2.39   2.73   2.96   3.14
10: 0.00  -1.55  -1.90  -1.50  -1.34
11: 0.00   2.75   2.80   2.71   2.96
12: 0.00  -2.54  -2.94  -3.28  -3.11
13: 0.00   0.14  -0.32  -0.52  -0.97
14: 0.00   1.92   1.64   1.94   1.96
15: 0.00  -0.39  -0.08   0.09   0.51
16: 0.00  -1.36  -1.61  -1.68  -1.73
17: 0.00  -0.70  -0.79  -0.80  -0.53
18: 0.00   1.67   1.60   2.02   2.08
19: 0.00  -0.19  -0.52  -0.31   0.13
Cluster 0: 0 3 16 18 19 Centroid: ( 0.00, -0.19, -0.36, -0.13, 0.10)
Cluster 1: 1 5 8 9 11 12 13 14 15 Centroid: ( 0.00, 0.37, 0.27, 0.26, 0.29)
Cluster 2: 2 4 6 7 10 17 Centroid: ( 0.00, 0.27, 0.35, 0.40, 0.58)      (continued)
```

```
Moving 0 from 0 to 2
Moving 1 from 1 to 2
Moving 5 from 1 to 0
Moving 6 from 2 to 0
Moving 9 from 1 to 2
Moving 10 from 2 to 0
Moving 11 from 1 to 2
Moving 12 from 1 to 0
Moving 13 from 1 to 0
Moving 14 from 1 to 2
Moving 15 from 1 to 0
Moving 17 from 2 to 0
Moving 18 from 0 to 2
Cluster 0: 3 16 19 5 6 10 12 13 15 17 Centroid: ( 0.00, -1.27, -1.41, -1.38, -1.24)
Cluster 1: 8 Centroid: ( 0.00, 0.49, 0.44, 0.07, 0.49)
Cluster 2: 2 4 7 0 1 9 11 14 18 Centroid: ( 0.00, 1.79, 1.83, 1.97, 2.06)
Moving 0 from 2 to 1
Moving 7 from 2 to 1
Moving 13 from 0 to 1
Moving 15 from 0 to 1
Moving 19 from 0 to 1
Cluster 0: 3 16 5 6 10 12 17 Centroid: ( 0.00, -1.75, -1.89, -1.86, -1.73)
Cluster 1: 8 0 7 13 15 19 Centroid: ( 0.00, 0.35, 0.31, 0.24, 0.41)
Cluster 2: 2 4 1 9 11 14 18 Centroid: ( 0.00, 2.01, 2.02, 2.24, 2.32)
Moving 6 from 0 to 1
Moving 17 from 0 to 1
Cluster 0: 3 16 5 10 12 Centroid: ( 0.00, -2.07, -2.34, -2.33, -2.27)
Cluster 1: 8 0 7 13 15 19 6 17 Centroid: ( 0.00, 0.02, 0.04, 0.01, 0.21)
Cluster 2: 2 4 1 9 11 14 18 Centroid: ( 0.00, 2.01, 2.02, 2.24, 2.32)
```

# KEY TERMS

genotype (8.4)

phenotype (8.4)

differential gene expression (8.4)

transcriptional profiling (8.5)

transcriptome (8.5)

sensitivity (8.5)

selectivity (8.5)

gridding (8.7)

segmentation (8.7)

information extraction (8.7)

spot intensity extraction (8.7)

background intensity
   extraction (8.7)

gene filtering (8.8)

perfect match (PM) (8.8)

mismatch (MM) (8.8)

$log_2$ transformation (8.8)

scaling (8.8)

hypothesis testing (8.10)

$p$-value (8.10)

gene expression matrix (8.11)

clustering (8.11)

Pearson correlation (8.11)

Euclidean distance (8.11)

SOM (self-organizing map) (8.11)

classification (8.11)

machine-learning technique (8.11)

supervised approach (8.11)

structured query language
   (SQL) (8.12)

probe (8.12)

metadata (8.12)

ontology (8.12)

# BIBLIOGRAPHY

1. L. Anderson and J. Seilhamer. A comparison of selected mRNA and protein abundances in human liver. *Electrophoresis,* 18:533–537, 1997.

2. M. Ashburner, C. A. Ball, J. A. Blake, et al. Gene ontology: Tool for the unification of biology. The gene ontology consortium. *Nat Genet,* 25:25–29, 2000.

3. Alvis Brazma. On the importance of standardisation in life sciences. *Bioinformatics,* 17:113–114, 2001.

4. Michael P. S. Brown, William Noble Grundy, David Lin, et al. Knowledge-based analysis of microarray gene expression data by using support vector machines. *PNAS,* 97:262–267, 2000.

5. Evelyn Camon, Michele Magrane, Daniel Barrell, et al. The gene ontology annotation (GOA) database: Sharing knowledge in uniprot with gene ontology. *Nucleic Acids Res,* 32 (Database-Issue):262–266, 2004.

6. K. D. Dahlquist, N. Salomonis, K. Vranizan, et al. GenMAPP, a new tool for viewing and analyzing microarray data on biological pathways. *Nat Genet,* 31:19–20, 2002.

7. J. M. Deutsch. Evolutionary algorithms for finding optimal gene sets in microarray prediction. *Bioinformatics,* 19:45–42, 2003.

8. S. Draghici. *Data Analysis Tools for DNA Microarrays.* Chapman and Hall/CRC, New York, 2003.

9. J. B. Fan, X. Chen, M. K. Halushka, et al. Parallel genotyping of human SNPs using generic high-density oligonucleotide tag arrays. *Genome Res,* 10:853–860, 2000.

10. Alan M. Frieze, Franco P. Preparata, and Eli Upfal. Optimal reconstruction of a sequence from its probes. *J Comput Biol,* 6(3/4), 1999.

11. Max H. Garzon, Vinhthuy T. Phan, Kiran C. Bobba, and Raghuver Kontham. Sensitivity and capacity of microarray encodings. In Alessandra Carbone and Niles A. Pierce, editors, DNA, volume 3892 of *Lecture Notes in Computer Science,* pages 81–95. Springer, 2005.

12. M. S. Giri, M. Nebozhyn, L. Showe, and L. J. Montane. Microarray data on gene modulation by HIV-1 in immune cells: 2000–2006. *J Leukocyte Biol,* 80:1031, 2006.

13. T. R. Golub, D. K. Slonim, P. Tamayo, et al. Molecular classification of cancer: Class discovery and class prediction by gene expression monitoring. *Science,* 286:531–537, 1999.

14. J. Heer, S. K. Card, and J. A. Landay. Prefuse: A toolkit for interactive information visualization. In CHI 2005: *Human Factors in Computing Systems,* 2005.

15. P. Heiter and M. Boguski. Functional genomics: It's all how you read it. *Science,* 278:601–602, 1997.

16. R. A. Irizarry, D. Warren, F. Spencer, et al. Multiple-laboratory comparison of microarray platforms. *Nat Methods,* 2:345–349, 2005.

17. Leping Li, Clarice R. Weinberg, Thomas A. Darden, and Lee G. Pedersen. Gene selection for sample classification based on gene expression data: Study of sensitivity to choice of parameters of the ga/knn method. *Bioinformatics,* 17:1131–1142, 2001.

18. MAQC. Cross-platform comparability of microarray technology: Intraplatform consistency and appropriate data analysis procedures are essential. BioMed Central Ltd., 2005.

19. R. Mei, E. Hubbell, S. Bekiranov, et al. Probe selection for high-density oligonucleotide arrays. *Proc Natl Acad Sci USA,* 100:11237–11242, 2003.

20. P. Mitchell P. A perspective on protein microarrays. *Nat Biotechnol,* 20:225–229, 2002.

21. D. Nam, S-B. Kim, S-K. Kim, et al. Adgo: analysis of differentially expressed gene sets using composite go annotation. *Bioinformatics,* 22:2249–2253, 2006.

22. NCBI Gene Expression Omnibus (GEO) http://www.ncbi.nlm.nih.gov/projects/geo/info/cluster.html

23. Taesung Park, Sung-Gon Yi, Seungmook Lee, et al. Statistical tests for identifying differentially expressed genes in time-course microarray experiments. *Bioinformatics,* 19:694–703, 2003.

24. Rhys Price Jones, S. J. Harrington, J. F. Naveda, et al. On the Structure of Style Space for Documents. Presented at the American

Association for Artificial Intelligence (AAAI) Symposium on Style and Meaning in Language, Art, Music, and Design, Washington DC, October 2004.

25. H. Primdahl, F. P. Wikman, H. von der Maase, et al. Allelic imbalances in human bladder cancer: Genome-wide detection with high-density single-nucleotide polymorphism arrays. *J Natl Cancer Inst,* 94:216–223, 2002.

26. J. Quackenbush. Computational analysis of microarray data. *Nat RevGenet,* 2:418–427, 2001.

27. S. Selvey, E. W. Thompson, K. Matthaei, et al. Beta-actin-an unsuitable internal control for RT-PCR. *Mol Cell Probes,* 15:307–311, 2001.

28. J. Seo and B. Shneiderman. Interactively exploring hierarchical clustering results. *IEEE Computer,* 35:80–86, 2002.

29. R. L. Stears, T. Martinsky, and M. Schena. Trends in microarray analysis. *Nat Med,* 9:140–145, 2003.

30. Dov Stekel. *Microarray Bioinformatics.* Cambridge University Press, 2003.

31. P. Tamayo, D. Slonim, J. Mesirov, et al. Interpreting patterns of gene expression with self-organizing maps: Methods and application to hematopoietic differentiation. *Proc Natl Acad Sci USA,* 96:2907–2912, 1999.

32. Stefan Tomiuk and Kay Hofmann. Microarray probe selection strategies. *Briefings Bioinformatics,* 2:329–349, 2001.

33. Huai-Kuang Tsai, Jinn-Moon Yang, Yuan-Fang Tsai, and Cheng-Yan Kao. An evolutionary approach for gene expression patterns. *IEEE Transact Infor Technol Biomedicine,* 8:69–78, 2004.

34. Willy Valdivia-Granda and Christopher Dwan. Microarray data management. An enterprise information approach: Implementations and challenges, 2006. In Zongmin Ma and Jake Chen, Jake (editors): *Database Modeling in Biology: Practices and Challenges.* Springer Sciences & Business Media.

35. V. E. Velculescu, L. Zhang, B. Vogelstein, and K. W. Kinzler. Serial analysis of gene expression. *Science,* 270:484–487, 1995.

36. Patricia L. Whetzel, Helen Parkinson, Helen C. Causton, et al. The MGED ontology: A resource for semantics-based description of microarray experiments. *Bioinformatics,* 22:866–873, 2006.

37. Y. H. Yang, M. J. Buckley, and T. P. Speed. Analysis of cDNA microarray images. *Brief Bioinform,* 2:341–349, 2001.

38. Michael Zuker. MFold web server for nucleic acid folding and hybridization prediction. *Nucleic Acids Res,* 31:3406–3415, 2003.

# 9

# Projects

*"The men of experiment are like the ant, they only collect and use; the reasoners resemble spiders, who make cobwebs out of their own substance. But the bee takes the middle course: it gathers its material from the flowers of the garden and field, but transforms and digests it by a power of its own."*

—Francis Bacon

In this chapter, we are touching on several different topics, many of them currently at the cutting edge of the field of bioinformatics. Each section begins by describing some accomplishments, at the end of which we turn it "over to you" by suggesting exercises or projects that venture further into the topics. Finally, each section ends with a list of annotated resources to encourage more exploration into the computational challenges.

## 9.1 VISUALIZATION AND EXPLORATION OF COMPLEX DATASETS

Like any lively flourishing science bioinformatics does not have all the answers. In fact, we don't even know all the questions! But thanks to truly amazing technological advances such as those described in Chapter 3 we *do* have huge, and we mean truly prodigious and colossal, quantities of data. The data are so vast and complex that we cannot effectively investigate it ourselves. For the science of bioinformatics to advance, we need to be able to examine those data and formulate the questions, frame the hypotheses, and test our conclusions, all in the context of unsolved biological problems. What makes bioinformatics really exciting is that sometimes, nay, often, we have no idea what we're looking for as we develop ways to examine the data. We cannot therefore write programs to perform that investigation.

Instead we need to work in an evolving partnership with our computers. Programs can be written to organize our data and present it to us in ways that enable us to make new discoveries. Only humans are capable of discovering new and unexpected patterns that eventually lead to new and testable science. Computers themselves are incapable of creative and original investigation. But because of their ability to process large amounts of data very quickly, suitably programmed computers will play an indispensable role in the advancement of our science.

What do we mean by "suitably programmed computers"? The smart aleck (and, incidentally, correct) answer to this question is that we do not know. We cannot in general know in advance precisely how computers can aid the process of scientific investigation. Here is our single most compelling reason for writing this book. Talented, curious, investigative scientists are needed who are comfortable enough with computing machinery and its capabilities that they can demand, obtain, or create the exact tools and data configurations to spur effective scientific research. We hope our readers are the scientists who will know what can be accomplished with computers and how to get it done.

Our first project looks at how computers have been used to arrange data so that scientists can immediately see important correlations and formulate valuable hypotheses.

## 9.1.1  Sequencing Gel Visualization

To illustrate the ways in which human investigators can use evolving computer algorithms to advance science, let's conduct a mind experiment and pay a visit to the year 1977. Pioneers including Maxam, Gilbert, and Sanger are developing sequencing techniques. Eventually it is possible to create a set of DNA fragments of varying lengths starting at a predetermined primer site in which the final terminating dideoxynucleotide is labeled such that each corresponding nucleotide fluoresces with a different color spectrum. These fragments are forced through a gel and arrive sorted by size. As they pass by a laser the laser excites the fragments, making each fluoresce within a measurable range of spectral intensities.

That's the theory. Now technology creates sequencing machines to speed up the process. Output from these machines creates a huge amount of numeric data indicating output intensities at different wavelengths in the spectrum as the fragments in strict order of size pass by a fixed reader.

Table 9.1 is a (very much simplified and reduced) set of such data. Each row shows the four intensity readings at a single time. Reading down a column shows how the intensity of each wavelength varies as time proceeds.

A human is hard pressed to detect and record the patterns in the data within any reasonable time frame. As we study the data we note that each wavelength varies as time proceeds. To truly understand what that variation means, however, we need to see the data displayed graphically. To paraphrase a great truism "A picture is worth a million numbers."

These days we'd just import the numbers into some standard software, maybe a spreadsheet, and click the right buttons to draw the graph. But remember this is a thought experiment and we are in the 1970s. So we write a program to read the data series for each wavelength and draw the graphs shown in Figure 9.1.

At each wavelength, we can see a series of peaks. Presumably a peak corresponds to the passage of a fragment and its corresponding terminal dideoxynucleotide past the detector. Looking at the four separate graphs does not help us determine the sequence. Perhaps we conclude that we need to superimpose

TABLE 9.1    Simplified sequencer output

| | | | |
|---|---|---|---|
| 10 | 12 | 11 | 12 |
| 12 | 14 | 7 | 14 |
| 11 | 8 | 6 | 13 |
| 12 | 3 | 7 | 28 |
| 13 | 2 | 6 | 16 |
| 10 | 3 | 7 | 32 |
| 17 | 1 | 6 | 12 |
| 25 | 2 | 7 | 13 |
| 14 | 1 | 5 | 12 |
| 15 | 3 | 6 | 13 |
| 12 | 11 | 7 | 12 |
| 10 | 2 | 21 | 13 |
| 11 | 3 | 29 | 11 |
| 12 | 1 | 16 | 13 |
| 10 | 2 | 8 | 32 |
| 9 | 1 | 7 | 35 |
| 10 | 3 | 6 | 31 |
| 6 | 12 | 7 | 14 |
| 10 | 13 | 6 | 13 |
| 11 | 7 | 5 | 13 |
| 10 | 3 | 6 | 18 |
| 12 | 2 | 5 | 28 |
| 11 | 1 | 7 | 13 |
| 10 | 5 | 16 | 12 |
| 10 | 1 | 30 | 14 |
| 10 | 2 | 22 | 12 |
| 9 | 2 | 31 | 13 |
| 11 | 1 | 15 | 12 |
| 18 | 3 | 7 | 13 |
| 28 | 1 | 6 | 13 |
| 25 | 2 | 7 | 14 |
| 16 | 1 | 6 | 12 |
| 12 | 3 | 27 | 14 |
| 11 | 1 | 6 | 13 |
| 9 | 2 | 7 | 17 |
| 10 | 3 | 8 | 29 |
| 10 | 1 | 7 | 17 |
| 9 | 2 | 8 | 15 |
| 11 | 1 | 6 | 33 |
| 12 | 3 | 7 | 14 |

the graphs and have a separate pattern for the graph for each column. Again (remember we're pretending to be in the 1970s) we need to write a simple program to produce the visual output that will let us figure out what is going on.

Figure 9.2 shows the output from our new program. Commercial base-calling software takes advantage of color to differentiate the graphs for each column.

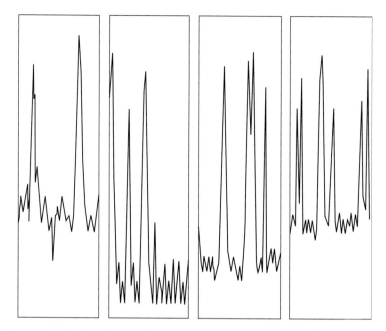

**FIGURE 9.1**    Graphs of each column of data. It is next to impossible to determine the order in which peaks occur.

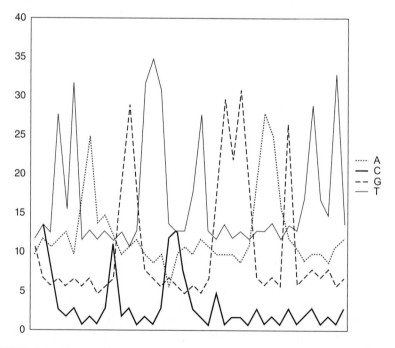

**FIGURE 9.2**    One graph for all four columns of data. It is difficult to identify the nucleotides corresponding to a consecutive sequence of peaks.

We can see that peaks of different nucleotides appear at different times. Unfortunately, it is very difficult to see the sequence of peaks because the intensities of the four frequencies vary in such different ranges. The C peaks occur at roughly the same level as the T troughs. This makes it very difficult to extract the information we need from the graph. We therefore need to **normalize** the data and scale each column's information so that peaks and troughs of each appear at roughly the same heights. That's not hard to do using current standard software, but since we're imagining this in the 1970s we need to write another program. It must normalize each column of data to establish maxima and minima at the same levels. You'll be asked for the formula in Exercise 9.1.

Figure 9.3 shows the result on our simplified dataset. The human researcher could conclude that the sequence for this piece of DNA was

CTTACGTCTGGAGTT
    1       234

The process is named "calling the sequence," and it is a good early example of cooperation between the experienced and skillful biologist and a far from perfect program analyzing perhaps noisy data. Notice that our call is by no means the

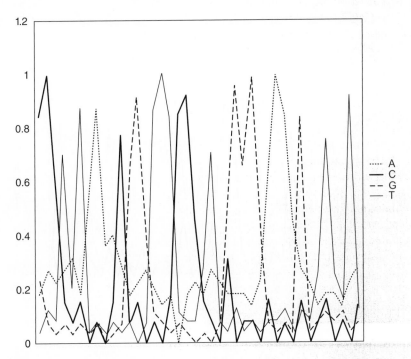

**FIGURE 9.3**    One graph for all four columns of normalized data. The sequence of bases is fairly discernible.

only possible reading of the data in the graph. As you scan Fig. 9.3 here are some legitimate questions raised by the data:

1. Could this be two successive A's or is it just one slightly fat A?
2. Is there a C peak ahead of this G peak?
3. Are we sure there are exactly two G peaks here?

This list is by no means exhaustive. Are the low C peaks just noise? Or are more real C nucleotides hiding there?

Sequence-calling software evolved along with improvements in the sequencing machines themselves. As the quality of the raw data improved, so did the opportunity for the base-calling software to succeed. By now, the programs are good enough to proceed with no human intervention. Not only do they do a good job of calling the bases, they actually associate a quality score with each of their calls. This quality score is based on such measurable quantities as the peak height, the distance between successive peaks, or the presence of multiple peaks in close proximity.

Perhaps our normalization procedure was too simplistic. Figure 9.4 shows the result of applying a transformation to the data that results in a mean of 0 and a standard deviation of 1 for the data in each column. Do you think that is better?

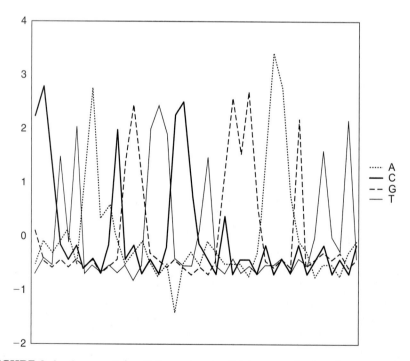

**FIGURE 9.4**   One graph for all four columns of data normalized to the same mean and standard deviation. The sequence of bases is readily discernible.

Do you think you could write software to call the bases unaided by any human expert?

## 9.1.2 Microarray Data Visualization

Microarrays are another example of the simultaneous evolution of software, human understanding, and technological developments to glean meaning from large datasets.

As discussed in Chapter 8, because studying the expression of one gene or even a few genes rarely captures the attention of grant reviewers, many researchers opt for whole-genome, system-wide studies instead. Unfortunately, carrying these studies to conclusion is rife with pitfalls and hurdles, not the least of which is the torrent of data produced by experiments. So much so that it seems devoid of any meaning. Fortunately, many data analysis tools are currently available, both free and commercial, to aid the researcher in transforming data into information and integrating that new information with current knowledge. The best of these tools use sophisticated data visualization techniques to help the researcher understand the data.

Recall the challenges with microarray datasets: they are large, they are noisy, and they are multidimensional. Today it is relatively easy to analyze thousands of variables at the same time but more difficult to gain insights into complex and dynamic biological processes from these data. Multivariate datasets are not unique to microarrays or even to biology. Indeed, they are also commonly found in physics, astronomy, geology, medicine, business, and the social sciences. In a lighter vein, multivariate analyses of baseball statistics are often featured in the national press. Think about using the same approach to analyzing data about the weather or stock market trends. What would you want to know? What are the challenges? Due to their size alone all of these datasets would be difficult to analyze without the help of computers. Another feature many large, multivariate datasets share is the way in which they are used. Typically, users of these datasets are explorers. That is, they are engaged in search activities in which the target may be undefined. We might not know which stocks will plummet after a devastating hurricane or which will soar after the Federal Reserve chairman speaks a few words before the Senate Banking Committee (although some people make their living claiming to know). We may not know which genes are important in the cell's defense against HIV attack. What is needed in all these circumstances is an open-ended, exploratory approach to multivariate data analysis. As discussed in Chapter 8, biologists often turn to computing techniques that allow them to discover relationships in microarray data without prior knowledge of what those relationships might be. Unsupervised clustering algorithms, such as hierarchical clustering, allow them to find groups based on the characteristics of the data alone. This is a useful first step but it is not usually sufficient to extract meaning from those groups; that is, to derive biological inferences.

The high dimensionality of the data makes it difficult to explore the many clusters, to find interesting patterns within those clusters, and to integrate any resultant biological knowledge. This is where data visualization tools come in.

## 9.1.3 Data Visualization Tools

A primary purpose of a data visualization tool is to provide domain-relevant insight into the data and support domain-specific data exploration strategies. Theoretically, the tool should allow an individual with expertise in a particular field to gain new insights and develop new hypotheses through data exploration and discovery [34]. This means that the developer of a visualization tool must understand the domain in which the tool is to be used. A developer in the field of biology, for instance, must understand how the biologist thinks and solves biological problems. How is a problem-solving task done and in what context? What other information will help elucidate the problem? Is a biologist similar to a computer scientist or a statistician in terms of experience, expertise, work habits, and error tolerance? Not surprisingly, some of the most innovative and effective visualization tools in bioinformatics have been designed by researchers in human computer interaction working with biologists and bioinformaticists. These teams have applied cognitive theory and understanding of human perception and problem-solving with analysis of biological tasks to create new visualization tools.[1]

### Sequence Visualization

The human genome sequence makes dull reading. It consists of about 3 billion base pairs. By comparison, let's work out how many letters occur in a typical novel.

One version of *The Picture of Dorian Gray* [41] extends over 193 pages. Each page has about 40 lines, and each line has about 60 characters. That makes a total of about 463,200 characters. To match the number of characters in the human genome, we would need about 6000 novels of the length of Oscar Wilde's 1890 gothic horror classic.

Put another way, if you could read one-novel's worth of the human genome every day, it would take you more than 17 years to get through the whole thing. That's assuming you could stay awake!

We need tools to help us visualize the information. The rate at which we humans can absorb information by scanning a scene is much faster than the speed with which we can read character-by-character. It is well established that the average person can recognize a face in about 170 milliseconds (ms). We don't need megapixel resolution to form a recognizable image of a human face. Let's conservatively estimate that 100-pixel resolution is adequate. On these assumptions, it seems that evolution has equipped us to process visual information at a rate of $100 \times 100$ units per 170 ms, or well over 50,000 units per second. By converting the human genome data into, say, 3 billion such visual units, we could

---

[1] See the resources in Section 9.1.4 for more information about such tools.

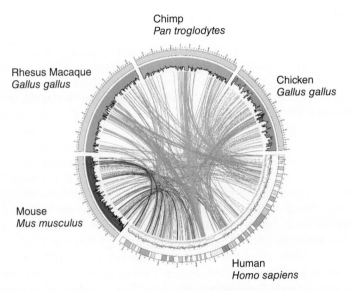

Chimp
*Pan troglodytes*

Rhesus Macaque
*Gallus gallus*

Chicken
*Gallus gallus*

Mouse
*Mus musculus*

Human
*Homo sapiens*

**FIGURE 9.5**   An image from Circos. This emphasizes gene similarities between human, rhesus monkey, chimp, chicken, and mouse genomes. Shaded arcs connect similar regions. Line charts and bar charts indicate the degree of similarities.
© M. Krzywinski (2005) Circos http://mkweb.bcgsc.ca/circos

expect to scan the whole thing in 51,000 seconds or slightly more than 14 hours. Contrast this with the 17 years it would take us to "read" the genome.

By contrast, computers are famously fast at processing character data and notoriously poor and slow at processing image data. A good solution is to have the computer process the raw character data of the genome into visual images for us humans to scan.

One such program developed in Canada by Martin Krzywinski is Circos [22]. Please visit the website to see the effectiveness of color in images like Figure 9.5. You will see the kind of visual image that can be produced by this freely distributed software. You will encounter more visualization tools as scientists recognize the need for help in absorbing and interpreting large datasets. The following two are currently in use for viewing genomic sequence data:

- Artemis (http://www.sanger.ac.uk/Software/Artemis/) is a free genome viewer and annotation tool written in Java and is available from the Sanger Institute of the Wellcome Trust.
- As mentioned earlier, the USCS Genome Browser is available at http://genome.ucsc.edu/

### Tools for Microarray Visualization

An example of a successful solution (albeit a continually improving one) to the microarray visualization problem is the Hierarchical Clustering Explorer (HCE) developed by Jinwook Seo and Ben Shneiderman in 2002 at the Human Computer Interaction Lab (HCIL) at the University of Maryland. This visualization tool, developed with a user-centered approach, extended and improved on the static visualization tools that were available at the time. Whereas a static tool allows researchers to visualize the outcome of hierarchical clustering via the dendrogram and employs useful visualization techniques such as color-coding, it falls short of supporting the biologists' needs for solving some important data analysis problems. Over more than three years of iterative development, Seo and Shneiderman have expanded the functionality of HCE based on users' needs [see following reference list 5–8]. This interactive tool allows researchers to explore clustering results and provides many useful visualization tools, including one-dimensional histograms, two-dimensional scatterplots, parallel coordinates, tabular views, and a gene ontology viewer, all as coordinated windows. Knowledge discovery strategies were investigated by interviewing users of high-dimensional data in many fields. Based on this, Seo and Shneiderman developed a set of guiding principles known as "graphics, ranking, and interaction for discovery" (GRID). GRID is a structured knowledge discovery strategy that supports analyses of multivariate datasets using low-dimensional projections. GRID is implemented in HCE and is known as the rank-by-feature framework. The basic idea is that the researcher starts with one-dimensional and then two-dimensional projections of the data (consider fewer variables at a time in order to find interesting patterns) and views them according to ranking criteria such as signal-to-noise ratios. Ordered one-dimensional histograms or two-dimensional scatterplots can then be interactively explored and integrated with other useful information through use of features such as the Gene Ontology viewer. Case studies of HCE in use by researchers have shown the rank-by-feature framework to be an effective support of the biologists' problem-solving strategies.

The HCIL Website (http://www.cs.umd.edu/hcil/) chronicles the history of HCE development. Related papers on visualization problems not limited to microarray or bioinformatics data, such as papers on the visualization of a variety of types of network, are also available. Another success in the campaign to help people visualize complex datasets is prefuse (prefuse.org), an extensible software framework developed by user interface research groups at the University of California at Berkeley, Xerox PARC, and the University of Washington [11]. Data modeling, visualization, and interaction can all be supported easily using the prefuse toolkit at http://prefuse.org.

### 9.1.4  Over to You

**Exercise 9.1**    If you take a set of numbers lying within an arbitrary range, say from $x_{min}$ to $x_{max}$, and subtract $x_{min}$ from each, you obtain a transformed set whose range is from 0 to some upper limit. What is that upper limit? Now if you divide each of the transformed numbers by that upper limit you obtain a set of numbers each of which lies between 0 and 1. Effectively what you have done is to *normalize* the original set of numbers to the range 0 to 1. Write a program to normalize a set of integers.

Visualization tools to aid the scientist in relating gene expression and other types of genomic data to knowledge about biological networks and pathways constitute another area of ongoing research and development in bioinformatics. For example, GenMapp (http:www.genmapp.org) and PathDb (http://www.intl-pag.org/8/abstracts/pag8684.html) are two such tools that have evolved to allow the visualization of varied data types in the context of multiple, user-defined or user-selected networks or pathways. For this project your tasks are

**Exercise 9.2**

1. Investigate the implementation of one or more network/pathway visualization tools.
2. Create a small prototype tool of your own.

The tool you investigate need not be for biological data, although that is okay, too. Start with some of the papers and Websites provided in this section and do whatever exploration is needed to develop an understanding of the computing technologies and methods used. Develop a small sample set of data, along with some gene ontology or network data. Use these to implement a prototype visualization tool that allows the user to input, visualize, and explore biological relationships.

## 9.1.5  Resources for Visualization

1. K. D. Dahlquist, N. Salomonis, K. Vranizan, et al. GenMAPP, a new tool for viewing and analyzing microarray data on biological pathways. *Nat Genet,* 1:19–20, 2002.

   *The original paper describing the conceptual framework for the GenMapp tool.*

2. Jeffrey Heer, Stuart K. Card, and James A. Landay. Prefuse: A toolkit for interactive information visualization, CHI '05: Proceedings of the SIGCHI conference on human factors in computing systems, ACM Press, ISBN 1-58113-998-5, 421–430, 2005.

   *Description of a usable Java-based tool for visualization.*

3. H. Javahery, A. Seah, and T. Radhakrishnan. Beyond power: Making bioinformatics tools user-centered. *Comm ACM,* 47:59–63, 2004.

   *An overview of the need for and value of user-centered design approaches for bioinformatics tool development. Provides several examples of tools developed with UCD.*

4. P. Saraiya, C. North, and K. Duca. An evaluation of microarray visualization tools for biological insight. *IEEE Trans Vis Comput Graph,* 11:443–456, 2005.

   *An empirical evaluation of five microarray visualization tools. The authors identify and quantify several characteristics of "insight" as a means of evaluating and comparing tools.*

5.  J. Seo and B. Shneiderman. Interactively exploring hierarchical clustering results. *Computer,* 35:80–86, 2002.

*The original paper describing the development of the HCE tool. Provides motivation for dynamic visualizations of microarray data.*

6.  J. Seo, M. Bakau, Y-W. Chen, et al. Interactively optimizing signal-to-noise ratios in expression profiling: Project-specific algorithm selection and detection p-value weighting in Affymetrix microarrays. *Bioinformatics,* 20:2534–2544, 2004.

*Description of a ranking feature used in HCE. This paper describes the idea that different mRNA profiling projects have varying sources and degrees of confounding noise which alter the choice of a specific probe set algorithm.*

7.  J. Seo and B. Shneiderman. A rank-by-feature framework for interactive exploration of multidimensional data. *Info Vis,* 4:99–113, 2005.

*Describes the support of knowledge discovery based on the GRID principles.*

8.  J. Seo and B. Shneiderman. Knowledge discovery in high dimensional data: Case studies and a user survey for the rank-by-feature framework. *IEEE Trans Vis Comput Graph,* 12:311–322, 2006.

*Evaluation of the HCE tool by users of high-dimensional data in diverse fields. Highlights tool features and demonstrates evaluation methodologies.*

## 9.2  RNA STRUCTURE AND FUNCTION PREDICTION

Much of the material in this book covers the use of computers to find and analyze signals embedded in DNA, RNA, or protein sequences. Since sequences contain most of the information content of a cell, it seems reasonable to focus our computational efforts in this area. However, keep in mind that the cell is more than a package for retaining information. Because cells carry out many complex activities to ensure their survival they rely on large molecules such as proteins to interact with one another in specific ways. So if we wish to truly model the ways in which cells work, we must look beyond the one-dimensional level of sequence information by considering the two- and three-dimensional **structure** of a molecule.

The three-dimensional structure, or shape, of a molecule is critical for determining its function in a biological context. As a result, biologists almost always talk about structure and function in the same breath. What they mean is that if we can identify the structure of a molecule, we almost immediately have a very good sense of its likely function.

To understand why this is the case, consider a simple example from a different realm. Archaeologists specialize in identifying artifacts from long-departed societies. They use these objects to conjecture about the ways in which those societies worked. When an archaeologist uncovers a settlement with many large jars, the shape of the jars can provide insights into what kind of goods could be stored in them. Low, flat jars were likely to hold grain, but jars with spouts were likely to be used to pour liquids. In other words, the structure of a jar indicates its likely *function*. Of course, we need to back up our ideas about the uses of the jars by considering other factors. If we know that the region around the settlement was especially good for growing grapes or wheat, we might be able to make more specific guesses about the function of a given set of jars. On the other hand, we cannot discount the possibility that what we consider "reasonable guesses" are in fact completely off track. For example, we could be looking at a society of practical jokers who put their rice in tall, fluted jars with spouts because it provided entertainment when a thirsty person tipped the grain out into a cup.

Where archaeologists consider jars and pots, biologists look at cellular machines: proteins, RNAs, and other molecules. The idea is that the shape of the molecule, its structure, dictates its function. In the same way that an archaeologist might argue that a jar with a spout would contain liquids, a biologist will argue that a protein with a rotary component is likely to be part of a cellular motor. Usually, the archaeologist is right about the spouted jar, and the biologist is right about the rotor protein. But we must always remember that evolution can be a prankster too.

## 9.2.1  Solving Structures for Functional RNAs: Early Successes

In Chapter 2 we introduced the idea of protein structure, but RNAs also exhibit a structure when the single-stranded molecules fold up on themselves through basepairing. Unlike proteins, which can form structures through many different types of bonds, most RNA structures are entirely the result of base-pairing. Because the structures are formed by specific interactions among the nucleotides, these interactions produce what is known as **secondary structure.** We will discuss the higher levels of structure, tertiary and quaternary structure, in Project 9.3.

Why are we talking about structure in RNAs? Isn't the function of RNA to act as a go-between, carrying information from DNA to protein as stated in the central dogma? The answer, like many things in biology, starts with, "Yes but. . ." Yes, a certain type of RNA, known as messenger RNA (mRNA) does indeed carry information copied from the DNA and directs the synthesis of proteins. But this is just one type of RNA. The cell has many other kinds of RNAs. In fact, mRNA makes up only about 1% of the total RNA content of a cell. The rest of the RNAs in a cell also play important roles in the translation of proteins and in many other cellular activities. These RNAs, sometimes referred to as structural RNAs, are tiny machines in their own right. Although they are made up of RNA, their structure drives their ability to do the work of the cell.

One of the most distinctive and well-studied examples of RNA structure is that of transfer RNA. Transfer RNA (tRNA) acts like a decoder ring, matching up nucleotide triplets on the mRNA with the appropriate amino acid during translation of the mRNA (see Chapter 2). The structure of the tRNA not only allows it to serve its function as a decoder, it is also critical for enabling the ribosome, the translation machine within the cell, to recognize the tRNA.

Given how important tRNAs are for cellular function, developing computational approaches to predicting their structure might seem reasonable. However, why is this needed? After all, we already know how the structure looks. The answer is that although we know how tRNAs look, we need to be able to locate them within the genome.

The challenge of finding RNA genes in a genome is threefold. First, because these genes do not code for proteins, many of the features we discussed in Chapter 7 are not applicable in this instance. For example, RNA genes do not have to contain start and stop codons. Indeed, RNA does not always follow the pattern of retaining the triple-nucleotide codon. Secondly, many RNA genes vary greatly at the sequence level, even if they all generate the same or similar structures. This may in part be because the selection pressure to retain a conserved sequence is not crucial as long as the structure remains conserved over time. Finally, most RNA genes tend to be small, and, in a surprising twist, are often found within the introns of other, protein-coding genes. These three aspects of RNA genes make them especially tricky to identify.

One method for identifying many classes of RNAs is to use structure to find the genes in a genome. It has been especially successful with the tRNAs because of their distinctive, well-conserved structure. An added advantage is that many tRNA genes do have some sequence conservation as well. Several algorithms have been developed to find tRNA structures in a given sequence. Most begin by comparing a putative tRNA sequence with known sequences to gauge the likelihood that the gene of interest is a tRNA gene. Following this, at least one method uses a hidden Markov model (HMM, see Chapter 7) to check whether the sequence can fold into the classic tRNA shape [6]. As you can see in Figure 9.6, the tRNA structure involves four regions of strong base-pairing, known as stems. Three of the stems end in a loop area, and the fourth ends with the distinctive nucleotide sequence that allows for amino acid attachment. So an algorithm can check to see if the sequence supports base-pairing in the areas where the stems should occur. The final step of the analysis is to check whether the sequence, when folded, would be thermodynamically stable. We will return to this issue in Section 9.2.3.

In terms of complexity, the prediction of the tRNA structure and its use in gene finding are probably the easiest problems to solve. In the next sections, we will consider the prediction of RNA structures for many different RNA genes, some of which are not nearly as well conserved or well understood as the tRNA. The success of RNA structure prediction in tRNAs stands as a small triumph in the structure prediction world, but it is just the tip of the structure–function iceberg.

## 9.2.2  Structural RNAs and Gene Regulation

An area of research that has dramatically expanded of late is the study of functional RNAs and their effect on gene regulation. Specifically, it now appears

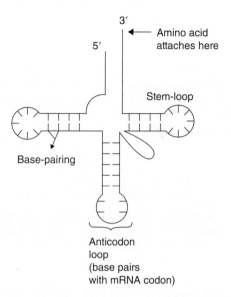

**FIGURE 9.6**   The structure of the tRNA forms a distinctive "cloverleaf" shape with four stem regions and three loops. The loop at the "bottom" of the structure contains the anticodon that will base pair with the appropriate codon in the mRNA. The 3' end of the tRNA sequence includes a distinctive set of nucleotides (the acceptor arm) that allow for binding to the correct amino acid.

that a variety of RNAs are actually involved in regulating when and how often a protein-coding gene is expressed. In most of these cases, the structure of the RNA is critical to its ability to regulate gene expression. In addition, as in the case of tRNAs, finding the genes that encode these RNAs requires searching the genome for structural rather than sequence conservation.

A relatively simple example comes from the viral regulation of gene expression in HIV. Several of the mRNAs that are generated by HIV have a special RNA secondary structure known as the Rev responsive element (RRE). This region allows the mRNA to bind to an HIV protein known as Rev. Rev helps transport these mRNAs from the nucleus, where they are synthesized, to the cytoplasm where they can be translated. The presence of the RRE structure is critical for the mRNAs that encode the viral capsid proteins. If these mRNAs are not translated, the virus cannot assemble new particles to spread to other cells. So in the absence of the RRE structure or the Rev protein, the virus stalls inside the first cell it enters.

The RRE is a distinctive structure. The key aspect seems to be a double stem around an internal loop. The Rev protein appears to bind to this region as a way of identifying the viral mRNA. This structure may also help keep the mRNA attached to the Rev protein as it is transported out of the nucleus. So the structure of the RRE serves two important functions: identification and a creation of a latch-on region for transport. Not much is known about the exact mechanics of the RRE–Rev interaction, but it is an area of active research [2].

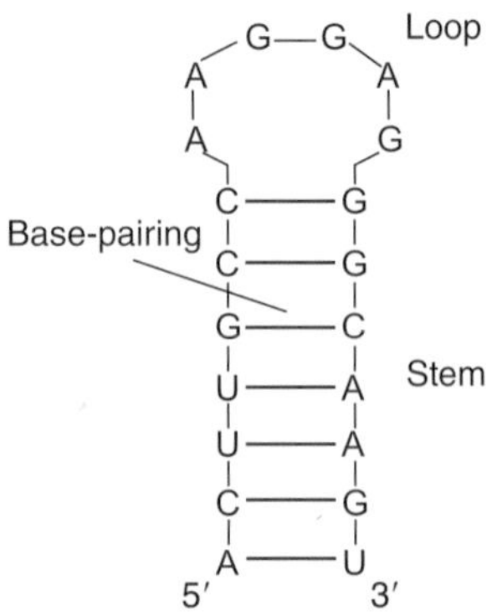

**FIGURE 9.7**   The typical hairpin structure of a RNA has two portions: a stem part where base-pairing occurs and a loop section where nucleotides are not paired. In miRNAs, the two halves of the miRNA gene base pair to form the stem region. A small section in the center of the gene yields the loop region.

Many viruses in the same family as HIV use RRE type signals to regulate the expression of their mRNAs. A recent computational survey of these viral genomes has yielded a large collection of putative RRE structures [23]. This represents an interesting example of how the computational prediction of RNA secondary structure can further our understanding of a biological structure and its putative function.

### Gene Regulation by RNAs in Higher Eukaryotes

The regulation of genes by RNA structures in HIV is perhaps not so surprising. Since HIV has a RNA genome, we might expect that many of its gene-regulatory operations would be adapted to take advantage of the RNA world. However, the recent discovery of regulatory RNAs in higher eukaryotes including humans suggests that such strategies are commonplace in organisms across the spectrum of life.

Researchers have identified a class of small, structural RNAs that may be involved in gene regulation. These RNAs, collectively known as microRNAs (miRNA), are found in humans. The miRNA transcript is about 70 nucleotides long, and once it is synthesized, it forms a simple hairpin structure (Figure 9.7). This hairpin structure is then cut, and a small fragment of about 20 to 25 nucleotides is released. The small fragment is the active miRNA. These short sequences are complementary to the 3′ ends of mRNAs that code for a variety of proteins. When the miRNA binds to the 3′ end of the mRNA, it can inhibit protein translation or trigger changes in the mRNA that affect protein synthesis. As a result, miRNAs can dramatically alter the production of a given protein. MicroRNAs seem to have a role in cancer as well, with some very aggressive tumors exhibiting many more miRNAs than normal cells. This is an area of active research, however, so there are still many unanswered questions about miRNAs, their role in healthy cells, and their potential role in disease [27]. Exercise 9.4 asks you how you might find miRNA genes within a genome.

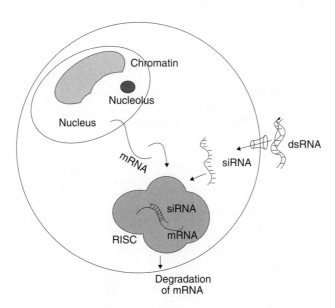

**FIGURE 9.8**   Small interfering RNAs (siRNAs) work by finding complementary sequences within the target mRNA. They base pair with these mRNAs, which triggers degradation through a complex known as the RNA-inducing silencing complex (RISC). The end result is that the mRNA is chopped up into small fragments rather than being translated.

MicroRNAs are actually just one member of a class of small RNAs that seem to be involved in gene regulation in eukaryotes. In plants and some lower eukaryotes, small interfering RNAs (siRNAs) can be used to eliminate expression of a given gene (Figure 9.8). This is known as RNA interference, or RNAi. In plants, researchers have been able to use siRNA to specifically target genes and exquisitely tweak their expression. They can almost play genes like a piano—sometimes dampening expression to negligible levels, then letting it ramp back up, then down again, and so on. They are able to do this because siRNAs are simply short stretches of RNA that are the reverse complement of the mRNA that a gene produces. If you add a specially designed siRNA to a plant cell, it finds its complementary mRNA, binds to it, and shuts down protein translation. If you wait for a while, the siRNA degrades, and gene expression surges back up. At which point, you can reintroduce the siRNA and snap the lid on expression again. Figure 9.8 shows how siRNAs might work.

To understand how siRNAs can shut down gene expression, we need to digress for a moment to talk about viruses. As you know from Chapter 2, many viruses including HIV have RNA genomes. When the RNA genome of a virus enters the cell, it hijacks the translation apparatus of the cell and uses it to make viral proteins. Cells have evolved ways to combat viral infection, chief among which is to be "on the lookout" for unusual RNA structures that might indicate the presence of a viral genome.

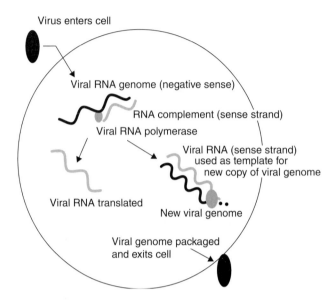

**FIGURE 9.9**   This schematic summarizes very briefly the life cycle of RNA viruses that have a negative sense genome. In order to make its proteins and replicate its genome, a negative sense virus must first generate the complement RNA. This sense strand serves two functions: it is the mRNA from which proteins are translated, and it is also the template for replication of the viral genome.

Viral RNA genomes can be either single- or double-stranded. HIV, for example, has a single-stranded RNA genome. The single-stranded RNA genome contains the coding sequences that need to be translated, and ribosomes translate this RNA strand as if it were mRNA. The problem is that ribosomes move in just one direction: starting at the 5′ end and heading toward the 3′ end of an RNA sequence. When the viral genes are organized in such a way that a ribosome can proceed in the 5′-to-3′ direction and actually translate the genes, the virus is said to have a "sense strand" genome. However, some RNA viruses have a different arrangement: their genes occur in the reverse orientation, requiring that a complementary copy of the RNA be made first before translation. They are known as "negative sense strand" viruses. These viruses use specialized RNA polymerases to make a complementary copy of their genome that contains the correct orientation for the translatable genes.

The upshot is that in the process of generating the complementary mRNA, there is a phase when the viral RNA polymerase generates double-stranded RNA (dsRNA) molecules. Figure 9.9 shows a brief summary of the life cycle of RNA viruses and why dsRNA is a critical step in the replication of the virus. Since dsRNA almost never occurs in normal, uninfected plant cells, the sudden appearance of such a construct triggers the plant's immune response. It targets the dsRNA for immediate degradation, thereby destroying the viral genome and its ability to further damage the cell.

With RNAi, researchers basically co-opt this mechanism to target specific genes for down-regulation. They generate complementary sequences to the mRNAs of the gene, and then inject those sequences, the siRNAs, into the plant cell. The plant then responds as if it has been infected by a virus, targeting both the siRNA and its complementary mRNA sequence in the double-stranded portion for degradation. In the process, it destroys the mRNA for the gene that was targeted, and, as a result, the gene's expression is suppressed. Because siRNAs are susceptible to degradation even when they are not in a double-stranded configuration, over time the cell clears out any remaining siRNAs. Eventually gene expression of the targeted gene regains its former level as the unused siRNAs are cleared out [5, 26].

What makes RNAi so attractive is that it offers researchers a simple, reversible, and exquisitely targeted suppressor of gene expression. Because siRNAs degrade over time, the cell's gene expression is not permanently altered. But for short periods a gene's protein products can be completely eradicated from the cell. Some pharmaceutical agents can stall protein synthesis in cells, but most of these drugs are broad-spectrum, turning off protein synthesis altogether. In contrast, siRNA can target a specific gene so that only its product is affected. The rest of the cell's activities continue unabated. These properties of siRNAs have made them very attractive to researchers trying to design drugs to treat a variety of diseases from genetic disorders to cancer [33].

RNAi presents some problems, however, as a therapy. Chief among these is that humans have a specialized signaling pathway, known as the interferon-signaling pathway, that is designed to spot dsRNAs. Whenever dsRNA is encountered, cells shut down all transcription and translation. They also signal to neighboring cells to shut down their transcription. The interferon system is present in animals including humans, and it is the corollary of the plant immune response to viral infection. The problem is that while plants target dsRNA for degradation, they do not shut down overall translation activity in the cell. The interferon pathway, in contrast, basically triggers complete cellular shutdown for a few hours or even days. So even though the siRNA targets a specific gene the unfortunate consequence is that it effectively shuts down cells altogether. Some promising new directions for siRNA research might one day find a path around the interferon obstacle, but for now, siRNA therapy in humans seems a more distant hope [5, 33].

Healthy cells also seem to use siRNAs to regulate their genes. This has been demonstrated in plants (where it is called post-transcriptional gene silencing, or PTGS) and in some eukaryotes including worms and fruit flies [26]. So it is possible that siRNAs are already a part of the arsenal of gene-regulatory methods that cells use to control gene expression and protein synthesis.

## 9.2.3   RNA Structures in Machines: Solving Complex Structures

So far, we have considered relatively simple secondary structures such as stems, loops, and hairpins. The algorithmic solutions to finding these structures are relatively straightforward. The challenge is to predict the structures of much more complex molecules.

One of the most complex structures involving RNA is the ribosome. This cellular machine translates proteins by linking tRNAs with their respective codons and then creating the special peptide bond that connects the amino acids brought to the site by the tRNAs. The ribosome is a complex mix of proteins and RNAs, but the key steps in the translation process are all handled by RNAs within the ribosome. Current research suggests that the critical function of peptide bond formation is catalyzed entirely by a single RNA—a **ribozyme.**

A number of other RNAs also show catalytic activity. For example, the splicing of introns from mRNA relies on RNA–protein complexes called small nuclear ribonucleoprotein particles (snRNPs) (see Chapter 2). As with the ribosome, the structure of specific RNAs within the snRNPs enables splicing to occur. Like the ribosomal RNAs, the RNA components of the splicing machinery are able to accomplish their function because of their unique structures.

### Solving Structures Through Minimum Free Energy

To solve the structures of these more complex molecules, we cannot rely solely on context-free grammars such as HMMs or sequence conservation. Rather, we must consider the physical and chemical properties of the RNA sequence and take these into consideration as we develop a prediction.

The first law of thermodynamics states that energy must be added to a system for it to do work. This seems about as obvious a statement as one could make, but it has some interesting consequences for our purposes. The measure of the amount of energy available to do work in a system is known as **free energy.** The free energy of a system is expendable, and it is ruled by the second law of thermodynamics. That law states that over time, systems tend toward entropy. In other words, a system devolves into chaos over time unless energy is put into the system to maintain order.

What does all this have to do with RNA structure? It turns out that, like all other physical systems, an RNA strand requires a finite amount of energy to maintain a particular shape. In the absence of that energy, the RNA strand will lapse into some simpler structure that does not require as much energy to maintain. The state with the least energy, of course, would be free nucleotides. Given enough time and a closed system where new energy cannot be added, the laws of thermodynamics predict that an RNA structure will eventually fall apart into its constituent nucleotides. However, long before an RNA strand disassembles, it can find certain structures and configurations that require a small amount of energy to maintain but not so much that it is impossible to retain the structure for an extended time. This known as the **minimum free energy configuration.** We say that molecules in their minimum free energy configuration are stable.

We can use this configuration to determine the structure of a given RNA sequence by assuming that an RNA structure is necessary for a given function. It is therefore in the cell's best interest to develop a structure that can be stable long enough to accomplish its task. Stability in the complex chemical soup that is the cell's interior requires that the molecule maintain its structure with the smallest possible input of energy. This ensures that the structure is not easily perturbed by small changes in the environment that might be the consequence of other, unrelated processes. What are the properties of such a structure? They are similar to, if not identical to, those of the minimum free energy configuration. Therefore, to predict the structure of an RNA sequence, we start by determining what the free energy is for each of thousands of possible structures. We then select the few shapes that require the least energy to maintain their configuration. One of these is the RNA structure we seek. In other words, *the structure that requires the least energy to maintain is the biologically relevant structure.*

The idea is simple. It requires more energy to form an open-ended loop than one that comes together to form a stem. This is because the base-pairing in the stem region increases stability and reduces the amount of energy needed to keep the structure intact. Similarly, a hairpin is more stable than a structure that tries to force every nucleotide on one side into a base-paired arrangement with a nucleotide on the other side. Some nucleotides simply can't base pair with each other, and forcing them right next to each other requires a good deal more energy than letting them drift apart in a loop.

This is where the idea and logic stop being so simple. The rules that govern how much energy is required to maintain a particular structure are incredibly complex and detailed. The good news for us is that most of the hard work of determining the amount of energy required to keep a particular string of nucleotides in a given shape has already been done.

What remains now is applying that information to structure prediction. To predict a structure, these rules about the amount of energy required for base-pairing and loop-and-stem formation are applied iteratively across a given RNA sequence. Computing every possible structure, however, is a difficult problem. Exercise 9.4 introduced you to some of the difficulties, even when we placed severe limits on the nature of the targets of our search. The number of possible structures is overwhelming when considering RNA sequences for complex RNAs such as the ribosomal RNAs. For the challenge we face here we need a shortcut through all possible structures to those most likely to minimize free energy.

The challenge here is remarkably similar to a problem we discussed earlier. In Chapter 5 we presented the problem of aligning two sequences and encountered the same challenge of finding an optimal solution without necessarily testing every combination of a query sequence with every member of a database of possible matching sequences. In that instance, we used dynamic programming to solve smaller parts of the problem and thereby approximate the optimal solution. The same approach has been used in RNA structure prediction. Using dynamic programming, we can search for some of the configurations that likely minimize free energy. We do this by filling a dynamic programming matrix not with scores for gaps, matches, and mismatches as we did in Chapter 5 but with scores for the amount of energy required to maintain a small section of the sequence in a given structure. By combining these small sections using the traceback of the dynamic programming matrix, we can identify a structure that is likely to minimize the overall free energy. We presume that this structure is then the biologically relevant one.

The original implementation of this approach, known as mfold, continues to dominate the field. Other approaches have been developed, but they tend to draw on mfold. For example, more recent algorithms use a graph theory approach to identify the minimum free energy structure and, of course, if something is known about the structure, then a context-free grammar can sometimes succeed in conjunction with minimizing free energy. Some of the references at the end of this project section will help you explore these other methods in more detail.

### Problems with the Minimum Free Energy Approach

How effective is this approach in predicting the structure of an RNA? It depends. The overall accuracy of these methods depends heavily on the evaluation set of sequences. When these sequences have relatively straightforward structures, such as those of the tRNAs, then the minimum free energy approach works extremely well. However, the longer and more complex a RNA sequence, the greater the likelihood that this approach fails to identify a relevant structure.

It is difficult to know why some sequences yield accurate predictions and others prove unproductive. At least four sources of error seem to be associated with the prediction of RNA structures using the minimum free energy approach. First, it is possible that the energy measurements for a particular base-pairing or structure are incorrect or not entirely reliable. Although every effort may be made to determine the exact energy required, making the actual experimental measurements is still something of an art as well as a science. As a result, the very first step of the algorithm, the calculation of the free energy of a given section of the sequence, may prove its undoing.

Second, having calculated a structure based on minimizing the free energy of the components of the sequence, the traceback through the dynamic programming matrix can yield more than one reasonable solution. The question then becomes, which of these possible solutions is the biologically correct one? Initially, methods such as mfold selected whichever structure seemed to require the absolute least free energy, but these predictions were rarely the biologically relevant ones. As a result, mfold now reports several structures, highlighting the configuration that has the least free energy, but also listing numerous "suboptimal" configurations. Sometimes the biologically relevant structure is found in these alternative structures.

This leads to the third problem with predicting structure by minimizing free energy. The argument can be made that structures probably evolve that require little energy to maintain their shape, but sometimes the longevity of a structure is not critical. For example, a component of a cellular machine may need to acquire a structure for just a fraction of a second to accomplish its function. After that, it might lapse into some other shape that does not require as much energy to maintain. In other words, there is no reason to expect that the **biologically active** configuration is the same as the one with the least energy. As a result, what is predicted by a minimum free energy approach may not have any correlation to the functional version of the RNA in the cell.

The final source of error is that some structures involve complex overlapping sections of the sequence that are difficult to model using a dynamic programming approach. One of the fundamental assumptions of the dynamic programming matrix is that a given nucleotide or set of nucleotides will be involved in just one structural component. However, this is not always the case. Chief among such structures is something known as the pseudoknot, the bane of RNA structure prediction in general. A **pseudoknot** is a double stem loop in which the first stem's loop forms part of the stem of a second stem loop. Because the loop and stem overlap, the nucleotides involved in the pseudoknot cannot be modeled in a traditional dynamic programming table. One way around this is to use a stochastic context-free grammar rather than dynamic programming to develop the structure. Alternatively, we can modify the dynamic programming scoring scheme to accommodate overlapping segments of structures. Both approaches have been reasonably successful. However, pseudoknots remain a very difficult problem for any RNA structure prediction approach to solve.

## 9.2.4  Over to You

### Project Activity

One solution to some of the challenges inherent with a pure minimum free energy approach uses hints from sequence conservation. Earlier, we said that many RNA genes have poorly conserved sequences. However, although two related RNA sequences are rarely identical, they often show a consensus. That is, although one sequence might have AGGA and the other GAGA, we might notice that these sequences are exclusively made up of purines (As and Gs). Since purines share certain chemical properties as well as certain preferences for base-pairing, the overall structural interactions possible will be similar for both sequences. In other words, although the sequences do not match exactly, the *properties* of the nucleotides in each sequence are generally similar. We can use these conserved properties of the sequence to help guide our structure prediction. Some of the references to this area of research are listed [7, 12, 14, 25, 32]. These papers will provide you with more insight into the algorithms that utilize sequence conservation to guide the prediction of RNA structures. Develop a description of these algorithms and methods and present this information in the form of a term paper or presentation to the class.

Explore the following hypothetical question: Do any cellular RNAs have RRE-like structures? What features would an RNA sequence need to form this distinctive structure? How might you determine such a structure given these sequence features?

**Exercise 9.3**

**Exercise 9.4**

Recall that an miRNA gene typically arises from a fragment that is approximately 70 nucleotides long, in which strict base-pairing occurs from the ends of the stretch extending inward to reach an inner portion that forms the loop portion of the hairpin. For this exercise, we assume that possible miRNA genes consist of a stretch of between 60 and 80 nucleotides, with strict base-pairing occurring from the ends except for a loop section between 2 and 8 nucleotides long.

1. Write a program to input an RNA sequence $s_1 s_2 \ldots s_n$. Your output must list pairs $(i_1, j_1)(i_2, j_2) \ldots (i_k, j_k)$, for which each $(i, j)$ pair corresponds to an miRNA gene candidate. Specifically:

   - $60 \leq j - i \leq 80$
   - $s_{i+p}$ is the complement of $s_{j-p}$ for each value of $p$ from 0 to $q$, where
   - $2 \leq j - i - 2q \leq 8$

2. Estimate the running time of your program as a function of $n$.

## 9.2.5  Resources for Structure Prediction

### General References and Reviews

1. Paul P. Gardner and Robert Giegerich. A comprehensive comparison of comparative RNA structure prediction approaches, BMC Bioinformatics, 5:140, 2004. http://www.biomedcentral.com/1471-2105/5/140

   *Excellent review of many different RNA prediction programs and their comparative strengths and weaknesses.*

2. Michael Zuker. Calculating nucleic acid secondary structure, *Curr Opin Struct Biol*, 10:303–310, 2000.

   *The original developer of mfold has produced a comprehensive review of RNA secondary structure and the many approaches to predicting these structures. This is probably the best resource for references to the primary literature and a comprehensive overview of the approaches, successes, and problems in the field. It is also, consequently, rather dense and somewhat difficult to access for the novice in the field. We recommend that you consider some of the other references in this list first, and once familiar with the area, plunge into this exegesis on RNA and DNA secondary structure.*

### tRNA Structure Prediction

1. Sean R. Eddy and Richard Durbin. RNA sequence analysis using covariance models. *Nucleic Acids Res*, 22:2079–2088, 1994.

   *One of the original papers that proposed a strategy for identifying tRNA genes in a genome, this paper is a classic in the field.*

## HIV RRE-Rev Interactions

1. K. Boris-Lawrie, T. M. Roberts T.M., and S. Hull S. Retroviral RNA elements integrate components of post-transcriptional gene expression. *Life Sci,* 69:2697–709, 2001.

   *This article is a more focused description of the biology of the Rev-RRE interaction and its role in HIV infections of cells.*

2. E. A. Lesnik, R. Sampath, and D. J. Ecker. Rev response elements (RRE) in lentiviruses: An RNAMotif algorithm-based strategy for RRE prediction. *Med Res Rev,* 22:617–636, 2002.

   *This paper describes a simple approach to predicting the secondary structure known as RRE (Rev response element) used by HIV to transport certain mRNAs out of the nucleus of infected cells. The exercise included in this project was inspired by the work done here.*

## MicroRNAs, Small Interfering RNAs, and RNA Interference

1. http://www.ncbi.nlm.nih.gov/books/bv.fcgi?rid=coffeebrk.chapter.33

   *More about microRNAs, small interfering RNAs, and RNA interference can be found through the short description and links here.*

2. Derek M. Dykxhoorn, Carl D. Novina, and Philip A. Sharp. Killing the messenger: Short RNAs that silence gene expression. *Nat Rev,* 4:457–465, 2003.

   *A detailed look at siRNA and RNAi from a biological perspective. This article is particularly commended by the wealth of references to the primary biological literature.*

3. Richard Robinson. RNAi therapeutics: How likely, how soon?" *PLoS Biol,* 2(1): e28, 2004.

   *An elegant review of the state of RNAi therapy to date, this review is more accessible to nonbiologists.*

4. Marjori A. Matzke and J. M. Antonius. Planting the seeds of a new paradigm. *PLoS Biol,* 2(5): e133, 2004.

   *A good introductory review of RNA interference in plants, and the contributions that plant researchers have made to the RNAi and siRNA fields. This is particularly recommended as a very easy introduction to the area for nonbiologists.*

## Original Papers on Structure Prediction Methods

1. Michael Zuker. On finding all suboptimal foldings of an RNA molecule. *Science,* 244:48–52, 1989.

   *This article describes the mfold algorithm in good detail.*

2. E. Rivas and S. Eddy. A dynamic programming algorithm for RNA structure prediction including pseudoknots. *J Mol Biol,* 285:2053–2068, 1999.

   *For a look at the best approach to predicting pseudoknots in RNA sequences using a variant on the standard dynamic programming approach to minimizing free energy, consider this article.*

3. Robert Gigerich, Bjorn Voss, Marc Rehmsmeier. Abstract shapes of RNA. *Nucleic Acids Res,* 32:4843–4851, 2004.
   http://nar.oxfordjournals.org/cgi/content/full/32/16/4843

   *This article suggests a different kind of approach to RNA structure prediction by classifying predicted structures into classes of shape. This simplifies the evaluation of the many structures generated by RNA structure prediction programs.*

# 9.3  RATIONAL DRUG DESIGN THROUGH PROTEIN STRUCTURE AND FUNCTION PREDICTION

## 9.3.1  A Pharmaceutical Fairy Tale

Once upon a late twentieth century decade, chemists at a major pharmaceutical company were working with a set of compounds that might be useful in controlling high blood pressure. The compounds were involved in a newly discovered signaling pathway that used the gas nitric oxide (NO). Cells release this gas into their vicinity, triggering the dilation (opening up) of blood vessels. The set of compounds the chemists were studying could mimic the effect of NO, causing blood vessels to dilate. The chemists theorized that by dilating the blood vessels, these compounds might reduce blood pressure. This in turn would make it easier for the heart to pump the blood and prevent the formation of clots. Clot formation is often a precursor to a heart attack or stroke. Since heart disease is one of the top killers of Americans every year, the potential to make a life-saving and very profitable drug was enormous.

After much study, a single compound that came to be known as sildenafil was selected for development as a drug to manage heart problems. The first step in evaluating its efficacy was to study its effects in research animals. Animal models are often used to evaluate the toxicity of a drug; many compounds are very effective at a local level, but have devastating systemic (across the body) effects.[2] So the first step in studying the effects of the drug was to inject it into mice and see what effect, if any, it had on the mouse's heart and blood vessels.

Unfortunately for the pharmaceutical company, the drug did not seem to elicit a sufficient response in mice. Some general blood vessel dilation did occur, but not nearly enough to help treat high blood pressure. It seemed that sildenafil would join the countless other compounds on the pharmaceutical junk heap. Then, an observant technician noticed something. The mice being treated with sildenafil might not have lower blood pressure, but unlike their counterparts receiving a placebo, they seemed pretty active. In fact, it looked for all the world like they were maybe having a little bit too much fun in their cages.

---

[2] One such example, the antibiotic Neosporin (a compound containing three other antibiotics: bacitracin, neomycin, and polymyxin B) found in over-the-counter antibiotic creams is a very effective antibiotic when applied on the skin. However, taken as a pill, it is deadly.

Further study, including clinical trials in humans, proved that sildenafil would never be a good medication for treating high blood pressure, but it did dilate the blood vessels of the male penis, helping men to achieve and maintain an erection. The pharmaceutical company was Pfizer, and the drug developed from sildenafil was Viagra. It went on to be a blockbuster drug, generating over a billion dollars in revenues for Pfizer and setting off an entire industry, not only in pharmaceuticals but in spam advertisements for variants of the drug.

## 9.3.2  Drug Development: One in a Million Chances

The story of the discovery of sildenafil's ancillary properties may seem to fit more into the realm of urban legend than scientific fact. Surprisingly, the general outlines of the story are more common than you might imagine. Many of the drugs available to treat diseases today are the result of serendipitous discovery. The search for new drugs usually starts with a known compound that has some demonstrated effect on a particular physiological condition. A large number are derived from natural sources and purified or modified to make them more effective. The list of such drugs is long and varied: aspirin is derived from a compound in willow bark, penicillin from the *Penicillium* mold, digitalis (for irregular heart activity) from the common garden flower, the foxglove. Many plants, fungi, bacteria, and even animals produce compounds with important medical benefits.

The traditional approach to drug development is to start with a panel of hundreds or even thousands of compounds. Each of these compounds is chemically similar, but has some minor modification to it. Usually the basic chemical structure is extracted from a source, such as a plant or a bacterium, known to have some medicinal properties. For example, penicillin comes in several varieties today, such as amoxicillin, ampicillin, and methicillin. Each of these compounds has the same basic chemical structure with some relatively small modifications. The drug panel that yielded sildenafil contained many different variants on a chemical compound that could trigger nitric oxide signaling in cells.

The entire panel of compounds is rigorously tested to identify those that are most effective in treating the specific problem of interest, such as blood vessel dilation. The best compounds, usually less than 10% of the initial panel, are selected and subjected to extensive screening for other concerns, such as toxicity and efficacy in animal systems. Most compounds are too toxic to be of any use; many compounds have so many side effects as to be useless; and a large number of compounds fail to have any efficacy at all when introduced into the complex environment of a living organism. As a result, less than 0.1% of the initial panel of compounds ever make it to the point where drug development can begin.

Beyond that initial screening, each candidate drug must pass through an extremely complicated set of hurdles, including numerous trials and evaluations in a variety of animal models. Each phase of screening is usually followed by more chemical tinkering to adjust the properties of the compound. Then another round of testing is conducted, followed by more adjustments, and so on. Eventually, the rare compound makes it to the point where human clinical trials can begin. The U.S. Food and Drug Administration (FDA) requires three levels of trials, starting with patients who are healthy volunteers. These individuals volunteer to take a drug at different dosages to help the researchers determine the correct dosage and to assess the likelihood of serious side effects.

If the drug makes it past the first round of trials, then it must still pass through two more levels of clinical investigation. When all the stages of clinical trials have been completed to the satisfaction of the scientists at the FDA, the drug can finally be made available to the general public. It remains under close scrutiny for a few years after that, as well, and any signs of trouble can cause the FDA to trigger a recall, such as what happened recently with Vioxx and some other drugs. The road to the blockbuster drug status of sildenafil and many other drugs is littered with obstacles. Few drugs make it.

The problems with this approach are immediately apparent. Obviously, screening thousands of compounds for one rare successful drug is incredibly inefficient. The cost of screening all those candidates alone is staggering, on the order of millions of dollars. The cost escalates with each step of the process, so that a drug that makes it to phase III clinical trials (the last step in the process) and then fails has already cost the developer an astronomical sum.

Aside from the cost, the process itself is inefficient because we must rely on chance to find that rare successful drug. It would be far more efficient if we could design a compound that had all the properties of the perfect drug. Such a process would shortcut the many thousands of hours of effort and simplify the entire drug manufacturing process.

The idea that we can design a drug to have a specific action within the body is the basis of an entire realm of research known as **rational drug design.** The theory behind this approach is to first identify the *target* of the drug, figure out how to control it, and then *design* a molecule that fits the target like a key in a lock. Then this specially designed molecule is used to control the target, usually a protein.

The wealth of knowledge and data generated in the past decade on the genomes and proteomes (the full complement of proteins) of myriad organisms should provide an excellent resource in the rational drug design effort. The idea is that given the full parts list of the human genome, we should be able to design drugs that specifically target a particular gene or protein. In other words, rather than waiting for a chance compound like sildenafil to fall into our laps, we should try to target a specific protein within cells and design a drug to control that individual protein's behavior. The challenge is to figure out what sort of drugs can interact with the target protein [13].

### 9.3.3  Structure-Based Drug Design

To design a drug based on a target protein, we must understand the protein's structure or shape. Determining protein structures is not easy. Researchers have traditionally taken one of two general approaches. They can try to determine the structure of a protein experimentally—the "gold standard" for protein structure analysis. However, experimental approaches are time-consuming and fraught with problems. As a result, researchers have also sought ways to computationally predict the structure of a protein based on a variety of criteria.

A common theme for all structure prediction, regardless of the type of molecule being studied, is that the shape of a molecule must be stable. That is, it must remain in a particular conformation for a significant period of time in order to accomplish its function. The laws of thermodynamics suggest that a conformation that requires little energy to maintain it is more stable, or lasts longer, than one that requires a great deal of energy to maintain. As a result, most molecules adopt a conformation that requires the least energy necessary. We call this shape the **minimum free energy conformation** (see Project 9.2 for more about the thermodynamics of structure prediction). The idea in protein structure prediction is to identify this minimum free energy structure because it is likely to be the biologically relevant conformation as well.

Predicting the structure of a protein can occur at many levels. As discussed in Chapter 2, the primary structure of a protein is its amino acid sequence. This sequence can form local bonds to create the secondary structure. The secondary structures can then form interactions with other secondary structures to yield the three-dimensional structure, known as the tertiary structure. Large tertiary structures can then further conglomerate into a protein's quaternary structure.

For the purposes of structure prediction, computational methods focus primarily on the secondary and tertiary levels of structure. Although secondary structures are important for determining some of the shape of the protein, they are rarely on their own sufficiently detailed to be relevant for drug design. We therefore focus on tertiary structure prediction methods.

It turns out that tertiary structures are so complex that we do not really have the computational methods in place to reliably predict more than a handful of complete tertiary protein structures. Instead, researchers have tried to identify something called **protein folds.** These groups of secondary structures create defined three-dimensional shapes but do not necessarily represent the entire tertiary structure of a protein. A protein fold can include the areas of the protein that are of specific interest to a drug manufacturer, and predicting the structure of the fold can help direct the design of the drug.

The process of rational drug design is somewhat akin to a criminal trying to pick a lock. The lock is the target protein in a cell or organism, and the key or keys are the molecules that can interact with that target protein. Sometimes we want to open the lock by designing a key that fits it. Other times, we want to gum up the lock. Either way, the drug (key) we want to design looks much like the natural keys that would ordinarily open the lock (protein). The natural keys are known as **ligands,** and the general idea is simple. After determining the structure of our lock, we computationally design a key to fit the keyhole. Just as the shape of a lock limits the size, shape, and orientation of the keys that can fit it, the target protein's structure limits the size, shape, and orientation of the molecules that it can bind.

Of particular interest is the keyhole of the lock, which in the case of a protein is usually its **active site.** Just like the keyhole, the active site serves to limit which ligands can interact with the protein. The right bits have to line up perfectly before the lock will turn or the protein will activate. In essence, we want to do what criminals in novels always do: pour some wax in a lock, extract the shape of the key and then make a new duplicate key that can open up the lock or gum it up so it cannot function.

### Early Success: HIV Protease Inhibitors

One of the first successes with rational drug design came in the development of new drugs to combat AIDS. As you know, AIDS is caused by HIV, which has a number of unusual proteins. A key compound is needed to enable the virus to infect a healthy cell—the HIV protease, an enzyme that chops up other proteins. The HIV protease is critical because it helps generate the coat proteins that HIV uses to bind to host cells and enter them. The coat proteins occur as one large protein, and the HIV protease then chops up this large protein at specific sites to generate the individual coat proteins. Without the HIV protease, the coat proteins cannot be made, and as a result, the virus remains trapped within the first cell it enters.

The HIV protease would make a great target for a drug because disabling this protein could directly affect the virus' ability to infect other cells. However, to disable the protease, researchers had to first determine its structure and mode of action.

Researchers took a two-pronged approach to the problem. One group of researchers tried to determine the structure of HIV protease using laboratory methods, which seek the precise locations of the individual atoms within a protein. The information about the positions of these atoms is then used to determine the three-dimensional structure of the protein. *X-ray crystallography* uses X-rays and *nuclear magnetic resonance* (NMR) imaging uses high-intensity magnetic fields to determine the locations of the atoms. Either approach is exacting and time-consuming, and X-ray crystallography can require large amounts of sample material.

While one group of researchers began the process of experimentally determining the structure of HIV protease, other investigators sought a faster route to developing a drug to interfere with this protein. The second group decided to use existing knowledge about proteases to try and develop an inhibitor drug. They sequenced the HIV genome and discovered that the HIV protease amino acid sequence looked a great deal like that of another virus protease, the Rous sarcoma virus protease. The structure of that protease had already been determined, so researchers decided to "guess" at the structure of the HIV protease based on what they knew about Rous sarcoma virus protease. In other words, they used sequence homology to develop a model for the structure of HIV protease.

Using sequence homology to model three-dimensional structures has been one of the best ways to predict the structure of a protein. This is because many proteins that have similar amino acid sequences acquire the same three-dimensional structures. The three-dimensional structure of a protein is determined by the kinds of chemical interactions that occur among its amino acids (see Chapter 2). If two proteins have similar amino acid sequences, it is reasonable to assume that they are able to form similar chemical bonds and thereby yield similar structures.

Using the Rous sarcoma virus protease structure as a guide, researchers at three pharmaceutical companies began developing drugs they hoped would interfere with the protease. They were looking for a molecule that could fit in the protease precisely at the active site and therefore prevent the viral proteins from being cleaved. The protein has two halves that come together, creating the active site in the center of the molecule.

Returning to our lock-and-key analogy, recall that the lock represents the HIV protease, and its keyhole can fit certain kinds of proteins (the keys). We need to inactivate this lock. One way is to gum up the keyhole. If we stuff the keyhole with a bit of bubble gum, no keys can enter it and nothing can unlock the lock. The researchers wanted to design a molecule that would act like a bit of gum in the lock. It would essentially sit inside the protease in the active site, preventing the protease from binding its usual ligands and cleaving the viral proteins.

While the researchers were developing the molecular "gum," the structure of HIV protease was published. And it proved to be nearly identical to the structure that had been predicted based on sequence homology with Rous sarcoma virus protease. As a result, the drug companies sped forward with the development of a collection of drugs, the HIV protease inhibitors. These were the first set of drugs devised specifically for HIV treatment, and they revolutionized the treatment of AIDS. Suddenly, a diagnosis of AIDS was not an immediate death sentence. Many millions of infected people were given the possibility of living out a normal life span [28].

### Other Approaches to Protein Structure Prediction and Drug Design

Since the HIV protease inhibitors were developed, this same approach of using predicted protein structure to design a molecule has been used in many other areas. In the case of HIV proteases, the sequence homology to Rous sarcoma virus helped simplify the process of predicting the structure. Unfortunately, a close homolog is not always available to enable this approach. From a computational perspective, one of the biggest complications in predicting protein structure is that two proteins with very different amino acid sequences can have the same three-dimensional structure. This is because many amino acids have similar chemical and physical properties and can be used interchangeably, at least to some extent. To model these proteins, we have to use other approaches [17].

One successful approach, known as homology threading, compares the structures of the proteins rather than analyzing them at the sequence level. A known structure is used as a *scaffold*. The amino acid sequence for the protein of interest, the structure of which is not known, is then "threaded" onto the scaffold. We then try to match up each amino acid in our protein with some part of the scaffold. At each step, we ask if the amino acid in our query protein "fits" into the structure at that position. For an amino acid to fit, it must satisfy some basic constraints of physics and chemistry. For instance, an uncharged amino acid cannot stably fit into a region of a protein that is highly charged. Similarly, a hydrophobic (water-hating) amino acid cannot remain stable in a region exposed to the watery environment of the cell. These considerations limit which amino acids can be present in a given part of a structure and can be used to quantitatively assess possible amino acid candidates [18].

We need to identify a structure for the amino acid sequence that requires the least amount of energy to maintain its structure. The optimal structure is one in which each amino acid of the sequence exists in an environment favorable to its particular chemical and physical properties. This should correspond to its minimum free energy conformation. For many proteins, the biologically active structure and minimum free energy structure are similar if not identical.

There are other methods for predicting the minimum free energy conformation of a protein, including ab initio approaches that try to determine the structure purely from the energetic constraints present at the amino acid sequence level. In these approaches, the structure of a region of a protein is determined by trying out many different conformations and identifying the one with the least energy requirements. Such approaches have some promise, but remain far too theoretical to be of much use in the rational drug design arena [1].

### 9.3.4  A Pharmaceutical Cautionary Tale

We focused here on the benefits of rational drug design and its potential to both simplify and accelerate the process of drug discovery. However, the road to successful drug development is littered with many promising compounds that turned out not to have much use in the complex systems of the human body. Other drugs have survived the complex process of selection only to fail spectacularly after being launched on the market. This is the story of Vioxx, the most famous failure of rational drug design in recent years.

The story begins about a decade ago, with researchers who were trying to better understand how pain is perceived. Several receptors on cells in the skin and organs communicate pain. One of the pathways that allows for pain signaling to occur begins at the surface of these cells with a specific receptor protein known as cyclooxygenase-2 (COX-2). One of the early success stories of rational drug design was the development of a compound that could bind to and block the signaling of COX-2 receptors. The COX-2 inhibitors, as these drugs were known, were developed based on computational modeling of the active site in COX-2 receptors.

When this class of drugs first made it to the market, they were hailed as a revolution in pain management. Instead of generally reducing perception of pain, which most other pain medications do, these new drugs directly targeted a specific pathway involved in pain regulation. As a result, they would have fewer side effects, they would be more effective, and patients would likely be able to take them for longer periods without developing tolerance to a given drug dosage. These were all considered critical features of the perfect pain management drug.

Unfortunately, the class of COX-2 inhibitors had some unforeseen serious side effects. The most infamous of the COX-2 inhibitors is a drug called rofecoxib, better known as Vioxx. Vioxx is exceptionally good at blocking COX-2 receptors, and as a result, it was considered an excellent treatment for the chronic pain associated with arthritis and other ailments. Unfortunately for Merck, the company that developed Vioxx, the compound also seems to trigger heart attacks and stroke in a significant minority of people who took it. As a result, Merck withdrew Vioxx from the market in September 2004, but the company is involved in litigation with many people who suffered ill effects from taking Vioxx.

The moral of this story is one of caution—that even the very best science is not always enough to predict what will happen in a complex system such as the human body. Nevertheless, rational drug design remains the best path forward in identifying drug targets and designing drugs to interact with those targets. It is certainly a more intellectually satisfying approach to developing drugs than the old-fashioned, trial-and-error approach. As a result, it is likely to remain a prominent aspect of pharmaceutical research and development for the foreseeable future. But for every success story such as the HIV protease inhibitors, there are cautionary tales like that of Vioxx. The search for the perfect drug is still as much about luck as it is about science and technology.

## 9.3.5  Over to You

As you learned in this chapter, synthetic chemists traditionally generated shelves full of compounds that are chemically similar to known active agents. These were then tested with the hope that one would be the next new drug or it would have fewer deleterious side effects than current drugs. Here we want you to consider how to harness the power of the computer to generate a series of potential new compounds. Evolutionary algorithms have been introduced in several contexts in this book, and their use in reducing the search space for computational chemistry is another. In this project you will apply some of what you have learned about evolutionary algorithms to explore their use for drug design.

First, you must address the fact that important drug targets (e.g., active sites of enzymes) or receptor-binding sites are functionally dependent on their three-dimensional structure. You need to represent structures in a fairly simple way so their quality can be evaluated. Find out what you can about pharmacophores. What are they? How might these compounds be used when designing an evolutionary approach to drug development?

Also, to make the problem tractable you need to convert the chemical and biological entities into formats that the computer can use. One approach to the formatting issue has been to convert the structure into a linear representation known as a simplified molecular input line entry system (SMILE) string. David Weininger created this representation based on concepts that should be familiar to you from graph theory. Atoms are nodes and bonds are edges, for example [40]. Find out what you can about SMILE strings. How might they be used in the design of an evolutionary algorithm? Is any information lost in the conversion? Here is a good starting point, and additional references follow. Start at: http://www.daylight.com/smiles/. This approach has been applied to the HIV-I protease, one of the major drug targets [37].

To complete this project you may either (1) propose a high-level design for an evolutionary algorithm to be used for rational drug design. Describe the components and how it will work, but you are not required to write code, or (2) find a paper describing the implementation and use of an evolutionary algorithm for rational drug design. Present this paper, the algorithm design, and its findings to the class.

### 9.3.6  Resources for Rational Drug Design

1. D. Weininger. SMILES, a chemical language and information system. 1. Introduction to methodology and encoding rules. *J Chem Inf Comput Sci,* 28:31–36, 1988.

   *A description of the language used to convert protein structures into the linear representations (strings) used by some computer programs*

2. http://www2.chemie.uni-erlangen.de/projects/sol/drugdesign.html

   *A discussion of the pharmacophore*

3. http://www.netsci.org/Science/Cheminform/feature02.html

   *A tool for pharmacophore searching*

4. A recent review of computer-based drug design appears in [36]. You can read about a genetic algorithm approach to drug design in [4].

## 9.4  INFORMATION-BASED MEDICINE

Emerging scientific fields are in constant flux. Terminology and methodologies change along with concepts and paradigms and even our understanding of what "the field" is. The emerging field of bioinformatics is no exception. Even the name *bioinformatics* means different things to different people. The term is applied to almost all the related fields of study that have arisen along with the advances in high-throughput technologies and computer analysis of their data. In this book we have focused mainly on "bioinformatics computing," the use of computers and algorithms to work with and understand basic biological data. Often, depending on the context, the terms *genomics, biomedical informatics,* and *medical informatics,* among others are used almost synonymously with *bioinformatics,* largely because the lines between these fields have blurred as new synergies among them arise.

It has become increasingly clear that most, if not all, human diseases and our response to them have a genetic component—from developmental disorders, to cancer, to immune system responses to the environment. Even some psychological disorders have genetic roots. From the very start, scientists and clinicians have seen the promise of molecular biology and genomics for health care. If we can find the genetic causes of disease and discover how these genes work, then the door is open to the development of therapies to target those genetic roots. By understanding individual genetic variation in disease-causing genes or in genes that determine how a person responds to a particular drug, precise targeting can lead to personalized effective health care. Treatments and medications based on an individual patient's genetic profile can maximize a medication's effectiveness while avoiding adverse side effects.

The convergence of life sciences, health care, and information technology today is revolutionizing the practice of medicine and the discovery of new treatments and has led to what is now known as information-based medicine. This is not entirely new. Physicians have always relied on a combination of knowledge, experience, and clinical observation to treat patients. Contemporary medical practice is expanding the traditional realms of knowledge and clinical observation to include new types of biomedical data, and doctors are being required to access this information via electronic patient health records. Another major change is in the way medications are developed and prescribed. The approach to drug development known as rational drug design is described in Section 9.3. In the past, new medicines were designed as "one size fits all" rather than customized for individual patients. The new paradigm of information-based medicine seeks to target medications and treatments based on each patient's complete medical profile.

What information is needed to achieve information-based medicine? Certainly all the bioinformatics topics in this book could conceivably contribute to a full understanding of human health. Knowledge of genes, their products (whether protein or RNA), their functions, and interactions are all important. Here our focus is identifying the genes associated with a disease or those involved in drug response pathways and characterizing individual variants of these genes in the population.

## 9.4.1  Identifying Simple Disease Genes

### Early Successes

Prior to the molecular biology revolution of the 1980s, genetic contributions to the relief of human disease were limited to those diseases whose biochemical basis was well understood because the defective gene product could be isolated and identified directly and its variants could be studied. The field of biochemical genetics waged an early war on disorders such as the hemophilias, diseases which are characterized by a failure of the blood to clot due to defective proteins. Unfortunately, in most cases we don't know which defective gene product or combinations of products are responsible for a specific human disease. Techniques were needed to find and characterize genes that had obvious effects on human health (a recognizable phenotype) even though the biochemical nature of the phenotype was not understood.

### Mapping the Genome

The advent of molecular biology and the ushering in of large-scale genome sequencing greatly changed the strategies for identifying disease genes. One of the early goals set out by the proponents of the Human Genome Project was to create a complete map of the human genome. Like a roadmap which shows the location of towns and cities and important landmarks and the spacing between them, a genetic map would show the locations and relative positions of all the genes, as well as other useful genetic landmarks. If we can navigate to those genes then we can begin to understand how they work or how to manipulate them to our advantage.

## Creating Maps

There are many strategies of mapping and different types of maps. Just as Mendel traced generations of peas to study vegetative traits, so today's investigators trace generations of human families to establish linkages between genes and inherited disorders and to discover informative DNA markers. **Linkage** means that genetic loci (such as a gene associated with an inherited disorder and some other specific DNA marker) are inherited together. The two are linked because they physically reside on the same chromosome. If two markers are very closely linked, the probability is low that DNA recombination can occur between them as a result of crossing-over during meiosis. An informative DNA marker is some characteristic of the DNA that we can recognize in the lab and that exists in two or more different forms in the population. The Human Genome Project has identified thousands of useful DNA markers.

Maps constructed by following inheritance patterns among related organisms, families, or populations are considered to be of low resolution because the identifiable markers are generally located fairly far apart in the genome. They are sometimes called genetic maps.

Physical maps are created by actually characterizing the physical nature of the genome. The contig map, constructed during fragment assembly discussed in Chapter 4, is a type of physical map. The ultimate high-resolution map, of course, is the complete and accurate sequence of the entire genome. From that, we can eventually identify and place all of the genes and other interesting sequences so that we can directly investigate the genetic basis of disease.

## Simple Genetic Disorders

The earliest success stories in mapping human disease genes came prior to the Human Genome Project and prior to high-throughput sequencing [39]. "Simple" genetic disorders, such as Duchenne muscular dystrophy, cystic fibrosis, and Huntington disease were among the first. These genetic diseases are relatively rare but are considered simple in the sense that they result from mutation in a single gene and are inherited in a Mendelian fashion. Passing on of genes and their variations can easily be followed from generation to generation for these human diseases. The first of these disorders to be mapped, Duchenne muscular dystrophy, is the most common of a group of related, but clinically and genetically distinct disorders, all of which are known as muscular dystrophies and are characterized by degeneration of skeletal muscle fibers. Duchenne muscular dystrophy is a lethal disease that affects 1 in 3500 males so it is not surprising that great attention has been paid to it in the scientific and medical communities.

The defective gene, named *DMD,* was the first gene to be identified, in 1987, through a process sometimes known as "reverse genetics" [42]. Contrary to the traditional genetic approach, the *DMD* gene was identified without first knowing anything about the structure, function, or pathological mechanism of the gene's protein product. Instead, the gene was identified using the strategy of positional cloning; that is, first mapping the location of a human disease gene by linkage analysis and then using the mapped location on the chromosome to clone (or copy) the gene. Only later was the protein product characterized. Positional cloning is an established approach today and has been used in the discovery of many other genes responsible for disease, including cystic fibrosis and Huntington disease.

How was mapping accomplished with no knowledge of the gene itself? Recall that we need two things—informative genetic markers and families—to follow inheritance. In the experimental organisms commonly used in laboratory-based genetic studies, such as the *Arabidopsis* plant or fruit flies, we can create and use phenotypic markers for genetic mapping of mutations. Since these are laboratory organisms with short generation times we can set up multiple crossings to examine the offspring in many generations. We can easily look for and count malformed flowers or red eyes, for example, and can generate sufficient data for reliable analysis. Obviously, this is not possible for mapping genes associated with diseases in humans. However, clever scientists realized that molecular DNA markers could be powerful tools for mapping genes. The initial mapping strategies took advantage of the new field of recombinant DNA technology and specifically of the discovery of restriction enzymes. One of the first types of commonly used DNA markers is referred to as a **restriction fragment-length polymorphism (RFLP).** RFLPs are variations among individuals in the length of restriction fragments produced from identical regions of the genome.

In all organisms natural DNA sequence variations occur throughout the genome. Some estimates place variations in human DNA every 200 nucleotides or so apart. These naturally occurring DNA variations are referred to as DNA polymorphisms. DNA polymorphisms may create or destroy restriction-enzyme recognition sites so that the pattern of restriction fragment lengths from a region of the genome may differ between two individuals or even between two homologous chromosomes of one individual. Recall that restriction enzymes recognize specific sequences and work like molecular scissors to cut DNA into fragments. The fragments can be isolated in the lab and their sizes measured. Loss of a site due to sequence variation results in the appearance of a larger fragment and the disappearance of the two smaller fragments. Gain of a new site results in the loss of a larger fragment and its replacement with two smaller fragments. Changes in the number and size of fragments can be detected by probing for specific single-copy regions (genes) in the DNA of interest. These inherited changes in DNA are used as polymorphic markers for mapping in a fashion analogous to the phenotypic markers used in classical genetic studies.

Multigenerational families of related individuals, some with and some without the disease, allow us to follow inheritance of the disease along with inheritance of informative markers. Generations are needed so that recombination frequencies between markers can be estimated (remember that recombination occurs during meiosis in formation of the gametes to produce the next generation). Once suitable families are identified, RFLP analysis is used to determine if members of the family who have the disease have particular DNA sequences at specific locations (marker locations) that healthy family members do not. This process involves collecting blood from family members for DNA isolation, genetic analysis of the RFLP markers, and statistical analyses to determine the significance of sequence differences between affected and nonaffected family members.

A particular DNA marker is said to be "linked" to the disease if, in general, family members with certain nucleotides at the marker always have the disease and family members with other nucleotides at the marker do not have the disease. The marker and the disease gene are so close to each other on the chromosome that the likelihood of crossover is very small. **Linkage analysis** in humans is difficult because in a family pedigree (a chart that displays all the known family members, their mates, siblings, and offspring over multiple generations) the number of progeny is low. Establishing linkage required the development of a method that combined data from different families and provided some statistical evidence for linkage. The LoD, or logarithm of the odds, score was developed for this purpose. Exercise 9.5 will ask you to find out more about LoD scores.

Once linkage is established more markers are examined until a small enough region of the chromosome is identified and the region can be cloned and sequenced. Today it is quite likely that the sequence is available immediately. The gene must also be definitely linked to the disease. This is usually accomplished by identifying and characterizing individual mutants in the gene and establishing the molecular connections among mutation, aberrant gene product, and disease. For example, a mutation that converts an amino acid codon to a stop codon results in a truncated, abnormal protein. A mutation in a splice site results in abnormal splicing and likely failure of translation of a pre-mRNA.

In the cases of Duchenne muscular dystrophy, cystic fibrosis, Huntington disease and many others, the positional cloning strategy was highly successful and led to great advances in understanding the disease physiology, in dissecting the many different mutations that result in gene defect, in early diagnosis, and in some cases in treatment. Check out OMIM, the Online Mendelian Inheritance in Man database at the NCBI for a detailed history of these and many other diseases. One of the great strengths of this bioinformatics resource is the integration of multiple types of data and information as well as organization of those data for easy access.

## 9.4.2  The Challenge of Mapping Complex Diseases

The genetic diseases discussed so far are "simple" because the correlation between genotype and phenotype is fairly complete. Most human diseases have a much more complicated genetic story. Common genetic diseases in humans tend to be more complex and cluster in families but do not follow Mendelian inheritance patterns [8, 16, 31]. Indeed they result from the action of multiple genes. Alleles of these genes are "susceptibility factors," and most factors are neither necessary nor sufficient to produce disease. Making the situation even more difficult, a complex interaction between the environment and these susceptibility alleles contributes to disease. Well-known examples of complex diseases include diabetes, asthma, cardiovascular disease, many cancers, hypertension, and Alzheimer disease.

The phenomena described in simple Mendelian studies are discontinuous; that is, a pea plant is either "short" or it is "tall." In contrast, complex traits don't fall into these discrete classes. Consider a breeding experiment involving corn. If corn with short ears is crossed with long-eared corn the first generation has ears of intermediate length. The next generation ranges from short to tall with intermediate lengths in a normal distribution. The values are in a continuous range, and accordingly we call these "continuous," or "quantitative, traits." In the agriculture industry and in agricultural bioinformatics, genes that contribute to complex phenomena are known as quantitative trait loci (QTL) [8].

The study of complex diseases is challenging because the contribution of multiple genes is coupled with environmental influences. To further complicate matters, conflicting theories seek to explain the evolutionary origin of common disease variants [16]. One theory, known as the common disease/common variant (CD/CV) theory, contends that most of the susceptibility alleles for common diseases existed prior to the global dispersal of humans or are alleles that are subject to positive selection. As a result we would expect the disease variants to be common, occurring throughout human populations. The opposing theory, known as the common disease/rare allele theory, argues that most mutations underlying common diseases occurred after the divergence of populations. We would then expect significant heterogeneity in the variations found among the disease genes. Which theory is to be tested has a major influence on the strategy we employ for searching for disease genes. Here we consider the CD/CV theory and the use of single-nucleotide polymorphisms (SNPs).

The CD/CV theory predicts that the susceptibility alleles should occur at relatively high rates in the population (at least 1%) and suggests that association studies in large cohort populations (unrelated individuals sharing the common disease) will be fruitful. Compare this to the strategy for simple disease traits where we need to look within families to find evidence of causative genes. Since each of the susceptibility alleles contributes only a portion of the risk, looking outside of families eliminates the background noise that arises from shared genes in closely related individuals and that have nothing to do with the disease of interest.

SNPs have greatly facilitated the search for common disease variants. Consider a single location on the human genome. If in about 99% of the population the base is, say, a C but in the remaining 1% of the population it is instead an A nucleotide, then we say that a single-nucleotide polymorphism occurs at that position of the genome. In other words, a SNP is a single base that is different in a small portion of the population than in most people. Each SNP occurs in approximately 1% of the population and is stable. Bear in mind that many SNPs occur, so they fit our need for informative DNA markers. It has been estimated that humans share about 99.9% sequence identity. Much of the other 0.1% (about 3 million bases) are SNPs. Although "hot-spots" occur with high densities of SNPs, it is thought that SNPs occur about every 1000 bases. Most SNPs have only two alleles (one of two different nucleotides at that position), but because SNPs are relatively close together, any given gene may have several SNPs or SNPs probably occur close by that serve as potential markers.

As a bioinformaticist it is important to be mindful of the origin and quality of SNP data. It comes from many different sources including genome-wide sequencing with multiple coverage, data mining of expressed-sequence tags (EST), sequencing within suspected disease genes, sequencing of BAC clones, and sequencing of individual chromosomes. Skepticism about the validity of SNP data is therefore prudent. Questions to consider are: Could the investigators be identifying sequencing errors rather than genuine SNPs? Is a suspected SNP simply a splice variant? Could recombination or other duplication of regions have occurred during the cloning process?

Note also that most SNPs are not in coding regions. The immediate value of studying SNPs is not so much in understanding changes to genes as it is in their use as polymorphic, informative markers to find and identify possible disease genes. As in the case of simple disease mapping, we look for a marker that is located near a gene associated with a disease. We try to find evidence of linkage disequilibrium, meaning that the disease and the marker are genetically associated at a higher frequency than would be expected if there were no relationship between them. We carry out what are known as association studies by comparing genome-wide SNP profiles from individuals who have the disease with those who do not have the disease. The difference identifies a putative disease profile that may eventually be used in diagnosis or prediction of disease and for the identification of new drug targets. We may also identify some of the susceptibility factors by using SNPs from known genes in the profile. One well-known example of this comes from association studies of patients with Alzheimer disease. One associated gene, the *ApoE* gene, has two SNPs. Between the variants of these two SNPs fall three alleles of the *ApoE* gene: *ApoE2, ApoE3,* and *ApoE4.* Inheritance of the *ApoE4* allele has been associated with Alzheimer disease, and the APOE4 protein has been found in brain lesions of patients with the disease [15, 38].

The high-throughput analysis and computing challenges in studying genetic diseases are not unlike those encountered when we studied gene expression microarrays. Genotyping of SNPs can be accomplished via oligonucleotide arrays by isolating DNA isolated from only a few drops of blood. For example, Affymetrix has 10-K and 100-K arrays. Knowing which individuals to study, which SNPs to study, and how to find patterns of inheritance are major hurdles. Like the gene expression problem, measurements across many, many genes can result. The fact that each of these genes contributes only an unknown measure of risk, and that environmental influences are also factors, necessitate the use of advanced statistical approaches for analysis. This is a prime example of the need for biologists, computer scientists, mathematicians and statisticians, among others, to work together as teams in bioinformatics.

One of the major bioinformatics efforts at mapping complex disease traits is the International HapMap Project. This multicountry effort seeks to characterize and categorize genetic differences in humans. It is a public resource designed to help researchers find genes that are not only associated with human disease but also genes that control an individual's response to drug treatments. Recall that SNPs occur rather close together in the genome. Those too close together are not useful individually as markers because the likelihood of recombination is low; that means they will always be inherited together. A set of closely linked genetic markers present on one chromosome that tend to be inherited together is known as a haplotype. This haplotype, or set of SNPs, can be used to look for evidence of disease association, as in the *ApoE* example. Knowing which SNPs are inheritied together effectively reduces the number of SNPs that need to be analyzed when genotyping individuals. This has greatly reduced the costs of running large association studies. To learn more about this interesting project, and about gene mapping, in general, check out the Website for the HapMap Project at http://www.hapmap.org.

This brings us to one of the other major components of information-based medicine: the field(s) known as **pharmacogenetics** or **pharmacogenomics.** Pharmacogenetics is the science of the influence of heredity on the response to drugs [29]. Pharmocogenomics refers to the general study of all of the many different genes that determine drug behavior. These related fields are concerned with research that identifies and characterizes polymorphic genes encoding drug metabolizing enzymes, transporters, receptors, and other drug targets in humans and animals. The driving force behind this field is that individual variation in response to drugs is a major clinical problem. Issues range from severe adverse reactions, to no reaction at all, to problems with drug interactions. Since much individual response to drugs is now believed to be inherited, it is hoped that pharmacogenetics can make a significant contribution to knowledge in drug design and refinement. It has been predicted that in the future guidelines will be established for prescribing drugs based on differences in metabolism established in clinical studies. Personal pharmocogenetic profiles will be established for individuals, doses and drug interactions will be determined on the basis of these profiles, and new drugs will be developed for individuals rather than the one size fits all approach. Already there have been successes in identifying genetic variants associated with adverse drug reactions and differences in drug metabolism. One of the best known, which was discovered before the age of genomics, is $CYP_2D_6$, the cytochrome $P_{450}$ 2D6 gene that is involved in the metabolism of many drugs. Variations in this gene cause some people to be slow metabolizers, some fast, whereas some don't metabolize well at all [29]. Advancement in this field will require the integration of many types of genomic and clinical data [35].

## 9.4.3  Over to You

Investigate the LoD score. Find a small set of sample data and write some code to generate the LoD score.

**Exercise 9.5**

Many computing challenges lie ahead in the effort to create individual genetic profiles for better managing and treating human disease and for supporting information-based medicine, in general. Many of the leading attempts involve collaborations between industry and academia. For example, IBM has partnered with the Mayo Clinic, and Providence Health Care is working with the University of British Columbia. For this exercise you must explore and report on one or more examples of major projects. What are the challenges? What solutions have been implemented?

**Exercise 9.6**

### 9.4.4  Resources for Information-Based Medicine

1. R. G. Worton and M. W. Thompson. Genetics of Duchenne muscular dystrophy. *Annu Rev Genet,* 22:601–629, 1988.

   *Reference [42] is a good review article describing an early example of mapping by positional cloning.*

2. Three review articles that cover theoretical and technical issues of complex disease mapping with examples are [8, 16, 31].

## 9.5  SYSTEMS BIOLOGY

### 9.5.1  Introduction

Anatomy can be thought of as the study of the component parts of the human body. Physiology can be thought of as the science of how one individual human works, what makes one human functionally different from another. Sociology is the science of how entire networks of individual humans work together and achieve complex ends. Up to this point our study of bioinformatics has concentrated on the anatomy of a genome: how small pieces can be discerned whose purpose we can infer. Now we embark on the "physiology" (how the same genome can achieve vastly different functionalities in different cells) and the "sociology" (how different components interact in networks to achieve communal goals) of genomic science. We use the term **systems biology** to cover both the functional differentiation and the collaborative aspects.

We have discussed ways of interpreting some of the information content of a genome in a localized and nonintegrated sense. For example, our study of genes has indicated how certain stretches of DNA lead to the generation of proteins that then fold into shapes that achieve a specific goal for the genome's organism. Our knowledge of the workings of many single genes is fairly advanced. A genome, however, contains the information necessary for the entire operation of the organism, including how to differentially regulate individual genes depending on the location of the cell within an organism. Every living form begins as just a single cell. That cell divides into two. Each of those divides into two more, each of which divides, and so on. This exponential growth results in over a thousand cells in the time required for 10 divisions, more than a million after 20, over a billion after 30, and trillions soon after that. Every one of those trillions of cells contains the same genomic sequence. Some of those cells become constituents of bones, some become part of an eye, some participate in the action of muscles, and some contribute to the working of a brain. Vastly different functionality, all deriving from essentially identical individual information units. The genome contains the information that enables differential expression of genes so that cells can achieve different functionalities in the appropriate settings, resulting in a successfully functioning complete organism. Differentiated cells are characterized by their specialized proteins, which constitute the specific structures, enzymes, networks, and pathways of a given cell type. These differentiated characteristics determine how a cell responds to its neighboring cells, the intercellular milieu, and to external influences. It is a complicated situation, but we already know a lot about the workings of such systems.

Decades of traditional biological research has taught us much about the nature of biological systems. See resources 5, 6, 7 at the end of this section for some reviews. We can draw generalities from this knowledge so that we can better model these systems. First, biology can be characterized by a notion of function, or "purpose," unlike the other natural sciences. This, of course, is related to natural selection and the relationship of function to fitness and selection [3]. Genetic variation and environmental perturbation are among the forces that influence cell function and its survival. Although, purpose in biology is not at the level of consciousness, it still differentiates a living being from an inanimate object (e.g., a rock) that nonetheless may be shaped by its environment. An understanding of biological function must always take this into account.

Biological systems are large and complex. Biological systems are set apart from most other large, complex systems by their large number of functionally diverse and multifunctional elements as opposed to large collections of simple and identical elements that occur in other familiar systems (e.g., computer networks, integrated circuits). Rather than creating complex behaviors, components of biological systems interact selectively to produce "coherent" behaviors [3]—the behavior makes sense given the biological context. An oft-used example is that of p53, the tumor suppressor protein [21]. This protein's function depends on the cellular context, and p53 itself is actively modified by other elements of its network. Sometimes p53 protein causes cells to stop dividing and sometimes it causes them to die. Each is a coherent behavior that arises from different selective interactions within the network.

Biological systems are robust [3, 20]. In computing we often refer to robust hardware or software systems, meaning that they are unlikely to crash under unexpected or unusual circumstances. Similarly, biological systems have evolved numerous mechanisms by which to adapt to environmental flux and also become relatively insensitive to alterations in internal parameters. We commonly refer to the ability of cells to maintain "homeostasis"—the normal, stable body state. Maintenance of a constant internal body temperature is a simple example. Certainly, you are most aware of the relatively rare times in which your body has failed in this respect when you have run a fever. Sometimes robustness is not a good thing. In fact, this property is often exploited by pathological mechanisms and can account, for example, for the resistance of some cancer cells to chemotherapy or radiation. One strategy for developing new therapeutic interventions for cancer treatment and for diseases such as AIDS is to find and target fragile points in the mechanisms controlling robustness.

Many different mechanisms contribute to the robustness of biological systems. One of these is feedback, which can be either positive or negative. Here, again, the p53 protein is an informative example. When DNA is damaged, for example when cells are exposed to ultraviolet light from the sun, p53 is activated by other proteins. Its role is to act like a brake to stop the cell cycle so that DNA can be repaired. Once DNA repair is complete a feedback loop causes p53 to be released and the cell cycle continues.

Another factor that contributes to robustness of biological systems is redundancy. Redundancy means that the same function may be accomplished in more than one way. This interesting characteristic has caused its share of surprises and disappointments in the research community. Redundancy occurs at many levels. For example, different genes encode similar proteins and multiple networks have complementary functions. Some of the surprises came from "knock-out" experiments. Although there are many ways to inactivate, or "knock out," a gene's function, one of the most time-consuming and expensive has been the generation of gene-targeted, or knock-out, mice in which both copies of a particular gene have been rendered inactive. The idea is that the gene's function may be elucidated by loss of function and study of the resultant new, abnormal phenotype. It is not at all unusual, however, for no new phenotype to arise because redundancy in genes and pathways takes over the function being studied. Some genes turn out to be not as indispensable as the researcher thought!

Modularity is another aspect of robust biological systems. Functional modules, composed of many types of interacting components such as DNA, RNA, and proteins, are considered by systems biology researchers to be a critical level of biological organization [3, 10]. The function of a module is a property of the whole rather than the individual components. The function is separable from other modules, but it may also interact with other modules. Modules may be isolated chemically in biochemical reactions or spatially by their cellular localization. Some examples of biological modules are networks and pathways such as a signal transduction pathway, or structural entities such as the mitotic spindle. Even organelles such as a ribosome might be considered as modules. Given some thought, one can imagine modules at many different levels of complexity.

Human beings originated as the result of a speciation event from an ancestral species. The precise moment of separation of one species from another is not an easily identifiable event, but we can be certain that soon afterwards the number of human individuals was small. Each had its own genome. As with modern humans, there were minor differences between the genomes of pairs of members of the new species. Because of the very nature of speciation, however, we know that the human genomes were sufficiently similar to allow breeding and replication between pairs, and sufficiently different from all other species' genomes to make breeding and replication impossible across species borders. Human society began with a small number of essentially identical individuals. Exponential growth occurred, not necessarily at a fixed rate, but exponential in the aggregate, over millennia. Now there are billions of essentially identical human beings. We are not trying to detract from the importance of individuality when we say that all humans are essentially identical. So few differences exist between pairs of human genomes that, prima facie, there is no obvious reason why one individual's role cannot be adequately filled by any other individual. In this sense, human society is composed of billions of people who all share essentially identical information units. Some of those individuals function as doctors, some as lawyers, some as farmers, some as artists. Vastly different functionality, all deriving from essentially identical individual information units. Just like cells, a large number of individuals each with the same instruction set, each interpreting those instructions differently to achieve different functionalities to contribute in different ways to a larger entity. Human society is a self-regulated system within which billions of essentially identical individuals each adopt a functionality that enables the entire human society to work.[3] A living entity is a self-regulated system within which trillions of essentially identical cells adopt a functionality that enables the entire organism to work.

One of the most fascinating aspects of this discussion is the self-regulatory nature of the collections of cells and the collections of individual humans. No "intelligent designer" directs each cell to develop in its own way. Except in the most extreme dictatorial societies, no paternalist presence tells each human being what role he or she must play in society at large. Collections of computers are different. They do not self-regulate. Although our knowledge of computer science may help us understand some of the networking and collaboration aspects of systems biology, it will not help us understand how one program, in the form of one genome, can lead to differential cell functionalities. We are tied to the determinism of current computers, and will need to shed that limitation. Who knows? We may contribute to a new understanding that will result in far more versatile computing networks.

Think of all the computers in the world today. Despite the claims of the manufacturers, they are all essentially identical individuals. They have different functionalities. Some contribute to air traffic control, some keep track of commercial inventory, some help to write homework essays, some attempt to extract information from intercepted telephone conversations. Each individual computer is capable of being used in any of these roles.[4]

Computers are similar to cells in this regard: They are a large number of essentially identical units, each of which can perform any of several different tasks within a system. One huge difference distinguishes computer networks from biological systems: Each individual computer in a network is deliberately *programmed* to achieve its functionality. It requires specific direction on how to achieve its own purpose. Each computer is given its own specific code controlling its actions, and that code is deliberately placed in that machine by a skilled software engineer who went to great lengths to calculate what steps were necessary to deterministically achieve the results desired by the customer. Most programmers are very frugal, or efficient, in that they provide a minimal sequence of actions to achieve one specific deterministic purpose. They avoid redundancy. Any slight mutation in the code results in a nonfunctional component. It is inconceivable that a computer programmed for one purpose will ever evolve into anything that can act, not even in a minuscule way, differently from its initial programming. This is not so for biological systems. No programmer tells one cell as opposed to another what to do. The program in every single cell, in the form of its DNA string, is identical to the program in every other cell. No "grand designer" specifies the

---

[3] Cynics might argue that human society can hardly be claimed to "work," considering all the struggle, war, and strife that beset us. We use the term *work* here in the same way that a predator species could be said to "work" even though the prey might disapprove of our use of the word.

[4] We are minimizing the importance of differences between "normal" computers and supercomputers: within a short period of time, today's supercomputer will be equivalent to tomorrow's normal computer.

cell's precise actions. In all likelihood, each cell will function correctly in its appropriate role. The information required for each functionality is contained in the one genome. The cell's environment somehow causes it to function in its appropriate way.

Computer programmers often aim for economy and efficiency. Indeed, these qualities are valued within the profession. It is clear that biological programming is different. Redundancy and the possibility of deviation from the "normal" functioning of components are built into the system. Diseases and malfunctions occur in cells. New functionalities evolve. And although analogies can be drawn between computer networks and biological networks, the analogy stretches only so far. The intelligent design of current computing is insufficient to maintain life on Earth. Lasting and robust life requires redundancy, inaccuracy, mutation, and, above all, self-regulation without any outside direction apart from the Darwinian effects of the environment. At times, our discussion of systems biology may remind you of something you know about computer networks. But remember that computer networks, being designed entities, are so very simple compared with evolved biological systems. Systems biology is a challenge.

## 9.5.2  Inputs

Earlier we raised the question of how a single program (genome) could produce vastly different behaviors in different circumstances. An obvious answer, at least in the case of computer programs, is by providing different inputs, tailored for each of the circumstances. Inputs need not be simple numeric or character data supplied by a user in a text field or selection box. Computers can be equipped with sensing devices that allow the environment direct input to the computation. Biological systems are also provided with ample sensory input devices.

An example of a computer with a sensing device we see in our own homes or dorms is the heating and cooling system controlled by a computer with an attached thermostat. When the thermostat indicates to the computer that the temperature is below a preset threshold, then the computer turns on the furnace, and if the ambient temperature rises above another threshold, the air conditioner is turned on. In this way, thermostatically controlled heating/cooling systems maintain an indoor temperature between two thresholds.

Such devices act differently depending on their environment. Evidence suggests that similar environmentally determined differences in functioning occur in biological entities. Many mammals respond to cold environments by increasing their metabolism to warm their bodies. Others respond by reducing their metabolism to minimal levels to survive during hibernation. Both indicate a modification of functional operation in response to environmental factors. Similarly, creatures respond to an unusually hot environment by modifying some function. Dogs, for example, can reduce internal temperatures by panting to enhance evaporation; humans achieve a similar result by sweating.

Both mechanical and biological thermostatically controlled systems work by causing functional or behavioral changes in response to detected environmental factors. The similarity is largely superficial, however. The important distinction between mechanical thermostats and their biological counterparts is that the behavior of a mechanical device is deterministically programmed by a designer who makes assumptions that necessarily limit the environmental potentialities to which the device responds well. If something unexpected happens, the mechanical device cannot be expected to respond well. If the whole structure of the house is removed by, say, a tornado, and the thermostat and heating/cooling system are left intact, the system will persist in wasting energy in impossibly attempting to maintain a nonexistent internal temperature!

Nature employs a much more robust strategy than the intelligent design of today's software engineers. Some program components (genes) occur in subtly different versions (alleles) between one device (creature) and another. Under normal circumstances these small differences have no effect on the survival characteristics of the devices. But when the unexpected happens, it may be that one allele causes a behavior in one device that leads to its destruction, whereas another allele leads to behavior that enables its survival. Darwinian selection ensures that in the long term devices respond sensibly to rare events. It even provides for adaptation to the completely unexpected.

The study of artificial life and genetic algorithms as discussed in Chapter 7 is an attempt by computer scientists to break loose from the limitations of predetermined computer behavior. We know that this science is in its infancy and has much to learn from the living world. The study of systems biology may have significant consequences for computer science as we learn more about the robustness and versatility of living forms.

## 9.5.3  Outputs

Every component of a biological system is capable of affecting the other components. Indeed, we would be very surprised if this were not the case. When we focus on just one component, it is natural to apply our computing experience and abstract that component into a device that transforms certain inputs into various outputs.

It is difficult to choose the appropriate level of detail (what programmers refer to as granularity) with which to approach biological systems. If the granularity is too coarse, we risk failing to understand the microeffects fundamental to the process. If the granularity is too fine, we expend too much effort on specific inputs and outputs of pieces when, in fact, the net input and net output of a group of these pieces is our true focus.

## 9.5.4  Modern Approach to Systems Biology

Systems biology builds on a long tradition of experiments and investigations that provide us with detailed information about small parts of life. In fact, only rare biological functions can be attributed to one or a few molecules; most are controlled by multiple interacting components. But biologists have always known that such detailed information is but a small step on the road to comprehending the vast landscape of how life operates.

Modern experimental techniques, including high-throughput devices, produce enormous quantities of data with an intricacy of detail that is unprecedented. In addition, powerful machines can now process, categorize, and share these large data resources. The paradigm of systems biology starts with data from high-throughput biotechnologies such as microarrays and mass spectroscopy, then creates models to simulate and predict system behaviors, and finally tests these models to measure their validity. The latter steps represent a return to hypothesis-driven research as opposed to the data-driven hypothesis-free data-mining approaches that have emerged along with the generation of almost unmanageable volumes of data.

Dr. Douglas Lauffenburger, who trained as a chemical engineer and who is one of the leaders in the field, refers to this process as the "four M's" of systems biology: measurement, mining, modeling, and manipulation. "Manipulation and measurement are on the experimental side. Mining and modeling are on the computational side. These four M's are part of an iterative process, beginning with manipulating the system. Once a system is perturbed, it is measured using a high-throughput, multivariate technology. The data are then mined to elucidate hypotheses that, when cast in terms of formal computational models, form the basis for a new manipulation of the system" [1].

Modeling and simulation bring a whole new set of complications to the problem. Some of these are computational and some are biological. One of the main challenges is the need to integrate different levels of information. It is not enough to study genes or proteins or pathways or cells in isolation to understand how biological systems function. An understandable model of a whole system will ultimately represent all of the relationships and interactions between the various and diverse parts of a biological system.

Although we emphasize the computing side in this book, it is important to remember that traditional experimental, lab-based methods continue to play a crucial role in systems biology. Many wet lab techniques help the scientist integrate findings from mining high-throughput data with biological "knowledge" to elucidate interactions and relationships. For example, individual, specific RNAs and proteins can be localized at the cellular and tissue levels using in situ hybridization and antibody localization techniques, respectively. These techniques provide an understanding of where, when, and sometimes even why a particular molecule is present and functioning in the cell. At another level, scientists study genetic variation, either natural or experimentally induced, to understand the relationships between genes and their functions in individuals and in populations. Studies of normal physiology and disease at the levels of cells, tissues, organs, organisms, and populations continue to set a foundation on which mathematical and computational models can be built.

### 9.5.5  Feedback, Equilibrium, and Attractors

As we shall see when we study the Rasp example in the Over to You in Section 9.5.7, one important aspect of genetic networks is that the expression of one gene (*Tym*) can affect the expression of another (*Haa*). But it omits another important and ubiquitous aspect of genetic networks. The Rasp system lacks any feedback mechanism. The incorporation of feedback into networks makes their analysis a good deal more complicated. Sometimes the resulting networks are amenable to mathematical analysis, albeit more complicated analysis than any required by the

Rasp network. Often however, the investigating scientists resort to using computer simulation to study the properties of a network. The main reason for this is that networks admitting feedback are susceptible to what mathematicians call **chaotic** behavior. Tiny differences in initial settings can quickly amplify, leading to enormous differences in the network performance in a short time.

A very simple feedback equation is the basis for the formation of the famously challenging **Mandelbrot set** described by Benoit Mandelbrot in [24] and depicted graphically in Figure 9.10. The figure's shading indicates the points $c$ of the complex plane for which the feedback equation $z_{\text{new}} = z^2 + c$ starting with $z = 0 + 0i$ produces a sequence of values that do not tend to infinity. The unexpectedness and the beauty of this set have been well described in books and articles. A simple description is given by James Gleick in [9], and Roger Penrose goes into more depth and raises questions about the decidability of the set in [30].

Let's look at how feedback can produce very complex behaviors in even the simplest of networks. Figure 9.11 indicates how the levels of product of each of four genes regulates each gene. The simplest gene in the network is $D$ whose activity produces a constant level $d$ of product. $B$'s output is such that it is $b = 1 - a$, so it is down-regulated by $A$. $C$'s activity is regulated by all three $A$, $B$, and $D$; indeed its level of production is given by $c = abd$. Finally note that $A$'s activity is controlled by $C$'s level, so that $a$ equals $c$. Levels $a, b$, and $c$ are numbers that stay in the range 0.0 to 1.0. We allow more flexibility for $d$.

Concentrating on what happens to the activity of $A$ within a given period, elementary algebra assures us that $a_{\text{new}} = da(1 - a)$. This is a feedback equation showing us how the level of activity of $A$ changes in the presence of this network acting as described. Let's investigate with some actual numbers.

Suppose $d$ is 3.0, and the initial value of $a$ is 0.5. After one iteration, the value of $a$ becomes $da(1 - a)$ or $3.0 \times 0.5.5 = 0.75$. The next iteration gives a new

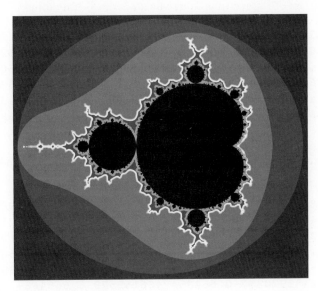

**FIGURE 9.10**  The Mandelbrot set.
© Stephen Gerard/Photo Researchers, INC

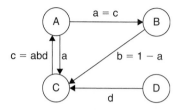

**FIGURE 9.11**   A simple genetic network with feedback. The level $a$ of protein from gene A regulates the level $b$ of protein from gene B to be $b = 1 - a$, and also regulates the action of gene C. C is also regulated by the level $b$ from B and the level $d$ from gene D so that the level of $c$ is given by $c = abd$. The feedback becomes apparent when we note that the activity of A is regulated by the level of $c$.

value for $a$ of 3.0.75 × 0.25, or 0.5625. It's easy to write a program to produce the successive values

```
0.5 0.75 0.5625 0.73828125 0.5796661376953125
0.7309599195141345  0.5899725467340735  0.7257148225025549
0.5971584567079203  0.7216807028704055  0.6025729979246489
0.7184363402902498  0.6068566957218066  0.7157449397382518
0.6103623629320143  0.713460446544187   0.6133039132834688
0.7114866697039566  0.6158201656125887  0.7097570677124175
0.6180059176340649...
```

We can continue for a few hundred iterations, and the sequence seems to settle down:

```
0.6590985347359144  0.6740629687346551  0.6591062487458353
0.6740556048300851  0.6591139392816997  0.6740482629787787
0.6591216064622096  0.6740409430706571  0.659129250405229
0.6740336449964098  0.6591368712277909  0.6740263686474885
0.6591444690461052  0.6740191139160997  0.6591520439755666
0.674011880695198   0.6591595961307606  0.6740046688784795
```

After tens of thousands of iterations, our program produces something like:

```
0.6648538916610314  0.6684695832126388  0.6648539985964792
0.6684694774402561  0.664854105513021   0.6684693716865052
0.6648542124106624  0.6684692659513806  0.6648543192894091
0.6684691602348767  0.6648544261492663  0.6684690545369883
0.6648545329902398  0.6684689488577098  0.6648546398123352
0.6684688431970357  0.6648547466155579  0.6684687375549606
```

and we are tempted to believe that the network is settling into a **steady state** in which the level of activity of gene $A$ resolves to a value close to .665.[5]

Try the same thing with a different value of $d$, say 3.3. Again starting with $a = 0.5$ the sequence begins with the following:

```
0.5  0.825  0.47643750000000007  0.8231678683593749
0.4803563452381904  0.8237266185310761  0.4791635522996359
0.8235672800758589  0.4795039103722253  0.8236137040229017
0.4794047628763067
```

After 10 thousand iterations, we see:

```
0.8236032832060689  0.47942701982423414  0.823603283206069
0.4794270198242338  0.8236032832060687   0.4794270198242346
0.8236032832060689  0.47942701982423414  0.823603283206069
0.4794270198242338  0.8236032832060687   0.4794270198242346
0.8236032832060689  0.47942701982423414  0.823603283206069
0.4794270198242338  0.8236032832060687   0.4794270198242346
```

It looks as if the value of $a$ alternates between two limits. Over time then, the activity of the gene $A$ rapidly alternates between two values. After 10 thousand iterations with the level of $D$ set at 3.5, we find that the activity of $A$ alternates between four values as seen in the following output:

```
0.8749972636024641   0.38281968301732416  0.8269407065914387
0.5008842103072179   0.8749972636024641   0.38281968301732416
0.8269407065914387   0.5008842103072179   0.8749972636024641
0.38281968301732416  0.8269407065914387   0.5008842103072179
0.8749972636024641   0.38281968301732416  0.8269407065914387
0.5008842103072179   0.8749972636024641   0.38281968301732416
0.8269407065914387   0.5008842103072179   0.8749972636024641
0.38281968301732416  0.8269407065914387   0.5008842103072179
0.8749972636024641   0.38281968301732416  0.8269407065914387
0.5008842103072179   0.8749972636024641   0.38281968301732416
0.8269407065914387   0.5008842103072179   0.8749972636024641
0.38281968301732416  0.8269407065914387   0.5008842103072179
0.8749972636024641   0.38281968301732416  0.8269407065914387
0.5008842103072179
```

What was one limit at $d = 3.0$ **bifurcated** by $d = 3.3$ into two limits and divided again by $d = 3.5$ into four limits. After 3.5 the behavior becomes even

---

[5] Mathematically astute readers may wish to prove that the value to which the sequence converges is, in fact $\frac{2}{3}$.

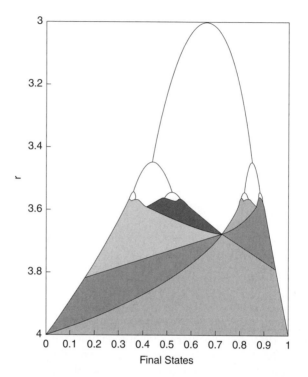

**FIGURE 9.12**   A graph indicating the onset of chaos in our simple feedback gene network. As the value of $d$ increases from 3.0 to 4.0, the ultimate behavior of $a$ after thousands of iterations of the feedback $a = da(1 - a)$ progresses from approaching just one limit, to two limits, to four, and so on. Then at about 3.56, chaos sets in.

more chaotic; splitting into 8 limits, then 16, and so on. Indeed, the term **chaos** is used by mathematicians to describe precisely the situation we are observing (Figure 9.12).

Exercise 9.8 will ask you to write programs to investigate this phenomenon further.

The set of values to which the value of $a$ ultimately gravitates is called the **attractor.** At $d$ values near 3.0, the attractor is a single point. By 3.3 the attractor becomes a set of two points, then a set of four, and so on until, somewhere around $d = 3.56$ the attractor becomes very strange. In chaos theory (an area of mathematics) such sets are called **strange attractors.**

Even the simplest of networks of genes can result in long-term behavior that is extremely difficult to predict. But the bioinformatics problem is even more difficult. It's almost the reverse of the chaos problem. Typically, we would *begin* with some rather chaotic data, perhaps the expression levels of various genes under many different conditions as indicated by a series of microarray experiments. The systems biology challenge is to reconstruct from that chaotic data what kind of relationships must exist between the genes in order to produce such chaotic data. In other words, can we discover what sort of network relationships between the genes produce the observed behavior? Chaos theory is good at displaying how even very simple dynamic systems can produce extremely complex outputs. Our challenge is to find simple networks that explain very complex data. We're following a generally accepted maxim that, in science, the most economical explanation for a set of observations is often correct. Compare this notion with Occam's razor as described in Chapter 6. The challenge of systems biology is to "reverse engineer" the biological networks to explain a flood of data. If you are interested in how dynamic systems can become chaotic, a good starting reference is James Gleick's book [9].

## 9.5.6  What Kind of Model?

How detailed a model do we need? Should we seek the simplest explanation possible for observed phenomena?

### Boolean

Earlier we saw how even four interacting genes, each having continuous possible expression levels, could easily lead to chaotic and unpredictable behavior. Some researchers have tried to simplify the situation by positing networks where gene activity can take on only one of two values: The expression of a gene in the network is either off (0) or on (1). On the face of it, this simplification would seem to make network behavior more amenable to analysis. In practice, it is still possible for chaotic behavior to emerge from even simple Boolean networks. Kauffman's [19] book discusses models based on Boolean logic.

### Differential Equations

In our simple example the levels of the various genes were expressed as simple functions of the expression levels of other genes. Is it more realistic to assume that the **rate of change** of the expression level rather than the expression level itself is a function of other genes' expressions? If so, we obtain a model based on differential equations. This has the advantage of being similar to many other dynamical systems that have been studied in other areas besides bioinformatics, such as thermodynamics. Nevertheless, the mathematics is complicated! A library or Internet search for terms like "reaction kinetics" may give you some leads on this topic.

### Stochastic Models

When the next configuration of a part of a network is determined from the current configuration according to some fixed probability vector, the model is called **stochastic.** We briefly entered into this domain earlier when we discussed evolutionary mutation matrices such as the PAM transition matrix and when we looked at hidden Markov models. If you postulate a stochastic model to explain a large dataset, it is possible to perform backpropagation, or Bayesian analysis, to guess at the probability vectors that best explain the observations. Library or Internet searches for **stochastic network model** should provide you with ample resources to pursue this issue.

### Hybrid Models

Of course, aspects of each modeling system can be combined with aspects of others, often with encouraging results.

### In Summary

Once again we observe that bioinformatics is a science in its infancy. Many huge questions still remain unanswered, so don't be afraid to follow even your craziest hunches if you think you have an explanation for some of the phenomena described here.

## 9.5.7  Over to You

### The Rasp

We now embark on an extended exercise, containing two specific smaller individual exercises, to help us understand the kinds of complex interactions that make systems biology such a fascinating study. The Rasp is an imaginary creature. The Rasp lives in an environment where its survival is largely governed by three factors:

- The temperature (given as a daily average),
- The availability of food (given as a 30-day average),
- The availability of water (given as a 30-day average).

For our exercise we rate the survivability of various minor mutations of the Rasp over a 360-day experimental period. Inputs are as follows:

- 360 integers, each representing a daily average temperature,
- 12 floating point numbers in the range 0.0 to 1.0, indicating the availability of food (0.0 = nonexistent, 1.0 = plenty),
- 12 floating point numbers in the range 0.0 to 1.0, indicating the availability of water (0.0 = nonexistent, 1.0 = plenty).

An example input file is provided on the book's Website as `rasp1.dat`. The following four genes and their products are of interest in this exercise:

1. *Tym,* whose product level controls two threshold temperatures at which production of *Haa* begin to be down-regulated. The product level of *Tym* is scaled to be a number *tym* in the range 0.0 to 1.0. The upper threshold temperature for down-regulation of *Haa* is given by the expression $hiThresh = 20tym + 10$, and the lower threshold temperature by $loThresh = 20tym - 10$.
2. *Gop,* whose product level determines the rate at which *Haa* is down-regulated. The level of *Gop* is a number *gop* again scaled to be in the range 0.0 to 1.0. The level of *Haa,* represented by the number *haa,* is given as a function of the day's average temperature $\theta$. Above *hiThresh* the level $haa = 1.0 - gop \frac{(\theta - hiThresh)}{(50 - hiThresh)}$; and below *loThresh* the level $haa = 1.0 - gop \frac{(loThresh - \theta)}{(loThresh + 10)}$.
3. *Haa,* whose product level *haa* determines the quantity of food required to flourish given a difference between ideal body temperature (30) and the average daily temperature (given as an input). The quantity of food required is

$foodNeed = \frac{haa|\theta-30|}{40}$, unless the temperature is below *loThresh,* in which case an additional $.02(loThresh - \theta)$ is needed.

4. *Pri,* whose product level determines the quantity of water needed to properly digest food and to achieve cooling if the day's temperature is below *loThresh.* The quantity of water necessary is *waterNeed = prifoodNeed* if the temperature is below *hiThresh* and *waterNeed = prifoodNeed + 0.03(\theta - hiThresh)* otherwise.

The "magic numbers" given in the preceding formulas are the result of levels of other gene products in the Rasp anatomy. As always in systems biology, we must simplify our model to achieve manageable computations. Some more magic numbers are required to formulate a survivability index for the Rasp.

The survivability index depends on the availability of food and water and on the Rasp's needs for food and water. If the availability exceeds the needs, the Rasp will survive very well. Problems arise when availability is low. To continue our simplified model, recall that the availability of food and water are both inputs to our experiment and are given as 30-day averages. A simple fitness function can be defined by

- If the Rasp needs more food than is available and more water than is available, then its fitness that day is −0.3.
- If its food needs are satisfied, but not its water needs, then its fitness is −0.05.
- If both its food and its water needs are provided for by the food and water availabilities, then the fitness that day is +0.2.

The fitness of the Rasp over a period of time is calculated by summing its daily fitness over each of the days in the period.

## Exercise 9.7

1. Write code for a Rasp class. A Rasp object is instantiated with four values for its levels of *Tym, Gop, Haa,* and *Pri.* Create a method to compute its food and water needs from the preceding formulas, and update the values of its *Tym, Gop, Haa,* and *Pri* for a given temperature $\theta$. This method will be called whenever we need an update step for the Rasp object. If you wish you may use the following code for the step method:

```
public void step(double theta) {
        hiThresh = 20*tym + 10;
        loThresh = 20*tym - 10;
        if (theta > hiThresh)
            haa = 1.0 - gop*(theta - hiThresh)/(50 - hiThresh);
        else if (theta < loThresh)
            haa = 1.0 - gop*(loThresh - theta)/(loThresh+10);
```

*(continued)*

```
        foodNeed = haa * Math.abs(theta - 30)/40.0;
        if (theta < loThresh) foodNeed += 0.02*(loThresh - theta);
        waterNeed = pri * foodNeed;
        if (theta > hiThresh) waterNeed += 0.03*(theta - hiThresh);
}
```

The Rasp class must also provide public accessor methods that return the values of *foodNeed* and *waterNeed*. We call these food( ) and water( ):

```
    public double food () {
            return foodNeed;
        }
        public double water () {
            return waterNeed;
        }
```

2. Write a program to:

   - Input four floating point numbers in the range 0.0–1.0;
   - Create a Rasp object whose initial levels of *tym, gop, haa,* and *pri* are the four values you just input;
   - Read 360 daily temperatures, 12 levels of food availability, and 12 levels of water availability from a file; (Recall that these levels of food and water persist over a 300-day period.)
   - Accumulate a total fitness for this Rasp over that 360-day period. We provide a method to do this based on the fitness functions given earlier, assuming the daily food and water availabilities have been entered into arrays foodAvail[] and waterAvail[] and the daily temperatures are in array temps[], is given by:

```
        public double fitness(Rasp r) {
            double fit = 0.0;
            for (int i = 0; i<360; i++) {
                r.step(temps[i]);
                fit -= 0.3;
                if (r.food() < foodAvail[i]) fit += 0.25;
                if (r.water() < waterAvail[i]) fit += 0.25;
            }
            return fit;
        }
```

3. Enter different values of the four initial settings for *Tym, Gop, Haa,* and *Pri* to find the fittest possible Rasp. In other words, find four numbers that when used to create a Rasp object produce a Rasp *r* such that fitness(*r*) is as large as possible.

For this exercise, find the parameters that create the fittest Rasp given a file of temperature and food and water availabilities. Do this by a process of trial and error, looping through many possible values for each parameter to the Rasp constructor and keeping track of the ones that produce the objects of highest fitness.

For a greater challenge, you can try to evolve the best Rasp by means of a genetic algorithm. Start with a population of, say, 50 Rasp objects, each of which has been constructed with random parameter values. Now introduce ways to:

1. Mutate one Rasp object into another slightly different object;
2. Take two Rasp objects and produce an "offspring" object that in some way is an aggregate of its "parents."
3. Measure the fitness of all 50 Rasps, keep the best, say, 40, of them, replace the worst, say, 10, of them by mutations and offspring of the fittest Rasps.
4. Repeat this step for hundreds or thousands of generations.

If your genetic algorithm is successful, you will end up with a population of fit Rasps. You will have simulated the process of evolution in a very oversimplified and artificial setting.

Write a program to input two numbers: $d$ and an initial value for $a$. Your program should run the feedback $a = da(1 - a)$ 10 thousand times and then print the next 40 values of $a$. (The 10 thousand iterations ensure that the system has settled into its ultimate behavior pattern.) Test the following propositions:

1. For a given value of $d$, it does not really matter what value of $a$ you enter as long as it is between 0.0 and 1.0. The behavior in the limit is the same.
2. There is a value for $d$ below which there is just one limit and above which there are more limits. Find this value.
3. What happens to the limits as $d$ gradually increases. Test if the graph in Figure 9.12 is accurate.

If you are adept at such things, you may be interested in adapting your program so you provide $d$ and $a$ via sliders and produce graphic output.

## 9.5.8   Resources for Systems Biology

1. Benoit B. Mandelbrot. *The Fractal Geometry of Nature,* W. H. Freeman, New York, 1982.

*This interesting coffee-table book contains more about fractals and beautiful designs generated by feedback equations.*

2. Roger Penrose. *The Emperor's New Mind,* Oxford University Press, Oxford, 1990.

*Penrose's masterly and approachable (though far from elementary) critique of hard artificial intelligence places the issues in the context of computability theory, which he describes very effectively.* Hard *is the term applied to the aspect of artificial intelligence (AI) that maintains that everything that goes on in the human brain can be reproduced in silicon. Penrose provides a well-reasoned case that the state of AI is nowhere near achieving such goals.*

3. James Gleick. *Chaos: The Making of a New Science,* Viking Adult, New York, 1987.

*Gleick's book provides an elementary introduction to how dynamic systems can become chaotic.*

4. S. A. Kauffman. *The Origins of Order,* Oxford University Press, Oxford, 1993.

*Kauffman's book discusses system models based on Boolean logic.*

5. Marie E. Csete and John C. Doyle. Reverse engineering of biological complexity. *Science,* 295:1664–1669, 2002.

*Describes similarities and differences between advanced technologies and biological systems.*

6. H. L. Hartwell, J. J. Hopfield, S. Leibler, and A. W. Murray. From molecular to modular cell biology. *Nature,* 402:C47–52, 1999.

*This paper presents the case that biological systems are modular and can be understood by applying principles that govern other modular systems.*

7. H. Kitano. Cancer as a robust system: Implications for anticancer therapy. *Nat Rev Cancer,* 4:227–235, 2004.

*A perspective of cancer from the point of view of systems biology.*

# KEY TERMS

normalize (9.1)
structure (9.2)
secondary structure (9.2)
ribozyme (9.2)
free energy (9.2)
minimum free energy
   configuration (9.2)
biologically active (9.2)
pseudoknot (9.2)
rational drug design (9.3)
minimum free energy
   conformation (9.3)

protein folds (9.3)
ligand (9.3)
active site (9.3)
linkage (9.4)
restriction fragment-length
   polymorphism (RFLP) (9.4)
linkage analysis (9.4)
pharmacogenetics (9.4)
pharmacogenomics (9.4)
systems biology (9.5)
chaotic (9.5)
Mandelbrot set (9.5)

steady state (9.5)
bifurcated (9.5)
chaos attractor (9.5)
strange attractor (9.5)
rate of change (9.5)
stochastic (9.5)
stochastic network model (9.5)

# BIBLIOGRAPHY

1. D. Baker and A. Sali. Protein structure prediction and structural genomics. *Science,* 294:93–96, 2001.

   *This is a good general review of protein structure prediction methods and the road ahead for computational approaches.*

2. K. Boris-Lawrie, T. M. Roberts, and S. Hull. Retroviral RNA elements integrate components of post-transcriptional gene expression. *Life Science,* 69:2697–2709, 2001.

   *This article is a more focused description of the biology of the Rev-RRE interaction and its role in HIV infections of cells.*

3. Marie E. Csete and John C. Doyle. Reverse engineering of biological complexity. *Science,* 295:1664–1669, 2002.

4. Dominique Douguet, Etienne Thoreau, and Gérard Grassy. A genetic algorithm for the automated generation of small organic molecules: Drug design using an evolutionary algorithm. *J Comput Aided Mol Des,* 14:449–466, 2000.

5. Derek M. Dykxhoorn, Carl D. Novina, and Philip A. Sharp. Killing the messenger: Short RNAs that silence gene expression. *Nat Rev,* 4:457–465, 2003.

   *A detailed look at siRNA and RNAi from a biological perspective. This article is particularly commended by the wealth of references to the primary biological literature.*

6. Sean R. Eddy and Richard Durbin. RNA sequence analysis using covariance models. *Nucleic Acids Res,* 22:2079–2088, 1994.

   *One of the original papers that proposed a strategy for identifying tRNA genes in a genome, this paper is a classic in the field.*

7. Paul P. Gardner and Robert Gigerich. A comprehensive comparison of comparative RNA structure prediction approaches. *BMC Bioinformatics,* 5:140, 2004.

   *This paper reviews several existing algorithms for RNA structure prediction using sequence conservation guidance. A good place to start in learning more about the existing approaches in this area.*

8. Anne M. Glazier, Joseph H. Nadeau, and Timothy J. Aitman. Finding genes that underlie complex traits. *Science,* 298:2345–2349, 2002.

9. James Gleick. *Chaos: The Making of a New Science.* Viking Adult, New York, 1987.

10. H. L. Hartwell, J. J. Hopfield, S. Leibler, and A. W. Murray. From molecular to modular cell biology. *Nature,* 402(SUPP):C47–C52, 1999.

11. J. Heer, S. K. Card, and J. A. Landay. Prefuse: A toolkit for interactive information visualization. In CHI 2005: Human Factors in Computing Systems, 2005.

12. I. Hofacker, M. Fekete, and P. Stadler. Secondary structure prediction for aligned RNA sequences. *J Mol Biol,* 319:1059–1066, 2002.

    *This paper describes a popular algorithm for the prediction of RNA structures using sequence conservation.*

13. A. S. Ivanov, A. V. Veselovsky, A. V. Dubanov, and V. S. Skvortsov. Bioinformatics platform development: from gene to lead compound. *Methods Mol Biol,* 316:389–431, 2006.

    *This comprehensive review of rational drug design proposes a more ambitious goal: the computational development of drugs directly from targets in sequenced genomes.*

14. Y. Ji, X. Xu, and G. Stormo. A graph theoretical approach for predicting common RNA secondary structure motifs including pseudoknots in unaligned sequences. *Bioinformatics,* 20:1591–1602, 2004.

    *This approach to RNA structure prediction uses an interesting algorithm drawn from graph theory. It offers a novel way of thinking about structures and the process of RNA folding.*

15. John M. Olichney, Lawrence A. Hansen, Richard Hofstetter, et al. Association between severe cerebral amyloid angiopathy and cerebrovascular lesions in Alzheimer disease is

not a spurious one attributable to apolipoprotein e4. *Arch Neurol,* 57:869–874, 2000.

16. G. C. L Johnson and J. A. Todd. Strategies in complex disease mapping. *Curr Opin Gen Dev,* 10:330–334, 2000.

17. D. T. Jones. Protein structure prediction in the postgenomic era. *Curr Opin Struct Biol,* 10:371–379, 2000.

    *A comprehensive review of protein structure prediction methods, with a wealth of references.*

18. D. T. Jones, W. R. Taylor, and J. M. Thornton. A new approach to protein fold recognition. *Nature,* 358:86–89, 1992.

    *The original paper describing the homology threading technique and its application to protein structure prediction.*

19. S. A. Kauffman. *The Origins of Order.* Oxford University Press, Oxford, 1993.

20. H. Kitano. Systems biology: a brief overview. *Science,* 295:1662–1664, 2002.

21. H. Kitano. Cancer as a robust system: Implications for anticancer therapy. *Nat Rev Cancer,* 4:227–235, 2004.

22. Martin Krzywinski. Circos. http://mkweb.bcgsc.ca/circos/

23. E. A. Lesnik, R. Sampath, and D. J. Ecker. Rev response elements (RRE) in lentiviruses: an RNAMotif algorithm-based strategy for RRE prediction. *Med Res Rev,* 22:617–636, 2002.

    *This paper describes a simple approach to predicting the secondary structure known as RRE (Rev response element) used by HIV to transport certain mRNAs out of the nucleus of infected cells. The exercise included in this project was inspired by the work done here.*

24. Benoit B. Mandelbrot. *The Fractal Geometry of Nature.* W. H. Freeman, New York, 1982.

25. D. Mathews and D. Turner. Dynalign: An algorithm for finding the secondary structure common to two RNA sequences. *J Mol Biol,* 317:191–203, 2002.

    *One of the best algorithms for RNA structure prediction using sequence conservation is Dynalign. This paper describes the algorithm in detail.*

26. Marjori A. Matzke and Antonius J. M. Matzke. Planting the seeds of a new paradigm. *PLoS Biol,* 2:e133, 2004.

    *An accessible review of RNA interference in plants and the contributions that plant researchers have made to the RNAi and siRNA fields. This is particularly recommended as a very easy introduction to the area for nonbiologists.*

27. NCBI Coffee Break on Micro RNAs. http://www.ncbi.nlm.nih.gov/books/bv.fcgi?rid=coffeebrk.chapter.33

    *More about microRNAs, small interfering RNAs, and RNA interference can be found through the short description and links here.*

28. National Institute of General Medical Sciences. Structure-based drug design: From the computer to the clinic. http://publications.nigms.nih.gov/structlife/chapter4.html

    *This short introduction to rational drug design through protein structure prediction is a good place to start in learning more about how HIV protease inhibitors were developed.*

29. Kevin M. O'Shaughnessy. Hapmap, pharmacogenomics, and the goal of personalized prescribing. *Br J Clin Pharmacol,* 61:783–786, 2006.

30. Roger Penrose. *The Emperor's New Mind.* Oxford University Press, Oxford, 1990.

31. Mayeux R. Mapping the new frontier: Complex genetic disorders. *J Clin Invest,* 115:1404–1407, 2005.

32. E. Rivas and S. Eddy. The language of RNA: a formal grammar that includes pseudoknots. *Bioinformatics,* 16:334–340, 2000.

    *This paper proposes a formal stochastic grammar for RNA structure prediction. It was also one of the first to specifically target the prediction of pseudoknots in RNA secondary structure.*

33. Richard Robinson. RNAi Therapeutics: How likely, how soon? *PLoS Biol,* 2(1):e28, 2004.

    *An elegant review of the state of RNAi therapy to date, this review is more accessible to nonbiologists.*

34. Purvi Saraiya, Chris North, and Karen Duca. An insight-based methodology for evaluating bioinformatics visualizations. *IEEE Trans Vis Comput Graph,* 11:443–456, 2005.

35. E. E. Schadt, S. A. Monks, and S. H. Friend. A new paradigm for drug discovery: Integrating clinical, genetic, genomic and molecular phenotype data to identify drug targets. *Biochem Soc Trans,* 31:437–443, 2003.

36. Gisbert Schneider and Uli Fechner. Computer-based de novo design of drug-like molecules. *Nat Rev Drug Discov,* 4:649–663, 2005.

37. Priyadarsini Soundararajan. *Ligevolver: A Tool for Ligand Formulation Using Genetic Algorithm.* Master's Thesis, Rochester Institute of Technology, 2006.

38. W. J. Strittmatter and A. D. Roses. Apolipoprotein e and Alzheimer disease. *Proc Natl Acad Sci U S A,* 92:4725–4727, 1995.

39. J. D. Terwilliger and H. H. Goring. Gene mapping in the 20th and 21st centuries: Statistical methods, data analysis, and experimental design. *Hum Biol,* 72:63–132, 2000.

40. D. Weininger. Smiles, a chemical language and information system. 1. Introduction to methodology and encoding rules. *J Chem Inf Comput Sci,* 28:31–36, 1988.

41. Oscar Wilde. *Plays, Prose Writings and Poems.* Everyman's Library, London, 1930.

42. R. G. Worton and M. W. Thompson. Genetics of Duchenne muscular dystrophy. *Annu Rev Genet,* 22:601–629, 1988.

# Index